*The Pro Android Wearables book is dedicated to everyone in the open source community who is working diligently to make professional new media application development software and content development tools freely available to rich application developers to utilize to achieve our creative dreams and our financial goals. Last, but not least, I dedicate this book to my father, Parker Jackson, my family, my life-long friends, and all my ranch neighbors, for their constant help, assistance, and those relaxing, late night BBQ parties.*

# Pro Android Wearables

## Building Apps for Smartwatches

Wallace Jackson

Apress®

**Pro Android Wearables: Building Apps for Smartwatches**

ISBN-13 (pbk): 978-1-4302-6550-4

ISBN-13 (electronic): 978-1-4302-6551-1

Managing Director: Welmoed Spahr
Lead Editor: Steve Anglin
Technical Reviewer: Jeff Tang
Editorial Board: Steve Anglin, Louise Corrigan, Jim DeWolf, Jonathan Gennick, Robert Hutchinson,
    Michelle Lowman, James Markham, Susan McDermott, Matthew Moodie, Jeffrey Pepper,
    Douglas Pundick, Ben Renow-Clarke, Gwenan Spearing, Steve Weiss
Coordinating Editor: Mark Powers
Copy Editor: Mary Bearden
Compositor: SPi Global
Indexer: SPi Global
Artist: SPi Global

Distributed to the book trade worldwide by Springer Science+Business Media New York, 233 Spring Street, 6th Floor, New York, NY 10013. Phone 1-800-SPRINGER, fax (201) 348-4505, e-mail orders-ny@springer-sbm.com, or visit www.springeronline.com. Apress Media, LLC is a California LLC and the sole member (owner) is Springer Science + Business Media Finance Inc (SSBM Finance Inc). SSBM Finance Inc is a Delaware corporation.

For information on translations, please e-mail rights@apress.com, or visit www.apress.com.

Apress and friends of ED books may be purchased in bulk for academic, corporate, or promotional use. eBook versions and licenses are also available for most titles. For more information, reference our Special Bulk Sales–eBook Licensing web page at www.apress.com/bulk-sales.

Any source code or other supplementary material referenced by the author in this text is available to readers at www.apress.com/9781430265504. For additional information about how to locate and download your book's source code, go to www.apress.com/source-code/. Readers can also access source code at SpringerLink in the Supplementary Material section for each chapter.

# Contents at a Glance

# Contents

# About the Author

**Wallace Jackson** has been writing for international multimedia publications about his content production work for major international brand manufacturers since the advent of *Multimedia Producer Magazine*, nearly two decades ago, when he wrote about advanced computer processor architecture for an issue centerfold (removable "mini-issue" insert) distributed at the SIGGRAPH trade show. Since then, he has written for a number of popular publications about his production work using interactive 3D and new media advertising campaign design, including *3D Artist Magazine, Desktop Publishers Journal, CrossMedia Magazine, AVvideo/Multimedia Producer Magazine, Digital Signage Magazine, and Kiosk Magazine.*

He has authored a half-dozen Android book titles for Apress, including four titles in the popular Pro Android series. This particular Pro Android Wearables application development title focuses on the Java 7 programming language that is used with Android 5 (and most other popular platforms as well) so that developers can "code once, deliver everywhere." Open source technologies such as Java, XML, WebKit, Gradle, SQL, and others used in Android 5 allow free for commercial use applications in an open environment that does not have to be approved and can make millions in profits.

He is currently the CEO of Mind Taffy Design, a new media content production and digital campaign design and development agency, located in North Santa Barbara County, halfway between its clientele in Silicon Valley to the north and in West Los Angeles, Beverly Hills, Hollywood, "The OC" (Orange County) and San Diego to the south.

Mind Taffy Design has created open source technology-based (HTML5, JavaScript, Java 8, JavaFX 8, and Android 5) digital new media content deliverables for more than a quarter century (since 1991) for a large number of leading branded manufacturers worldwide, including Sony, Tyco, Samsung, IBM, Dell, Epson, Nokia, TEAC, Sun, Micron, SGI, and Mitsubishi.

He received his undergraduate degree in business economics from the University of California at Los Angeles (UCLA). He received his graduate degree in MIS design and implementation from the University of Southern California (USC). He also received his postgraduate degree in marketing strategy at USC, and completed the USC graduate entrepreneurship program. His USC degrees were completed while at the USC night-time Marshall School of Business MBA program, which allowed him to work full time as a programmer while he completed his graduate and his postgraduate business degrees.

# About the Technical Reviewer

**Jeff Tang** has successfully developed mobile, web, and enterprise apps on many platforms. He became a Microsoft-certified developer and a Sun-certified Java developer last century; had Apple-featured, top-selling iOS apps in the App Store; and was recognized by Google as a top Android market developer. He has a master's degree in computer science with an emphasis on artificial intelligence and believes in lifelong learning. He loves playing basketball (he once made 11 three-pointers and 28 free throws in a row), reading Ernest Hemingway and Mario Puzo, and fantasizing about traveling around the world.

# Acknowledgments

I would like to acknowledge all my fantastic editors and the support staff at Apress who worked long hours and toiled so diligently on this book to make it the ultimate Pro Android Wearables title.

Steve Anglin, for his work as the Lead Editor for this book, and for hiring me to write all of these Android and Java programming titles over the past decade.

Matthew Moodie, for his work as the Development Editor on the book, and for his experience and guidance during the process of making this book one of the truly great Pro Android smartwatch software development titles.

Mark Powers, for his work as the Coordinating Editor for this book, and for his constant diligence in making sure I hit, or surpassed, my always looming writing and editing deadlines.

Mary Bearden, for her work as the Copy Editor on this book, and for her close attention to every detail, and also for conforming the text to the current Apress book writing standards.

Jeff Tang, for his work as the Technical Reviewer on the book, and for making sure I didn't make any programming mistakes. Java code with mistakes does not run properly, if at all, unless they are very lucky mistakes, which is quite rare in computer programming these days.

Finally, I'd like to acknowledge Oracle for acquiring Sun Microsystems and for continuing to enhance Java, so that it remains the premiere open source programming language, and Google, for making 64-bit Android 5 the premiere open source operating system and for acquiring ON2's VP8 video codec and making it available to multimedia producers on both the Android 5 and HTML5 interactive content development platforms.

# Introduction

Welcome to the *Pro Android Wearables* book, where you will learn how to develop applications for smartwatch devices. There will be a follow-on book called *Pro Android IoT* (Internet of Things), which will cover the other Android APIs such as Android TV, Android Auto, and Android Glass, so in this book I can focus only on an exploring the smartwatch device market.

The reason that smartwatches, along with iTV sets, are continuing to explode is a case of basic economics. There are now dozens of manufacturers, including traditional watch brands, such as Citizen, Rolex, Casio, Tag Heuer, Timex and Fossil, making smartwatches, as well as all of the major consumer electronics giants, including Sony, Samsung, LGE, ASUS, Huawei and Motorola, who now have multiple smartwatch models. This generates incredibly massive competition, which drives down pricing, making this value proposition difficult to argue with. I Google searched Android Wear watches today and found two of the most impressive smartwatches, the Motorola MOTO 360 and the ASUS ZenWatch, priced at less than $200. For a computer on your wrist, made with rose gold and calf leather (ZenWatch) or a beautiful carbon black steel bracelet (MOTO), that is an exceptionally reasonable price point. I expect smartwatches to range from $150 to $450 and to continue to generate increasing sales into the future, while adding screen resolution (480 to 640 pixels), processor cores (two to four), and system memory (1 to 2 GB).

This book will cover how to develop applications for an exploding smartwatch market, and it includes the new **Watch Faces API** released by Google that allows developers to create their application as the watch face design itself! Since that is what a watch is used for, I will discuss the Watch Faces API in detail, so that your smartwatch applications can offer their functions to the users while also telling them the time, date, weather, activity, notifications, and so forth. You will learn how to use Google Play Services and make Android Wear applications that have components running on your smartwatch, as well as on the smartphone or tablet, called a **companion activity application**.

Chapter 1 looks at Android Wear and wearable concepts and design considerations, before you set up the Wear production workstation, including your IDE, SDKs, and New Media Content Development applications in Chapter 2. I will discuss the new features of Android Wear in Chapter 3, before you learn about the IntelliJ IDEA, and create a foundation for your Wear project in Chapter 4. In Chapter 5 you will set up the IntelliJ IDEA, also known as Android Studio, for production readiness, by making sure all the SDKs and emulators are up to date and creating AVDs to use for round or square watch face testing.

In Chapter 6, you will get ready to start coding by looking at the Android Watch Faces API and all of its functionality and UI design considerations. In Chapter 7, you will actually code your Watch Face Service and Watch Face Engine classes. These drive the Watch Face infrastructure which you will be putting into place in subsequent chapters.

In Chapter 8 you will put your Watch Face Timing Engine into place, learning about the Time and TimeZone classes, as well as implementing a BroadcastReceiver object to manage the implementation of these classes (objects). In Chapter 9, you will implement core Watch Faces API methods that control different watch face rendering styles and event processing.

In Chapter 10 you will learn about vector graphics and how to "render" designs on the smartwatch face using the onDraw() method, and in Chapter 11 you will learn about raster graphics and how to use BitmapDrawable objects along with PNG32 bitmap assets to add digital imagery to your smartwatch designs. In Chapter 12 you will learn digital imaging techniques that will allow you to optimize the number of colors used to accommodate different smartwatch display color limitations, so you can get the most photorealistic results for your smartwatch application design.

In Chapter 13 you will learn about the Google Mobile Services (GMS) APIs and how to access Google Play Services so that your Wear apps can do even more than they can using the native Android and Android Wear APIs. In Chapter 14 you will implement Android Wear Data APIs in your code to create a Watch Face Utility class to manage your users' settings.

In Chapter 15 you will learn how to set up a testing environment for real-world hardware devices and learn about the Android Debug Bridge, or ADB, as well as how to implement USB device drivers for your hardware devices.

In Chapter 16, you will learn how to dealing with API deprecation and class and method call code updates, as you remove the deprecated Time class and replace it with the Calendar and GregorianCalendar class code to make your application more efficient.

Finally, Chapter 17 goes over the Android IoT APIs and other Wear API features to consider for your smartwatch applications, such as voice recognition and location tracking using the Speech and GPS APIs, respectively. With the information in this book, you will be well on your way to developing smartwatch applications using Android Wear and Android Watch Faces APIs!

# Introduction to Android Wearables: Concepts, Types, and Material Design

Welcome to the *Pro Android Wearables* book! This book will show you how to develop Android Studio applications for those Android devices that are outside your normal smartphones and tablets. This book also includes Android development for devices that can be worn on your person, which is why these Android devices are commonly called "wearables."

If you are looking to develop for Android appliances, such as iTV sets, 4K iTV, game consoles, robots, or other appliances, then the book you want is the *Pro Android IoT* (Apress, 2016) book. That title covers development for Android devices known as "Internet of Things," which include devices that are not worn on your person and are beyond the more normal tablets and phones.

This chapter will look at the different types of wearables, as well as their features and popular usage, and you will learn about the terminology, concepts, differentiating factors, and important technology surrounding wearables and take a closer look at what types of Android applications you can develop for wearable devices. I'll get all of this wearables-related learning out of the way here so you can focus on setting up your workstation in Chapter 2, and then get into Android wearables features in Chapter 3. I will also explain the distinction between wearable devices and Android wearable peripherals.

I'll also discuss the new material design features that have been added to Android 5, as these are available for wearables' application development, and you will see all the cool things you can do with these!

# Wearable Technology Defined: What Is a Wearable?

The term *wearables*, as well as the terms *wearable technology* and *wearable devices*, is indicative of consumer electronics technology based on embedded computer hardware that is built inside products that are worn on the outside of one's body. This includes clothing and accessories, including jewelry, such as watches, and protective wear, such as glasses, as well as items of clothing such as socks, shoes, hats, and gloves and sports, health, and fitness products that can be comfortably worn somewhere on your body.

Wearable devices often have some modicum of communications capability, and this will allow the device wearer to access information in real time. Data input capability is a necessary feature for wearable devices, as it allows users to access the features of the wearable device and use it to run the applications you are going to be learning to develop over the course of this book. Data input is usually in the form of touch screen interfaces, voice recognition (also known as voice input), or sometimes through use of hardware buttons built right into the wearable device itself.

Thanks to the cloud, local storage is not necessary for a wearable device, although some feature micro SD (secure digital) cards or store data on linked, companion devices. Wearable devices are able to perform many of the same application tasks as mobile phones and tablets; in fact, many wearable devices require that the wearable device be "married" to another Android device (more on this later on in the chapter) within the operating range of Bluetooth 4.x technology.

Android wearable devices tend to be more sophisticated on the "sensor input" side of the equation than hand-held technologies on the market today. This is because wearable devices will provide sensory and scanning features not typically seen with smartphone or tablet devices. Examples of this include features such as biofeedback and the tracking of physiological functions, such as pulse, heart rate, workout intensity, sleep monitoring, and so on.

Examples of wearable hardware devices include smartwatches, smartglasses, textiles, also called smart fabrics, hats, caps, shoes, socks, contact lenses, ear rings, headbands, hearing aids, and jewelry, such as rings, bracelets, and necklaces. Wearable technology tends to refer to things that can be put on and taken off effortlessly. It's important to note that there are versions of the wearables concept that are more radical in nature, for instance the implanted devices, such as microchips or even smart-tattoos. I will not be covering application development for any of these nonmainstream device types in this book. Because the general public will primarily be using smartwatches, I'll be focusing on that type of wearable device. Ultimately whether a device is worn on, or incorporated into, the body, the purpose of these Android wearable devices is providing constant, convenient, portable, seamless, and hands-free access to consumer electronics.

## Wearable Application Development: What Types of Apps?

The uses of wearable technology are limited only by your imagination, and the implications of these applications will be far reaching, which is why you have purchased this *Pro Android Wearables* book in the first place!

Wearable applications will influence a wide spectrum of industry verticals in a large number of ways. Some of the many industries that are embracing Android wearable devices include the health care, pharmaceutical, education, fitness, entertainment, music, aging, disability, transportation, finance, enterprise, insurance, automotive, and gaming industries, and the list grows larger daily.

The goal of wearable applications in each of these industries should be to seamlessly incorporate functional, portable electronics and computers into an individual's daily life. Prior to their presence in the consumer market, wearable devices were primarily utilized in military operations as well as in the pharmaceutical, health care, sports, and medicine industries.

More than ten years ago, medical engineers started talking about a wearable device that could monitor the health of their patients in the form of a smart-shirt or smart-wristband. At least one of these is a mainstream technology today, and its aim is to monitor vital signs and send that biofeedback information to an application or a web site for data tracking and analysis.

The types of Android applications that you can create for use on wearable devices is limited only to your imagination. This is because wearables are "paired" with more advanced hardware and thus have those same hardware capabilities that smartphones or tablets have, plus some sensors that smartphones and tablets do not have!

One of the logical application verticals is health and welfare monitoring; because of these heart-rate sensors, Android wearables applications can be created that help with health-related areas of users' lives, such as their work out in the gym, tracking their diet on the go while working or traveling, getting enough sleep, walking or running enough miles in a day, and similar applications that will help users improve their health or at least stay healthy.

Another logical application vertical is social media, as the current trend these days is staying connected to everyone at all times of the day, while also making new friends or business associates. Androids are connected to the Internet, via Wi-Fi or 4G, at all times, so these types of wear apps are also going to be very popular for use on wearable devices.

Of course, games, watch faces or skins, and entertainment consumption will also be a massive application vertical for wearable devices. Let's look at this aspect so you can get some idea about how to apply what you'll be learning!

# Android Wearable Fun: Augmented Reality, Edutainment, and Gamification

Although wearables technology could potentially have a significant impact in the areas of social media connectivity, health, dieting, or fitness, the area of wearable technology also promises to have a major impact on the casual gaming, audio video (AV) entertainment, edutainment, and augmented reality (AR) markets. Wearable applications that make everyday tasks into fun to play games, commonly termed *gamification*, is also a major market opportunity.

AR, originally called mixed reality, can leverage wearable technology. AR uses i3D OpenGL capabilities, found in the Android platform, to create a realistic and immersive 3D environment that syncs up with the real world around you in real time, thanks to Java 7 code in your Android 5 application. Whereas Android 4.4 and earlier used Java 6, Android 5 uses

Java 7. Mixing virtual reality or interactive 3D (i3D) with actual reality, using digital video, digital imaging, or global positioning satellite (GPS) location-based technology, is not new by any stretch of the imagination. AR apps are the most advanced type of wearable apps.

AR delivered through the use of wearable devices has been contemplated since before the turn of the century. What's important is that AR hardware prototypes are morphing from bulky technology, such as the massive goggles used by the Oculus Rift, into small, lightweight, comfortable, highly mobile 3D virtual reality systems.

The next most complex type of application that will soon be appearing on a wearable device will be wearable games. You can expect to see casual games created for smartwatches and smartglasses on the market very soon. Careful optimization is the key to creating a game application that will work well on a wearable device, and I will be covering that topic within this book.

Another complex type of entertainment application for a wearable device is the AV application. Playing digital audio or digital video on a wearable device also requires careful optimization, as well as a user who owns a good pair of Bluetooth audiophile headphones, which fortunately are made by more than a dozen major electronics manufacturers these days.

Finally, one of the more complex types of wearable applications is custom smartwatch faces or skins. These turn the watch face that a user looks at all day long into something they want their watch to look like. Of course you can also create loads of text-based apps, like office utilities or handy recipe managers, for instance; these will work great on wearables!

The future of Android wearables applications needs to reflect the seamless integration of fashion, functionality, practicality, visual, and user interface (UI) design. I'll discuss how to do this throughout the book, after you have put together the development workstation in Chapter 2 and created the emulators in Chapter 5, so you have a foundation in place for wearable development.

# Mainstream Wearables: Smartwatches and Smartglasses

There are two primary (i.e., mainstream) types of wearable devices that popular consumer electronics manufacturers are scrambling to manufacture.

The smartwatch is currently the most popular type of wearable device, with hundreds of affordable models already available in the marketplace. As the centuries have passed by, watches have become the international fashion statement. Thus, it is no surprise that this is the most popular and useful type of Android wearable device.

The other type of popular wearable genre is smartglasses, and dozens of products have already been released by companies such as Google (Glass) and Vuzix (M100). Let's take a closer look at these two types of wearables hardware, since they are going to be the majority of the device types that run the pro Android wearables applications you will be creating during the course of this book.

# Smartwatches: Round Watch Face vs. Square Organic Light-emitting Diode

The smartwatch wearable genre of consumer electronics has the most products out there, with dozens of branded manufacturers and actual product models numbering in the hundreds, with all but one (Apple Watch) running one flavor of Android or another. For this reason, I'll focus on these in this book.

There is also a smartwatch from Samsung, the Galaxy Gear 2, which uses the Tizen OS, utilizing Linux, HTML5, JavaScript, and CSS3 for app development. I won't be covering these in this book, instead focusing on the Samsung Gear S.

Android 5 Wear Software Development Kit (SDK) supports two different smartwatch face types, round and square, as watches normally come in these two configurations. You'll create Android virtual devices (AVDs) (software emulators) for both of these smartwatch types in Chapter 5.

# Smartglasses: Glasses and Other Smartglasses Manufacturers

The smartglasses wearables consumer electronics product genre is the next fastest growing wearables products genre. Brand eyewear manufacturers are scrambling to get into this wearables space, so look for smartglasses from Luxottica soon. For this reason, this will be the secondary focus in this book.

Smartglasses will generally run the Google Glass Development Kit (GDK) or Android 4.x, and you can expect Android 5 smartglasses wearables in 2015. There are a number of smartglasses companies, including Google, Vuzix, GlassUp, Sony, six15, and Ion. Google has of course stopped producing the glasses, promising new and better products in the future.

# Wearable Application Programming Interfaces

There are two primary application programming interfaces (APIs), both of which run under Google Android Studio, that can be used to access features for wearable devices that are not yet standard in the version of Android 5 that spans across mainstream devices, such as smartphones and tablets. The smartwatch API is called *Wear SDK* and the smartglasses API is called *Glass GDK*. It's important to note that some wearable devices can run the full Android operating system (OS).

The smartwatch example of this would be the Neptune Pine Smartwatch, which runs a full Android OS, and the Google Glass product does not require that you use Glass GDK unless you need to use special features of Google Glass or want to develop "native" glass apps. In other words, Google Glass will run Android apps that run on normal smartphones and tablets.

This means that Neptune Pine and Google Glass can run the same application you develop for other Android devices. Newer versions of this Neptune Pine product line will utilize the Wear SDK, which is largely what I will be covering within the scope of this book.

# Android Studio 1.0: Android Wear SDK

Android Wear SDK is the API created by Google for use with Android wearables (wearable devices that run on Android).

It was launched at the beginning of 2015 via the Android developer web site along with several customized "vertical" APIs, including Android Auto SDK (for automobiles), Android TV SDK (for 2K or 4K iTV sets), and an Android Wear SDK (for smartwatches). For now, Wear SDK is targeted at smartwatches, but later it may expand to other wearables such as shoes, hats, and the like.

Android Wear SDK provides a unified Android wearables development platform that can span across multiple smartwatch products. Before the Wear SDK was available, a smartwatch manufacturer had to either provide its own APIs, like the Sony SmartWatch One and Two did back in 2014, or support the full Android 4 OS, like the Neptune Pine did during 2014.

It is important to note here that this Android Wear SDK does not provide a separate operating system, but in fact is an extension of the Android 5 OS that requires a portion of the Android wearable application to run on your host Android device. This would normally be an Android smartphone, as that is the most portable device and the device type that connects to a wide variety of networks and carriers.

Because the Android smartwatch represents the majority of the wearable application marketplace, I will focus the majority of this book on that area of wearable application development, although I'll also cover Google Glass in Chapter 17.

# Google Glass Development Kit: GDK for Android or Mirror

When developing Google Glass wearable applications, you have two different GDK API options. You can use these separately or in conjunction with each other. Additionally, there is a third option of simply using the Android OS without either of the APIs. Let's take a closer look at Glass development.

## Google Glass's Android Studio GDK: The Glass Development Kit

The Google Android GDK is an add-on to the Android OS APIs (also known as the Android 5 SDK), which allows you to build what Google terms *Glassware*. Glassware comprises the Google Glass wearable apps that run directly on Google Glass hardware.

In general, you would want to use this Android GDK development approach if you need direct access to unique hardware features of the Google Glass, real-time interaction with the Google Glass hardware for your users, or an off-line capability for your application if no Internet, Wi-Fi, 2G, 3G, or 4G cellular network is available.

By using the Android SDK in conjunction with the GDK, you can leverage the wide array of Android APIs while, at the same time, designing a great user experience for Google Glass owners. Unlike the Mirror API, Glassware built using this Android GDK runs on Glass itself. This allows access to Glass hardware's low-level, proprietary (unique to Google Glass) product features.

## Develop Google Glass Apps Using Only the Android Environment

Google designed the Glass platform to make their existing Android SDK work on Glass. What this means is that you may use all of the existing Android development tools, which you'll be downloading and installing in Chapter 2, and your Glassware can be delivered using the standard Android application package (APK) format.

This opens up a lot of those other pro Android development book titles, such as *Pro Android Graphics* (Apress 2013) or *Pro Android UI* (Apress 2014), which will show you how to make visual Android applications that work well on Google Glass devices. This is because the Google Glass product is designed to run the full Android OS, and, therefore, any applications that will run on it. This means you can develop an application that will run across all of the Android devices out there, including Google Glass. This allows a code once, deliver anywhere (highly optimized) development work process for your app, as long as users don't need to run on smartwatches, other than Pine!

## Using RESTful Services with Google Glass: The Mirror API

There's another API that works with Google Glass and is not tied to Google Android OS at all. This is what is known as the Google Glass Mirror API, and it is what is commonly known as a RESTful API.

The Mirror API allows developers to build Glassware for Google Glass using any programming language they choose. RESTful services provide easy access to web-based APIs that will do most of the data transfer heavy lifting for the application developer.

In general, you would want to utilize this Mirror API if you need to use a cross-platform infrastructure such as HTML or PHP, need to access built-in functions for the Google Glass product, or need platform independence from the Android OS. This would be how you would use Google Glass with iOS or Windows, for instance.

## Hybrid Glass Applications: Mixing Android GDK and the Mirror API

Finally, it's interesting to note that developers can also create "hybrid" Google Glass applications. This is because, as you may have suspected, the Google Glass Mirror API can interface with the Google Glass Android GDK.

This is done by using a menu item to invoke Mirror API code that sends an Intent object to the Android GDK API and then to the GDK application code. I'll be using Intents, which are an Android platform-specific Java Object type, in this book. Intents are used to communicate among applications, menus, devices, activities, and APIs, such as the Mirror API. You can even use this hybrid development model to leverage existing web properties that can launch enhanced i3D experiences that run directly on Google Glass.

# True Android or Android Peripheral: Bluetooth Link

In the world of pro Android wearables, and in some cases even in the world of pro Android appliances, there is often a distinction that you will need to be aware of as a developer that the marketers of Android products will have a tendency to want to hide. This is because the cost to manufacture one type of Android device will be quite high (miniaturization), while the cost to manufacture another type of Android device will be quite low, so profit margins will be higher, especially if the public can be convinced the product is running an Android OS, when in fact it's not actually doing so!

This is quite evident in Android wearables product segments, which include smartwatches and smartglasses, such as Google Glass. A couple of smartwatches are True Android devices; that is they have a computer processing unit (CPU), memory, storage, an OS, Wi-Fi, and the like, right inside of the smartwatch. A good example of one of these True Android devices is the Neptune Pine.

True smartwatch devices would actually be like having a full smartphone on your wrist and would be offered by telecommunications carriers just as smartphones currently are. This True Android smartwatch would be your only Android device, you would not need to carry a smartphone anymore. Embedded computer miniaturization advances will eventually allow all smartwatches to do the same things that the Neptune Pine did in 2014, placing a full-blown Android device on someone's wrist.

In case you are wondering, I borrowed this "true" Android description from the TrueHD (HDTV) industry term. TrueHD is 1920-by-1080 resolution, and it is a necessary descriptive modifier because there is another lower 1280-by-720 resolution in the marketplace that is called just HD (I call it pseudo-HD).

Other smartwatches are not True Android devices and could be described as more of a "peripheral" to your existing smartphone, phablet, or tablet, and these use Bluetooth technology to become an *extension* of an Android device that has the CPU (processor), memory (application runtime), data storage, and telecommunication (Wi-Fi access and 4G LTE cellular network) hardware.

Peripheral Android devices would obviously require a different application development work process and have different data optimization and testing procedures to achieve an optimal performance and user experience.

Obviously, because this book will be looking at developing for some of these more popular Android wearable devices, I will be getting into this "remote Android peripheral" development issue in greater detail and taking a look at how to design and optimize wearable peripheral apps.

I just want you to be aware that there are two completely different ways to approach Android development now: on-board, or native Android apps, and remote or two-way (back-end) communication Android app functionality.

With the advent of Bluetooth wearables and second-screen technology (which is covered in the book *Pro Android IoT* [Apress, 2016]), this is going to become an important distinction in Android applications' development as time goes on, and these extension Android products continue emerging into the market.

The bottom line is that you need to know which consumer electronics device is hosting the CPU, memory, storage, and telecommunications hardware, which consumer electronics device is hosting the touch screen, display, and input, and which technology (and how fast it is) is connecting those two together. This is important for how well you'll be able to optimize app performance, as user experience (UX) is based on how *responsive* and easy an app is to use.

# Wearable Apps Design: Android 5 Material Design

Android 5, released in 2014 along with the Android TV, Wear, and Auto SDK add-ons, features an all new UI paradigm. Google calls it *Material Design* because it is more 3D savvy. Texturing or "skinning" a 2D or 3D object involves using what are commonly termed *materials* in the media design industry.

Google created Material Design to be a far-reaching UI design guideline for end-user interaction, animated motions, and visual design across the Google Chrome OS and Android OS platforms, as well as across consumer electronics devices that run Chrome OS (HTML5, CSS3, and JavaScript on top of Linux) or Android 5 OS (Java 7, CSS3, and XML on top of a 64-bit Linux Kernel).

One of the cool features in the Android 5 OS, which you may have learned about if you read the book *Android Apps for Absolute Beginners* (Apress 2014), is support for Material Design in apps across all types of Android 5 devices.

You will learn about using Material Design for Android wearables apps in this chapter, as well as throughout the rest of this book. Android 5, also known as Android API Level 21 (and later), offers some new components and new OS functionality, specifically for Material Design.

This includes a new Android 5 theme, Android View widgets for new viewing capabilities, improved shadows and animation APIs, and improved Drawables, including better vector scaling, 32-bit PNG tinting using the 8-bit alpha, and the automatic Color Extraction API. I will be covering all of these in more detail during the rest of this chapter.

# The Android Material Design Themes: Light and Dark

This Android 5 Material Design Theme provides the new Android 5 conforming style to use for your Android 5 apps. Because the Android Wear SDK is a part of Android Studio 1 (Android 5 plus IntelliJ), these new themes will apply to pro Android wearables as well. You will be installing Android Studio, as well as some other open source content development software in Chapter 2, and exploring Android Studio 1.x and IntelliJ in Chapter 3 and Java 7 in Chapter 4. If you're developing for Android 4, you will use the HOLO Theme; if you are developing for Android 5, you will use the Material Theme.

Both Theme.Holo and Theme.Material offer a dark and a light version. You can customize the look of the Material Theme to match a brand identity using the custom color palette you define. You can tint an Android Action Bar as well as the Android Status Bar by using Material Theme attributes.

Your Android 5 widgets have a new UI design and touch feedback animations. You can customize these touch feedback animations, as well as the Activity transitions for your app. An Activity in Android is one logical section or UI screen for your application. I am assuming you already have knowledge of Android lingo, because this is an intermediate to advanced level (pro) book.

## Defining the Wearable Material Theme: Using the Style Attribute

Just as in the previous versions of Android, the material theme is defined using the Android Style attribute. Examples of the various material themes would be defined using XML, using the following XML 1.0 markup:

```
@android:style/Theme.Material                     (the default dark UI version)
@android:style/Theme.Material.Light               (the light UI version)
@android:style/Theme.Material.Light.DarkActionBar (a light version with a dark version
                                                   Actionbar)
```

As I mentioned, the Theme.Material UI style (or theme) is only available in Android 5, API Level 21 and above. The v7 Support Libraries provide themes with Material Design styles for some pre-5 View widgets and support for customizing the color palette prior to Android 5.

## Defining the Wearable Material Theme Color Palette: The Item Tag

If you wanted to customize your Material Design theme's primary color to fit your wearables app branding, you would define your custom colors using the **<item>** tag, nested inside a **<style>** tag, nested inside a **<resources>** tag inside a **themes.xml** file. You create an **AppTheme** with parent attributes inherited from the **Theme.Material** parent theme and add your custom color references using the **colors.xml** file that holds the hexadecimal color data using an XML markup structure. This should look something like this:

```
<resources>
    <style name="AppTheme" parent="android:Theme.Material">
        <item name="android:colorPrimary">@color/primary</item>
        <item name="android:colorPrimaryDark">@color/primary_dark</item>
        <item name="android:colorAccent">@color/accent</item>
    </style>
</resources>
```

Again, I assume you know basic Android (Java and XML) development here. The style name used for the app here is **AppTheme**, it references a **parent** style of **Theme.Material** and sets custom color values, set in a **colors.xml** file, using **<item>** tags containing your main theme style constants—**colorPrimary**, **colorPrimaryDark**, and **colorAccent**. Android is hard wired to use these theme constants, so all you have to do is reference custom color values to them.

## Customizing a Wearable Material Theme Status Bar: *statusBarColor*

You can also easily customize the application Status Bar for **Theme.Material**, and you can specify another color that fits the wearable application brand and will provide a decent amount of color contrast to show the white status icons. To set the custom color for your application Status Bar, add an **android:statusBarColor** attribute when you extend a **Theme.Material** style definition. Using the previous example, your XML should look like this:

```
<resources>
    <style name="AppTheme" parent="android:Theme.Material">
        <item name="android:colorPrimary">@color/primary_color</item>
        <item name="android:colorPrimaryDark">@color/primary_dark</item>
        <item name="android:colorAccent">@color/accent_color</item>
        <item name="android:statusBarColor">@color/status_bar</item>
    </style>
</resources>
```

The **statusBarColor** constant will *inherit* the value of the **colorPrimaryDark** constant if you do not provide one specifically, as is seen above. You can also can draw behind the Status Bar using the *alpha channel* component of an Android 5 **#AARRGGBB** 32-bit hexadecimal color data value. If you want to delve into Android graphics, check out the book *Pro Android Graphics* (Apress 2013).

For example, if you wanted to show the Status Bar as completely transparent, you would use an **@android:color/transparent** constant, which sets the alpha channel to zero (off or **#00000000**). However, this would not be a good UI design practice, as you could have a background with white in it behind the Status Bar, which would then render the Status Bar icons invisible.

So what you would really want to do is create a **tinted** Status Bar over a background (image, photo, 3D, 2D, artwork). You should use a dark gradient to ensure the white status icons are visible. To do this, you would set the **statusBarColor** to transparent and also set the **WindowManager** object's **windowTranslucentStatus** attribute to a data value of true using an Android **WindowManager.LayoutParams** class (objects) **FLAG_TRANSLUCENT_STATUS** constant. You can also use the **Window.setStatusBarColor()** method with Java code to implement Status Bar animation or translucency fade-in or fade-out.

As a UI design principle, your Android Status Bar object should always have a clear demarcation against an Action Bar, except in cases where you design custom UI images or new media content behind these bars, in which case you should use your darkening gradient, which will ensure that icons are still visible. When you customize both UI navigation (Action Bar) and a Status Bar, you should make them both transparent or only change the transparency for the Status Bar. The navigation bar should remain black in all other cases.

## Customizing a Wearable Material Theme: Individual View Themes

Android Styles and Themes can not only be used for customizing a look and feel for your entire wearables application globally, but they can also be used to style and theme *local screens*, which are components of your application.

Why would one want to go to the trouble of developing a style or theme for an *individual* View object or Activity object in Android 5, you might ask?

The answer can be found in the concept of UI design *modularity*, which is a cornerstone of Android wearables app development. Once you develop a Style and Theme using an XML file, you can apply it whenever necessary, which will probably be multiple times during your wearables app development process. In this way, you do the UI design work once (create a module) and apply it many times thereafter. This also ensures that the theme or style is applied in exactly the same way every time. If you need to get into UI design for Android 5 development in greater detail, the book *Pro Android UI* (Apress 2014) covers all of the Android UI design issues in depth.

UI elements (Android *widgets* subclassed from View) in your XML user interface layout container definitions (Android layout containers are subclassed from **ViewGroup**) can reference an **android:theme** attribute or an **android:style** attribute. This allows you to reference your prebuilt style and theme resources in a modular fashion.

Referencing one of the prebuilt style or theme attributes will then apply that UI element as well as any child elements inside that UI design element. This capability can be quite useful for altering theme color palettes in a specific section of your wearables application UI design.

# Android Material Design View Widgets: Lists and Cards

The Android 5 API provides two completely new View subclasses (widgets). These can be used for displaying information cards or recyclable lists using the Material Design themes, styles, animation, and special effects.

The **RecyclerView** widget is a plug-and-play enhancement of Android **ListView** class. It supports many layout types and provides performance improvement. The **CardView** widget allows your wearable application to display contextual pieces of information using "cards" that have a consistent look and feel.

Let's take a closer look at the new UI design tools before I move on to dropshadows, animation, and special effects like Drawable tinting and Color extraction.

## Android *RecyclerView* Class: Optimized (Recycled) List Viewing

The Android RecyclerView is a UI design widget that is a more feature-filled version of the Android ListView widget. The RecyclerView is used to display extensive lists of applications data. What is unique about the class is that the data contained in the View can be scrolled extremely efficiently. The way this is done is through the RecyclerView ViewGroup (a layout container) subclass. It holds a limited number of data (View) objects inside its ViewGroup layout container at any single moment in time.

This memory optimization principle is quite similar to how digital video streaming works, keeping only the currently utilized portion of your data list in the system memory, which makes this class faster and more memory efficient. You would want to utilize Android's RecyclerView widget when you have data collections where the data inside are going to be changed at runtime, based on the actions of your application's end users or by network transactions.

The RecyclerView class accomplishes all this by providing developers a number of software components that wearable developers can implement in their code. These include layout managers, for positioning data View items in the List, animation to add visual effects to data View item operations, and flexibility in designing your own custom layout managers and animation for your wearable application's implementation of this RecyclerView widget.

## Android *CardView* Class: The Index Card Organization Paradigm

The Android **CardView** class is a ViewGroup layout container class extending the **FrameLayout** class. The Android FrameLayout class allows you to display a single View UI element (widget) so the CardView would be a collection of FrameLayout individual Views in the paradigm of a stack of 3-by-5 index cards. This class allows you to show any informational data for your wearable application on virtual cards that have a consistent look across the Android (application, wearable, TV, or auto SDK) platforms.

Your CardView widget can also feature shadows and rounded corners for each card in this CardView layout container, although it is the CardView itself that is dropshadowed and rounded, not each individual card. To create a card with a shadow, you need to use a **card_view:cardElevation** attribute.

The CardView class accesses the actual elevation attribute and creates the dynamic shadowing automatically if your user is using Android 5 (API Level 21) or later, and for earlier Android versions, it will create a programmatic shadow implementation based on earlier versions.

If you wanted to enhance the appearance of your CardView widget, you would provide a custom *corner radius* value, say 6dip, which would create rounded corners for each card in your CardView using a **cardCornerRadius** attribute.

If you wanted to show a background image, behind your CardView widget, you would provide a custom *background color* value, like #77BBBBBB, which would create a light gray transparent background color for each card that is in your CardView, using the **cardBackgroundColor** attribute.

If you wanted a dropshadow behind the CardView widget, you would provide a custom *elevation* value, say 5dip, which would create a nice, highly visible dropshadow behind each card in a CardView using a **cardElevation** attribute. Before you use the **cardElevation** attribute, you will need to set a Padding compatibility constant, called **cardUseCompatPadding**, to a value of true in order for the dropshadowing (elevation) effect to be computed by CardView.

To access these CardView attributes, you must import a custom XMLNS (or XML naming schema) for both your LinearLayout parent layout container class as well as for the nested CardView child layout container class. This is done by using the following XML parameter inside each layout container tag:

```
xmlns:card_view=http://schemas.android.com/apk/res-auto
```

Once you have this in place, you can use the attributes specified above by prefacing them with a **card_view:** modifier, so that your **cardCornerRadius** attribute would be then be written as **card_view:cardCornerRadius**, for example.

To implement the three examples I outlined previously in this section, the markup for the LinearLayout parent layout container containing a CardView containing a TextView object would look something like the following XML:

```
<LinearLayout xmlns:android="http://schemas.android.com/apk/res/android"
          xmlns:tools="http://schemas.android.com/tools"
          xmlns:card_view="http://schemas.android.com/apk/res-auto" >
    <android.support.v7.widget.CardView xmlns:card_view="http://schemas.android.com/apk/res-auto"
        android:id="@+id/my_card_view"
        android:layout_gravity="center"
        android:layout_width="180dip"
        android:layout_height="180dip"
        card_view:cardCornerRadius="6dip"
        card_view:cardBackgroundColor="#77BBBBBB"
        card_view:cardUseCompatPadding="true"
        card_view:cardElevation="5dip" >
        <TextView android:id="@+id/info_text"
                android:layout_width="match_parent"
                android:layout_height="match_parent" />
    </android.support.v7.widget.CardView>
</LinearLayout>
```

Now let's look at special effects applications in Material Design and learn about dropshadowing and animating the View widgets.

# Android Material Design Effects: Shadows and Animation

Although Android has always had a shadows and animation feature set, which works with Android View objects (called Android widgets), Material Design takes these effects to a new level by providing more advanced shadows so that everything on a screen has a 3D z axis element to it. For instance View objects other than Text objects can now access dropshadows, and there are now advanced transition animation effects, such as curve interpolation motion and things that simulate 3D effects on the screen such as ripples.

## Android Material Design 3D Effects: Automatic View Shadowing

In addition to the x and y properties, Android widgets, which are subclassed from the View class in Android, now feature a third, z axis property. This property, which is called an *elevation* property, defines the height of the View object, which in turn determines the characteristics of its shadows.

As many of you who are familiar with 3D know, this takes Android UI design from a 2D place into the exciting 3D realm. This allows photo-realistic i3D UI designs, whereas before, only "flat," 2D UI designs were possible.

This new elevation property was added to represent the elevation or height of a View object, relative to other View objects above and below it in the UI design. The elevation property (or if you prefer, attribute or characteristic) will be used by the Android OS to determine the size of the shadow, so a View object (widget) with a larger elevation value should cast a wider shadow, making the widget appear to be at a higher elevation.

The View widgets in the UI design will also obtain their drawing order via the z values. This is commonly called the *z order* or *z index*, and your UI View objects that have been assigned a higher z value will always appear on top of other View objects (widgets) that have been assigned lower z values.

## Android Material Design Animation: Touch Feedback for Your UI

The upgraded Animation API in Android 5 lets you create custom animation for touch feedback for your UI controls (widgets). These allow for triggering these animation effects based on changes in the View widget state, and also allow Activity transitions when the user navigates between Activity screens in your application.

The Material Design–related enhancement to the Animation API allows you to respond to touch screen events on your View widget using new *touch feedback animations*. These implement the new *ripple* element (**RippleDrawable** class), and can be defined as *bounded* (contained within the View) or as *unbounded* (emanating beyond a View bounds). Defining this using XML is fairly straightforward, although it can also be defined using Java 7.

To define a bounded ripple touch feedback animation, reference it inside the **android:background** parameter in your View widget tag, like this:

```
<Button android:id="@+id/my_rippling_muscles_I_mean_button"
        android:layout_width="wrap_content"
        android:layout_height="wrap_content"
        android:background="?android:attr/selectableItemBackground" />
```

To define an unbounded ripple touch feedback animation, again reference it using the **android:background** parameter in your View widget tag, like this:

```
<Button android:id="@+id/my_rippling_abs_I_mean_button"
        android:layout_width="wrap_content"
        android:layout_height="wrap_content"
        android:background="?android:attr/selectableItemBackgroundBorderless" />
```

Touch feedback animations are now integrated inside several standard View widget subclasses, such as the Button class. A new API lets you customize these touch feedback animations so you can add them to your custom View.

Users can now hide and show View widgets using a circular reveal animation, which adds another level of wow-factor to the Android operating system. Those of you familiar with 2D and 3D graphics will know that this is being accomplished by applying an animated circle (ShapeDrawable) clipping shape into the rendering pipeline between the two UI widget visuals.

## Android Material Design Transitions: Enhanced Activity Transitions

In the area of activity transitional animation, you can now switch between activities with custom activity transition animations. The custom Activity transitions will be applied by the Android OS whenever the user transfers from one Activity to another using an Intent object.

These Activity animations are intended for usage in conjunction with other Material Design animation effects. I suspect that these were added so that the Material Design UX is uniform across the entire Android 5 wearable application. Now, both View and Activity objects offer prebuilt animation! You can also create custom transitional animation, as you could before Android 5.

There are four different types of prebuilt Activity animations in Android 5 Material Design: *enter* and *exit* control full-screen animation effects, and *SharedElementEnter* and *SharedElementExit* control localized UI elements effects for UI elements, which are *shared* (on both Activity screens).

The enter Activity animation will be triggered when a user switches into a new Activity screen from another Activity screen in a wearable application and, thus, this enter transition determines how View widgets in an Activity enter the screen. For example, in an *explode* transition, View widgets enter the screen from the outside of the screen, flying in toward the center of the screen. Be sure to use graphic designs for your Activity that enhance this transitional special effect.

Conversely, an exit type of Activity animation can be triggered when users exit an Activity screen in their wearable application. The exit transition will determine how View widgets in your wearable Activity exit the screen. For example, using the explode transition example, in the exit transition, your wearable application View widgets will exit the screen traveling away from the center, the opposite of an enter explode transition animation.

If there are shared UI elements between two Activity screens, then the *shared element* transitions can be applied for this UI design scenario. As you may have guessed, these are called the SharedElementEnter and SharedElementExit transitions. The SharedElement transition determines how View widgets that are shared between two Activity screens will handle the transition between these Activity screens.

For example, if two Activity screens have the same digital image, but it's in a different position or resolution, the changeImageTransform shared element transition will translate (reposition) or scale (resize) the image smoothly between the two Activity screens.

There are other shared element transitions such as the changeBounds shared element transition, which will animate any changes in the layout bounds of any target Activity View widgets. There is also a changeTransform shared element transition that can animate any changes in the scale (size) and rotation (orientation) of target View widgets between two Activity screens being transitioned. Finally, there is a changeClipBounds shared element transition, which will animate any changes in the clipping path boundary for target Activity View widgets that have clipping paths assigned to them.

Android 5 now supports three primary enter and exit transitions; these can also be utilized in conjunction with a shared element transition. There is the *explode* transition, which moves View widgets in or out from the center of the screen, the *slide* transition, which slides View widgets in from, or away from, the edges of the scene, and the *fade* transition, which adds, or removes, the View widgets from the screen by changing their opacity value.

You're probably wondering if there's any way to create custom transitions. This is done by creating a custom transition subclass using the Visibility class, a subclass of the `Transition` class, created for this exact purpose.

## Android Material Design Motion: Enhanced Motion Curves or Paths

Those of you who are experienced with 3D animation software such as Blender3D or digital video editing software such as Lightworks are familiar with the concept of using *motion curves* to control the rate of change in speed for things like video clips or 3D object movement in scenes.

This is called a motion curve because it allows you to precisely control the way in which something moves over time, which is important in film making, character animation, and game design. There is another closely related tool that is called a *motion path*. A motion path defines how an object will move through a 2D or 3D space.

Therefore, a motion curve is a tool that will be used for defining *temporal animation attributes* (changes in animation speed over time), while a motion path is a tool that will be used for defining *spacial animation attributes*.

Animation in Android OS, as well as in the new Android 5 Material Design, relies on these motion curves using the Interpolator class. This class can now be used to define more complex 4D motion curve interpolation (a fourth dimension, or 4D, means change over time). Material Design now adds motion paths to support 2D spatial movement patterns, so now not only the rate of movement can be controlled, but also where that movement occurs.

The **PathInterpolator** class is a new Interpolator subclass based on Bézier, which is a complex type of curve definition mathematics. Bézier curves have been implemented in Android 5 as Path (class) objects. This Interpolator class can specify Bézier motion curves in a 1-by-1 square, with anchor points at 0,0 and 1,1 and with custom *x,y control points*, which developers specify using the **pathInterpolator** class's constructor method parameters. You will usually define a **PathInterpolator** object using an XML resource, like this:

```
<pathInterpolator
    xmlns:android="http://schemas.android.com/apk/res/android"
    android:controlX1="0.5"
    android:controlY1="0"
    android:controlX2="1"
    android:controlY2="1" />
```

This Android 5 operating system provides XML resources for three basic new motion curves in the Material Design specification. These would use markup and would be referenced in your XML markup, or Java code, using the `@interpolator/` path referencing header, like this:

```
@interpolator/linear_out_slow_in.xml
@interpolator/fast_out_linear_in.xml
@interpolator/fast_out_slow_in.xml
```

# Android Material Design Animate State Change: *StateListAnimator* Class

Android state changes, such as the signal meters on your phone, can now be animated using the new Android 5 Material Design feature set. This will allow wearable applications developers to add even more detail to the wow-factor elements inside their Android wearables' applications design.

The new Android StateListAnimator class lets developers use ObjectAnimator objects that are triggered (run) by the Android OS whenever the state of a View object changes. The way you would set up your StateListAnimator as an XML resource leverages the **<selector>** tag (selects among different states) and the **<set>** tag (creates selection set), along with **<item>** tags defining the states and the **<objectAnimator>** tags defining the Object Animation. A simple **pressed=true** and **pressed=false** StateListAnimator Selector object is set up in this fashion, by using a four-level (deep) nested XML construct:

```
<selector xmlns:android="http://schemas.android.com/apk/res/android" >
   <item android:state_pressed="true" >
      <set>
         <objectAnimator android:propertyName="translationZ"
             android:duration="120"
             android:valueTo="5dip"
             android:valueType="floatType" />
      </set>
   </item>
   <item android:state_pressed="false"
         android:state_enabled="true"
         android:state_focused="true" >
      <set>
         <objectAnimator android:propertyName="translationZ"
             android:duration="120"
             android:valueTo="0"
             android:valueType="floatType" />
      </set>
   </item>
</selector>
```

To attach custom state change animations to the View, define an ObjectAnimator using the <selector> element in an XML resource file as shown above. Next, reference it inside the View object XML tag you want to be effected by it using the **android:stateListAnimator** XML parameter.

To assign this state change in animations StateListAnimator to a View in your Java code, you should utilize an **AnimationInflater.loadStateListAnimator()** method call, and then remember to assign this ObjectAnimator to your View, using the **View.setStateListAnimator()** method call.

It is important to remember that whenever your wearables application theme extends a Theme.Material Material Design theme, UI Button objects have a z animation enabled (setup and activate) by default. To avoid this behavior in your UI Button objects, set this **android:stateListAnimator** attribute to a data value of **@null** in the XML markup, or "**null** in Java code.

Next let's look at what Android 5 added to a plethora of Android Drawable classes already in Android 4.x to be able to provide this greatly enhanced Material Design capability via animated vectors, bitmap graphics, tinting capabilities, color extraction, and new state animation graphics.

# Android Material Design Graphics Processing: Drawables

There are also some new Drawable API capabilities for Material Design that make it easier to use Android Drawable objects to help you implement sleek material design wins for your applications. New Android Drawable classes include a VectorDrawable, AnimatedVectorDrawable, RippleDrawable, Palette, and AnimatedStateListDrawable, all of which I'll discuss in this section.

These new Android 5 Drawable classes add Scalable Vector Graphics (SVG) path support, morphing, i3D ripple special effects, palette color extraction, and animated transitions for multistate Drawable objects to Android OS. Android 5 has added some very powerful classes, where 2D vector and bitmap graphics are concerned!

## Android 5 Drawable Tinting: *.setTint()* and *.setImageTintMode()*

With Android 5 and above, you can *tint* BitmapDrawable objects as well as NinePatchDrawable objects. You can tint the digital image objects in their entirety or limit this tinting effect to certain pixels. This is done by defining an alpha channel to "mask" the tinting effect.

You can tint these Drawable objects using Android Color class resources or using Android Theme attributes that reference these Color class resources. Usually, you would create these assets once, and then use them across your wearable applications, using the tint capability to tint them as needed to match your theme. As you might imagine, you can use this for optimization, as you would use far less graphic image assets across an entire application.

You can apply a tint to BitmapDrawable or NinePatchDrawable objects in the Java code for your wearable application using a **.setTint()** method. You can also set the tint color and the tint mode in the XML UI layout container definition. This is accomplished by using the **android:tint** and an **android:tintMode** parameters (attributes) inside your View object tags.

## Android 5 Vector Drawable Objects: The *VectorDrawable* Class

The new Android 5 VectorDrawable class and the object created using this class can be scaled up or down without losing any quality. This is because, unlike the bitmap image, a vector image is made up of code and mathematics (lines, curves, fills, and gradients) and not pixels. Therefore, if scaling occurs, the vector image will actually be rendered to fill the amount of pixels available to display it. A vector image is not being resampled like a pixel-based image is when it is scaled, but rather *rerendered* to fit the new screen resolution, whether it's a 320-by-240 smartwatch or 4096-by-2160 iTV.

For this reason, vector imagery can be used from wearables all the way up to 4K iTVs, with the same exact visual quality. This is not possible using bitmap images. Because vector imagery is text based, it will be at least one order of magnitude more data compact than bitmap imagery, because vectors are code (math and text), not an array of data-heavy pixel values.

As you might imagine, vector imagery would be perfect for single-color app icons. You only need one image asset for a vector image, as opposed to the bitmap image format, where you would need to provide an asset file for each screen density. To create a vector image, you would define SVG data for the shape inside of a <vector> XML parent tag. The XML markup to define an SVG vector image of a color filled square would look like the following:

```
<vector xmlns:android="http://schemas.android.com/apk/res/android"
        android:height="320dip"
        android:width="320dip"
        android:viewportWidth="160"
        android:viewportHeight="160" >
        <path android:fillColor="#AACCEE"
              android:pathData="M0,0 L0,100 100,100 100,0 Z" />
</vector>
```

SVG imagery Is encapsulated in Android 5 using VectorDrawable objects. For information about SVG Path command syntax, see the SVG Path reference on the W3C web site (http://www.w3.org/TR/SVG/paths.html). I also cover this in depth in the book *Beginning Java 8 Games Development* (Apress 2014), since Java 8 and JavaFX have extensive **SVG Path** support.

You can also simulate the popular multimedia software genre called *warping* and *morphing* by animating the SVG path property of VectorDrawable objects, thanks to another all new Android 5 class called AnimatedVectorDrawable.

Next let's take a closer look at all of the new Android 5 (automatic) color extraction capabilities, which are provided by the Android Palette class.

## Android 5 Automated Color Palette Extraction: The *Palette* Class

Android 5 added a new Palette class that facilitates a *colors extraction* algorithm, which allows developers to automatically extract prominent colors from a bitmap image asset in your application. The Android Support Library r21 and above includes the Palette class, which lets you extract prominent colors from an image in Android application versions previous to version 5, such as Android 3.x and Android 4.x applications. Palette will extract the following types of prominent colors from a bitmap image's color spectrum:

- Vibrant
- Vibrant dark
- Vibrant light
- Muted
- Muted dark
- Muted light

The Palette class is a helper class, which helps developers extract six different classifications of colors (listed above). To use this helper class, you would pass the bitmap object you want palettized to the Palette class's **.generate(Bitmap image)** method, using the following method call:

```
Palette.generate(Bitmap imageAssetName);
```

Be sure to do this in a background thread where you load the image assets. If you can't use a background thread, you can also call the Palette class's **.generateAsync()** method, providing a listener instead, like this:

```
public AsyncTask<Bitmap, Void, Palette> generateAsync (Bitmap bmp, Palette.
PaletteAsyncListener pal)
```

You can also retrieve the prominent colors from the image using the *getter* methods in the Palette class, like **.getVibrantColor()** or **.getMutedColor()**. A **.generate()** method will return a 16-color palette. If you need more than that, you can use another (overloaded) **.generate()** method with this format:

```
Palette.generate(Bitmap image, int numColorsInPalette);
```

I looked at the source code for this Palette class and there does not seem to be any maximum number of colors you can ask this class to provide (most palettes max out at 8-bit color, or 256 colors). This allows for some very interesting applications for this class, as it is not tied to 8-bit color. The more colors you ask for in a palette, the longer your processing time. This is why there's an **AsyncTask<>** version of the **.generate()** method call!

To use the Palette class in your wearables application's IntelliJ project, you will need to add the following Gradle dependency to your app's module:

```
dependencies { ... (default Gradle dependencies remain in here)
            compile 'com.android.support:palette-v7:21.0.+'  }
```

## Android 5 State Animation: An *AnimatedStateListDrawable* Class

Besides the new Android RippleDrawable class, which creates the effects discussed in the past couple sections, and VectorDrawable class, there's also an all new AnimatedStateListDrawable class that allows you to animate the transition between StateListDrawable objects.

The Android AnimatedStateListDrawable class lets you create an animated state list of drawable objects (hence the class name), which calls animations between state changes for the referenced View widget. Some of these system widgets in Android 5 will use these animations by default. The following example shows how to define an AnimatedStateListDrawable by using an XML resource:

```
<animated-selector xmlns:android="http://schemas.android.com/apk/res/android">
    <item android:id="@+id/pressed"
          android:drawable="@drawable/drawable_pressed"
          android:state_pressed="true" />
```

```
    <item android:id="@+id/focused"
        android:drawable="@drawable/drawable_focused"
        android:state_focused="true" />
    <item android:id="@id/default"
        android:drawable="@drawable/drawable_default" />
    <transition android:fromId="@+id/default"
            android:toId="@+id/pressed" >
        <animation-list>
            <item android:duration="85"
                android:drawable="@drawable/asset1" />
            <item android:duration="85"
                android:drawable="@drawable/asset2" />
        </animation-list>
    </transition>
    <transition android:fromId="@+id/pressed"
            android:toId="@+id/default" >
        <animation-list>
            <item android:duration="85"
                android:drawable="@drawable/asset2" />
            <item android:duration="85"
                android:drawable="@drawable/asset1" />
        </animation-list>
    </transition>
</animated-selector>
```

The top part of the **<animated-selector>** XML definition defines the states, using **<item>** tags specifying each state, and the bottom part defines your transitions, using (surprise) **<transition>** tags with **<animation-list>** tags nested inside them.

# What You Will Learn from This Book

This book will focus on those features of the Android 5 operating system and the IntelliJ IDEA, which are used to create Android wearable apps, using Android Studio and the Wear SDK. If you require foundational Android 5 apps development knowledge or want to learn how to create a wearable application for Neptune Pine (or another smartwatch that does not use Wear SDK), take a look at my book *Android Apps for Absolute Beginners* (3rd edition, 2014, Apress).

The first part of this book will create the foundation for the rest of the book, including this chapter covering wearable types, concepts, and the new Android 5 Material Design additions to the Android OS. Then you'll set up a development workstation, go over the wearables features of Android, and learn about the new IntelliJ IDEA. You'll also set up the emulators that will be used to test the wearable applications during the book.

The second part of the book will show you how to create wearable apps for smartwatches using the Wear SDK. You will learn about areas of Android technology that are important for wearables application developers to master, such as creating and delivering a wearable application, notifications, data layer, synchronization, and user interface layout design, using cards, and lists.

The third part of the book will explain how to create smartwatch faces using the Android Watch Faces API. You'll learn how to create a Watch Face Service, how to draw your Watch Faces to the screen, how to design Android Watch Faces, how to optimize your Watch Faces for best performance, how to display information (data) inside of your Watch Faces designs, and finally how to create Watch Faces app configuration screens for your Watch Faces.

## Summary

In this first chapter, you took a look at wearables' types and concepts, and learned about the many new features that Google added to Android 5 OS. You looked at Bluetooth LE, Material Design, new Drawable types, and advanced 3D such as OpenGL ES 3.1.

In the next chapter, you'll put together your development workstation and all of the open source software that you will be able to use to develop your advanced pro Android wearables application.

# Chapter 2

# Setting Up an Android 5 Wearables Application Development Workstation

Now that you have some foundational knowledge about wearables and what Android 5 has added to make the wearable applications memorable, this chapter will help you put together another type of foundation. Your development workstation is the most important combination of hardware and software for reaching your goal of Pro Android Wearables application development. Here I will spend some time upfront considering the hardware you'll need and the software infrastructure that you will need to put together a professional, well-rounded, Android software development workstation with a dozen arrows in your software development quiver right off the bat (strange analogy mix isn't it? Robin Hood and baseball). Then you will have everything you need for the rest of the book, no matter what type of wearable app you develop!

We'll also get all of those tedious tasks out of the way regarding putting together a 100% professional **Pro Android Wearables production workstation**.

Because readers of this book will generally want to be developing using an identical Android Wearables Applications Software Development Environment, I will outline all of the steps in this chapter to put together a completely **decked-out** Android Studio Development Workstation. You'll need to do this because everything you will be learning over the course of this book needs to be experienced equally by all of the readers of this book. You'll learn where to download and how to install some of the most impressive open source software packages on the face of this planet!

# Work Process for Creating an Android Workstation

The first thing that you'll do after taking a look at hardware requirements is download and install the entire Java **software development kit** (SDK), which Oracle calls **Java SE 7 JDK** (Java Development Kit). Android OS uses the Java Standard Edition (SE) Version 7 update 71, as of Android Studio 1.0. Android Studio 1.2, which I just upgraded to as I went over my second edit on this book, uses Java 7 update 79. When you read this, it may well use a later version than that! That is the nature of software development.

It's important to note that Java Version 8 also exists and was released in the second quarter of 2014. Java 8 includes powerful JavaFX APIs that turn Java programming language into a powerful new media engine. Java 7 support for JavaFX does exist outside of Android OS, and if you want to use JavaFX, there is a work process for getting a JavaFX new media application to work under Android 5. Thus the future of open source development (Android OS, XML, Java7, Java8, JavaFX, HTML5, CSS, JavaScript, and OpenGL) has arrived!

The second thing that you will download and install is **Android Studio**, which you'll get from Google's **developer.android.com** web site. Android Studio 1.0, which is actually a software bundle, consists of **IntelliJ IDEA** (Integrated Development Environment for Android) along with an Android Developer Tools **ADT 5 plug-in**. Prior to Android 4.4, the Eclipse IDE, Android SDK, and ADT Plug-Ins were all installed separately, which made the install difficult.

This ADT plug-in, which is now an integral part of Android Studio, **bridges** the **Android SDK**, which is also part of the Android Studio download, with version 14 of the IntelliJ IDEA. ADT plug-in makes this IntelliJ Java IDEA into the IntelliJ Android Studio IDEA. It is important to note that IntelliJ could still be used for straight Java SE 7 application development as well. IntelliJ also supports Java 8 and JavaFX.

After your Android Studio wearables application development environment is set up, you'll then download and install the **new media asset development** tools, which you will utilize in conjunction with (but outside of) Android Studio for things such as digital image editing (GIMP), digital video editing and special effects (EditShare Lightworks), digital audio mix-down, sweetening and editing (Audacity), and 3D modeling, rendering, and animation (Blender).

All of these software development tools, which you will be downloading and installing, will come close to matching all of the primary feature sets of expensive paid-for software packages such as those from Apple (Final Cut Pro), Autodesk (3D Studio Max), or Adobe (Photoshop, Premiere, or After Effects).

Open source software is free to download, install, and even upgrade, and is continually adding features and becoming more and more professional each and every day. You'll be completely amazed at how professional open source software packages have become over the past decade or two; if you have not experienced this already, you are about to experience this in a major way!

# Android Development Workstation: Hardware Foundation

Because you will be putting together in this chapter what will be the foundation of your Pro Android Wearables Application Development workstation used for the duration of the book, let's take a moment to review Android Studio 1.0 development workstation hardware requirements first, as that is the factor that will influence your development performance (speed). This is clearly as important as the software itself, since the hardware runs the software.

Minimum requirements for Android Studio include **2GB** of memory, **2GB** of hard disk space, and 720p **HD** (**1280 by 800**) display. Next let's discuss what you need to make the Android Studio Wearable Workstation usable, starting with upgrading that 1280-by-800 HD display to a **1920-by-1080** True HD display!

I recommend using at a bare minimum an **Intel i7 quad-core** processor, or an **AMD 64-bit octa-core** processor, with at least **8GB** of **DDR3 1600** memory. I'm using the octa-core **AMD 8350** with **16GB** of **DDR3 1866**. Intel also has a six-core i7 processor. This would be the equivalent of having 12 cores, as each i7 core can host two threads; similarly, the i7 quad-core should look like eight cores to a 64-bit operating system thread-scheduling algorithm.

There are also high-speed **DDR3 1866** and **DDR3 2133** clock-speed memory module components available as well. A high number signifies faster memory access speed. To calculate the **actual megahertz speed** that the memory is cycling at, divide the number by **4** (1333 = 333Mhz, 1600 = 400Mhz, 1866 = 466Mhz, 2133 = 533Mhz clock rate). Memory access speed is a major workstation **performance factor** because your processor is usually "bottlenecked" by the speed at which the processor cores can access the data (in memory) it needs to process.

With all this high-speed processing and memory access going on inside your workstation while it is operating, it is also important to keep everything cool so that you do not experience "thermal problems." I recommend using a wide **full-tower** enclosure, with **120mm** or **200mm** cooling fans (one or two at least), as well as a **captive liquid induction cooling fan** on the CPU. It's important to note that the cooler a system runs, the faster it can run and the longer it will last, so load the workstation with lots of silent fans!

If you really want the maximum performance, especially while emulating AVDs (Android virtual devices) for rapid prototyping or testing, which I will be covering in Chapter 5, install an **SSD** (solid-state disk) drive as the main disk drive, where your applications and operating software will load from. Use legacy **HDD** (hard disk drive) hardware for your **D:\** hard drive, for slower data storage.

As far as OS goes, I am using a **64-bit Windows 8.1** operating system, which is fairly memory efficient. Linux 64-bit OS is extremely memory efficient. I recommend using a 64-bit OS, so you can address more than 3GB of memory!

## Android Development Workstation: Software Foundation

To create a well-rounded Android Applications Development Workstation, you will be installing all of the primary genres of open source software that I'm going to be exposing you to later on in the book. First, you'll install JavaSE 7, Android Studio, and Gimp, Lightworks, Blender3D, and Audacity, which are also all open source software packages and programming languages (Android uses Java, XML, CSS, and HTML5). Thus, you'll be putting together a 100% open source workstation (unless you are using the Windows 8.1 OS, which is paid software). I also recommend other free software at the end of the chapter, so you can put together a mega-production workstation!

Because open source software has reached the level of professionalism of paid development software packages, and because I want all of you to be able to participate, I'll also use open source. Using open source software packages, such as Java, IntelliJ, Blender3D, GIMP, Audacity, Lightworks, and others, you can put together a free new media applications development workstation that rivals paid software workstations, which can cost several thousands of your country's units of currency (just to make this book international).

For those of you who have just purchased their new Pro Android Wearables development workstation PC and are going to put an entire development software suite together completely from scratch, I'll go through an entire work process, starting with Java 7, then adding Android Studio, and finally various media content development software packages from each major genre: digital imaging, digital video editing, 3D, and digital audio editing. If you have Macintosh, most of the open source software supports that platform as well as the popular Linux distributions and even Oracle's Open Solaris.

## Java 7: Installing the Foundation for Android Studio

The first thing you'll want to do is to visit the **Oracle** web site and download and install the latest **Java 7 JDK** environment, which, at the time of the writing of this book, was **Java SE 7u71**, as is shown in Figure 2-1.

*Figure 2-1. Oracle TechNetwork web site Java SE 7 download section; find the latest Java SE 7 JDK for your OS*

The URL is in the address bar of Figure 2-1, or you can simply Google **Java SE 7 JDK Download**. This will give you the latest link to the Java web page, which I will also put here, in case you wanted to simply cut and paste it:

`www.oracle.com/technetwork/java/javase/downloads/jdk7-downloads-1880260.html`

You will pull your scrollbar on the right side of the web page halfway down the page, to display the **Java SE Development Kit 7u71** (or later **version 7u79**) download links table, as can be seen on the very bottom of Figure 2-1. You can also read the explanation of the new CPU and PSU Java release versions located right above the download link table; for examples in this book I'll be using Java 7u71.

Once you click the **Accept License Agreement** radio button on the **top left** of this download links table, the links will become **bolded** and you will be able to click the link you wish to use. If you are on Windows and your OS is 64-bit, use the **Windows x64** link, otherwise use the **Windows x86** link. I am using what is described in these links as "Windows x64," which is the 64-bit versions of Windows, for my Windows 7 and Windows 8.1 workstations.

Make sure that you use this **Java SE Development Kit 7u71** downloading link, and do not use a **JRE** download (Java Runtime Edition) link. The JRE is part of the JDK 7u71, so you do not have to worry about getting the Java Runtime separately. In case you're wondering, you will indeed use the JRE to launch and run the IntelliJ IDE, and you will use the JDK inside of that software package to provide the Java core class foundation, which is used as the foundation for the Android OS Java-based API classes.

Make sure **not** to download a JDK 8u25 or the JDK 8u25 Bundle, which includes NetBeans 8.0 from the normal (current, latest Java) download page, because Android 5 uses Java 7u71 and the IntelliJ IDEA, **not** the NetBeans 8.0.1 IDE, for its ADT plug-ins, so be very careful regarding this particular initial Java 7 JDK foundational software installation step in your work process!

I actually use a different Windows 7 workstation for my JavaFX development which has Java SE 8u25 and NetBeans 8, and I have another HTML development workstation that has Java SE 8u25 and NetBeans 8.0 (only) installed on it.

Before you run this installation, you should remove your older versions of Java, using your Windows **Control Panel**, via the **Add or Remove Programs** (XP and older) or **Programs and Features** (Windows Vista, 7, and 8.1) utilities.

This will be necessary especially if your workstation is not brand new, so that your latest Java SE 7u71 and JRE 7u71 are the only Java versions that are currently installed on the Android Studio wearables workstation.

Once the installation executable has downloaded, open it and install this latest Java SE 7u71 JDK on your system by double-clicking the EXE file to launch a **Setup** dialog, as shown on the left-hand side of Figure 2-2. Click the **Next** button to access the **Custom Setup** dialog, shown in the middle of Figure 2-2. Click the Next button again to access the **Extracting Installer Progress** dialog, as shown on the right-hand side of Figure 2-2. Once you have extracted the installation software, you can select an installation folder.

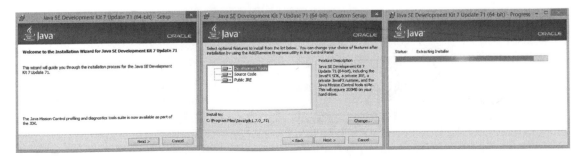

*Figure 2-2. Java SE 7 JDK extraction; click on Next button to proceed to extraction*

Use the default **C:\ProgramFiles\Java\jre7** in the Destination Folder dialog shown on the left-hand side of Figure 2-3, and then click the **Next** button. This will install the Java Runtime Edition (JRE) edition in that folder.

*Figure 2-3. Java 7 JDK install; click on Next button to install, then Close button*

Interestingly, the installer does not ask you to specify a JDK folder name for some reason, probably because it wants the Java JDK to always be a set or fixed (locked in the same location) name. This JDK folder will be named **C:\ProgramFiles\Java\jdk1.7.0_71**, and you will notice that internally Java 7 is actually referred to as being Java 1.7.0. Thus Java 6 would be 1.6.0, and Java 8 would be 1.8.0. This is useful to know, in case you are looking for Java versions using a search utility, for example, or just to show off!

Once you click the Next button, you'll get the **Java Setup Progress** dialog, shown in the middle of Figure 2-3. Once Java 7 is finished installing, you will finally see your **Complete** dialog, which can be seen on the right-hand side of Figure 2-3. Congratulations! You have successfully installed Java!

Remember that the reason you did not download the JRE is because It is part of this JDK installation. This Java Runtime Edition is the executable (platform) that runs your Java software once it has been compiled into an application, and thus the latest JRE will be needed to run IntelliJ, which as you now know is 100% completely written using the Java SE platform.

Once Java 7u71 (or later) JDK is installed on your workstation, you can then download and install the latest **Android Studio** software installer from the developer.android.com web site. This is getting more and more exciting with each layer of Pro Android Wearables development software you install!

You can also use that same **Programs and Features** or **Add or Remove Programs** utility in the Control Panel, which you might have recently used to remove older Java versions or even to confirm the success of a new Java install, to remove any older versions of any Android 4 development environments that might be currently installed on your Android development workstation.

Now you are ready to add the second layer of Android wearables applications development software (Android Studio 1.0 and IntelliJ) on top of Java 7.

# Android Studio 1.0: Download the Android 5 IDEA

The second step in this process is to visit the developer.android.com web site and
download and install an Android Studio software installer file from the /sdk/ folder of the
Android developer web site, at the following URL:

**https://developer.android.com/sdk/index.html**

From the Android Developer web site's home page, this page can be reached by clicking the
**Get the SDK** button found on the bottom left of the web site's home page. This will take you
to the SDK section of this web site, as can be seen on the right-hand side in Figure 2-4. You
can also get to the web page from an **Android Studio Overview** page, seen on the left-hand
side of Figure 2-4. The Android Studio Overview page is located at the following URL:

**http://developer.android.com/tools/studio/index.html**

Once you are on the **Android Studio SDK** page, click the **Download Android Studio** sage
green button on the lower left and download Android Studio for Windows, as shown in
Figure 2-4. This will take you to a downloading page.

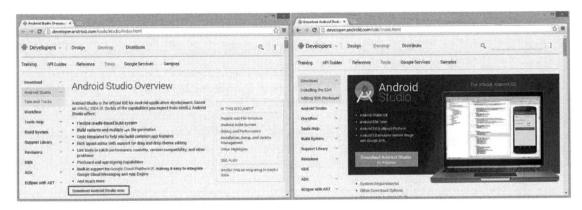

**Figure 2-4.** *Android Studio download link (left) and download page (right); click the green Download Android Studio button*

The actual Android Studio downloading page, seen in Figure 2-5, contains a section at the
top, outlining the **Android Software Development Kit License Agreement**. This agreement
is what is commonly termed an End-User Licensing Agreement (EULA), and it stipulates
what you can and cannot do with Android 5 Studio SDK, IDEA, Software, Tools, Codecs,
and APK (Application Package).

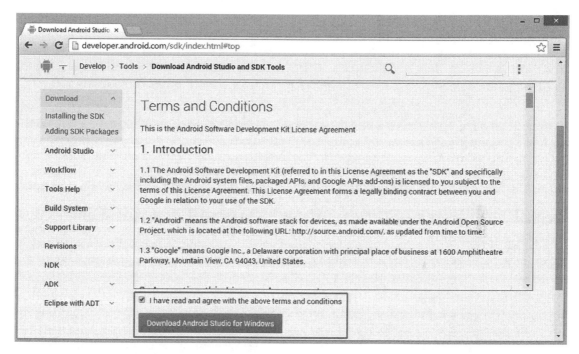

*Figure 2-5.  Select the "I have read and agree with the terms and conditions" check box and click the blue Download Android Studio for Windows button*

Review the **Terms and Conditions** section of this web page carefully, along with your legal department, if necessary, and then click the check box next to the statement at the bottom, which reads: **I have read and agree with the above terms and conditions**, as is shown highlighted in red in Figure 2-5.

Once this check box has been activated (checked), you should now be able to see a blue Download Android Studio for Windows button. The download site automatically detects your operating system, as well as the bit-level (32-bit or 64-bit) that your operating system supports. This should match the workstation, so if you have a 64-bit processor (CPU), you should also have a 64-bit OS.

If you downloaded the Java 7u71 JDK for Windows x64 or Linux x64, you would thus have the 64-bit version of Android Studio; conversely, if you selected Java 7u71 for a 32-bit x86 OS, you would have a 32-bit version of Android Studio.

Click the **Download Android Studio** blue button once it is activated and begin the download process. If you have a slow Internet connection (modem, or ISDN), this could take an hour or two. If you have a DSL or 4G connection, it will take about half an hour. If you have a fiber-optics connection, it should only take a minute or two.

Once this download is complete, you'll launch a software installer, which will set up the Android 5 SDK and integrated development environment (IDE) for use on your Pro Android Wearables Development Workstation. These files used to be installed using a ZIP file, so this is a big improvement! It is important to note that these file sizes change from time to time as well, so they may be different if an SDK has changed between the time of writing this book and when you do this.

Before this Android Studio "Bundle" became available in Version 4, setting up this Android IDE was a complicated and involved process, taking some 50 or more steps. These included installing Java SDK, then Android SDKs, then Android plug-ins, and then configuring the plug-ins to see an Android SDK. Setting up the Android 5 development environment is so much simpler now!

The new bundling approach accomplishes all of this Android SDK and plug-in configuration by including the IntelliJ IDE, along with all of the Android SDK and plug-in components, which allows all this configuration work to be done in advance by the people at Google, instead of by developers at home.

# Installing Android Studio: IntelliJ IDEA and Android SDK

The first thing you'll need to do once your download is complete is to find the file you just downloaded. It should be in your operating system's **Downloads** folder, or in my case, I specified my **Software** folder for this download, so I navigated to that folder to find and then launch it.

If you don't know where your browser put your file after it downloaded it, you can also right-click the downloaded file, located in the browser's download progress window, and select the **View in Folder** option. If a right-click does not work, there should be a down-arrow next to the file name that will give you a drop-down menu item list.

Download progress tabs are usually located on the bottom status bar area of each browser or can be accessed via a download menu option or an icon in the upper right of the browser (usually this is three black bar stripes indicating a menu list can be accessed via that icon).

In my case, this file was called **android-studio-bundle-135.1641136.exe** (I told you it was a software bundle), which I will use for my 64-bit Windows 8.1 workstation. Once you find the EXE file, **right-click** it and select the **Run As Administrator** option from the context sensitive menu. This will launch an Android Studio Setup dialog, as seen on the left side of Figure 2-6.

*Figure 2-6. Launch Android Studio installer (left), choose default components (middle), agree to licensing (right)*

Once you have the **Welcome to the Android Studio Setup** dialog, click the **Next** button, which will take you to the **Choose Components** dialog, shown in the middle of Figure 2-6. Accept the default component install selections, and then click the **Next** button. This will take you to a **License Agreement** dialog, seen on the right side of Figure 2-6. Click the **I Agree** button, which will take you to the **Configuration Settings** dialog, which is seen on the left side of Figure 2-7. Accept the default installation locations for Android Studio and Android SDK, and then click the **Next** button to proceed.

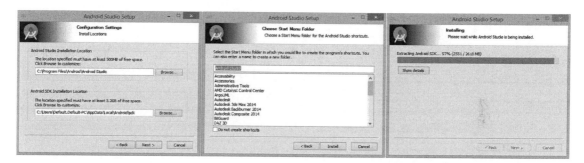

*Figure 2-7.  Accept default locale (left), accept Android Studio name, click Install (middle), Installing dialog (right)*

In the **Choose Start Menu Folder** dialog, shown in the middle of Figure 2-7, make sure the folder is named **Android Studio** and then click the **Install** button to begin the installation process. You will then see an **Installing** dialog, shown on the right in Figure 2-7, which will show you what components are being extracted and installed on your workstation. If you want to see more detail than the progress bar, click the **Show details** button in this dialog.

Once the extraction and installation processes have been completed, you'll see the **Completing the Android Studio Setup** dialog, shown on the left side of Figure 2-8. Leave the **Start Android Studio** option selected. Next, click the **Finish** button, which will then launch the Android Studio so that you can make sure the installation created a usable IDE. The startup screen and a Setup Wizard are shown in the middle and right portions of Figure 2-8. You can see that Android SDK was installed and is up to date, so you are done!

*Figure 2-8.  Select Start Android Studio check box (left), startup screen (middle), confirm install components (right)*

Click the **Finish** button, and then launch Android Studio, which is shown on the left side of Figure 2-9. At the bottom left of the dialog, you will see a **Check** for updates now link, and you should click this in order to make sure that your Android Studio IDEA is completely up to date, which it should be, as you just downloaded and installed it! As you can see at the top right of Figure 2-9, I clicked the link and got a **Checking for updates** progress bar, and then the **Update Info** dialog, seen at the bottom right of Figure 2-9, telling me that I have the latest version of Android Studio.

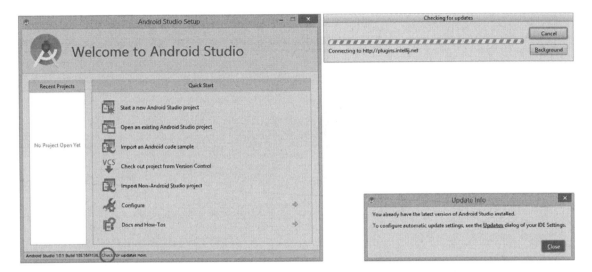

*Figure 2-9.  Check for updates (bottom left highlighted), progress bar (top right), Update Info dialog (bottom right)*

For the remainder of this chapter, you will download and install other tools that you will need.

# Professional Digital Imaging Software: GIMP 2.8.14

The GIMP is a **digital imaging** software package that's similar to Photoshop, which is currently at version 2.8.14. Version 3.0 is expected out in 2015.

GIMP has a number of important tools for the creation of the digital image assets you will need for your Pro Android Wearables application, including digital image manipulation, masking, alpha channel transparency, auto path creation, vector (SVG) path manipulation, layer compositing, and so forth.

To get to the GIMP web site, you would either enter GIMP into your Google search box or you can type in a URL for the web site to go directly to the GIMP home page. The URL for the nonprofit (.ORG) GIMP 2.8.14 web site takes the following format:

`www.gimp.org/`

When the GIMP 2 home page appears, as shown in Figure 2-10, you will see an orange **Download** button in the top middle of the page, as well as an orange **Downloads** link on the top right of the web site home page. You will click either one of these to access the GIMP 2.8.14 `www.gimp.org/downloads` page.

*Figure 2-10.* Go to the gimp.org *site, and click the orange Download button to get the latest version of GIMP*

You can download versions of GIMP compiled specifically for Windows Vista, XP, 7, and 8.1, Linux (generic), Mac OS/X, BSD, Solaris, Debian, Mandriva, Fedora, Open SUSE, and Ubuntu. GIMP supports 32-bit and 64-bit versions of each of these OSs. Simply click a download link for an OS and download the software onto your Pro Android Wearables apps development workstation.

Until recently, GIMP 2 was hosted on SourceForge, but the company made the decision to self-host on HTTP and Torrent servers, due to some activity regarding advertiser opt-ins that the creators of the GIMP didn't support. I used the standard HTTP link to start the 64-bit Windows 8.1 GIMP 2.8.14 download, and it works great. Next, let's take a look at the Lightworks 12 digital video editing and special effects open source software package.

Once your download is complete, launch your installer EXE, which should be named **gimp-2.8.14-setup-1.exe**, unless a later version has become available (version 2.10 is expected out in Q1 2015, and version 3.0, later in 2015). You can right-click an installer and **Run as Administrator** to launch it.

# Professional Digital Video Editing: Lightworks 12

EditShare Lightworks used to be a (expensive) paid digital video editing and special effects software, and to this day, it competes head-to-head with leading digital video editing packages (FinalCut Pro X and After Effects).

You can find out more about this leading digital video editing FX software package on the EditShare web site at www.editshare.com or the Lightworks web site at www.lwks.com, where you can also sign up to get a copy of the software, and once you do that, you can download it for your own free use.

When EditShare made Lightworks open source, it became the third, free open source software (the first was GIMP, the second was Blender3D) to be able to compete feature-for-feature with the paid software package in its new media production genre (digital video editing, compositing, special effect applications, and compression). In fact, EditShare won an NAB "Best of Show" award for its speed of processing and innovative user interface approach.

Lightworks was one of the first software packages to rewrite their code to run on the GPU (graphic card, like an nVidia GeForce or AMD ATI Radeon). A GPU will process effects and encoding at an order of magnitude faster rate than a CPU will, and many other software packages, including GIMP, are now moving to implement GPU-based processing in their code as well.

Once you register on this Lightworks web site, you will be able to create a video editor profile for your company and log in to be able to download a copy of Lightworks 12.1 for the content development workstation you are putting together in this chapter. Because EditShare Lightworks is such a valued piece of software, you'll need to register to get it, which I didn't object to, given that this software previously had a four-figure price tag.

Once you are signed up as a proud Lightworks 12 user, you can click the **Downloads** button located at the top right of the site menu, and you'll see tabs for the three different OS versions—Mac, Linux, and Windows—and tabs for tools and documentation for the software.

Click the red Download button that matches the bit level of your OS, or the blue Download button if you want the latest beta version that is in development. After you download it, install it using the default settings, create a quick launch icon for it, and launch it to make sure it's working properly with your workstation, as you have done with your other software.

This Downloads page for EditShare Lightworks version 12, released in Q4 of 2014, can be seen in Figure 2-11. Click the tab that represents your OS and then download the 75MB software installer. I downloaded the Lightworks 64-bit version 12.0.2 for Windows 8.1.

*Figure 2-11. Go to the lwks.com web site, register, and click an OS tab and Download button matching your system*

Now that you have 2D image and video editing software packages in place, you probably should also get 3D and digital audio editing software packages!

# Professional 3D Modeling and Animation: Blender

Next let's get one of the most popular open source software packages in the world, the **Blender**3D Modeling, Rendering, and Animation software package, which can be found on the Blender web site at the following URL:

www.blender.org/

Blender has an extremely active development community and has updates that come out on a monthly basis or even more frequently than that sometimes. I would imagine that there will be a later version of the software available by the time you get to this in this book, however, everything in this section should still apply. There are also 3D movies that are made with Blender, just in case you wanted to master the software and then become a major filmmaker!

As you can see in Figure 2-12, there is also a **Download Blender 2.72b** blue button on the Blender.org home page, which will also take you to a Blender download page, where you can select a 32-bit or 64-bit version of Blender for Windows. Blender is also available for Linux, Mac, Unix, and Solaris.

*Figure 2-12. Go to the blender.org web site, and click the blue Download button from the cloud icon*

This site will **auto-detect** the OS version you are currently running, and since I am running Windows 8, you will see in Figure 2-13 that Blender for Windows tab is selected showing a blue primary software download area.

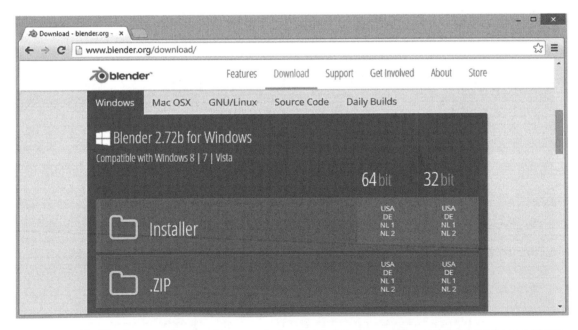

*Figure 2-13. The blender.org/download/ page; select an OS tab at the top, and click an Installer link for your OS type*

As you can see there are a number of different download servers around the world that host this incredibly popular software package, so if you are in the Netherlands (NL) or Germany, you can click those links to download the software faster (or at least closer to you).

Because I have new media content production workstations running Windows XP (32-bit), Windows Vista (32-bit), Windows 7 (64-bit), and recently Windows 8.1 (64-bit), I have downloaded both of these versions of Blender, as you can see if you look back at the screenshot shown in Figure 2-13. Click the version (the OS bit-level) that matches your OS configuration (32-bit or 64-bit) and then download the appropriate version of Blender.

Once your download is completed, launch the installer EXE, which should be named **blender-2.72-windows32.exe** or **blender-2.72-windows64.exe**, unless the later revision has become available (version 2.8 is expected out in 2015). Once your installation is complete, right-click the icon or executable file and select the **Pin to Taskbar** option to create a Quick Launch Icon.

# Professional Digital Audio Editing: Audacity 2.0.6

The **Audacity** project is hosted on sourceforge.net, an open source software development web site, which you might find extremely interesting to search for software that interests you, if you didn't already know about this site! To reach the Audacity project, go to the audacity.sourceforge.net URL and you will see a **Download Audacity 2.0.6** link, as shown in Figure 2-14.

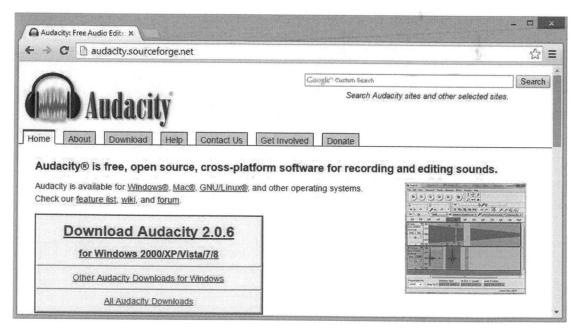

*Figure 2-14. Go to the audacity.sourceforge.net page on the SourceForge web site and click Download Audacity*

Notice that the 32-bit Audacity supports decades-ancient operating systems such as Windows 2000, well over a decade old, and Windows XP, now almost a decade old. I am hoping that you are using either a Windows 7 or a Windows 8.1 operating system for your Android Wearables development workstation as Windows 8.1 is getting to be almost as memory efficient now as Linux is!

Once an Audacity installer file has been downloaded, you can launch it and proceed to install this feature-filled digital audio editing software. The first thing that it asks you is what language you want to run the software in, I selected the default, **English**. Then I clicked a **Next** button and read the information. Then I clicked the Next button again, accepting a default installation location, and created the desktop icon. Finally, I clicked the **Install** button and got the **Installing** progress bar dialog, as well as more information regarding the Audacity project, and a final dialog where I could click the **Finish** button to exit the installer software.

If you like, you can follow the same work process that I did with Blender and place a quick launch short-cut icon on your taskbar by right-clicking the Audacity 2.0 icon and selecting **Pin to Taskbar**. You can reposition launch icons by dragging them into any position you prefer on the taskbar.

Now that Audacity is installed, you can launch the audio editing software and make sure it is working on your system. Launch Audacity via your quick launch icon or by double-clicking the icon on the desktop. You should see a new blank project, as shown in Figure 2-15, opened up on the desktop. You will be using Audacity later in this book to add sound effects to your Android UI element objects, such as your buttons and ImageButton objects.

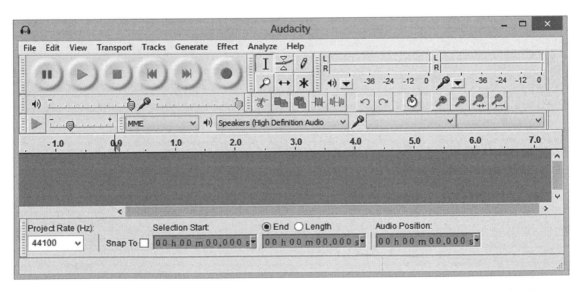

*Figure 2-15.* *Launch Audacity to make sure that it's running properly on your wearables development workstation*

Next let's download the leading, open source, user interface design prototyping software package, Pencil 2.0.5. This is available for Windows, Linux, and Macintosh and supports both Android and HTML5 user interfaces in the form of what are termed "stencil" packages, which are offered for Android 4, iOS, Dojo JS, Ext JS Neptune, and probably at some point in the future, Android 5. If you like to diagram UI designs, you'll love Pencil!

# Professional UI Design Wireframing: Pencil Project 2.0.5

Next, you will download and install a user interface (UI) **wireframing** or **prototyping** tool called **Pencil**, which is currently at revision 2.0.5. Do a Google search for Pencil or go directly to the following URL, which can be seen at the top of Figure 2-16:

```
http://pencil.evolus.vn
```

*Figure 2-16.* Go to the pencil.evolus.vn web site and click the orange Download button to download Pencil 2.0.5

When the Pencil Project home page appears, click the orange **Download** button and download the 22MB software installer executable file. This should be named something like **Pencil-2.0.5.win32.installer.exe**. Pencil only uses a 32-bit binary, as the software does not need the capabilities offered by 64-bit.

Once the download is complete, launch the installer and when it's finished, right-click your desktop icon or Start Menu icon (or even on an executable file) and select the **Pin to Taskbar** option to create the **Quick Launch Icon** shortcut for the software. My Windows 8.1 taskbar is shown in Figure 2-17; notice I have added **font**, **calculator**, **text**, and **file management** utilities.

*Figure 2-17.* Showing the Quick Launch taskbar, with key OS utilities, new media software, and the Android Studio

Now, just to be thorough, let's install a full business production software suite, just in case you need to put together quotes, spreadsheets, and even contracts for a future Android wearables software development project!

# Professional Business Software Suite: OpenOffice 4

To make 100% sure your Android development workstation has everything installed you will need for your Pro Android Wearables Applications Development business, let's finish off this impressive run of professional software installation with yet another package, called OpenOffice 4, which was originally from Sun Microsystems, the makers of Java, and was acquired by Oracle and then handed over to Apache, after it was made open source.

Do a Google search for Apache Open Office, or go to the www.openoffice.org web site, and then click the **I want to download OpenOffice 4** link or go to the Open Office 4.1.1 downloads page, which is located at the following URL, if you want to type the URL into your browser directly:

`https://www.openoffice.org/download/index.html`

As you can see in Figure 2-18, the web site can detect the OS and bit level that you are using, as well as the language you are speaking (using)!

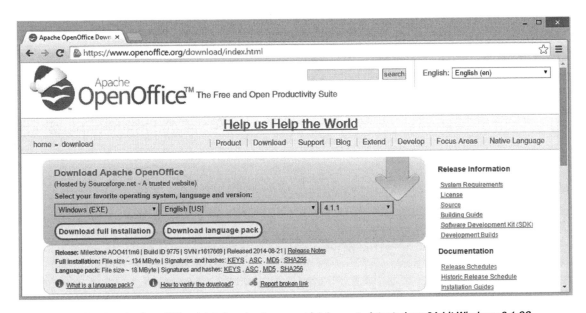

*Figure 2-18. The Apache OpenOffice 4.1.1 download page, which has autodetected my 64-bit Windows 8.1 OS*

Once you are on the /download/ page, shown in Figure 2-18, click the green arrow to download the most recent version of the office suite for your OS, which in my case was Windows 8.1 (which the site autodetected for me). This download is almost 135MB and includes more than half a dozen productivity software packages, including a word processor, a spreadsheet, and a database.

Once the download has completed, launch your installer EXE, and when it is finished, right-click the icon or executable file and select the **Pin to Taskbar** option to create the **Quick Launch Icon** shortcut for the software.

Next, I will tell you about some of the other open source and affordable 3D software packages that I use to create new media content for my clientele.

# Other Open Source and Affordable Media Software

There are lots of other open source software packages, which are available if you want them, including **SketchUp** (architectural rendering), **TerraGen3** (virtual world creation), **TrueSpace** (3D), **Wings** 3D, **Bishop** 3D, **POV Ray** 3.7 (3D Rendering), **Rosegarden** (Music Composition, MIDI and Scoring), **Qtractor** (Sound Design and MIDI), **DAZ Studio** 4.6 (Character Modeling), and this list of amazing open source software just goes on and on!

There are also some very affordable 3D software packages you should take a look at as well, including NeverCenter **SILO** 2.3 (Quad 3D Modeling), **Moment of Inspiration** 3 (NURBs 3D Modeling), **Vue 3D** (3D world generation), **Hexagon** 2.5 (Polygon 3D Modeling), Auto-Des-Sys **Bonzai** (3D Modeling), and NewTek **Lightwave** 3D (3D Modeling, 3D Animation, and 3D Special Effects).

I install each of these professional open source software packages on each of my new media content production workstations. This allows you to create fully loaded 3D production workstations for all of your producers, and the only cost is the hardware, which you can get at Walmart for $300 to $600.

Congratulations! You have now assembled a professional-grade, Android Wearable Applications and New Media Content Development Workstation you can now utilize to create Pro Android Wearable apps and develop user interface designs and user experiences hither before unseen by the world!

Next, let's take a quick overview of some of the things that you are going to learn about over the course of the book, now that you have learned about wearables, Android 5 Material Design, and set up the Pro Android Wearables development workstation you're going to use to develop wearable apps.

# Summary

In this chapter, you completely set up your comprehensive Pro Android Wearables Android Studio application development workstation, learning the hardware requirements (and what you should really have) and all about open source software, which over the past decade or two has ultimately become as professional as paid software packages that could have easily cost thousands!

You downloaded and installed Java SE 7, to Android Studio, to new media content production software, to (optional) User Interface Design prototyping, to business productivity tools, and you downloaded and then installed the most impressive open source software packages that can be found on the planet.

You did this to create the foundation for your Pro Android Wearables and Appliances application development work process, which you will undertake during this book. Rather than install these software packages as you went along, I decided to have you set up all this software first. I did this in case you wanted to explore some of the many features of these powerful, exciting new media content production software packages before you actually have to use them during the book. I think that's only fair.

The best thing about the process was that you accomplished it by using open source, 100% free for commercial usage, and professional-level application software packages, which is pretty darned amazing if you think about it.

You started by downloading and installing Oracle's **Java SE 7u72 JDK** or **Java Development Kit**, which is the Java 7 programming language's SDK. This Java JDK is required to use Eclipse, as well as to develop application software for the Android operating system platform for consumer electronic devices.

You then visited the **Android Developer** web site and downloaded and installed the **Android Studio Bundle**, which built the **IntelliJ IDEA** complete with all of the **Android Developer Tool** plug-ins on top of your Java SE 7 programming software development environment.

Next you downloaded and installed **GIMP 2.8.14**, the powerful digital image editing package that is available for Windows, Linux, and Macintosh OSs.

Then you downloaded and installed **Lightworks 12**, a digital video editing and special effects package, which was recently released as open source and is currently available for all of the popular OSs.

You then downloaded and installed **Blender 2.72**, a professional 3D modeling, rendering, and animation tool available for Windows, Linux, and Mac OSs.

Next you downloaded and installed **Audacity 2.0.6**, an open source digital audio editing tool available for the Windows, Linux, and Mac OSs.

Then you downloaded and installed **Pencil 2.0.5**, the popular UI wireframing and prototyping tool that is available for Windows, Linux, and Mac OSs.

Finally, you installed Apache **Open Office 4.1.1**, just to make sure that you have a completely well-rounded open source workstation at your disposal.

In the next chapter, you will learn all about the new features in Android 5 so that you have a firm foundation on what Android 5 OS offers for your custom wearables application development.

# Chapter 3

# A Foundation for Android Wearables: New Wearable Features in Android 5

Now that you have an Android Development Workstation assembled, with those valuable (but free), professional-level, open source packages installed on it, it is time to take a look at all of the new things that Android 5 adds for wearable development. I discussed the Material Design additions thoroughly in Chapter 1 along with wearable types and concepts, so this chapter will be covering more technical and "under-the-hood" additions, such as new media hardware and codec support, new technologies such as the latest **Bluetooth**, **OpenGL**, **WebKit**, **WebAudio**, and **WebRTC** platforms, and other things you will want to be advised of and up to speed on so that your Android wearables applications feature everything that users need them to.

I will of course attempt to utilize as many of these Android 5 features as I can during this book to add a plethora of features to your wearables application. That said, I only have a few hundred pages here to accomplish this, and Android OS has thousands of classes, methods, and constants, so I am going to focus on the Android 5 features, and how these will apply to wearables applications. I'm approaching it this way primarily because this is a book about Pro Android wearables, and as such, I am assuming that you're already up to speed on Android 4, as well as previous Android OS versions. This chapter will take a look at Android 5 power management, network connectivity, video, audio, and 3D new media, web media rendering, ultra high definition camera support, data storage, LockScreen notification and notification metadata, screen sharing, screen capturing, and the Android Extension Pack.

# Android's Project Volta: Power Management Tools

One of the most critical areas for wearables applications currently is the area of **power management**. Many smartwatch models are still struggling with the issue of **battery life**. Smartwatch manufacturers are trying to make the products last for weeks or months without charging; however, better battery technology, or maybe a simple smartwatch stand that charges your battery when the smartwatch is on it, during the night, while users are sleep, is likely to result in a better solution in the end. Regardless, Android 5 addresses the power issue in its **Project Volta**, a focus on making Android more power efficient by using task scheduler (power management) and task minimization (power optimization) APIs.

# Android 5 Process Scheduler: JobScheduler and JobInfo

Android 5 adds a new **android.app.job** package, which contains **JobScheduler**, a class (object) that lets you optimize wearables' battery life by defining **jobs** (task processing) for the Android operating system to run asynchronously. **Asynchronous processing** allows tasks to be processed "out of sync" (out of order), possibly at a later time, so that the operating system can optimize memory and CPU usage at a lower level. Because you as a wearable application developer do not know which apps, and in what order, the user will be running, you will not be able to implement this level of optimization as a wearable apps developer, and this job API allows Android to do it for you.

These jobs (tasks) can also be scheduled for processing under more optimal conditions, such as when the Android device is charging and has access to unlimited power or under other types of conditions that can be specified by the wearable applications developer, such as when video is streaming.

This JobScheduler class is used to guarantee an Android wearable device's power optimization in wearables development scenarios where the wearable app has non-user-facing tasks (background processing) that you can defer or where the application has tasks that a developer prefers to have processed when the wearable device (and host) is plugged into a power source (charging).

Developers can also schedule task processing based on the availability of external resources, for example, telecommunication (4G LTE) network access, a Bluetooth host device, or the availability of a local Wi-Fi connection.

You can also use this JobScheduler class for batch processing. This allows developers to group scheduled tasks together, so that they can be run in a "batch." Batch processing became popular back in the days of mainframe and minicomputers, which is currently called enterprise computing and servers!

Batch processing is where a computer processes tasks all at the same time. This is usually done on a regular schedule, such as hourly, daily, weekly, or monthly. Back in the early days of mainframe computing, batch processes were scheduled at night, when the IT department was resting and all of the computer power could be focused on that processing. Note that you can also schedule time-based tasks one at a time as well, so the JobScheduler class can also be used to perform routine or time-based task processing as well.

The JobScheduler object runs inside of the **JobService** object (class), which is an Android service subclass, which manages all of your jobs that need to be scheduled. Each "unit of work" to be processed by a JobScheduler object is defined using a **JobInfo** (class) object. Android OS will also generate a JobParameters object. This contains job identification, configuration, and parameters. These are generated by Android OS based on all scheduled jobs.

The JobInfo object is used to specify how a developer wants the scheduling criteria to be handled by the Android OS. This object is created using the **JobInfo.Builder** class, which allows developers to use Java Builder syntax and to easily configure how the scheduled task should run.

You can schedule your JobInfo task objects to run under precise (exacting) or specific conditions. These include starting the task when the device is charging or only processing that task when the device is charging, running or starting the task when the device is connected to an unmetered network, starting the task processing whenever the device is idle (not being actively used), or processing the task before a certain deadline occurs or with a minimum delay before the processing of the task is started.

For example, the following Builder Java code structure will, in this order, create a JobInfo object that will persist across device reboots, require that the device be on the charger, run the task periodically, delay the running of the task by a certain latency factor, and require the device to be connected to an unmetered network (such as home Wi-Fi or DSL [digital subscriber line] service).

```
JobInfo uploadTask = new JobInfo.Builder( mJobId, mJobServiceComponent )
                        .setPersisted( true )
                        .setRequiresCharging( true )
                        .setPeriodic( intervalUsingLongDataValueInMilliseconds )
                        .setMinimumLatency( minimumLatencyUseLongData
                        ValueMilliseconds )
                        .setRequiredNetworkCapabilities( JobInfo.NetworkType.
                        UNMETERED )
                        .build();

JobScheduler jobScheduler = (JobScheduler) context.getSystemService(Context.JOB_SCHEDULER_
SERVICE);
jobScheduler.schedule(uploadTask);
```

It is important to note that if the device has "stable" power—that is, it has been plugged in (for more than two minutes) and the battery life is at a healthy level—the system will run any scheduled job that is ready to run if that JobInfo object's task processing deadline has not expired.

## Android 5 Battery Optimizer: The BatteryHistorian Tool

There is also a new **adb shell dumpsys batterystats** command that generates statistical data regarding the battery usage on your Android devices. These data are organized using a **unique user ID** (UID). The statistics, which will be collected whenever the command is invoked, include a history of battery-related events and global power-related statistics for that Android hardware device, an approximation of power usage per UID, and for system components, per-application mobile milliseconds per data packet, UID system aggregated statistics, and UID application aggregated statistics.

If you would like to learn more about the various command-line options for tailoring the output of the utility, you would want to use a switch called **--help** (command-line utilities use switches, or options, prefaced by a pair of minus signs or dashes). I would use the following command-line format:

```
$ adb shell dumpsys batterystats --help
```

For example, if you wanted to print out the battery usage statistics for a given application's package since the Android device was last charged, you would run this command-line format to accomplish that:

```
$ adb shell dumpsys batterystats --charged <your-package-name-here>
```

You can use the Google **Battery Historian** tool on the output of the dumpsys batterystats commands. This will generate an HTML5-based visualization for your power-related events from the command logs. This information makes it easier for you to understand, and diagnose, your battery-related wearables' application programming issues. You can download a copy of Google's Battery Historian tool on GitHub if you like, at the following URL:

**https://github.com/google/battery-historian**

Next, I'll explain the different types of networks Android 5 can connect with. This is obviously very important for wearables applications.

# Android's Network Connection: NFC and Bluetooth

Another critical support area for Android wearables hardware devices currently is the area of **multiple data networks support**. Wearables that support more telecommunications networks are going to be connected to the world better and thus feature more useful wearable applications. When your wearable Android devices can find and tap into a variety of different data networks, such as 4G LTE, Wi-Fi, Bluetooth, and NFC (near field communication), your wearable applications become more valuable to both businesses and consumers alike.

## Android 5 Multiple Network Support: ConnectivityManager

Android 5 provides an all new **multinetworking API** that will allow your wearable application to dynamically scan for available networks with specific capabilities. Once the API finds a network, you will be able to establish a connection to it to provide data for your wearable application's features.

The functionality provided by the Android **ConnectivityManager** class can be quite useful when the wearable application requires a specialized network. Networks that are currently supported by Android can be found inside a constant list in the ConnectivityManager class, which includes **TYPE_BLUETOOTH** (Bluetooth data connection), **TYPE_DUMMY** (Dummy connections), **TYPE_ETHERNET** (an Ethernet connection), **TYPE_MOBILE** (Mobile connection), **TYPE_MOBILE_DUN** (DUN Mobile connect), **TYPE_MOBILE_HIPRI** (High Priority Mobile connection), **TYPE_MOBILE_MMS** (MMS Mobile data), **TYPE_MOBILE_ SUPL** (a SUPL Mobile data), **TYPE_VPN** (a Virtual Private Network), **TYPE_WIFI** (WIFI connection), and the **TYPE_WIMAX** (a WiMAX data connection). This class can also be useful if you wanted to transfer your data with a particular type of transport protocol.

To select and connect to a data network dynamically from your app, you will first need to create a ConnectivityManager object. Next, you'll use a builder class called **NetworkRequest.Builder** to create the **NetworkRequest** object and then specify the network features and transport type that the wearable app is interested in connecting with (network type) and utilizing (the protocol).

To scan for various supported data networks, you can use **.requestNetwork()** and then you can pass the NetworkRequest object into the method call along with a **ConnectivityManager.NetworkCallback** object. This should be done via the following .requestNetwork() method call to the Java programming structure:

```
.requestNetwork( NetworkRequest, ConnectivityManager.NetworkCallback )
```

You can also set up Android to notify your application of detected network availability by using a **.registerNetworkCallback()** method call to set up a listener in your Java code for networks as they come into range. This should be done using the .registerNetworkCallback() method call with the following Java programming structure:

```
.registerNetworkCallback( NetworkRequest, ConnectivityManager.NetworkCallback )
```

You would use the requestNetwork() method if you wanted to actively switch to a suitable network, once it has been detected. If you wanted to receive only notifications for scanned networks without actively switching over to them, then you would want to use a .registerNetworkCallback() method call.

When the Android operating system detects a suitable network, it will then connect to the network and invoke an **.onAvailable()** callback method call.

You can poll this network object that is returned from the NetworkCallback object if you want to ascertain additional information about the available network(s). After you do this, you can then direct your applications to use one of these selected networks to perform your data transfer operations.

## Android 5 Low Energy Bluetooth: The Bluetooth LE API

You probably remember that in 2014 Android 4.3 introduced platform support for **Bluetooth Low Energy** (a Bluetooth LE API), to support the Wear SDK. In Android 5, your user's Android hardware device can act as a Bluetooth LE peripheral device as well, allowing it to "socialize" with other Bluetooth devices. In essence, this turns the Android hardware into a Bluetooth hub!

Android 5 wearables applications could use this capability to make their presence known to any Bluetooth-capable consumer electronic device nearby. Using this new capability, you can build wearables apps that allow a device to function as a pedometer or heart monitor, if the wearable hardware can support these features, and then communicate the resulting health care data with another Bluetooth LE device that happens to be nearby.

This new Bluetooth LE API is contained in an Android package that is named **android. bluetooth.le**, as you may have already guessed. This new API enables your wearables applications to do things like broadcasting advertisements, scan for a response, and form connections with other Bluetooth LE devices.

If you want to use these new advertising or scanning features, you need to add the **BLUETOOTH_ADMIN** permission into the AndroidManifest.xml file. When your end users download (or update) your wearable app from the Google Play Store, they will be asked to grant this "**Bluetooth connection information**: *Allows the app to control Bluetooth, including broadcasting to, or getting information about, nearby Bluetooth devices*" permission for your wearables application. This gets the permission from the user before the application is used to connect to (going in either direction) other Bluetooth devices.

To begin Bluetooth LE advertising so any Bluetooth-capable devices will be able to detect the wearable application, call a **.startAdvertising()** method and then pass it an implementation of the Android **AdvertiseCallback** class.

This AdvertisingCallback object will receive the report regarding success, or failure, of Bluetooth LE advertising operations. Android 5 also added a **ScanFilter** class so that wearables can scan for only the specific types of devices they are interested in connecting to. To begin a Bluetooth LE device scan, you would call a **.startScan()** method, passing in your list of ScanFilter objects. You must also provide a reference to your **ScanCallback** object. The ScanCallback object will report back to a wearable application whenever any specified Bluetooth (device) advertisement has been detected.

# Android 5 NFC Improvements: Near Field Communication

Android 5 has also added enhancements to their NFC technology implementation. These additions will enable a wider range as well as a more flexible application of this powerful NFC technology.

The **Android Beam** technology, which was added in Android 4 but never really had a solid user experience design applied to it because the technology was difficult to initiate relative to the two different Android users, has been added to the Android Share Icons area for the Android 5 OS.

Your wearable application can invoke this Android Beam application on your user's Android hardware whenever you want a user to share data. This would be accomplished by calling the **.invokeBeam()** method.

Setting things up using this method call circumvents the need for the user to manually tap their device against other NFC-capable devices in order to complete a data transfer, making this technology easier to use from a user-experience standpoint.

To transfer data over an NFC connection, you'll need to create and utilize an **NDEF** (NFC Data Exchange Format) Record, which uses a light-weight binary format. This NDEF format was specified by the NFC Forum and can be used to encapsulate typed data for transmission and storage using an NFC connection. It is interesting to note that NDEF is transport agnostic.

This NDEF is used to define messages and data records. Your **NDEF Record** will contain typed data, such as a URL or URI (uniform resource identifier), MIME-typed media, a text message, or a custom application data transfer "payload." An **NDEF Message** is a container for one or more of the NDEF Record structures. This might take a little getting used to, as normally, a data record would contain a message, not the other way around. I would have called it a NDEF Packet, but as long as you know that NDEF Messages are collections of NDEF Records, then you are good to go if you want to develop apps that use NFC!

For instance, if you wanted to create an NFC messaging application, you can use the new **.createTextRecord()** method to create an NDEF Record containing UTF-8 text data. This Android NdefRecord class also has a **.createUri()** and a **.createMime()** method for creating URI and MIME data record types, respectively.

If you are developing a credit payment application, you now have the ability to **register** your NFC **Application ID (AID) dynamically**. This can be accomplished by calling a **registerAidsForService()** method. You can also use a **setPreferredService()** method call to set a preferred card emulation service. This method would always be called when a specific activity is in the foreground (in use by an end user). Next, let's look at Android Media!

# Android 5 Media: Adding Wow-Factor to Wearables

Unless your wearable applications are all purely functional, a lot of your wearable applications' success in the marketplace will be based on how you implement media elements to achieve a level of wow-factor. This will allow you to have buyers choose your application over other (competing) wearable applications. This section will look at all of the new media assets, such as digital video, digital audio, and 3D, as well as other areas, such as web browser support (WebKit), WebAudio, WebGL, WebRTC, MediaBrowser, and the new ultra high definition (UHD) savvy Camera 2 API.

## Digital Video Playback: MediaController and MediaSession

Android 5 adds an entirely new package for media control that is called **android.media. session**. The package contains the all new **MediaController** and **MediaSession** classes, as well as nested classes for these two classes, and the **MediaSessionManager** and **PlaybackState** classes, which also have nested classes.

Use the new notification and media APIs to ensure that the system UI knows about your media playback and can extract and show album art. Controlling media playback using a UI Design with a MediaSessionManager Service is now a seamless developer experience thanks to the MediaSession, PlaybackState, and MediaController classes, along with their nine utility nested classes.

You would use a **Context.getSystemService(Context.MEDIA_SESSION_SERVICE)** call in order to obtain an instance of the MediaSessionManager object (class) and call the .getSystemService(Context.MEDIA_SESSION_SERVICE) method off of your **Context** object. This conveniently gives a MediaSessionManager Service class the context (object) showing what the wearable application is doing.

The MediaSession class replaces the now deprecated **RemoteControlClient** class and provides a unified set of callback methods. These handle the transport controls as well as the media buttons. If your wearable app provides media playback, you'll need to use the MediaSession class (object) to handle the transport controls using these callback methods. It's important to note an app coded in this fashion can run on both Android TV and Android Wear SDK.

You can even create your own MediaController wearable application with the MediaController class. This class provides a "thread-safe" approach so you can monitor and control your media asset playback from inside the wearable application's UI process (primary UI thread). To create a media controller, you specify a MediaSession.Token object. Once this has been done, your app can interact with the MediaSession object. You will call the **.play()**, **.stop()**, **.skipToNext()**, or **.setRating()** method to control the media asset playback.

This is done by using the **MediaController.TransportControls** object (nested class), which, as you may notice from the class name, provides a UI Transport Control object to use with your MediaController object, which is a part of your MediaSession object.

Another MediaController nested class, **MediaController.Callback**, will allow you to register a MediaController.Callback object. This will listen for an asset's **metadata** and will report any **state changes** for the MediaSession to the wearable application in real time so your code can respond to it.

You can create **multimedia notifications**, which allow your playback controls to be tied to a media session using the new **Notification.MediaStyle** class. This class is a part of the **android.app** package and is subclassed from the Notification.Style class, and it allows you to mix your media with multimedia designs, for instance, showing your album cover along with a transport UI.

# Digital Audio Playback: Enhanced AudioTrack Precision

The Android 5 **AudioTrack** class is also in the android.media package, and it manages and plays a single audio resource for Java applications. It allows developers to stream (dynamic) or play (static) PCM (pulse-code modulation) audio buffers directly from the system memory to the audio hardware for a low-latency user experience.

This is achieved by loading data to the AudioTrack object in the system memory by using one of the three .write() method call parameter list structures:

```
.write( byte[],  int, int )
.write( short[], int, int )
.write( float[], int, int, int )
```

In stream (dynamic) mode, a wearable application writes a continuous stream of data into an AudioTrack object using one of the three .write() methods. A dynamic stream mode is useful when playing blocks of audio data that are too data heavy to be able to fit in memory at one time, either because the duration of the audio is too long or because of the digital audio asset data compression characteristics (high-frequency sampling rate at 24-bit sample resolution, for instance, like THX, 48Khz 16-bit or 24-bit digital audio).

A dynamic audio stream is also flexible as it can be received or generated while previously queued (loaded in system memory) digital audio plays.

A static audio mode should be utilized when dealing with short sounds that will easily fit into system memory that need to play back using the smallest amount of latency (delay) for synchronization accuracy.

The static audio mode should thus be utilized when implementing UI or game audio assets that need to be played often, or rapidly, several times in a row, using low latency and the smallest amount of system memory possible.

Once you create an AudioTrack object, Android OS initializes an associated audio buffer for an AudioTrack object. The size of the buffer is specified during the construction of the AudioTrack object. This determines how long an AudioTrack object will play from memory before running out of data. For an AudioTrack object that uses static mode, the buffer size is the maximum size of the sound that can be played using the AudioTrack object.

The AudioTrack class offers three overloaded constructor methods that can take the following constructor method call parameter list formats:

```
AudioTrack( int streamType, int sampleRateInHz, int channelConfig, int audioFormat,
            int bufferSizeInBytes, int mode )
AudioTrack( int streamType, int sampleRateInHz, int channelConfig, int audioFormat,
            int bufferSizeInBytes, int mode, int sessionId )
AudioTrack( AudioAttributes attributes, AudioFormat format, int bufferSizeInBytes,
            int mode, int sessionId )
```

For the streaming mode, data will be written to the audio sink in chunks less than or equal to the total buffer size. AudioTrack is not final and thus permits subclasses, but such use is not recommended. This release includes a number of changes of note to the Android AudioTrack class.

Your app can now supply audio data using the high-precision floating-point format with the new Android constant **ENCODING_PCM_FLOAT**. This is to permit increased dynamic range for your PCM (also known as WAVE audio) audio data format. This allows high-definition (24-bit and 32-bit) WAVE digital audio (.WAV files) to have more consistent precision as well as more "headroom."

The reason for this is because floating-point precision can be very useful for providing more accurate results in the types of calculations used with digital audio assets. The playback endpoints still use integer data format for digital audio assets and, therefore, utilize a lower bit depth. As with Android 5, portions of the internal digital audio pipeline have not yet been fully recoded to utilize 100% floating point data representations.

There are also some powerful digital audio processing algorithm classes in Android 5, held inside the **android.media.audiofx** package. Those of you who are familiar with audio engineering will tremble with anticipation as I simply mention some of the class names, which reveal what each process does. Some of these impressive audio processing algorithms that are implemented as classes include BassBoost, EnvironmentalReverb, Equalizer, Virtualizer, PresetReverb, Visualizer, LoudnessEnhancer, NoiseSuppressor, and, finally, AcousticEchoCanceler and AutomaticGainControl.

As you can see, Android is focusing quite a bit on the professional multimedia genres of digital video, digital audio, digital illustration, and 3D rendering and animation, which I'll explain next. Hold on to your hats folks, we're about to venture into the third dimension!

# Real-Time 3D Rendering: OpenGL ES and Extension Pack

Android 5 adds a plethora of powerful interactive 3D, also known as i3D, features. These are intended to increase the wow-factor of the Android OS so that it can compete with all of the other 64-bit operating systems that are in the marketplace, such as iOS 8 and the upcoming Windows 9.

It's commonly said that "flat UI design" is the popular trend; however, the Android 5 OS seems to be bucking this trend by including things like 3D ripple effects, fine-tune controls for dropshadow (shadow height, Z layer order, View autoshadowing), OpenGL ES 3 support, and OpenGL 4.4 emulation.

These features target placing Android 5 on a level playing field with Xbox and PlayStation game consoles. Much of this i3D capability is utilized for the new Android 5 Material Design schema, which I discussed in exacting detail in Chapter 1. Let's learn about OpenGL and Android Extension Pack!

## Open GL ES 3.1: Enhanced 3D Rendering Technology for Android 5

One of the most powerful 3D features added in Android 5 is the inclusion of the latest version of **OpenGL ES 3.1**. As you may have guessed, this "ES" stands for **embedded systems**. This version of OpenGL is optimized to run in browsers and on embedded devices, such as smartwatches and smartglasses.

OpenGL ES 3.1 is the latest version of this real-time i3D rendering technology. OpenGL is often used in popular 3D video games. Most of the new features are related to the "skins" that make a 3D object look realistic. These are called "texture maps" in the 3D modeling or animation industry. These texture maps are made up of different "shading attributes," which are commonly called "shaders."

Advanced effects such as animated surfaces or surfaces that are responsive to game play or position can be created using the "Shader Language" in each shader "slot" in a surface material. This is somewhat akin to using layers in image compositing, only shaders are far more mathematically complex, as they contain a number of attributes that allow them to achieve photorealism. Some of them include **color**, **transparency**, **luster** (shininess), **illumination** (glow), **reflectiveness** (reflection), and **bump mapping** (surface height).

Loan Receipt
Liverpool John Moores University
Library Services

**Borrower Name: Selvaraj,Malarvizhi**
**Borrower ID: **********7418**

Beginning android programming :
31111014848947
**Due Date: 26/05/2016 23:59**

Java made simple /
31111010147732
**Due Date: 09/06/2016 23:59**

Pro Android wearables :
31111014660516
**Due Date: 09/06/2016 23:59**

Total Items: 3
19/05/2016 16:11


Please keep your receipt in case of
dispute.

OpenGL ES 3.1 supports **Enhanced Texture Mapping** functionality, including a "Multi-Sample" texture capability, which can yield higher edge quality, in texture map applications. This is similar to the anti-aliasing you will be learning about later on during this book.

Also supported in OpenGL ES 3.1 is **stencil texture mapping**, which is used to enhance an illusion of depth in your texture map. These can be created using depth buffer textures, rather than actual 3D geometry (the underlying mesh or 3D polygon model). These advanced features allow 3D game output quality that rivals the traditional game platforms such as PlayStation 4 or Xbox.

It's apparent that Google is going after their 3D game console competitors with Android 5. There are already several Android-based game consoles on the market, including the $99 OUYA, the Amazon Fire TV, and the $199 nVidia Shield. These will all most likely be upgraded to Android 5 during 2015.

OpenGL ES 3.1 also supports something called a "compute shader." These are not actually texture maps or shaders at all, but rather they are a programming construct that allows developers to use the graphics processing unit (GPU) to perform non-3D-related calculations. Using the GPU, rather than the CPU, for math calculations is faster and more efficient, as the GPU is optimized for floating-point math, whereas a CPU is better suited (optimized) for integer-based mathematics.

In game applications, the popular implementation for a compute shader will be to use the compute shader to offload game **physics** calculations onto the GPU. This is done because current GPU technology is more powerful than CPU technology, at least when it comes to solving highly complex mathematical calculations, which are commonly utilized inside i3D game applications.

Many open source software packages, such as GIMP 3 or EditShare Lightworks 12, leverage compute shaders to make their software perform complex special effects and pixel filter applications at lightning fast speeds.

A wearable application can also utilize compute shaders as long as a user has an nVidia GeForce or AMD Radeon GPU in their Android device. There are Android devices that feature the **Tegra K1** microprocessor (manufactured by nVidia and currently in the nVidia Shield and the Amazon Fire TV) and can therefore take advantage of this ability to use the GPU for non-3D-centric computation by using these OpenGL ES 3.1 compute shaders.

OpenGL ES 3.1 is also backwardly compatible with OpenGL ES 2 and OpenGL ES 3, so rest assured that none of your existing 3D wearable application code will be broken. OpenGL ES 3.1 will offer optional "extensions," which allow third-party manufacturers (like nVidia) to add things like advanced blending modes (a texture layer compositing special effect) and fine-tuned shading effects such as those that are found in the full OpenGL 4.4 specification.

In fact, the Android Extension Pack (AEP), which I'll discuss next, is a prime example of this third-party extension feature.

Android 5 adds Java interfaces and native support for OpenGL ES 3.1. The Java interface for OpenGL ES 3.1 on Android is provided via **GLES31**. If you use OpenGL ES 3.1, be sure to declare it in the Android Manifest file with the **<uses-feature>** tag, along with the **android:glEsVersion** attribute, like this:

```
<manifest>
        ...
        <uses-feature android:glEsVersion="0x00030001" />
</manifest>
```

Next, let's take a look at how to upgrade Android 5 to OpenGL 4.4!

## Android Extension Pack: Simulate OpenGL 4.4 Using OpenGL ES

There is an additional extension to the OpenGL ES 3.1 standard called AEP (**Android Extension Pack**). AEP allows features such as those found in the full OpenGL 4.4 release. This means 3D console games with 3D graphics that are similar to those seen in Madden Football, Unreal 4, and Halo 4 will be able to run on Android 5 and later hardware devices supporting GPU hardware such as the nVidia Tegra K1.

Primary features of the AEP include **Tesselation Shaders**, **Geometry Shaders**, and **Adaptive Scalable Texture Compression (ASTC™)**, all of which I'll cover in this section. A geometry shader was the first feature to come out in OpenGL, so let's look at that concept first.

The geometry of a 3D object is the underlying 3D model, like a shape, only in three dimensions instead of two. Geometry is also sometimes referred to as the "mesh," because without any texture mapping, this is exactly what it looks like. Another term for 3D geometry, called a "wireframe," also comes from what this mesh-like 3D geometry looks like. Geometry is modeled using "polygons," each of which are triangular (called "tris") or quadrilateral (called "quads").

A geometry shader allows an underlying mesh to become more refined without adding any more polygons. This allows 3D models to be created using a "low polygon" modeling approach, which lowers the data footprint (smaller file size). Geometry shaders allow low-poly meshes to look like high-poly meshes, which are smoother. Geometry shaders use the GPU to apply a refinement algorithm called "tesselation," which adds more "vertices."

Each polygon is made up of "vertices" (points in space), which are elements connected with "edges." A triangular polygon has three vertices and three edges, and a quad polygon has four vertices and four edges. It is important to note that a quad polygon can be split in half (diagonally), making two triangle polygons. An example of a quad modeler is the NeverCenter SILO2 software, and an example of a triangular modeler would be the Blender3D software.

The rendering pipeline (a 3D layer stack, if you will) usually goes from a "Vertex Shader" on the top, or skin, of the 3D mesh (model) down through the "Tessellation Shader," which provides fine-tuned tessellation control over how the underlying geometry shader will be tessellated.

How this all works is beyond the scope of a Pro Android programming title, but I wanted to cover it briefly here so you have a good idea of how advanced the AEP is.

Finally, ASTC is akin to a more advanced 3D version of the advanced WebM and WebP codecs added in Android 4. ASTC is in OpenGL 4.4 as well as in OpenGL ES 3.1, so it is an advanced technology that is used in popular 3D video games. ASTC allows even better 3D texture map optimization, allowing both an application's data footprint and the amount of memory used for these texture maps to be applied to your 3D polygonal mesh to be reduced significantly.

In addition to OpenGL ES 3.1, Android 5 provides this extension pack and Java interfaces and native support for using AEP's incredibly advanced i3D graphics functionality. The AEP extensions are treated as a single package by Android. If the **ANDROID_extension_pack_es31a** extension is present, your wearables apps can assume all extensions in this package are present. This will enable shading language features using a single **#extension** statement.

A Java interface for Android extension pack is provided with **GLES31EXT**. In your wearables application manifest, you can declare that your app must be installed only on devices that support the extension pack, just like this:

```
<manifest>
        ...
        <uses-feature android:glEsVersion="0x00030001" />
        <uses-feature android:name="android.hardware.opengles.aep" android:required="true"
/>
</manifest>
```

Next, let's take a look at browsing media related to the World Wide Web.

# WebKit Media: WebView, WebAudio, WebGL, and WebRTC

One of the super powerful features of Android is a WebKit API, which you can use to display HTML content or even to create your own browser. The Android WebView uses the WebKit Rendering Engine to display a web site, and Android 5 upgrades this to the latest version of Chromium, which is the equivalent of Google Chrome Browser version 37. I just looked at my Chrome browser, and it is at version 39, so this is fairly recent. I would expect Google to keep this part of Android 5 recent, so with each of the Android 5.x updates, expect this version number to advance (increase), as it has already increased to Android 5.1 during the writing of this book.

## Android WebView Class: The PermissionRequest Class

Besides updating the Android 5 WebView implementation to Chromium M-37, Android 5 takes security enhancements to a new level, increasing stability of the WebView class and WebKit Rendering Engine, via numerous bug fixes.

Your default user-agent string for running a WebView on Android 5 has been updated to incorporate **37.0.0.0** as your latest version numbering schema.

Android 5 adds a new **PermissionRequest** class. This class allows your app to grant a WebView object permission to access protected resources such as the camera or a microphone. This is accomplished using WebKit APIs such as **getUserMedia()**. The app must declare the correct Android permissions to be able to use these resources in the first place before you then grant these permissions over to the WebView object for its usage.

The PermissionRequest class creates your permission request object and is required when you wish to request access to web content that has protected resources incorporated into the web site. There are three constants in this class that relate to the types of data you will need permission to access.

The **RESOURCE_AUDIO_CAPTURE** resource permission will allow access for audio capture devices such as microphones. There's a **RESOURCE_PROTECTED_MEDIA_ID** resource permission that will allow you to access a protected media asset, and the **RESOURCE_VIDEO_CAPTURE** will allow you access to video capture devices, such as an HD digital video camera.

The PermissionRequest class's permission request events are delivered with an **onPermissionRequest(PermissionRequest)** method call and can be canceled by using an **onPermissionRequestCanceled(PermissionRequest)** method call.

The PermissionRequest class has the **.grant()** and **.deny()** methods for granting or denying permission, respectively. You will call either a .grant() or a .deny() method in your application's UI thread to respond to a permission request.

There's also a new **.onShowFileChooser()** method, which allows you to use an input form with a files field in a WebView that will launch a file chooser, allowing the end user to select images or files from their Android device.

This Android 5 release also adds support for several powerful new media-related open source standards, including **WebAudio**, **WebGL**, and **WebRTC**. I'll cover what these three technologies are and what capabilities they'll give to your wearables application development next.

## WebAudio: Digital Audio Synthesis and Real-Time Processing

Until the advent of this WebAudio API, web browsers have not had powerful digital audio processing and synthesis capabilities. An introduction of an <audio> tag in HTML5 started it all off, allowing for basic streamed audio playback support. Whereas the audio tag was powerful enough to allow audio streaming, all processing of this digital audio stream had to be done on the server side (or before posting the digital audio on the server).

To really have powerful digital audio processing, the digital audio must be able to respond to complex digital audio (programming) applications on the client side, that is, inside the web browser or embedded OS browser itself.

The WebAudio API provides this client-side processing capability. The API has been designed to support a plethora of digital audio processing uses. The API has been designed in a modular fashion so that much more advanced capabilities can be added as time goes on.

WebAudio API supports a wide range of complex digital audio applications, including games and interactive audio design and synthesis applications. I would include virtual synthesizers, audio sequencers, and music composition software in the types of digital audio applications that could be created using the WebAudio API, which makes it extremely impressive. Any wearable with the right hardware support would be able to take advantage of these!

WebAudio provides a great synergy with the more advanced graphic features offered by WebGL, which I'll cover in the next section. The WebAudio API features modular digital audio sample routing (in analog audio, this would be termed signal routing), providing the ability to create complex mixing and allowing developers to create highly detailed special effects pipelines.

This WebAudio API will allow developers to program multiple digital audio data "send" (sources), as well as submixing. The API supports high dynamic ranges by using the 32-bit floating point data format for internal processing.

The API allows audio developers to utilize sample-accurate scheduled sound playback that features a very low latency. This is necessary for musical applications that require a high degree of rhythmic **precision**, such as drum machines and audio sequencers. Low latency (delays) allows the possibility of dynamic (real-time) creation of digital audio special effects.

The API allows for the automation of audio parameters for features such as envelopes, fade-ins, fade-outs, granular (noise) effects, filter sweeps, or LFOs (low-frequency oscillations). Developers are afforded flexible ways to handle audio input channels, allowing input audio to be split apart, or merged together, in real time.

You can process audio sources extracted from audio or video media elements or process live audio input via a MediaStream obtained using a method call to **.getUserMedia()**. You could also integrate WebAudio and WebRTC, which I'll be covering after I cover WebGL. You can process audio received from a remote peer by using the **MediaStreamAudioSourceNode** method with WebRTC.

Developers can perform digital audio synthesis or digital audio processing using JavaScript and can even send a generated (or processed) audio stream to a remote peer by using the **MediaStreamAudioDestinationNode** method.

The 3D audio is also supported through spatialized audio, which supports a wide range of 3D games and immersive environments. There are also several audio panning models, including HRTF (heat-related transfer function), equal power, and pass-through panning.

Other notable features include distance attenuation, Doppler shift, sound cones, support for obstruction (or occlusion), and a linear convolution engine that allows you to create a range of high-quality special effects such as simulating audio in different types of rooms (ambient sound spaces) like an amphitheater, cathedral, concert hall, hallway, tunnel, caves, and forests.

The WebAudio API also supports oscillators (tone generation); waveshaping effects for sound design; distortion; nonlinear audio processing effects; real-time, time-domain, and frequency analyses; music visualization support; highly efficient bi-quad filters that can be used for lowpass, highpass, and other common filter applications; comb filter effects; sample reverse; and dynamics compression for overall control and sweetening of a mixdown. Whether or not the smartwatch can take advantage of this is an issue that pertains to audio hardware feature support.

Next let's take a look at **WebGL**, which is even more powerful than WebAudio and applies to the **i3D** genre of media rather than the digital audio genre.

## WebGL Support: Interactive 3D Rendering, Shading, and Animation

WebGL is exactly what it sounds like, OpenGL ES for the web (browser). The initial WebGL (1.0) supports the OpenGL ES 1.1 and 2.0 specifications, and the next WebGL 2 (2.0) specification will support OpenGL ES 3.0 and 3.1 as well as 1.1 and 2.0. Both WebGL and OpenGL are managed by the **Khronos Group**, a group of developers who manage open source specifications for i3D-related technology, such as OpenGL, OpenGL ES, OpenCL, OpenSL, OpenSL ES, Collada, WebGL, WebCL, OpenMAX, glTF, and a number of other 3D-related technologies.

You can find out more about the WebGL specification on the Khronos web site as well as the W3C web site. These sites are located at the following URLs:

```
https://www.khronos.org/webgl/
www.w3.org/community/declarative3d/wiki/Related_technologies
```

Until WebGL 2.0 is supported using WebKit, Pro Android wearables developers will want to use the OpenGL ES 3.1 discussed earlier (with AEP if needed) and not use WebGL, as using Android's native OpenGL ES will render faster.

## WebRTC Support: Real-Time Communication for Your Wearables

The **WebRTC** standard is a free, open source project that provides browsers and mobile applications with **real-time communications** (RTC) capabilities.

The WebRTC API offers web application developers an ability to write rich, real-time multimedia applications (such as chat, audio chat, or video chat) on the web, without requiring plug-ins, downloads, or installs. Its purpose is to help build a robust free RTC platform that works across multiple web browsers, as well as across multiple operating system platforms.

Like WebAudio and WebGL, this is accomplished by using the **WebRTC API**. The WebRTC components have been optimized for serving the purpose of real-time audio and video telecommunications inside of web browsers and inside of CE (consumer electronics) devices (also called embedded devices) such as iTV, smartwatches, smartphones, tablets, e-readers, game consoles, and the like.

A WebRTC API allows robust, professional quality RTC applications to be developed for web browsers, mobile platforms, tablet or e-reader platforms, and IoT devices such as smartwatches and smartglasses.

This WebRTC API allows each of these consumer electronics device genres to communicate with one another using a common set of protocols that have been agreed upon by all of the platform software and hardware manufacturers.

The WebRTC initiative is an open industry project that is currently agreed upon, and supported by, Google, Mozilla, and Opera. The WebRTC API web site is being maintained by the Google Chrome team.

# Android MediaBrowser Class: Browsing Third-Party Media

Android 5 introduces the ability for wearable applications to browse the media content library of other applications using an **android.media.browse** API. To expose the media content that is inside your wearable apps, extend the **MediaBrowserService** class.

Your custom class's implementation (subclass) of MediaBrowserService would provide access to the **MediaSession.Token** nested class. This should be done so your wearable applications can play media content provided through your MediaBrowserService Service class, which is scheduled via Android OS.

To interact with this MediaBrowserService object, you use the **MediaBrowser** class (object). To do this, you would first specify the component name for your **MediaSession** class (object). This would be done at the same time that you create your MediaBrowser instance, by using the constructor method.

Using your MediaBrowser object instance, your apps can then connect to the MediaBrowserService object, which you have "wired up" or referenced to it. This MediaBrowserService object will obtain a **MediaSession.Token** object to play the new media content, which is exposed through that Android Service.

# Android Camera 2 API: UHD Image Processing Support

Android 5 introduced a new **android.hardware.camera2** package, and its API (classes, interfaces, methods, properties and constants) allows developers to implement **HDRI** (high dynamic range images) photographic capture as well as HDRI processing. There's already one smartwatch model with an HDRI camera in the crown, the Hyetis. You can expect HDRI camera support to take wearable application development by storm as more products add in these cameras.

You can now access an HDRI camera device available to the operating system in your Java code. You would use a **.getCameraIdList()** method to ascertain the cameras are available to the user's hardware device, and then connect to a specific camera hardware device, using the **.openCamera()** method call.

Once this has been done, you can start to capture HDRIs, by creating a **CameraCaptureSession** object and then specifying **Surface** objects to send the captured images into for display in your wearable applications. These CameraCaptureSession objects can be configured to either capture a **single image shot** or to capture multiple HDRIs in a single **burst image shot**.

To notify the wearable application when a new image has been captured, you implement the **CameraCaptureSession.CaptureCallback** listener and set it in your capture request. When the system completes the image capture request, the CameraCaptureSession. CaptureCallback listener will receive the call to **.onCaptureCompleted()**, which will provide your wearable application with an image capture metadata object encapsulated inside a **CaptureResult** object.

There is also a **CameraCharacteristics** class (object), which will allow your wearable application to detect which HD camera features are available on a given hardware device. The object features a **INFO_SUPPORTED_HARDWARE_LEVEL** property, which will contain data representing the level of functionality.

All camera-compatible Android devices are required to support at least the **INFO_SUPPORTED_HARDWARE_LEVEL_LEGACY** hardware support data variable level. This property contains support for non-HDRI camera capabilities, which are essentially equivalent to that of the "deprecated" (discontinued but still supported) camera APIs. So basically this Camera 2 API replaces the original camera (Camera1) API. Android devices that support the **INFO_SUPPORTED_HARDWARE_LEVEL_FULL** hardware support data variable level are capable of **manual control** of image capture and image **postprocessing**, as well as capturing **high-resolution images**, using **hyperfast frame rates**.

# Android 5 Notifications: LockScreen and MetaData

Android 5 adds some new notification features to its lockscreen feature as well as its MetaData capabilities. Let's take a look at these next.

## LockScreen Notifications: Privacy Safeguard Control APIs

Android 5 LockScreen APIs now have the ability to present notifications. Users of your application can now choose, via Android OS settings, whether to allow "sensitive" (private) notification content to be seen on a secure (locked) Android device screen. Developers can control the level of detail that is visible on the LockScreens when notifications are displayed on a user's LockScreen, representing a much needed increase in flexibility when developing LockScreen applications, which are growing in popularity.

To control the visibility level, call the **.setVisibility()** method and then specify one of the visibility constants: **private**, **public**, or **secret**.

The **VISIBILITY_PRIVATE** constant tells the LockScreen that it can show only the most basic information, such as the notification's icon, but hides the notification's full content from view (as it is deemed to be private). The **VISIBILITY_PUBLIC** constant tells your LockScreen that it is allowed to show a notification's full content (as it is deemed to be public), and the **VISIBILITY_SECRET** constant tells the LockScreen that it must show nothing, excluding any notification text and even a notification icon (Shhh, it's a secret). When you set a visibility constant as VISIBILITY_PRIVATE, you also have the option of providing a "redacted" (limited or abridged) version of your LockScreen notification content, which will hide any personal details.

Say that you wanted to create a texting (SMS; short message service) wearable application and you wanted to display a notification showing "5 new SMS text messages arrived" and you needed to hide the actual message text as well as sender identity.

To provide this alternative notification, first create the replacement notification using Notification.Builder. When you create the private notification object, attach the replacement notification to it through the setPublicVersion() method.

# Notification MetaData: Intelligent Notification Classification

Android 5 now supports metadata properties, which you can associate with your wearables application notifications. This allows your applications to sort these notifications more intelligently. To install this metadata, you would call any (or all) of three methods in your **Notification.Builder** when you construct your Notification object using an associated Builder object.

The first of the three methods, a .setCategory() method, instructs Android regarding how to handle your wearable application's notifications when the Android device happens to be in the priority mode. You can, for example, add categories for your notification that represent an instant message, an incoming call, or an alarm notification. Categories are String constants.

The .setPriority() method sets a priority level for a Notification object. You can set the Notification object's priority to be either more or less important than a normal system notification. Notification objects with the priority field set to **PRIORITY_MAX** or to **PRIORITY_HIGH** appear in a small floating window if your Notification object features sound (or vibration).

The .addPerson() method call will allow wearables developers to add one or more people to a Notification object. These individuals should be relevant to your Notification objects. Your wearable application might utilize this to signal to the Android operating system that Notification objects should be grouped together after they arrive from persons added using this method call. You could also use this method call to rank notifications from these people as being more important or less important based on a priority flag.

# More Android 5 Operating System Enhancements

Finally, let's look at a few other areas that were improved in Android 5 and can be leveraged in Pro Android wearables application development. The **recent applications and documents** area of Android 5 OS has been completely overhauled, as has the **file management by directory structure**. In addition, there are the all-important **second screen capabilities** that allow Android devices to cross-dress one another (had to spin something in the book controversially) so that smartwatches or smartglasses can control things like UHD 4K iTVs!

# The Recents Screen: Concurrent Document Support

In Android OS releases prior to 5, the "recents" screen will only display one single task for each application an end user has interacted with recently. This provided limited multitasking capability and needed to be upgraded significantly in Android 5. This allows Android 5 to be able to better compete with all of the other popular OSs.

With Android 5, your wearable applications can open more tasks, as needed for additional concurrent activity screens for application documents. This feature will add in the much needed multitasking support by letting users efficiently switch between individual activity screens (which contain user documents) simply using the new recents screen. This provides a consistent task-switching user experience across Android 5 apps currently being used.

Examples of concurrent tasks that might be utilized in the recents screen would include multiple open tabs in any mobile web browser, any concurrent gameplay sessions in a game application, business documents in one of your business productivity applications, or text messages in any messaging app.

Your wearables applications can manage its tasks for the recents screen by using an Android **ActivityManager.AppTask** class (or object). This is one of eight nested classes for the ActivityManager class, which is part of the **android.app** package. This class is important as it allows your application to see all of the other Android apps that may be running alongside yours!

This Android ActivityManager class allows wearables developers to interact in various ways with all of the currently active Activity objects that are running in the Android operating system. This class has eight nested class structures, which will allow you to interface with what is running on your users' incarnation (current memory or processor deployment) of Android OS. I'll cover them here as it's important for you know about what they can do to allow your wearables applications to know what is going on around them!

The ActivityManager.AppTask class allows you to manage your application's tasks (hence its name). There is also an **ActivityManager.MemoryInfo** class, which allows you to poll operating system information regarding available memory by using a .getMemoryInfo(ActivityManager.MemoryInfo) method call.

The **ActivityManager.ProcessErrorStateInfo** class will allow developers to retrieve information regarding OS processes (threads) that are in an error condition. The **ActivityManager.RecentTaskInfo** will allow you to retrieve information regarding tasks that a user has most recently started or visited.

The **ActivityManager.RunningAppProcessInfo** class will allow you to retrieve system information regarding what processes are currently running, and the **ActivityManager. RunningServiceInfo** class will allow you to retrieve system information regarding a particular service that's currently running inside the Android OS.

The **ActivityManager.RunningTaskInfo** class will allow you to process system information regarding a particular task that is currently running in the OS thread manager. The **ActivityManager.TaskDescription** class will allow you to retrieve information regarding a current activity within the recent task list.

To insert a logical break, so that the system treats the activity as a new task, you can use your **FLAG_ACTIVITY_NEW_DOCUMENT** constant when you launch your activity using the .startActivity() method call. You can also achieve this behavior by setting your <activity> XML element's **documentLaunchMode** attribute to "intoExisting" or "always" in your AndroidManifest XML file.

To avoid cluttering your user's recents screens, you could set the maximum number of recent tasks to show from inside your applications, which limits the tasks that can appear inside that screen. To do this, you would set the <application> parent tag's parameter called **android:maxRecents**.

The current maximum that can be specified is 50 tasks per user, unless you are on a low-memory Android device, in which case it's set to 25. Tasks in users recents screen can also be set to **persist across reboots**. To control this task-persistence behavior, use the **android:persistableMode** parameter.

You can also change the visual properties of the activity in the recents screen. This includes your activity's color, label, and icon. This is done by calling the **.setTaskDescription()** method of the activity.

# Data Storage: Directory Structure Selection Support

Another impressive Android 5 upgrade has to do with data storage access. The Android Storage Access Framework capability has been expanded to allow developers (as well as their users) to select an entire directory subtree. This will allow your wearable applications to have read, as well as write, data storage access to all documents contained in a given directory folder structure, without requiring user confirmation for each item to boot!

To select an entire directory subtree, you will want to create and send an **OPEN_ DOCUMENT_TREE** Intent object. An Android operating system will display any and all **DocumentsProvider** object instances that will support a subtree selection. This allows the end users to browse and select a directory. The returned **URI** object will reference access to the selected subtree. You can then use the **.buildChildDocumentsUriUsingTree()** method call in conjunction with the **.buildDocumentUriUsingTree()** method call, and then use a **.query()** method call to explore the data inside of the subtree.

There is also a new **.createDocument()** method call, which lets you create a new document or directory structure anywhere underneath a subtree. If your wearable application needs to manage an existing document, you will want to use a **.renameDocument()** or a **.deleteDocument()** method call. You can also check the **COLUMN_FLAGS** constant to verify provider support for these calls before issuing them.

If you wanted to implement your DocumentsProvider object and also want to support subtree data selection, you will want to utilize the method called **.isChildDocument()** and then set the **FLAG_SUPPORTS_IS_CHILD** constant in the **COLUMN_FLAGS** attribute, asking Android OS to grant child document support.

Android 5 also introduced the new package-specific directory on shared storage. Your app can place media files there for inclusion in MediaStore.

A new **.getExternalMediaDirs()** method call will return a **path reference** for the external MediaStore directories across all the shared storage devices.

No additional permissions will be needed by the app to access any returned paths, which is similar to the functionality of the **.getExternalFilesDir()** method call. The Android OS will periodically scan for media located in these directories. You could also force the operating system to perform one of these media asset scans by using the **MediaScannerConnection** object (class), which will allow developers to scan to detect the existence of new media content at any time. The class implements a **ServiceConnection** interface and also features two nested helper classes.

A **MediaScannerConnection.MediaScannerConnectionClient** nested helper class will provide developers with the interface needed for notifying clients of MediaScannerConnection objects whenever any connection to the MediaScanner Service has been established or when the scanning of a file has completed.

Another **MediaScannerConnection.OnScanCompletedListener** nested helper class provides a listener interface, which can be used to listen for, and notify any clients of, the results of the scanning for a requested media file.

## Second Screen: Screen Capturing and Screen Sharing

Finally, Android 5 OS has ratcheted up its **second screen** capabilities by allowing developers to add both screen-capturing as well as screen-sharing capabilities to their Pro Android wearables applications using the all new android.media.projection package and its powerful APIs.

Second screen functionality could be very useful, especially for wearables applications, as you might well imagine! For example, if your users wanted to enable screen sharing in a video conference app, they could see another party in life-sized splendor, using a 2K or 4K Android TV capable iTV set.

There's also a **.createVirtualDisplay()** method that is new that allows your wearables application to capture the contents of your main screen (default display) and put that screen capture data inside a Surface object. Your application can then send those data across a network. This API only allows the capture of screen content that has not been secured and will not work for system audio captures.

To begin the screen capturing process, your application must first request the user's permission by launching a screen capture dialog using an Intent, which is obtained by using the **.createScreenCaptureIntent()** method call. A call to this method will then return an Intent object, which must be passed to the **.startActivityForResult()** method in order for the screen capture to be initiated. To retrieve screen captures, use a **.getMediaProjection()** method.

By using the **.getMediaProjection(int resultCode, Intent resultData)** method call, you can then access the **MediaProjection** object that will be obtained from a successful .createScreenCaptureIntent() screen capture request.

Congratulations! You have just updated yourself on the key things that the Android 5 OS has added that will bring you up to speed from your Android 4.4 (and prior) knowledge base. Many of these can be used creatively in one way or another for Pro Android wearables application development.

## Summary

This chapter looked closely at all of the features other than Material Design, which was covered in detail in Chapter 1, in Android 5. This included everything from OS features to new media features, to a new version of OpenGL, and far beyond (Hey, to infinity and beyond!).

First, I discussed the Android Project Volta, which aims to allow the developer community to take power management, and optimization, into their own hands. This can be done by using the **JobScheduler** and **JobInfo** classes, in conjunction with the **Battery Historian Tool**.

Next, I discussed the new Android Network Connection technology improvements, both to NFC and Bluetooth, as well as to the new Bluetooth LE APIs. You learned all about the Android **ConnectivityManager** class, as well as **NDEF**, and **Android Beam** technology, and how to implement them in Java 7.

Next, I discussed all of the new wow-factor opportunities afforded by all of the cool multimedia additions to Android 5. I discussed the **MediaSession** and **MediaController** classes, for digital video playback, and **AudioTrack** for digital audio, and you learned how to use these for new media playback.

Next, I delved into **Open GL ES 3.1** and the **Android Extension Pack** and explained how to implement these, to take OpenGL from 3.1 to 4.4, adding all new real-time i3D rendering power into your Android i3D applications.

Finally, I discussed **WebKit** support and **WebView** class, as well as the new support for the latest **WebAudio**, **WebGL**, and **WebRTC** APIs. Then I finished up by looking at what is new with the Android **recents screen**, the new file (directory) management capabilities, and the new **second screen** and **screen capturing** capabilities, as well as how to implement these cool new features in your Pro Android wearables applications.

In the next chapter, you will get up to speed on the software development environment, the IntelliJ IDEA, which you will be using over the rest of this book to develop Android 5 Wear SDK applications. This is presented so you will have a solid foundation regarding the tools you will be using to write your Java 7 code, and XML markup, during the duration of this book.

# 4

# Exploring Android Studio: Getting Familiar with the IntelliJ IDEA

Now that you have a comprehensive overview of the new features in Android, including the new Material Design paradigm and other new Android 5 features, this chapter will take a look at the **integrated development environment** for Android Studio, **IntelliJ IDEA.** You took care of getting your Development Workstation assembled during Chapter 2, so all that is left to do now is to get you up to speed regarding the ins and outs of the IDE software tool that you will be using from here on out during this book. Once this is out of the way, you can then focus on Java 7 coding or XML markup for the duration of the next 13 chapters in this book.

Let's start by looking at how IntelliJ allows you to learn about all of its features, and then take a look at how to find out exactly which of the Android APIs are currently installed, using the Android **SDK Manager**. I want to show you how to make sure that all of the latest APIs for Wear and Android TV are installed, so you have some practice in upgrading your IDE.

After that, you'll spend the rest of this chapter learning about how your IntelliJ IDEA will be laid out and its various functioning components. I'll then explain how to use some of the IDEA features and functions, as well as the IDEA interfaces with the Android SDK to build wearables applications. I'll show you how to use the SDK Manager so you can install APIs that will allow you to develop Google cloud wearable apps. Then I'll show you how to create Wear smartwatch apps and how the Wear components work.

# Updating IntelliJ IDEA: Using the Update Info Dialog

If you have not done so already, go ahead and launch the Android Studio environment with the quick launch icon you created in Chapter 2. This will launch the IntelliJ IDEA, which is the foundation for Android Studio, replacing the Eclipse ADT IDE used in Android version 4.x and previously.

As you can see in Figure 4-1, if there is an update to Android Studio, your Welcome to Android Studio launch screen will have a lime green Update Info message in the upper right corner. Fortunately, when I launched today there was an update from 1.0.1 to 1.0.2, so I can show you the work process that is involved in updating, as you will most likely encounter this at some point in your wearable application development.

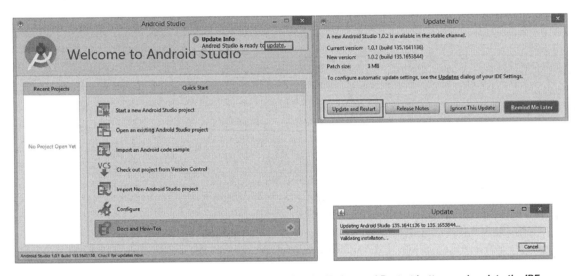

**Figure 4-1.** *Launch Android Studio, click the update link, click the Update and Restart button, and update the IDE*

Click the blue update link, highlighted in a red box in Figure 4-1, and launch the Android Studio update process. This will open a dialog shown in the top right corner of Figure 4-1, which will give you the current build, the current version number, and the size of your patch. This patch will only update those parts of your Android Studio installation that have changed. This is called an incremental update, and it is preferable to having to download the full one gigabyte (maybe more) Android Studio development environment again, which would be redundant. Click the **Update and Restart** button and you will see the Update Progress Bar dialog, shown in the lower right side of Figure 4-1, and you will be updating to the latest version of Android Studio.

# Exploring IntelliJ IDEA: Help, Tips, and Keymaps

After you have updated and relaunched Android Studio (IntelliJ IDEA), the lower left part of the Welcome to Android Studio screen will show the latest version number, which is 1.0.2, as shown in Figure 4-2. Click the Docs and How-Tos option, seen on the bottom left side of Figure 4-2. This will open the Docs and How-Tos panel, shown on the right-hand side of Figure 4-2.

*Figure 4-2.   Once Android Studio restarts, click the Docs and How-Tos option to explore the IntelliJ documents*

As you can see, there are a number of helpful areas for you to explore for your IDEA learning curve climb, including the **Read Help** documents, which you'll look at next, **Tips of the Day** dialog, **Default Keymap Reference,** and, if you have unlimited bandwidth, **JetBrains TV**.

JetBrains is the developer of this IntelliJ IDEA. If you wanted to develop **third-party plug-ins** for IntelliJ, which is beyond the scope of this book, there is also an option to get educated about that endeavor.

Click the **Read Help** option at the top of the Docs and How-Tos panel and open the IntelliJ IDEA Help section of their web site, which can be seen in Figure 4-3. There are logically grouped areas of information regarding new features, the Help system, a Quick Start Guide, the basic IDEA concepts, a tutorials section, and similar reference materials.

*Figure 4-3.   Clicking the Read Help option opens up the JetBrains IntelliJ IDEA version 14 Web Help web site*

I would suggest that you read through all of this material at some point if you want to master the integrated development environment that you'll be using to develop Pro Android Wearables applications over the course of this book. I'll also cover the basics of the IntelliJ IDEA during this chapter.

Click the **Getting Help** link and see what options you have for Help with the IntelliJ IDEA. As you can see in Figure 4-4, clicking the link will open a subpanel in the left content navigation pane of the web site that shows more detail in the form of links that you can click to explore different areas of the IntelliJ IDEA Help system.

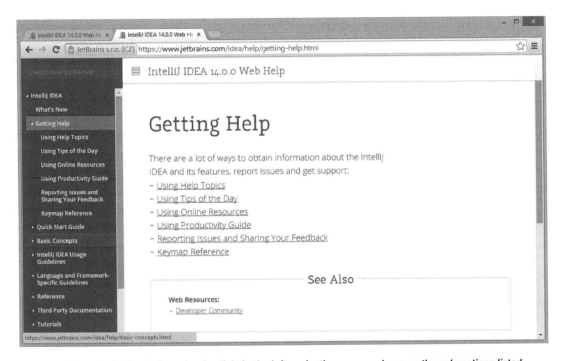

*Figure 4-4. Click the Getting Help navigation link, in the left navigation pane, and peruse the subsections listed*

This includes information on how to use Help Topics, how to use the Tip of the Day dialog, how to use the IntelliJ online resources, how to use IDEA productivity guidelines, how to report any issues you are having with your IntelliJ IDEA installation (or functionality), how to submit your feedback regarding which features you would like to see in future versions, and your keymapping references, in case you like to use keyboard shortcuts instead of the mouse and IDEA menuing system.

Later in this chapter, I will go over some of these core IntelliJ IDEA concepts that are expounded on in the Concepts section, as shown highlighted in gray in Figure 4-4. I will do this so you have some core concepts regarding the IDEA under your belt before you start to use these in earnest in Chapter 5 and throughout the duration of this book.

If you are the curious type, go ahead and look through some of this online material now so that you're familiar with it when I start to cover it in earnest later in the book.

Next, let's take a look at the Configure menu on the Android Studio startup screen to learn how to use your SDK Manager tool to customize your IDEA.

# Configure Android Studio: Using the SDK Manager

Because this is a Pro Android title, you probably have some experience using the Eclipse ADT IDE for Android 4.4 (and earlier) application development, which includes an **Android SDK Manager** menu option and dialog. This utility can also be accessed in IntelliJ IDEA by using the **Configure ➤ SDK Manager** panel sequence, which is shown in Figure 4-5.

*Figure 4-5. Click the back arrow to return to the Quick Start, and click the Configure option and SDK Manager option*

The Android Studio Configure panel also accesses dialogs for your IntelliJ IDEA **settings**, manages **plug-ins** for IntelliJ IDEA, and sets **Import** and **Export** parameters.

You should really take some time to explore these dialogs. You will be using some of these dialogs during this book as well so that you will get some hands-on experience using IntelliJ IDEA to its fullest capacity for your Pro Android Wearables development work process.

Once you click the SDK Manager option, as shown at the top of Figure 4-5, this will open the Android SDK Manager dialog, which is seen in Figure 4-6. Notice that there is a Fetching URL progress bar at the bottom of the dialog that goes out to a repository at the download secure socket layer (dl-ssl) Google server and checks everything in your IDEA against the latest APIs on the Android 5 Google server. This is so that the next dialog can recommend packages for you to install, so that you can bring your Android Studio (IntelliJ 14 IDEA) up to the latest capabilities, or hardware platform (Wear SDK, Android TV, Auto SDK, etc.) support levels.

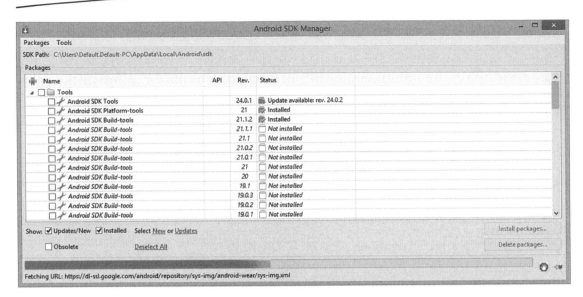

*Figure 4-6.  Once you launch the Android SDK Manager, you will see the Fetching URL progress bar loading APIs*

As you can see in Figure 4-7, this Android SDK Manager will populate those check boxes that it thinks you should check to invoke updates or new APIs.

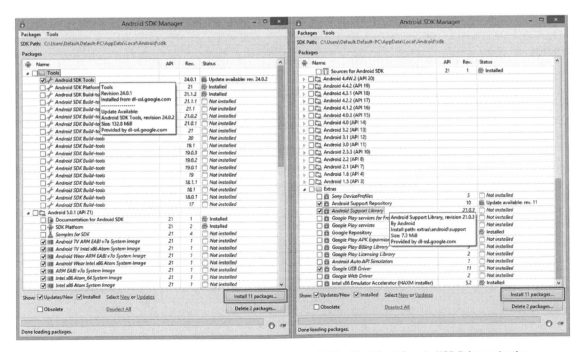

*Figure 4-7.  Android SDK Manager dialog (top on left, bottom on right) with default Google USB Driver selection*

There are updates to Android Studio 1.0.2, or you could view this as a new API for Android Studio 1.0.2 delineated here as Android SDK Tools version 24.0.2, which is an **internal numbering schema** and is shown in the Rev(ision) column.

There are also seven new system images for Android Wear or Android TV, for both the ARM and Intel (Atom) processor hardware. I left them checked as they are suggested because they will be needed in the examples in Chapter 5, where I will be covering your AVD (Android virtual device) emulator creation. These can be seen on the bottom left of Figure 4-7, which I had to cut (the dialog) in half to fit on the page.

On the right side of Figure 4-7, you can see at the bottom that there are new Android 5 Support Tools (a new Support Repository and a new Support Library), as well as a new Google USB Driver (version 11). The support library and its repository are important as they provide backward compatibility. Using the support library allows you to develop for Android 5 and still support earlier versions of the OS, such as 2.3.7 (Kindle Fire) and 4.x.

You can also use this Android SDK Manager dialog to install the "extras," like Google Web Driver, which are shown on the bottom right in Figure 4-7.

Once you click the (in this case) **Install 11 Packages** button, these will all be installed (or updated) in your Android Studio, which as you now know is the fusion of version 14 of the IntelliJ IDEA and the Android 5.0.2 SDK. If Android Studio is at 1.0.2, Android OS would be at 5.0.2.

Before you can install any of the APIs, which are essentially new software packages, you must agree to each of their licensing "terms and conditions," which are shown in this **Choose Packages to Install** dialog in Figure 4-8. Select the Accept License radio button, shown highlighted in red, and click the **Install** button to continue with the installations.

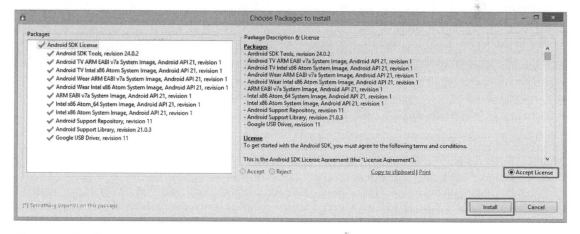

*Figure 4-8. The Choose packages to Install dialog and the Accept License agreement*

I clicked on the Install button, and what should have been a fairly long install process went by in less than five seconds! The dialog as shown in Figure 4-9 appeared a few seconds after I clicked the Install button. This was somewhat puzzling to me, so I waited to see if a download log dialog would pop up. Sure enough it did, and filled with errors to boot! Oh boy!

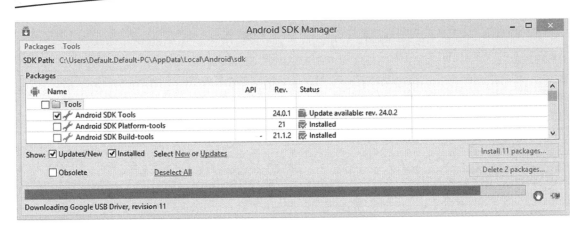

*Figure 4-9.  Showing the Downloading SDK updates progress dialog bar, located at the bottom of the dialog*

I got a "Download interrupted: bad record MAC" error for each of the packages I selected for installation, as can be seen in Figure 4-10.

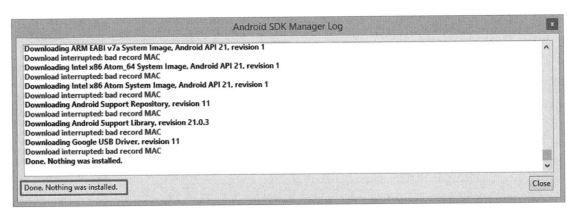

*Figure 4-10.  Showing the Android SDK Manager Log dialog and Download interrupted: bad record MAC error*

Notice at the bottom left of the Log dialog, shown highlighted with red in Figure 4-10, that the installation is done and **Nothing was installed**! Thus my premonition was correct, and when I Googled this error, I didn't find a solution to this problem, so I then decided to try launching Android Studio as a **System Administrator**, so I have top-level admin privileges. I will show you this work process, as this is always the second approach I'll try when a software install does not work, because sometimes a file is trying to write to the hard disk drive but does not have the authority to do so!

# Run As Administrator: Installing Using Admin Privileges

There are two ways to invoke the **Run as Administrator** command in Windows, which are shown in Figures 4-11 and 4-12. The cool shortcut way that few developers know about is to right-click the Android Studio Taskbar Launch Icon and select **Android Studio ➤ Run as Administrator**. This is shown in Figure 4-11, along with a far more involved **Android Studio ➤ Properties** approach, which I'll explain next.

*Figure 4-11.* *Right-Click on the Android Studio icon and select Run as administrator*

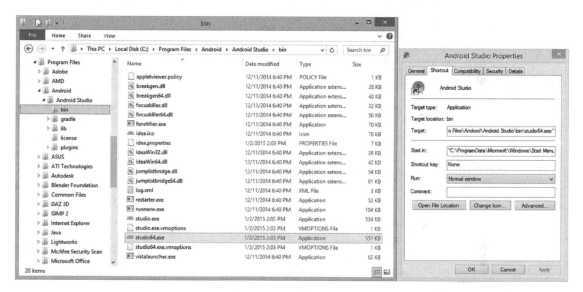

*Figure 4-12.* *Look in the bin subfolder to find the studio64 executable file; right-click and select Properties to review its properties dialog (seen at right)*

From that same menu, you could also select the Properties menu option and open the properties dialog for the Android Studio file that would tell you the EXE file name and where it is located on your hard disk drive.

Armed with this information, you would then right-click that file in the Windows Explorer (or Linux OS file management utility) and then select the **Run as Administrator** option. From that point you launch Android Studio as an Administrator before you again use a **Configure ➤ SDK Manager** sequence. Then try the update (upgrade) again, this time, with admin privileges!

Figure 4-12 shows the **Android Studio Properties** dialog with the target file folder and the fact that you want to use the **studio64.exe** (64-bit version) as the file you will right-click and launch using the very same menu sequence shown in Figure 4-11.

As you can see in Figure 4-13, the installation is now creeping along at an exceedingly slow pace, which means that this time around, I am getting a very different result! What this means is that the update will probably be successful, so if no Log dialog pops up, Run as Admin will solve the problem.

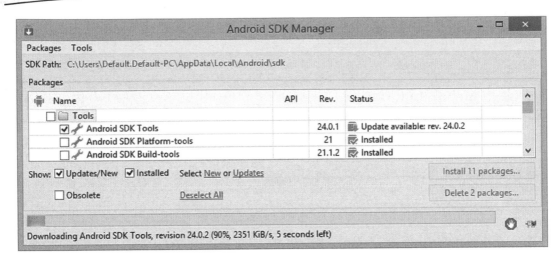

*Figure 4-13. Use the SDK Manager dialog to download any new Android SDK updates*

I wanted to show you the solution to this SDK Manager API update quagmire in case you encountered it, as there are not a lot of web sites that feature this quick and simply variant on how to launch IntelliJ IDEA as an admin!

It is important to note that you do not always have to launch your Android Studio 1.0.2 (IntelliJ IDEA 14) as an administrator to use the development environment, only when you are trying to update your SDK environments and encounter errors that relate to reading or writing files on your operating system hard disk drive areas that are deemed "sensitive" (or privileged).

After this second attempt, I did not have an Android SDK Manager Log dialog (window) pop open! Instead, at the end of this installation process, I was presented with the **Android Tools Updated** message dialog, which can be seen in Figure 4-14.

*Figure 4-14. Once you update your SDK you will get the Android Tools Updated dialog*

This dialog recommends closing the SDK Manager window and reopening it. I took the suggestion to the next level and closed Android Studio (IntelliJ IDEA) and relaunched it to load the latest version into memory. I did this to make 100% sure everything in memory was Android Studio 1.0.2 "clean."

Let's again use the **Configure ➤ SDK Manager** option pane sequence, and you will see that the Android SDK Manager shows that it is now installed. This is shown in Figure 4-15, and as you can see there, there is a folder-check Installed icon next to everything you were attempting to update or install.

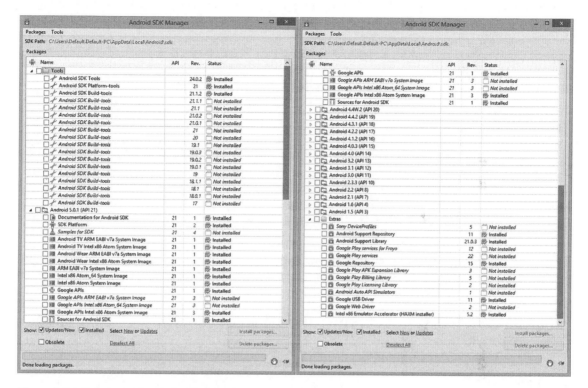

*Figure 4-15. Use the Configure ➤ SDK Manager sequence to launch the SDK Manager and confirm installations*

You will want to perform this work process anytime you get the little green Update dialog upon launching your Android Studio (reference Figure 4-1).

This green dialog (more of an alert post-it, actually) will tell you that Android Studio (IntelliJ IDEA) has an update waiting. This will alert you that you also need to use your **Configure ➤ SDK Manager** panel sequence, because updates to the SDK, drivers, libraries, repositories, services, and system images almost always happen in lockstep with every major (and minor) update to the IntelliJ IDEA itself!

Next I want to give you a quick overview of IntelliJ IDEA as well as present the concepts pertaining to how it works so you have a bird's eye view before I dive into actually using the IDEA later in this chapter to create an Android project, as well as in Chapter 5 when you will create AVD emulators (virtual device), so you know how to create and test Android projects.

# Learning the IntelliJ IDEA Basics: Projects and SDK

There are two major levels covered in the IntelliJ IDEA documentation. You will see this if you review it in detail. Some of it will apply to you as an Android application developer and some of it will apply to Google's Android Studio development teams, as it pertains to integrating customized SDKs and plugging them into IntelliJ IDEA to create platforms such as the Android Studio 1.0.2 (or later version) platform you just upgraded to.

## IntelliJ Project Level: Developing Android Applications

When you use the IntelliJ IDEA, you need to create a "project" for each of your applications. You will be doing this a bit later on in this chapter so you can see the work process that is involved. An IntelliJ project is used to organize your application into functional development component assets. As you know as a Pro Android developer, this includes things such as Java code, XML markup, digital images, digital video, digital audio, your build.gradle and AndroidManifest.xml file, and the components that you just installed in the SDK Manager that also need to be in your application to provide the foundation for what you code (and markup) on top of the Java or Android SDK code base.

A finished, or "compiled," wearable application's APK (Application PacKage) may look like a single file, but it actually contains a plethora of discrete or "isolated" modules that provide code organization similar to a package in Java. The IntelliJ IDEA projects define which modules are to be utilized within any given wearable application.

This project approach allows a highly visual way for developers to bring a project together inside an IDE (integrated development environment) and ties these functional modules together using a visual development editor. This is similar to a word processor, but it is optimized for writing code rather than business documents and is popularly known using the abbreviation IDE.

Just to clarify, this IntelliJ IDEA "Project" does not contain your actual development assets, called "artifacts" in IntelliJ terminology, like media assets, Java code, XML markup, compilation build scripts, documentation, and the like. These projects are the highest level of organization for the IntelliJ IDEA, and they define project-wide settings, a collection of what are termed modules and libraries, and references to various assets (files) that you use within the project to create the application. As you can see, this IntelliJ Project really ties everything together in one project file, which is, of course, going to be necessary for the IDE to generate an app!

## IntelliJ Project File Formats: Files, Folders, and Configuration

The IntelliJ IDEA will store the configuration data for a project, as well as its component parts, using a plain text XML file format. This will make it easier for you to manage, as XML is a relatively simple format to edit, or debug, if needed, and you can also share the project configuration data with others more easily using this XML data format. There are two types of configuration data formats that are available to IntelliJ developers that can be used for storing your Android Studio wearables applications project configuration data. These include directory-based and file-based formats.

## The IntelliJ IDEA Directory-based Data Format

When a directory-based data format is being utilized for the IntelliJ IDEA project, you will find the **.idea** directory in your IntelliJ project folder structure. This .idea subdirectory will contain a collection of the XML configuration files mentioned in the previous section.

Each of these XML files will contain only a logical portion of the overall project configuration data. The names of the files reflect the functional areas within your IntelliJ IDEA project. In this way, what you are looking for will be easy to find, using this logical file-naming approach.

As an example, you might see the **compiler.xml** file containing XML markup that relates to how your project is to be compiled, an **encodings.xml** file that would relate to how your project implements encoding, or a **modules.xml** file that contains the modules that are required for your Android Studio application project.

Almost all of these files will contain information that is central to the project itself. This would include things such as file names and locations for the component modules and libraries needed, or maybe compiler settings or other IDEA configuration settings. These files can (and should) be kept under version control, just like all the other files in your project.

There is, however, one exception to this file-naming approach, which is named **workspace.xml**. This XML file will contain all of your preference settings, such as the placement of IDEA editing panes and the positioning of various editor UI windows. This file also contains your VCS (version control system) and History settings.

This workspace file can also contain any additional data pertaining to the IntelliJ IDEA integrated development environment. For this reason, you may not wish to share this file publicly, unless you want folks to mimic your IDE!

## The IntelliJ IDEA File-based Data Format

There is also a file-based configuration format, which should be used with IntelliJ, when you wish to place only two configuration files in a project directory. One of these files features an **.ipr** extension, which stands for **IntelliJ Project**. This file will store the primary IntelliJ IDEA project's configuration information.

The other more secondary file will use an **.iws** extension, which stands for **IntelliJ WorkSpace**, and this file stores your personal workspace settings. This .iws file should not be placed under version control, while your .ipr file can (and should) be placed under version control, if you are using version control.

A file-based configuration file format can additionally be converted into a directory-based configuration file format (see "Converting Projects into Directory-Based Format" on the JetBrains website for further information).

# IntelliJ Features: SDK, Language Support, and Auto-Coding

To develop any kind of application, you will always need to use a Software Development Kit (SDK). An example that pertains to Android Studio would be the Android SDK, which you updated earlier in this chapter, which runs on top of the Java 7 Software Development Kit, which Oracle calls the JDK.

The IntelliJ IDEA does not in and of itself contain any SDK; however, this Android Studio 1.x bundle of IntelliJ IDEA and Android SDK is based on the Java 7 JDK, as you know, from Chapter 2. Usually, before you start writing any application code, you would have to download and install one of the supported SDKs and then configure it for use in the IntelliJ IDEA.

You can specify an SDK when you first create your application project, and you could even specify an SDK at a later time. To define an SDK in an IntelliJ IDEA, what you'll have to do is to specify the SDKs name and its location.

The location on the hard disk drive is the disk letter and directory path, which is commonly referred to as your SDK's "Home" directory, similar to the terminology that Java uses. This would be the directory that you installed the SDK into, and since you've already installed the Java 7 JDK in Chapter 2, you may remember that for Java it was **C:/ProgramFiles/Java/jdk1.7.0_71**.

Let's take a look at some of the popular development environments that can be supported by (used with) an IntelliJ IDEA, just in case you're planning to develop applications in Flash (using Flex or AIR) as well as Java SE or Java ME, and, of course, using Android Studio 1.0.2 (Android 5.0.2). There are third-party plug-ins that allow other development platforms as well.

## Popular SDKs Supported by IntelliJ: Android, Java, and Flash

Some of the most widespread software development platforms that are used with the IntelliJ IDEA include open source Java 8 SE, Java 8 ME, Java 7 SE with Android Studio on top, and the paid software from Adobe called Flash, which is not really supported on many of the embedded devices (smartphone, tablet, smartwatch, smartglasses, iTV sets, game consoles, set-top boxes, e-book readers, home media centers) these days, as Flash is very data-heavy and is also expensive for manufacturers to implement (it is not open source).

The Java 7 or 8 SDK (JDK) covers the development of Java desktop (Java SE) and Enterprise (Java EE) applications, as well as Java mobile (Java ME) or Java Embedded (Java SE Embedded and Java ME Embedded) applications. JavaFX is also now a part of Java 7 and Java 8, so this is included in all of the versions of Java. I wrote *Beginning Java 8 Games Development* (Apress 2014) that covers this topic if you happen to be interested.

The Android SDK, which once it is preintegrated with IntelliJ using the Android Studio 1.x Bundle, is used to develop applications for Android 5 and earlier devices (using the Android Support API backward compatibility library discussed earlier).

There are also Adobe Flex and Adobe AIR SDKs that are used to develop applications for the Adobe Flash platform, which has been declining in popularity for a decade now. Free for commercial use, open source platform usage has surged ahead, taking away market share from paid platforms such as Apple, Adobe, and MS Windows due to a similar level of functionality at zero cost to the media developer. This is why you see so many devices based on HTML5 and Android.

There is also support for the Flexmojos SDK, which will launch the Adobe Flex compiler and debuggers. It is important to note that this SDK will be created by IntelliJ IDEA automatically when a Flexmojos project is opened.

Finally, there are "native" IntelliJ IDEA platform plug-in SDKs that are used to develop customized plug-ins for the IntelliJ IDEA. A IntelliJ IDEA installation will inherently act as an IntelliJ IDEA platform plug-in SDK.

## Popular Languages Supported by IntelliJ: Java 8, XML, and Groovy

The development of modern software applications currently involves the use of several (unrelated) programming languages within one single development infrastructure. This describes a development environment called a **polyglot** programming environment. Android Studio 1.x is the perfect example of this as it uses Java 7 for coding and XML markup for quick object definition.

As you know as a Pro Android developer, these objects are later "inflated" and the XML markup structures are transformed into Java objects. IntelliJ IDEA is the professional IDE for polyglot programming, which is why Google adopted it for Android Studio 1.x and Android 5 (and earlier) development.

The primary programming languages that are supported by this free version of the IntelliJ IDEA include Java 8 (and lambda expression) as well as the earlier Java support, including Java 7 (without lambda expression support) used with Android Studio, as well as XML and XSL. XML is used extensively for Android application development, so IntelliJ is perfect for Android 5. IntelliJ also supports **Groovy**, which is not usually used for Android apps development, but as you might imagine, the Groovy crowd has found a way to make Groovy development for Android a reality, so if you groove on Groovy then you are in luck, and all supported IntelliJ languages work together! The Gradle build system in Android Studio uses Groovy syntax.

An "Ultimate" edition of the IntelliJ IDEA supports a plethora of advanced languages, such as Java Server Pages (JSP and JSPX), Flex, ActionScript, HTML5, CSS3, JavaScript, SQL, PHP, Spring, and a number of other languages.

Ultimate costs are around $500 to purchase (first time) or $300 to upgrade. There are 50% discounts for startups, as well as free versions for students and teachers. There is a free open source license available to noncommercial OS software projects that meet the definition of open source software and a set of additional criteria defined on the IntelliJ licensing and upgrade (the "buy" page) web page. There are also free versions for educational and training purposes, so it turns out JetBrains is quite a generous company!

## IntelliJ Auto-Coding Features: Highlighting, Formatting, and Folding

Like the NetBeans (JavaFX, HTML5) or Eclipse (Java) IDE software packages, IntelliJ IDE has a number of advanced features, just like a word processor has for writing, only these features are used to assist in code programming.

### IntelliJ Code Highlighting, File Templates, Code Completion, and Code Generation

The most obvious feature, which a word processor doesn't do to your words, is **highlighting** different words using different colors based on their use. Syntax and error highlighting are common in all of the IDEs, but IntelliJ seems to have the most professional appearance of any of these, because of the Ultimate (or paid) version that the free version was created from. You can also change your code-coloring color values, if you like, although the default colors used in the IntelliJ IDEA are the industry standard colors.

Code highlight colors can be configured in the **Colors and Fonts** section of the **Settings** dialog, which you can see on the right-hand side of Figure 4-5, second from the top, which you have probably already explored, as I suggested that you do earlier.

There's another cool feature called "file templates," which allows IntelliJ to create what I call **bootstrap**, or partially coded (these are also called **stubs**), for languages supported in the IDE. This enables IntelliJ to create "empty" classes and methods, for instance, for Java 7, or XML 1.0 markup.

There is another popular feature that is found in all IDE software that is called **code completion**, which looks at the context of what you are coding and finishes portions of that code for you. There is also **code generation**, which is closely related to the file templates' function that provides your bootstrap code "snippets" that you can then modify as needed.

### IntelliJ Code Formatting, Code Folding, Search and Replace, Macros and Documentation

Not only does IntelliJ IDEA write and color your code for you, in order to make things easier, it also formats, hides (and shows), and automates your programming in other cool ways.

One of the features that helps you organize and get a better overview of your program logic is called **code folding**. Code folding will generally use plus (+) or minus (-) icons at the left side of major blocks of code, such as classes and methods in Java 7, to allow you to "collapse" these program structures so you are able to have more room on your screen to work on other code structures or to get a bird's eye view of your code structure for the Java class you are working on.

As you might expect, IntelliJ allows you to rapidly access the Android API documentation so you can research constants, interfaces, methods, or classes quickly and easily. The Android 5 API has become so vast that this feature becomes an important addition to your wearable apps development.

Another automation feature that becomes more and more valuable as your code becomes more complex includes the use of macros in the editing pane. Macros are automated work processes, which go all the way back to the early days of mainframe computing, DOS, and batch processing.

There are other useful features such as console windows you can open so you can execute commands interactively without leaving the IntelliJ IDEA.

Besides code editing assistance features, IntelliJ IDEA enables debugging, for Java, JavaScript, PHP, and Adobe Flash (Flex) applications. Debugging for JavaScript-related applications is currently supported in the Mozilla Firefox and the Google Chrome browsers. Now, let's create a wearables app!

## Creating an Android Wearable App: Using IntelliJ

It's time to fire up Android Studio using the quick launch shortcut and this time instead of the Configure or Docs and How-Tos options, click the Start a new Android Studio project option, as shown selected in Figure 4-16.

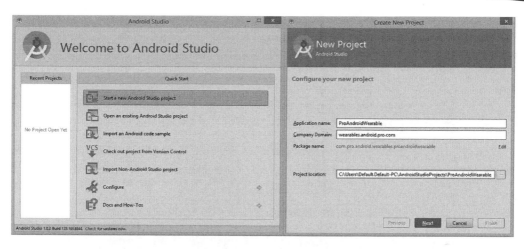

*Figure 4-16.  Select Start a new Android Studio project; name your application ProAndroidWearable*

Name your application **ProAndroidWearable** and set **wearables.android.pro.com** as
your domain, then click the **Next** button. In the next dialog, as shown in Figure 4-17, select
**Android 4.3 Jelly Bean API Level 18** from the drop-down, and then check the Wear check
box option. Leave the Phone and Tablet check box option checked (as this is the default
application development option).

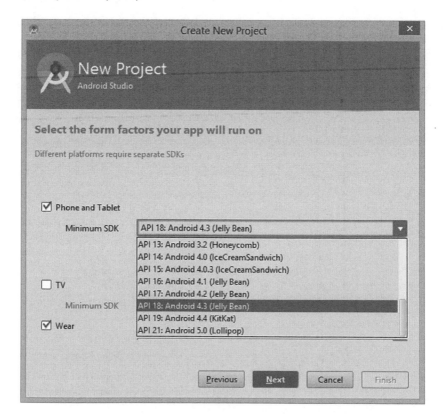

*Figure 4-17.  Select API 18, Wear, Phone and Tablet*

Once you click the **Next** button, you will then be taken to an **Add an activity to Mobile** dialog, as shown in Figure 4-18. Select the **Add No Activity** option, shown in the upper left corner of this dialog, so as to not create an Activity for the Phone or Tablet option portion of the previous dialog.

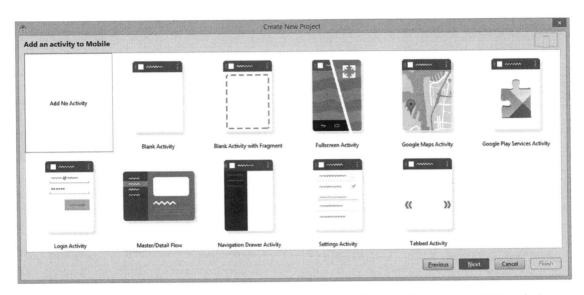

*Figure 4-18.* *Select an Add No Activity option in the Add an activity to Mobile dialog (for Phone and Tablet option)*

Once you click the **Next** button, you will get the fourth dialog, the **Add an activity to Wear** dialog, which is where you will select your **Blank Wear Activity** option, which as you can see in Figure 4-19, shows both the round and square Android Wear smartwatch screen (Activity) configurations. Click the **Next** button, after you have selected the Blank Wear Activity and you can name the Main Activity for the wearable application, and have IntelliJ set up (generate the code for) the bootstrap XML files in the next dialog.

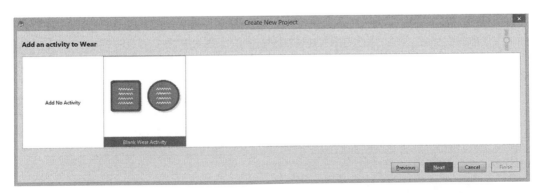

*Figure 4-19.* *Select the Blank Wear Activity option in the Add an activity to Wear dialog and click the Next button*

In the **Choose options for your new file** dialog, which can be seen in Figure 4-20, accept the suggested Android 5 Java and XML file-naming conventions that are suggested by Android Studio and name your primary Java bootstrap **MainActivity.java** and the primary

XML user interface layout container file **activity_main.xml**. The Wear UI layout container XML files preface the file names with round_ and square_, respectively, which seems logical to me.

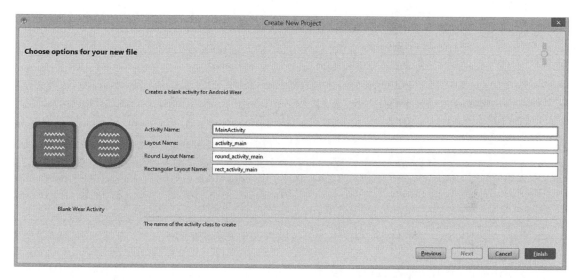

*Figure 4-20. Accept standard Java and XML file name conventions in the Choose options for your new file dialog*

After you click the **Finish** button, you will get a Windows Security Alert dialog, which is shown on the left side of Figure 4-21. Click the Allow access button so that Android Studio can continue to launch, building a project with Gradle, as shown in the build dialog on the right side of Figure 4-21.

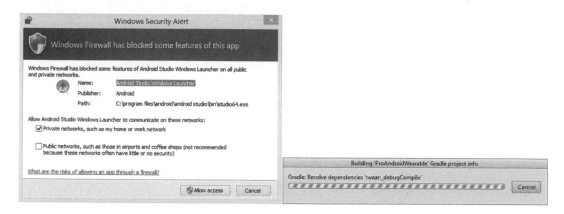

*Figure 4-21. Click the Allow access button in the Windows Security Alert dialog to unblock Windows Firewall*

Once Android Studio (IntelliJ IDEA) launches with your bootstrap project, you will see the Tip of the Day dialog, which could also be accessed using the **Docs and How-Tos ➤ Tip of the Day** panel sequence, as shown in Figure 4-22.

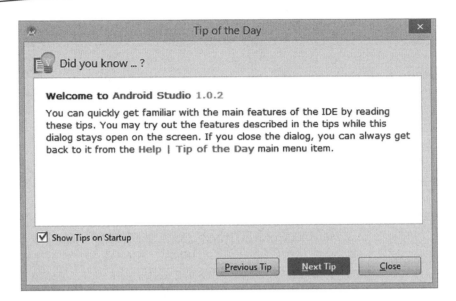

*Figure 4-22. Upon IntelliJ launch, the Tip of the Day dialog will open*

You can either click the **Next Tip** button, shown in blue in Figure 4-22, or you can click the **Previous Tip** button to the left of it to cycle the tip queue backward, if you're a nonconformist, and read all of these hot tips regarding IntelliJ IDEA, which I vigorously recommend.

After you have finished with the Tip of the Day, click the **Close** button on the right of the Next Tip button and close the Tip of the Day dialog. Then open the Android Studio IntelliJ IDEA full screen, so you can look at it next, now that it has your Pro Android Wearables project open in it for the first time! This hands-on usage is getting quite exciting!

As you can see in Figure 4-23, there is a Project pane on the left that has your ProAndroidWearable project structure. The middle editor pane features two tabs currently, one for the Java 7 code used in Android 5, which you'll look at next, and another for the XML user interface layout markup, which is the default tab that opens with any IDEA startup.

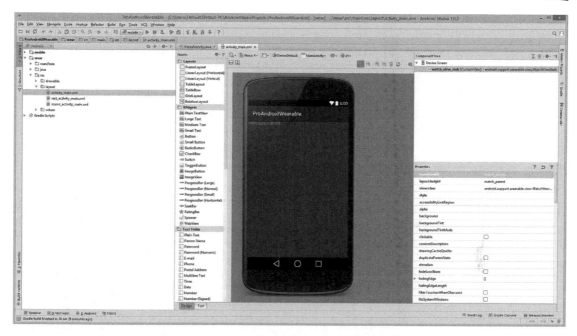

*Figure 4-23. Once you finish the project creation process the new project will open*

The XML tab has a design mode, the default shown on startup, and indicated at the bottom left of the editing pane using a blue tab, labeled "design." On the right of that there is a white tab labeled "text," which you will be using to write your XML markup by hand (from scratch), since this is a Pro Android title! The design tab has a rendering engine that is used to show what the XML markup will probably look like on an Android hardware device. This is not as accurate as an AVD emulator, which you will be setting up in Chapter 5, where you'll learn how to create and configure emulators.

The Design Editor in IntelliJ provides a drag-and-drop user interface for adding UI widgets and setting their properties (attributes or parameters, if you prefer those terms). The widgets are on the left in a **Palette** pane and can be dragged to the smartphone preview to add them to the design.

The properties for each widget are shown on the bottom right of Figure 4-23, when a given UI widget has been selected for editing. The pane is called **Properties** and will contain any **attributes** (or **parameters**, also known as properties) that the selected user interface widget supports for further customization.

There is also the **Component Tree** pane, on the top right of the XML editing area in Figure 4-23, that shows the widget components that are currently being used, such as those UI widgets that have been added to the current design preview.

This pane gives you a bird's eye view, essentially the top-level UI design hierarchy structure. This is provided for complex UI design hierarchy use, just as code folding is provided in the Java editing pane to make things easier when your code gets more complex.

Next, click the Text tab at the bottom left of the XML editor pane so that it turns blue and shows you the XML markup structure that creates the preview, which you will notice in Figure 4-24 is now being shown on the right side of the XML editing area this time instead of in the middle.

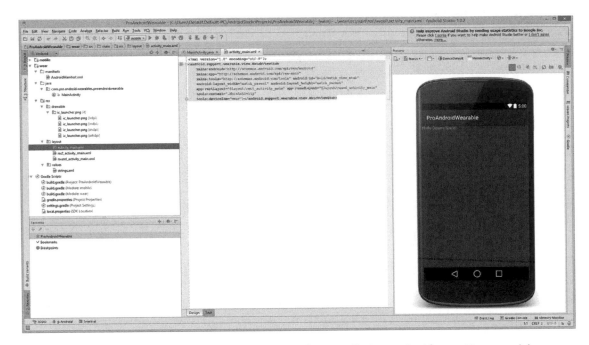

*Figure 4-24.  Click the Text tab at the bottom, expand the Project pane file tree, and opt in or out to usage stats*

Next, use the right-facing arrowhead icons in the Project pane on the left of IntelliJ to open all of the folders in that pane that are closed. Your project already has one Java file, four PNG image assets, three XML layout files, one XML file with String values in it, and six Gradle scripts, which are used to "build" your wearables application.

When I get to the Java code and XML markup in Chapter 7, you will start to learn the details regarding what this Java code (and XML markup) is doing.

Next, click the MainActivity.java tab at the top left of the edit pane in the middle of the IntelliJ IDEA and take a look at the Java code that was created for you using the new Android project series of dialogs.

Let's take a look at the bootstrap Java code that Android Studio has created for you and see where it was taken from. Your first Java package statement came from the dialog shown in Figure 4-16 on the right side, and it concatenates your Company Directory field with your Application Name field to create the following Java package statement:

```
package com.pro.android.wearables.proandroidwearable;
```

Then you have import statements. These import four Android classes: **Bundle, Activity, TextView,** and **WatchViewStub**. These are needed to create Activity objects, save the application state, and create UI widgets (View objects). The Java code for these four initial import statements (there will be more added later as you add more widgets and functions) look like the following:

```
import android.app.Activity;
import android.os.Bundle;
import android.support.wearable.view.WatchViewStub;
import android.widget.TextView;
```

The important part of the Java code that was generated is the **MainActivity** class, which is your **subclass** of the Android Activity class. The way that you know this is the **class hierarchy** is because it is being indicated through the usage of the Java **extends** keyword:

```
public class MainActivity extends Activity {
    private TextView mTextView;
    @Override
    protected void onCreate(Bundle savedInstanceState) {
        super.onCreate(savedInstanceState);
        setContentView(R.layout.activity_main);
        final WatchViewStub stub = (WatchViewStub) findViewById(R.id.watch_view_stub);
        stub.setOnLayoutInflatedListener(new WatchViewStub.OnLayoutInflatedListener() {
            @Override
            public void onLayoutInflated(WatchViewStub stub) {
                mTextView = (TextView) stub.findViewById(R.id.text);
            }
        });
    }
}
```

Let's go through what is inside the body of this Java code, which is shown in Figure 4-25. I will go over this here so you know how everything interconnects between these Java classes and the XML markup in your files. The first line of code declares a TextView widget named mTextView, so half the import statements are now used, as the Activity import is used for the MainActivity subclass and the TextView import for this Text View Widget.

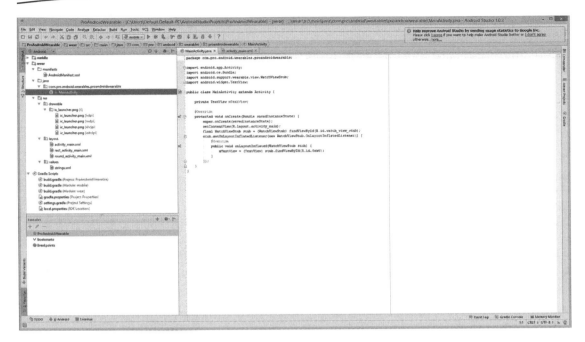

*Figure 4-25. Click the MainActivity.java tab at the top, expand Project pane file tree, and opt in or out to use stats*

As you probably know as a Pro Android developer, you must always @Override an **onCreate()** method for Activities you create for an Android application. If you need to review Android development, I just wrote the third edition of *Android Apps for Absolute Beginners* (Apress) in Q3 2014 that covers it all in great detail. This method call uses the **Bundle** class you imported to create state memory (all states or settings related to the Activity instance in memory) Bundle, which is appropriately named **savedInstanceState**. If Android has to swap your Activity out of memory for any reason, this little Bundle object will allow Android OS to reconstruct your Activity exactly as the user had left it, so the user does not even know that the Activity was removed from the system memory temporarily.

The first thing that you see inside this .onCreate() method structure is the **super.onCreate (savedInstanceState);** statement. This creates (or re-creates using the Bundle object if the Activity has been removed from memory by Android) the Activity object by using the parent Activity class .onCreate() method, which is called from the parent Activity class using a Java **super** keyword.

The next code statement is one that every Android application must have to set up your user interface layout container. This is your setContentView() method call, which references the activity_main.xml file, which you looked at earlier in the activity_main.xml tab. This is how the XML UI definition is connected to the Java 7 code for your wearable application.

The next line of code is what bridges the Android application part of your wearable app to the wearable itself, using the fourth WatchViewStub import statement, so that now you've used all of the imported classes. You create a WatchViewStub object named **stub** and load it with the **watch_view_stub** UI widget, which has been defined in the activity_main.xml file, by using the **findViewById()** method call.

Next a Listener is attached to the WatchViewStub object named stub using a .setOnLayoutInflatedListener() method. The code inside this method will be **triggered** after the watch_view_stub XML layout definition is inflated.

This construct will ensure that the wearables UI definition is in place before any Java statements inside the .onLayoutInflated() method structure are executed. Notice inside of this .setOnLayoutInflatedListener() method, a **new** .onLayoutInflatedListener() object is created in the parameter area.

This .onLayoutStubListener() method is called by using a path reference to the WatchViewStub class that contains this method. This is very dense Java code, and it sets up your entire Listener structure, as well as what it is going to do, after a UI layout has been inflated. This is all accomplished using only a half dozen lines of Java code.

Inside the onLayoutInflated() method, the mTextView TextView object will be loaded using the XML definition of the TextView UI widget with an ID of **text**. As you can see, there is no TextView widget or any other widget with an ID of text, so you need to open one of the other XML UI layout container files. This is done by **right-clicking** the **rect_activity_main.xml** file name in the Project pane and selecting the **Jump to Source** menu item, which in IntelliJ lingo means "open file in a tab in the central editing area."

As you can see in the rect_activity_main.xml tab in Figure 4-26, there's a TextView widget named **@+id/text**, which is what the Java code is referencing inside the .onLayoutInflated() method structure using findViewById().

*Figure 4-26.  Right-click the rect_activity_main.xml file, select a Jump to Source menu option to open in a tab*

If you want to see how the UI definition in the rect_activity_main.xml tab is referenced in your activity_main.xml UI definition, as shown in Figure 4-24, look at line number 7. If you want to turn on line numbering in IntelliJ, right-click in the gray column just at the left of the XML markup pane and select a **Show Line Numbers** option. Line 7 looks like the following markup:

```
app:rectLayout="@layout/rect_activity_main" app:roundLayout="@layout/round_activity_main"
```

These two app: references to a rectLayout and roundLayout property are the properties that Android Wear looks at to determine which UI design to use for smartwatches that are rectangular (square) or round.

So now that you know how everything connects together in the bootstrap project, the next thing you need to do is to make sure your AVD emulators are in place and ready to use for the rest of this book. Congratulations! You are making great progress.

# Summary

In this chapter, you learned all about the IntelliJ IDEA as well as how Android Studio combines their Android 5 SDK and Java JDK to turn it into a customized Pro Android wearables application integrated development environment software tool.

You also learned how to use the **SDK Manager** to see which SDKs are installed as well as to install the other features that you'll be needing during this book. You learned that little-known **Run as Administrator** trick, which can also solve many other failed installation scenarios besides the one encountered when you tried to update Android Studio 1.0.1 to Android Studio 1.0.2. Luckily an update was available so I was able to show you that little trick that gives you read or write privileges across the OS board.

You learned all about version 14 of your IntelliJ IDEA: how to update it, how to learn about its features, and about its projects structure, files, folder hierarchies, and configuration files. You learned what SDKs IntelliJ will support and what versions of IntelliJ (free versus paid) support which programming languages. You learned about myriad programming features that will make your coding job easier.

Finally, you created your **ProAndroidWearable** application so you could explore the IntelliJ IDE. You looked at the Java 7 and XML markup and went through what the Java code does and how it links into (is wired up with) the XML markup UI definition files.

In the next chapter on AVDs, you will learn exactly how to set up an Android **AVD emulator** for custom wearables devices and get some experience with AVD creation, configuration, set up, and customization.

# Chapter 5

# Android Virtual Devices: Setting Up Wearables Application Emulators

Now that you have an overview of the features in Android Studio, this chapter will discuss Android virtual devices (AVD), which are software emulators.

The reason that these are important is because they allow you to test your Pro Android wearables application more rapidly, without having to transfer your APK file to a hardware device via a USB cable (although you did install the latest USB driver in Chapter 4 in case you want to do this) every time you want to test your application's Java code or XML markup.

Let's start out by creating AVDs for both square and round Wear hardware (smartwatch peripherals). You will do this for both the Intel x86-based smartwatches as well as ARM EABI7-based smartwatches. This is possible due to the x86 and ARM system images, which you installed in Chapter 4, using the SDK Manager, when you updated to Android OS 5.0.2.

After that, you'll spend the rest of this chapter learning how your AVDs interface with the rest of the Android 5 wearables application development project inside the IntelliJ IDEA. You'll learn how to select which AVD emulator you will use to test your application at any given time during the development. This is important for Wear application development as you will need to create both square and round versions of your UI design, as discussed in detail in Chapter 4, when you learned how the WatchViewStub object allows Android OS to detect and serve the correct UI design for the user's smartwatch shape.

## Using the AVD Manager: Creating Wear Emulators

If you've not done so already, launch the Android Studio development environment with the quick launch icon you created in Chapter 2. This will launch IntelliJ IDEA and display the

ProAndroidWearable project you created in Chapter 4. Click the **Tools** menu at the top of the IDE, as is shown in Figure 5-1, and click the **Android** menu to display the submenu that has the **AVD Manager** option on it. Also notice that underneath the AVD Manager is your SDK Manager option, so if you were wondering how to access an SDK dialog once you're inside IntelliJ in Project mode, this is how you would accomplish that.

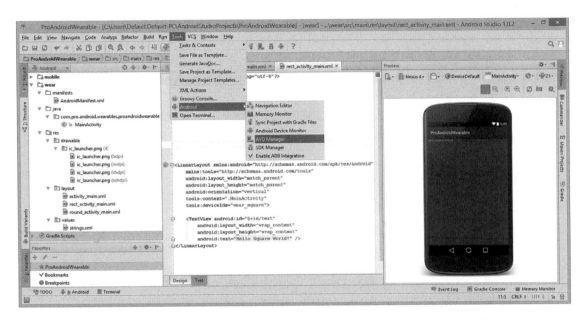

*Figure 5-1.  Use the Tools ➤ Android ➤ AVD Manager menu sequence in IntelliJ and launch the AVD Manager*

This will open the **AVD Manager** dialog and a list of currently installed AVD emulators called the **Your Virtual Devices** screen, as shown in Figure 5-2.

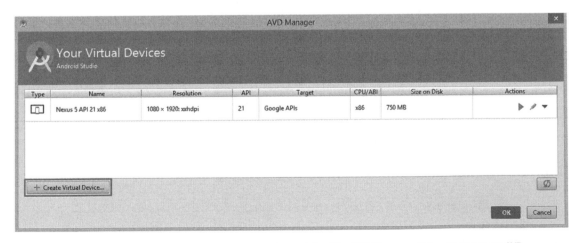

*Figure 5-2.  Use the Create Virtual Device button on the lower left of the AVD Manager dialog to create an AVD*

This dialog lists the basic AVDs that are currently installed in IntelliJ IDEA with the default software installation, including Motorola's Android 5 OS compatible **Nexus 5** API Level 21 for Intel Atom x86 processor emulation. For those of you who did not hear the industry news, Google bought Motorola several years ago.

On the bottom left of the dialog there is a button labeled Create Virtual Device. Clicking this button brings up a second level of AVD creation.

This second level dialog in your AVD Manager is used to **Select Hardware** in the **Virtual Device Configuration** dialog, as shown in Figure 5-3. It lists all of the currently predefined **Phone**, **Tablet**, **Wear,** and **TV** hardware and classifies and organizes these by **Category** buttons on the left side of the dialog. As you can see in Figure 5-3 "True SmartWatches," which are not smartwatch peripherals, are listed in a Phone section, since they act as a phone strapped to your wrist. I've highlighted the **Neptune Pine SmartWatch** in Figure 5-3 so you can see how the **attributes** are listed on the right.

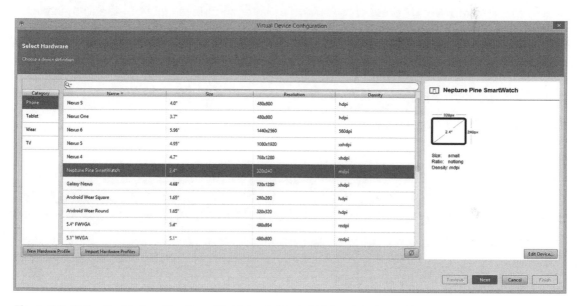

*Figure 5-3. Notice the Neptune Pine SmartWatch is a full Android (phone) device and is not under Android Wear*

Click the **Wear** button on the left side of the dialog and see what built-in Android Wear device options there are listed for use in the IntelliJ IDEA.

There are predefined SmartWatch emulators for Android Wear Square, as well as Android Wear Round, as shown in Figure 5-4. Let's start by creating the Android Wear Round AVD emulator for Intel Atom (x86) processors.

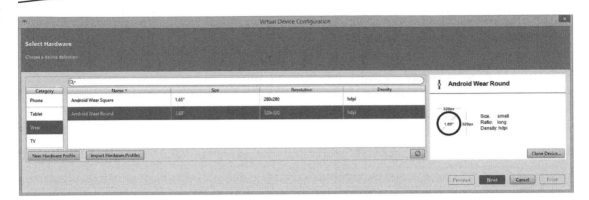

*Figure 5-4.  Select the Android Wear Round Hardware Emulator and click the blue Next button to define it for use*

Select the **Android Wear Round** entry, shown selected in blue in Figure 5-4, and then click the blue **Next** button. This will then take you to a third level, to a **System Image** dialog, which is shown in Figure 5-5. Notice that there are two different hardware versions, ARM and Intel processors, listed in this dialog. You will be creating emulators for both types of Wear hardware, since some smartwatch products are ARM based and others are Intel based. Select the **Lollipop x86 API Level 21** option and click **Next** to proceed to the next dialog in the series, where you can define the emulator options for the Intel Atom x86 Android Wear Round SmartWatch AVD emulator.

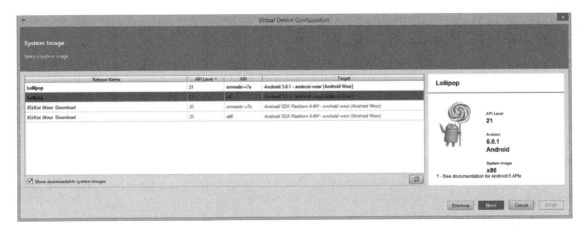

*Figure 5-5.  Select an Intel x86 Lollipop System Image for Android Wear, which you installed using SDK Manager*

The fourth level down in the series of dialogs is the **Verify Configuration** dialog, which is shown in Figure 5-6. You will see two check boxes under the **Emulated Performance** section, one for **GPU emulation** and one for storage of a **memory snapshot** for the last emulator state, which is used for faster loading of the emulator. I assume that you took my advice in Chapter 2 and have an SSD hard drive, so the **Use Host GPU** option is more valuable to select as it allows 3D **OpenGL** to be emulated. It's important to note that both of these check boxes cannot be selected at the same time. You'll have to choose between these two important emulator perks, so choose carefully!

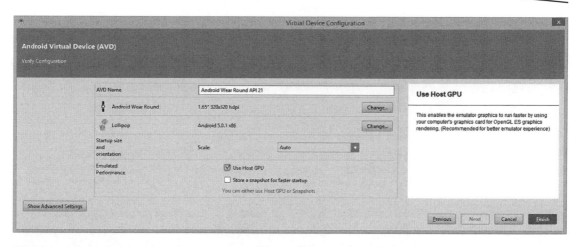

*Figure 5-6.   Select the Use Host GPU to enable emulator graphics to run on your workstation's graphics adapter and click Finish*

Once you click the **Finish** button, as shown on the bottom right of Figure 5-6, you will be taken to the **Your Virtual Devices** dialog, as shown in Figure 5-7.

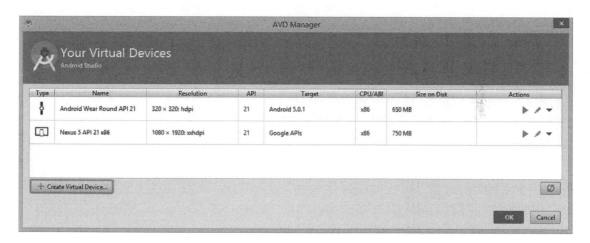

*Figure 5-7.   Once you click Finish, the Android Wear Round API 21 x86 AVD will be listed in the Virtual Devices*

Again, click the **Create Virtual Device** button on the bottom left of the dialog as shown in Figure 5-7, and let's create an Android Wear Square API 21 AVD next. In the Select Hardware dialog, as shown in Figure 5-8, this time select the **Android Wear Square** device, as shown selected in blue. Notice again on the right that information is listed about the specifications of this AVD emulator, in this case a **small** size, **long** ratio, **HDPI** density, and **280 DP**.

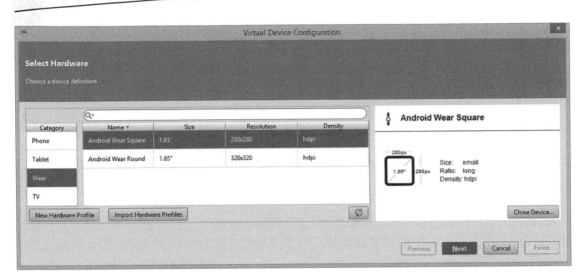

*Figure 5-8. Select the Android Wear Square Hardware Emulator, and click the Next button to define it for use*

Click the blue **Next** button, which will open the **System Image** dialog, as shown in Figure 5-9. Again select a **Lollipop API Level 21 x86** system image.

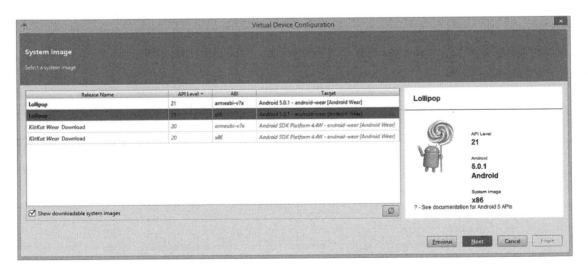

*Figure 5-9. Select an Intel x86 Lollipop System Image for Android Wear, which you installed via SDK Manager*

Click the blue **Next** button and proceed to the **Verify Configuration** dialog, as shown in Figure 5-10. I am again using the **Use Host GPU** option because I have an advanced 3D graphics card and I am a 3D modeler and animator who is planning to eventually use OpenGL in my Android applications. It is important to note that many of your dialogs "lag" a version in the upgrade process. So even though you made sure that you were 5.0.2 "clean" in Chapter 4, details such as updating the dialog text feedback information, for example, the Android 5.0.1 x86 that is now Android 5.0.2 x86, didn't get into an update of the dialog UI labels that are being used currently!

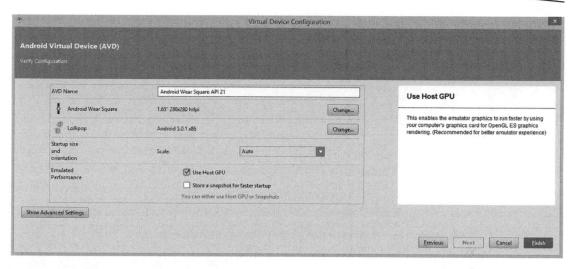

*Figure 5-10. Select the Use Host GPU to enable emulator graphics to run on the workstation's graphics adapter*

Click **Finish** and return to the **Virtual Devices** dialog, as shown in Figure 5-11.

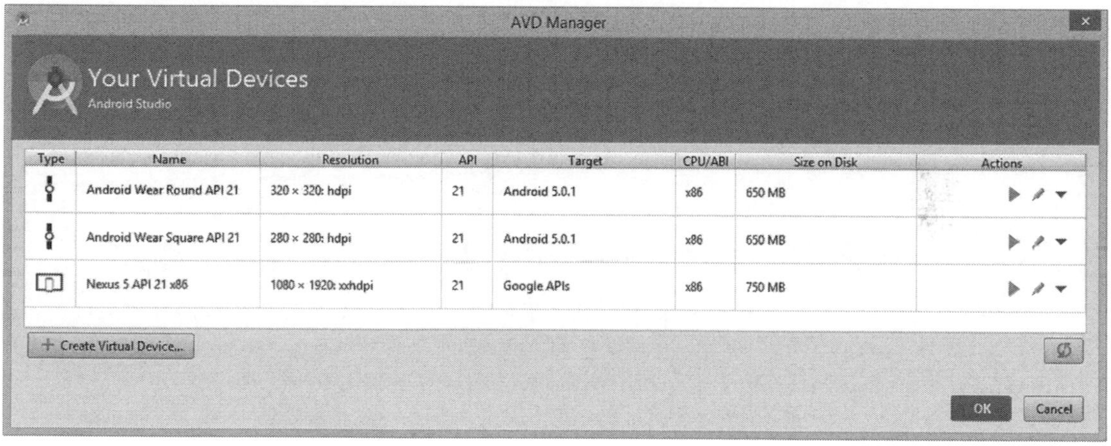

*Figure 5-11. Intel Atom Android Wear AVD emulators for Round and Square SmartWatches have been created*

I would suggest using the exact same work process you did for Intel Atom–based SmartWatches, which can also be seen in Figures 5-4 through 5-11, and creating AVD emulators that use the ARM processor technology. If you do this, you will have all four of the emulators at your disposal later on when you need them for Android Wear Round and Android Wear Square testing. During this book, I will be following the "do it right the first time" work process, so get everything done you will need when you're in that dialog.

Figure 5-12 shows the **Your Virtual Devices** dialog, after all four of these Android Wear AVD emulators have been created.

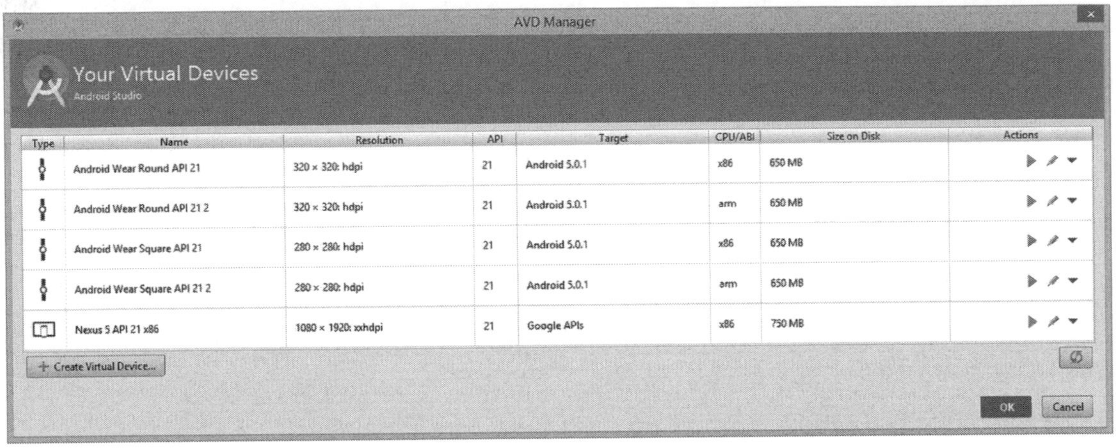

*Figure 5-12.* *Intel Atom or ARM Android Wear AVD emulator for Round or Square SmartWatches ready for use*

Now that you've gotten some practice creating ARM and Intel AVD emulators for your Android Studio IntelliJ IDEA, you will be prepared when it comes time to test your Pro Android wearable application.

Next, let's take a look at how these AVD emulators can be used to test the ProAndroidWearable app you created in Chapter 4.

# Using Wear Emulators: Testing Your Wearable App

The emulator settings in Android Studio IntelliJ IDEA are accessed via the **Run/Debug Configurations** dialog, which you may have perused when you were looking at the Configure dialogs in Chapter 4 when you updated and explored the IntelliJ advanced integrated development environment for Android 5.

As you can see in Figure 5-13, this could also be accessed from the inside of your project, by using a **Run ➤ Edit Configurations** menu sequence, which is seen highlighted in blue. Click the **Run** menu at the top of the IntelliJ IDEA and select the Edit Configurations menu item to open the dialog.

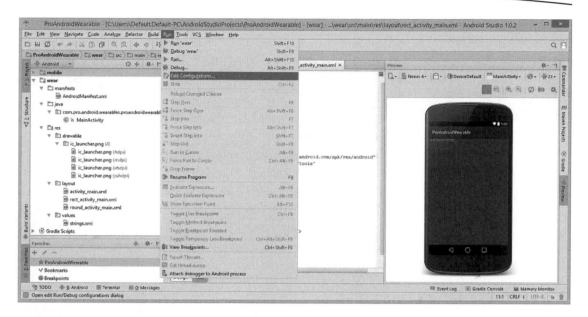

**Figure 5-13.** *Use the Run ➤ Edit Configurations menu sequence to set the AVD emulator that you want to use*

As you can see in Figure 5-14, there are three main tabs: **General**, **LogCat**, and **Emulator**. Here you will be looking at how to use LogCat (Logger-Cataloging) as you start to generate errors that need to be corrected over the course of this book. LogCat is something that you really need to look at in the context of the development work process, which is why I didn't discuss the LogCat functionality in Chapter 4.

You might think the Emulator tab is where you need to set your AVD emulator, however, in fact there is a **Target Device** section located at the bottom of the General tab where this functionality is set up for use with IntelliJ.

As you can see in Figure 5-14 at the bottom, there are several options for setting up the Target Device that will be used for testing your wearables applications in IntelliJ. These range from using the emulator AVD to using the USB Driver you updated in Chapter 4 to instructing IntelliJ to poll you regarding which device (emulator or real hardware) to utilize to test your Android Wear application's Java code and XML markup.

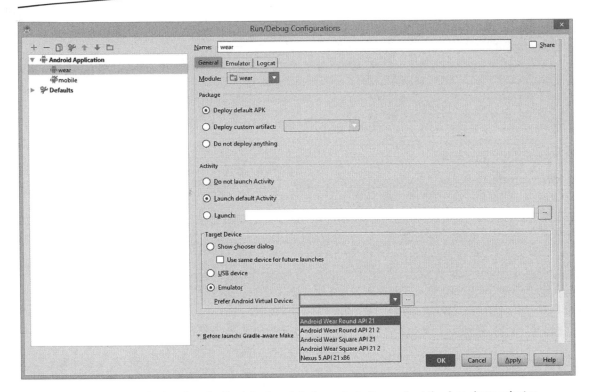

*Figure 5-14. In the General tab, select the Emulator target device radio button, and set the drop-down selector*

If you want to select a target device manually, every time you use the Run or Run Wear icon or menu sequence, you will want to select the radio button that is next to the **Show chooser dialog** option. Each time you start a Run Wear or Debug operation in IntelliJ with this configuration setting, Android Studio IntelliJ IDEA will display a **Choose Device** dialog for you.

If you choose the USB Device option, IntelliJ will detect a plugged-in USB device upon your application start up, which will then be used for testing purposes. This would be your optimal option if you own a Wear SmartWatch!

Because I cannot make the assumption that all of the readers will own a Wear SmartWatch, I will primarily be using the Android Wear Square and Android Wear Round AVD emulators during the course of this book for the wearables application testing purposes. That brings you to the third emulator option.

If you select the third Emulator radio button, you will be able to select the **Prefer Android Virtual Device** setting from a drop-down menu. This is populated with the AVD emulators that you created earlier in the chapter.

I am going to initially select the **Android Wear Round API 21** (Intel Atom), which you will be testing next, to make sure that it works. You will also be testing your ARM AVD emulators and the Android Wear Square AVD during this chapter so you can see how they look and work as hardware emulators.

If you intend to change AVD emulators and go back and forth between a USB driver (external hardware device) and using AVD emulators, you'll want to experiment with using the Show chooser dialog radio button option. This will allow you to select how you want to test a wearables application each time you click that **Run icon** (looks like a green video Play transport button) or use the **Run ➤ Run Wear** menu sequence to test your application.

## Using IntelliJ Run: Running Wearable Apps in Round Wear

Let's use the **Run ➤ Run** menu sequence and execute the bootstrap wearables application called ProAndroidWearable, which you created in Chapter 4. I get an error, which is shown in Figure 5-15, at the bottom left of the screenshot. I also show the **Run ➤ Run** menu sequence in this screenshot as well. As you can see, my system, which happens to be an AMD FX-8350, seems to be having trouble running the Intel HAXM x86 emulation. This may be due to the intense competition in the CPU and GPU market between Intel and AMD, therefore, it is not surprising that this is happening.

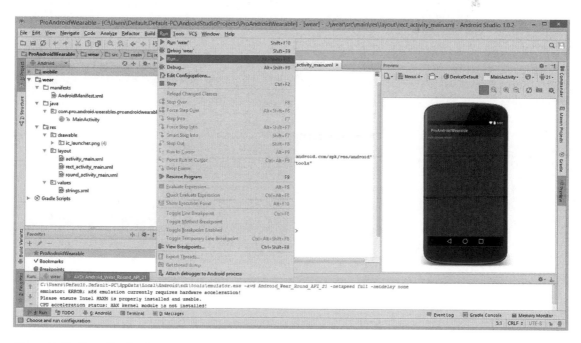

*Figure 5-15. Use a Run ➤ Run menu sequence to try and launch the AVD; notice the error in the output (bottom)*

Let's take a look at the proper work process to get Intel HAXM working properly, just in case the HAXM error message happens to you!

## Installing the Intel Hardware Extension Manager: The intelhaxm.exe

Open your OS file management utility and use the Search Bar, and enter the **intelhaxm** or **intelhaxm.exe** search term, as highlighted in red at the top of Figure 5-16. This will locate the **intelhaxm-android.exe** file for you.

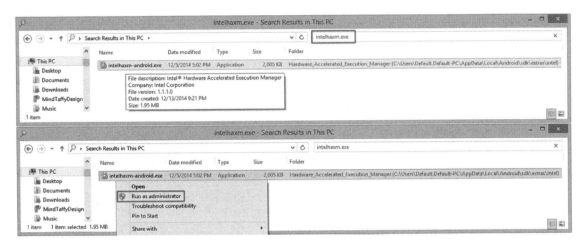

*Figure 5-16. Use your file management tool to search for intelhaxm.exe file, then right-click it and select Run as administrator*

You can actually right-click the file (result), as shown in Figure 5-16, and use the Run as administrator menu option to install the Intel **Hardware Accelerated Execution Manager** (HAXM) on your system to get rid of the HAXM error you are getting inside of the Android Studio IntelliJ IDEA.

On my system, I received the dreaded "This computer does not support Intel Virtualization Technology" error message inside a **VT not supported** dialog, as shown on the left side of Figure 5-17. Fortunately for me, specifically, in this case, I installed all of the AVD types and can still use an ARM AVD in my Android Wearable application development. I can continue writing the book!

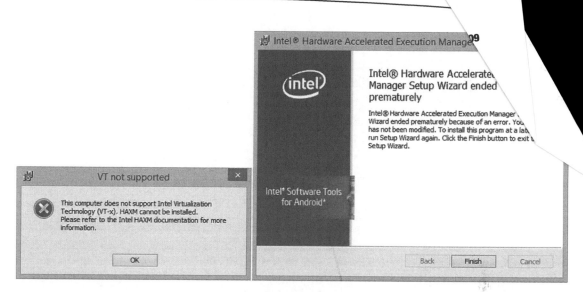

*Figure 5-17. If you are using a powerful AMD 8-core FX processor like I am, you are going to be out of luck!*

Once I clicked the **OK** button, shown on the left in Figure 5-17, I received this "Intel Hardware Accelerated Execution Manager Setup Wizard ended prematurely" dialog, as shown on the right side of Figure 5-17, so I clicked **Finish**.

If you do not get the dialog shown in Figure 5-17, install the Intel HAXM, and that should take care of any error messages you may be getting inside the IntelliJ IDEA in the Run/Debug/Compile output pane and tabs at the bottom of the IDEA (these are shown in Figure 5-15).

## Switching AVDs: Running Apps in Round Wear ARM AVD

Because I cannot emulate this Intel Atom Android Wear Round AVD, I went back into the Run/Debug Configurations dialog, as shown in Figure 5-18, using that **Run ➤ Edit Configurations** menu seen in Figure 5-13. I selected the **Android Wear Round API 21 2** option from the drop-down. Because I just created all of these AVDs a few minutes ago, I know that this is the ARM version, so I can use this emulator to show you how to test your ProAndroidWearable app.

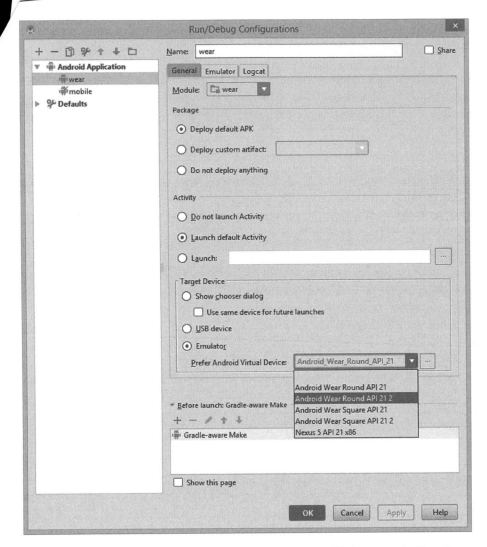

*Figure 5-18.* Select your ARM Android Wear Round API 21 2 AVD (notice Intel AVD is now marked in red)

This time I am going to have you click the **green Play (Run) icon** at the top of IntelliJ. As you'll see during this chapter, there are several ways to Run your wearables application. Once you click the Run icon, you'll see the output pane shown at the bottom of Figure 5-19, which shows a plethora of technical information related to running your application inside the AVD emulator. The last line says "creating window" (contains the emulator) at **30,30** (upper right corner of your OS desktop) sized for a **320x320** Round AVD emulator. If you want to take a peek at what this looks like, it is shown in Figure 5-20, starting up for the very first time on my system!

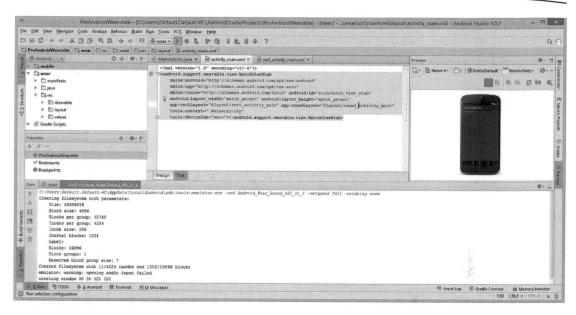

**Figure 5-19.** *Click the green Run (Play) icon at the top to run ARM emulator; notice the stats in output tab (bottom)*

When you first run and launch the Android Wear AVDs, it simulates exactly what you would experience with any smartwatch product when you run it for the first time. The sequence of screens you will see can be seen in Figure 5-20, including a screen that says that the Android Wear app is not on your phone.

**Figure 5-20.** *First time launch displays accurate Wear emulation; SmartWatch shows this when you first turn it on*

If you swipe the emulator screen to the side, using your mouse, you'll see other screens that advise you to install the Android Wear application from the Google Play Store, so that the Wear SmartWatch Peripheral can function properly. It's important to note that this is not needed; this is just the emulator being exceptionally accurate in an attempt to simulate real-world Android Wear experiences. Also notice on the far right side of Figure 5-20 that there is also a Project Volta Power off (shutting down) screen that's displayed if you don't do anything with the AVD emulator (after a minute).

If you shut down the AVD emulator, click the **red X** to close the window and simply restart it using a Run process in IntelliJ. I will show you another way to directly run your application using a right-click context-sensitive menu-based work process. Click the **MainActivity.java** tab, as shown in the top middle of Figure 5-21, and then right-click, in the right side of your editing pane, and select a **Run 'MainActivity'** menu option to again launch the AVD you chose in the **Run ➤ Edit Configurations** Run/Debug dialog.

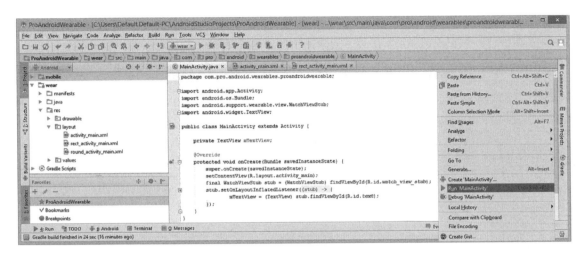

*Figure 5-21. Another way to launch an AVD from the project is to right-click in the code area and select Run 'MainActivity'*

The second time you launch the AVD, you will get a different series of AVD start-up screens, which tell you the number of apps that are being loaded, optimized for Wear devices, starting, and the like. You will also see a Wear start-up logo screen, and a SmartWatch screen with the time and indicators for cloud and charge, as well as the "Ok Google," as shown in Figure 5-22.

*Figure 5-22. AVD optimizes and starts apps, shows the Android Wear start-up logo, and Ok Google time screen*

Once you get the default Android Wear Home Screen (the time), you can swipe your mouse over the screen and pull down different watch faces, as shown on the far left side of Figure 5-23. You can also swipe up or down; this will scroll through different options, as shown in the second pane of Figure 5-23.

*Figure 5-23. Once emulator starts, swipe screen to find the Start button, then swipe to find the ProAndroidWearable app*

Scroll down and find the blue Start option, then click that to get your applications screen, which can be seen in the third pane in Figure 5-23.

You can scroll up and down through that Start Application screen until you find your **ProAndroidWearable** application, which will launch when you click it. This will run the bootstrap application and display the Hello Round World! message. This text String object is contained in a TextView widget, which can be found in your **round_activity_main.xml** file that is referenced inside your activity_main.xml file.

I highlighted the markup reference in Figure 5-19 using light blue. I did this by clicking my mouse cursor on the XML file reference, so look for an insertion bar inside this reference. This is where the Android OS looks at which emulator (or smartwatch hardware) you are using and then calls the correct UI layout design XML definition file which will fit with that type of SmartWatch face! You as the developer will define that upfront, and I will be focusing on SmartWatch UI design during the course of this book.

## Switching AVDs: Running Apps in Square Wear ARM AVD

Go into IntelliJ and use the **Run ➤ Edit Configurations** work process, which was shown in Figure 5-13 (I'm not going to duplicate screenshots here), and select the **Android Wear Square API 21 2** (ARM, unless your Intel AVDs are working, your choice). Then use one of the **Run** methods shown in Figure 5-15, Figure 5-19, or Figure 5-21 and this time run the wearable application in the Android Wear Square AVD emulator so that you can see how the user experience compares with the Android Wear Round AVD emulator.

Notice that whenever you change an Android Virtual Device emulator, you'll get a "Waiting for adb" progress bar dialog, because IntelliJ IDEA will need to load that new AVD emulator system image definition into the system memory. This progress bar is shown in Figure 5-24, and if you have a fast multiple core system with an SSD hard disk drive, it should only display for a few seconds at the most.

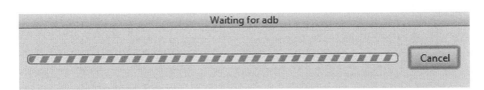

*Figure 5-24. If you switch to a different AVD emulator in IntelliJ, you will get the Waiting for adb progress bar*

After this progress bar disappears, your Android Wear Square emulator will appear at the same location (upper right of your desktop) as the Android Wear Round emulator did earlier. As you can see in Figure 5-25, there is a Just a minute (loading) screen that will appear, and then you will see the same connect screen that you saw on the Android Wear Round emulator.

*Figure 5-25. When you first launch an AVD it emulates what a real smartwatch will do*

With the Android Wear Round AVD emulator, if you do not use your emulator, just like how Project Volta works with your SmartWatch, your AVD will shut itself down if you don't use it within a minute or so of launch.

For this reason, I'd suggest testing the ProAndroidWearable application as soon as it launches in your Android Wear emulator! One would assume that a developer would be eager to see if their Java programming logic, or XML UI Design, works anyway, so letting the AVD go into "power-saving" mode will seldom be a problem.

Once your emulator has loaded, you will get a "Paired!" screen, simulating the pairing of a Wear device with a smartphone or tablet, as shown on the left side of Figure 5-26. After that screen disappears, you will see a **You're all set!** screen, telling you to **Swipe up to get started**, which is shown on the right side of Figure 5-26.

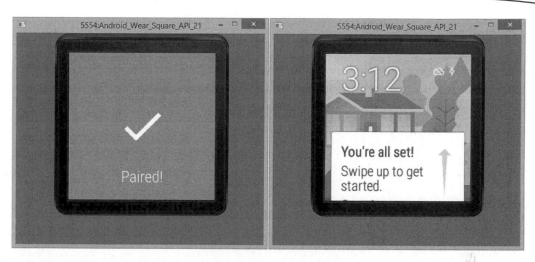

*Figure 5-26.*  *Once you get the Paired screen and You're all set! screen, swipe up!*

If you swipe down the screen at this point, you see a list of the various things you can do with the wearable, just like you did with the Android Wear Round AVD, and as shown in Figure 5-27 in the left-hand pane. Find the Start icon and click it to load the applications that are on the device. Next, find your ProAndroidWearable application and click it. Once you do, you will see your application running, as shown on the right pane in Figure 5-27.

*Figure 5-27.*  *Find the Start menu and the ProAndroidWearable app and start it to run*

Because there are both round and square smartwatches, you need to test your applications on each of these emulators to make sure your app works on both types of screens. Some top manufacturers, such as LG (Lucky-Goldstar) Electronics, even have both types of screens. LG has G (square) and R (round) smartwatch products being offered currently.

# Summary

In this chapter, you learned about how to create **software emulation** for your Pro Android wearables IntelliJ development environment. These are called **Android virtual devices**, also known as **AVDs**, created using the Run/Debug dialog in your IntelliJ IDEA and accessed using your **Run ➤ Edit Configurations** menu sequence.

First, you learned how to use the AVD Manager to create AVD emulators to be used inside Android Studio (IntelliJ IDEA). You created an Android Wear Round and Android Wear Square AVD emulator for the Intel Atom processor as well as for the ARM processor. This was done so that you have four different emulators to use for your Android development work process.

When I tried to run the Android Wear Round AVD for the Intel Atom, I got an error message in an output pane in IntelliJ. So I took that opportunity to show you exactly how to find and install Intel's Hardware Accelerated Execution Manager (**HAXM**) on the workstation in case you encounter this same problem.

I found out Intel does not support AMD processors (no surprises there), so I will have to use those ARM AVDs for my Pro Android wearables development work process. Next, you learned how to actually use these AVDs to run your ProAndroidWearable application and how to navigate the AVD emulation mode.

In the next section of this book, you will start learning the ins and outs regarding how to develop Android wearables apps and add wearable features.

# Chapter 6

# Introduction to Android Watch Faces Design: Considerations and Concepts

Now that you have some "foundational knowledge" in place regarding Android 5 and its new features, Material Design, Android Studio IntelliJ IDEA, and AVD emulators and have set up, updated, and configured an open source Pro Android Wearables application development workstation, the time has come for you to get down to business and learn about the various parts of the Android 5 API that directly apply to and affect wearables application development.

You have already learned how to create a brand new ProAndroidWearable application in Chapter 4 (I wanted to give you a head start), so in this chapter you will begin to learn about the most popular type of Android Wear SDK application. This is called the Watch Faces API, released by Google to enable developers to create custom watch faces that will work across all smartwatch models.

Because there is so much interest in how to create Watch Faces in Wear SDK and although it is complex, it provides a foundation for creating some of the other more advanced types of wearable applications, so I'm going to cover Watch Faces in detail during this book. I'll cover more advanced Android Wearable development topics in Chapter 17. Let's start by looking at watch face design considerations; after that, you'll be learning some of advanced graphic design concepts over the next few chapters.

# Watch Face Design: Considerations and Guidelines

Google's Android Wear SDK recently introduced a **Watch Faces API** in Android Studio 1.x that allows developers to create customized watch faces. This allows developers to create smartwatch "skins" or "faces" using customized designs that are based on a combination of Java code, XML user interfaces, and new media assets such as SVG (Shapes), PNG (Images), and UI widgets.

These Watch Faces applications can simply tell the user what time it is in a new and unique fashion, and they can also show contextually relevant information to the watch wearer, like notifications, the weather, health information, incoming text messages, phone caller names, and similar information that users would want to access in real time to improve their day-to-day lives. The Watch Faces API allows Android 5 developers to create a design that integrates all of these data into one seamless user experience.

## A Watch Faces UI: Seamless Blending of Art and Function

Your Watch Faces UI Design will start with your **activity_main.xml** file, which you created in Chapter 4, and then progress from to the more customized designs in the **square_activity_main.xml** and **round_activity_main.xml** files. As you know, these hold your different watch faces UI design types, which I'll be getting to shortly.

As you might imagine, a watch face design will optimally feature a perfect blend of graphics, algorithms, and data, creating a visual user experience that informs users of various types of information in a beautiful fashion without requiring any additional viewing effort.

Your goal as a Watch Faces API developer will be to create elegant, clear, organized, and attractive user interface layouts that are able to adjust to different smartwatch display types, screen shapes, and bezel sizes.

Throughout this chapter, and the remainder of this book, you'll learn how to design the Watch Faces UI as well as provide your users with options for color and presentation. This will empower your users to create their own personalized Watch Faces user experience using a Wear smartwatch device that fits their lifestyle.

You will also need to consider how Android OS user interface elements will interact with your Watch Faces application design, including system icons such as battery power, Bluetooth, or 4G LTE signal indicators. I'll discuss the various options for positioning these within the UI design layout for your watch face design a bit later in the chapter.

## Watch Faces Power Usage: Interactive and Ambient Modes

The Android Watch Faces API requires that developers provide two different power usage modes for their Watch Faces applications. These are called the interactive (color) mode and the ambient (grayscale) mode. Your watch face UI designs will need to take these different power consumption modes into account. I'll discuss how to optimize designs for both of these modes.

Usually if a watch face design looks professional in ambient mode, it will look even more pristine in the interactive (color) mode. The opposite will not always be the case, as certain colors that contrast in the interactive mode may exhibit the same shades of gray in a grayscale mode, and for this reason, Watch Faces API graphics design will be a lot more tricky than you might expect it would be.

## Watch Faces Interactive Mode: Full Color with 30 FPS Animation

The highest level mode in your Watch Faces smartwatch skin UI design is the **interactive mode**, which allows full color and animation for your Watch Faces design. In interactive mode, when users move their wrists to glance at their watch faces, their screen switches into interactive mode.

Your watch faces (or skins) graphic design can use full color pixels along with high frame rate animation in interactive mode. This is not to say you should use high frame rate animation, if you can avoid doing so, as it uses power at a much faster rate than a static interactive mode watch face design would.

## Watch Faces Ambient Mode: Grayscale with Per Minute Updates

The next highest level mode in your Watch Faces smartwatch skin UI designs will be the **ambient mode**. This mode will help a smartwatch device conserve power by using fewer colors (on a select few models) or using grayscale or black and white to represent your Watch Face UI Design. Your UI design can make it obvious to your user that their smartwatch screen is in an ambient mode by using only grayscale colors for that Watch Face Design component.

It's important not to use a lot of pure white (full on #FFFFFF white pixel color value) in ambient mode. This is because it can drain battery life and can be distracting to the user compared to just a black background color.

In ambient mode, a smartwatch display screen will only be updated one time every minute. For this reason, the Watch Face UI Design should only update hours and minutes when it is in ambient mode. You should only show seconds when it is in interactive mode, and only if the watch face requires it.

The Android OS will alert your watch face applications when the smartwatch device switches into ambient mode, as you will see during this section of the book. you can create a Watch Face ambient mode design to be used in this mode specifically. So, if you are serious about designing Watch Faces applications, you will need to design your graphics at the pixel level to fit all of these different modes, including those super low power modes, which I'll cover in the next section of this chapter.

## Watch Face Power Conservation: Low-bit and Burn Protect

All of today's latest Android Wear smartwatch devices utilize a wide array of different display screen hardware technology. These include **LCD** (liquid crystal display), **LED** (light-emitting diode), **OLED** (organic light-emitting diode), **AMOLED** (active matrix organic light-emitting diode), and Qualcomm's **Mirasol** front-lit technology.

Each of these display pixel array manufacturing approaches that come with their own advantages and power conservation considerations. An important consideration for designing an ambient mode display for your watch face is how it affects battery life and even screen burn-in, which can affect some screen technologies such as AMOLED and OLED.

You can configure your watch face application to display different ambient design graphics depending on the kind of screen available on each device, if you want to get that detailed in your Java coding and XML design. I'll be discussing all of these screen type constants and more complex Watch Faces API considerations during this section of the book so you can craft the best overall design for your watch faces across all screen types.

## Low-bit Ultra Power Conservation: Considerations and Techniques

Pixels in some display screen technology such as OLED or transflective LED will either be "on" or white, or "off" or black, when in ambient mode. The ambient mode in these situations, that is, on these screen types, such as the ASUS ZenWatch, is commonly known as a "low-bit" ambient mode.

When designing for a low-bit ambient mode, use only black and white colors and avoid using grayscale values, as they do not work on low-bit displays. Make sure to test your UI design on devices that use low-bit ambient mode.

This means that you'll need to disable anti-aliasing in your paint styles, which I'll discuss later in the book, which covers the graphics design concepts, such as anti-aliasing, alpha channels, blend modes, and the work processes that are needed to implement these concepts.

## Burn-in Protection and Prevention: Considerations and Techniques

When designing for display screens such as AMOLEDs and OLEDs, which can produce pixel burn-in, much like the old cathode ray tube (CRT) screens would get from displaying the same image for prolonged periods of time, you should minimize white pixel coloration, both for power efficiency and to minimize the display screen burn-in effect.

When these types of display screens are operating in the ambient mode, the operating system will shift the content of the display screen periodically by a few pixels, which will help to avoid this pixel burn-in phenomenon.

The key to minimizing screen burn-in for low-bit ambient mode design is to keep 90% of your pixels black. Replace solid grayscale shapes in a regular ambient mode design with outline shapes in low-bit ambient mode to provide burn-in protection.

Another good idea is to replace grayscale image areas that are filled with pixel (matrix) patterns. For analog (round) watch face designs, hollow out a center (where the hands meet) area so you can avoid pixel burn-in in the center of the watch when it is in low-bit ambient mode.

# Watch Faces UI Design Shapes: Square vs. Round

If you're going to be a Pro Watch Faces API developer, then you will need to learn how to optimize your Java code, XML markup, UI designs, and graphics design to fit both square and round devices. This can be done by using one single design that fits both shapes or by providing two different designs.

If you provide two different designs, then you can use the Android operating system's capability to detect face shapes to your advantage. I'll discuss how to do this in your Java code and XML markup in this part of the book.

Some Watch Face Design concepts may work better in one or the other format, as you might expect. However, with a little clever designing, you can create a hybrid design that will allow users to utilize the watch faces regardless of the display screen format that their smartwatches use.

Let's go over some of the Watch Faces API design guidelines that will help your watch face applications span across both square and round devices.

## Watch Faces Concept Design: Create a Flexible Design Concept

A visual functionality for the watch face design should work in both round and square formats. The visual functions for your watch face should always be flexible enough to be viewable in either format without any adjustment.

However, some watch face design concepts will ultimately require different executions, that is, different Java code, different XML markup, different graphics design, and different animations, across square and round screens.

## Watch Faces Style Design: Use a Common Set of Design Styles

Similar to what you would do using CSS3 with your HTML5 apps and web sites, or using Styles, Themes, and Material Design with your Android application, use a stylized collection of colors, line thicknesses, shading, gradients, graphic design elements, animations, and other design elements to draw the visual connection between your square and round Watch Faces apps versions.

By using similar color palettes or consistent visual elements, your overall UI design's look and feel for your square and round watch face will appear to be customized for each watch face shape while still retaining a feeling that the watch faces application design is part of the same visual system.

## Watch Faces Design Type: Round Analog vs. Square Digital

Some of your Watch Faces Design concepts would probably take the format of the traditional analog clock, since that is the most popular look and feel for time telling throughout the centuries, and it uses a radial (round) approach featuring a center pivot point with hands for hours, minutes, and seconds.

Using this traditional Watch Faces Design scenario, developers will have an opportunity to assimilate the rounded-corner areas that will inevitably be present when translating this design into the square Watch Faces format.

This will give your Watch Faces Design process a creative spark as you try to discover innovative and attractive ways of extending and exploring this additional Watch Faces screen "real estate." This might involve decorative elements, operating system indicators, animated elements, functioning user interface elements, date-related indicators, or calendar dates information.

# Watch Faces Integration: Assimilating OS Functions

The Android Watch Faces API requires that you assimilate all necessary OS features within your watch faces' design, so that your design accommodates basic Android Wear UI elements, such as states, status, and notifications.

These OS-rendered (controlled) UI elements give your Watch Face user their status information regarding their wearable hardware (power, signal, etc.) and show various types of notifications from services on the user's phone, or tablet, which is running the Wear peripheral application.

For this reason, it is important to have a Watch Faces Design work process that displays critical operating system UI elements in a logical location and clearly defined within the watch face design. For instance, ensure the OS-provided UI elements and messages are not obscured by any of your Watch Faces graphic design or UI design elements.

## Android Notifications: CardView UI Layout Messaging

Android "Cards" is a new notification system in Android 5 that bridges information between a wearable peripheral and its host mobile device. This is how most wearable applications are going to notify end users of various things. A user might be notified on their wearable regarding things such as e-mails or text messages. As a watch face developer, you'll be required to support large as well as small Cards in your design. Your watch faces applications can specify your preference for the Card size, but users can override this setting. A user can also temporarily hide a Card by swiping it downward.

A **Peek Card** is the top Card in the notification stream and will be visible at the bottom of your smartwatch screen. A **Variable Peek Card** has a height attribute, which is determined by the amount of text within a notification. A **Small Peek Card** will leave more room for the watch face design. Watch faces with round analog hands usually use the Small Peek Card. If the time is clearly visible above the maximum height of the Variable Peek Card, you can choose to use a Variable Peek Card if you wish. A Variable Peek Card will display more notification information, however, Watch Faces with information on the bottom half of it should optimally utilize a Small Peek Card.

It is important to note that your Android 5 operating system will notify your watch face design (Java code) when the Bounds (dimensions) of a Peek Card changes. For this reason, your Java code will interactively rearrange the user interface and graphic design elements in the watch face design if the Peek Card Bounds object changes and make an interactive rearrangement necessary.

# Android Hardware State Indicators: Hardware Mode Status

Android **State Indicators** are used to tell users the status of the wearable device, such as how much power it has left, if it's currently charging, or if it's in airplane mode. When creating your watch faces design, you need to consider how these indicator icons will fit into your watch face visual design composition.

Android status indicators on a smartphone or tablet are in the Status Bar, no surprises there; however, in a Watch Faces Design, these can be placed in several fixed locations around the display screen for the wearable device.

An Android CardView class is used to create the new "cards" paradigm under material design. If you need to support a larger Peek Card, your indicator placement for your status indicator icons should go near the top or on the center of your Watch Faces Design. If you instead position the hardware status icons on the bottom of a Watch Faces Design, the operating system will be forced to use Small Peek Cards.

If the perimeter of the watch face contains important visual elements, for instance, decorative elements, ticks, or numbers, place your indicators in the center of your Watch Faces Design.

# Android Hotword Placement: The OK Google Phrase

Another important consideration to keep in mind for integrating Android OS functionality into your Watch Faces UI Design is to include spacing for the Android "hotword." The Android hotword is the phrase **OK Google**, which is shown on startup and tells the user that they can interact with the watch by using voice recognition technology, including predefined vocal commands.

When your user turns on their wearable device, this hotword appears on the smartwatch display screen for a few seconds. The hotword no longer appears after the user says OK Google five times, and for this reason, placement of this Android OS UI element is not as critical as the status icons or cards.

You should avoid covering up important UI elements of a watch faces design using the Android hotword location. There are also "background protection" UI element settings for the hotword and state indicators that can help to **increase contrast** (readability). These UI element options should be turned on, unless your design is tailored to have the UI element appear on top of it with maximum contrast (e.g., using dark colors with no patterns).

# Android Peripheral Connection: The Wear Companion App

The Android Wear companion app is the bridge between the "host" smartphone or tablet and the "peripheral" Android Wear smartwatch hardware. This app will give your users access to all of the watch face designs in your app, and allow them to select from the included designs and to change their settings, such as color, numbers, style, animation, features, and the like.

## Watch Faces Manifest: You Don't Have to Provide a Launcher Icon

All available Watch Faces apps are accessed from an Android Wear companion app or from your bundled third-party app. For this reason, your application launcher icon is for the bundled peripheral (smartphone or tablet) app and not for the Watch Faces app.

For this reason, there's no need for a standalone app launcher icon to be declared inside your AndroidManifest.xml file for any of your Android Wear Watch Faces applications.

## Watch Faces Control Panel: Your Settings Dialog Panel

Your Watch Faces Design can also have a Watch Faces Settings panel if your design has useful options that need to be set using a Settings dialog. The settings dialog (or panel) can be made accessible using a Watch Face itself or by using the (larger) display screen on the companion application that is installed on the user's smartphone or tablet.

You should design your Watch Faces settings on the watch face itself to be limited to on or off (termed binary) selections. You can also use **ListView** objects (class) to implement scrollable lists of settings.

Settings on the Wear companion application on a smartphone or tablet might include more complex configuration items in addition to the basic settings you make available on the watch face UI design.

You can use the standard UI layout container classes (UI components), such as the Android **CardView** class, to design a settings dialog or the settings panel in most cases, as you will learn later in this book.

As you become a more advanced Android Watch Faces API developer, you might also want to explore other, more complex, creative settings option designs once you have built a solid work process for designing your watch faces.

# Watch Faces Function: Functional Data Integration

Now that I have covered the Watch Face Design rules and Form, I'll cover Watch Faces functions. Your Watch Faces Design can show users "contextually relevant" data, such as the weather outside, the phases of the moon, or colors representing nighttime, sunrise, midday, or sunset and similar textual data representations, which will turn raw data into Watch Faces Design graphics.

Watch Face Designs will usually visualize different types of external data by changing colors, styles, or graphic designs for the Watch Faces Designs. This is done using Java code and XML markup. Let's take a look at some of the many considerations for adding function to form for Watch Face Design.

# Data Visualization: The Data You Want a User to See

The first step in Watch Faces Design where data integration is involved is the graphic design that will bring to life, or visualize, the data themselves.

Decide how your watch face is going to define your viewer's perceptions of the data you want to display as part of your watch face design. Your visual conceptualization of the data should be easy to recognize or figure out by the user. Additionally, the data your watch design is trying to visualize need to be supported by a real user's day-to-day requirements and the need to put these data to real-world usage.

You need to think about what you want the end users to know after they look at the watch faces' design. Will they understand what your design is trying to convey using the colors, style changes, or graphic design you've chosen?

Once you have designed your data visualization and tested it to make sure that users can identify how your design is visualizing the data they are interested in, the next thing you will need to do is determine how the watch face is going to obtain the data you are going to visualize.

# Data Integration: A Fusion of Watch Face Design and Data

If you are going to visualize data other than just the time of day, design the watch faces application so that it includes other useful types of data that relate closely to the time data that are central to the watch face.

Logical types of data to include with time data would include the date, of course, and maybe a timer (stopwatch), alarms, calendar appointments, time zone features, weather forecasts, moon phases, and maybe even location or fitness data.

You also need to find a way to seamlessly integrate the data visualization with your Watch Faces Design in a way that creatively inspires the viewers when they glance quickly at the watch face application to consume the data you're visualizing using color, text, style, or custom graphic design.

The brilliance with which your design both visualizes and integrates the external data will directly relate to the popularity of a watch face app. For this reason, you will want to avoid overlaying a time-based watch face with extra data, without seamlessly integrating it into the overall design in a clever fashion, using an inspired design.

When designing your data integration, you need to consider how that type of data can be expressed through the design you are using for your watch face. As an example, if you're designing a weather-related watch face, use color gradients that reflect the current temperature range for the day, so a range of 80 to 100 degrees can be represented using orange to red color or 20 to 40 degrees might be represented using white to light blue colors.

# Data Assimilation: Use a Simple, Unified Design Objective

Once you have decided how you are going to visualize your data and have reached your watch face concept decision, it is time to use Java code, XML markup, and digital imaging (GIMP for instance) to achieve your desired UI design.

The most popular watch face designs are ultimately going to be the designs that are, at the same time, both simple and elegant. Watch Faces that can convey a lot of information with one simple glance are going to be in high demand in the Wear market. Watch Faces that are able to deliver a unified design that expresses different types of data are going to be considered to be the most "genius" watch faces in the Google Play Store.

In order to craft one singular watch face data visualization "message," you will have to rank the most important data you want to visualize within the design. For instance, instead of trying to put a comprehensive weather forecast on the watch face, you might use a graphic design that shows what the sky will look like if you go outside (sunny, cloudy, stars, rain, snow, and the like).

If you're displaying text-based information, try to minimize the number of characters on the screen at any one given time. For instance, if you are adding calendar features, instead of trying to display an entire month of calendar events, your design should only display one or at the most two upcoming events.

Utilize the process of "reverse reduction," which I'll discuss next, and you'll be able to craft one singular expression of data in the design.

## Watch Face Development: Start Basic and Add as You Go

Make sure your watch faces design work process begins with careful thought regarding what your Watch Face will provide to your end user. This should give you the insight into the needs and expectations of your end users so you can construct a winning watch face application, which is the topic of discussion over the course of this book.

It's always a good idea to run a concept by other smartwatch aficionados to see if the consensus regarding the design concept is a good and popular one. You should also test your watch face design thoroughly as you develop it, and even implement a "beta test program" and include other smartwatch users who can confirm any of the design assumptions you've made about your watch face design.

It might even be a great idea to start your watch face design work process by drawing out a rough sketch of the watch face design on a napkin and ask a smartwatch end user or two to tell you what they think of the design, as well what they would use it for.

Don't make the assumption that you are going to develop an epic Watch Face Design on the very first try, as that is not likely to happen. You'll need to try the watch face design and data combination with different types of data in conjunction with different design scenarios. You should also be sure to test your watch face design with an actual watch screen before you start coding.

## Watch Faces Graphic Design: Multimedia Concepts

Let's take a look at the different types of graphics concepts and support in Android 5 that you're likely to use in your Watch Faces Design. The primary assets you will be using in Watch Faces Design are **vector illustration**, called Shapes and Gradients in Android, and **bitmap images**, which use graphic file formats such as JPEG, WebP, and PNG, and

**Animation**, which support both **vector animation** and **bitmap animation** and brings both of these types of multimedia into a fourth dimension (movement over time).

Let's start by learning about the most data compact graphic technology, vector illustration, which is done using only code, then cover bitmaps and graphic formats supported in Android and core digital image concepts, and then finish by examining how animation is implemented in Android, using XML markup in conjunction with bitmap image assets and vector code. After I've covered all of this, you'll be ready to dive into Java coding, XML markup, and the graphic design work process needed to create Watch Faces!

## Vector Watch Faces: Using SVG, Shapes, and Gradients

The most data-optimized type of new media asset that can be used in Watch Face Design is **digital illustration**, commonly known as **vector graphics**. If you are familiar with Adobe Illustrator or InkScape, then you already know that vector graphics involves **lines**, **curves**, **strokes**, **fills**, and **gradients**.

The major open source file format for vector graphics is called **SVG**, which stands for **Scalable Vector Graphics**. All the popular open source platforms support SVG data, including Android, as well as HTML5 and JavaFX (Java 8).

As a Pro Android developer, you know that multimedia assets in Android are represented using **Drawable** objects. Vector shapes will use a **ShapeDrawable** class to create an outline of the vector shape and can fill the shape with a gradient use of the **GradientDrawable** class. Your Watch Faces app can create these scalable vector graphic elements on the smartwatch screen using only Java code, or using Java code in conjunction with XML definition files.

It's important to note that entire Watch Faces applications can be created only using SVG, which means that they'll be 100% Java code and XML markup. For this reason, the file size for these application APK files will be exceptionally small, as there will be no new media asset (digital image file) storage inside the APK file.

Certain Watch Faces Design elements are especially well suited to scalable vector elements. Lines can be used for hour, minute, and second hands, text can be used for numbers and Roman numerals, or circle elements can be used for the watch rim or chronograph elements, for instance.

Usually there will be some combination of vector graphic elements, bitmaps, and animation used for a Watch Faces Design, so let's look at the BitmapDrawable object for Android next, as well as other supported digital image formats and even a few important digital imaging concepts so that you will better understand what I am talking about during the remainder of this book.

## Bitmap Watch Faces: Bitmap Formats and Image Concepts

Because you'll be using digital images for your Watch Faces Design and digital images are also the foundation of your AnimationDrawable objects in Android, I will spend some time providing those of you who are not professional digital image editors with the foundational knowledge that is needed to understand the concepts in this book. Android 5 supports a number of popular open source digital image file formats, some of which, such as GIF, have been around for decades. Let's look at those next.

# Android Digital Image Format Support: PNG, JPEG, WebP, and GIF

Digital image formats supported by Android 5 range from your decades-old Compuserve Graphic Information Format (**GIF**) and ancient Joint Photographic Experts Group (**JPEG**) formats, to the more recent Portable Network Graphics (**PNG**) and Web Photo (**WebP**) formats. I will cover these in order of origin, from the older (and much less desirable) GIF, to the newest WebP format.

Compuserve GIF is still supported by the Android 5 OS, however, it is not recommended for everyday use. GIF is a **lossless** digital image file format, as it does not throw away any image data to achieve its better compression result. The GIF compression algorithm, called a **codec** (Coder-DECoder), is not as refined (read: powerful) as the other formats. It only allows **indexed color**, which I'll cover later in this chapter. That said, if all your image assets are already created and they use GIF format, you'll still be able to use them without any problems, other than decreased visual quality in a Watch Face.

The next oldest digital imagery file format that Android supports is JPEG, which uses a **truecolor** depth instead of an indexed color depth. JPEG is a **lossy** digital image file format. The term comes from the fact that it "throws away" or loses original image data, in order to be able to achieve this smaller file size. JPEG format can compress imagery up to, or greater than, an order of magnitude (or ten times, if you are wondering) smaller.

It's important to note that the original image data, which is known by the term "raw," or uncompressed image data, is unrecoverable after compression by a JPEG codec encoding has taken place. For this reason, you should make sure to save your original (uncompressed) image before you run your image through this JPEG digital image compression algorithm.

If you zoom into JPEG images after compression, you'll see discolored areas, which clearly were not present in the original image. These degraded areas in JPEG image data are termed **compression artifacts** in the digital imaging industry. Compression artifacts occur when using lossy image compression.

This is a primary reason that JPEG file format is not a highly recommended digital image format for use in Android. The most recommended image format for use in Android 5 application development is the PNG file format. PNG is pronounced "ping" in the digital image industry. PNG has both its indexed color version, called **PNG8** (or PNG5, if you only need to use 32 colors), as you'll discover later in this chapter, and truecolor versions, which are called **PNG24** (no alpha channel) or **PNG32** (with alpha channel). I'll discuss the concept of a digital image alpha channel later in the chapter as well, as it's very important.

The PNG8 and PNG24 numbering extensions I am using represent the **bit-depth** of color support, so truecolor PNG with an alpha channel could technically be referred to as a PNG32. Similarly, a PNG using 16 colors should be said to be a PNG4, a PNG using 64 colors should be referred to as a PNG6, and a PNG using 128 colors should be referred to as a PNG7 and so on. The reason PNG is the recommended format for use with Android 5 is because it uses lossless compression. This will provide high image quality as well as good digital image data compression efficiency.

The most recent image format was added to Android 5 when Google acquired ON2, the WebP image format. This format is supported with Android 2.3.7 for image read or playback support, and in Android 4.0 or later for image writing or digital image file saving support.

Image writing support in Android, in case you might be wondering, would be used with your Android camera, so your users can save or write images to their SD card or to the cloud via remote web server. WebP is a static image version of the WebM video encoder file format. WebM is also known in the industry as the ON2 VP8 video codec, which was acquired by Google, and then declared for (also termed "released into") open source availability.

## The Foundation of Watch Faces Digital Imagery: The Pixel

Digital imagery is made up of 2D arrays or grids. These contain data elements commonly referred to as **pixels**. This industry term is a conjugation of the word **picture** (some people call these "pix") and **element** (if you shorten the word elements you get the hip word "els").

The number of pixels in your digital image asset is expressed using a term called **resolution**. This is the number of pixels in both the **width** (denoted using a W or an X for the x axis), and the **height** (denoted using an H or a Y for the y axis) dimensions of an image. Resolution for image assets is usually expressed using two (X and Y) numbers, with an "x" in the middle, or using the word "by," such as **800x480** or as **800 by 480** pixels.

To find the total number of pixels in a 2D image, simply multiply the width pixels by the height pixels. For instance, HDTV resolution, 1920-by-1080 images contain 2,073,600 pixels, or over two million pixels. This is also referred to as **two megapixels**. The more pixels in an image, the higher its resolution can be said to be, giving higher visual quality.

Just like digital cameras, which range from three-megapixel smartphone cameras to 75-megapixel DSLRs (digital single-lens reflex), the more megapixels in your digital image grid or array, the higher the quality level that can be achieved using the image. This is why 4K **UHDTV** screens, which have a resolution of 4096 by 2160, are becoming popular. Android supports smartwatch resolution through 4K UHDTV.

## The Shape of a Watch Faces Digital Image: The Image Aspect Ratio

A more complicated aspect (no pun intended!) of digital imagery resolution would be the **image aspect ratio**, a concept that also applies to Android 5 device hardware displays. Aspect ratio is the **ratio of width to height**, or **W:H**, or if you like to think in terms of an x axis and y axis, it would be **X:Y**. The aspect ratio will define the **shape** of an image or display screen, that is, how square or rectangular (popularly called widescreen) the image or the display screen might be. Watch Faces have a square aspect ratio.

A 1:1 aspect ratio display (or digital image) is perfectly square, as is a 2:2 or a 3:3 aspect ratio image. It is important to notice that it is the **ratio** between these two numbers that defines the shape of the image, or of a screen, not the numbers themselves. That is why this is called an aspect ratio, although it is often called the image "aspect" for short.

The image aspect ratio is usually expressed as the **smallest set or pair** of numbers that can be achieved (reached) on either side of the aspect ratio colon. If you paid attention in high school, when you learned about lowest (or least) common denominators, the aspect ratio math will be very easy.

I perform the mathematical matriculation by continuing to divide each side by two. Taking a fairly common **1280-by-1024 SXGA** resolution as an example, half of 1280:1024 is 640:512; half of that, would be 320:256; half of that would be 160:128; half of that again is 80:64; half of that is 40:32; half of that is 20:16; half of that is 10:8, and half of that is 5:4, so an SXGA screen uses a **5:4 aspect ratio**.

Interestingly, all the above aspect ratios are the same aspect ratio, thus all are valid! So if you want to take the really easy way out, replace the "x" in your image resolution with a colon and you have an aspect ratio for the image, although distilling it down to the lowest format, as I did here, is far more useful and is the industry standard way to do things.

The original PC screens used a more square 4:3 aspect ratio, and early 2:3 aspect ratio CRT television sets were nearly square as well. The closer these numbers on either side of the colon are to each other in size, the more square the image or the screen aspect ratio is. Always remember that identical numbers represent a square aspect ratio, unless one of the numbers is a one. The 2:1 aspect is a widescreen display, and a 3:1 aspect display would be downright panoramic, if and when it comes into existence that is!

The current display market trend is certainly toward widescreens as well as ultra high resolution displays. Android 5 Watch Faces could change this trend back toward a square aspect ratio. Square screens are being used in a variety of new consumer devices, one of which is Android 5 smartwatches.

## Coloring Your Digital Images: RGB Color Theory

Now that you understand digital image pixels, how they are arranged in 2D rectangular arrays, and about aspect ratio, which defines a rectangular shape, the next logical aspect (again no pun intended) to look into is how each of the pixels is assigned a color value. Pixel colors are defined by an amount of three colors: red, green, and blue (or RGB). These are present in varying amounts in each pixel. Android display screens utilize **additive** color, which is where the wavelength of light for each RGB **color plane** can be summed together. Additive colors are used to create tens of millions of different color values. This is used in popular LED, LCD, and OLED displays, which are used in smartwatches, smartphones, iTV sets, or tablets. Additive color is the opposite of subtractive color, which is utilized in printers.

The amounts, or numbers, of RGB "shades" or intensities of light that you have available to mix together determined the total amount of colors you will be able to reproduce. In today's digital devices, we can produce 256 levels of light intensity for each RGB color. Colors are generated for each image pixel, so every pixel in an image will have 256 levels of color intensity for each of the RGB data values. Each of these RGB "plates" or "planes" would use one byte of data per RGB color.

## Amount of Color in Watch Faces Digital Imagery: The Color Depth

The **number of bits** that are used to represent color data in digital image assets is referred to as the **color depth** of that image. It is important to note that in digital images, fewer than eight bits can be used to represent an amount of color in an image. This only applies when you're using "indexed" color models, which I'll be discussing in this section.

There are several common color depths used in the digital imaging industry, and I will outline the most common ones here, along with the digital image file format that uses them in Android OS. The lowest color depth exists in the eight-bit indexed color digital image formats. An indexed color image will use **256 total color values** per pixel and will use the **GIF** or a **PNG8** image format to contain these indexed color digital image data.

Indexed color imagery does not have (RGB) color planes, so it is generally **three times smaller** than a truecolor RGB image will be. Instead, it uses a "palette" of up to 256 maximum color values to represent all of the colors in a digital image. This **palette** is "culled" using a compression algorithm (codec), which finds the most frequently used colors in that digital image.

A **24-bit** color or **truecolor** depth image features the full eight-bit color data values for each of your RGB **color plates** (also called **color planes**). These truecolor images are capable of displaying 16 million potential colors per pixel. This is calculated as 256 × 256 × 256 and equals 16,777,216 colors.

Using a 24-bit color depth will give you the highest digital image quality level, which is why Android prefers the use of the PNG24 or the JPEG image file format. Because PNG24 is lossless, which means that it loses no quality during its compression process, it offers the highest quality compression and lowest original data loss, along with the highest quality color depth.

For this reason, the PNG24 is the preferred digital image format to use as far as Android is concerned. This is because the use of PNG produces the highest quality visual results across any and all Android 5 applications.

It's important to note that higher color depth (16 bits of data in each of the RGB channels) imagery currently exists, made popular by the i3D gaming industry. This color depth is called HDRI (high dynamic range imagery).

## Representing Color in Watch Faces: Using Hexadecimal Notation

Now that you know what color depth is and that colors are represented as a combination of three different color channels within any given image, let's look at how, as programmers, we are going to represent these three RGB color values inside Android apps so we'll be able to create any color in the visible color spectrum.

It's important to note that in the Android 5 OS, color is not only used in digital image assets known as BitmapDrawable objects, but also in scalable vector graphics such as color fills and gradients, which you learned about earlier. Color data values are also used for setting UI color, such as the background color value utilized in your user interface screen or for your textColor values, for instance, that fill your font outlines with color.

In Android 5, different levels of RGB color intensity are represented as data values using **hexadecimal notation**. Hexadecimal notation is based on the original **Base16** computer notation used decades ago to represent 16-bit data values. Base10 notation will count from zero through nine, whereas Base16 notation will count from zero through F, where F would represent a Base10 value of 15. Counting from zero through 15 gives you 16 total data values.

To tell Android that you're giving it the hexadecimal value, you would preface the Base16 values using the **pound sign**, also known as the **hash tag**, like this: **#FFFFFF**. This hexadecimal notation data value represents a color of **white**, because if you blend red, green, and blue light wavelengths together, your resulting light color will be white, sometimes considered no color at all!

Because each slot in this 24-bit hexadecimal representation represents one Base16 value, to get the 256 values you need for each RGB color will take two of these slots, as 16 × 16 equals 256. Therefore, for a 24-bit image, you would need six slots after your hash tag, and for a 32-bit image, you would need eight slots after your hash tag. I'll be covering what 32-bit images are, and what they are used for, in the next section of this chapter.

The hexadecimal data slots represent the RGB values in the following format: **#RRGGBB**. Thus, for the color white, all red, green, and blue channels in this hexadecimal color data value representation are at a **maximum luminosity** of fully on, or FF, which would be 16 × 16, and a full 256 data value for each RGB color channel. As you can see, I'm using the different industry terminology (color channels, color planes, color plates) that you will find being utilized currently in the graphics design industry. All these digital imaging terms can be used interchangeably, if you so desire.

If you additively sum all of the colors together, you will get white light. In differing amounts, they will create colors! The color **yellow** is represented by the red and green channels being on and the blue channel being off, so the hexadecimal notation representation for the color yellow would be **#FFFF00**, where both red and green channel slots will be fully on, using FF for a color intensity (level) value of 256, and the blue channel slots being fully off, using 00, indicating a zero value.

As I mentioned earlier in this section, there is also a **32-bit** image color depth whose data values are represented using an **ARGB** color channel model. In this model, A stands for **alpha**, which is short for **alpha channel**. I'll be going over the concept of image alpha and alpha channels in far greater detail in the next section of the chapter, and I'll also cover the more advanced (and related) concept of **pixel blending**.

The hexadecimal notation data slots for your ARGB color channel model data values will hold data in the following format: **#AARRGGBB**. Thus, to represent the fully opaque color white, all the alpha, red, green, and blue channels in your hexadecimal color data value representation should be at a maximum luminosity (and maximum opacity). The alpha channel is set to fully opaque by using an FF value, so the full hexadecimal value would be **#FFFFFFFF**.

A **100% transparent alpha channel**, on the other hand, is represented by the alpha slots being set to zero. Thus, a fully transparent image pixel could be configured as #00FFFFFF, or #00000000, or even #00F7D9C4, if you like.

It is important to notice here that if an image alpha channel is set to be transparent, then it follows that each pixel color data value, represented by the last six hexadecimal data slot values, does not even matter! This is because a 100% transparency data value will override any color value using what a "pixel needs to be composited with a completely transparent setting" for that particular pixel's ARGB (alpha channel plus color) data value.

# Representing Transparency in Watch Faces: Using Alpha Channels

This section will look at how digital images are **composited** together in a process known as **image compositing**. This is done by a professional graphic artist who is called a digital image **compositor**.

Digital image compositing is a process of **blending** together more than just one single layer of digital imagery (a photograph). This is done to obtain a more complex image. A composite image on a display screen will appear as though it were one single image. In reality, an image composite is actually a collection, in a stack, of more than one, seamlessly composited digital image **layers**. To be able to accomplish seamless image compositing, the images used in each layer need to use an alpha channel (a transparency level) data value that is associated with each of the pixels in the image.

You can use an alpha value for each pixel in the image to precisely control the **blending** of the pixel with other pixels with the same image **coordinate** or location, but on other layers, above or below that particular image layer. It is because of this layer-stacking paradigm that I refer to this compositing as 3D, as these layers are stacked along a **z axis** and can be said to have a particular **Z order**. Do not get this confused with 3D modeling software such as Blender3D, as the end result of a digital image compositing (layer) stacking is still a resulting 2D digital image asset.

Like all channels, alpha channels also support 256 levels of transparency. These are represented using your first two data slots within a hexadecimal representation for the ARGB data value, which has eight slots (32-bits) of data, rather than the six slots used to represent a 24-bit image. A 24-bit image can be thought of as being a 32-bit image, with opaque alpha channel data. Don't use a 32-bit image format unless you need transparency values!

To relate this to image compositing, 24-bit imagery doesn't use an alpha channel and is not going to be used for image compositing, unless it is the bottom plate (or back plate) in an compositing layer stack. A 32-bit image, on the other hand, is going to be used as a compositing layer on top of something else that will need the ability to show through (via transparency values) in some of the pixel locations. These 32-bit composite image layers on top of a 24-bit back plate use pixel transparency to create a final composited digital image. So you might be wondering how having an alpha channel and using digital image compositing factor into Watch Faces graphic design.

A primary advantage is the ability to split what looks like a single image into a number of **component layers**. The reason for doing this is to be able to apply Java code logic to individual layer elements in order to control **component parts** of Watch Face Designs you can't individually control.

# Algorithmic Image Compositing in Watch Faces: Blending Modes

There is another more powerful aspect of image compositing called **blending mode**. If you are familiar with Photoshop or GIMP, you know that each layer in a digital image composite will be set to use a different blending mode. Blending modes are **algorithms** that specify how the pixels for a layer are blended (mathematically) with the previous layers (underneath that layer).

These pixel blending algorithms take into account your transparency level, and they can be used to achieve virtually any compositing results you are trying to achieve. Blending modes can be implemented in Android 5 using the **PorterDuff** class. This PorterDuff class gives Watch Face designers the same blending modes Photoshop (or GIMP) affords to digital image artisans.

The major difference with Android is that blending modes can be controlled interactively, using custom Java 7 programming logic. This is the exciting part for us Watch Faces developers. Some powerful Android PorterDuff class blending modes include **XOR**, **SCREEN**, **OVERLAY**, **DARKEN**, **LIGHTEN**, **MULTIPLY**, or **ADD**. Apress's *Pro Android Graphics* (2013) title covers how to implement PorterDuff blending modes inside a complete image compositing pipeline, if you are interested in diving into this area of Android 5 in far greater detail.

## Masking Watch Faces Digital Imagery: Leveraging Alpha Channels

One of the most popular uses of the alpha channel is to "mask" out an area of a digital image. This creates a layer that can be utilized in the image compositing layer stack. This is clearly important to Watch Face Design as components such as hands, numerals, or decorative components will use this.

**Masking** is a process of extracting subject matter, essentially cutting the subject matter out of your source image, so that it can be placed (pasted) onto its own transparent layer. I'll explain the work process for performing this masking process using GIMP during the course of this book.

A masking process yields a part of your image on its own layer. The masked subject will be isolated from the rest of the source image, but because of the layer transparency, it will appear as if it were still in the final image composite. Once the masked image element has its own alpha channel, you'll be able to do things such as rotate, tint, scale, or move this element and not affect the rest of your image composite.

The implications for Watch Faces Design are fairly obvious, which is why I'm covering this foundational material here and why you'll be using a masking work process later on in this book, so you'll get some masking experience.

A masking work process allows you to put image elements (subject material) to use inside other imagery, such as Watch Faces or to use for special effects applications. Digital image software (Photoshop and GIMP) has many tools and features that are specifically there to be used for masking, and later in image composites. You can't really do effective image compositing without creating a mask, so it is an important area to master for graphics designers, and for Pro Android Wearables (and Watch Faces) developers.

The major important consideration in a masking process is getting a smooth but crisp edge around a mask object, so that when you "drop it into" a new background image, it looks as though it belonged there in the first place.

The key to masking is a proper **selection** work process. Using digital image software selection tools (there are a half-dozen of these in GIMP 2.8) in the proper way with an optimal work process is the key to "pulling" the "clean" image mask (an additional cool industry term for you to toss around, to make you appear both artistic as well as tech savvy).

If there are areas of uniform color around a subject that you want to mask, it makes the masking process easier. You can shoot subjects on bluescreen, or on greenscreen, and then you can use the "magic wand tool" along with a threshold setting to select everything except the object and then invert a selection set, in order to obtain a selection set containing the object.

Other GIMP selection tools contain complex algorithms that can look at the color changes between pixels in an image. These can be very useful in edge detection, which you can use for other types of selection work processes.

The GIMP Scissor edge-detection selection tool will allow you to drag your cursor along the edge of the object you wish to mask, while the edge-detection selection tool's algorithm lays down the precise, pixel-perfect placement of the selection edge automagically (based on its algorithms).

## Smoothing Watch Faces Edges: The Concept of Anti-Aliasing

Anti-aliasing is an imaging technique that is usually implemented using an algorithm. What it does is find where two adjacent colors meet in an image and blend the pixels around that jagged edge. Anti-aliasing will add blend colors along the edge between two colored areas to visually smooth blended colors together along that (formerly) jagged edge. This makes jagged edges appear to be smoother when the image is zoomed out, when the pixels aren't individually visible. What anti-aliasing does is it tricks your eyes into seeing smoother edges, to eliminate what is commonly called the "jaggies." Anti-aliasing provides impressive results, using very few (seven or eight) intermediary averaged color values for the pixels that lie along an edge that needs to look smoother.

By intermediary or averaged I mean some colors or spectrum of colors, which is partway between the two colors that are intersecting along an edge. I created a visual example of anti-aliasing to show you the effect. As you can see in Figure 6-1, I created a seemingly smooth red circle against a yellow background. I zoomed into the edge of that circle and grabbed a screenshot. I placed this alongside the zoomed out circle to show the anti-aliasing (orange) values for colors between (colors which are made using) the red and yellow color values that border each other on the edge of the circle. Notice that there are seven or eight average color values.

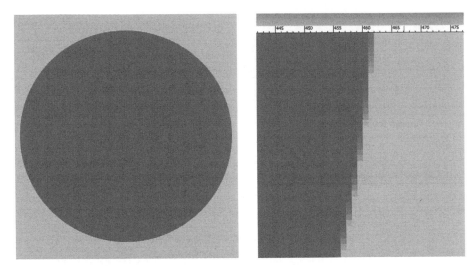

*Figure 6-1. A red circle on a yellow background (left) and a zoomed in view (right) showing the anti-aliasing*

The best way to get great anti-aliasing results is to use the proper image masking work process, using proper settings with any given selection tools you might be using. One of the other tricks for implementing your own anti-aliasing effect is to use the **Gaussian blur** tool with a very low blur value (0.15 to 0.35) on the transparency layer containing the object that has jagged edges. This will provide the same anti-aliasing you see in Figure 6-1, and not only that, it will "blur" your transparency values for the alpha channel (mask) itself as well. This will allow you to anti-alias that 32-bit image object with any background imagery you may be attempting to seamlessly composite it against. I'll be showing you these cool digital image compositing techniques using GIMP 2.8 later in this book in Chapter 12, so get ready to learn how to be a digital image compositing Android Wearables Watch Faces designer and developer! Next, let's look at image optimization!

## Optimizing Your Watch Faces: Digital Image Compression Factors

There are several technical factors affecting digital imagery compression, which is the process of using a codec that an algorithm looks at for your image data and finds a way to save it as a file that uses less data. A codec's encoder essentially finds "data patterns" in the image and turns them into a form of data that the decoder part of a codec can use to reconstruct an original image.

There are some approaches that can be used to obtain higher quality image compression results, which should result in a smaller file size along with higher image quality. The image with a small file size and a high level of quality can be said to have achieved a **highly optimized data footprint**.

This is a primary objective in optimizing digital imagery, to get the very smallest data footprint possible while at the same time achieve a high quality visual end result. Let's start by discussing the image attributes that affect data footprint the most and examine how each of these aspects can contribute to data footprint optimization for a given digital image. Interestingly, these are similar to the order of digital imaging concepts that I covered thus far during the second half of this chapter!

The most critical contributor to your resulting image file size (your data footprint) is the number of pixels or the **resolution** of the digital image. This is logical, because each of the pixels needs to be stored, along with the color values for each of these pixel's RGB color channels. Therefore, the smaller you can make your image resolution, while still having it look detailed, the smaller your image file size will be, as there are less data.

Raw (uncompressed) image sizes can be calculated using this formula: width × height × color channels. So for 24-bit RBG images, there are three (RGB) color channels, and there are four (ARGB) color channels for 32-bit images. Thus, an uncompressed, truecolor (24-bit), VGA image will have 640 × 480 × 3, equaling 921,600 bytes, of original uncompressed data. If you divide 921,600 by 1,024 (number of bytes in a kilobyte), you will get the number of kilobytes that are in a raw VGA image (an even 900 KB).

As you can see, color depth is therefore the next most critical contributor to data footprint in the image, because the number of pixels in that image is multiplied by one (eight-bit) or two (16-bit) or three (24-bit) or four (32-bit) color data channels. This may be a primary reason indexed color imagery is still being widely utilized, usually via PNG8 image format. Lossless compression algorithms like PNG8 lose no image data (quality), and PNG8 will generally utilize four times less data than a PNG32 and three times less data than a PNG24, so using PNG8 alone can reduce your data footprint 200% up to 300%.

The final concept that can increase the data footprint of the image is the alpha channel, as adding an alpha adds another eight-bit color channel (transparency) to the image being compressed. If you need the alpha channel to define transparency, in order to support future compositing needs with your image, there is no other choice but to include these alpha channel data. Just make sure you do not use a 32-bit image format to contain a 24-bit image that has an empty (unused) alpha channel.

It is interesting to note that most alpha channels, which are used to mask objects in your image, will compress extremely well. This is because alpha channels contain fill areas of white (opaque) or black (transparent) color with very few gray values. The only gray values are in the pixels along edges between the black and white colors. These anti-alias the mask. These gray values in an alpha channel are anti-aliasing values, and, as you know, they are used to provide visually smooth edge transitions for image composites.

The reason for this is because in your alpha channel image mask, the eight-bit transparency gradient is defined with a white to black spectrum (gradient) that defines the alpha channel transparency levels. The gray values along the edges of each object in your mask are essentially averaging (blending) the color of your object with colors in your target background image. This essentially provides **real-time anti-aliasing** using any background imagery.

## Using Indexed Color Images in Watch Faces: Dithering the Pixels

Indexed color images can simulate truecolor images if the colors that are used to create an image do not vary widely. Indexed color images use eight-bit data to define the image colors, using a palette of 256 optimally selected colors, rather than three RGB color channels. Depending on how many colors are used in the image, using only 256 colors to represent your image can cause an effect called **banding**, where the transfers between adjoining colors are not smooth. Indexed color image codecs have an option to correct for this, called "dithering." **Dithering** is a process of creating **dot patterns** along the edges between two adjoining color areas in the image. This tricks your eyes into thinking there is a **third color** being used. Dithering gives us a perceptual amount of colors of 65,536 colors (256 times 256), only if each of the 256 colors borders on each of the other 256 colors (otherwise less).

You can see the potential for creating additional colors, and you would be amazed at the results an indexed color image can achieve in some scenarios, that is with certain images. I took a truecolor image, such as the one shown in Figure 6-2, and saved it as an indexed color image to show you the dithering effect. Look at the dithering effect on the driver's side rear fender in this Audi 3D image, as it contains a gradient of color that will show a dithered effect when I saved it as indexed color.

*Figure 6-2. A truecolor source image uses 16,777,216 colors that are optimized to eight-bit PNG8*

I set the codec to encode the **PNG8** image, as shown in Figure 6-3, using **five-bit** color (32 colors), so that you can clearly visualize the dithering effect. As you can see, many dot patterns are added between adjacent colors by the dithering algorithm, which creates the perception of additional colors.

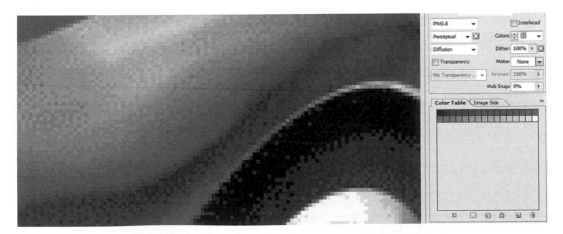

*Figure 6-3. Showing the dithering effect in an indexed color image with compression set to 32 colors (five-bit color)*

It is interesting to notice that you have the option to use less than 256 colors when compressing an eight-bit indexed color image. This is usually done to reduce your data footprint. For instance, an image that can attain good results using 32 colors would actually be a five-bit image (PNG5), even though the format is generally termed PNG8. Notice you will also set a **percentage** of dithering used. I usually select either the 0% or 100% setting, but you may fine tune your dithering effects anywhere in between those two extreme values. You may also select your dithering algorithm type. I use **diffusion** dithering, as it may yield a smoother gradient effect along an irregularly shaped gradient, such as the one you see in Figure 6-3 on the Audi fender.

Dithering, as you might imagine, adds data patterns to the image that are more challenging for the codec's algorithms to compress. Because of this, dithering increases the data footprint by a few percentage points. Be sure to compare the file sizes with and without dithering applied to make sure dithering provides improved the visual results.

Now that I've covered static digital imagery concepts and techniques, a will provide a little information on how Android 5 uses the Animation and AnimationDrawable classes (objects) to allow you to take the digital imagery you learned about to the next level using animation before I finish this chapter.

# Animated Watch Faces: Animation and AnimationDrawable

Android 5 OS has both **bitmap animation**, also known as **frame animation**, and **vector animation**, commonly known as **procedural animation**. Vector animation is referred to as **tween animation** in Android jargon. Animation in Android is handled by two different sets of classes. The **AnimationDrawable** class handles frame animation using the **/res/drawable** project folder to hold your animation assets, and the **Animation** class handles vector animation, using the **/res/anim** project folder to hold the procedural animation definitions.

## Frame Animation for Watch Faces: The AnimationDrawable Class

The Android AnimationDrawable class is the way you implement what are commonly referred to as "flipbook" animation, allowing you to play a range of bitmap frames in rapid succession to create the illusion of motion. The AnimationDrawable class gives developers the ability to create animation assets **outside** of Android 5, using powerful third-party tools like Blender or Lightworks. If you wanted to create animation inside Android, you would use procedural Animation classes using only Java code with XML. Apress's *Pro Android UI* (2014) title covers both animation topics in great detail.

Using the AnimationDrawable class is fairly easy, since all you have to do is define your bitmap frames using GIF, JPEG, WebP, or PNG image assets. This is done using an XML format to define what the file name of each frame asset is and what the duration is for it to be displayed on the screen. This XML file is then "inflated" into an AnimationDrawable object, using Java 7 code, and then Java 7 methods can be used to control playback for your frame animation's new media asset and from that point on in your Watch Faces apps. Frame animation assets use more memory and less processor than vector animation, because it's easy to "flip" through frames, but these must be held in memory to be able to do this. Vector animation uses very little memory to hold the code for the animation "moves," but the processor needs to compute and "render" the moves, creating animated digital illustration.

## Tween Animation for Watch Faces: The Animation Classes

The Android Animation class is a different way to implement animation with code (procedures) rather than with pixels. This type of animation allows a definition of what are called **transformations**. These include **translations** (movements), **rotations** (directional changes), and **scaling** (size changes).

Vector animation allows developers to define complex "sets" of transforms, using an **AnimationSet** class. These include logical grouped transformations including movements (**translate**), orientations (**rotate**), and sizing (**scale**).

The Android OS renders these to the screen using the processor on the user's device, creating an illusion of motion. An Animation class gives developers the ability to create animation assets **inside** Android 5, using only XML and Java code, with no external new media assets needed. It is interesting to note that procedural animation can not only be used to animate a vector shape, gradients, and text, but will also transform bitmap assets as well, including while your frames are animating. I'll cover this in the next section of the chapter, under what I like to term "hybrid animation."

Using the Animation class is not as easy as using AnimationDrawable, because you have to define fairly complex transformational structures using either XML markup or Java code. This is usually done with an XML definition file, which is used to define a hierarchy of grouped rotate, scale, and movement transformations. These harness the power of the Android Animation classes, which include an **Animation**, **AnimationSet** (used for grouping), and of course the **RotateAnimation**, **ScaleAnimation**, **TranslateAnimation**, and **AlphaAnimation** classes. As you may have guessed from the previous section of the chapter, this AlphaAnimation class allows you to also procedurally animate opacity, which will allow you to fade in and fade out components of your animation! These five specialized transformation classes are all **direct subclasses** of an Animation superclass, so all six classes will work together seamlessly.

Your procedural animation XML definition file will also be "inflated" into an Animation object, using Java 7 code, and after that, Java 7 methods can be used to control playback for your vector animation's new media asset from that point on in your Watch Faces application. Remember, Android 5 uses Java 7.

Vector animation assets use more of the CPU processing resources and less of the system memory resources than frame animations use. This is because the user's hardware device processor is rendering a vector animation using math, data, and code in real time. This takes a lot of processing, but very little memory to hold vector and code variables being processed over time.

## Hybrid Animation for Watch Faces: The Power of Combination

It is also interesting to note here, before I finish this chapter, that it is possible to combine your AnimationDrawable frame animation XML definition with your Animation class-based vector animation XML definition.

This is accomplished by applying a vector animation to the UI element that contains the running frame animation. If you set it up correctly, you will be able to achieve even more complex and fantastic animation results using all of the Android animation classes in conjunction with one another.

# Summary

In this chapter, you learned about Watch Faces Design considerations and guidelines, which you will need to create Watch Faces during the remainder of this book.

You learned about important Watch Faces power conservation considerations and about **interactive** mode and **ambient** mode, as well as **low-bit** mode, used by some smartwatch manufacturers, such as ASUS. You looked at Watch Faces Design shapes and how to assimilate Android 5 OS features such as hardware state icons, hotwords, and notification card messages in your Watch Faces Designs. You also looked at advanced Watch Faces settings dialogs and data integration considerations that you will need to create professional apps.

Next, I took some time to make sure you are up to speed on multimedia concepts that I will be using to help you create your Pro Android Wearables applications. In this way, I presented all of the foundational learning you need in this one chapter.

In the next chapter, you will start to learn how to put Java code and XML markup in place to form the foundation for your Watch Faces Design and Watch Faces applications.

# Chapter 7

# Program Watch Faces for Wear: Creating the Watch Face Code Foundation

Now that you have the foundational knowledge in place regarding Android Watch Faces Design and Digital Imaging and Android Animation concepts, you are ready to start coding your Watch Face application, using the bootstrap Java code and XML markup you started in Chapter 4.

Because there was no New Android Project work process included in the earlier coding to create a Watch Face Bootstrap Project infrastructure, this chapter will show you how to morph a standard Wear Project bootstrap infrastructure, turning it into a Watch Faces project. Along the way you'll learn how a Watch Face is set up in Android, what permissions it needs, how Watch Faces AndroidManifest XML files are different from a standard app, and much more.

Let's start by taking a look at the Gradle Build Configuration files and the repositories and dependencies they references, and then add permission entries to your Wear and Mobile app AndroidManifest.xml files.

Once these are in place, you will learn how to create a **New Java Class**. This will create the **Watch Face Service** and **Engine**, which will be the foundation of your Watch Face Design and Watch Face Processing Code. After that, you will create a new **/res/xml** resource directory and create a **watch_face.xml** file. This file is needed to create the living wallpaper paradigm, which is used to make the Watch Faces API operational. Next you'll modify some Watch Face Preview drawable assets and add your Service class and a dozen related parameters to your AndroidManifest XML file. Let's get started!

# Gradle Scripts: Setting Gradle Build Dependencies

If you've not done so already, launch the Android Studio development environment with the quick launch icon you created in Chapter 2. This will launch IntelliJ IDEA and display the ProAndroidWearable project you created in Chapter 4. Click the arrow next to the **Gradle Scripts** folder in the left panel of the IDE to open it, as shown in Figure 7-1.

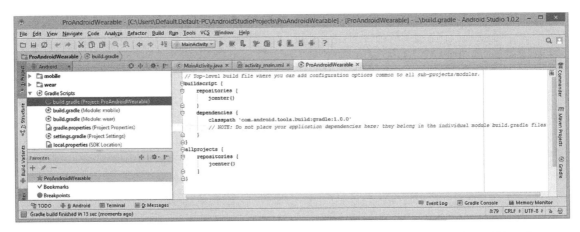

***Figure 7-1.** Open the Gradle Scripts folder in your ProAndroidWearable project and open the Project build.gradle*

Right-click the master **build.gradle (Project: ProAndroidWearable)** file, as shown highlighted in blue at the left of Figure 7-1, and select the **Jump to Source** menu option, or simply use an **F4** function key shortcut if you wish. This will open the top-level (master) Project Gradle Configuration file in the editing area of the IDEA, as shown on the right two-thirds of Figure 7-1.

This top-level build.gradle file will use a (green) classpath reference in the dependencies section, referencing the **Android Gradle Build Tool** on the Android repository server, by using **com.android.tools.build:gradle:1.0.0**.

If the Android Gradle Build Tool has been updated, then the version numbering may be different. This was all set up correctly by the Android New Project series of dialogs; the important thing to note in Figure 7-1 is an important message: *Note: Do not place your application dependencies here; they belong in the individual module build.gradle files.* Because an Android Wear project has a **Wear** as well as a **Mobile** component, as you can see in the IntelliJ Project Navigator Pane on the left, each of the app components will have their own unique Gradle Build Script files, which I will discuss next.

It's important that you place Gradle Build Dependencies in a file matching each Wear and Mobile app component, so that Gradle build works correctly.

Next, right-click the mobile **build.gradle (Module: mobile)** file, shown highlighted in blue at the left of Figure 7-2, and select a **Jump to Source** menu option, or simply use the **F4** function key shortcut if you prefer.

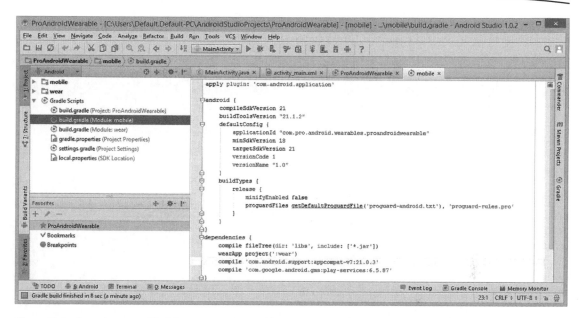

*Figure 7-2.  Open the second build.gradle Module: mobile Gradle Build Script in the ProAndroidWearable project*

This is the build.gradle file for your Mobile application component, which will contain your **application ID**, a concatenation of your package name and class name, which is **com.pro.android.wearables.proandroidwearable**, as well as the **Minimum SDK Version** specification set at **API Level 18** (Android 4.3) and **Target SDK Version** of **API Level 21** (Android 5), as shown in the **android** section of the build.gradle file in the top half of Figure 7-2.

At the bottom of Figure 7-2, you will see the Gradle **dependencies** section, referencing the **wearApp project (':wear')** project type and the compilation dependencies for **Android Support Library**, which you installed in Chapter 4, denoted using **com.android. support:appcompat-v7:21.0.3**, and the **Google Play Services Support Library**, denoted using the **compile** statement setting that specifies **com.google.android.gms.play-services:6.5.87**.

It is important to note that you'll see some projects, such as those that are still using Eclipse ADT IDE, that set the Google Play Services in the Android Manifest file. This can be done using the following **meta-data** tag:

```
<application>
    <meta-data android:name="com.google.android.gms.version"
               android:value="@integer/google_play_services_version" />
</application>
```

Because you are setting this compile dependency in the build.gradle file, you will not need to include this <meta-data> tag in your Android Manifest XML file, which you will be transforming to work with WatchFaces API during this chapter. I will explain what **<meta-data>** tags do later!

Finally, right-click the wear **build.gradle (Module: wear)** file, as seen highlighted in blue at the left of Figure 7-3, and select a **Jump to Source** menu option, or simply use the **F4** function key shortcut if you prefer.

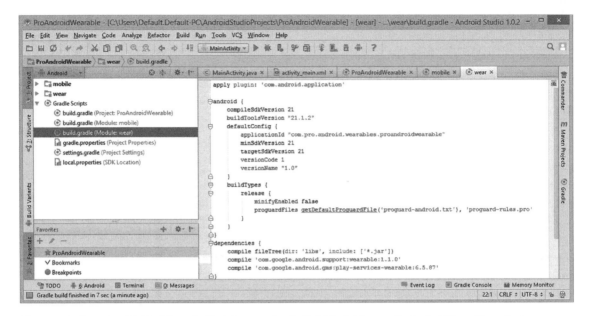

*Figure 7-3. Open the third build.gradle Module: wear Gradle Build Script in your ProAndroidWearable project*

This is the build.gradle file for the SmartWatch (Wear SDK) app component, which as you can see will also contain your **application ID** as well as the **Minimum SDK Version** specification. Note in this Gradle Build specification file that this is set for Wear, at **API Level 21** (Android 5), the same as the **Target SDK Version** of **API Level 21** (Android 5), as shown in the **android** section of the build.gradle file in the top half of Figure 7-3.

At the bottom of Figure 7-3, you will see the Gradle **dependencies** section. Instead of referencing the **Android Support Library**, this Wear Gradle Build specification will instead reference the Android Wear Support Library with the com.google.android. support:wearable:1.1.0 repository path and file and version string concatenation. It's interesting to note the Android Support Library is at com.android.support; Wear is also at com.google.android.support!

Notice you'll need to again reference the **Google Play Services Support Library** using the same **compile** statement you used in the mobile Gradle build.

# Android Permissions: Watch Face Uses-Permission

Click the down arrow, next to the **Gradle Scripts** folder in the left panel, to close that, and then click the arrow next to **wear** to open that folder. Next click the arrow next to the **manifests** folder to open that folder as well, revealing the AndroidManifest.xml file, as shown in Figure 7-4. Right-click the **/wear/manifests/AndroidManifest.xml** file, as shown highlighted in blue at the left of Figure 7-4, and select a **Jump to Source** menu option, or simply use the **F4** function key shortcut if you prefer. As you can see, this opens the AndroidManifest.xml file that was created by a New Android Studio Project series of dialogs you used in Chapter 4.

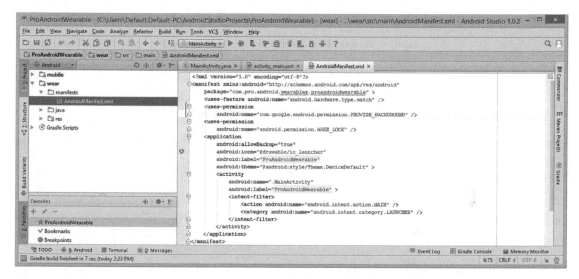

*Figure 7-4. Add two <uses-permission> tags for PROVIDE_BACKGROUND and WAKE_LOCK to wear Manifest*

Add two **<uses-permission>** tags right after (or even before, if you prefer) the <uses-feature> tag specifying smartwatch hardware. The uses-permission attribute is set using this XML tag and defines which permissions your app will request for use from the Android operating system.

Notice that these child tags need to be "nested" inside your **<manifest>** parent tag. This is because the <uses-permission> tag will access constant values that are contained in the Android **Manifest.permission** class. If you are the curious type and would like to see all of the permissions that are allowed by the Android OS in one single location, visit the following URL:

**http://developer.android.com/reference/android/Manifest.permission.html**

One of the permissions you will be using is not listed, and I'll explain why next!

The uses-permission attribute uses the **android:name** variable to set up the predefined operating system constants used to specify permissions required for the use of certain hardware (or software) features in the Android OS.

If you use a constant that is not a part of the Manifest.permission class, then that constant will need to be prefaced by the repository path, so you will notice that the **PROVIDE_ BACKGROUND** constant, shown highlighted at the top of Figure 7-4, uses a **com.google. android.permission.PROVIDE_BACKGROUND** constant reference, whereas a WAKE_ LOCK permission constant reference uses an android.permission.WAKE_LOCK, which is a shorter reference path directly accessing the constant that can now be seen in the Manifest. permission class inside of the Android OS (SDK).

If you visit the Manifest.permissions URL that I included earlier, you will see that the WAKE_LOCK constant is used to enable a permission that allows using an Android PowerManager WakeLocks feature that keeps hardware device processors from sleeping and keeps your (smartwatch) screen from dimming. The XML tags you need to add to the Manifest should look like this:

```
<uses-permission android:name="com.google.android.permission.PROVIDE_BACKGROUND" />
<uses-permission android:name="android.permission.WAKE_LOCK" />
```

Next, click the arrow next to **mobile** to open that folder. Next click the arrow next to your **manifests** folder to open that folder, revealing another Android Manifest file, as shown in Figure 7-5. Right-click this **/mobile/manifests/AndroidManifest.xml** file, as seen highlighted in blue at the left of Figure 7-5, and select a **Jump to Source** menu option or simply use your **F4** function key shortcut if you wish. Add these same two tags to this Manifest file as well, because your wearable permissions need to be a subset of (or equal with) the mobile (phone or tablet) permissions set.

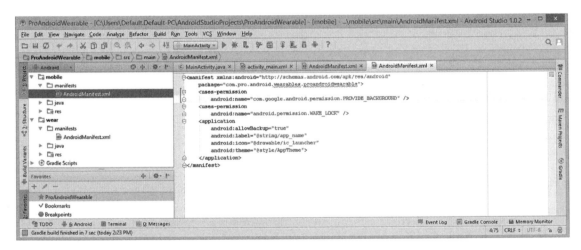

**Figure 7-5.** *Add <uses-permission> tags for PROVIDE_BACKGROUND and WAKE_LOCK to mobile Manifest*

Now you're ready to create the core class for your Watch Faces application, which you will call ProWatchFaceService.java and will use the Android CanvasWatchFaceService class as its superclass. This is getting exciting!

# Canvas Watch Face Service: A Watch Face Engine

This section will look at the classes that drive the foundation of a Watch Face Service, **CanvasWatchFaceService** and **CanvasWatchFaceService.Engine**, as well as where they come from in the Java and Android class hierarchies. You'll also learn how they are implemented in your current ProAndroidWearable project code base, which you'll be morphing into a Pro Watch Face project, so that you know how to do this if you wanted to develop using the Android 5 WatchFaces API.

# The CanvasWatchFaceService Class: An Overview

The Android **CanvasWatchFaceService** class is a **public abstract class**, which means that you must subclass it in order to be able to use it. You will be doing this in the next section of the chapter, after I provide a bird's eye view of the class itself and where it comes from, which will tell you quite a bit about what it is doing and where it gets the capabilities to do so.

The Java class hierarchy is fairly complex and looks like the following:

```
java.lang.Object
  > android.content.Context
    > android.content.ContextWrapper
      > android.app.Service
        > android.service.wallpaper.WallpaperService
          > android.support.wearable.watchface.WatchFaceService
            > android.support.wearable.watchface.CanvasWatchFaceService
```

Of course every class and object in Java is based on **java.lang.Object**, and in Android, a **Service** class is based on the **Context** class, because a Service will need contextual information regarding what your Service, in this case the **WatchFaceService**, is trying to accomplish. Notice the WatchFaceService is subclassed from **WallpaperService**, which tells you that the Watch Face API is based on the Android Wallpaper API, which is why you have to implement Wallpaper objects and BIND_WALLPAPER capabilities during this chapter.

The CanvasWatchFaceService class is a base class used to create watch face apps that uses a **Canvas** object to draw a Watch Face on your display screen. This class provides an invalidate **screen refresh** mechanism that is similar to an **invalidate()** method call. The method call is foundational to Android and is found in the **View** class, and it allows View objects to be refreshed.

# Creating a ProWatchFaceService Subclass: extends Keyword

Now let's put this abstract CanvasWatchFaceService class to use and create an all new Java class in this ProAndroidWearable project. Open your **/wear/java** folder by clicking the right-facing arrow icon. Next right-click the **com.pro.android.wearables.proandroidwearable** (package) folder and then select the **New ➤ Java Class** menu sequence, as shown in blue in Figure 7-6. I also placed the **Create New Class** dialog in the screenshot at the right side to save space. Select the **Class** option from the **Kind** drop-down menu selector, enter the **Name** of **ProWatchFaceService**, and finally click the **OK** button to create your new ProWatchFaceService WatchFace Service and Engine subclass.

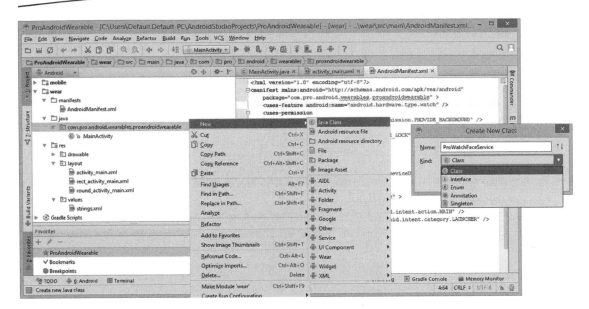

**Figure 7-6.** *Right-click your package folder and use New ➤ Java Class to create the ProWatchFaceService class*

Once you have created the new Java class, it will be opened for you in an editing tab, as seen in the right two-thirds of Figure 7-7. The bootstrap class is provided for you with the following "empty" public class Java code:

```
package com.pro.android.wearables.proandroidwearable;
public class ProWatchFaceService {...}
```

The first thing you will need to do is add your Java **extends** keyword, which you'll insert after your ProWatchFaceService class name, referencing the CanvasWatchFaceService superclass, and giving your ProWatchFaceService class all of the power, algorithms, methods, variables, and features of the Android CanvasWatchFaceService superclass.

If you type in the Java extends keyword and the first few letters of this superclass name, the IntelliJ IDEA will drop down a helper selector dialog for you, as shown in Figure 7-7, and you can find and double-click your CanvasWatchFaceService (android.support.wearable. watchface package) option and have IntelliJ finish writing the code for you. Now you have your empty ProWatchFaceService subclass and are ready to code an Engine inside of it.

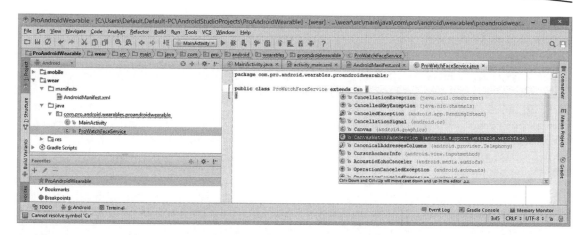

*Figure 7-7.  Use an extends keyword to subclass a ProWatchFaceService class from CanvasWatchFaceService*

Before you code your WatchFaceService **Engine** class, let's take a quick look at the
**CanvasWatchFaceService.Engine** to get an overview of what it can do.

# The CanvasWatchFaceService.Engine Class: The Engine

The **CanvasWatchFaceService.Engine** is a **public class** that provides the Draw
Engine that calls the **onDraw()** method to actually do the heavy lifting of drawing (or
animating in some instances) your Watch Face on the smartwatch screen. The Java class
hierarchy still comes from **WallpaperService.Engine**, however, it is far less complex than
CanvasWatchFaceService and looks like the following:

```
java.lang.Object
   > android.service.wallpaper.WallpaperService.Engine
      > android.support.wearable.watchface.WatchFaceService.Engine
         > android.support.wearable.watchface.CanvasWatchFaceService.Engine
```

This class provides an actual implementation of a Watch Face that draws on a Canvas
using onDraw(). You will need to implement the **.onCreateEngine()** method in your code in
order to get your class to return the usable Engine implementation. This class's constructor
method will be combined with this onCreateEngine() method to get Android OS to return the
new Engine object.

This is done using the following Java constructor method structure, which you will be
implementing in the next section of this chapter:

```
public CanvasWatchFaceService.Engine onCreateEngine() { return new Engine(); }
```

The class has a number of powerful methods that you will be using in your advanced Watch
Face Java code development, which you will be adding over the remainder of this book
once you put a Watch Face Code Foundation in place later in this chapter.

One of the most important methods is the **invalidate()** method, which causes the Engine to redraw the watch face screen. The method will schedule calls to the **onDraw(Canvas, Rect)** method requesting that an Engine draw the next frame of either animation or time update.

There are several **onSurface()** method calls that handle the surface of the canvas, including your **.onSurfaceChanged(SurfaceHolder holder, int format, int width, int height)** method, where you can define what happens when a Watch Face Surface changes, and the **.onSurfaceCreated(SurfaceHolder holder)** method, where you can define what happens whenever a Watch Face Surface is created. There is also the **.onSurfaceRedrawNeeded (SurfaceHolder holder)** method, where you can define what happens whenever the Watch Face Surface needs to be redrawn.

There is also the **.postInvalidate()** method, which requests that the Android OS post a message that schedules a call to the .onDraw(Canvas, Rect) method, requesting that it draw the next frame. Let's create that Engine class now!

# Creating a Private Engine Class: Using onCreateEngine()

Inside the ProWatchFaceService class (inside the curly braces), you need to implement a CanvasWatchFaceService() constructor method, using the Java @Override keyword. Type the @Override and then press the Return key to enter a new line of code, then type the Java public keyword and start to type the constructor method name CanvasWatchFaceService().

When IntelliJ pops up the method insertion helper dialog, as shown in Figure 7-8, choose the **CanvasWatchFaceService(android.support.wearable.watchface)** option and have IntelliJ IDEA write the Java code statement for you. Type a period and the word Engine, to access the complete CanvasWatchFaceService.engine class path.

At this point, all you have to do is add in the onCreateEngine() method call discussed in the previous section after a public keyword and the class name. Inside the curly braces, add the **return new Engine();** statement, and the construct that creates your Watch Face Engine will be created. This would be done using the following Java code structure:

```
public CanvasWatchFaceService.Engine onCreateEngine() {
    return new Engine();
}
```

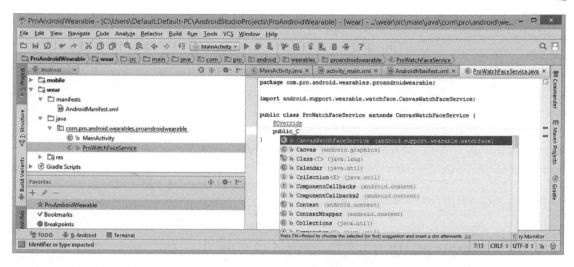

*Figure 7-8.  Add @Override, type the Java keyword public and the letter C, and select CanvasWatchFaceService*

Once you put this public CanvasWatchFaceService.Engine onCreateEngine() in place, as
shown error-free in Figure 7-9, you can code a structure for your Engine **private inner class**,
which will hold the onDraw() method structure.

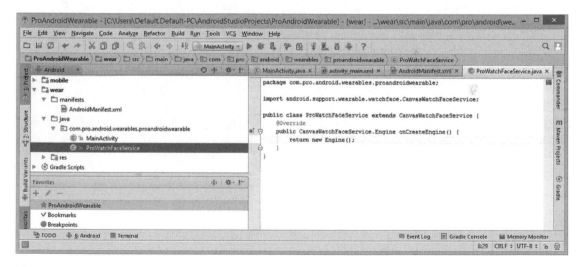

*Figure 7-9.  Add the onCreateEngine() method call and return new Engine(); statement inside the structure*

Create a private inner class inside the ProWatchFaceService class named **Engine**
using the Java private keyword, and use the Java extends keyword to subclass the
CanvasWatchFaceService.Engine class. Your resulting structure should look like the
following Java code:

```
private class Engine extends CanvasWatchFaceService.Engine {  // An Empty Class Structure  }
```

As you can see in Figure 7-10, the code is error-free, and you're ready to code your **public void onDraw()** method inside this private Engine class.

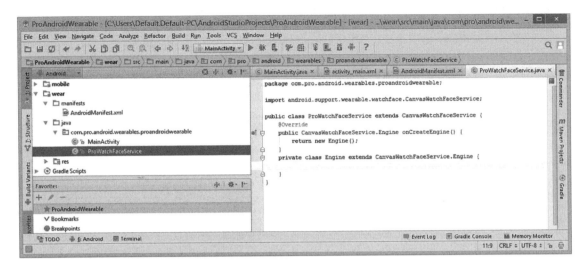

*Figure 7-10.* *Code an empty private class named Engine extending the CanvasWatchFaceService.Engine class*

Inside the Engine class (inside the curly braces), you need to implement a public void onDraw() method, again using the Java Override keyword. Type the @Override and then press the Return key to enter a new line of code. Then type the Java **public** keyword and a **void** Java return type, the **onDraw()** method name with a Canvas object parameter named **watchface**, the Rect object parameter named **rect**, and your two curly braces, as shown in Figure 7-11.

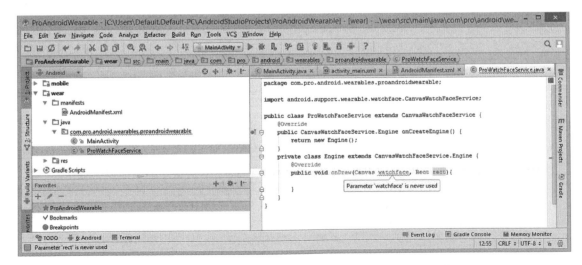

*Figure 7-11.* *Code an empty public void onDraw method with Canvas watchface and rect object parameters*

As you can see at the bottom of Figure 7-11, there's a wavy green underline highlight under **watchface**. If you mouse-over it, you'll see the "Parameter 'watchface' is never used" concern that IntelliJ has. You can ignore this green (mild warning level) code highlighting for now, because you are going to call a .drawColor() method off this watchface Canvas object later.

Also notice the red color that IntelliJ had added to your Canvas and Rect objects (classes). This means that you will need to write an import statement before you use these in your code. After you pass Canvas and Rect objects into the .onDraw() method in your CanvasWatchFaceService.Engine superclass using the Java **super** keyword, you will see how to get IntelliJ to code these import statements for you. Patience is a virtue!

Inside the body of the onDraw() method, that is, inside the open and the close curly braces, type the Java super keyword and a period character to bring up the IntelliJ helper dialog, showing methods in your superclass that can be utilized. Figure 7-12 shows the onDraw(Canvas canvas, Rect bounds) selection; once you double-click this, IntelliJ will write a Java code statement for you, generating a wavy red (severe error level) line, which I will discuss next (this is why I took this specific work process).

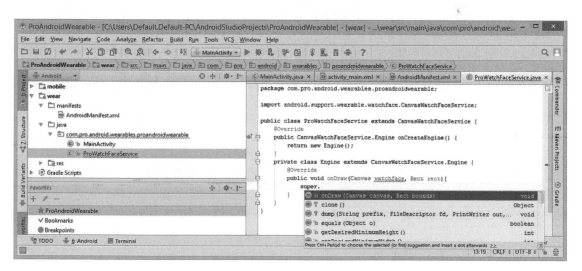

*Figure 7-12.  Inside the onDraw method, use the Java super keyword to call the onDraw(Canvas, Rect) method*

As you can see in Figure 7-13, if you mouse-over the wavy red error highlights, IntelliJ will tell you what your problem is. In this case, the package and class for **android.graphics. Canvas** and **android.graphics.Rect** are shown and an error "onDraw(Canvas,Rect) in Engine cannot be applied" is being shown.

The fact that the package and class name parts of the import statement are being used here should trigger an "import statement" in your thought process, so the only thing you need to know is how to get IntelliJ to code these.

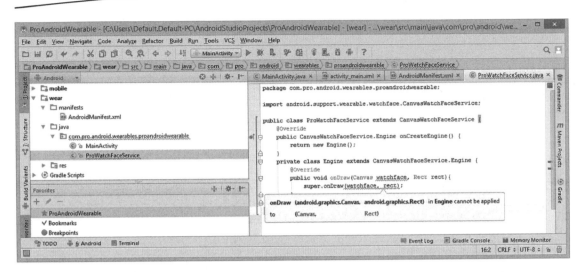

**Figure 7-13.** *Mouse-over the wavy red error highlighting to see the problem with the Canvas and Rect classes*

As you can see in Figure 7-14, if you mouse-over the Canvas or the Rect in your public void onDraw(Canvas watchface, Rect rect) method declaration, a somewhat cryptic, abbreviated "? android.graphics.Rect? Alt+Enter" message will appear. I would translate this cryptic message to "Question: Import your android.graphics.Rect package and class for you? If yes, press the Alt key, and at the same time, press the Enter key, and I'll code it!" You will find that if you mouse-over each of these red-colored class names and press the Alt-Enter keystroke sequence as suggested, IntelliJ will code both of the import statements for you, as you'll see in Figure 7-15.

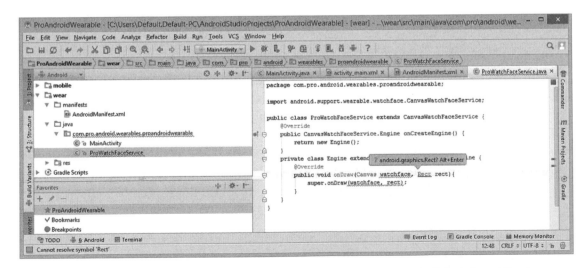

**Figure 7-14.** *Mouse-over the red Canvas and Rect class names in the code and use Alt+Enter to import the classes*

Now the time has come to use the watchface Canvas object in the body of the onDraw() method. You will be calling a **.drawColor(int color)** method off this object to set the color of the Canvas to black. This optimizes power use for the Watch Faces Design, of course, as black pixels use zero power!

Type in the **watchface** object name and then a **period** key and then type in a few characters of drawColor, which will provide you with the pop-up helper dialog containing the draw methods that start with the letter C, as shown in Figure 7-15, at the bottom right of the screenshot. Double-click in the **drawColor(int color)** option to call the method off the watchface Canvas object. Now all you have to deal with is your **Color** class parameter, which you will be passing into the method call, and you will be done coding the basic Engine structure, which will draw the black (empty) watch face!

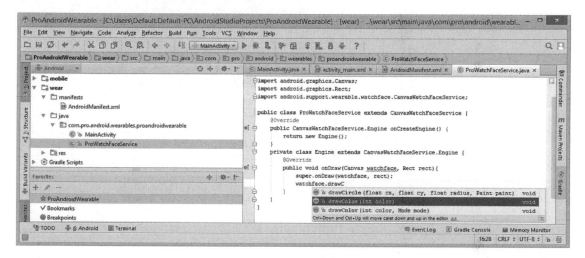

*Figure 7-15. Type in the watchface Canvas object and use a period and drawC to bring up the method helper dialog*

You might have noticed that my approach has been to get an empty Java code structure in place and working before trying to get more complicated code in place. This is because Java is a complex language, and Android 5 is a complex operating system; therefore, I usually start out with the lowest level of functionality coding.

My development approach is to build up gradually from empty but error-free code constructs that have all of the needed import statements and coding syntax (keywords, parenthesis, curly braces, etc.) properly in place.

As you can see in Figure 7-16, I have typed in a **Color** class name (object) and pressed the **period** key to bring up the Color constants helper dialog, so I can find the color I want to use for the Watch Face background color.

For power conservation reasons, I have selected the Color class constant of **Color.BLACK (android.graphics)**, as seen selected with blue in Figure 7-16.

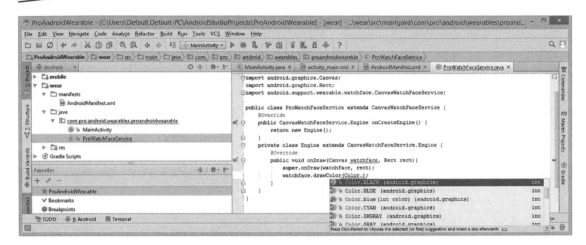

*Figure 7-16.*  *Inside the watchface.drawColor() method type the Color class and select BLACK*

Once you've double-clicked the Color.BLACK constant in the helper dialog, you will see a **lightbulb** in the left margin of the Java code editor pane, as shown on the left side of Figure 7-17. You can either mouse-over the icon or click the drop-down arrow next to it to open the solutions IntelliJ has to offer you regarding this line of code you've just generated.

This message says "Add static import for android.graphics.Color.BLACK," so it looks like IntelliJ IDEA (or Android Studio) wants you to add an import statement not for the Color class but for the Color.BLACK constant itself!

A Java static import statement was created to provide a type-safe mechanism for including constants in your Java code, without the need of referencing the entire (Color in this case) class originally defined as a constant.

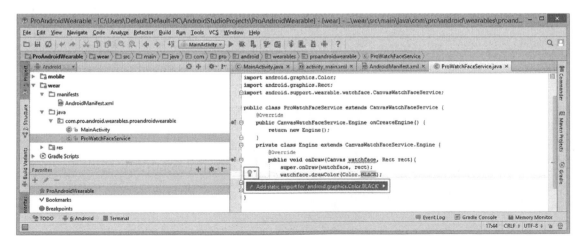

*Figure 7-17.*  *Click the lightbulb drop-down arrow, and add the suggested static import*

Congratulations! You have now put in place a Java code foundation for your ProWatchFaceService and its accompanying Engine class, including your core onDraw() method, which currently draws a blank, black, empty watch face to the smartwatch display screen.

This core .onDraw() method will ultimately update your Watch Face whenever it's necessary. It is true that this is currently an empty Java structure, although it does provide a blank black screen (a Canvas) for you to create your Watch Faces Design on, so it is still significant that you have put it into place and that you're taking baby steps to learn how this Watch Faces API is implemented as well as how it all works under the hood.

Your code is now error-free, which can be seen in Figure 7-18. You can see the three import statements, one static import statement, and one unneeded (shown in IntelliJ using gray color) import statement for the Color class. This shows the Color class is referenced, but that a full import statement is not needed. IntelliJ has a **Code ➤ Optimize Imports** feature that you can use to remove all unnecessary import statements once the app is developed.

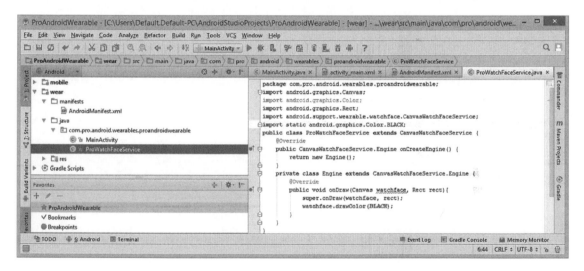

*Figure 7-18. Completed private class Engine and five import statements, one static*

Now that you have the Java code in place that provides the core Watch Face processing functionality, let's finish putting all of the XML foundational markup in place. There is still a lot of setup work to do!

The XML part of the Watch Faces API set up will include an all new **/res/xml** directory, the XML Wallpaper object definition, and you'll finish morphing both the mobile application and wear application AndroidManifest.xml files from the default Wear application bootstrap to the Watch Faces API application compatibility. After you do this, you'll be able to create watch face image previews.

# Watch Face XML Assets: Create and Edit XML Files

Even though you've added Watch Faces API-related permissions and created a Watch Faces rendering engine using Java 7 code, there are still a number of pieces of the puzzle that you'll need to put in place using XML markup.

These include creating an XML resource folder, Wallpaper object definition, and adding the <service> declaration into the AndroidManifest.xml file. You'll also add (or delete) some other XML tag and parameter entries to make some key adjustments in both of the (mobile and wear) Android Manifest XML definition files. This will show you how to "morph" the bootstrap Wear app into a Watch Faces API application, which is what this chapter of the book is all about! Let's get to work on all of this XML markup so you can finish up this foundational chapter and then start to create the Watch Faces Design!

## Watch Face Wallpaper: Creating a Wallpaper Object in XML

The next thing you need to create is the **/res/xml/watch_faces.xml** file that defines your Wallpaper object and contains the Watch Faces Design. As you can see in Figure 7-19, a **/res/xml** folder doesn't exist in the project folder yet, so you need to right-click the **/wear/res** folder and use the **New ➤ Android resource directory** menu sequence to create the directory that is needed to hold the watch_faces.xml file you will be creating next to hold the XML **<wallpaper>** object parent tag and xmlns referencing.

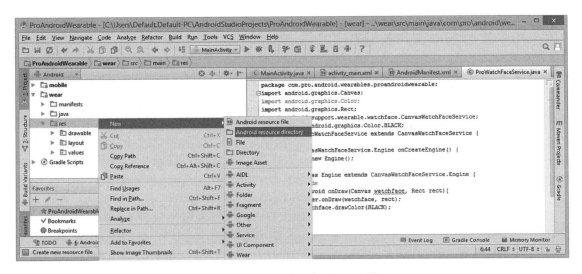

*Figure 7-19. Right-click on /res folder and select New ➤ Android resource directory*

After you invoke this menu sequence, you will see a **New Resource Directory** dialog, which can be seen in Figure 7-20. Select your **Resource type** as **xml** and set the **Directory name** to **xml**. It is important to notice that IntelliJ will name the directory for you if you select a Resource type first. Leave everything else set as is, and then click the **OK** button to create the XML folder, which as you can see has been created successfully in Figure 7-21.

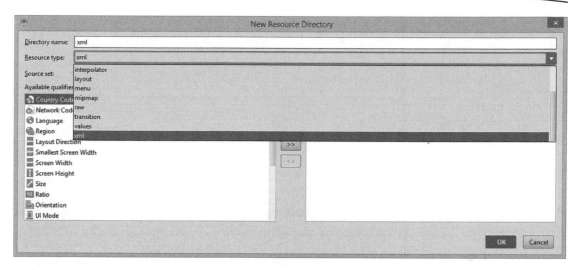

*Figure 7-20. Select an xml resource type, which will name this directory /res/xml*

Right-click the new /res/xml folder and select **New ➤ XML resource file**, as shown in Figure 7-21, to create the new **watch_faces.xml** wallpaper file.

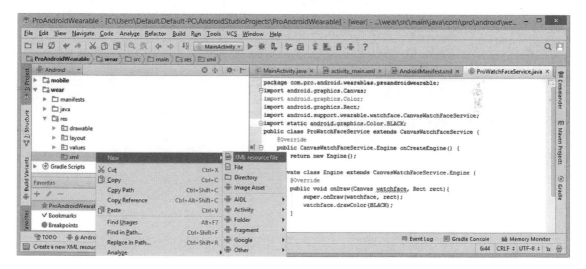

*Figure 7-21. Right-click on /res/xml directory, and select New ➤ XML resource file*

After you invoke the menu sequence, you'll see a **New Resource File** dialog, which can be seen in Figure 7-22. Select your **Source set** as **main**, then set the **File name** to **watch_face.xml**. Leave everything else set as is, and then click the **OK** button to create the watch_faces.xml definition file, which, as you can see in Figure 7-23, has been created successfully and has been opened for you in an editing pane inside the IntelliJ IDEA for editing.

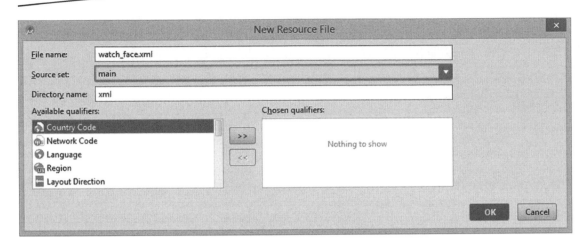

*Figure 7-22. Name the file watch_face.xml and set Source set to main (leave the defaults)*

Enter the **<xml>** version container tag and **<wallpaper>** parent tag using the following XML markup, which can be seen in the right half of Figure 7-23:

```
<?xml version="1.0" encoding="utf-8"?>
<wallpaper xmlns:android="http://schemas.android.com/apk/res/android" />
```

This creates the Wallpaper object in Android for use with your watch face.

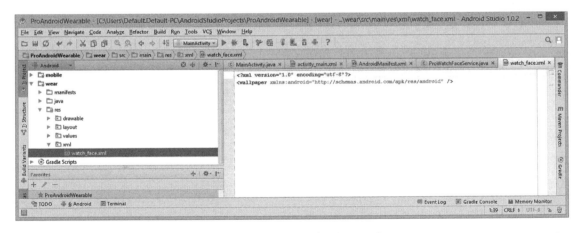

*Figure 7-23. Right-click on watch_face.xml to view it in a tab using Jump to Source*

Now you have put everything into place that is needed to be able to create the <service> declaration in the wear Android Manifest XML file, which will declare your ProWatchFaceService (and Engine) for use and reference all of the various other watch face image previews and a wallpaper object using <meta-data> child tags inside the parent <service> tag.

# Declaring a WatchFace Service: The XML <service> Tag

Click the **AndroidManifest.xml** tab for your **wear** app in IntelliJ so you can declare your **Service** for use in the Watch Face application. As you can see in the **title bar** of IntelliJ in Figure 7-24, it shows you the path to the file you are currently editing. Use this feature to make certain you are editing the correct (wear) AndroidManifest and not the mobile AndroidManifest. I have made the **<uses-feature>** and **<uses-permission>** tags and their parameters fit on one line of code to make room for a <service> parent tag and its child tag structure, which you will create next.

The **<service>** tag itself has nearly a half-dozen parameters that configure it for use, starting with the **BIND_WALLPAPER** permission, which allows your Service object to "bind." **Binding** means establishing a "real-time refresh" or real-time updating connection with the Wallpaper object you created in the previous section. You'll also need to give the <service> tag a Service class name, which is **.ProWatchFaceService**, as well as a label of **Pro Watch Face**. Finally, you will need to set a **true** (on) flag for the **allowEmbedded** option, as well as add an **empty string value** to a required **taskAffinity** parameter (attribute). This would be done using the following XML markup:

```
<service
    android:permission="android.permission.BIND_WALLPAPER"
    android:name=".ProWatchFaceService"
    android:label="Pro Watch Face"
    android:allowEmbedded="true"
    android:taskAffinity="" >
    <meta-data
      android:name="android.service.wallpaper"
      android:resource="@xml/watch_face" />
    <meta-data
      android:name="com.google.android.wearable.watchface.preview"
      android:resource="@drawable/preview_pro_square" />
    <meta-data
      android:name="com.google.android.wearable.watchface.preview_circular"
      android:resource="@drawable/preview_pro_circular" />
    <intent-filter>
      <action android:name="android.service.wallpaper.WallpaperService" />
      <category android:name="com.google.android.wearable.watchface.category.WATCH_FACE" />
    </intent-filter>
</service>
```

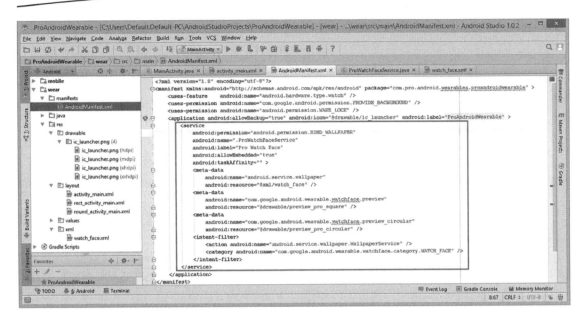

*Figure 7-24. Add a <service> parent tag and <meta-data> child tags defining Service*

There are also three <meta-data> child tags inside the <service> parent tag as well as an <intent-filter> child tag. I'll cover the Intent Filter first, as there is only one of these and because it is very important. The Intent Filter child tag has two of its own (nested) child tags. One is for an **action**, which is a **WallpaperService** class, that is a superclass of the WatchFaceService class. This is a superclass to the CanvasWatchFaceService superclass for the ProWatchFaceService class. The other child tag is for a **category** for the action, which, not surprisingly, is a **WATCH_FACE** constant.

The reason I went into detail here covering the CanvasWatchFaceService class (and its nested Engine class) is so that when it comes time to look at the Intent Filter set up you will understand that the WallpaperService is the uppermost type of bindable Service class and that the WATCH_FACE category is really pointing out a WatchFaceService subclass type for this WallpaperService superclass.

Next, you'll need to add in **<meta-data>** child tags that define certain things for this Watch Faces Service declaration. The most important of these will define the Wallpaper object, which you created in the previous section with your watch_face.xml file and is referenced in a meta-data tag named android.service.wallpaper that references an XML resource file in /res/xml using the **android:resource="@xml/watch_face"** parameter referencing syntax.

The other two <meta-data> child tags will provide the Drawable assets for the Watch Face Round and Square version previews. Let's create those next.

The <meta-data> child tag for the square watch face preview will use a name value of **com. google.android.wearable.watchface.preview** with a reference to an XML resource file that you'll be creating in the next section that uses the **android:resource="@drawable/ preview_pro_square"** parameter referencing syntax. Notice in the name parameter that the default watch face screen shape type is square, whereas round would be coded as **preview_circular**.

Notice in Figure 7-24 that IntelliJ is wavy green underline highlighting the word watchface, just like it was doing with the Java object name. It turns out IntelliJ thinks that this is a spelling error, so, hopefully, at some point IntelliJ will update its dictionary and add in the watchface and WatchFaces API correct spellings!

The <meta-data> child tag for your round watchface preview will have the name value of **com.google.android.wearable.watchface.preview_circular** and an XML reference to a Drawable resource file that you'll be creating in the next section using the **android:resource="@drawable/preview_pro_round"** parameter referencing syntax.

Next, you'll need to create and add these watchface.preview assets into the correct /res/ drawable folders, so, before I end this chapter with a fully loaded (but empty) and configured Watch Face API application, let's look at some digital image asset placement work to show you how this is done.

# Watch Face Image Preview: Using Drawable Assets

The next thing that you need to do to get rid of those red error indicator text highlights in the <meta-data> tags for the watch face preview imagery shown in the bottom half Figure 7-24 is to copy both (square and circular) watch face preview **PNG** images into the correct /res/ drawable folder in the **wear** portion of your project. I will be using preview images from a later chapter in Part 2 covering graphic design asset creation and integration into the Watch Face design, code, UI design, XML markup, and application.

The preview imagery needs to be **320 x 320 pixels** in image resolution. This means that the images are HDPI (high-density pixel images) resolution and will therefore need to go into the **/wear/src/main/res/drawable-hdpi** folder in order for Android 5 to locate them. This folder can be seen on the left-hand side of Figure 7-25, as well as on the left-hand side of Figure 7-26.

Find the **preview_pro_square** and **preview_pro_circular** PNG images in the Pro Android Wearables archive in the book's repository and copy them into the **/AndroidStudioProjects/ ProAndroidWearable/wear/src/main/res/drawable-hdpi/** folder, as seen in Figure 7-25. These preview images will be used with the watch faces companion app that runs on phones or tablets to show the users what a watch face looks like pixel for pixel (watch faces use 320 pixels).

*Figure 7-25.  Copy the preview_pro_circular and preview_pro_square files to drawable-hdpi*

Once the digital image assets have been properly copied into place in your /wear/src/
main/res/drawable-hdpi/ folder, that red error code highlighting that was present in
Figure 7-24 will vanish. This can be seen on the right side of Figure 7-26, and now the
AndroidManifest.xml markup is also error-free. You have made a significant amount of
progress during this chapter!

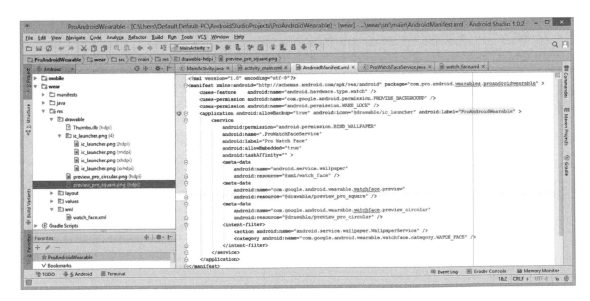

*Figure 7-26.  Once PNG assets are copied into a /res/drawable folder, errors go away*

# Summary

In this chapter, you learned about how to create the foundation for your **Watch Face Application** by taking your Pro Android Wearable bootstrap application and morphing it into a Watch Face App using the IntelliJ IDEA.

First, you learned how the Gradle Scripts in the project need to be stratified, as well as how they should be set up in order to have a successful watch faces application hierarchy. You learned about dependency and repositories and how to set up the Google Play Services using Gradle.

Next you added the Android Permissions, which are necessary to create Watch Faces applications, and learned that there are two Android Manifest XML files that you need to deal with: one for the wearable peripheral device and one for the phone or tablet "master" mobile device.

After that you learned about the Android CanvasWatchFaceService class and its Java class hierarchy, which describes how it's an Object that uses Context to start a Service that creates a Wallpaper that is used to create a Watch Faces Engine that uses the Canvas to Draw to the smartwatch display. It is interesting how one Java hierarchy can show us exactly how Google has implemented their WatchFaces API in Android 5 OS, isn't it?

Then you learned about the Android CanvasWatchFaceService.Engine class and its hierarchy and how to implement it as a private class for your ProWatchFaceService class. You learned how to implement the .onDraw() method and created an empty Watch Face Service Engine that will be used for the rest of Part 2 of this book covering Watch Faces API.

Next, I discussed Watch Face XML definitions and you created a /res/xml folder and then a watch_face.xml file, which defined a Wallpaper object to use for our Watch Faces Design.

Then I discussed the Wear Android Manifest and you crafted the Service entry, which defined the new ProWatchFaceService.java class as well as other key things like the Wallpaper object, Intent Filter, and preview imagery.

Finally, you put the Watch Face Preview Images into place in a drawable HDPI folder, so that all of the Java code and XML markup became green and thus error-free!

In the next chapter, you will start adding Watch Face features to the public ProWatchFaceService class and private Engine class.

# Chapter 8

# A Watch Faces Timing Engine: Using TimeZone, Time, and BroadcastReceiver

Now that you have your CanvasWatchFaceService subclass and private Engine class in place and have your Gradle Scripts, XML assets, Wallpaper object, and preview assets installed where they're supposed to be, you're ready to start getting into learning more advanced Java utility classes and Android classes and methods that implement the WatchFaces API.

Topics will get more advanced as you progress through the watch face creation process throughout this book. During this chapter, you'll be taking an in-depth look at the drawing surface, setting up your watch face styling, time zone management, the Time object, and the time zone broadcasting class that will need to be implemented in order to create a functional watch face design application.

You'll also be taking a detailed look at the **WatchFaceStyle** class and its **WatchFaceStyle. Builder** nested class. These classes will allow you to build, and configure, the required parameters that you learned about in Chapter 6.

You'll also be taking a look at Android time-related classes and methods, such as **Time** and **TimeZone**, as well as the Android **SurfaceHolder** class, and finally at the Android **BroadcastReceiver** class and methods. This chapter is full of information about Java and Android classes, so, let's get started!

# Your WatchFace Surface: Android SurfaceHolder

Your Watch Faces Design will be "hosted" by using an Android **SurfaceHolder** object. This object is compatible and works in conjunction with the Android **Canvas** object and your **.onDraw()** method, both of which you have put into place in your code and will be expanding your use of as you progress through this chapter.

I want to give you an overview of this SurfaceHolder interface before you implement it in your code. Then I will go over the WatchFaceStyle class and finally cover the key WatchFaceService and WatchFaceService.Engine classes, which contain most of the important WatchFaces API methods you will implement during the course of the next few chapters.

## Android SurfaceHolder Interface: The Watch Face Surface

The Android WatchFaces API uses a **SurfaceHolder** object as the lowest-level object to hold your Watch Faces Design. The SurfaceHolder is a **public abstract Java interface**, so it defines methods or constants you will need to implement in order to create Watch Face Apps. It's a member of the **android.view.SurfaceHolder** package because it is a type of Android View.

The SurfaceHolder object was designed to facilitate holding (hosting) a display screen drawing surface. This interface allows you to control the display drawing surface format or sizing as well as edit the pixels on its surface.

There are methods that can be used to monitor any changes to the surface. This interface is usually accessed using a **SurfaceView** class, however, the WatchFaces API accesses it through the **.onCreate()** method. I will be covering this method in the WatchFaceService. Engine section of the chapter after a brief discussion on the SurfaceHolder and WatchFaceStyle classes.

An Android SurfaceHolder interface contains three nested classes: two that are interfaces that can be utilized in order to determine when changes to a WatchFace Surface have occurred and one that is a class that is utilized for bad Surface type exception error handling.

The **SurfaceHolder.Callback** interface can be implemented in your Java code, and it allows your Watch Face app to receive information about changes to the SurfaceHolder object. There is a second **SurfaceHolder.Callback2** interface that implements the SurfaceHolder. Callback interface, providing additional callbacks that can be received.

The **SurfaceHolder.BadSurfaceTypeException** class provides an exception that is thrown from the .lockCanvas() method when that method is called from a SurfaceHolder object whose type has been set to **SURFACE_TYPE_PUSH_BUFFERS**.

This constant usually will not affect Watch Faces Design and Application development, and I am including it here only for the sake of completeness in covering the class across all of its implementations in the Android OS.

The interface also contains about a dozen public methods, several of which can be used in Watch Faces Design. These methods are abstract, so you must implement them with your own unique code. They are listed in Table 8-1. You can familiarize yourself with them here so you know what they can do.

*Table 8-1. SurfaceHolder Interface Methods along with Data Type, Method Call Structure, and Purpose*

| Method Type | Method Structure | Method Purpose |
| --- | --- | --- |
| abstract void | addCallback(SurfaceHolder.Callback callback) | Add callback interface |
| abstract Surface | getSurface() | Access the Surface object |
| abstract Rect | getSurfaceFrame() | Get current dimensions |
| abstract boolean | isCreating() | Surface being created? |
| abstract Canvas | lockCanvas() | Edit surface pixels |
| abstract Canvas | lockCanvas(Rect dirtyRect) | Dirty Rect lock Canvas |
| abstract void | removeCallback(SurfaceHolder.Callback cback) | Remove the callback |
| abstract void | setFixedSize(int width, int height) | Make surface fixed W×H |
| abstract void | setFormat(int format) | Set the pixel format |
| abstract void | setKeepScreenOn(boolean screenOn) | Keep ScreenOn option |
| abstract void | setSizeFromLayout() | Allow surface resizing |
| abstract void | unlockCanvasAndPost(Canvas canvas) | Finish editing surface |

Now that you have an overview of the SurfaceHolder interface, let's take a real-world look at how SurfaceHolder is used to provide a Surface (Holder) for the Canvas object that you will be using for your Watch Faces API Design.

## A SurfaceHolder Object: onCreate(SurfaceHolder surface)

If you've not done so already, launch the Android Studio development environment with the quick launch icon you created in Chapter 2. This will launch the IntelliJ IDEA and display the ProAndroidWearable project you created in Chapter 4, where you added Watch Faces to in Chapter 7.

Close all of the editing tabs except for the **ProWatchFaceService.java** tab, as shown in Figure 8-1, because you are going to be working on this tab during this chapter. You'll be adding the methods from the WatchFaceService.Engine class, which you're going to be learning about later on in this chapter, the first of which will be the **.onCreate()** method, as shown in Figure 8-1.

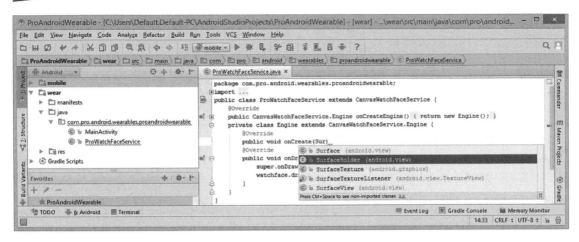

***Figure 8-1.*** *Add a public void onCreate() method to the private Engine class and type Sur in the parameter list*

Type in the @Override public void onCreate() {} method infrastructure, and inside the parameter area type in **Sur** to trigger IntelliJ to bring up a helper dialog with all of the object (class) types that can be utilized with the method call. Find the **SurfaceHolder (android. view package)** option and double-click It to insert the SurfaceHolder object into the method call and name it **surface**, because that is what it is acting as (holding).

The public void onCreate() method structure that creates the SurfaceHolder object, which is named surface, will take the following Java structure, as can also be seen in Figure 8-2:

```
@Override
public void onCreate(SurfaceHolder surface) { Your Java method body will go in here }
```

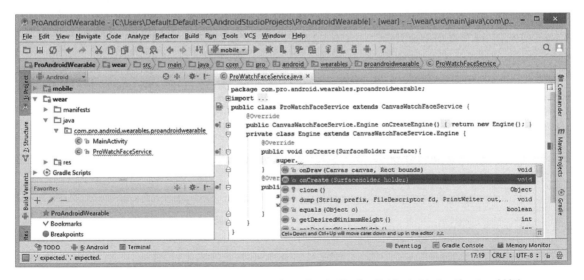

***Figure 8-2.*** *Type in the Java super keyword and select the onCreate (SurfaceHolder holder) option to add it in*

As you can see in Figure 8-2, if you simply type in the Java keyword **super** and the **period** key inside of the method body, IntelliJ IDEA will provide a method helper dialog. You can use this dialog to peruse all of the methods that can be used with the .onCreate() method.

Double-click the **onCreate(SurfaceHolder holder) void** option and insert the .onCreate() method call to your superclass, using the **surface** object you created inside of the public void onCreate(SurfaceHolder surface) method construct. This passes your SurfaceHolder object, named surface, up to the superclass .onCreate() method for processing at that higher level. This is how you create a SurfaceHolder and implement it in your WatchFace.

You will notice in Figure 8-3 that if you start to type your SurfaceHolder object name (surface) inside the super.onCreate() method call parameter area, IntelliJ will find this object name, along with every other compatible object types that are available, and put them together into one big helper dialog for you to select from.

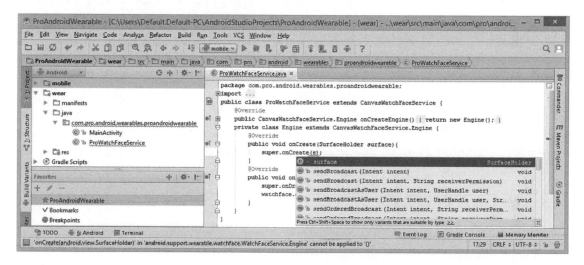

*Figure 8-3. Type an s in the .onCreate() method parameter area, and select the surface object from the dialog*

Now that you have put your SurfaceHolder into place using this .onCreate() method call, let's build a WatchFace Style using the WatchFaceStyle class.

# Setting Watch Face Style: WatchFaceStyle.Builder

The WatchFaces API contains your WatchFaceStyle and WatchFaceStyle.Builder classes, which are used to build and configure the Watch Faces Design with the many Android design requirements you learned about in Chapter 6.

These considerations define how your WatchFace will assimilate the Android OS considerations such as placement of the Status Bar indicators, peek card support, placement of the Google hotword indicator, and so forth.

# Android WatchFaceStyle Class: Styling Your Watch Face

The Android **WatchFaceStyle** class is a **public** class that **extends** the Object class and implements the Java **Parcelable** interface. This class is part of the **android.support.wearable** package. The hierarchy of this WatchFaceStyle class indicates (due to a lack of any other classes in the hierarchy) that it was "scratch-coded" by Google's Android development team. The class was created to provide Watch Faces Styles, and the hierarchy looks like this:

```
java.lang.Object
  > android.support.wearable.watchface.WatchFaceStyle
```

It is important to note that the Wearable Support Library classes that are found in this android.support.wearable package are subject to change. The WatchFaceStyle class provides constants and methods allowing a Watch Face to be described and configured. The parameters outlined in this class define how the WatchFaceService will draw Android's operating system user interface (UI) elements over your custom watch face design.

An instance of this class will be passed into a method that you will be using in the next section, called **setWatchFaceStyle(WatchFaceStyle)**, for the **onCreate** method in your private **Engine** class in the **ProWatchFaceService.java** class.

To construct your WatchFaceStyle object instance, you will use the Java **new** keyword to create a new WatchFaceStyle.Builder object. This is done inside this setWatchFaceStyle() method using a **Context** object from your class.

The WatchFaceStyle class thus contains one solitary nested class, which is named **WatchFaceStyle.Builder**. I'll be covering this in detail during the next section of this chapter. You will also be using this nested class, in the section of the chapter after that, when you build a WatchFace Style.

The WatchFaceStyle class holds 11 important watch face constants that you will be using in your watch faces design and applications development. These are shown in Table 8-2, along with the proper name and a description of what they do.

*Table 8-2. WatchFaceStyle Class Constant Names along with Their Intended Functionality*

| WatchFaceStyle Constant Name | WatchFaceStyle Constant Function |
|---|---|
| AMBIENT_PEEK_MODE_HIDDEN | Hides the peek cards when the watch is in ambient mode |
| AMBIENT_PEEK_MODE_VISIBLE | Displays a peek card when the watch is in ambient mode |
| BACKGROUND_VISIBILITY_INTERRUPTIVE | Shows the peek card Background briefly on Interrupt |
| BACKGROUND_VISIBILITY_PERSISTENT | Shows the peek card Background always for Interrupt |
| PEEK_MODE_SHORT | Displays the peek cards using a single line of text |
| PEEK_MODE_VARIABLE | Displays the peek card using multiple lines of text |
| PEEK_OPACITY_MODE_OPAQUE | Displays the peek card using opaque/solid background |
| PEEK_OPACITY_MODE_TRANSLUCENT | Displays the peek card with a translucent background |
| PROTECT_HOTWORD_INDICATOR | Use Semi-Transparent Black background in Hotword |
| PROTECT_STATUS_BAR | Use Semi-Transparent Black background StatusBar |
| PROTECT_WHOLE_SCREEN | Use Semi-Transparent Black background for Screen |

This WatchFaceStyle class contains public methods that allow you to access information about a WatchFaceStyle. Most of these are **.get()** methods, which match up with the .set() methods you will access later using a nested WatchFaceStyle.Builder class. I will be covering that class next.

There is a **.describeContents()** method to describe WatchFaceStyle contents, as well as an **.equals(Object otherObject)** method, which is used to compare WatchFaceStyle objects. There's a **.getComponent()** method that gets a value for a component of the watch face whose style is being specified, and your standard inherited **.toString()**, **.hashCode()**, and **.writeToParcel()** methods.

The getter methods include a **.getAmbientPeekMode()** method that shows how a primary peek card will be displayed while the watch is in ambient mode, and a **.getBackgroundVisibility()** method that shows how the background display is set for the primary peek card. The **.getCardPeekMode()** method shows how far into your watch face display screen the primary peek card will go, and the **.getHotwordIndicatorGravity()** method shows where you have positioned an OK Google hotword on the watch face screen. The **.getPeekOpacityMode()** shows a Peek Card Opacity setting, and a **.getShowSystemUiTime()** shows whether your WatchFaceStyle is configured to show the system time over your watch face.

There is also a **.getStatusBarGravity()** method call that allows you to poll and find out the position of the Status Bar icons on your screen, as well as a **.getViewProtectionMode()** that allows you to poll the setting pertaining to adding a transparent black background color to elements on your watch face screen so they are readable on the watch face.

Finally, there's a method called **.getShowUnreadCountIndicator()** that polls the WatchFaceStyle object to find if the WatchFaceStyle object contains an indicator that, if set to the true value, shows how many **unread peek cards** are left to be read by the user from their unread peek cards input stream.

Next, let's take a look at the WatchFaceStyle.Builder nested class and its many watch face styling methods. You are going to be using most of these methods in the section of the chapter that follows this next section as you create and build a WatchFaceStyle object.

# Android WatchFaceStyle.Builder Class: Building the Style

The Android **WatchFaceStyle.Builder public static** class also has an **extends Object** indicating that it was also scratch-coded for building your WatchFaceStyle objects. This class provides the "builder methods" that are used to create WatchFaceStyle objects. The Java class hierarchy looks like the following:

```
java.lang.Object
  > android.support.wearable.watchface.WatchFaceStyle.Builder
```

This is another one of the Wearable Support Library classes that can be found in the **android.support.wearable** package, and like the WatchFaceStyle class, it is also subject to change in the future as smartwatch manufacturers change the way their products function. For instance, more smartwatches will inevitably switch from being peripherals to full Android devices (like the Neptune Pine) as consumer electronics component miniaturization progresses and as these miniaturized component prices continue to decline over time.

The **public Constructor method** for your WatchFaceStyle.Builder object takes a **Service**, specifically your WatchFaceService subclass, in this case, a **ProWatchFaceService** class, and it's Context object (this), as its parameter, using the following format:

```
WatchFaceStyle.Builder(Service service)        // This is the Generic Constructor Method Format
WatchFaceStyle.Builder(ProWatchFaceService.this) // This is our specific Constructor Method Format
```

A Java **this** keyword contains the **Context** of the ProWatchFaceService class, and that Context object contains all of the **relevant information** about the class.

This WatchFaceStyle.Builder class contains **ten** public method calls. I will show you how to implement each of these in your **private Engine** class's **.onCreate()** method. You'll do this in the next section of the chapter, when you add your WatchFaceStyle object into the **ProWatchFaceService.java** class.

The core method in the WatchFaceStyle class is your **.build()** method, which actually builds the WatchFaceStyle object, using a **read-only** data (object) format. This is because the WatchFaceObject is meant to be "configured" at start up using an .onCreate() method, and then simply read from during the watch face application's execution.

The **.setAmbientPeekMode(int ambientPeekMode)** method allows you to specify the **visibility** setting for peek cards. This will determine whether Peek Cards will be displayed while your watch face is in an ambient mode. This method uses the first two constants listed in Table 8-2 to determine whether Peek Cards will be displayed or hidden while the watch face is in ambient mode. Here you will set this to display peek cards in ambient mode.

The **.setBackgroundVisibility(int backgroundVisibility)** method allows you a way to specify how you want to display your background for your peek card. This method uses the second two constants listed in Table 8-2 to determine whether or not Peek Card backgrounds will be displayed persistently.

The **.setCardPeekMode(int peekMode)** method allows you to specify just how far onto a watchface a peek card will overlay while a watchface is displayed. This method uses the third two constants listed in Table 8-2 to determine how much of the Peek Cards will be displayed over your watch face screen.

The **.setPeekOpacityMode(int peekOpacityMode)** method allows you to specify a Peek Card Background Opacity as being a solid or translucent background. This method uses the fourth two constants listed in Table 8-2 to determine whether Peek Cards backgrounds are solid (nontranslucent) or translucent.

The **.setViewProtection(int viewProtection)** method allows you to add a dark translucent background effect to UI elements over your watch faces screen. This method uses the last three constants listed in Table 8-2 to determine whether a Status Bar, hotword, or both (whole screen) will be "protected."

The **.setHotwordIndicatorGravity(int hotwordIndicatorGravity)** method allows you to set a position constant (or constants) to position a hotword over a watch face. A parameter uses one or more standard Gravity constant values.

The **.setStatusBarGravity(int statusBarGravity)** method allows you to set the position of the Status Bar icons on the watch face screen. This parameter also uses one or more standard Android Gravity constant values.

The **.setShowSystemUiTime(boolean showSystemUiTime)** method call allows you to specify if the operating system will draw the time over your watch face design. The parameter for the method is a simple **true** or **false** value.

The **.setShowUnreadCountIndicator(boolean show)** method allows you to set if an indicator showing how many unread cards there are waiting to be read is showed along with the StatusBar icons. The parameter for this method is a simple **true** or **false** value. You will use a true value in the watch face app developed in this chapter.

# Building Your Watch Face: Using .setWatchFaceStyle( )

Let's build the WatchFaceStyle object next, so you can learn how to create this required watch face object that defines how your watch face is going to assimilate the Android OS functionality. You will put this object right after the **super.onCreate(surface);** line of code, which creates the SurfaceHolder object for the Watch Face.

Add a line of code, and type the word set to initiate the IntelliJ method helper dialog, as can be seen in Figure 8-4. Locate your **setWatchFaceStyle (WatchFaceStyle watchFaceStyle)** method and double-click it to add it to the Java code you are creating to implement a WatchFaceStyle object.

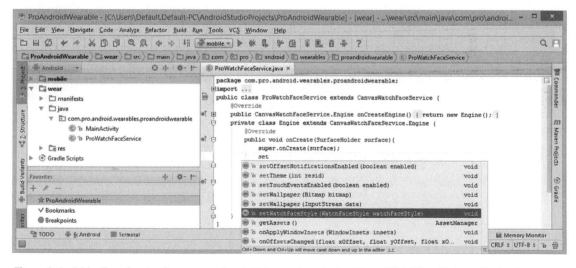

*Figure 8-4.  Add a line of code after super.onCreate(), type set, and select the setWatchFaceStyle method option*

Inside the setWatchFaceStyle() method parameter area, you will nest your constructor method for this WatchFaceStyle.Builder object using a Java **new** keyword. This creates a more dense (and complex) Java construct, but it is also more compact, allowing you to construct and configure a WatchFaceStyle object using less than a dozen lines of Java programming logic. This could even be one single (extremely long) line of Java code; however, I'll format it using a dozen lines in the IntelliJ IDEA for much improved readability!

The primary Java construct for the setWatchFaceStyle() method call and the new WatchFaceStyle.Builder() constructor method nested inside it will look like the following Java code, which is also shown in Figure 8-5:

```
setWatchFaceStyle( new WatchFaceStyle.Builder(ProWatchFaceService.this) );
```

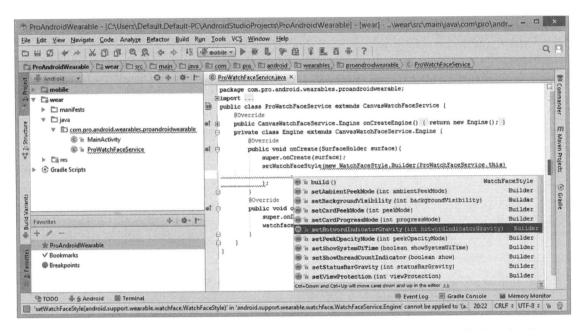

*Figure 8-5.  Add a line, type a period to bring up the method helper dialog, and select setHotwordIndicatorGravity*

Add a line of code by pressing the Return key with the cursor placed after your WatchFaceStyle.Builder() method's closing parenthesis, and before the setWatchFaceStyle statement's terminating parenthesis and semicolon, press the **period** key and select a **.setHotwordIndicatorGravity(int hotwordIndicatorGravity)** method from the IntelliJ pop-up method helper dialog, as shown in Figure 8-5.

In the parameter area, type **Gravity** and a **period**, as shown in Figure 8-6.

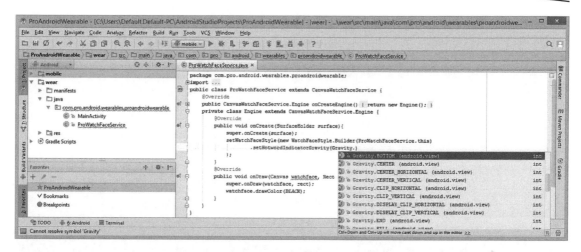

**Figure 8-6.** *Type Gravity object inside of the parameter area, and use the period key to bring up the helper dialog*

Double-click the **Gravity.BOTTOM** constant to place the OK Google hotword at the bottom of the watch face design, as shown in Figure 8-6. Next use a vertical bar | character to add another **Gravity.CENTER_HORIZONTAL** constant to the method call parameter area. What this will do is center the hotword horizontally at the bottom of your watch face design. Make sure that there are **no spaces** between the vertical bar separator and the Gravity constants because that will be perceived by the compiler as multiple parameters rather than one single "unified" Gravity **concatenation parameter**.

Next, let's add in another line of code. Press the period key and select the **setShowSystemUiTime(boolean showSystemUiTime)** option from the pop-up helper dialog, then enter the value of **false**, as you will want to control all of the watch face time displayed using application code. The setWatchFaceStyle() method structure should now looks like the following Java 7 programming logic:

```
setWatchFaceStyle( new WatchFaceStyle.Builder(ProWatchFaceService.this)
        .setHotwordIndicatorGravity(Gravity.BOTTOM|Gravity.CENTER_HORIZONTAL)
        .setShowSystemUiTime(false)
);
```

Next, let's set up the Peek Card configuration settings, starting with the background visibility method and constant value, as shown in Figure 8-7.

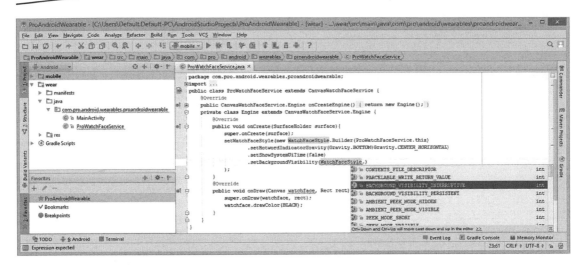

***Figure 8-7.*** *Add a setBackgroundVisibility() method and type WatchFaceStyle inside and select*
*BACKGROUND_VISIBILITY_INTERRUPTIVE*

Add a line of code under the .setShowSystemUiTime() method and add in your
**.setBackgroundVisibility()** method call. In the method parameter area, type **WatchFaceStyle**,
and press the **period** key to open your helper dialog. Use the **BACKGROUND_VISIBILITY_**
**INTERRUPTIVE** constant value with this method to allow your watchface design to be at
least partially visible when a Peek Card appears. This would be done using the following
Java code structure:

```
setWatchFaceStyle( new WatchFaceStyle.Builder(ProWatchFaceService.this)
        .setHotwordIndicatorGravity(Gravity.BOTTOM|Gravity.CENTER_HORIZONTAL)
        .setShowSystemUiTime(false)
        .setBackgroundVisibility(WatchFaceStyle.BACKGROUND_VISIBILITY_INTERRUPTIVE)
);
```

Next, let's add in the **.setCardPeekMode()** and **.setPeekOpacityMode()** method calls to
finish configuring how the Peek Cards will work in interactive mode. After that, you can add
the other four configuration methods. The Peek Card method call configuration using the
WatchFaceStyle constants covered in Table 8-2 is shown in Figure 8-8 and should look like
the following Java code:

```
setWatchFaceStyle( new WatchFaceStyle.Builder(ProWatchFaceService.this)
        .setHotwordIndicatorGravity(Gravity.BOTTOM|Gravity.CENTER_HORIZONTAL)
        .setShowSystemUiTime(false)
        .setBackgroundVisibility(WatchFaceStyle.BACKGROUND_VISIBILITY_INTERRUPTIVE)
        .setCardPeekMode(WatchFaceStyle.PEEK_MODE_SHORT)
        .setPeekOpacityMode(WatchFaceStyle.PEEK_OPACITY_MODE_TRANSLUCENT)
);
```

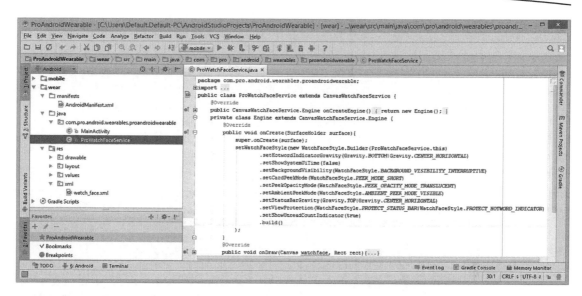

*Figure 8-8. Add the .build() method call to the end of the method chain to build the WatchFaceStyle object*

Let's add the last four WatchFaceStyle configuration methods and constants so you can get some hands-on experience implementing and utilizing all of the WatchFaceStyle object attributes for your Watch Faces API.

Next you will enable Peek Cards when the watch face is in ambient mode, position the Status Bar at the top center of the watch face design, turn on the View protection feature for the Status Bar and Hotword, and show the unread Peek Card messages counter.

The very last method call that must end the method call chaining that uses Java dot notation is the .build() method. Notice that you could chain each of these separate lines together as one long line of code. I'm just lining up the methods in the chain using the dot connector for better readability, as can be seen in the final Java construct, which is shown in Figure 8-8:

```
setWatchFaceStyle( new WatchFaceStyle.Builder(ProWatchFaceService.this)
    .setHotwordIndicatorGravity(Gravity.BOTTOM|Gravity.CENTER_HORIZONTAL)
    .setShowSystemUiTime(false)
    .setBackgroundVisibility(WatchFaceStyle.BACKGROUND_VISIBILITY_INTERRUPTIVE)
    .setCardPeekMode(WatchFaceStyle.PEEK_MODE_SHORT)
    .setPeekOpacityMode(WatchFaceStyle.PEEK_OPACITY_MODE_TRANSLUCENT)
    .setAmbientPeekMode(WatchFaceStyle.AMBIENT_PEEK_MODE_VISIBLE)
    .setStatusBarGravity(Gravity.TOP|Gravity.CENTER_HORIZONTAL)
    .setViewProtection(WatchFaceStyle.PROTECT_STATUS_BAR|WatchFaceStyle.
    PROTECT_HOTWORD_INDICATOR)
    .setShowUnreadCountIndicator(true)
    .build( )
);
```

Next, let's take a look at the Android (and Java) timing-related classes as these provide the functionality for getting the system time and updating the watch face design, so it shows the correct time all in real time!

# Setting Watch Face Time: The Time-Related Classes

Now that you have fully satisfied the operating system feature assimilation requirements that you learned about in Chapter 6 and created the Watch Faces SurfaceHolder and WatchFaceStyle objects that are needed to form the core surface of the WatchFace Design and display the required operating system features on top of it using those CanvasWatchFaceService and CanvasWatchFaceService.Engine classes you put in place in Chapter 7, it is time to learn about the time-related features in both Java 7 and Android 5 classes and packages.

This is the next level of foundation you'll need to put in place so your watch faces design can take system time and time zone values and convert them to display on the surface of your watch face design using whatever visual design paradigm you have decided to implement.

## Java Time Utility Classes: TimeUnit and TimeZone

Because this WatchFaces API is meant to create applications that tell time, let's take a closer look at the time-related classes. These would be found in the java.util and java.util. concurrent packages, and they control conversion of time units such as hours, minutes, seconds, milliseconds, microseconds, nanoseconds, and the like, as well as conversions between GMT time zones.

### Translating Between Units of Time: Using the TimeUnit Class

The **public enum TimeUnit** class is a subclass of a **java.lang.Enum<TimeUnit>** class, and it is part of the **java.util.concurrent** package. The class is an enumeration class, which is used to enumerate, that is, provide the numeric representation for, units of time that are used in your Java 7 applications.

The Java class hierarchy for this TimeUnit class looks like the following:

```
java.lang.Object
  > java.lang.Enum<TimeUnit>
    > java.util.concurrent.TimeUnit
```

The TimeUnit class (and object) is used to represent time durations at any specified unit of time duration granularity. You'll be using it for SECONDS and MILLISECONDS in the WATCH_FACE_UPDATE_RATE constant, which you will put into place after a brief discussion covering these Java 7 TimeUnit and TimeZone classes.

This class provides developers with utility methods that can convert time across discrete time units, hence its class name. You can use these methods to implement timing and delay operations using these time units.

It is important to note that a TimeUnit does not maintain time information itself! It simply helps developers organize or use time representations that are maintained separately across various Context objects. So TimeUnit objects could be thought of as a real-time time conversion filter, for all you sound designers, video special effects editors, or animators out there.

The TimeUnit properties that are supported are expressed in this class as Enum Constants. These include **DAYS**, **HOURS**, **MINUTES**, **SECONDS**, **MILLISECONDS**, **MICROSECONDS**, and **NANOSECONDS**.

A nanosecond is defined as one-thousandth of a microsecond, a microsecond is defined as one-thousandth of a millisecond, a millisecond is defined as one-thousandth of a second, a minute is defined as 60 seconds, an hour is defined as 60 minutes, and a day is defined as 24 hours.

The TimeUnit class contains over a dozen methods that are used for controlling and converting time, including **.toMillis(long duration)**, which you will be using in the ProWatchFaceService.java class.

There are also a half-dozen other .to() methods in this class, including .toDays(), .toHours(), .toSeconds(), .toNanos(), and .toMicros(). All of the .to() TimeUnit class methods take a long data value in the parameter area.

Next, let's take a look at the TimeZone class, so you can not only convert time into different units, but you can also convert time around the Earth! This is important for the international compatibility of the watch face design.

## Transitioning Between Time Zones: Using the TimeZone Class

The Java **public abstract TimeZone** utility class extends a **java.lang.Object** class. This signifies that the TimeZone utility class was scratch-coded to provide time zone support. The class is part of the **java.util** package. This TimeZone class has one known direct subclass called SimpleTimeZone, but you'll be using this top-level TimeZone class. In case you're wondering what a **known direct subclass** is, it is a direct subclass that has been made a part of the Java API. Thus, your direct subclasses would be **unknown direct subclasses**, until Oracle officially makes them a permanent part of Java 9!

The Java class hierarchy for this TimeZone class looks like the following:

```
java.lang.Object
  > java.util.TimeZone
```

The TimeZone class creates an object that is used to represent a **Time Zone Offset**. It is important to notice that the TimeZone class will also figure out daylight saving time adjustments for you as well, which is convenient.

Typically you get the TimeZone object by calling the **.getDefault()** method, which creates a TimeZone object based on a time zone where your Watch Face application is running currently. For example, for a WatchFace application running in Santa Barbara, where I live, the .getDefault() method creates a TimeZone object based on Pacific Standard Time, also known as PST. You can get the ID of a TimeZone object using the **.getID()** method call, like this:

```
TimeZone.getDefault().getID()
```

You can also get a TimeZone object for a specific Time Zone if you like by calling the .getTimeZone() method, in conjunction with the .getID() method call, using the following Java dot chaining method call structure:

```
TimeZone.getTimeZone().getID()
```

You will need to know what the TimeZone ID values are in order to use this approach correctly. For instance, the TimeZone ID for the Pacific TimeZone is "America/Los_Angeles." If you wanted to create a TimeZone object loaded with Pacific Standard Time, you would use the following Java statement:

```
TimeZone timeZone = TimeZone.getTimeZone("America/Los_Angeles");
```

If you don't know all of the supported TimeZone ID values, you can use the **.getAvailableIDs()** method, and then iterate through all the supported Time Zone ID values. You can choose a supported TimeZone ID and then obtain that time zone. If a TimeZone ID that you want to use is not represented by one of the currently supported TimeZone ID values, then a custom TimeZone ID can be specified by a developer in order to produce a custom TimeZone ID. The syntax of a custom TimeZone ID is **CustomID: GMT Sign Hours : Minutes**.

When you create the TimeZone object, it will create your custom TimeZone ID attribute. This **NormalizedCustomID** will be configured using the following syntax: GMT Sign (OneDigit, or TwoDigit) Hours: (TwoDigit) Minutes. Other acceptable formats include **GMT Sign Hours Minutes** and **GMT Sign Hours**.

The sign will be either a + or a - minus (hyphen) sign, and the TwoDigit Hours will range between 00 and 23. The Minutes always use two digits, from 00 to 59.

Digits will always be one of the following: 0, 1, 2, 3, 4, 5, 6, 7, 8, 9.

Hours need to be between 0 to 23 and Minutes must be between 00 to 59. For example, "GMT+10" means ten hours ahead of the GMT, where "GMT+0010" means ten minutes ahead of the GMT, so "GMT+1010" would be ten hours ten minutes ahead of the GMT, and so forth.

The TimeZone data format is location independent, and digits must be taken from the **Basic Latin** block of the **Unicode** standard. It's important to note that you cannot specify a custom daylight savings time transition schedule using a custom TimeZone ID. If your specified String value does not match the required syntax, then the "GMT" String value will be utilized.

When you create the TimeZone object, it will create your custom TimeZone ID attribute. This **NormalizedCustomID** will be configured using the following syntax: GMT Sign TwoDigitHours : Minutes.

The sign will be either a + plus or a - minus sign, and the OneDigit Hours will range from 1 through 9, and the TwoDigit Hours will range between 10 and 23. The Minutes also use two digits, ranging from 00 through 59. As an example, `TimeZone.getTimeZone("GMT-8").getID()` will return a GMT-08:00 data value.

The TimeZone class has **21** methods, which I will not go into great detail here, but you will be using the .getID() and .getDefault() methods in your Watch Faces application code. These will allow you to obtain the current time zone in use by an Android user and its ID, so that you can switch time zones in your Watch Faces application if the user's host device (phone or tablet) does so at any time. The watch face design will then reflect this time zone change as well.

If you want to dive more deeply into all these powerful time zone methods, you can visit the TimeZone URL on the **docs.oracle.com** web site:

http://docs.oracle.com/javase/7/docs/api/java/util/TimeZone.html

Next, let's start to implement some of these classes you have been learning about by using some time-related Java 7 code in your ProWatchFaceService class. After that, you will learn about Android BroadcastReceiver and how it allows you to broadcast (and receive) time-related data from the host phone that can be used to set the timezone (in real time no less) on a watch face.

## Keep Watch Face Time: WATCH_FACE_UPDATE Constant

Let's get started by adding the timing-related Java code to the watchface app by adding the constant that defines the update rate for the watch face. A TimeUnit will be used to do this, and you will use one-thousand (millisecond) timing resolution for the watch face, because you will be using a second hand.

As you know, the TimeUnit class methods use a long data type, and because this is a constant that will only be used inside the class, let's make this a private static final long variable. You can name this WATCH_FACE_UPDATE_RATE, because that's what it will represent within the context of this application.

You will set this constant equal to a TimeUnit value of 1000, where you will use the TimeUnit. SECONDS.toMillis(1) construct to set this value. A SECONDS constant in the TimeUnit class represents that you are dealing with seconds as the time unit, and the .toMillis(1) method call (and parameter) converts one second to its milliseconds value, which, as I already mentioned, is 1000.

The Java code for this constant declaration statement should go at the top of the ProWatchFaceService.java class, as shown in Figure 8-9, and should look like the following:

```
private static final long WATCH_FACE_UPDATE_RATE = TimeUnit.SECONDS.toMillis(1);
```

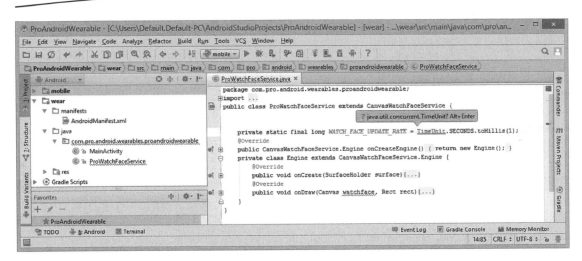

*Figure 8-9.* *Add a private static final long WATCH_FACE_UPDATE_RATE variable and convert it to MILLISECONDS*

# Android Classes: Time, Handler, and BroadcastReceiver

Besides the WatchFaceService and WatchFaceService.Engine classes, which you already subclassed in Chapter 7 and whose methods I will be delving into in great detail in Chapter 9, there are a few other important Android classes that are utilized in Watch Faces Design. I want to cover these in detail during this section, as well as implement some of their key methods in the public ProWatchFaceService and the private Engine classes to show you how these classes are used in Watch Faces App Design.

First, let's start with the Android **Time** class, which is used to hold the current time value and is accurate to the second. Next, I'll discuss the Android **BroadcastReceiver** class, which is used to receive time zone changes, and finally, I'll discuss the **Handler** class, which is used to send messages containing the updated timezone value.

## The Android Time Class: Time Processing Using Seconds

The Android **Time** class is a **public** class that extends the java.lang.Object class. The class hierarchy for the Time class looks like the following:

```
java.lang.Object
  > android.text.format.Time
```

This Time class is the Android alternative to the **java.util.Calendar** and the **java.util. GregorianCalendar** classes. This is why you're going to utilize it with the Watch Faces API. A Time object (an instance of the Time class) is used to represent a single moment in time and specifies time using **SECONDS** as far as time precision is concerned, which works well for Watch Face app usage. It is important to note that the Time class is not thread-safe and does not consider leap seconds. None of these feature limitations presents any problems for a watch face application implementation, however.

The Time class has a number of calendar (day and date specific) issues, and if you're using it for a calendar-centric usage, it is recommended that you use the GregorianCalendar class for calendar-related applications.

When performing time calculations with the Time class, arithmetic currently uses 32-bit integer numeric representation. This limits your reliable time range representation from 1902 through 2037, meaning if you use this class for Calendar-centric watch face design, you will need to rewrite your code around two decades from now. Much of the formatting and parsing of Time objects uses ASCII text, and, therefore, this class is also not suitable for use with non-ASCII time processing, which doesn't apply to WatchFace apps.

The Time class features three overloaded constructor methods. One of these allows you to specify a TimeZone for the Time object, and it looks like this:

`Time(String timezoneId)`

The constructor method, which you will be using, allows you to construct a Time object in the current, or default, time zone and will look like this:

`Time( )`

The third constructor allows you to make a copy of an existing Time object by passing an existing Time object as a parameter. This should be used for "nondestructive editing" purposes, for instance, and it will look like this:

`Time(Time other)`

The Time class contains 26 methods, which I am not going to cover in detail here. Because you are only going to be using the **.clear()** and the **.setToNow()** method calls with your Watch Faces application, I will cover those methods in detail here. If you're interested in learning about the other two dozen methods in the Time class, you can find this information on the Android Developer web site:

`http://developer.android.com/reference/android/text/format/Time.html`

The **public void clear (String timezoneId)** method was added into Android in API Level 3 and, when called, it resets (clears out) all current time values and sets the time zone to the TimeZone value, which is specified inside the method call parameter area using a String object and its data value.

The .clear() method call will also set the **isDst** (is daylight saving time) attribute (or property) of the Time object to have a **negative** value, which signifies that it is "unknown" if daylight saving time is active (or not).

This .clear() method call is usually used before the .setToNow(), or other set() method call, is used. This will ensure that a Time object is cleared and that it is set to the current time zone before a time value is loaded.

The **public void .setToNow()** method has no parameters, and when it is called it sets the Time object to the current time, using the settings being used in your user's Android operating system and hardware devices. This method was also added in API Level 3, and you'll be using it after the clear() method call, using the following Java programming statements:

```
watchFaceTime.clear(intent.getStringExtra("time-zone"));
watchFaceTime.setToNow();
```

Next, let's create a Time object in the Watch Face application. After you do that, I will get into how TimeZone data values will be broadcast between a Host (smartphone or tablet) and a smartwatch, using the Android BroadcastReceiver class. Then, I will get into how the system time itself is sent to the smartwatch, using the Handler class, and custom messaging that you'll create in an **updateTimeHandler** object.

## Adding the Watch Face Time Object: watchFaceTime

Add a **Time** object as a first line of code in your Engine class. Select the **android.text. format** Time version seen in the helper dialog in Figure 8-10.

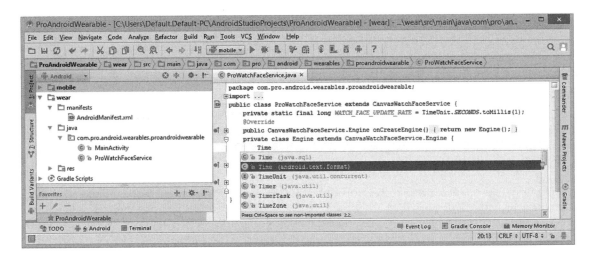

*Figure 8-10. Add a Time object declaration at the top of your Engine class; select the android.text.format version*

Name the Time object that you're declaring for use **watchFaceTime**. Once the Java statement is in place, use the **Alt+Enter** shortcut and **import** the Time class. Select an **android.text.format.Time** version, as shown in Figure 8-11.

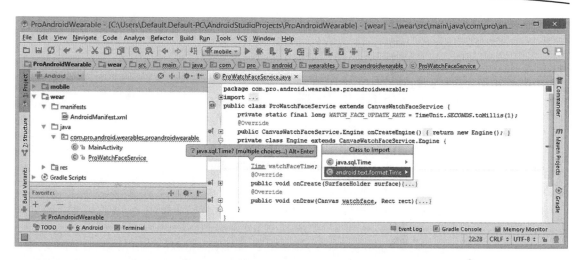

*Figure 8-11. Name a Time object watchFaceTime, use Alt+Enter to import Time class; select android.text.format.Time*

Now that you've declared your watchFaceTime Time object, the time has come to construct the object using the Java **new** keyword. You will do this inside the onCreate() method, because this is where it is best to create things for use in the watch face application.

The Java programming statement to construct the Time object is simple, as shown highlighted in Figure 8-12, and it should look like the following:

```
watchFaceTime = new Time();
```

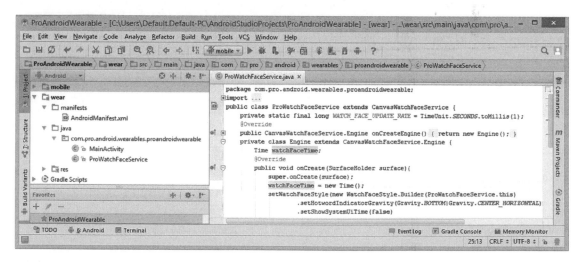

*Figure 8-12. Inside the Engine class, construct your watchFaceTime Time object by using the Java new keyword*

Now that the Time object that will hold your Time value is in place, let's take a look at how to broadcast the current TimeZone setting. You will do that so that if the user is traveling, or manually changes the time zone, it will immediately be reflected in the Watch Face Time Display.

## Android's BroadcastReceiver Class: Broadcasting Time Messages

Android's public abstract BroadcastReceiver class extends java.lang.Object and has four known direct subclasses: WakefulBroadcastReceiver, AppWidgetProvider, DeviceAdminReceiver, and RestrictionsReceiver. The Java class hierarchy for this BroadcastReceiver class looks like the following:

```
java.lang.Object
  > android.content.BroadcastReceiver
```

A BroadcastReceiver class provides Intent broadcasting (delivery) methods. This class provides the infrastructure that will allow your watch faces to receive Intents sent by the Android OS whenever the time zone has changed.

You will dynamically register an instance of this class in your watch face app by implementing a **private void registerTimeZoneReceiver()** method. This method will be called whenever a watch face goes to sleep (is not visible) and then wakes up, setting the **updateTimeZoneReceiver** flag and sending out an **Intent** object loaded with an **ACTION_TIMEZONE_CHANGED** constant.

This TimeZoneChange Intent will then ascertain if your user's time zone has changed (since their watch went to sleep and woke up), and then calls the **timeZoneReceiver** BroadcastReceiver object by using the .registerReceiver() method. You will be creating this timeZoneReceiver BroadcastReceiver in the next section of this chapter. The timeZoneReceiver BroadcastReceiver object will set your Time object to the TimeZone object. This will ensure that the time zone your watch face is using is always current.

This BroadcastReceiver class has one basic **BroadcastReceiver()** constructor method call, and it has **18** methods. I will not be covering all of these in detail here, however, I will cover the **.onReceive()** method, which you will be using in the Watch Face application. If you want to research this class in detail, you can visit the Android developer web site at this URL:

**http://developer.android.com/reference/android/content/BroadcastReceiver.html**

This **public abstract void onReceive(Context context, Intent intent)** method takes two parameters. The first is the Context object named context, which contains the Context object for your (private) Engine class, in which this BroadcastReceiver is running. The second is the Intent object named intent, which is the Intent object that will be received by your timeZoneReceiver object. This method is an original Android method originating in API Level 1, since BroadcastReceiver objects were a core building block for Android.

The method that calls out to this .onReceive() method, when you wish your BroadcastReceiver object to receive Intent broadcasts, is registerReceiver. The **.registerReceiver (BroadcastReceiver, IntentFilter)** method also has the **.unregisterReceiver (BroadcastReceiver)** counterpart, both of which you will be implementing during this chapter to create a Time Zone Broadcast System.

It is also important to note that you can't launch any pop-up dialog in the implementation of the .onReceive() method, and that implementations of the .onReceive() method should respond only to **known operating system actions**, such as the **ACTION_TIMEZONE_ CHANGED**, that you will be using. Implementations should ignore any "unexpected" (unknown to the operating system) or custom Intents that your .onReceive() method implementation might receive.

Now let's implement timeZoneReceiver BroadcastReceiver and its **public void .onReceive()** method on the inside of your private Engine class.

## Adding a Time Zone BroadcastReceiver Object: timeZoneReceiver

Let's add a final BroadcastReceiver object named timeZoneReceiver after the Time object named watchFaceTime and use the Java new keyword and type the first few letters of BroadcastReceiver to bring up the method helper dialog. Double-click the BroadcastReceiver (android.content) option and insert that constructor method into your Java code, as shown in Figure 8-13.

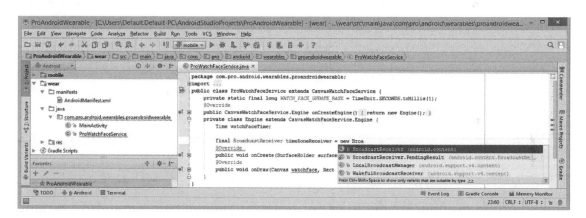

*Figure 8-13.* Add a final BroadcastReceiver object, named timeZoneReceiver, after your watchFaceTime object

Click the drop-down arrow indicator located next to the red error lightbulb on the left side of that line of Java 7 code. Select the **Implement Methods** option, as seen on the left side of Figure 8-14, and in the **Select Methods to Implement** dialog, as shown on the right side of Figure 8-14, select the **onReceive(context:Context,intent:Intent):void** and click the **OK** button.

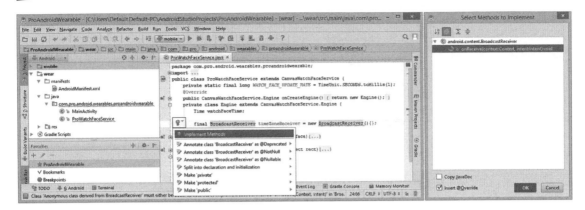

**Figure 8-14.** *Add a Java new keyword and BroadcastReceiver() constructor method; select Implement Methods*

After you click OK, the IntelliJ IDEA will create an empty bootstrap method structure for this **public void onReceive(Context context, Intent intent){}** method implementation for you. Now all that you need to do is clear the watchFaceTime Time object and load it with the new TimeZone information in an Intent object named intent, which is passed into the method. The TimeZone String is accessed using the **.getStringExtra()** method called off of intent using the extra data field named "time-zone" to access this TimeZone data.

After that is done, all you have to do is set your watchFaceTime object to the current system time by using the **.setToNow()** method call, and your Time object is now set to the correct time zone and time information. This Java code for your .onReceive() method implementation should look like the following Java 7 method structure:

```
@Override
public void onReceive(Context context, Intent intent) {
    watchFaceTime.clear(intent.getStringExtra("time-zone"));
    watchFaceTime.setToNow();
}
```

As you can see in Figure 8-15, the code is error free, and you are ready to add in a boolean flag variable, which will tell you when your watch face has gone to sleep and that it needs to check your OS Time Zone setting when it wakes back up! Let's do that next, and then I will explain more about the Android Handler class.

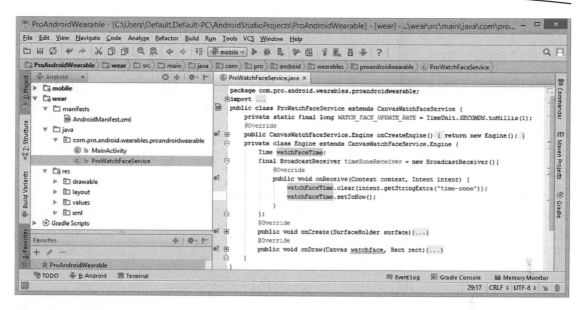

**Figure 8-15.** *Inside the onReceive() method add .clear() and .setToNow() method calls off the watchFaceTime object*

The final thing you need to do relative to this timeZoneReceiver is to create a boolean "flag" variable that tells you when you need to update this timeZoneReceiver.

Let's name the flag **updateTimeZoneReceiver** and set it to an initial value of **false**, as shown in Figure 8-16, because the assumption is that a watch face has not initially gone to sleep, and that the .onReceive() method in your timeZoneReceiver object does not need to be called (as it would be if this were set to true). This boolean flag needs to start out as false. Later on, in **.registerReceiver()**, this boolean flag will be set to true, and in **.unRegisterReceiver()**, this boolean flag will be set back to false to unregister a BroadcastReceiver.

```
boolean updateTimeZoneReceiver = false;
```

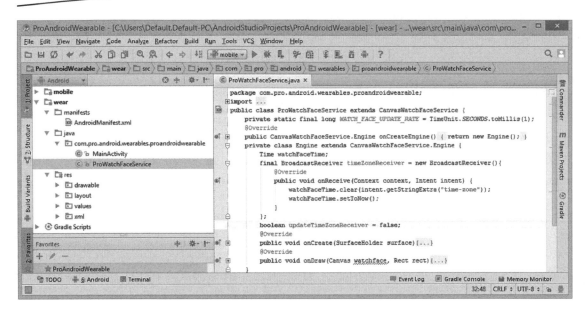

*Figure 8-16. After the timeZoneReceiver add a boolean updateTimeZoneReceiver variable set to a value of false*

This boolean updateTimeZoneReceiver, being set to a false value initially, indicates that a BroadcastReceiver is not registered for use. In this next section, you will create the **.registerTimeZoneReceiver()** method, which will set this value to **true**, indicating that a BroadcastReceiver is being used.

Your timeZoneReceiver BroadcastReceiver object will then update a TimeZone object value and then your **.unregisterTimeZoneReceiver()** method, which you will also be creating during this chapter, will set this boolean value back to false.

Let's get to work creating your register, and unregister, TimeZoneReceiver methods, so I can get into the Handler class and more time-related code!

## Calling Your timeZoneReceiver Object: registerTimeZoneReceiver()

Underneath the boolean updateTimeZoneReceiver variable, create the **private void registerTimeZoneReceiver()** method structure, and inside it, create an **if() conditional statement**. Inside the evaluation area of this if() statement, type the first few letters of the updateTimeZoneReceiver object, and then select it from the pop-up helper dialog by double-clicking it. This selection is shown highlighted in blue, at the bottom of Figure 8-17.

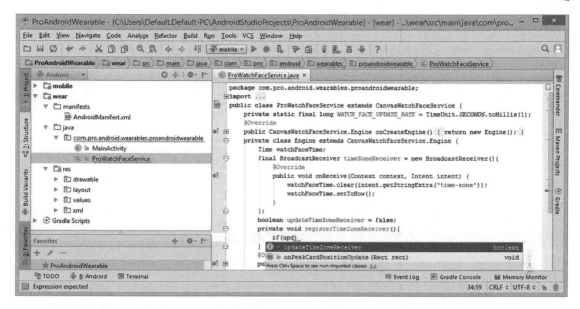

***Figure 8-17.*** *Create a private void registerTimeZoneReceiver() method and add an if condition by typing the first few letters of update*

Finish the initial conditional if() structure for the method, providing an exit to this method if your updateTimeZoneReceiver boolean flag is already set to a true value. The **if(updateTimeZoneReceiver)** construct would equate to true, whereas the **if(!updateTimeZoneReceiver)** construct would equate to false, as you'll be doing inside your .unregisterTimeZoneReceiver() method.

Therefore, the following conditional if() statement structure will "break" out of this method, that is, exit this method without doing anything else, if the updateTimeZomeReceiver boolean flag is already set to a true value:

```
if( updateTimeZoneReceiver ) { return; }
```

So the logic here is, if the receiver is already registered, the method is not needed, so let's get back out of it by using the Java **return** keyword.

Once you have ascertained that your updateTimeZoneReceiver boolean flag is set to a false value, as it will be on the start of the application thanks to your variable creation and the initialization statement you put into place in the previous section, you'll set the boolean flag to a **true** value by using the following Java statement, which can be seen in Figure 8-18:

```
updateTimeZoneReceiver = true;
```

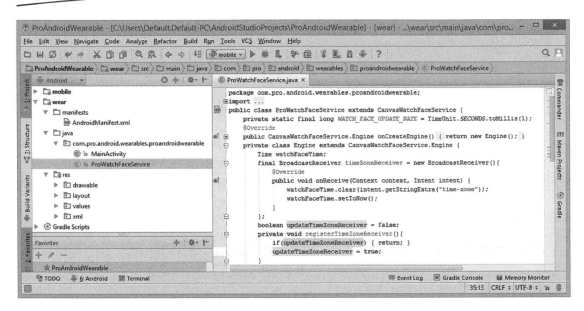

*Figure 8-18. If updateTimeZoneReceiver is true, return (exit the method); then set updateTimeZoneReceiver to true*

The next thing you need to do is create your Intent object that is loaded with the **ACTION_TIMEZONE_CHANGED** Intent, which will tell the Android OS what you are looking to ascertain from the user's system settings area.

This can be done using an Android **IntentFilter** class, so you will need to create a complex IntentFilter Java statement that declares that class for usage, names the IntentFilter object **intentFilter**, constructs that object using a **IntentFilter()** constructor method, and finally loads it with a Changed Time Zone Intent by using the **Intent.ACTION_TIMEZONE_ CHANGED** reference to that Intent class (object) constant value.

Type in the Java statement as shown in Figure 8-19, using a pop-up helper dialog to find the correct Android operating system Intent constant. These Intent constants that populate the helper dialog list when you type in the word ACTION_ are what I was referring to earlier as known operating system actions, as they're "hard coded" inside the Android OS using the **Intent** class. This is the reason that a "reference path" to the constant uses the format Intent.ACTION_TIMEZONE_CHANGED because the constant is in that class.

The Java code, shown at the bottom of Figure 8-19, should look like this:

```
IntentFilter intentFilter = new IntentFilter( Intent.ACTION_TIMEZONE_CHANGED );
```

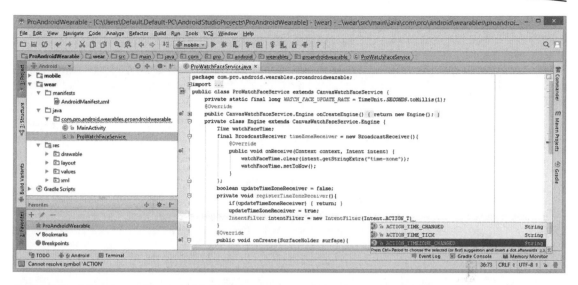

*Figure 8-19.  Add an IntentFilter named intentFilter, construct it using a new keyword, and type Intent.ACTION_T*

Finally, you need to use the **.registerReceiver()** method call to register your timeZoneReceiver BroadcastReceiver object. This enables the timeZoneReceiver object for a one-time use and will also send it over the Intent object you just created in the IntentFilter class.

This is done by using the following Java 7 statement, which can be seen in Figure 8-20, as it's being created using the IntelliJ pop-up helper dialog:

```
ProWatchFaceService.this.registerReceiver( timeZoneReceiver, intentFilter );
```

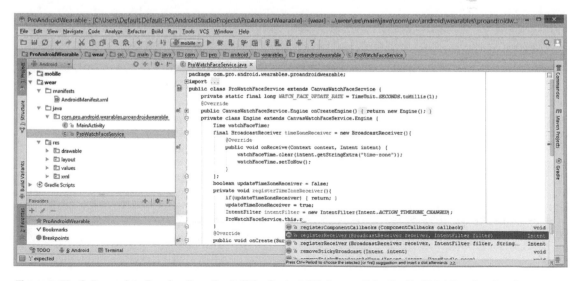

*Figure 8-20.  Call a .registerReceiver() method off the Context (this keyword) for the ProWatchFaceService class*

This calls the **.registerReceiver** method, off the **Context** object for your **ProWatchFaceService** class, using the Java **this** keyword and dot notation to reference a Context object, using **ProWatchFaceService.this** at the first part of the programming statement. Inside your method call parameter area, you will pass a **timeZoneReceiver** BroadcastReceiver object, as well as the **intentFilter** object you created and loaded with the **ACTION_TIMEZONE_CHANGED** Intent object in your previous line of code.

To create this, type **ProWatchFaceService.this** and a **period**, and select the **.registerRece iver(BroadcastReceiver receiver, IntentFilter filter)** option, and insert the method call into your programming statement, as shown at the bottom of Figure 8-20.

Now all you have to do is specify the timeZoneReceiver object as your BroadcastReceiver for the method and specify the intentFilter object you created holding the ACTION_TIMEZONE_CHANGED Intent object. After you have done this, your Java code will be error-free, as shown in Figure 8-21, and you will have your .registerTimeZoneReceiver() method ready for use!

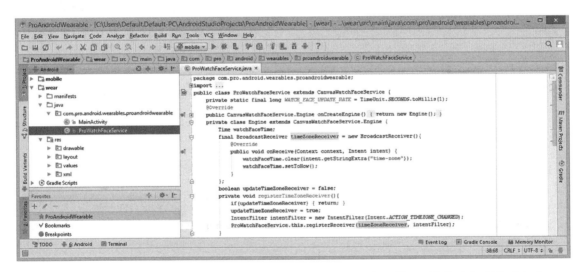

*Figure 8-21. In the .registerReceiver() parameter area, call a timeZoneReceiver object with the intentFilter Intent*

Next, you need to create the **.unregisterTimeZoneReceiver()** method that will unregister the BroadcastReceiver object and set the updateTimeZone boolean flag variable back to its original false value.

## Calling Your timeZoneReceiver Object: registerTimeZoneReceiver()

Underneath your private void .registerTimeZoneReceiver() method, create an empty **private void unregisterTimeZoneReceiver()** method structure, with the following Java keywords and code, as shown at the bottom of Figure 8-22:

```
private void unregisterTimeZoneReceiver() { your custom method code will go inside here }
```

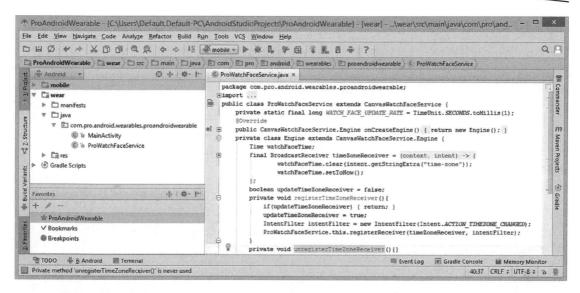

*Figure 8-22. Add a private void unregisterTimeZoneReceiver() method after a registerTimeZoneReceiver method*

Inside this method, create another **conditional if() structure**. Inside the evaluation area of the if() statement, type in the false value for the updateTimeZoneReceiver object, which would be **if(!updateTimeZoneReceiver)**, and then a return statement inside the curly braces for the body of the conditional if() statement. This will exit the method if your boolean flag is already false. Otherwise, the next line of code sets the flag to false, so that it is set back to false when you unregister the receiver. The code structure should look like the following, and can be seen in Figure 8-23:

```
private void unregisterTimeZoneReceiver() {
    if(!updateTimeZoneReceiver) { return; }
    updateTimeZoneReceiver = false;
}
```

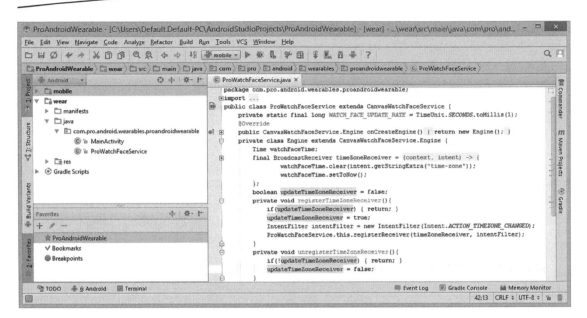

***Figure 8-23.*** *Add a conditional if(!updateTimeZoneReceiver) statement inside the method with a return statement*

Next type in the **ProWatchFaceService.this** Context object and a **period**, and select the
**unregisterReceiver(BroadcastReceiver receiver)** dialog option, as shown in Figure 8-24.

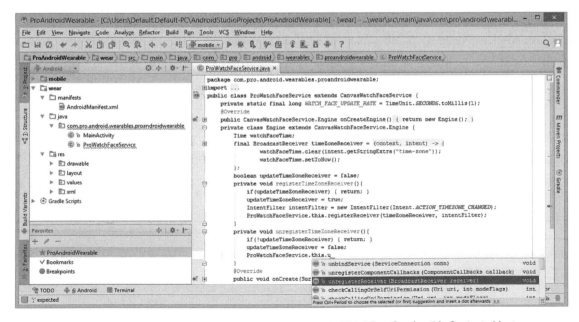

***Figure 8-24.*** *Add the method call to .unregisterReceiver() off your ProWatchFaceService.this Context object*

Inside the .unregisterReceiver() method call, pass the timeZoneReceiver BroadcastReceiver object. This will then unregister that BroadcastReceiver object and will therefore allow this BroadcastReceiver object to be used, again, to poll for the current time zone in use by your watch face user, as shown in Figure 8-25.

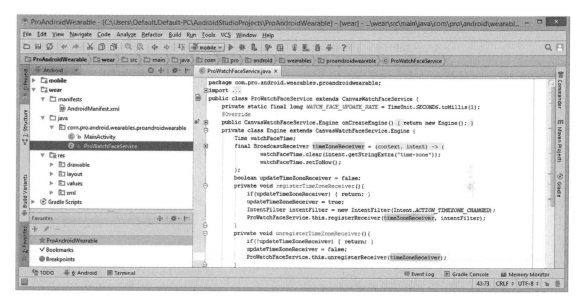

*Figure 8-25. Pass the timeZoneReceiver BroadcastReceiver object as your parameter for .unregisterReceiver()*

You'll be implementing these two methods in the next chapter, when I will cover the core WatchFaceService classes and methods used for the Watch Faces API.

# Summary

In this chapter, you learned about some of the Java utility classes and Android classes that are used for Watch Faces application development. They included the **SurfaceHolder** class, which you used to create the surface for your watch face, and the **WatchFaceStyle.Builder** class, which you used to style the watch face with the required Android UI elements.

Next, I delved into Android time-related classes, including **Time**, **TimeUnit**, and **TimeZone**. I also explained the **BroadcastReceiver** class as well as **Intent** objects, and you learned how to use the **.registerReceiver()** and **.unregisterReceiver()** methods to control a BroadcastReceiver object. You'll use this TimeZone broadcasting system in the next chapter to check on the user's time zone every time a watch face goes to sleep.

In the next chapter, you'll learn about the core **WatchFaceService.Engine** methods.

# Chapter 9

# Implement a WatchFaces Engine: Core WatchFaces API Methods

Now that you have put the Canvas SurfaceHolder, WatchFaceStyle, TimeZone, TimeUnit, Time, and BroadcastReceiver objects into place for your WatchFace application, you are ready to start getting into the advanced core methods that implement the WatchFaces API.

This chapter will take an in-depth look at the superclasses for the CanvasWatchFacesService and the CanvasWatchFacesService.Engine on which you based your ProWatchFaceService class and Engine class. It is important to learn about the **WatchFaceService** and **WatchFaceService.Engine** classes because these contain the methods, attributes, and constants you'll need to know about to correctly implement the WatchFaces API.

The WatchFaceService class contains the constants you'll utilize in your Watch Face applications, and the WatchFaceService.Engine nested class contains 14 methods, more than half of which you'll be implementing in your **ProWatchFaceService** public class inside the private Engine class.

The majority of this chapter's discussion will focus on these methods, which will need to be implemented inside the private Engine class for the core Watch Faces API Engine functionality. First, I'll explain how to use the Android **Handler** class to update the watch face time once per second in interactive mode. Then I'll explain Android **Message** and **System**. There are a ton of Android classes and methods that you will learn about during this chapter, so let's get started implementing the core WatchFaces API methods.

# WatchFace Seconds Time Engine: Using a Handler

Before I get into those core WatchFaceService.Engine methods, there are a few more objects and methods that you need to implement relating to the second hand time animation.

The way you update a second hand each second in Android is by using a Handler object. For this reason, I'll give you an overview of the Android Handler class, and after that you will create the **updateTimeHandler** Handler object and a **.handleMessage()** method structure that implements the watch face second hand time update programming logic.

## Android's Handler Class: Handling Time Update Messages

The Android Handler class is a public class that extends java.lang.Object, which means it was scratch-coded to implement thread and message handling for Android OS. The class hierarchy for the Handler class looks like this:

```
java.lang.Object
  > android.os.Handler
```

This Handler class has four known direct subclasses: HttpAuthHandler, AsyncQueryHandler, AsyncQueryHandler.WorkerHandler, and SslErrorHandler.

The Handler class (object) will allow you to send, and process, **Message** or **Runnable** objects that are associated with the application thread and its **MessageQueue**. You will be using a Message object to implement the updateTimeHandler Handler object and its **.handleMessage()** method.

Each Handler object instance will be associated with one single Thread and that Thread object's MessageQueue object. When you create your new Handler object, it is "bound" to a Thread object and MessageQueue object belonging to the Thread object that created the Handler object. Once the Handler is constructed, that Handler object will deliver messages (and runnables) for that MessageQueue object, processing them as they leave the MessageQueue.

There are two primary uses for the Handler object: scheduling messages to be processed or runnables to be executed at some time in the future, and queuing an action that needs to be performed on a thread other than the application's primary thread. You'll use the former in the Watch Faces API implementation in the next section of this chapter. Scheduling a message is accomplished using a .post(Runnable) method, .postAtTime(Runnable, long) method, .postDelayed(Runnable, long) method, .sendEmptyMessage(int) method, .sendMessage(Message), .sendMessageAtTime(Message, long) method, or sendMessageDelayed(Message, long) method.

Here you will be using the **.sendEmptyMessage()** method call in the **.updateTimer()** method, which you will be writing after you implement the Handler object.

The **post** version of these methods will allow you to queue Runnable objects to be called by a MessageQueue object after they are received, whereas the **sendMessage** version of these methods allows developers to queue up Messages containing data Bundle objects that can be processed by a Handler object's **handleMessage(Message)** method, which you are required to implement in the Handler object. You will be doing that in the next section of this chapter.

When posting or sending to a **Handler** object, you can either allow the item to be processed as soon as the MessageQueue object is ready, or you could specify a delay (before it gets processed) or an absolute time for it to be processed. Here you will use the former, however, the latter two will allow you to implement timeouts, ticks, or other time-based behaviors.

When a process is created for your WatchFaces application, the **main thread** is dedicated to hosting this MessageQueue object. This object manages the "top-level" application objects (Activity, BroadcastReceiver, Service) and any of the display windows they might need to create.

You can create your own thread and communicate with your main application thread using a Handler. In the example in this chapter, you will be creating an **updateTimeHandler**. This is done by calling the same post or sendMessage methods as before but from a new thread. A Message (or Runnable) will then be scheduled in your Handler object's MessageQueue object and processed whenever it is requested using a Message object, at least as far as the implementation for the example in this chapter goes.

The Handler class has one nested class, the **public static interface** called Handler.Callback in the android.os package. This nested class provides the Handler callback interface you will use when instantiating the Handler to avoid having to implement your own custom subclass of Handler. This nested class has one method, **.handleMessage(Message message)**, which you'll be using in the Java code for the updateTimeHandler Handler object you'll be coding.

The Handler class has four overloaded public constructor methods that you'll be using for the Watch Faces API implementation in this chapter. The simplest one you'll be using looks like the following, including the Java new keyword:

```
final Handler updateTimeHandler = new Handler() { Message Handling code will go in here }
```

If you construct the Handler.Callback object, you would use the following constructor method format:

```
Handler(Handler.Callback callback)
```

You could also provide your own customized Message Looper object using the following Handler constructor method format:

```
Handler(Looper looper)
```

Custom Looper objects, which allow you to create a MessageQueue for custom Threads, are not needed for Watch Faces API implementation, so I will not cover this in depth in this book. That said, I'll cover the Handler constructor methods in detail here for the sake of completeness.

The fourth and final constructor method provides the Message Looper object and accepts a Handler.Callback object in the same constructor method call, as shown in the following code:

```
Handler(Looper looper, Handler.Callback callback)
```

The Handler class supports 30 methods, which I clearly cannot cover in detail here, so I'll be covering the three methods you will be using in the code in the next section of this chapter. If you wanted to research all 30 in detail, you can visit the following developer web site URL:

```
http://developer.android.com/reference/android/os/Handler.html
```

The main method you'll be implementing inside the updateTimeHandler object to handle messages is the, you guessed it, **.handleMessage()** method. This **public void handleMessage(Message msg)** method will take the .handleMessage(Message yourMessageNameHere) generic format. The method was added in API Level 1, as it is a core feature and function for Android OS.

You will be using two other Handler class methods to talk to the Handler object from "outside" the updateTimeHandler object and to remove the Message object from the MessageQueue object, when it is no longer needed.

The **public final boolean sendEmptyMessage(int what)** sends an empty Message object with the **what** data value. This method was also added in API Level 1 and it returns a **true** value if a Message object is successfully placed into the MessageQueue object. As you may have surmised, it will return the false value upon failure.

The **public final void removeMessages(int what)** method, on the other hand, will remove any and all pending scheduling of Message objects that use the integer code for the what attribute of the Message object. In the watch faces application case, this will be zero, which is currently inside the MessageQueue object. Let's look at the Android Message class next so you'll get an overview of all of the object types you'll be using.

## Android's Message Class: Create a Time Update Message

Android **Message** is a **public final** class that extends the java.lang.Object master class, meaning that it was scratch-coded for holding Message objects for use with the Android OS. The class hierarchy looks like the following:

```
java.lang.Object
  > android.os.Message
```

The Message class allows you to create, define, and instantiate the Message object that will contain your Message description as well as any arbitrary data that need to be sent to your Handler object. In this watch face case, that would be your updateTimeHandler.

The Message object contains two extra **int** fields and an **extra object** field that allow you to avoid using any additional memory allocation in most uses. Whereas the constructor method for the Message class is public, as required by the Java programming language, the best code to create a Message object is to call Message.obtain(), or in the example here, the **Handler.sendEmptyMessage()** method call. This will pull the Message object from a "pool" of "recycled" Message objects.

The Message object has a number of data fields. These provide attributes, properties, or data fields (select a term most comfortable for you to use) that you can use to describe the content of the Message object, including arg1, arg2, obj, replyTo, sendingUid, and what. Here you'll be using the **what** attribute to send the **update time message code** inside a Message object.

The **public int arg1** attribute is a "low-overhead" alternative to using the **Message. setData()** method if you only need to store a few integer values. A **public int arg2** is also used to provide two integer data values.

The **public Object obj** gives you an arbitrary object as part of the Message object so you can send an object to the Message object recipient. The **public Messenger replyTo** provides you with an (optional) Messenger object. A Messenger object is another type of object that allows for the implementation of interprocess message-based communication. This allows creation of a Messenger object pointing to (referencing) a Handler, all in one process, and allows that Handler to handle the Messenger object across another process.

The **public int sendingUid** affords you an optional field indicating the UID (user identification) that sent the Message object in the first place. The **public int what** is used to provide a developer-defined message code. You'll be using this in your code to allow a recipient (Handler object) to be able to identify what the Message is all about, in this case, watch face timing.

The Android Message class has one public constructor method, the **Message()** constructor; however, the preferred way to get a Message object is to call Message.obtain() or one of the Message.sendMessage() method calls, which will construct the Message object for you.

This Message class has close to two dozen public methods, none of which you will be using in the watch faces development here, but if you are interested in learning more about these methods, detailed information can be found at the developer's web site:

http://developer.android.com/reference/android/os/Message.html

## Creating a Second Hand Timer: The updateTimeHandler

Let's create the final **updateTimeHandler** Handler object by typing the Java keyword **final** and the class name (object name) **Handler** and selecting the **Handler (android.os)** option from the pop-up helper dialog, as shown in Figure 9-1. Note there is also a java. util.logging.Handler class, which is why I used this work process, so be sure to select the correct Handler.

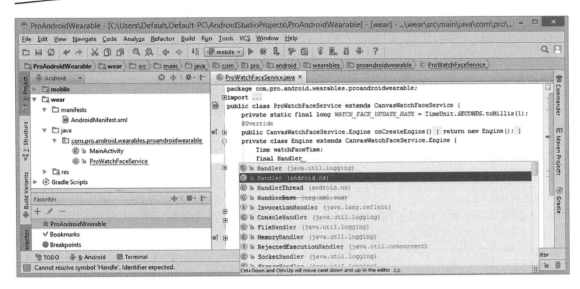

*Figure 9-1. Add a final Handler object declaration using the pop-up helper dialog to find the android.os Handler*

Once you double-click the **android.os.Handler** class to insert it, you've declared the Handler object as being final. This makes sure that it's only assigned (to memory) once and thus fixes it in the system memory, at the same memory location, for the duration of the running of your application.

Next, you will finish the Handler object named **updateTimeHandler,** using the Java new keyword and the Handler() constructor method call. The resulting empty Handler object structure should look like the following Java code:

```
final Handler updateTimeHandler = new Handler() { // An Empty Handler Object Structure };
```

As you can see in Figure 9-2, the updateTimeHandler Handler object's code is error free and you are ready to code the **public void .handleMessage()** method. This message handling method is created inside curly braces for the final updateTimeHandler Handler object implementing the Message object handling capabilities for the updateTimeHandler handler object. As mentioned earlier, this is the method that is required for implementation. Once this is done, a Handler object is "viable" and other methods can be called off it.

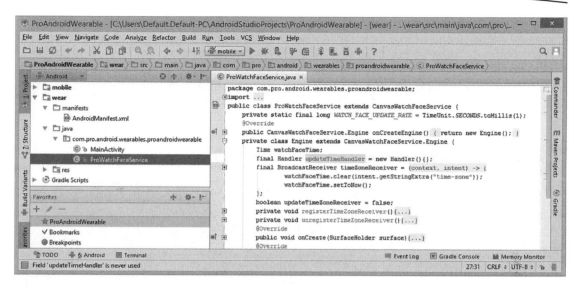

*Figure 9-2. Use the Java new keyword and Handler() constructor method to create an empty updateTimeHandler*

Inside the updateTimeHandler object, you'll add an **@Override public void handleMessage(Message)** method structure, selecting the **android.os.Message** option in the pop-up, as shown in Figure 9-3, using the following Java code:

```
@Override
public void handleMethod(Message updateTimeMessage) { // Message object evaluation goes in
here }
```

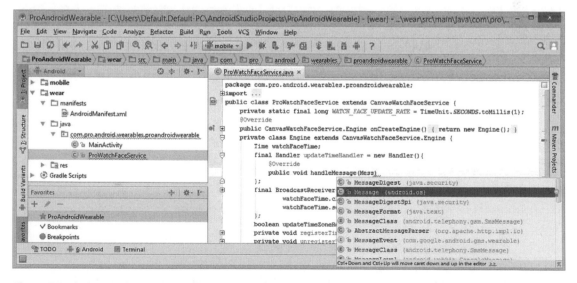

*Figure 9-3. Code a public void handleMessage(Message) method, using the pop-up to select android.os Message*

Once you have created the empty .handleMessage() method structure, as shown in Figure 9-4, you will need to create some Java code that will evaluate the Message object named updateTimeMessage. This Message object is going to be automatically passed into the .handleMessage() method whenever the Handler object is referenced with the .sendEmptyMessage() method call. An example of this referencing can be seen in this line of Java code:

```
updateTimeHandler.sendEmptyMessage(UPDATE_TIME_MESSAGE); // Send TimeZone Update Message
to Handler
```

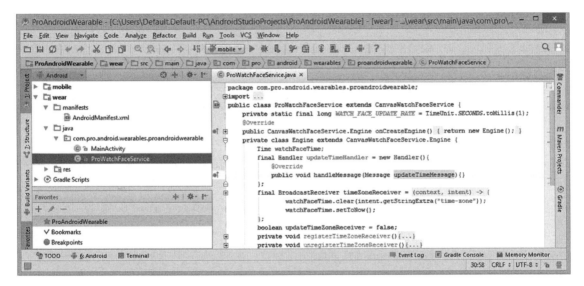

*Figure 9-4. The (empty) updateTimeHandler Handler object with handleMessage() processing construct is now in place*

You will actually be creating this line of code a bit later in the chapter.

The next step in this process is to evaluate the **updateTimeMessage** Message object that is passed into the .handleMessage() method using a Java **switch** evaluation structure. This structure will have case statements for each of the Message object's **what** attributes.

The Message object what attribute or property can be referenced using Java dot notation. For an updateTimeMessage Message object, this would look like **updateTimeMessage.what** and would be later referenced within the switch() statement's evaluation parameter area, using the following Java structure:

```
switch(updateTimeMessage.what) { your case statements evaluating what attributes will go
in here }
```

As you can see in Figure 9-5, once you type in the switch() statement and the updateTimeMessage Message object inside the evaluation parameter area and press the period key, you will be presented with a pop-up helper dialog containing the attributes you learned about in the previous section of this chapter. Double-click the what attribute to add it to the switch.

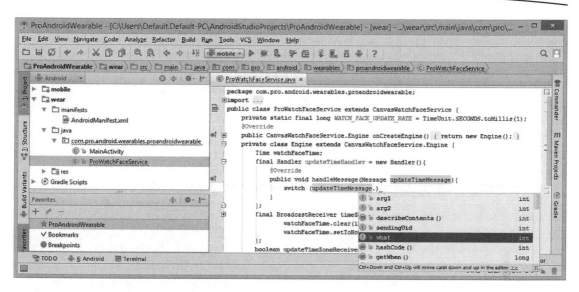

**Figure 9-5.** *Add a Java switch statement that will evaluate updateTimeMessage object's what attribute*

The next thing you'll need to do is create an update time message's **what** attribute integer data constant at the top of the private Engine class so that you have that in place before you add a case evaluation statement. The Java keywords used to define a constant are **static** and **final**, so your Java programming statement declaring an **integer** constant set to an initial **zero** data value and named **UPDATE_TIME_MESSAGE** should look like the following:

```
static final int UPDATE_TIME_MESSAGE = 0;
```

Create a Java switch statement evaluating the what attribute, called off of the updateTimeMessage object, and inside the UPDATE_TIME_MESSAGE constant case evaluator, call the invalidate() method, and then break out of the switch statement.

```
switch(updateTimeMessage.what) {
    case UPDATE_TIME_MESSAGE:
        invalidate();
        break;
}
```

As you can see in Figure 9-6, your Java code is now error free, and you are ready to implement more advanced features that kick in when the smartwatch enters ambient mode.

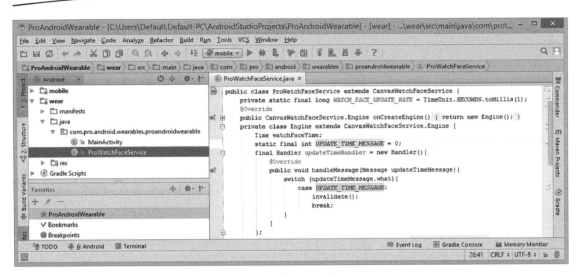

*Figure 9-6. Declare an UPDATE_TIME_MESSAGE integer valuable and add in your switch case statement for it*

Now it's time to use the watchface Canvas object in the body of the onDraw() method. You'll be calling a **.drawColor(int color)** method off this object to set the color of the Canvas to black. This optimizes power use for the watch faces design, of course! You learned well in Chapter 6!

# Watch Faces Time Calculation: Using System Time

The next Java code constructs you will be crafting will look at watch face modes (visible or on vs. off, and ambient vs. interactive), and you'll then determine if the updateTimeHandler is needed to update the watch face design second hand if a watchface is visible and in interactive mode. If the updateTimeHandler is needed, the system time in milliseconds will be used to calculate the next whole second (which equates to an exact value of 1,000 milliseconds), and moves the second hand in an .onDraw() method, which you'll be coding in Chapter 10.

## Java System Class: Accessing Time in Milliseconds

The Java **public final System** class extends a java.lang.Object master class and provides access to system-related information and resources, including system time functions, which you'll be using, as well as standard system IO (input and output). The System class hierarchy looks like the following:

```
java.lang.Object
  > java.lang.System
```

All of the methods in this class are accessed in a static fashion, and the class itself can't be instantiated. So you can't have any System objects, but you will reference system functions by using a System.methodCallName() approach. So, to reference the System Time using milliseconds, your method call structure would look like the following Java code, which you'll be using in the next section of this chapter:

```
System.currentTimeMillis()
```

Next, let's put the code in place that ascertains when the second hand, or seconds value, needs to be calculated for your watch face using the custom **isTimerEnabled()** method. After you do that, you can implement this method to tell you when you need to calculate second hand timing inside the Handler object's handleMessage() switch statement's Java programming structure.

## Watch Face Seconds: Calculating Second Hand Movement

The first thing you'll need to do is create a method that will return a true value if the watch face is currently visible and not using ambient mode, which means that it is in interactive mode and being viewed by the user. Add a line of code under the updateTimeHandler object and declare a **private boolean isTimerEnabled()** method, as shown in Figure 9-7. Inside the method body, type the Java **return** keyword and then the word **is**, and then double-click the **isVisible()** method option to insert it into your code when it appears in the IntelliJ pop-up method selector helper dialog.

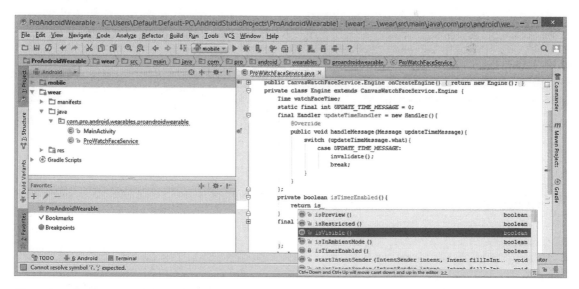

*Figure 9-7. Creating the private boolean isTimerEnabled() method with return statement, by typing is and then selecting isVisible()*

Next, type in the Java logical AND operator (&&) and the Java logical NOT (!) operator, and then type the word is. This will bring up an IntelliJ pop-up method helper dialog where you can then select an **isInAmbientMode()** method option, as seen selected with blue in Figure 9-8. Next, double-click the method to insert it into your code and add a semicolon to finish the return statement. Your code should be error free, as shown in Figure 9-9.

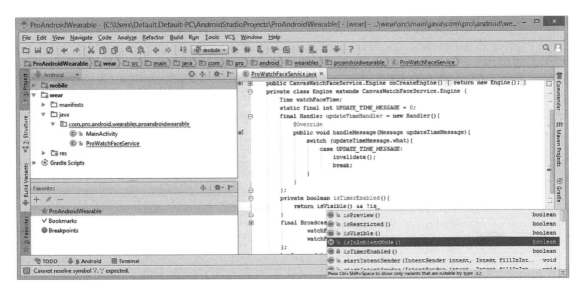

**Figure 9-8.** *Type a Java && Logical AND operator, and the not ! symbol, and is, then select isInAmbientMode()*

Now you can call this isTimerEnabled() method, inside a conditional if() structure, to ascertain if the smartwatch is operating in interactive mode. If this method returns a true value, you can calculate the system time to the nearest even whole second (exactly 1,000 milliseconds) value, moving the second hand as the second occurs precisely in the system clock.

Add a line of code inside the switch construct for the case statement for the UPDATE_TIME_ MESSAGE, after the invalidate() method call and before the Java break keyword. You will need to first put the empty conditional if() statement in place and then create the whole second timing logic after that.

The empty conditional if() statement that evaluates whether or not second timing needs to be calculated should look like the following Java code:

```
If( isTimerEnabled() ) { Your Whole Second Timer Programming Logic Will Go In Here }
```

As you can see in Figure 9-9, your code is error free and you are ready to add the body of the conditional if() statement to calculate system time to the nearest whole second value, which will then trigger the second hand to tick one more time on the user's watch face design.

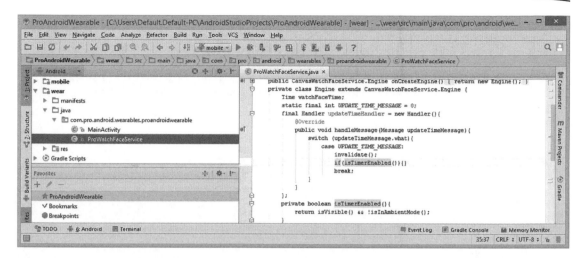

*Figure 9-9.  Add an if(isTimerEnabled()){} evaluation construct after the invalidate() and before the break keyword*

The first thing you'll need to do for this nearest whole second time calculation is to get the system time using the System.currentTimeMillis() method call and assign it to a long variable, which you'll name **msTime**.

Inside the body of the conditional if() statement, declare a **long msTime** variable and then type the **equals** (=) operator and the **System** class name. Then press the **period** key to bring up the IntelliJ pop-up method helper dialog, which is shown in Figure 9-10. Double-click the **currentTimeMillis()** method option and insert it into your Java code to complete the statement, declaring, naming, and setting the value for this msTime variable.

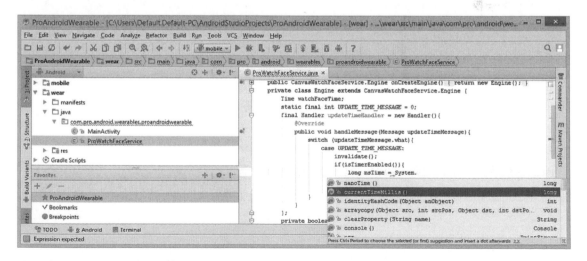

*Figure 9-10.  Declare a long variable named msTime by typing equals, System, and period; then select currentTimeMillis()*

Next, you'll need to calculate a **delay value** that represents the number of milliseconds that exist between the current system time and the next even 1,000-millisecond value. This would represent the next even (exact) second, which is precisely the time value you will want to advance the second hand in your watch face design to the next tick mark on the watch face.

As you can see in Figure 9-11, you need to add another **long** variable named **msDelay**, which will hold the calculated delay value. This will represent the amount of milliseconds until the next even millisecond will occur.

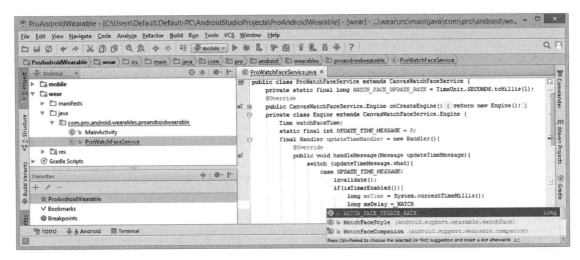

*Figure 9-11. Declare a long variable named msDelay and then type = WATCH, select WATCH_FACE_UPDATE_RATE*

Type in the Java long variable type and the msDelay variable name, as well as the equals operator and the first few letters of WATCH_FACE_UPDATE_RATE, which is the variable seen at the top of Figure 9-11 that holds the Time resolution value of 1,000 milliseconds for every full second.

Find the **WATCH_FACE_UPDATE_RATE** option, which IntelliJ will most likely put at the top of the list, and double-click it to insert it into your Java code. Now all you have to do is find a "delta" or millisecond difference between the current time and the next full second, and you'll be finished.

The key to finding the delta, or time delay value, lies in the Java **modulo** operator. To calculate this msDelay time to wait before calling the next full second hand advance, take the 1,000-millisecond WATCH_FACE_UPDATE_RATE and subtract the modulo (which calculates a leftover, or delta, time value) of the current millisecond time value and 1,000-millisecond time resolution, which will give you the amount of milliseconds until the next full second. This can be done using the following Java code, as shown in Figure 9-12:

```
long msDelay = WATCH_FACE_UPDATE_RATE - ( msTime % WATCH_FACE_UPDATE_RATE );
```

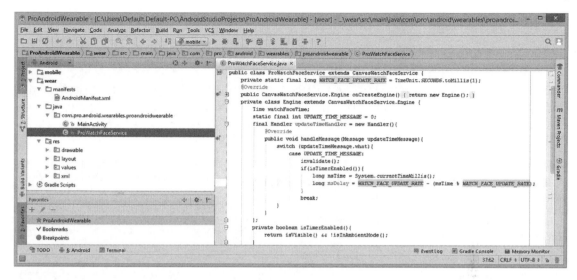

*Figure 9-12.* *Calculate the offset to the next full second using the msTime modulo % WATCH_FACE_UPDATE_RATE*

As you can see, the code is now complete and error free and you're ready to start implementing the core methods for the **WatchFaceService** class and the **WatchFaceService.Engine** class. I'll present an overview of the class and its nested Engine class, and then you'll implement some of these methods.

# WatchFaces API: Core Methods to Implement

This section will look at the core WatchFaces API methods that are held within the WatchFaceService and WatchFaceService.Engine classes.

## Android WatchFaceService Class: Core Constants

A **public abstract WatchFaceService** class extends a **WallpaperService** class, which then extends a Service class, which extends a ContextWrapper class, which extends a Context class, which extends a java.lang.Object class. Two known direct subclasses include the CanvasWatchFaceService you'll be using and Gles2WatchFaceService. The class hierarchy for this looks like the following:

```
java.lang.Object
  > android.content.Context
    > android.content.ContextWrapper
      > android.app.Service
        > android.service.wallpaper.WallpaperService
          > android.support.wearable.watchface.WatchFaceService
```

WatchFaceService and WatchFaceService.Engine, which I'll cover next, are subclasses of WallpaperService and WallpaperService.Engine, respectively. If you want to create watch faces for wearables, you will use this instead of the more vanilla WallpaperService, which you would use for wallpaper apps for smartphones, tablets, e-readers, and iTV sets.

The WatchFaceService object, just like a WallpaperService, must implement one important method, onCreateEngine(), which you implemented in Chapter 7. As you did in Chapter 7, here you must also create the (inner class) **private class Engine**, extending either WatchFaceService.Engine or one of its known direct subclasses.

This class also provides the "wake lock," which will be held so the device doesn't go to sleep until a watch face finishes drawing. This is intended for watch face updates that occur while the smartwatch is in ambient mode.

This class has one nested class named WatchFaceService.Engine, which is the actual implementation of the Watch Faces API. I will cover this next.

This class has five constants that control things such as watchface design interruptions (what notifications are shown) and hardware features such as screen burn-in protection and the low-bit (power saving) ambient mode. Two of these constants are String values and three are integer values:

- The **INTERRUPTION_FILTER_ALL** Integer constant is returned by a call to the .getInterruptionFilter() method. It can also be passed as the parameter in the .onInterruptionFilterChanged(int) method, which you'll be implementing.

- The **INTERRUPTION_FILTER_NONE** integer constant is returned by a call to the .getInterruptionFilter() method. It can also be passed as the parameter in the .onInterruptionFilterChanged(int) method, which you'll be implementing.

- The **INTERRUPTION_FILTER_PRIORITY** integer constant is returned by a call to a .getInterruptionFilter() method. It can also be passed as a parameter in the .onInterruptionFilterChanged(int) method, which you'll be implementing.

- The **PROPERTY_BURN_IN_PROTECTION** String constant will pass a Bundle object to .onPropertiesChanged(Bundle) to indicate whether burn-in protection is supported on the smartwatch hardware.

- The **PROPERTY_LOW_BIT_AMBIENT** String constant will pass a Bundle object to .onPropertiesChanged(Bundle) to indicate whether there is hardware-device support for implementation of a low-bit ambient mode.

Next, let's implement variables that can hold these constants in your Watch Face application. After that, I'll cover the WatchFaceService.Engine nested class, and you can implement the core methods that are required for a Watch Faces API–based application. After that, you can focus on drawing your Watch Faces Design on the surface of the watch face, which I cover in Chapter 10, and how to draw watch face element ShapeDrawable objects.

# Adding WatchFaceService Constants: Burn-In and Low-Bit

Because you want to support burn-in protection and low-bit ambient mode, and since the WatchFaces API does not currently have methods for this (like the .isInAmbientMode() method), which you have already utilized in the custom isTimerEnabled() method, let's add boolean variables to hold these flags.

You can declare both boolean flag variables by using a **compound** declaration statement, because you are not specifically setting any default values. It is important to note that if you don't declare any boolean values, Java's default initialization value for any boolean variable will be **false**.

Let's provide logical names for these boolean flags that signify what they do: let's name them **lowBitAmbientModeFlag** and **burnInProtectModeFlag**. Your Java compound statement should look like the following, which is error free and shown highlighted in the bottom half of Figure 9-13:

```
boolean lowBitAmbientModeFlag, burnInProtectModeFlag;
```

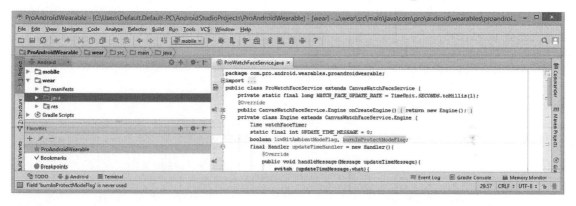

*Figure 9-13. Add boolean variables in your Engine class for lowBitAmbientModeFlag and burnInProtectModeFlag*

The time has come for you to implement several of the most important Watch Faces API methods from the WatchFaceService.Engine nested class. You'll be adding **.onDestroy()**, which is in the CanvasWatchFaceService.Engine class, because it needs to "destroy" (remove from memory) your Canvas and any related .onDraw() components that are in system memory as well.

From the WatchFaceService.Engine class, let's implement four methods: **.onTimeTick()**, **.onVisibilityChanged()**, **.onAmbientModeChanged()**, and **.getInterruptionFilter()**. Remember, you already implemented **.onCreate()**, although you'll be adding to this method later on when you learn about the graphics and .onDraw() portions of your watch faces design, which I will be covering in detail in Chapter 10.

# Android WatchFaceService.Engine Class: Core Methods

The Android **WatchFaceService.Engine** class is a **public abstract** class that extends the WallpaperService.Engine class, which means that Google Android developers created a Watch Faces API primarily by using the Wallpaper API.

This class represents the core Java code implementation of the Watch Faces API. You will need to implement the .onCreateEngine() method, as you did in Chapter 7 (see Figure 7-9), to return the Watch Face Engine implementation. The Java class hierarchy for this class will look like the following:

```
java.lang.Object
    > android.service.wallpaper.WallpaperService.Engine
      > android.support.wearable.watchface.WatchFaceService.Engine
```

The Android WatchFaceService.Engine class has two known direct subclasses: a **CanvasWatchFaceService.Engine**, which you are currently using for the ProWatchFaceService class, and the **Gles2WatchFaceService.Engine**, which is used to implement **OpenGL ES 2.0** WatchFaceService.Engine functionality.

The class has one public constructor method, **WatchFaceService.Engine()**, and 14 public methods, which I'll discuss here, along with one method from the CanvasWatchFaceService. Engine (onDestroy()) so you'll know what all of the core Watch Faces API methods are capable of providing.

You have already created the **void .onCreate(SurfaceHolder holder)** method, which is used to create variables and objects in memory on the Watch Face Service Engine creation.

The **void .onDestroy()** method is actually described in the documentation for the CanvasWatchFaceService.Engine class, on the Android developer web site, but I will include it here, because it will be implemented in this chapter. This method will remove the WatchFaceService.Engine from memory, and it can also remove Message objects from the MessageQueue object. Be sure to do this before calling the **super.onDestroy()** statement. The uses for the three void methods are:

> The **void .onTimeTick()** method is called one per minute when the watch face is in **ambient mode** to update the watch face's time (hour and minute hands).

> The **void .onPropertiesChanged(Bundle properties)** method is called when the properties of the hardware device are determined. This method will be used to set the low-bit and burn-in flags you created in the previous section.

> The **void .onVisibilityChanged(boolean visible)** method is called to inform you of the watch face becoming visible or hidden. You'll be using this to send a Message object to make sure the TimeZone object is in sync with the Time object. What the logic does is set the Time object to the TimeZone object value. This ensures the TimeZone is always set correctly.

Two of the methods in this class relate to setting attributes that affect the logic in the .onDraw() method. Since I cover the Draw logic in Chapter 10, you'll implement the next two methods in that chapter:

A **void .onAmbientModeChanged(boolean inAmbientMode)** method will be called whenever the user's hardware device enters or exits its ambient mode.

The **void .onInterruptionFilterChanged(int interruptionFilter)** method will be called when the user changes the interruption filter setting (constant).

You've already implemented some of these methods in this class, such as the .isInAmbientMode(), and there's also a method you can use to modify a Watch Face Style object, which you've already created as well. I'll cover these two methods next, just to be thorough:

The **final boolean .isInAmbientMode()** method will return your boolean value, which will tell the app whether the watch face hardware is in ambient mode.

The **void .setWatchFaceStyle(WatchFaceStyle watchFaceStyle)** method will set WatchFaceStyle attributes so you can change UI settings dynamically.

There are also three getter methods for this class, which allow developers to ascertain the current state (setting) for the interruption filter, Peek Card positioning, and the unread Peek Card count:

The **final int .getInterruptionFilter()** method returns interruption filter constants that have been selected by the user and are currently in force.

The **final Rect .getPeekCardPosition()** method returns the screen location X and Y coordinates of your first peeking card using the Rect object.

A **final int .getUnreadCount()** method will return a number for notification cards that are currently in a "to be read queue" that have not been read.

There are also three other .on() methods that will not be implemented, but I will mention them here just for the sake of completeness:

The Bundle **.onCommand(String action, int x, int y, int z, Bundle extras, boolean resultRequested)** implements Android's Live Wallpaper capability for intercepting a touch event from the surface of the watch face design.

The **void .onPeekCardPositionUpdate(Rect rect)** method is called whenever a first Peek Card positions itself on the watch face screen, giving its position using a Rect object.

The **void .onUnreadCountChanged(int count)** method is called when the number of unread notification cards in the "to be read queue" has changed.

I'll spend the remainder of this chapter discussing the core watch face methods that have not yet been added so you can then work on the .onDraw() method.

# Adding WatchFaceService.Engine Methods: Core Function

Over the rest of the chapter, I'll discuss the other core watch face methods that have to do with time and memory optimization. They allow you to detect whether a watch face is visible and the power saving and screen burn-in protection modes that are available for the smartwatch device hardware configuration the user is currently using.

Once all of these core watch face creation, styling, timing, and broadcast receiver objects and methods have been put into place in your code, you can then focus on how to draw your watch face design, which is covered in Chapter 10.

## Telling Time While in Ambient Mode: The .onTimeTick() Method

The simplest core method to implement is the **void .onTimeTick()** method, so let's start with that and add it at the top of the private Engine class.

Add the Java **@Override** keyword, signifying that you are about to override the superclass method, and type in **public void onTimeTick()**. Inside the method body, use a Java **super** keyword to pass the **.onTimeTick()** method call to the CanvasWatchFaceService.Engine superclass. Your code for the basic method body, as shown in Figure 9-14, should look like the following:

```
@Override
public void onTimeTick() {
    super.onTimeTick();
}
```

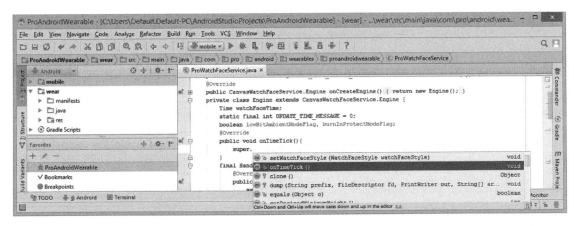

*Figure 9-14. Add public void onTimeTick() method; inside it, use the Java super keyword to call the parent method*

Use the pop-up helper dialog, as shown in Figure 9-14, to select the method call.

You'll also need to update the watch face time in this method, using the .invalidate() method call, so that Android knows to update the time on the watch face. Make sure to put this after the super.onTimeTick() superclass method call. This is so everything else that needs to be done by the superclass for the .onTimeTick() method is processed before you call this .invalidate() method call. The .onTimeTick() method structure should look like the following code, which can be seen in Figures 9-15 and 9-16:

```
@Override
public void onTimeTick() {
    super.onTimeTick();
    invalidate();
}
```

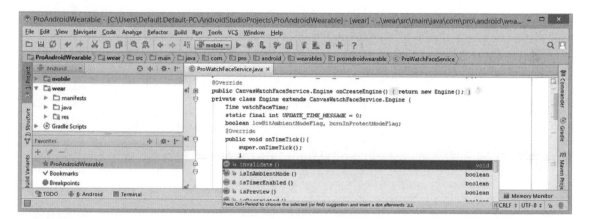

*Figure 9-15.* Add an .invalidate() method call to update the watch face once the super.onTimeTick() has been called

If you want IntelliJ to write the code for you, you can simply type in an "I" and select the invalidate() method from the pop-up helper method dialog or you can double-click the method you want IntelliJ to write for you, as shown in Figure 9-15.

Let's code another relatively simple method next, the .onDestroy() method.

## Removing a Watch Face from Memory: The .onDestroy() Method

Add another Java **@Override** keyword after the .onTimeTick() method, again signifying that you are about to override the superclass method, and type in **public void onDestroy()**. Inside the method body, use a Java **super** keyword to pass this **.onDestroy()** to the CanvasWatchFaceService.Engine superclass. If you have not implemented an updateTimeZoneReceiver function in the watchface application, this would be all that you would need to do.

The code for the basic .onDestroy() method body would therefore look like the following Java method structure:

```java
@Override
public void onDestroy() {
    super.onDestroy();
}
```

Because you are using a BroadcastReceiver object, you'll need to remove the Message object from the MessageQueue object by using the **.removeMessages()** method call. This will need to be done **before** the super.onDestroy() method call, or this will never occur because the WatchFaceService.Engine object will no longer exist and the Message object will still be in the queue.

So add the **@Override public void onDestroy(){}** empty method structure and then add the reference to the updateTimeHandler Handler object. Next, press the period key, to initiate the pop-up helper dialog, and select the **removeMessages(int what)** option, as shown in Figure 9-16.

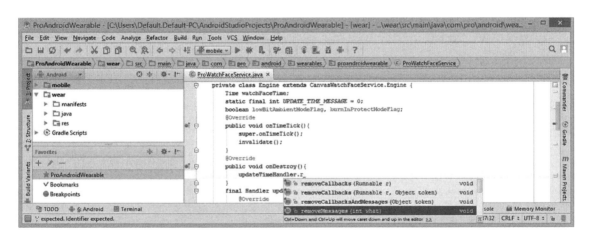

*Figure 9-16. Add public void onDestroy() method; inside it, use the updateTimeHandler.removeMessages() method*

Inside the resulting **updateTimeHandler.removeMessages()** method call's parameter area, type in the **UPDATE_TIME_MESSAGE** Message object constant, or type in a "U," and select it from the pop-up helper dialog list. Then you can add the **super.onDestroy();** Java code statement, and you will be finished!

The .onDestroy() method structure, shown error free in Figure 9-17, should look like the following Java code structure after you are finished:

```java
@Override
public void onDestroy() {
    updateTimeHandler.removeMessages(UPDATE_TIME_MESSAGE);
    super.onDestroy();
}
```

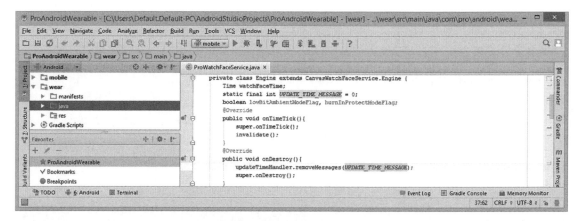

*Figure 9-17.  After using removeMessages() to remove Message object from MessageQueue, call super.onDestroy()*

Next, you'll implement the **.onPropertiesChanged()** method, which, at six lines of code, is a little more complicated than the previous two methods.

## Determining Low-Bit and Burn-In Modes: .onPropertiesChanged()

The next thing you need to do to is to implement an **.onPropertiesChanged()** method, using the Java **@Override** keyword. This can be seen at the bottom of Figure 9-18, and it results in the following empty Java method structure:

```
@Override
public void onPropertiesChanged(Bundle properties){ // The method implementation will
go in here }
```

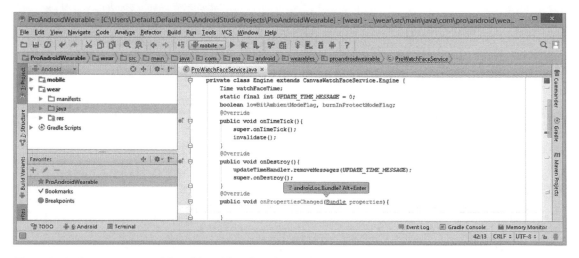

*Figure 9-18.  Create an empty @Override public void onPropertiesChanged(Bundle properties) method structure*

This method uses the Android **Bundle** object, named **properties**, to pass a bundle of smartwatch properties into the method for processing. As you can see, at the bottom of Figure 9-18, the Bundle class will most likely need to be imported, so click your mouse inside the empty method and use the Alt+Enter work process to have IntelliJ write the **import android.os.Bundle** import statement for you. Now you're ready to code the body of the method.

Inside the .onPropertiesChanged() method, type the Java **super** keyword and a **period**, and then select the **onPropertiesChanged(Bundle properties)** option from the pop-up helper dialog and double-click it to insert it into the Java statement, as shown at the bottom of Figure 9-19.

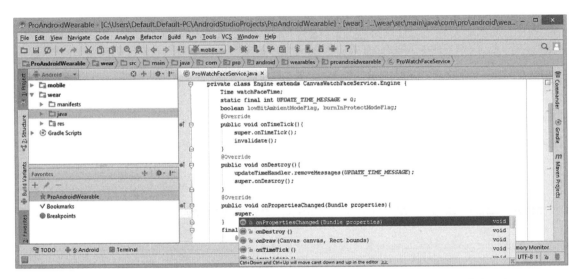

*Figure 9-19. Type in the Java super keyword, and select the onPropertiesChanged(Bundle properties) option*

This will pass a Bundle object named properties to the superclass, and you will be ready to set the properties contained in the Bundle object in the boolean variables for low-bit and burn-in that you declared at the top of the private (inner) Engine class.

Under the **super.onPropertiesChanged(properties);** Java programming statement, type the **lowBitAmbientModeFlag** boolean variable name, the equals sign, and then the properties Bundle object, which you're going to use to invoke a method call. Right after properties, press the period key to get the pop-up method helper dialog.

When the pop-up method helper dialog appears, select the **getBoolean(String key, boolean defaultValue)** option, or double-click it, which will insert the .getBoolean() method call structure into the Java statement you are coding, as shown in Figure 9-20. Once you are done using the IntelliJ pop-up helper dialog, the Java statement will look like this:

```
lowBitAmbientModeFlag = properties.getBoolean(PROPERTY_LOW_BIT_AMBIENT);
```

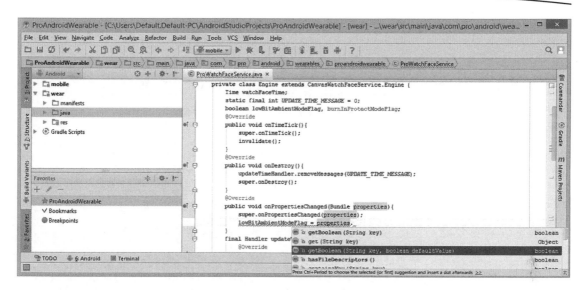

*Figure 9-20.  Type in your lowBitAmbientModeFlag variable, an equals sign, and the word properties and a period*

Inside the .getBoolean() method parameter area, type a "**P**" and select the **PROPERTY_LOW_BIT_AMBIENT** constant, as shown in Figure 9-21, which I discussed earlier in the chapter. Double-click this to set the lowBitAmbientModeFlag variable to the value of this LOW_BIT constant.

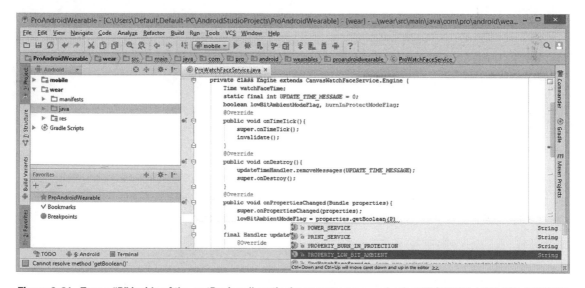

*Figure 9-21.  Type a "P" inside of the .getBoolean() method parameter area, and select PROPERTY_LOW_BIT_AMBIENT*

Now that you have extracted the low-bit ambient mode flag setting from the properties Bundle object and set it to the lowBitAmbientModeFlag variable, you'll need to do the exact same thing for the burnInProtectModeFlag variable.

Underneath the lowBitAmbientModeFlag Java programming statement, type in the **burnInProtectModeFlag** boolean variable name, an equals sign, and then the properties Bundle object, which you're going to use to invoke a method call. Right after properties, press the period key to initiate the pop-up method helper dialog.

When the pop-up method helper dialog appears, select the **getBoolean(String key, boolean defaultValue)** option, or double-click it, which will insert the .getBoolean() method call structure into the Java statement you are coding, as was shown in Figure 9-20. Once you are done using the IntelliJ pop-up helper dialog, your Java statement will look like this:

**burnInProtectModeFlag** = properties.**getBoolean**(PROPERTY_BURN_IN_PROTECTION);

Inside the .getBoolean() method parameter area, type a "**P**" and select the **PROPERTY_ BURN_IN_PROTECTION** constant, as shown in Figure 9-22. Double-click the constant, which will set the burnInProtectModeFlag variable to the value of this BURN_IN constant, so your app knows if the user's smartwatch supports (requires, actually) burn-in protection.

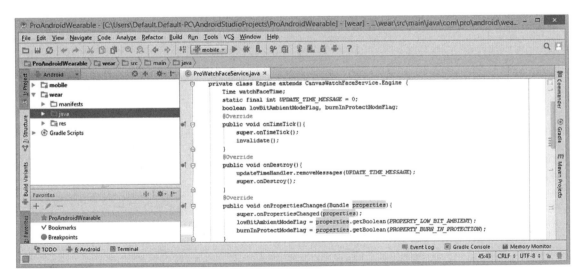

*Figure 9-22. Type in a burnInProtectModeFlag, set it equal to properties.getBoolean(BURN_IN_PROTECTION)*

Now that you know what special screen (display) modes your user's smartwatch hardware supports, the next most complex (and important, for that matter) method you need to implement is the **.onVisibilityChanged()** method. This method will take 10 lines of code to implement, so, let's get started now!

## Determining if the Watch Face Is Visibile: .onVisibilityChanged()

With the exception of .onDestroy(), you will call a super method call using the Java super keyword and the method name first, and then implement any custom programming logic, as you did with the previous method structure.

Let's do that here by adding the Java **@Override** keyword and the **public void onVisibilityChanged(boolean visible){}** empty method structure. Inside it, type the Java super keyword and a period character, and then select the onVisibilityChanged(boolean visible) option, as shown in Figure 9-23. The basic method structure should look like the following Java code:

```
@Override
public void onVisibilityChanged(boolean visible) {
    super.onVisibilityChanged(visible);
}
```

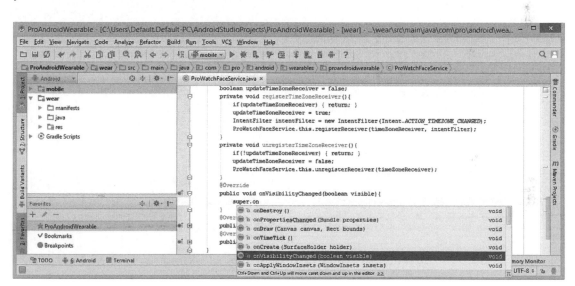

*Figure 9-23.  Create an onVisibilityChanged() method, type a Java super keyword, and call onVisibilityChanged()*

The rest of this method will consist of the if-else conditional structure, which will tell the watch face application what to do if the watch face is visible or not visible. The empty if-else conditional statement looks like the following and is shown error free in Figure 9-24:

```
public void onVisibilityChanged(boolean visible) {
    super.onVisibilityChanged(visible);
    if(visible) { visible=true statements here } else { visible=false statement here }
}
```

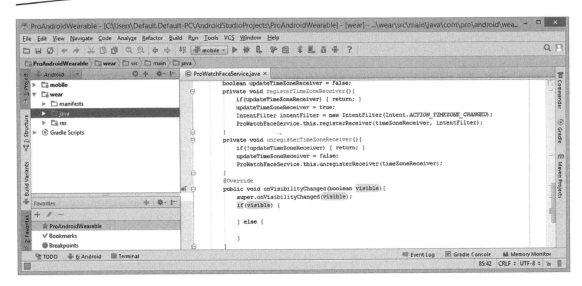

*Figure 9-24. Add an empty if(visible){ } else { } conditional structure after the super.onVisibilityChanged() method*

The first thing to do if the watch face comes alive (visible = true) is to call the **registerTimeZoneReceiver()** method to check whether the time zone has changed since the watch went to sleep. Inside an **if(visible){}** portion of the if-else conditional construct, type the "r" character and select a registerTimeZoneReceiver() option from the helper dialog, as shown in Figure 9-25, and insert this method call into the conditional if-else statement.

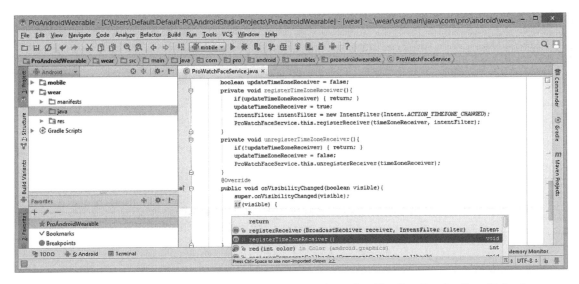

*Figure 9-25. Inside the if(visible) structure, type an "r" and select the registerTimeZoneReceiver() method call*

The next thing you want to do is to make sure the time zone is set in a Time object correctly by calling a **.clear()** method off the **watchFaceTime** object. Inside the parameter area, type "Ti" and then select a **TimeZone (java.util)** class from the pop-up helper dialog, as shown in Figure 9-26.

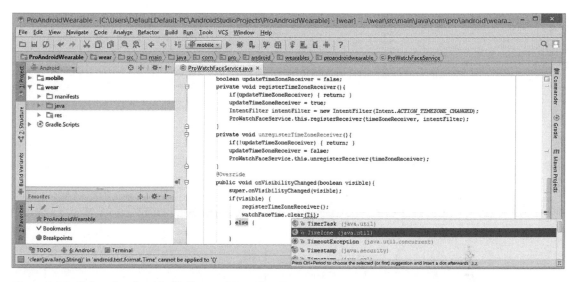

**Figure 9-26.**  *Call a .clear() method off a watchFaceTime Time object and select the TimeZone (java.util) option*

After the TimeZone, press the **period** key and select the **getDefault()** method, as shown in Figure 9-27.

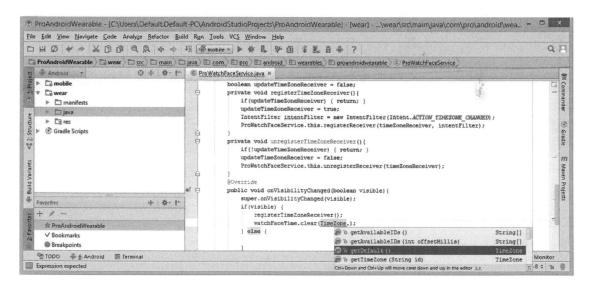

**Figure 9-27.**  *Type a period after the TimeZone object and select the getDefault() TimeZone method from the pop-up helper*

After you double-click the **.getDefault() TimeZone** option in the pop-up helper dialog, type a **period**, which will initiate another pop-up helper dialog, where you can select a **getID()** method. Double-click that, which will give you the final Java statement, reloading the TimeZone into the Time object. The final Java statement, as shown in Figure 9-28, should look like the following:

```
watchFaceTime.clear( TimeZone.getDefault().getID() );
```

The next thing that you will need to do, now that you have loaded a current TimeZone object into the Time object, is to use the **.setToNow()** method call to set the Time object to the current time using the newly loaded TimeZone as the guide to what the time value should be set to. The Java code, which is shown error free in Figure 9-28, should look like the following:

```
watchFaceTime.setToNow();
```

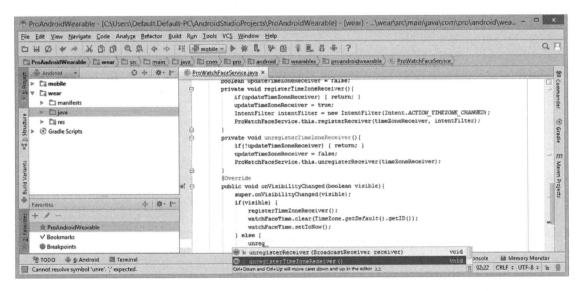

***Figure 9-28.*** *Type a first few letters of the unregisterTimeZoneReceiver() method and double-click it in the pop-up*

Now all you have left to construct is the else{} portion of this if-else conditional statement. This is what you want the watch face application to do when the user's smartwatch is asleep (the watch face is not visible).

Just like you call a .registerTimeZoneReceiver() method when the watch face is visible (true), you will similarly call an **.unregisterTimeZoneReceiver()** method when the watch face is invisible (false), as shown in Figure 9-28.

Type a "u" inside the else{} structure, and when the method helper pop-up appears, select the unregisterTimeZoneReceiver() method that you created in Chapter 8. Double-click this to have IntelliJ write the Java statement for you. Your error-free method is now complete, as shown in Figure 9-29.

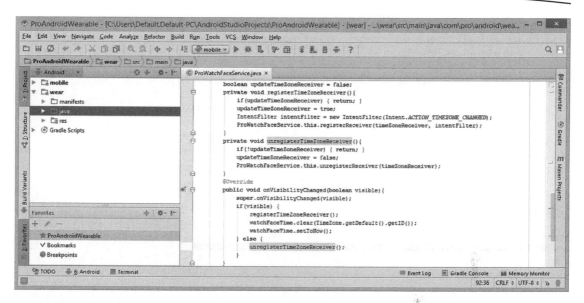

*Figure 9-29.* *The onVisibilityChanged() method with both the if(visible) and else{ } portions coded and error free*

Congratulations! You have now implemented all of the nongraphics portions of your WatchFaces API application! You are now ready to get into the **.onDraw()** method!

# Summary

In this chapter, you learned about how to create the core WatchFace Service Engine class methods for your **Watch Face Application**. There are a few more that relate to the .onDraw() related code that I am saving for the next chapter, when you'll start learning about vector graphics watchface design.

First, I discussed how to implement a second hand on your watch face using a Handler object and Message object. You created an updateTimeHandler, which will allow you to update the second hand on the watch every second.

Next, I discussed the core WatchFaces API classes: WatchFaceService and WatchFaceService.Engine. After I went over these classes in detail, you started implementing the constants and methods that you learned about inside the ProWatchFaceService and Engine classes.

In the next chapter, you will start adding vector graphics 2D design elements to the Watch Face application, and you will learn how to create a watch face using only code, because vector graphics are created using only an SVG or Shape class, that is, using only math or code. In Chapter 11, you'll learn how to use bitmap graphics for your watch faces design.

# Chapter 10

# WatchFaces Vector Design: Using Vector Graphics for WatchFaces

Now that you have most of the WatchFaces API infrastructure in place that does not directly relate to the Canvas object you will be "painting" on using **vector graphics**, you are ready to start implementing the **.onDraw()** method and learning about vector graphics as well as the Android classes that implement them.

This chapter will take an in-depth look at the Android classes that are used with a Canvas object, primarily the Android **Paint** class and nested classes, as you might have guessed, since one paints on a canvas!

You will also learn about the Android **Canvas** class and the **.drawLine()** method it contains, which you will be using to draw all the components of your watch face design.

The vector graphic draw methods, such as the .drawLine() method you'll be using during this chapter, use the Paint class (and object) to paint the vector (Shape) objects onto your Canvas. In your watch face implementation thus far, this is the **SurfaceHolder** object that holds this Canvas Surface object.

I will spend the majority of this chapter discussing the onDraw() method as well as methods that will need to be implemented in order to support all of the different modes you learned about in Chapter 6, such as low-bit ambient mode or burn-in protection mode. Once these are in place, you will be able to finish the last few WatchFaceService.Engine method implementations.

# WatchFace Painting Engine: Using the Paint Object

Before I get into the coding you will need for the objects and methods you will use to draw the vector graphics-based watch face design on the Canvas (screen), let's take an in-depth look at the Android **Paint** class.

The way that you stroke, color, style, and anti-alias your watch face design components is all done using constants and method calls that are from this Android Paint class and its **six nested** "helper" **classes**.

For this reason, let's take a close look at the Paint class, and after that, you'll create the Java code that draws the watch face with vectors.

## Android's Paint Class: Paint Vector Shapes on the Canvas

The **public** Android **Paint** class extends the java.lang.Object master class and was scratch-coded to provide all the digital paint functionality for the Android OS. The Java class hierarchy code for the Paint class looks like this:

```
java.lang.Object
  > android.graphics.Paint
```

The Paint class has one known direct subclass—the **TextPaint** class. A Paint class creates a Paint object that contains information regarding the **style** and **color**. This information guides the Android graphics engine when it comes time to draw the vector **Shape** objects, also known as "geometries," as well as **Text** objects (and **Font** objects), and it even guides how to render any **BitmapDrawable** objects, which I will discuss in Chapter 11.

The Paint class has six nested classes. I will cover only two of them in detail in the chapter, since you will be using these for the example's Watch Faces Design, as well as in the Watch Face Application's Java code.

> The **enum Paint.Align** nested class allows developers to specify how the **.drawText()** method should align a **Text** object relative to the **X,Y coordinates**.

> The **enum Paint.Cap** nested class allows developers to specify the treatment of (square ends or rounded ends) the beginning and ending of **stroked lines** and paths. This will allow you to define the look and feel for your second hand, minute hand, and hour hand for your watch, as well as the tick marks.

> The **class Paint.FontMetrics** nested class describes the **metrics** for **Font** object implementation at any given **floating point** size property for Text objects.

> The **class Paint.FontMetricsInt** nested class provides **convenience methods** for developers who wish to define **FontMetrics** values as **integers**.

The **enum Paint.Join** nested class allows developers to specify how lines or curve segments will "join" together (straight or curved join) on a stroked path. This is similar to the Paint.Cap function, except that it is applied at the **join** or **intersection** of two or more lines or paths, rather than on the open (unjoined) end of a line or path.

The **enum Paint.Style** nested class specifies how vector Shape objects, also known as primitives, are to be drawn. This can be specified with a **FILL**, a **STROKE**, or **FILL_AND_STROKE**. You will be using **FILL** and **STROKE** in your code.

The Paint class specified a dozen constant values, although one of them is no longer used by the Android OS. I'll mention them all here so you have a decent overview of what this Paint class can achieve, since the graphic design is one of the key components for your watch faces application design process.

The **int ANTI_ALIAS_FLAG** is a Paint flag constant that enables anti-aliasing when your Paint object is being drawn on your Watch Face Canvas object.

The **int DEV_KERN_TEXT_FLAG** is a Legacy Paint flag used to affect the kerning of Font objects relative to Text objects. It is no longer used.

The **int DITHER_FLAG** is a Paint flag that enables **dithering when rendering**. Turning dithering on enables true color graphics to be emulated on **hicolor** (15-bit 32,767 color, or 16-bit 65,536 color) or **indexed color** (8-bit or 256 color) smartwatch device hardware display screens (low color support).

The **int EMBEDDED_BITMAP_TEXT_FLAG** is a Paint flag that enables you to use **Bitmap Font** objects when you are drawing Text objects onto the Watch Face.

The **int FAKE_BOLD_TEXT_FLAG** is a Paint flag that allows developers to apply a **synthetic bolded effect** to a Text object. This is used with custom Font definitions that do not support (come with) a Font-Bold component.

The **int FILTER_BITMAP_FLAG** is a Paint flag that enables **bi-linear sampling** on BitmapDrawable objects if (and when) they are scaled. This should be in use in your Watch Face application if you want the highest quality results. (This will be covered in Chapter 11 when you learn how to use BitmapDrawable.)

The **int HINTING_OFF** and the **int HINTING_ON** Paint flag constants disable or enable, respectively, the Font object hinting option. Font Hinting is the equivalent of anti-aliasing. Therefore, if you are rendering Font objects in a Watch Face application, turn HINTING_OFF when in low-bit ambient mode!

The **int LINEAR_TEXT_FLAG** is a Paint flag that enables a smooth, linear scaling of Text objects and their Font objects. This is analogous to the filtering of BitmapDrawable objects, and therefore you would want to turn this on.

The **int STRIKE_THRU_TEXT_FLAG** is a Paint flag that applies strike-through decoration to the Text object if the Font object that Text object is using does not include the Font-StrikeThrough Font definition component.

The **int SUBPIXEL_TEXT_FLAG** is a Paint flag that enables subpixel positioning capability for the Text objects.

The **int UNDERLINE_TEXT_FLAG** is a Paint flag that, when enabled, allows an underline decoration to be applied to rendered Text objects if Font objects that the Text objects are using do not include a Font-Underline definition component.

The Paint class has three public constructor methods, including the default **Paint()** constructor, which creates a new Paint object with default settings. There is also a "flag-savvy" constructor that creates the new Paint object while at the same time setting those flag constants I just mentioned. This constructor uses the format **Paint(int flags)** to create your new Paint with specific flag constants (features) enabled.

There is also a "copycat" Paint object constructor method that uses a form of **Paint(Paint paint)** to create a new Paint object, and it initializes this using the attributes of another Paint object by using that specified Paint object inside the parameter list area of the constructor method call.

The Paint class supports 92 methods, which I obviously can't cover in detail here, so I will only be covering those methods that you will be using in the code during this chapter. If you want to research all 92 methods in detail, you can visit the following developer web site URL:

```
http://developer.android.com/reference/android/graphics/Paint.html
```

The **public void setARGB(int a, int r, int g, int b)** method is a helper for the .setColor() method. This .setARGB() method takes four color plates (or color planes) and configures the 32-bit Color object using those data. The A or alpha component supports 256 levels (8-bit) of transparency (opacity), the R or red component supports 256 levels (8-bit) of red color value, the G or green component supports 256 levels (8-bit) of green color value, and the B or blue component supports 256 levels (8-bit) of blue color value.

The **public void setAlpha(int a)** method is also a .setColor() helper method, however, it only assigns the Color object's Alpha value, leaving RGB values unchanged. The .setAlpha() 8-bit (integer) value must range from 0 to 255.

The **public void setAntiAlias(boolean aa)** method is a helper for the .setFlags() method. This method allows you to set or clear a Paint constant called ANTI_ALIAS_FLAG, which I mentioned earlier. A true value sets anti-aliasing on and a false value turns anti-aliasing off.

The **public void setColor(int color)** method sets a Paint object's color. An integer parameter holds a numeric value that contains the Alpha as well as the RGB data values. This 32-bit value is not premultiplied, meaning that the alpha can be independently set to any value via .setAlpha() regardless of the RGB data values. You can research the Android Color class for more details.

The **public void setStrokeCap(Paint.Cap cap)** method sets the Paint object's Cap style constant. This can be **BUTT** (the default value), **ROUND**, or **SQUARE**.

The **public void setStrokeWidth(float width)** method sets the pixel width with which to stroke a line or path Shape object. Pass a zero to stroke in **hairline mode**. Hairline always draws a single pixel independent of a Canvas matrix. The **width** parameter sets a Paint object's **stroke width**. This would be used whenever the Paint object's style is set to **STROKE** or **STROKE_AND_FILL**.

The **public void setStyle(Paint.Style style)** method sets the Paint object's style. This is used for controlling how vector Shape primitive geometry is interpreted. An exception to this is drawBitmap, which always assumes FILL.

Now that you know about the basic Paint class methods and their constants, you can start to implement the core methods and constants from this class in watch face design with only Java code, vector (Shape) objects, and Paint objects.

# WatchFaces Painting: Creating Watch Face Paint Objects

The first thing you'll need to do is declare those Paint objects that will define how the watch face components are going to look on the screen. The basic watch face components are the ticks and the watch hands.

## Declare Multiple Paint Objects: Using Compound Java Declarations

Now let's add a Paint object declaration after the low-bit and burn-in boolean flag variable declarations and name four paint objects **pHourHand**, **pMinuteHand**, **pSecondHand**, and **pTickMarks**, as shown (highlighted) at the bottom of Figure 10-1. Click anywhere inside the red Paint error message and use **Alt+Enter** to have IntelliJ write the **import android. graphics.Paint;** declaration for you.

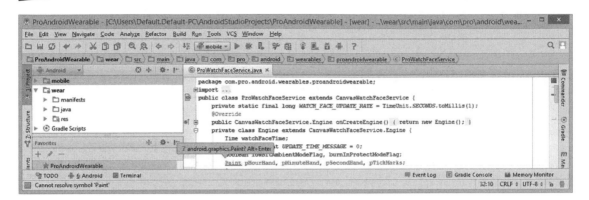

*Figure 10-1. Add a compound Paint object declaration for pHourHand, pMinuteHand, pSecondHand, and pTickMarks*

## Creating a WatchFace Component Method: Configuring the Paint

The next thing you want to do is create four logical method bodies to hold the Paint object construction (instantiation), configuration, and programming statements. I am constructing the Java code in this fashion in case you ever wanted to go back and make each Paint object more complex. A more organized code structure will pay off as an application becomes more complex, and this will allow you to use expand and collapse functions.

You'll work from the top (hour) to the bottom (second and ticks) and start with the creation of a **.createHourHand()** method. The Java code will look like this:

```
public void createHourHand() {   pHourHand = new Paint();   }
```

Add a line of code under the compound Paint declaration and type in the public void createHourHand(){} empty method structure. Then, inside it, add a **pHourHand = new Paint();** Java object instantiation statement to create the first Paint object you will be configuring to paint the hour hand. As you can see in Figure 10-2, you can select the **Paint (android.graphics)** option from the pop-up helper dialog and see the nested helper classes as well underneath it. Double-click the Paint class to insert it into the code.

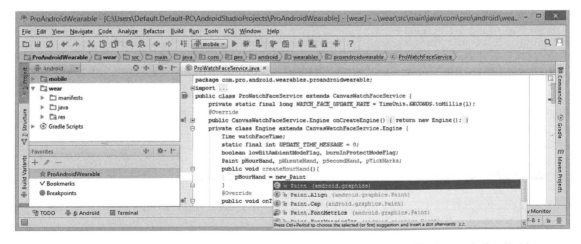

*Figure 10-2. Create a public void createHourHand() method; instantiate a new Paint object named pHourHand*

Now that you've instantiated the Paint object named pHourHand, you can start to configure it using attributes such as color and drawing style. The most important attribute is color, so let's add the **.setARGB()** method call that will configure the HourHand Paint to be fully opaque and to use full blue as a color. The Java statement is shown in Figure 10-3 and should look like this:

pHourHand.**setARGB**(255, 0, 0, 255);

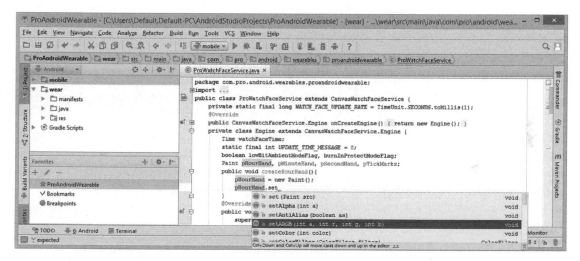

*Figure 10-3. Call a .setARGB() method off the pHourHand Paint object using the IntelliJ pop-up helper dialog*

Type in the pHourHand Paint object and then a period. When the pop-up helper dialog appears, select the **.setARGB(int a, int r, int g, int b)** option, as shown in Figure 10-3, to insert this method call into the Java statement, and then enter **255, 0, 0, 255**.

The next most important characteristic of the hour hand is how thick it is, which is configured using the **.setStrokeWidth()** method, which you'll set to 6 pixels (6/320 is .01875 or **1.875%** of the screen). The Java statement, as shown in Figure 10-4, should look like the following in the code base:

pHourHand.**setStrokeWidth**(6.f);

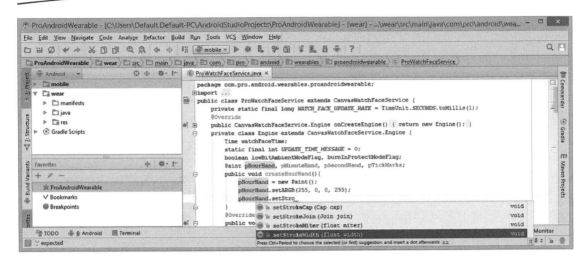

**Figure 10-4.** *Call a .setStrokeWidth() method off the pHourHand Paint object using the IntelliJ pop-up helper dialog*

You are configuring the Paint object as a default for the interactive watch face mode and then detecting ambient, low-bit, and burn-in, as these arise, depending on a user's watch model and what it is doing at any given time. So you'll turn **anti-aliasing on** for the default mode, for optimal visual quality, and make the tip of the hour hand **rounded** as well.

The Java statements to accomplish this are shown in Figure 10-5 and will look like the following code:

```
pHourHand.setAntiAlias(true);
pHourHand.setStrokeCap(Cap.ROUND);
```

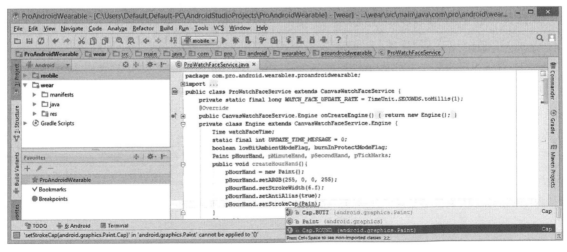

**Figure 10-5.** *Call a .setAntiAlias() method and a .setStrokeCap() method off the pHourHand Paint object using Cap.ROUND*

As you can see in Figure 10-5, if you type any portion of the Paint class (or object) name in the parameter area of the .setStrokeCap() method call, you will get the Paint.Cap nested (helper) class constants in this dialog.

Double-click the **Cap.ROUND (android.graphics.Paint)** option in the pop-up helper dialog, as shown in Figure 10-5, and finish the configuration code for a public void .createHourhand() method structure configuring a Paint object.

The finished .createHourHand() method structure, which is shown in Figure 10-6, which you will be copying and pasting below to create the other three methods, should look like the following Java method structure:

```java
public void createHourHand() {
    pHourHand = new Paint();
    pHourHand.setARGB(255, 0, 0, 255);
    pHourHand.setStrokeWidth(6.f);
    pHourHand.setAntiAlias(true);
    pHourHand.setStrokeCap(Cap.ROUND);
}
```

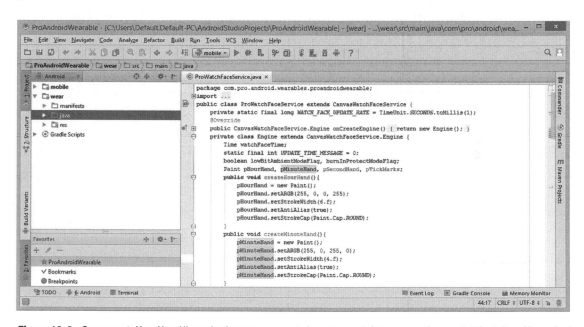

*Figure 10-6.* Copy createHourHand() method structure; paste it underneath it to create the createMinuteHand() method

## Creating Minute, Second, and Tick WatchFace Component Methods

As you can see in Figure 10-6, your Java code is now error free, and you're ready to block copy and paste a .createHourHand() method underneath it to create a **.createMinuteHand()** method. I have bolded the parameters you will be changing in the Java code listing just prior to this paragraph.

Because you will be using a rounded minute hand as well, you only need to change parameters for two of the six lines of code. However, do not forget to change the method name and the Paint object names from **pHourHand** to **pMinuteHand**. Change the .setARGB() method call, to paint the minute hand **green**, by turning the green data parameter fully on (255), and the red and blue parameters fully off (0), and then make the minute hand **4 pixels wide** instead of 6 pixels wide (**4/320** will represent **1.25%** of a display screen). The code for a .createMinuteHand() method structure should look like this:

```
public void createMinuteHand() {
    pMinuteHand = new Paint();
    pMinuteHand.setARGB(255, 0, 255, 0);
    pMinuteHand.setStrokeWidth(4.f);
    pMinuteHand.setAntiAlias(true);
    pMinuteHand.setStrokeCap(Cap.ROUND);
}
```

Because you're going to use a square second hand, you'll need to change three parameters in three of these six lines of code (bolded in the code above). Don't forget to change the method name and the Paint object names from **pMinuteHand** to **pSecondHand**.

Change the .setARGB() method call to paint the second hand **red** by turning a red data parameter fully on (255), with green and blue parameters turned off (0). Let's make the second hand **2 pixels wide** instead of 4 pixels wide (**2/320** will represent **0.625%** of the display screen). The Java code for the **.createSecondHand()** method structure should look like the following code:

```
public void createSecondHand() {
    pSecondHand = new Paint();
    pSecondHand.setARGB(255, 255, 0, 0);
    pSecondHand.setStrokeWidth(2.f);
    pSecondHand.setAntiAlias(true);
    pSecondHand.setStrokeCap(Cap.SQUARE);
}
```

As you can see in Figure 10-7, the code is error free and you are ready to create the final method that will create and configure a Paint object to be used to paint tick marks around the perimeter of the watch face.

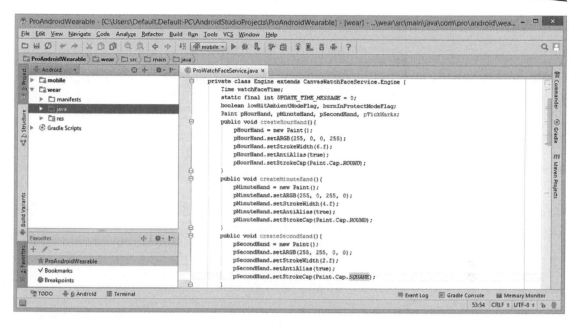

*Figure 10-7. Copy createMinuteHand() method structure; paste it underneath it to create the createSecondHand() method*

Copy and paste the CreateSecondHand() method underneath it to create a **createTickMarks()** method. The only method call you'll need to edit is your **.setARGB()** method call, setting all values to **255**, to make the tick marks a white color. The Java code for the method structure should look like this:

```
public void createTickMarks() {
    pTickMarks = new Paint();
    pTickMarks.setARGB(255, 255, 255, 255);
    pTickMarks.setStrokeWidth(2.f);
    pTickMarks.setAntiAlias(true);
    pTickMarks.setStrokeCap(Cap.SQUARE);
}
```

As you can see in Figure 10-8, the code is error free and you are ready to invoke the four methods you created inside the .onCreate() method that are required to be implemented by the WatchFaces API.

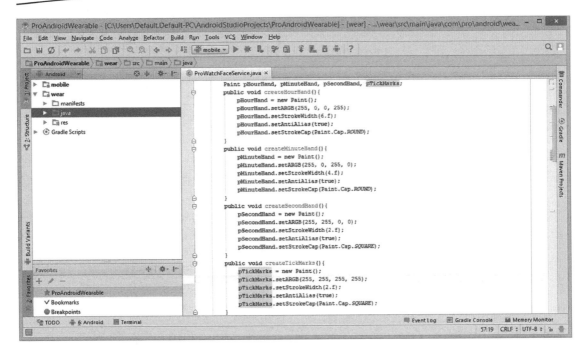

**Figure 10-8.** *Copy createSecondHand() method structure; paste it underneath itself to create the createTickMarks() method*

You've already implemented part of the method, including a super.onCreate() superclass method call, as well as created a WatchFaceStyle object, using the WatchFaceStyle.Builder class, that you learned about in Chapter 8.

After you've called these methods from an **.onCreate()** method to set up the Paint objects for the hour, minute, second hand and ticks, you can start working on the **.onDraw()** method. You can create the logic that uses these paint objects to draw watch face design components onto the Canvas by using the **.drawLine()** method from the Android **Canvas** class, which I will discuss in detail in the next section of the chapter.

## Calling the WatchFace Component Paint Methods from .onCreate()

Open the .onCreate() method implementation and call a .createHourHand() method before the WatchFaceStyle object's construction and configuration, or after it, if you prefer. As you can see in Figure 10-9, if you type in the word **create**, all the methods you just created are now part of the IntelliJ pop-up helper dialog. Double-click each, inserting all four.

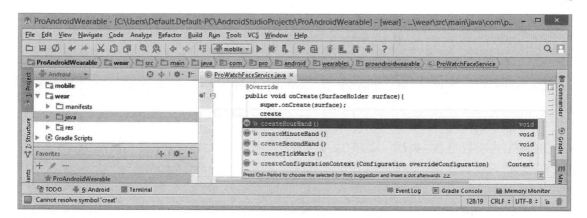

*Figure 10-9. Add a createHourHand() method call in the public void onCreate() method to create the first Paint*

Once you type in the word "create" four times and double-click the first four method calls, your code will look like that shown in Figure 10-10.

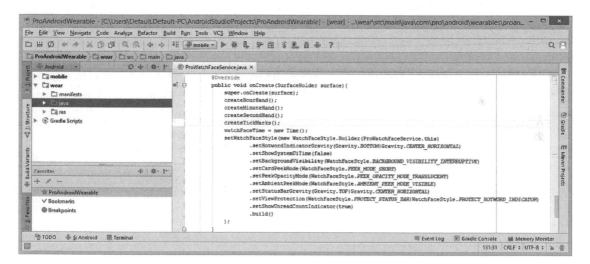

*Figure 10-10. Add all four Paint object creation method calls at the top of the public void onCreate() method*

Next, let's take a quick look at the Android Canvas class, which is the class that hosts (contains) the .onDraw() method. After that you will code the statements in the .onDraw() method to draw the watch face components.

# WatchFace Drawing Engine: The .onDraw() Method

The Android WatchFaces API uses the Android Canvas class as a drawing surface and the .onDraw() method, which applies Paint objects to a Canvas object. In this section, you will take a closer look at these classes objects, and see how they function in conjunction with one another.

## The Android Canvas Class: Your Canvas Drawing Methods

The Android **Canvas** public class extends the java.lang.Object master class, meaning it was scratch-coded for usage as a drawing canvas. This class is in the **android.graphics** package. The Java class hierarchy for the Android Canvas class looks like the following:

```
java.lang.Object
  > android.graphics.Canvas
```

The Canvas class is designed to create a Canvas drawing surface object to hold the .onDraw() method calls. In order to be able to draw on the Canvas object, you will need to have four basic components. The first is a **Bitmap** object, which holds the actual pixels that represent the Canvas surface.

The second is a **Canvas** object itself, which hosts, or provides, an interface for the .onDraw() method calls, which write data values into this bitmap object. The third is a "drawing primitive," such as vector (**Shape**) subclass objects like Rect, Path, Text, or Line, or a raster BitmapDrawable object. The fourth is the **Paint** object, which I covered in the previous section of this chapter, which is used to describe the colors and styles for the drawn components.

This Canvas class has two nested, also known as helper, classes. One is an **enum Canvas.EdgeType**, which defines edge constants AA (anti-aliased), or BW (black and white), which is not anti-aliased. The other nested class is the **enum Canvas.VertexMode**, which deals with 3D OpenGL ES, which I'm not going to be covering in this book.

The Canvas class has 90 methods, almost as many as the Paint class. You'll be using the **public void drawLine(float startX, float startY, float stopX, float stopY, Paint paint)** method to draw line segments using the specified start and stop X,Y coordinates. The line will be drawn using the specified Paint object(s), which you created in the previous section of this chapter.

## Drawing Your WatchFace: Using the .drawLine() Method

Next, let's collapse the .onCreate() method by clicking the **minus** sign to the left of the method, and expand the .onDraw() method by clicking the **plus** sign to the left of the method. You're going to first add the basic integer and floating point variables to set the center of the watch face design. Then you'll get the system time from the Time object, and then calculate the rotations for all of the watch face design components.

## Finding the Center of the WatchFace Design: centerX and centerY

Let's first create an **integer** variable named **width** and get the width of the Canvas using a .width() method call off a Rect object, which defines the Canvas bounds, or boundaries. To determine the vertical center, you would divide this number, which is going to be 320 pixels if the smartwatch uses the entire screen, by two. You will do this for the **height** (Y) value as well, using the following Java code, which is also shown in Figure 10-11:

```
int width = rect.width();
float centerX = width / 2.f;
int height = rect.height();
float centerY = height / 2.f;
```

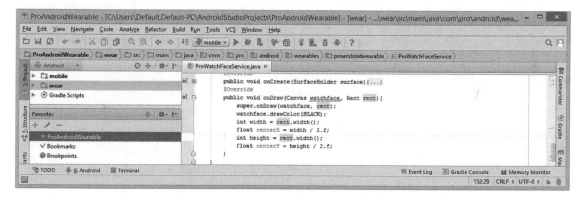

*Figure 10-11. Get the width and height of onDraw() Rect object and use them to calculate centerX and centerY*

You will be using these **centerX** and **centerY** values for everything you do in this section of the chapter. These values are used to provide the origin coordinate of the watch face hands and the center point around which ticks can be arrayed. The next thing you need to do is create **integer** variables, which have the time values for hours, minutes, and seconds in them. You do this because the Time object uses integer values.

## Finding the Current Time: Hours, Minutes, and Seconds Integers

One of the most important things an **.onDraw()** method will need to do every second is **rotate** all of these hands (hours, minutes, and seconds) to point in the correct direction, based on the current system time value. This is held in the **watchFaceTime** Time object, which you have already put into place in the code. All you have to do is create **integer** variables to hold the hours, minutes, and seconds components of the current system time, so you can perform calculations on them using PI, Sine, and Cosine to find out what direction each of your watch face hands should be pointing.

This can be done using the following Java code, also shown in Figure 10-12 in the construction of the first of these three statements using IntelliJ:

```
int hours = watchFaceTime.hour();
int minutes = watchFaceTime.hour();
int seconds = watchFaceTime.hour();
```

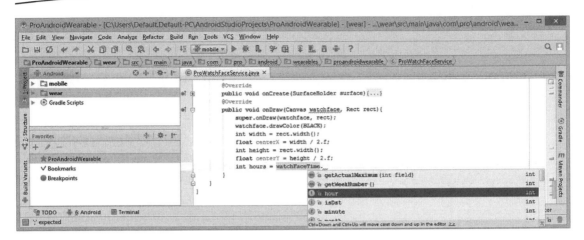

*Figure 10-12. Create an integer variable named hours and set it to the watchFaceTime object hour attribute*

If you type in **int hours =**, along with the name of the **watchFaceTime** Time object, and then a **period**, you will access the IntelliJ pop-up helper dialog where you can see the hour, minute, and second method calls.

As you can see, the variable declaration and initialization code so far is error free and takes only seven lines of code, as shown in Figure 10-13. I clicked a watchFaceTime object reference in the Java code to show its usage, which is tracked by IntelliJ using a purple tint. The watchFaceTime that I clicked is indicated by IntelliJ using a pale yellow highlight.

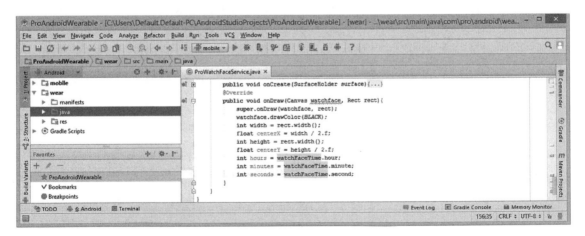

*Figure 10-13. Create integer variables for minutes and seconds and set it to the watchFaceTime object attributes*

I'll do this throughout this section to help you see the usage of the Time object. Now you're ready to calculate rotation via Sine, Cosine, and PI methods.

Now that you have the variables holding the watch face center point coordinates as well as the current hours, minutes, and seconds of your Time object, the time (no pun intended) has come for you to implement Java code that will rotate all of the basic watch faces components into position every second.

## Rotating an Hour Hand: Using the Math Class PI, Sine, and Cosine

Declare a **float** variable named **hourRot** to hold the hour hand rotation. The hour hand will show the **hours** value from the Time object, and it will also show a fractional component between each hour. You would take the **minutes** value from the Time object and divide that by 60, and then add it back onto the hours value using this equation format: **(hours+(minutes/60))**.

Because you're using the Sine Wave Function of the Java Math class, and PI defines one full cycle (wave facing up and wave facing down) of a Sine Wave, you need to divide the number of hours (12) in a full circle in half, and then divide the refined hours value by six, using the following equation format: **((hours+(minutes/60))/6)**. Now all you have to do to get the rotation angle is multiply this by PI, which is accessed using the Math.PI method. This will be **cast** to a floating point value using **(float)Math.PI**, so you don't get a compiler error. The Java code for an hour hand rotation, which is shown in Figure 10-14, should look like the following:

```
float hourRot = ((hours + (minutes / 60.f)) / 6.f) * (float) Math.PI;
```

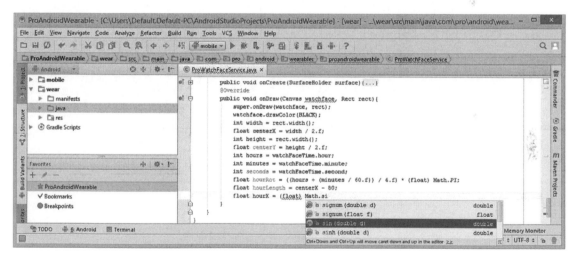

*Figure 10-14. Create an hourRot to hold the HourHand rotation calculation and a hourLength to hold the length*

The code for the hour hand length is considerably easier and involves the declaration of a **float** value named **hourLength**, which is set to the centerX (the watch face radius) value minus 80 pixels to make the hour hand shorter.

Remember that the centerX value is the radius of a watch face surface area because it is the Rect.width() divided by two. The code for the hour hand length, which is shown in Figure 10-14, should look like the following Java programming statement:

```
float hourLength = centerX - 80;
```

Next, you need to calculate the end of your Line Shape object, which you are going to draw from the centerX end of the Line to the hourX coordinate, so that an Hour Hand Line will be pointing in exactly the correct declination (direction). The Sine function takes the hourRot value and turns it into a rotational vector value for the X coordinate. You'll need to do the same thing for your Y coordinate in the next line of code. The Java statement should look like the following Java code:

```
float hourX = (float) Math.sin(hourRot) * hourLength;
```

As you type the line of code into IntelliJ, you should use the pop-up helper dialog, as shown in Figure 10-14, to select a Math class **sin(double d)** option, and insert that into the code, specifying **hourRot** as the double parameter.

To find the hourY value, you simply need to invert the Sine wave by using a Cosine wave instead, and then flip that value around the other axis with a minus sign to change this value into a negative value. Your Java statement should look like the following code, which can be seen in Figure 10-15:

```
float hourY = (float) -Math.cos(hourRot) * hourLength;
```

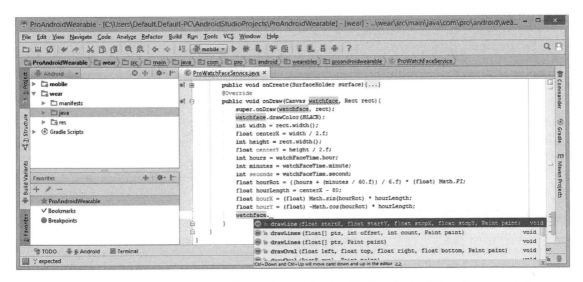

*Figure 10-15. Type in the watchface Canvas object and select the drawLine() method call from the pop-up helper*

You now have the hour hand **offsets** that determine X and Y coordinates for the outer end of the Hour Hand Line. You also have all the variables you need to be able to call the .drawLine() method to draw the Hour Hand line.

The .drawLine() method is called off of the **Canvas object** named **watchface**, which is declared in your **public void onDraw(Canvas watchface, Rect rect)**, as shown in Figure 10-15. As you can see, if you type in the watchface Canvas object and then the period key, your IntelliJ method pop-up helper dialog should appear. Double-click the **drawLine(float startX, float startY,**

**float stopX, float stopY, Paint paint) void** method option to insert it into the code, which should look like the following Java statement, as shown in Figure 10-16:

```
watchface.drawLine( centerX, centerY, centerX+hourX, centerY+hourY, pHourHand );
```

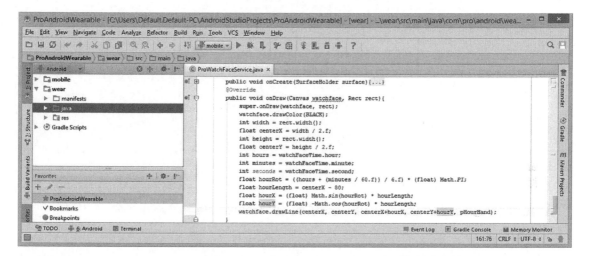

*Figure 10-16. Call a .drawLine() method off a watchface Canvas object; pass in hour Paint object and coordinates*

The method call structure for this .drawLine() method should include the start of the line in the center of the watch face, represented by using the **centerX** and **centerY** variables, and the end of the line would use the **centerX+hourX** and **centerY+hourY** data values, which are calculated inside this method call as a shortcut. The final parameter is the **pHourHand** Paint object that you created and configured in the first section of this chapter, which defines exactly how the Hour Hand Line is to be drawn.

## Rotating a Minute Hand: Using the Math Class PI, Sine, and Cosine

The Minute Hand Line drawing logic is very similar to the Hour Hand Line drawing logic, except that it does not have to adjust for partial minutes, as the hour hand needs to for hour accuracy. A minute hand is longer than an hour hand, so you'd only subtract 40 pixels from the half-screen value instead of 80. The Java code for the drawing of a Minute Hand Line is seen error free in Figure 10-17 and should look like the following:

```
float minuteRot = minutes / 30f * (float) Math.PI
float minuteLength = centerX - 40;
float minuteX = (float) Math.sin(minuteRot) * minuteLength;
float minuteY = (float) -Math.cos(minuteRot) * minuteLength;
watchface.drawLine( centerX, centerY, centerX + minuteX, centerY + minuteY, pMinuteHand );
```

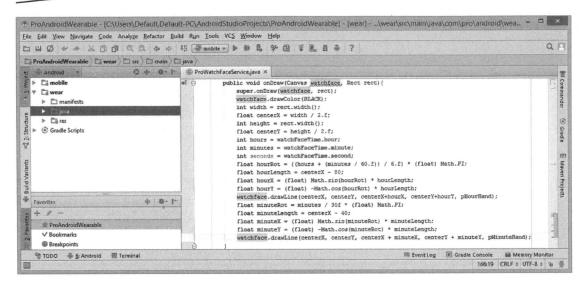

*Figure 10-17. Call a .drawLine() method off of a watchface Canvas object; pass in minute Paint object and coordinates*

Next, you'll code the Second Hand Draw Logic. This is very similar to the Hour and Minute Hand Logic, except it only draws when it is in interactive mode.

## Rotating Your Second Hand: Using the .isInAmbientMode() Method

The Second Hand Line logic is quite similar to the Minute Hand Line logic, with two exceptions. The line that is drawn is longer and is calculated as **centerX - 20**, and the Math.sin, Math.cos, and Canvas.drawLine() methods are only called if a smartwatch is in **ambient mode**. Your Java code for the Second Hand Line, including a conditional **if(!isInAmbientMode())** statement, which isolates the processing of the Math and Canvas method calls, should look like the following Java code structure, and is shown in Figure 10-18:

```
float secondRot = seconds / 30f * (float) Math.PI;
float secondLength = centerX - 20;
if ( !isInAmbientMode() ) {
    float secondX = (float) Math.sin(secondRot) * secondLength;
    float secondY = (float) -Math.cos(secondRot) * secondLength;
    watchface.drawLine( centerX, centerY, centerX + secondX, centerY + secondY, pSecondHand
);
}
```

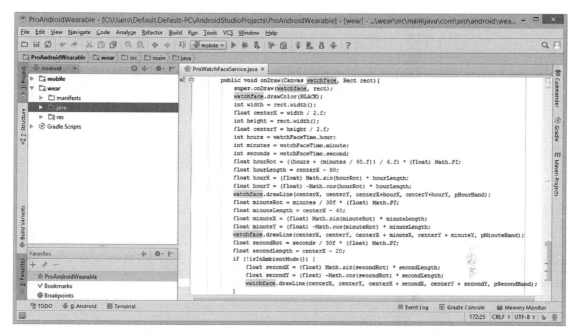

*Figure 10-18. Implement Second Hand Line drawing logic using a conditional if(!isInAmbientMode()) structure*

The Second Hand Line drawing code does not draw the line at all if a watch face is in ambient mode, as per the Android Watch Face API rules, and does not call any math functions if the watch is in Ambient mode, so the logic also serves to optimize processor usage involving second hand calculation.

## Creating Watch Face Tick Marks: Using a Java for Loop Structure

The code for drawing tick marks for each hour around the perimeter of the screen is similar to that used for Hand drawing code as far as the math is concerned. You'll still use the **PI** constant (3.14159) and **Math.sin** and **-Math.cos** to position the ticks around a watch face perimeter, using the **for loop** to position all 12. The code for this, shown at the bottom of Figure 10-19, looks like the following:

```
float innerTicksRadius = centerX - 10;
for (int ticksIndex = 0; ticksIndex < 12; ticksIndex++) {
   float ticksRot = (float) (ticksIndex * Math.PI * 2 / 12);
   float innerX = (float) Math.sin(ticksRot) * innerTicksRadius;
   float innerY = (float) -Math.cos(ticksRot) * innerTicksRadius;
   float outerX = (float) Math.sin(ticksRot) * centerX;
   float outerY = (float) -Math.cos(ticksRot) * centerX;
   watchface.drawLine(centerX+innerX, centerY+innerY, centerX+outerX, centerY+outerY,
pTickMarks);
}
```

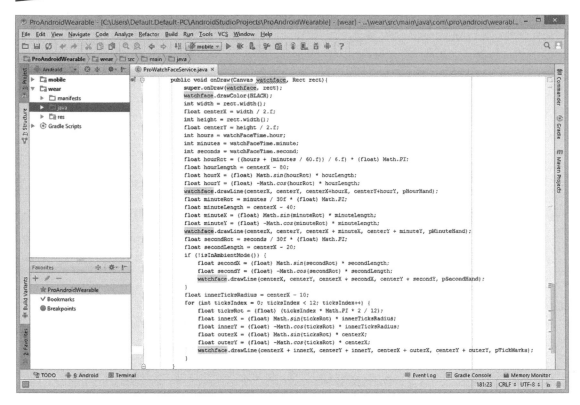

*Figure 10-19.* *Create a for loop to draw tick marks using an innerTicksRadius and centerX as the outer radius*

Now you are ready to implement some of the code that controls how the Paint objects will be modified when the different smartwatch hardware modes have been put into play. This will implement the required specialized drawing modes that you learned about in Chapter 6. The next section of this chapter will show you how to support the modes using only Paint constant settings code.

# Advanced Mode Support: Dynamic Paint Methods

This section will explain how to create several methods that can set Paint object characteristics **dynamically** based on the different modes that are supported on, and which are active in, the user's smartwatch hardware.

These modes include ambient mode, low-bit ambient mode, and burn-in protect mode, and they provide different graphic design characteristics, as discussed in Chapter 6. Interactive mode uses full (bright) colors, ambient mode uses a dimmed color or grayscale, depending on the hardware support, low-bit mode uses black and white, and burn-in protection uses only "edge-pixels" to define the watch face design, so that as few of the pixels are on (burning) as possible.

# Controlling Anti-Aliasing: Creating a setAntiAlias() Method

Now add a line of (new) code above the .onCreate() method and create a **private void setAntiAlias(boolean antiAliasFlag)** method. It is important to notice that Java is smart enough to let you use this method name in the watchface application ProWatchFaceService. java class because it references things by using dot notation between packages, classes, and methods, so it knows that this **ProWatchFaceService.Engine.setAntiAlias()** that you are about to create is completely different from the **android.graphics.Canvas. setAntiAlias()**.

This fact allows you to call this method setAntiAlias(), even though there is already an Android Canvas.setAntiAlias() method in the android.graphics package. It is interesting to note here that you'll actually be using this (Canvas) .setAntiAlias() method call inside the .setAntiAlias() method code as well. This is the reason I set it up this way, to show that it can be done, and that your IntelliJ (Java + Android) compiler is good with it!

If this bothers your sensibility, you can always name the method something different, such as .setAntiAliasingMode(), if you like. Inside the method, call the Canvas class's .setAntiAlias() method off the pHourHand Paint object, as shown in Figure 10-20. Your Java code should look like this:

```java
private void setAntiAlias(boolean antiAliasFlag){
    pHourHand.setAntiAlias(antiAliasFlag);
}
```

If you want to use the IntelliJ pop-up helper dialog, type in pHourHand.set, as shown in Figure 10-20, and double-click the **setAntiAlias(boolean aa)** option to insert this method call into the Java statement.

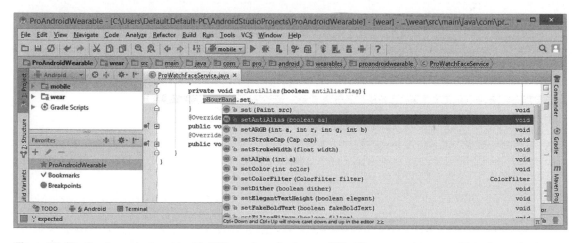

*Figure 10-20. Create a private void setAntiAlias using a boolean antiAliasFlag parameter passed into the method*

Add this **.setAntiAlias(antiAliasFlag)** method call off all of your Paint objects, which will set an on/off (true/false) setting on all of the Paint objects, allowing you to turn anti-aliasing on or off for the watch face. The Java code, which is shown in Figure 10-21, should look like this:

```java
private void setAntiAlias(boolean antiAliasFlag){
    pHourHand.setAntiAlias(antiAliasFlag);
    pMinuteHand.setAntiAlias(antiAliasFlag);
    pSecondHand.setAntiAlias(antiAliasFlag);
    pTickMarks.setAntiAlias(antiAliasFlag);
}
```

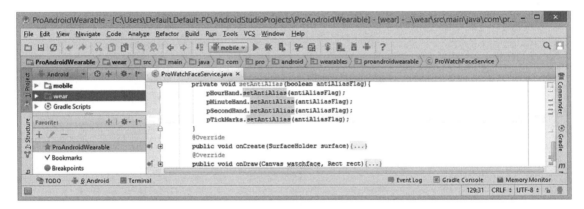

*Figure 10-21. Call a .setAntiAlias() method off each of the Paint objects and pass in the boolean antiAliasFlag*

Now that you have created the method that allows you to turn anti-aliasing on and off for your watch face design, you can create another method that draws only the edges of the hour hand and minute hand for burn-in protect mode. Finally, let's create a third method that implements low-bit ambient mode (black and white pixels only), and you'll then be in conformance with all of the Watch Faces API you learned about in Chapter 6.

# Controlling Burn-In: Creating a setBurnInProtect() Method

The next method you need to create deals with smartwatch hardware that requires **screen burn-in protection**, which is implemented using **edge render** code that only renders (draws onto the canvas using custom paint options) the edges of the watch face components.

Create the **private void setBurnInProtect(boolean enabled)** method structure and declare a **Paint.Style** object named **paintStyle**, and set it equal to the default value of **Paint.Style. FILL** because that is what the watch face vector shape needs to use in every other mode except for this burn-in protection mode.

As you type this statement in, an IntelliJ pop-up method helper dialog will appear, and you can select the **Paint.Style.FILL** option, or double-click it, which will insert it into the Java statement.

The Java method structure, which is shown in Figure 10-22, should look like this, once you are done using the IntelliJ pop-up helper dialogs:

```
private void setBurnInProtect(boolean enabled) {
    Paint.Style paintStyle = Paint.Style.FILL;
}
```

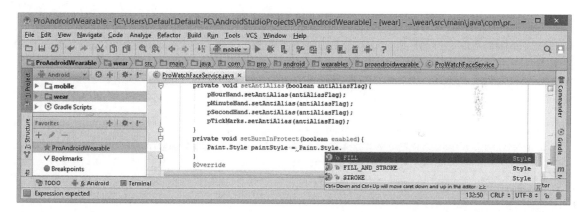

*Figure 10-22.  Create a private void setBurnInProtect using a boolean enabled parameter passed into the method*

The next thing you need to add is a **conditional if-else** structure that will handle if burn-in protection needs to be turned on (enabled) or else turned off (!enabled) if it is not needed. The **if(enabled)** part of the if structure should set the Paint.Style object named paintStyle to the **STROKE** constant, as shown in the pop-up helper dialog in Figure 10-23. The first part of the if() structure should look like the following Java code:

```
private void setBurnInProtect(boolean enabled) {
    Paint.Style paintStyle = Paint.Style.FILL;
    if(enabled) {
        paintStyle = Paint.Style.STROKE;
    } else {
        // an empty else structure for now
    }
}
```

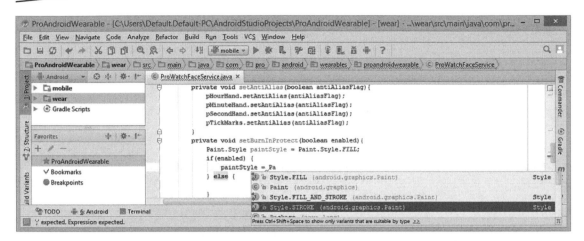

*Figure 10-23.  Add an if(enabled) { } else { } empty conditional structure and inside it set paintStyle to STROKE*

The else portion of the if-else conditional statement will set the default Paint.Style value of **FILL**, which you'll also set at the head (beginning) of the method, so that if this burn-in mode is not needed (false), the vector components will be filled and not stroked, making them filled with color instead of filled with black. This ensures that the only way STROKE will be used is if **enabled** is **true**. The Java code for the method so far should look like this, as shown in Figure 10-24:

```
private void setBurnInProtect(boolean enabled) {
    Paint.Style paintStyle = Paint.Style.FILL;
    if(enabled) {
        paintStyle = Paint.Style.STROKE;
    } else {
        paintStyle = Paint.Style.FILL;
    }
}
```

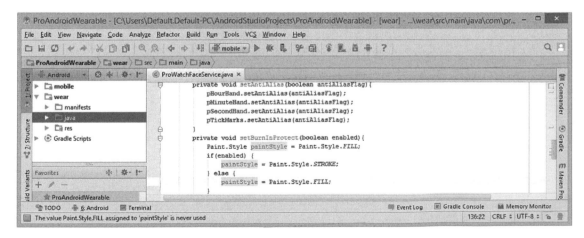

*Figure 10-24.  Add paintStyle object set to FILL in an else portion of the conditional if statement for enabled = false*

The final thing that the method will need to do is set the Paint object for the hour hand and second hand components of the watch face to use this paintStyle. This is done by calling a .setStyle() method and passing the paintStyle that has either been set as a default to FILL or changed to STROKE in the if(enabled) conditional structure.

The Java method structure should look like the following code after you are finished:

```java
private void setBurnInProtect(boolean enabled) {
    Paint.Style paintStyle = Paint.Style.FILL;
    if(enabled) {
        paintStyle = Paint.Style.STROKE;
    } else {
        paintStyle = Paint.Style.FILL;
    }
    pHourHand.setStyle(paintStyle);
    pMinuteHand.setStyle(paintStyle);
}
```

The final method is shown error free in Figure 10-25. I have selected the paintStyle attribute so you can see its use through this method body.

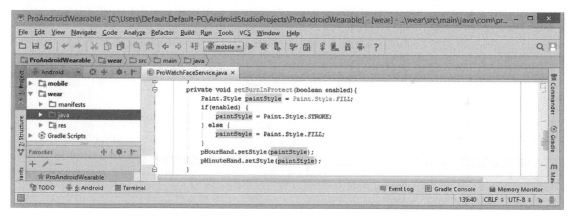

*Figure 10-25. After the if-else, set pHourHand and pMinuteHand Paint objects to the paintStyle, using .setStyle()*

It's important to note that this method will only change the value of the Paint objects to STROKE if the **.onPropertiesChanged()** method detects that the screen burn-in protection flag has been set for the user's smartwatch hardware. This method will be called in the .onAmbientModeChanged() method, which you will be creating later in this chapter (which is why you're creating it here now, so that it is available for use later when you need it).

The next thing you want to do is make sure that the Paint objects are configured correctly for the low-bit ambient and ambient modes, so let's create the **.ensureModeSupport()** method next, which controls the color and Alpha values, which in turn will control how bright (or dim) the watch face components are drawn on the screen against a black background color.

# Ensuring Mode Support: An ensureModeSupport() Method

Add a line of code underneath the .setBurnInProtect() method and create a **private void ensureModeSupport()** method. Declare the boolean flag variable named **enableLowBitAmbientMode** and set it **equal** to the Logical **AND** of the **lowBitAmbientModeFlag** boolean flag variable and the value that is returned from the **isInAmbientMode()** method call. The code for this is shown in Figure 10-26.

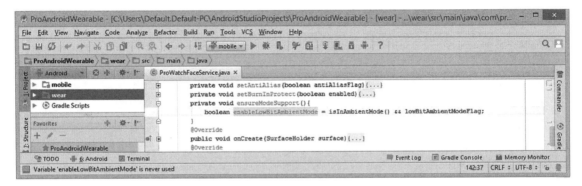

*Figure 10-26.   Create a private void ensureModeSupport, and add a boolean enableLowBitAmbientMode parameter*

Once you have created this enableLowBitAmbientMode boolean flag variable, create an empty **if{}else-if{}else{}** structure by using the following Java code structure, which is also shown in Figure 10-27:

```java
private void ensureModeSupport() {
    boolean enableLowBitAmbientMode = isInAmbientMode() && lowBitAmbientModeFlag
    if( enableLowBitAmbientMode ) {    // Low-Bit Ambient Mode Java Statements
    } else if( isInAmbientMode() ) {    // Ambient Mode Java Statements
    } else {                            // Interactive Mode Java Statements
    }
}
```

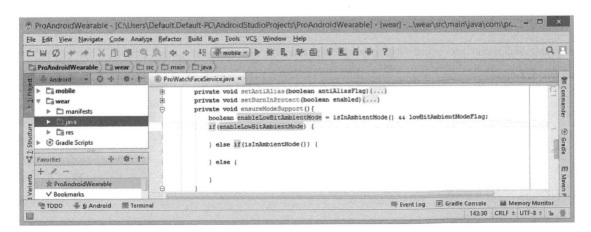

*Figure 10-27.   Add an if(enableLowBitAmbientMode) { } else if(isInAmbientMode) { } else { } conditional structure*

The characteristic of low-bit ambient mode is that it only uses **one bit** of data per pixel, which means full white on full black. Thus, you will have to set the Alpha to **255** (so that white has no black tint, from the background color) and the Color values to **Color.WHITE** as well.

The **.setAlpha()** method calls off the Paint objects, which is shown in Figure 10-28, and it should look like the following Java statements:

```java
private void ensureModeSupport() {
    boolean enableLowBitAmbientMode = isInAmbientMode() && lowBitAmbientModeFlag
    if( enableLowBitAmbientMode )  {
        pHourHand.setAlpha(255);
        pMinuteHand.setAlpha(255);
        pSecondHand.setAlpha(255);
        pTickMarks.setAlpha(255);
    } else if( isInAmbientMode() ) {  // Ambient Mode Java Statements
    } else {                          // Interactive Mode Java Statements
    }
}
```

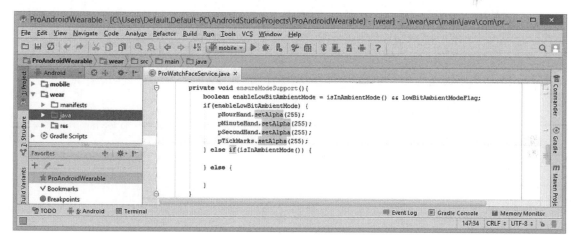

*Figure 10-28. Add .setAlpha(255) method calls, setting all Paint objects to paint using 100% of their color values*

The next thing you will need to do is set the color of all the watch face design elements to white with a **.setColor(Color.White)** call off the Paint objects. The Java code, as shown in Figure 10-29, looks like this:

```java
pHourHand.setAlpha(255);
pMinuteHand.setAlpha(255);
pSecondHand.setAlpha(255);
pTickMarks.setAlpha(255);
pHourHand.setColor(Color.WHITE);
pMinuteHand.setColor(Color.WHITE);
pSecondHand.setColor(Color.WHITE);
pTickMarks.setColor(Color.WHITE);
```

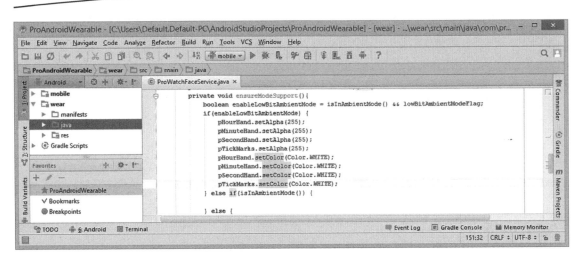

*Figure 10-29. Add .setColor(Color.WHITE) method calls setting all Paint objects to paint using white color value*

Now that you have ensured that only black and white values are used on the watch face screen in low-bit ambient mode, you need to implement an else-if section of the conditional logic that dims the color used in the component parts of the watch face by 50%. This is done using the Alpha value of **127**, which has the same effect as **dimming** the color values **50%** due to the black (zero value) background color. The Java code, as shown in Figure 10-30, looks like the following:

```java
private void ensureModeSupport() {
    boolean enableLowBitAmbientMode = isInAmbientMode() && lowBitAmbientModeFlag
    if( enableLowBitAmbientMode )  {
        pHourHand.setAlpha(255);
        pMinuteHand.setAlpha(255);
        pSecondHand.setAlpha(255);
        pTickMarks.setAlpha(255);
        pHourHand.setColor(Color.WHITE);
        pMinuteHand.setColor(Color.WHITE);
        pSecondHand.setColor(Color.WHITE);
        pTickMarks.setColor(Color.WHITE);
    } else if( isInAmbientMode() ) {
        pHourHand.setAlpha(127);
        pMinuteHand.setAlpha(127);
        pSecondHand.setAlpha(127);
        pTickMarks.setAlpha(127);
    } else {
        // Interactive Mode Java Statements
    }
}
```

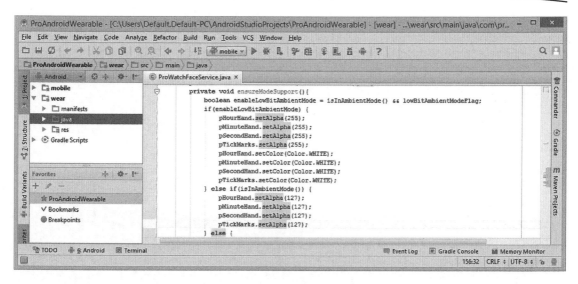

*Figure 10-30. Add .setAlpha(127) calls in else-if(), setting all Paint objects to paint using 50% of their color values*

Using the Alpha value as a dimmer (due to the black background color) will allow you to support smartwatches that **support color in ambient mode** and still allow you to dim the screen 50% for ambient mode support in the code.

The final else portion of the conditional if-else statement is the code that will be executed if the smartwatch is not in ambient mode at all (not in low-bit ambient mode and not even in ambient mode), which means it is in **interactive mode**.

What you want to do in interactive mode is turn the Alpha value back up, so that full brightness is used (because there is no blending with a black background color, which serves to dim color values and reduces brightness).

To do this, you will use the same four statements you used at the head of the if(enableLowBitAmbientMode) section of the conditional statement, where you called the .setAlpha() method with a fully-on value of 255.

Your finished ensureModeSupport() method structure, which is shown in Figure 10-31, should look like the following Java code:

```java
private void ensureModeSupport() {
    boolean enableLowBitAmbientMode = isInAmbientMode() && lowBitAmbientModeFlag
    if(enableLowBitAmbientMode)  {
        pHourHand.setAlpha(255);
        pMinuteHand.setAlpha(255);
        pSecondHand.setAlpha(255);
        pTickMarks.setAlpha(255);
        pHourHand.setColor(Color.WHITE);
        pMinuteHand.setColor(Color.WHITE);
        pSecondHand.setColor(Color.WHITE);
        pTickMarks.setColor(Color.WHITE);
```

```
    } else if(isInAmbientMode()) {
        pHourHand.setAlpha(127);
        pMinuteHand.setAlpha(127);
        pSecondHand.setAlpha(127);
        pTickMarks.setAlpha(127);
    } else {
        pHourHand.setAlpha(255);
        pMinuteHand.setAlpha(255);
        pSecondHand.setAlpha(255);
        pTickMarks.setAlpha(255);
    }
}
```

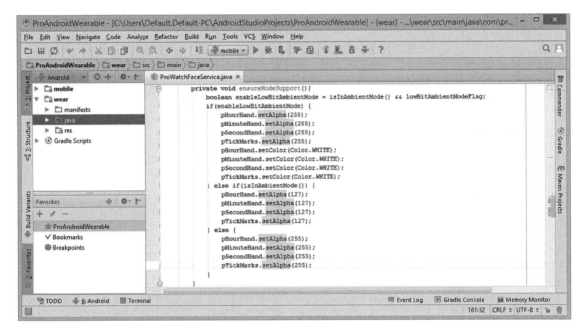

*Figure 10-31. Add .setAlpha(255) calls in else { } setting for all Paint objects to paint using 100% of their color values*

As you can see, for the most part, this method controls the alpha channel data, which you are using to act as a dimmer in ambient mode and to ensure fully white (or fully colored) pixel values for low-bit ambient and interactive modes, respectively. You are taking advantage of the watch's black background color to use Alpha values to darken or brighten pixels, so you can leave color values in place (except for low-bit ambient mode).

Now you have the methods in place that are needed for (and called from) the .onAmbientModeChanged() method from the WatchFaceService.Engine class, which you will be implementing next to make sure all of these various modes are supported when the smartwatch hardware goes into ambient mode.

# Invoking Mode Methods: onAmbientModeChanged()

Add a line of code after the .onVisibilityModeChanged() method and add the **@Override public void onAmbientModeChanged(boolean ambientModeFlag)** method structure, so that you can implement the watch face programming logic, which covers what you want to happen when the user's smartwatch hardware switches into ambient mode from interactive mode (to save battery power).

Inside the empty method structure, use a Java super keyword to call the superclass's .onAmbientModeChanged() method, passing up an **ambientModeFlag** boolean variable that is being passed into the method you're coding. The method structure so far is shown in Figure 10-32, and the code looks like this:

```
@Override
public void onAmbientModeChanged(boolean ambientModeFlag) {
    super.onAmbientModeChanged(ambientModeFlag);
}
```

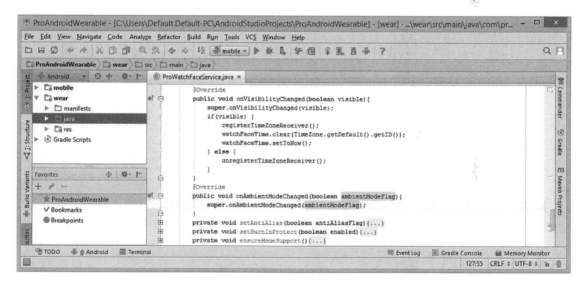

*Figure 10-32.  Create a public void onAmbientModeChanged() method, and call it off the Java super keyword*

Next, add a conditional **if(lowbitAmbientModeFlag){}** structure. If you want, let IntelliJ write it for you by typing an "l" inside the if() and then selecting the **lowBitAmbientModeFlag** boolean option, as shown in Figure 10-33, by double-clicking it to have IntelliJ write the conditional statement for you. Your Java conditional if() structure should look like the following:

```
if(lowBitAmbientModeFlag) {
    // Java statements to be processed for low-bit ambient mode will go in here
}
```

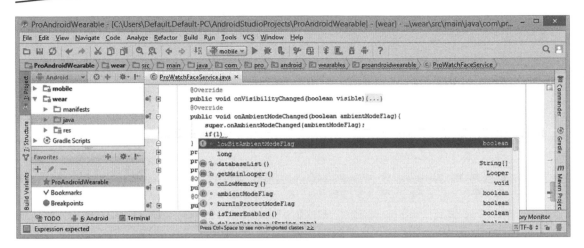

*Figure 10-33.  Add an if(lowBitAmbientModeFlag){} conditional structure and use a helper dialog to write the code*

Inside the conditional if structure, call the setAntiAlias() method, as shown in Figure 10-34, using the opposite of an ambientModeFlag value that was passed into this method. This uses the **setAntiAlias(!ambientModeFlag)** method call format. The Java code, thus far, should look like this:

```
if(lowBitAmbientModeFlag) {
    setAntiAlias(!ambientModeFlag);
}
```

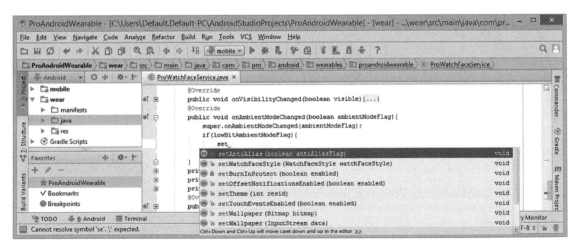

*Figure 10-34.  Inside the conditional structure, type set and double-click the setAntiAlias(antiAliasFlag) method*

Create another **if(burnInProtectModeFlag)** conditional structure that calls the **setBurnInProtect()** method you just coded, using the same value as ambientModeFlag, which will turn **Burn-In Protection on** if the flag is set that tells the watch face the smartwatch hardware needs this feature.

So far, the onAmbientModeChanged() method makes sure that if the smartwatch supports low-bit in ambient mode, **anti-aliasing is turned off**, and if the user's smartwatch needs burn-in protection, the components of the watch face are **stroked** (only the edges are shown) rather than filled. The Java code thus far, as shown in Figure 10-35, should look like the following method structure:

```
@Override
public void onAmbientModeChanged(boolean ambientModeFlag) {
    super.onAmbientModeChanged(ambientModeFlag);
    if(lowBitAmbientModeFlag) {
        setAntiAlias(!ambientModeFlag);
    }
    if(burnInProtectModeFlag) {
        setBurnInProtect(ambientModeFlag);
    }
}
```

*Figure 10-35.  Create two conditional if structures that will call the setAntiAlias() and setBurnInProtect() methods*

The next thing the .onAmbientModeChanged() method needs to do is call the **ensureModeSupport()** method, as shown in Figure 10-36, which you just created. After all of the Paint attributes have been reconfigured (reset), you can **redraw** the watch face design by calling the **.invalidate()** method.

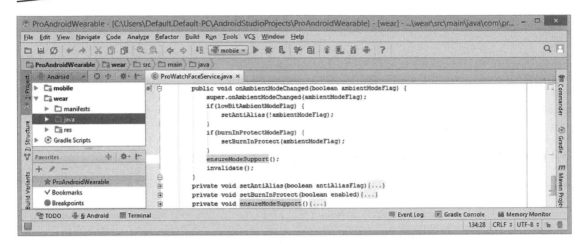

*Figure 10-36. Call the ensureModeSupport() method, then refresh a watch face by calling the invalidate() method*

The one final thing you need to do is create a **.checkTimer()** method. This will reset the updateTimeHandler and reset the timer logic so that it knows how long to wait until it can read the next even (1,000 millisecond) second value to set the watch face second hand, because the ambient mode might have changed back to interactive mode!

# Returning to Interactive Mode: checkTimer() Method

There is one last thing you need to put into place that applies to the .onVisibilityChanged() and .onAmbientModeChanged() methods. You'll need to make sure to **reset the second hand timer logic**, using an isTimerEnabled() method, in case the visibility or ambient mode changes back to interactive.

Add a line of code underneath the onAmbientModeChanged() method and create a **public void checkTimer()** method structure. Inside this structure, type in the **updateTimehandler** object, and then press the **period** key. Then select the **removeMessages(int what) void** option from the pop-up helper dialog, by double-clicking it, as shown in Figure 10-37.

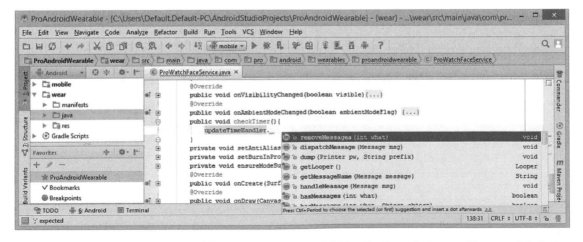

*Figure 10-37. Create a public void checkTimer() method, type updateTimeHandler, select removeMessages(int what)*

Add an **UPDATE_TIME_MESSAGE** constant as the parameter to remove any Message objects that might have been left in the MessageQueue when the watch face went into ambient mode or went into invisible (not visible) mode.

The Java method structure, thus far, should look like the following code:

```
public void checkTimer() {
    updateTimeHandler.removeMessages(UPDATE_TIME_MESSAGE);
}
```

The next part of this method needs to check the .isTimerEnabled() boolean return value with a conditional if structure. If the value equals true, it needs to call the **.sendEmptyMessage()** method off the **updateTimeHandler** object, using the following Java code structure, as shown in Figure 10-38:

```
If( isTimerEnabled ) { updateTimehandler.sendEmptyMessage(UPDATE_TIME_MESSAGE); }
```

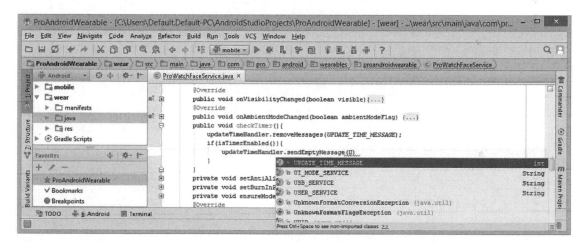

*Figure 10-38. Add an if(isTimerEnabled) condition and call the .sendEmptyMessage() off of the updateTimeHandler*

Now all you need to do is add a checkTimer() method call to the end of the onAmbientModeChanged() method, as shown highlighted in Figure 10-39.

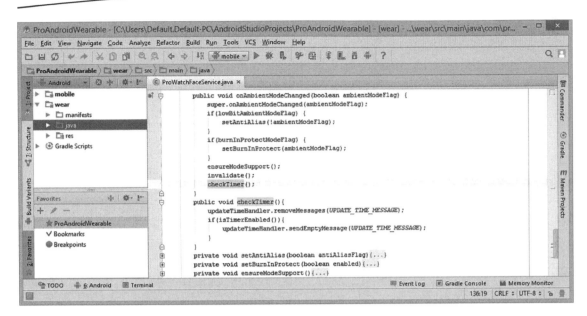

*Figure 10-39. Open the onAmbientModeChanged() method, and add the checkTimer() method call at the end*

Finally, you need to also add a checkTimer() method call to the end of the onVisibilityChanged() method, as shown highlighted in Figure 10-40. This call will be needed when a watch turns back on. To get the value, the Timer will have to wait until it can get the next even second (even 1,000 millisecond).

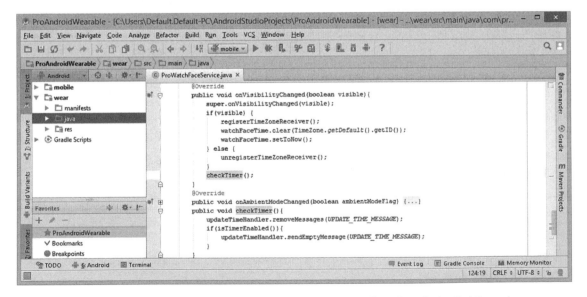

*Figure 10-40. Open the onVisibilityChanged() method and add in the checkTimer() method call at the end*

Now you have the basic methods in place for rendering a watch face!

# Summary

In this chapter, you learned how to create "vector" watch face designs using methods from the Android Paint and Canvas classes. First, I presented an in-depth look at the Paint class, nested classes, constructors, and methods that you were going to be using in the watch face design Java code. After that, you created your Paint objects for the hour hand, minute hand, second hand, and tick marks. I then discussed the Canvas class and the .drawLine() method, which you used to draw all of the watch face components.

Next, you created the .onDraw() method logic to draw the watch face component parts onto the Canvas, and then you developed Advanced Mode Support, using Paint methods, to implement special watch face API modes using methods that dynamically adjust the Paint characteristics based on boolean flag values. After that, you implemented these new methods in the onAmbientModeChanged() and onVisibilityChanged() methods, which are the core WatchFaceService methods.

In the next chapter, you will start adding bitmap graphics and 2D design elements to the Watch Face application, and you will learn how to create a watch face that uses both new media assets as well as vector code. You will also start to test your code using AVD emulators.

# Chapter 1

# WatchFaces Bitmap Design: Using Raster Graphics for WatchFaces

You now have enough of the WatchFaces API code in place to be able to test your Java code, which means that this is going to be a busy chapter. You'll learn how to get the emulators working, test the code, and make any additions, and after you have a working vector watch face application, you'll then look at how to incorporate a BitmapDrawable asset to create a background image for the watch face application. Most watch face designs will utilize a combination of bitmap assets and vector drawing code to create a design.

After you get the AVD emulators working and test the code base you have put in place thus far, you will make sure each of the Java statements that are needed to make the watch face work are in place. Advanced warning, I left one or two out, so you can see how to use the AVDs to test the WatchFaces API Java code!

After you get your basic watch face code working, you will add a method that detects whether a watch face is round or square, and then you will get into the different bitmap image–related classes that are needed to implement background imagery behind the vector watch face design.

I will discuss the Android WindowInsets class used to access inset information, as well as the Android Bitmap and Resources classes you will need to obtain the digital image assets. I will also discuss the Android Drawable and BitmapDrawable classes that are needed to wrap your digital image resource and raw Bitmap data into a format the onDraw() method can utilize to write the Bitmap Image Asset to your watch face background.

# Testing a WatchFaces Design: Using the Round AVD

Since you now have enough code in place to test the watch face application, open the Android Studio ProAndroidWearable project and let's run the code through the Watch Face Round 2 (ARM) emulator. I have collapsed all of the code to show around 60 top-level lines of code, as shown (marked with a 1) on the left side of Figure 11-1. Use the **Run** menu at the top of the IDE to access the **Run...** submenu (marked with a 2), which will open the **Run floating menu** (marked with a 3). If you are selecting this for the first time, your **Edit Configurations** dialog will open, which is what you want, because you'll need to select the **Do not launch Activity** option shown (marked with a 4).

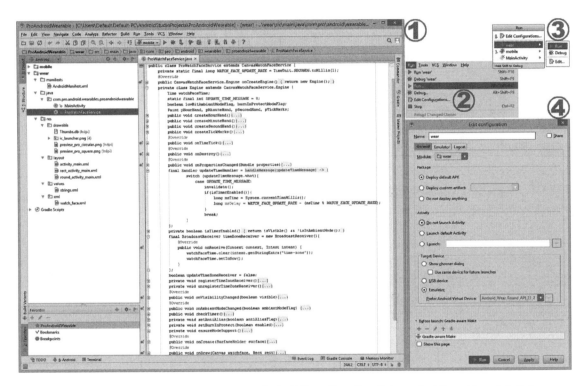

*Figure 11-1. Use the Run ➤ Wear menu sequence; in the Edit configuration dialog, select Do not launch Activity*

Once you select the Do not launch Activity option, because the WatchFace app does not use an Activity object (as it is a Wallpaper object), click the Apply button (at the bottom right of the dialog) and then the Run button.

This will start a **Waiting for adb** progress bar dialog, as shown at the top of Figure 11-2. Eventually, your Android_Wear_Round AVD emulator will appear.

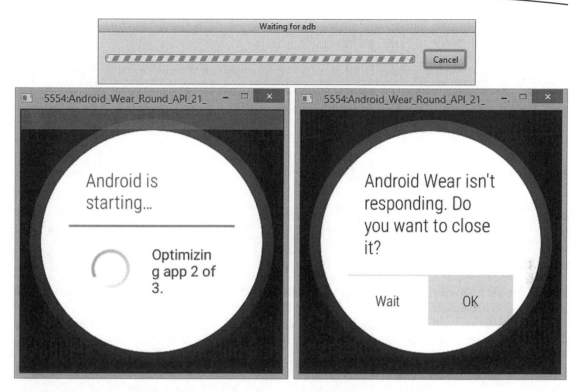

*Figure 11-2. Launch the Android Wear Round AVD to try to test the application. AVD crashes, click OK to close*

As you can see on the left side of Figure 11-2, the emulator will load and optimize its components into memory, telling you that Android is starting, and then your Android OS will appear. In my case, Android seemed to know I was writing this book, and the AVD crashed on me, so I took this opportunity to show you, on the right side of Figure 11-2, that an Android development environment is no more bulletproof than an operating system is! This will be especially true in new versions of software, such as Android 5 (Android Studio 1.x), as they are not yet perfected. You should expect hiccups, like the AVDs not working correctly, to happen, and do not let them deter you!

If you ever get this "Android Wear isn't responding" screen, as shown in Figure 11-2 on the right, simply click the **OK** button, make any changes, and try again! I encountered some problems with both the Square as well as the Round AVD emulators, so I'll show you some of the things that I did to rectify these problems in the first section of this chapter.

When I used the **Run ➤ Run Wear** menu sequence to try again, I got the **wear** tab seen at the bottom left in Figure 11-3. This section of the IDEA shows you what is happening with the AVD, including placement and any problems.

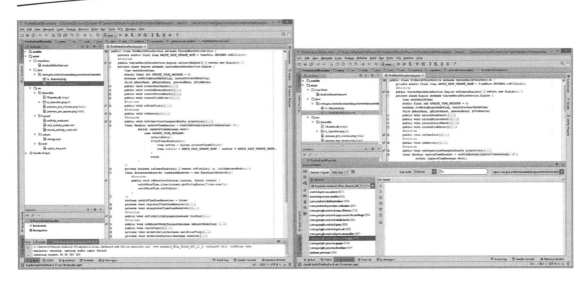

*Figure 11-3.  Try launching AVD again with Run ➤ Wear menu sequence; Android DDMS panel shows processes*

This time when I ran the AVD emulator, the **Android DDMS** also popped open a panel, showing **process info** in the left-hand pane and a **logcat**, which is short for **Error Log Catalog**, in the right-hand pane, as shown in Figure 11-3. The logcat pane is currently empty, so no errors have been logged, at least for the time period that includes the launch of the code. Once you start using an Android application, errors may appear inside this pane to inform you about any problems in your code.

Once your AVD launches, as shown in Figure 11-4, find the **Settings** option, click it, and find the **Change watch face** option, then click that and scroll sideways through the watch faces until you find your **Pro Watch Face** option. Once you click your preview image, Android launches the Pro Watch Face design, which is shown on the far right side of Figure 11-4. It appears that the onDraw() method is drawing a watch face design correctly, but the second hand is not advancing, so you will need to check the timing code.

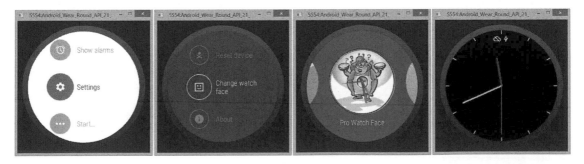

*Figure 11-4.  Find the Settings ➤ Change watch face sequence, select Pro Watch Face, and run your watch face*

## Sending the Whole Second Delay to Your Handler Object

Because the second hand is frozen in place, a logical place to start looking at the code is the Handler object named updateTimeHandler, since this code is where the watch face application starts the timer logic each second.

Inside the **.handleMessage()** method, will notice that within the conditional **if(isTimerEnabled())** structure you have calculated the **msDelay** (the time until the next whole second offset value). However, you have not sent that msDelay data value over to the Handler object so it can trigger the next time-related Message object.

This is done by using the **.sendEmptyMessageDelayed()** method call, and the Java programming statement to accomplish sending the msDelay value to the handler object will go right after the msDelay calculation. The Java code can be seen in Figure 11-5 and should look like the following statement:

```
updateTimeHandler.sendEmptyMessageDelayed(UPDATE_TIME_MESSAGE, msDelay);
```

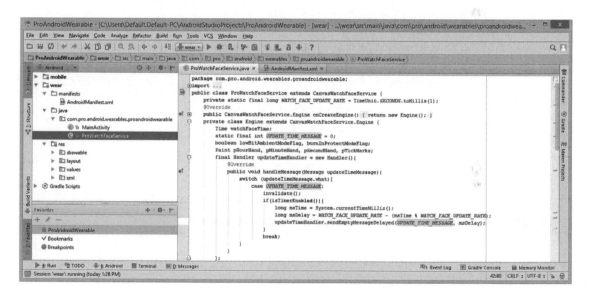

*Figure 11-5. Add a call to a .sendEmptyMessageDelayed() method off the updateTimeHandler object*

What this does is send the UPDATE_TIME_MESSAGE value and the delay value in milliseconds to the updateTimeHandler using the method call that specifies (by its very name) for it to send an empty message (a trigger) at that exact msDelay value, which represents the next whole (1,000ms) second.

Use a Run ➤ Run Wear menu sequence to launch an AVD to test the watch face. The second hand is still frozen, so there must be something else missing!

# Setting a Time Object to a Current Time in the Draw Logic

Now that the Handler object is broadcasting the correct whole second time, the next logical place to check that timing-based logic is in the **.onDraw()** method. Notice that you use the **watchFaceTime** Time object to calculate the hour, minute, and second hand angle positions. You need to make sure that the Time object is set accurately before these calculations are performed. Thus, you need to call the **.setToNow()** method, off the watchFaceTime Time object, at the top of the .onDraw() method.

I put this after the super.onDraw() method call and after the .drawColor() method call that sets the background color to black. The Java programming statement should look like the following:

```
watchFaceTime.setToNow();
```

As you can see in Figure 11-6, the Java code is error free and you're are now ready to test the code again using the Round AVD. I clicked the watchFaceTime object reference in the Java code to track its use in the onDraw() method.

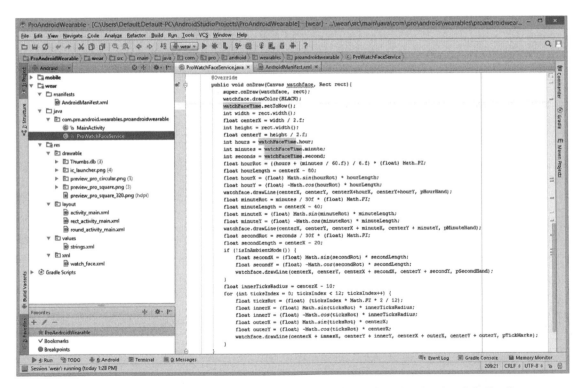

*Figure 11-6. Add a call to the .setToNow() method off the watchFaceTime object after the .drawColor() call*

After the watchFaceTime Time object updating line of Java code is added to the code, test the watch face again in the Round AVD. Now the second hand should be ticking away, and you're ready to test the code in the Square AVD emulator to get some experience working with the Android_Wear_Square AVD.

# Testing a WatchFace Design: Using a Square AVD

Use the **Run ➤ Edit Configurations** menu sequence (as shown in Figure 11-1) and set the Emulator to the Android Wear Square AVD, as shown in Figure 11-7.

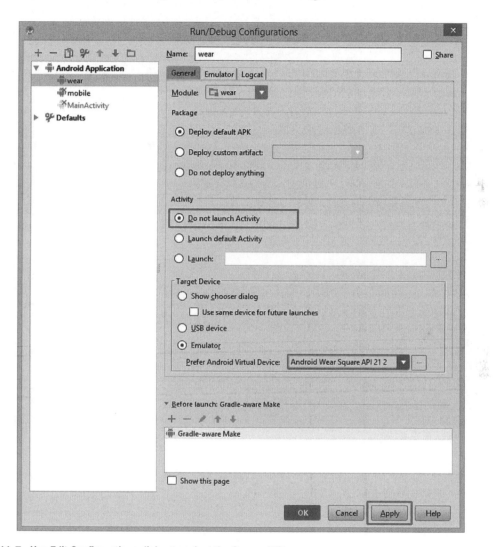

*Figure 11-7.* *Use Edit Configurations dialog to select the Square AVD*

I went into **Settings ➤ Change watch face** to find a square watch face preview, and it was not included! I checked my **AndroidManifest.xml** file to make sure the correct image asset was referenced, and then I used Google to see if anyone else had encountered this problem with the square watch face emulator. The one suggestion I saw related to the AVD **Use Host GPU** option. Some suggested deselecting this option, and others suggested selecting it!

So I tried both; neither setting worked! So I tried **Landscape Orientation**, which turned my content sideways in the emulator, but it didn't reveal the square watch face preview, so I tried increasing the **RAM** to **1GB** as well as the **Internal Storage** to **500MB**, the results of all of these can be seen in Figure 11-8.

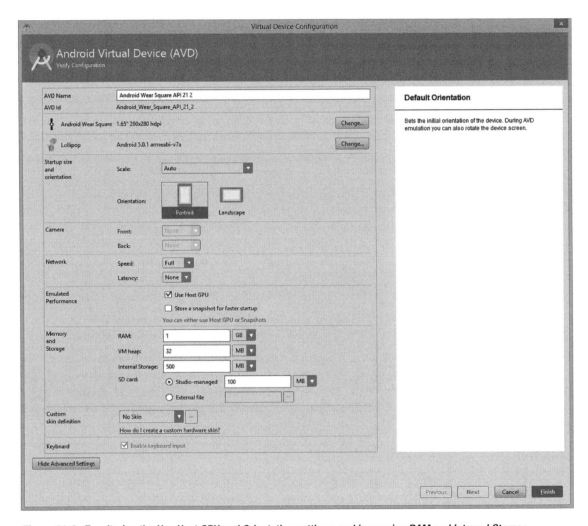

*Figure 11-8. Try altering the Use Host GPU and Orientation settings, and increasing RAM and Internal Storage*

Neither of these settings worked, and I spent a few days trying to get the square preview to appear in the emulator so I could test the code. I wanted to make sure that these AVD emulators worked because not all of you will have Smartwatch hardware to test on! I kept on trying different things to figure out why the square Pro Watch Face preview was not showing up in the Square AVD emulator.

Because this might happen to you at some point (not only with the emulator), I will tell you some of the things I tried and what finally worked!

After the suggested Use Host GPU didn't work and giving an AVD more system resources didn't work either, I wondered if a 320 pixel square preview was too big for the standard 280 DIP square watch face, as Android's documentation recommended 280 DIP dimensions for use with square watch face designs.

As I iterated among all of these different AVD settings and image asset dimensions, I had a couple of crashes of the Android Square ARM AVD, which gave me the dialog shown in Figure 11-9. I did not let this discourage me, as Android Studio and Android 5 are all new platforms, and bound to have numerous bugs, at least for a while. I simply closed the AVD (if it didn't vanish due to an **emulator-arm.exe** error dialog) and kept on trying.

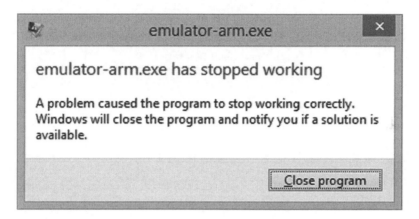

*Figure 11-9. The Square AVD crashed during the process showing this dialog*

I found a solution, at least for my hardware setup and installation, under the **Emulator** tab in the **Run/Debug (Edit) Configurations** dialog. The tab is shown selected in Figure 11-10, and underneath this tab is an option that was checked as a default in my Installation called **Additional command line options**. I thought it was strange that this option was checked, as well as being empty, so I **deselected** it. I also selected the **Wipe user data** option to make sure that I was getting a "clean" load of this ARM AVD into my system memory each time it was launched.

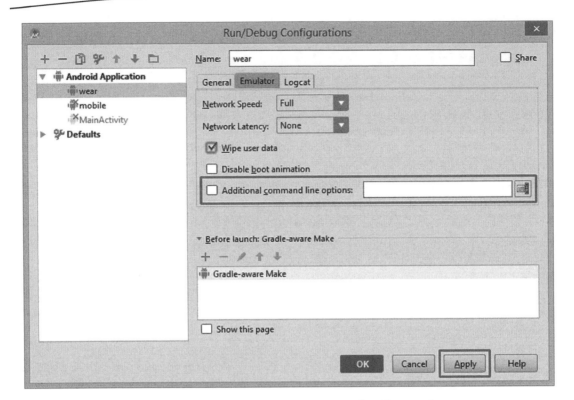

*Figure 11-10. Deselecting the Additional command line options and selecting Wipe user data*

My thought process here was that there was something that was being loaded into the AVD emulator code in system memory that was preventing the square watch face preview from loading into, or being displayed in the UI of, the Android Square ARM AVD emulator. As it turns out, this solved the problem, which is great, as I need this AVD emulator to work for those who do not have physical smartwatch hardware but want to learn about Android Wear.

The advanced emulator options are shown in the middle of Figure 11-10, including the **Wipe user data** option, which I have now selected (as shown).

There is also a **Disable boot animation** you could select, if you wish, to speed up the AVD load sequence, also shown in Figure 11-10.

Now when I launched a Square AVD and selected the **Settings ➤ Change watch face** option, I could scroll and find the Pro Watch Face square watch face preview image, which can be seen in the third pane from the left in Figure 11-11. It is important to note that this work process can also solve the same problem in the Round AVD emulator if you happen to encounter it.

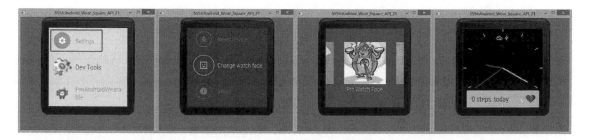

**Figure 11-11.** *Select the Settings ➤ Change watch face dialog, find the (square) Pro Watch Face, run and test it*

When I click the Pro Watch Face preview image, I now get the watch face design and the second hand is ticking, so the basic watch face code works!

You are now ready to test the various special modes (low-bit, burn-in) that have been implemented in the program logic, which kick in when the watch face enters ambient mode. Before I get into testing the custom hardware modes, I want to take a look at how to work with the AVD emulators, which tend to crash a lot because they are relatively new, and how to use the F7 key, which toggles the ambient mode on and off in the AVD emulator.

## AVD Crashes: Can't Connect and Not Responding Panels

When I was testing the watch faces code as I was writing this chapter, I had a ton of crashes as well as the problem mentioned in the previous section, where I could not even get a square watch face preview to select so I could test my Java code. Once I got this figured out, I still had a lot of problems with "hanging" AVD emulator software, so let's look at the two scenarios I encountered in this section so you know how to resolve the situation if you ever happen to encounter it. Hopefully, these issues will be fixed by the time this book is out, but you never know, so I'll include it here just to be thorough.

These crashes took the form of either a "Can't connect to the Android Wear app on your phone" screen or an "Android Wear isn't responding" screen. A "Can't connect" error, which can be seen in Figure 11-12 on the left, will often allow you to "Retry" or "Reset device" and continue the testing. To get into these two screens, use the "Swipe for some tips" option, as shown on the first screen (on the left) in Figure 11-12. This presents buttons you can click; be sure to try the **Retry** (green) button first before using a **Reset** (red) button as your last resort.

**Figure 11-12.** *If you get a Can't connect to the Android Wear app screen, swipe left a few times to get the Retry and Reset panes*

I have used both of these buttons successfully, to "save" the AVD session, so that I did not have to **exit** (by using a square red X in the upper right corner of dialog window) the AVD emulator software and start all over.

If the Retry or Reset device button works, you will see the startup screen shown in the middle pane of Figure 11-13, and you can then proceed to test your watch face application.

**Figure 11-13.** *If you get an Android Wear isn't responding pane, click Wait and you'll get the start screen. Press F7 for Ambient Mode*

Another show-stopper error screen you might encounter is the **"Android Wear isn't responding"** screen, which can be seen on the far left-hand side in Figure 11-13. If you click the Wait button, you may eventually get the startup screen shown in the middle of Figure 11-13. If you click the **OK** button, the AVD emulator will close, just as if you had used the square red X in the upper left corner of the dialog window.

Also shown on the right-hand pane in Figure 11-13 is the AVD ambient mode, which you invoke by pressing the **F7** key (Function key 7, along the top of your keyboard). As you can see, the code that dims the color to **50%** of its brightness, by using the **.setAlpha(127)** technique, is working well. If you want to use **grayscale** instead of color in ambient mode, you should add the **.setColor(Color.WHITE)** method call inside that section of the Java code.

Now that you know how to use the F7 key to put the AVD emulator into ambient mode, you can move on and test the **low-bit ambient mode** code.

# Special Screen Modes: Testing the Low-Bit Ambient Mode

There are a number of ways you can test the low-bit ambient mode code by forcing the lowBitAmbientModeFlag to be turned on by adding the line of code that does this somewhere inside the application programming logic.

The **lowBitAmbientModeFlag=true;** toggle statement would logically go either in the **onAmbientModeChanged()** method or the **onPropertiesChanged()** method; you'll be using both during this chapter so you can see how this works in each.

Add a lowBitAmbientModeFlag=true; Java statement in the onAmbientModeChanged() method after the superclass method call, as shown in Figure 11-14.

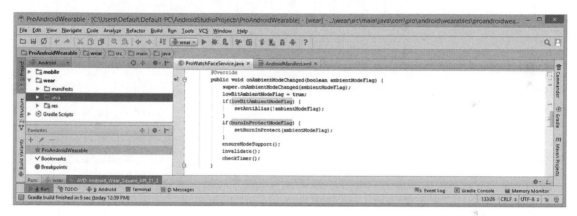

*Figure 11-14.* *Add lowBitAmbientModeFlag=true setting to the onAmbientModeChanged() method to test low-bit ambient mode*

Once you artificially set the value of the low-bit flag to true, you will use the Run ➤ Run Wear menu sequence to launch the AVD emulator. Next, use the Settings ➤ Change watch face ➤ Pro Watch Face sequence and launch your watch face application. The watch face in low-bit ambient mode can be seen on the far right in Figure 11-15, and it uses a white color for everything as well as no anti-aliasing (as indicated by the jagged edges) on any lines.

*Figure 11-15.* *Use Settings ➤ Change watch face ➤ Pro Watch Face series, and F7 to test low-bit ambient mode*

Because burn-in is usually used with low-bit mode, let's add the burn-in flag setting next, and you can test both of these flags in their "on" setting.

## Special Screen Modes: Testing Low-Bit and Burn-In Modes

Add a **burnInProtectModeFlag=true;** statement right before the if() statement that evaluates that flag, as shown in Figure 11-16. A lightbulb icon popped up in IntelliJ, so I dropped down the suggestion menu and double-clicked the "Remove braces from 'if' statement" suggestion. This allowed IntelliJ IDEA to streamline the Java code a bit. If IntelliJ gives you a reasonable code optimization suggestion, it is often wise to take it and see how it works!

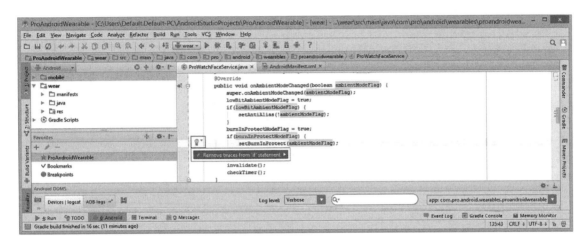

*Figure 11-16. Add a burnInProtectModeFlag=true, and take the IntelliJ suggestion to streamline the if() constructs*

In this case, it reduced the lines of code for this method from 12 to six, or a 50% code reduction, once you remove the flag forcing lines of code, which you will put into the **.onPropertiesChanged()** method next.

The Java code for the revised onAmbientModeChanged() method (sans the true flag settings) can be seen error-free in Figure 11-17 and would look like the following Java method structure:

```
@Override
public void onAmbientModeChanged(boolean ambientModeFlag) {
    super.onAmbientModeChanged(ambientModeFlag);
        if(lowBitAmbientModeFlag) setAntiAlias(!ambientModeFlag);
        if(burnInProtectModeFlag) setBurnInProtect(ambientModeFlag);
    ensureModeSupport;
    invalidate;
    checkTimer;
}
```

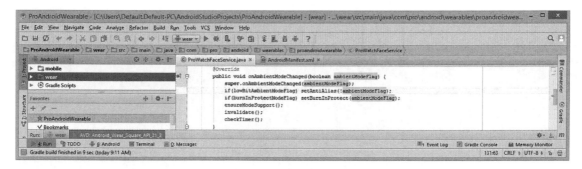

*Figure 11-17.  Once you implement the IntelliJ if() refinement suggestion, the method is reduced to six lines of code*

Next, let's put these special mode flag "forced true" settings into the onPropertiesChanged()
method, at the end of the method, as shown in Figure 11-18. The new Java code for this
method structure should look like this:

```
@Override
public void onPropertiesChanged(Bundle properties) {
    super.onPropertiesChanged(properties);
    lowBitAmbientModeFlag = properties.getBoolean(PROPERTY_LOW_BIT_AMBIENT, false);
    burnInProtectModeFlag = properties.getBoolean(PROPERTY_BURN_IN_PROTECTION, false);
    lowBitAmbientModeFlag = true;
    burnInProtectModeFlag = true;
}
```

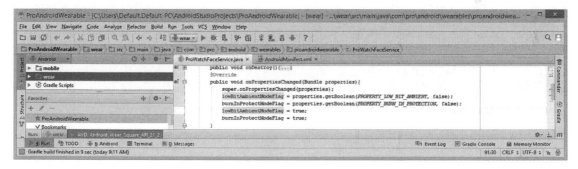

*Figure 11-18.  Move special mode flags set to true values to the bottom of the onPropertiesChanged() method*

Now let's test the watch face again using the Settings ➤ Change watch face ➤ Pro Watch
Face sequence. As you can see in the third pane from the left in Figure 11-19, when you
press the F7 key to toggle the watch face into ambient mode, the low-bit flag logic is
working, as you know already.

*Figure 11-19. Test your watch face Java code thus far by using the Android_Wear_Square_API_21 AVD emulator*

However, your burn-in programming logic is not placing that outline around the hands of the watch face as you expected it to. Press the F7 key again to toggle back into interactive mode, as shown in the fourth pane at the far right of Figure 11-19. As you can see, the RBG color values for the watch face hands are not being restored, so you will also need to take a look at the **ensureModeSupport()** method as well as the **setBurnInProtect()** method. Let's fix the switch back into interactive RGB color mode first.

Because you configured the watch face hands color in the .onCreate() method by calling the custom .createHand() methods, you need to set the color back in the final else section of the ensureModeSupport() method.

You're already setting the alpha value back to 255 (fully opaque) using the .setAlpha() method call, so, you need to use the **.setColor()** method call to reconfigure the Paint objects to use the BLUE, GREEN, RED, and WHITE Color class constants. I'm coding this in this way using a different method call to show you a different way to set color values. Remember that you used the .setARGB() method to set the color value in the .createHand() methods. The Java code, shown error-free in Figure 11-20, should look like the following:

```
} else {
    pHourHand.setAlpha(255);
    pMinuteHand.setAlpha(255);
    pSecondHand.setAlpha(255);
    pTickMarks.setAlpha(255);
    pHourHand.setColor(Color.BLUE);
    pMinuteHand.setColor(Color.GREEN);
    pSecondHand.setColor(Color.RED);
    pTickMarks.setColor(Color.WHITE);
}
```

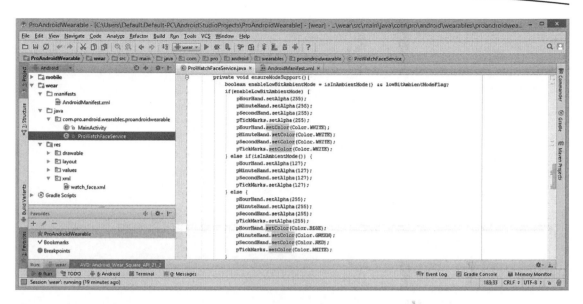

*Figure 11-20. Add .setColor() method calls in the else portion of the if-else loop in ensureModeSupport() method*

Now let's take a look at why the .setStyle(Paint.Style.STROKE) approach is not stroking the single pixel outline around the hour hand and minute hand watch face components. As you can see in Figure 11-19, the .setBurnInProtect() method is clearly having zero impact on what is being drawn to the screen.

As you saw in Figure 10-25, you're trying to use the **STROKE** Paint.Style constant to create the outline effect around the hour and minute hand vector objects and a **FILL** Paint.Style to create a solid, or filled, effect. Whereas this approach will work well with just about any of the **2D ShapeDrawable** objects in Android, including Text, Circles, Rectangles, and other "closed" line or curve-based shapes, it will not work with **1D** "open" line or curve-shaped objects because they have **no interior**! So in the case of a 1D vector "ray" object, STROKE and FILL will yield the exact same effect!

What you need to do to get this working is use the **.setStrokeWidth()** method call with the Line Shape objects, which will allow you to optimize the burn-in method, by not having to declare a Paint.Style object named paintStyle, and simplify the if-else conditional structure to use **three pixels** for the hour hand, which needs to be thicker than the minute hand, and **two pixels** for the minute hand, which is the same value you're using for the tick mark elements, so they can be easily seen on the watch face display.

Using one single pixel for drawing watch face elements will not allow the end user to easily read the watch face time, even though that would be the most optimal setting for the screen burn-in protection. You can experiment with using 1.f stroke width data values in your watch face applications if you would like to see how it looks! In this case, the hour hand would need to be 2.f to differentiate it, and the minute hand and tick marks would use a 1.f setting.

A new method structure, which sets the **StrokeWidth** attribute for the Paint objects, can be seen in Figure 11-21 and should look like this:

```
private void setBurnInProtect(boolean enabled) {
    if(enabled) {
        pHourHand.setStrokeWidth(3.f);
        pMinuteHand.setStrokeWidth(2.f);
    } else {
        pHourHand.setStrokeWidth(6.f);
        pMinuteHand.setStrokeWidth(4.f);
    }
}
```

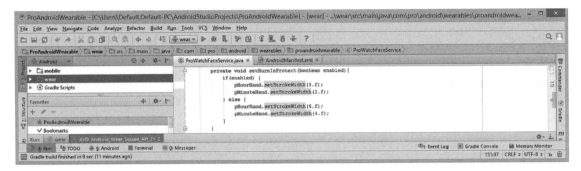

*Figure 11-21.  Remove the Paint.Style logic from setBurnInProtection method, and instead use .setStrokeWidth( )*

Now when you use the Run ➤ Run Wear and launch the AVD emulator and use the Settings ➤ Change watch face ➤ Pro Watch Face ➤ F7 key, you will get the ambient mode with low-bit and burn-in modes enabled, as shown on the far right pane in Figure 11-22.

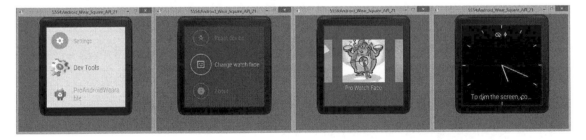

*Figure 11-22.  Use Settings ➤ Change watch face ➤ Pro Watch Face series, and F7 to test low-bit ambient mode*

As you can see, the watch face is still attractive, readable, and completely usable, even when using zero anti-aliasing. The watch face design is using very few pixels to draw in the watch face design elements, which serves to provide screen burn-in protection, which is the objective of this mode.

The next thing you need to do is learn how to detect whether the user has a square or round watch face, using Android's **WindowInsets** class. After you put that watch face shape detection code in place, you will learn about the Android **Bitmap**, **Drawable**, and **BitmapDrawable** classes, as well as how to use these to implement bitmap background images with your vector watch face components, taking your Android watch faces to all new levels.

# Android WindowInsets Class: Polling Screen Shape

The Android **WindowInsets** class is a **public final** class that extends the java.lang.Object class. The class hierarchy looks like this:

```
java.lang.Object
  > android.view.WindowInsets
```

This class is part of the **android.view** package because it is used with **View** objects. A WindowInsets object can be used to describe a set of insets for the application window content. In this case, this object holds watch face characteristics such as the shape of the watch face and whether it has a shelf, as the Motorola MOTO 360 does currently.

These WindowInsets objects are "immutable" (fixed or not changeable). They may be expanded (by Google's Android Team) to include other inset types in the future. Here you'll be using the WindowInsets object in conjunction with the **.onApplyWindowInsets(Window Insets)** method, which you will be coding next.

This WindowInsets class has one public constructor method, which takes the format **WindowInsets(WindowInsets insets)** and constructs a (new) WindowInsets object. It does this by copying the data values from a source WindowInsets definition, in this case, this would be from each SmartWatch manufacturer.

This WindowInsets class has 18 methods, two of which you would want to know about for WatchFaces API development. The **.isRound()** method will tell you if the watch face is round (or not round, which would be square), and the **.getSystemWindowInsetBottom()** method will tell you the size (integer) for the "shelf" the MOTO 360 uses to connect its watch face screen.

Next, let's create the **onApplyWindowInsets()** method, which is one of those WatchFaceService.Engine classes whose implementation I saved until now when you are learning about something that could actually "leverage" what it provides!

# Detecting WatchFace Shape: Using WindowInsets

Add a **public void onApplyWindowInsets(WindowInsets insets){}** empty method structure in the Engine class after the onTimerTick() method. As you can see in Figure 11-23, you will have to use **Alt+Enter** and have IntelliJ code the **import android.view.WindowInsets;** statement for you at the top of your class.

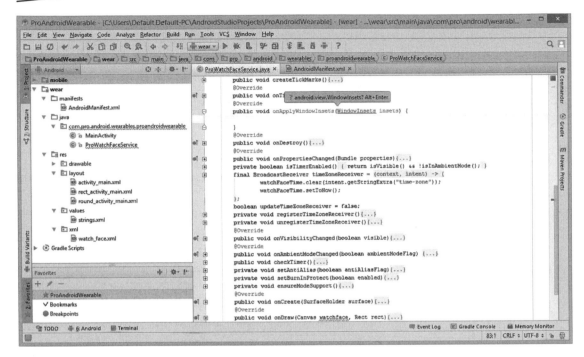

*Figure 11-23.  Add the public void onApplyWindowInsets(WindowInsets insets){ } empty method structure*

The next step is to add the **roundFlag** boolean variable to the end of the compound boolean statement (at the top of the private Engine class) using the following Java variable declaration statement, as shown (highlighted) at the top of Figure 11-24:

**boolean** lowBitAmbientModeFlag, burnInProtectModeFlag, **roundFlag**;

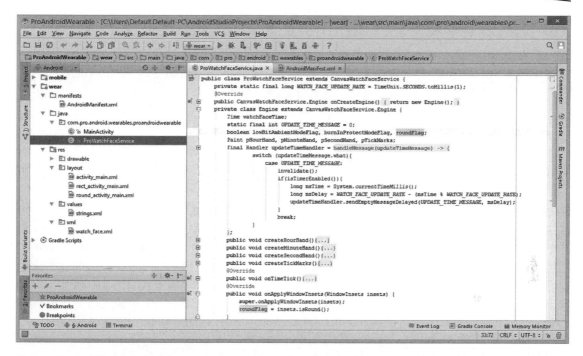

**Figure 11-24.** *Add a boolean variable named roundFlag to the Engine class and set it equal to insets.isRound() inside of the onApplyWindowInsets() method*

Inside the empty onApplyWindowInsets() method, call the superclass using the Java **super** keyword and pass the WindowInsets object named **insets** up to the parent class. Next, set the **roundFlag** boolean variable equal to boolean value of the **.isRound()** method call off the **insets** WindowInsets object.

The Java method, as shown at the bottom of Android Studio in Figure 11-24, should look like the following Java method construct:

```java
@Override
private void onApplyWindowInsets(WindowInsets insets) {
    super.onApplyWindowInsets(insets);
    roundFlag = insets.isRound();
}
```

Now you have a way to find out if the user's smartwatch is using round or square display hardware. This boolean value will be used in the next part of the chapter when you learn how to place bitmap imagery behind the vector watch face components. First, however, let's take a look at Android's Bitmap and Resources classes, which you will use to load your image data.

# Android Bitmap Class: Using Digital Image Assets

The Android **Bitmap** class is a **public final** class that implements the Java **Parcelable** interface and extends the java.lang.Object master class. The Bitmap class hierarchy looks like the following:

```
java.lang.Object
  > android.graphics.Bitmap
```

The Android Bitmap class has two nested (helper) classes. The first is the enum **Bitmap.CompressFormat** class, which specifies known image file formats these Bitmap objects can be compressed into using codecs, which are part of the Android OS. Enum values include **JPEG**, **WEBP**, and **PNG**.

The second is an enum **Bitmap.Config** class, which specifies possible bitmap configurations. These include **ALPHA_8**, which is the **8-bit** 256 transparency level alpha channel–only format, as well as **ARGB_8888**, which is the **32-bit** format using 8-bits of data per color plane (and alpha channel).

There is also a 16-bit bitmap format called **RGB_565**, which is interesting, because there is no 16-bit codec support (BMP, TIF, and TGA all support 16-bit color) currently in Android. There is also the deprecated (meaning, no longer supported) ARGB_4444 format, which you should not use because it was deprecated in Android API Level 13.

The Bitmap class has more than 50 methods, so clearly I can't cover these in detail here, but I will cover those methods that you will be utilizing to implement bitmap assets in the WatchFaces API designs in this chapter, as well as in the next chapter, when I will discuss digital imaging techniques used to create the other watch face mode bitmap assets.

The **.getWidth()** method call will return the width attribute of the Bitmap object and, similarly, the **.getHeight()** method call, which will return the height attribute of the Bitmap object.

The **public static Bitmap createScaledBitmap (Bitmap src, int dstWidth, int dstHeight, boolean filter)** method, added in Android API Level 1, creates a new Bitmap object by scaling image data from the source Bitmap object. The method parameters include a **src**, the source Bitmap object, a **dstWidth**, or the destination Bitmap object's target width, a **dstHeight**, the destination Bitmap object's target height, and a boolean **filter** data value, which will be set to **true** if you want Android to apply Bi-Linear Interpolation to the image scaling algorithm. You'll be using this option to achieve the highest quality image scaling result. This is especially important if you're going to be up-sampling (going from a lower resolution to a higher resolution).

The method returns a scaled Bitmap object, or if no scaling was performed, it would then logically return the source Bitmap object. The method throws an IllegalArgumentException if the source Bitmap object width is less than (or equal to) zero or if the Bitmap object height is less than or equal to zero. You'll be using this method later on in the chapter in the .onDraw() method to make sure that your Bitmap object fits your watch face display.

Next, let's take a look at the Android Resources class, because you will have to use this to load the digital image resources into the Bitmap object.

# Android Resources Class: Using Your Res Folder

The public Android **Resources** class extends java.lang.Object and is part of the **android.content.res** package. It has one known direct subclass, which is called MockResources. The Java class hierarchy looks like the following:

```
java.lang.Object
  > android.content.res.Resources
```

The Resources class is used to create objects that allow you to access the application resources that are stored in the **/res** folder. This Android "R" resource system (for instance, the images that are stored in **/res/drawable-hdpi** and referenced as **R.drawable.imagename**) keeps track of all noncode assets associated with your Android application. You can use this class to access these application resources, as you will be doing in the next section.

You can acquire a Resources object that is loaded with all the references to your external project assets (resources) within your application by using the **.getResources()** method call off the application's primary **Context**, which is accessed using the Java **this** keyword. In this application scenario, it would look something like the following Java statement:

```
Resources watchFaceResources = ProWatchFaceService.this.getResources();
```

The Android SDK tools installed in IntelliJ IDEA compile the application resources into the application binary at build time, where they go from the /res/drawable reference path to the **R.drawable** reference path. This is why you would use R.drawable.image_asset_name in Java method calls rather than /res.

To be able to use an external asset as a resource, you must locate it in the correct source subfolder inside the project res/ directory, so the **images** or **shapes** would go into **/res/ drawable** (R.drawable) and the **vector animation** would go into **/res/anim** (R.anim), for instance.

As part of your application build (compilation) process, Android SDK tools will generate R. symbols for each asset resource. You can then use these R. references inside the application's Java code to access the resources. Make sure to use R. references in Java code to access assets at runtime.

Using an external application resource allows developers the capability of changing the visual characteristics of their applications without modifying the Java code or the XML markup. Additionally, providing these alternative resources will allow developers to optimize their applications, across the exceptionally wide (and rapidly growing) collection of consumer electronic device hardware configurations. An ability to dynamically access different new media resources will allow developers to accommodate scenarios such as different end-user languages, disparate screen sizes, shapes and densities, and, in this case, round watch faces versus square watch faces!

Being able to access various assets dynamically at runtime is an essential aspect of developing Android Watch Faces (and other) applications that are compatible across a wide range of disparate types of hardware devices.

The Resources class has two nested (also called helper) classes. There is the Resources. NotFoundException class, which handles throwing an exception for the Resource API when your requested resource (or its path) cannot be found. There is also a Resources. Theme class, which holds current attribute values for the particular OS Theme that was implemented in the app.

There is one public constructor method for creating Resource objects, which takes this parameter format: **Resources(AssetManager assets, DisplayMetrics metrics, Configuration config)**. Note that if you use .getResources(), this Resource object will be created for you, and you do not have to explicitly use this constructor method call and format.

This is the case with an implementation that you will be utilizing later on in this chapter in the Java statement, which was outlined earlier in this section. Now let's create the Bitmap and Resources objects for the watch face application.

# Accessing Imagery: Using Bitmap and Resources

The first thing you need to do at the top (declarations area) of the private Engine class is create the compound statement that declares and names two Bitmap objects. One of these Bitmap objects will hold the image asset (the original image data) and the other will hold the scaled version of the image data if for some reason the smartwatch hardware is using some resolution other than 320 by 320 pixels.

This approach would allow you to use higher resolution digital image assets, if higher resolution watch faces were developed in later years. The Java code for the compound statement can be seen in Figure 11-25 and should look like the following:

```
Bitmap watchFaceBitmap, scaleWatchFaceBitmap;
```

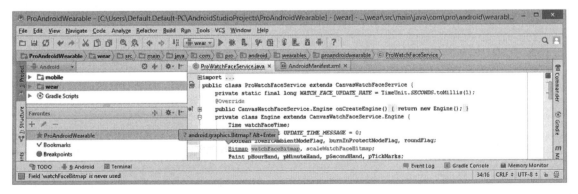

*Figure 11-25.  Add a compound Bitmap object declaration naming watchFaceBitmap and scaleWatchFaceBitmap*

Click anywhere in the line of code, shown highlighted in Figure 11-25, and use the **Alt+Enter** keystroke sequence to tell IntelliJ to write the import statement for you.

The next thing you want to do is create the Resources object. Your most logical method for doing this is the onCreate() method, because it only needs to be done once on application startup. You could declare Resources watchFaceResources at the top of the Engine class with other declarations, or you can declare, name, and load this object **locally** in onCreate(), using the following Java statement, which can also be seen in Figure 11-26:

```
Resources watchFaceResources = ProWatchFaceService.this.getResources();
```

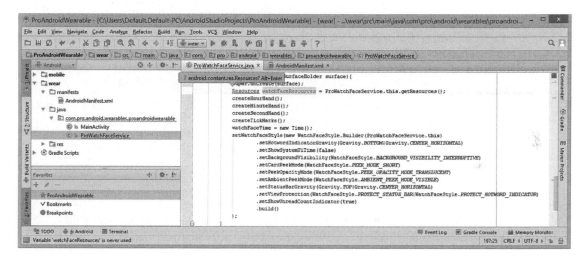

**Figure 11-26.** Create a Resources object named watchFaceResources; load it using the .getResources() method

Click in the Resources line of code and use the **Alt+Enter** work process to direct IntelliJ to code the import statement, as shown in Figure 11-26.

Before you continue coding, let's take a minute to get an overview of the Android Drawable class, because you will be implementing the Drawable object in your code to hold one of these Bitmap objects.

# Android Drawable Class: Creating Drawable Objects

The Android **public abstract Drawable** class was scratch-coded for creating Drawable objects in Android, so it directly extends the java.lang.Object, as shown in the following code:

```
java.lang.Object
  > android.graphics.drawable.Drawable
```

A Drawable is an Android term for something that can be drawn on a screen. The Drawable class provides the generic API for dealing with an underlying visual asset (resource), which might be any one of a plethora of graphics-related drawing element types, such as a nine-patch, vector, color, shape, gradient, inset, layer, clip, or a bitmap, which is what you will be using in the next section of this chapter.

The Drawable object does not have any ability to receive or process events or directly interact with the user, so you must "wrap" the Drawable object with a **View** object (widget) of some sort in able to be able to do this.

There are 15 known direct subclasses of drawable. You will be working with the **BitmapDrawable** subclass, but there are also others you could use in application development, including: VectorDrawable, GradientDrawable, NinePatchDrawable, AnimatedVectorDrawable, PictureDrawable, LayerDrawable, ClipDrawable, ColorDrawable, ScaleDrawable, RotateDrawable, ShapeDrawable, InsetDrawable, RoundedBitmapDrawable, and there's also a DrawableContainer.

There are seven known indirect subclasses; these are the subclasses of the direct subclasses and include: AnimatedStateListDrawable, RippleDrawable, AnimationDrawable, PaintDrawable, LevelListDrawable, StateListDrawable, and TransitionDrawable.

Drawables are not directly visible to Android applications until they are wrapped in a View. Drawables take on a variety of graphic element formats:

> The **BitmapDrawable** is the drawable you'll be using here; it is a map of "bits," or pixels, and uses the GIF, PNG, WEBP, or JPEG digital image "codecs" to compress and decompress the digital image data assets into system memory.

> The **NinePatchDrawable** is an extension to the PNG data format, allowing the image to specify how to stretch and scale perimeter areas.

> The **ShapeDrawable** contains simple vector drawing commands instead of a raw Bitmap object, allowing the vector artwork to "render" to any screen size.

> The **LayerDrawable** allows developers to create an image composite drawable. This type of drawable is like having a mini-GIMP in Android, where you can stack multiple bitmap drawables on top of one another using z-order layers.

> The **StateDrawable** is another type of compound drawable that selects one of a given set of drawables based on the state setting for the StateDrawable. A great example of this would be a multistate Android ImageButton widget.

> The **LevelDrawable** is another type of compound drawable that selects one of a given set of drawables, based on the level setting for the LevelDrawable object. A good example of this is the signal level icon on the Status Bar.

There are a plethora of other Drawable object types in Android, so if you are interested in learning about all of these in greater detail, check out the Apress *Pro Android Graphics* (2013) title.

Now it's time to create the watch face Drawable object and use it to load a Bitmap object, so that you can start adding background imagery to the watch face design. You will also incorporate the roundFlag boolean so that if you have different designs for the square versus round watch face, you'll know how to set up your watch face code to use the correct version.

# Loading the Drawable: Using the roundFlag Boolean

The first thing you need to do, at the top of the private Engine class, is declare, and name, your Drawable object. Let's use the logical name **watchFaceDrawable** for this Drawable object, so you know exactly what it is when you use it in the code. The Drawable object declaration can be seen in Figure 11-27, and should look like the following Java object declaration:

```
Drawable watchFaceDrawable;
```

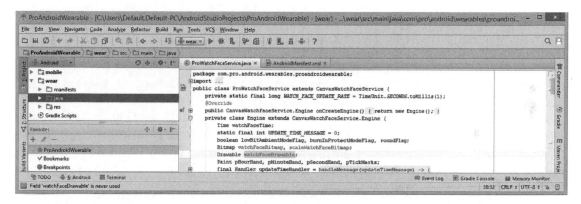

*Figure 11-27. Add a Drawable object declaration in the Engine class, and name the object watchFaceDrawable*

The next thing you'll want to do is add an empty conditional if-else structure at the top of the onCreate() method, after the Resources object declaration and instantiation line of code.

The conditional structure will evaluate the **roundFlag** boolean variable and load the watchFaceDrawable object with the correct digital image resource. The empty statement, which can be seen under construction in Figure 11-28, should look like the following Java conditional if-else (empty) structure:

```
if(roundFlag) {
        // Round Watch Face Java Statements
} else {
        // Square Watch Face Java Statements
}
```

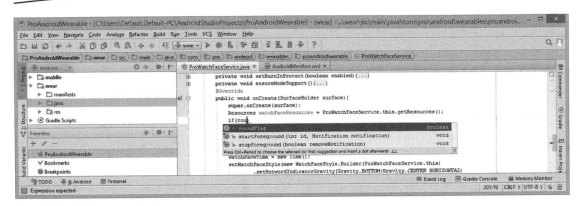

*Figure 11-28. Add an if(roundFlag) conditional structure in onCreate() method; choose roundFlag from the pop-up*

Inside the if part of the conditional statement, set the **watchFaceDrawable** object equal to a **getDrawable(R.drawable.preview_pro_circular)** method call off the **watchFaceResource** object. This preview_pro_circular PNG can be seen highlighted in blue in Figure 11-38. The Java code, as shown in Figure 11-29, should look like the following once you've coded the entire conditional if-else structure:

```
if(roundFlag) {
    watchFaceDrawable = watchFaceResources.getDrawable(R.drawable.preview_pro_circular);
} else {
    watchFaceDrawable = watchFaceResources.getDrawable(R.drawable.preview_pro_square);
}
```

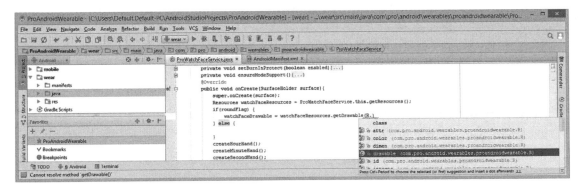

*Figure 11-29. Add a watchFaceDrawable object in the if, and load it with the watchFaceResources.getDrawable()*

As you can see in Figure 11-29, as you're coding the .getDrawable() method call, IntelliJ will list your Resources (R.) object assets for you, as you type in each period character. Type in the R and then a period, then select the drawable type (folder). Next, type in another period, and then select the **preview_pro_circular** PNG image reference to complete the Java programming statement. Now all you have to do is repeat this in the else structure.

Once you finish creating this if(roundFlag)-else structure that loads your watchFaceDrawable object with the correct Resources object reference, your code should be error-free, as shown in Figure 11-30, with the square watch face digital image asset reference in place (and highlighted).

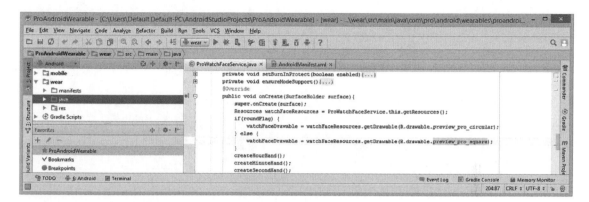

*Figure 11-30.* Add a different watchFaceResources.getDrawable() method call in the else portion of the if-else statement

Next, let's take a quick look at the Android **BitmapDrawable** class, which you will be using in the next line of Java code to "cast" the Drawable object, which has now been loaded with the correct image asset Resource reference, based on the setting of the roundFlag boolean variable, which you've culled from the WindowInsets object using the .isRound() method call. Whew!

I wanted to give you an overview of this class because BitmapDrawables are one of the most powerful and often used types of Drawable objects in Android application development, both for the UI design as well as for the graphics design for applications. If you are looking for more advanced material covering 2D Android UI design, check out the Apress title *Pro Android UI* (2014) when you have a chance.

# Android's BitmapDrawable Class: Image Drawables

Android's **public BitmapDrawable** class extends the Drawable class and is included in the **android.graphics.drawable** package. The Java class hierarchy looks like the following:

```
java.lang.Object
  > android.graphics.drawable.Drawable
    > android.graphics.drawable.BitmapDrawable
```

A BitmapDrawable is a Drawable object that contains a Bitmap object, which can be tiled, stretched, rotated, tinted, faded, or aligned. You can create a BitmapDrawable using one of **three** overloaded constructor methods, of the eight original constructor methods, introduced in Android API Level 1:

```
BitmapDrawable( )                            // This constructor was deprecated in API 4
                                             // and can be ignored

BitmapDrawable(Resources res)                // This constructor was deprecated in API 18
                                             // and can be ignored

BitmapDrawable(Bitmap bitmap)                // This constructor was deprecated in API
                                             // level 4 and can be ignored

BitmapDrawable(Resources res, Bitmap bitmap) // Creates Drawable using an external bitmap
                                             // resource

BitmapDrawable(String filepath)              // This constructor was deprecated in API
                                             // level 5 and can be ignored

BitmapDrawable(Resources res, String filepath) // Create a Drawable by decoding from a
                                             // file path

BitmapDrawable(InputStream is)               // This constructor was deprecated in API
                                             // level 5 and can be ignored

BitmapDrawable(Resources res, InputStream is) // Create Drawable decoding bitmap from input
                                             // stream
```

Because you will be casting the BitmapDrawable object, I will not cover all of these constructor methods here; however, suffice it to say that you can create a BitmapDrawable object by using an image file path, using an input stream, using another Bitmap object, using XML definition inflation, using another Bitmap object, or using a Resources object, as you will be doing.

If you want to define a BitmapDrawable using an XML definition file, use a <bitmap> XML tag to define this element. BitmapDrawable would be used with a Bitmap object, which handles management and transformation of raw bitmap graphics and ultimately will be the object that is used when drawing to the Canvas object, as you will notice in the code used in this chapter.

There are a number of XML properties, parameters, or attributes that can be used with Bitmap objects, which are outlined in Table 11-1.

*Table 11-1. BitmapDrawable Attributes Accessible Using XML Tag Parameters*

| Bitmap Attribute | Description of Bitmap Attribute Function |
|---|---|
| antialias | Enables or disables anti-aliasing (edge smoothing algorithm) |
| dither | Enables bitmap dithering for color-depth mismatch (ARGB8888 to RGB565) |
| filter | Enables or disables bitmap bilinear filtering for high-quality scaling |
| gravity | Defines the gravity constant setting to be used for the Bitmap object |
| mipMap | Enables or disables the mipMap hinting feature |
| src | Bitmap asset file identifier resource path |
| tileMode | Defines the overall Bitmap object tiling mode |
| tileModeX | Specifically defines the horizontal tiling mode |
| tileModeY | Specifically defines the vertical tiling mode |

# Using BitmapDrawable Object: Extract and Scale

Next, let's implement a BitmapDrawable object to obtain the Bitmap object data needed from the Drawable object that contains it. The Java statement **casts** the watchFaceDrawable Drawable to a **(BitmapDrawable)** with the following code, which can be seen error-free in Figure 11-31:

```
watchFaceBitmap = ( (BitmapDrawable) watchFaceDrawable ).getBitmap(); // Cast to a
(BitmapDrawable)
```

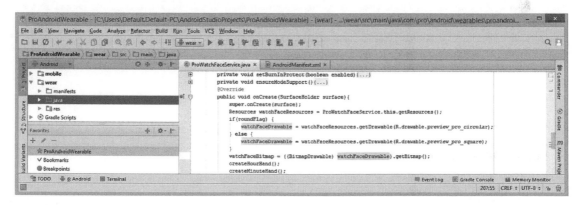

*Figure 11-31. Add a watchFaceBitmap object, and set it equal to the bitmap asset inside the watchFaceDrawable object*

This one compact line of Java code has the **watchFaceBitmap** Bitmap object, the **watchFaceDrawable** Drawable object (which contains your image resource), an undeclared BitmapDrawable object that is acting as a bridge between the Drawable asset in the APK file, and the raw bitmap that needs to live in the end-user's Android hardware device system memory.

What this statement is doing is setting the watchFaceBitmap Bitmap object equal to the result of a **.getBitmap()** method call, which was called off the casting structure, where the watchFaceDrawable object is cast into a BitmapDrawable using a **(BitmapDrawable) watchFaceDrawable** casting structure, which magically turns the Drawable object into a BitmapDrawable object.

Once the Drawable is cast into a BitmapDrawable, this .getBitmap() method call will work, that is, it will be a valid method call and will not throw an exception.

Now that you have the methods in place that will be needed for (and called from) the .onAmbientModeChanged() method from the WatchFaceService.Engine class, you'll need to make sure all of these various modes are supported when the smartwatch hardware goes into ambient mode.

## Scaling Bitmaps: Using the .createScaledBitmap() Method

The next area where you need to put code in place is inside the onDraw() method, where you need to insert a Bitmap object into the draw pipeline. Create an empty conditional if structure after the width and height value calculations, because you'll be using these values to determine if scaling is needed. The code, which is shown under construction in Figure 11-32, should look like this:

```
if(scaleWatchFaceBitmap) {
    // an empty conditional if statement thus far
}
```

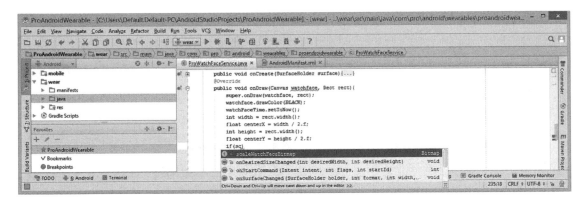

*Figure 11-32.  Add an if(scaleWatchFaceBitmap) conditional structure to ascertain if you need to scale the bitmap*

Inside the conditional if structure, evaluate if the scaledWatchFaceBitmap is unused (empty or null) or if it has different dimensions than a source bitmap. The Java code, as shown in Figure 11-33, should look like the following:

```
if ( scaleWatchFaceBitmap == null ||
     scaleWatchFaceBitmap.getWidth() != width ||
     scaleWatchFaceBitmap.getWidth() != height  ) { // Java code to be processed will go in here
     }
```

*Figure 11-33.* Add the boolean OR logic that determines if the scaleWatchFaceBitmap object is empty or needs setting

Inside the conditional if structure, if the bitmap needs scaling, call the **.createScaledBitmap()** method, off the Bitmap class, as shown in Figure 11-34, and load the scaleWatchFaceBitmap object with this result. The Java code, thus far, should look like this:

```
if ( scaleWatchFaceBitmap == null ||
     scaleWatchFaceBitmap.getWidth() != width ||
     scaleWatchFaceBitmap.getWidth() != height  ) {
     scaleWatchFaceBitmap = Bitmap.createScaledBitmap(watchFaceBitmap, width, height, true);
}
```

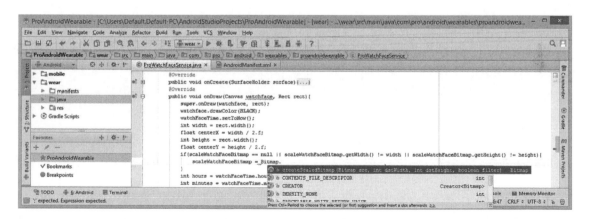

*Figure 11-34.* Inside the conditional if, call a Bitmap.createScaledBitmap() method off the scaleWatchFaceBitmap

As you can see in Figure 11-34, if you type in the **Bitmap** class name and press the **period** key, IntelliJ will give you a helper dialog pop-up, filled with all of the methods that apply. You can select the option that applies to what you want to do, in this case, **.createScaledBitmap(Bitmap src, int dstWidth, int dstHeight, boolean filter)**. The Java code, thus far, is error-free, and is shown in Figure 11-35.

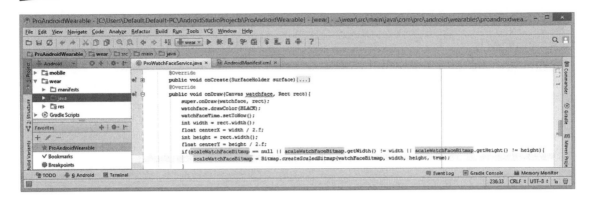

*Figure 11-35.  Pass the watchFaceBitmap object and watchface width and height into the .createScaledBitmap()*

Notice that if the scaleWatchFaceBitmap has not been used (null), this
.createScaledBitmap() method call will transfer the watchFaceBitmap object into the
scaleWatchFaceBitmap object, even if the width and height are the same! As you learned
in the previous section, this is how the method works, as it will return the original Bitmap
object if no scaling was required.

The next thing you need to do is draw the bitmap as the background, at the top left (0,0)
corner of the watch face screen. This is done using the .drawBitmap() method call. The Java
statement, as shown in Figure 11-36, should look like the following:

```
watchface.drawBitmap(scaleWatchFaceBitmap, 0, 0, null);
```

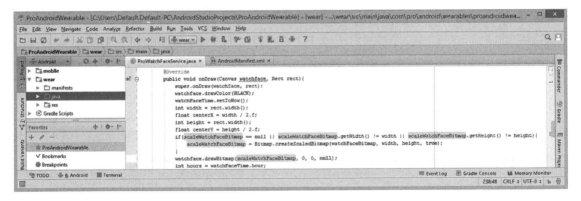

*Figure 11-36.  Call the .drawBitmap() method off the watchface Canvas object, using the scaleWatchFaceBitmap*

In case you're wondering, the null at the end of the method call parameter area references a
Paint object. If you have not defined a Paint object, to apply more screen drawing options to
your bitmap, then this would be null, as in empty or undefined. If you want to define further
options regarding how the Bitmap object is drawn (painted) on the screen, you would create
this Paint object, name it, load it (configure it), and use its name in the method call's last
parameter slot.

# Testing Background Bitmaps: Round vs. Square

Let's test the application using both AVD emulators to make sure that your Bitmap assets are now rendering where they should be behind the watch face design. As you can see on the right-hand side of Figure 11-37, your bitmap background for the round watch face seems to be using a square watch face bitmap asset, which means that the **roundFlag** is not getting set to **true**.

*Figure 11-37.  Test bitmap code in both AVD emulators*

Of course, there could also be some problem with the Bitmap object scaling, as this round watch face AVD seems to be zoomed in quite a bit. Let's make sure and create a couple of test images with text in them that says round and square. I'll use alpha channel transparency in the PNG32 image assets, so you will be able to see the Canvas object background (BLACK) color, since that line of code was left in the .onDraw() method and is currently being overdrawn by a Bitmap object. This will show you another level of flexibility; that is, seamlessly combining bitmaps and vector approaches to watch faces design. I'll include a round perimeter hoop in the round watch face image.

Copy the **round_face_text.png** and **square_face_test.png** image assets to the **/AndroidStudioProjects/ProAndroidWearable/wear/src/main/res/drawable-hdpi/** folder, the result of which can be seen on the right side of Figure 11-38.

*Figure 11-38. Add test bitmaps into the wear/src/main/res/drawable-hdpi folder using an OS file management utility*

Next, change the references to the watch face preview images that you were using to test the if(roundFlag) code to the watch_face_test images, as shown (highlighted) in Figure 11-39, using the following Java code:

```java
if(roundFlag) {
    watchFaceDrawable = watchFaceResources.getDrawable(R.drawable.round_face_test);
} else {
    watchFaceDrawable = watchFaceResources.getDrawable(R.drawable. square_face_test);
}
```

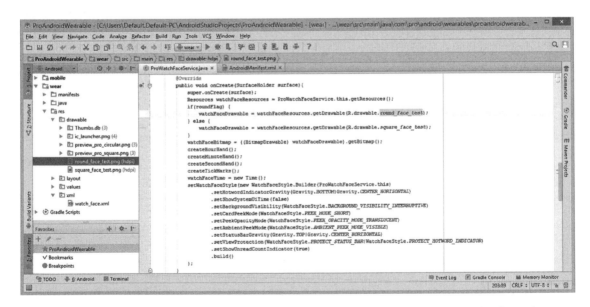

*Figure 11-39. Add if-else conditional structure that evaluates if the round watch face is being used and gets the correct resource*

Let's run this new configuration in both AVD emulators to confirm what is happening. As you can see in Figure 11-40, the scaling is being performed correctly, as the 320 pixel source is in the Round AVD pixel for pixel and the Square AVD is down-sampling to the 280 pixels that Android says a square watch face uses. You can tell by looking at the text (font) sizing.

*Figure 11-40. Test your Java code thus far in the Square and Round AVD emulators and make sure the code is working*

I Googled this ".isRound() not being set correctly" problem and found that a ton of developers are having problems with this issue, both on the AVDs as well as on actual smartwatch hardware. One of the solutions involved UI layout design workarounds using XML, but these do not apply to what you're doing here, which is writing directly to the Canvas object (admittedly an advanced approach). Therefore, I'm going to try to figure this one out for myself!

## Solving the roundFlag Problem: onCreate() to onDraw()

I am going to make the assumption that the onApplyWindowInsets() method is working and is setting the roundFlag variable correctly, and that the real problem I am having is with the timing of this method's execution. If the onCreate() method is being called first, then the roundFlag is not set to anything other than its default (false) value. So, the first thing that I am going to try is to put the code that is in the onCreate() method into the onDraw() method, after the width and height variable calculations.

As you can see in Figure 11-41, I am leaving some space around this code I moved so I can either move it back or refine it further, if needed.

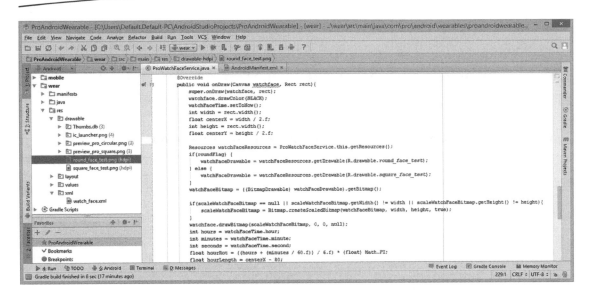

**Figure 11-41.** *Move the Bitmap and Drawable related code from the onCreate() method inside of the onDraw() method*

I tested the app in both AVDs to see if this was the problem, and it was, indeed, the problem, and the watch face now uses the correct bitmap asset, as shown in Figure 11-42.

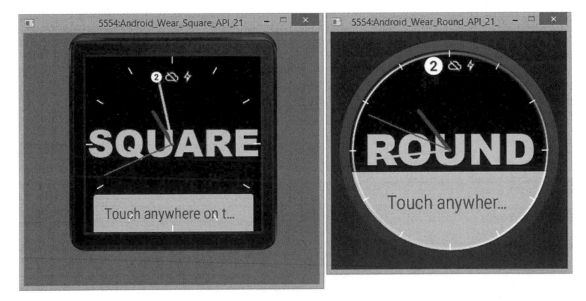

**Figure 11-42.** *Test new Bitmap code located in the .onDraw() method in both Round and Square AVD emulators*

This is great news because you will want to do all of the watch face design using the Android Canvas and Java 7 code, but this also causes some new optimization problems, as the onDraw() method is called frequently, and you only want to do these things one time, before the first draw, which is why I optimally tried to place these code statements in the onCreate() method.

Hopefully, the Android OS developers will change this method call order in the future so an onApplyWindowInsets() is called before onCreate(). I will show you how to make sure that these bitmap setup statements are only performed one time, so your app does not do all these operations more than one time, which would not be very optimal, because you only want to load a Resources object, determine the image resource to use (round or square), and then scale that resource, one single time, at application startup.

Let's optimize the bitmap portion of the .onDraw() method to implement the firstDraw boolean variable, so that these operations are only performed on the first onDraw() method call.

## Optimizing Your onDraw(): First Draw vs. Every Draw

At the top of the Engine class, create a boolean variable named **firstDraw** and set it equal to a **true** value, because, if you do not explicitly set this boolean variable, it will default to the false value. The Java code, which is shown (highlighted) in Figure 11-43, should look like the following:

```
boolean firstDraw = true;
```

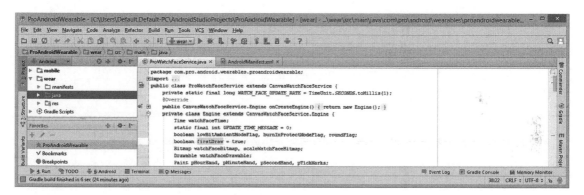

*Figure 11-43.   Create a boolean firstDraw variable at the top of the Engine class and set it equal to a true value*

The next thing you need to do is wrap the **if(firstDraw)** conditional statement around bitmap-related code, which you copied from the .onCreate() method into the onDraw() method. This will ensure that these statements are only executed one time, so that you do not waste memory or CPU cycles.

Because this will be true the first time you run the app, all you have to do is put the code you want executed one time in this structure, then set the firstDraw boolean value to be false at the end of the conditional statement, before the statement is exited. This will lock the statement to any future use, effectively allowing you to simulate .onCreate() functionality inside this .onDraw() method structure, as shown in Figure 11-44.

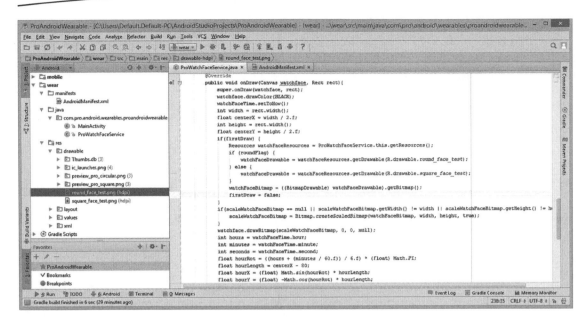

**Figure 11-44.** *Add an if(firstDraw) structure around the bitmap code, so that it is only performed on the first draw*

Because I'm kind of an optimization freak, I immediately started wondering if there were other statements inside this .onDraw() method that should be locked within this "only processed one time" box.

I decided to put the if(scaleWatchFaceBitmap) conditional structure that's after the if(firstDraw) statement inside the statement as well, so that all of the Bitmap object–related image processing is only done once, because hardware characteristics (screen resolution and shape) don't change during runtime, so you can do all of this processing on the first onDraw() cycle.

Copy the if(scaleWatchFaceBitmap) conditional structure from the outside of the if(firstDraw) conditional structure to the inside of it, after the if(roundFlag) in-else structure. Make sure that you paste this before the Java statement that sets the firstDraw boolean variable equal to false, at the end of the structure. Be sure to indent the if(scalewatchFaceBitmap) structure, as shown in Figure 11-45. If you test this in the AVD, you will see your second hand ticking away, which means this code is working.

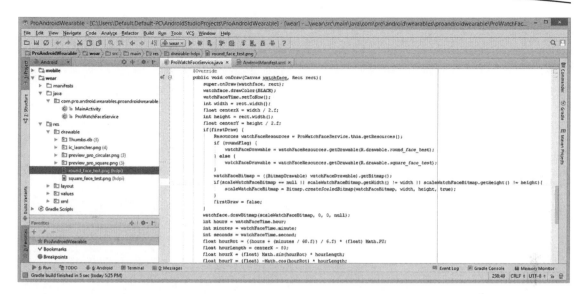

*Figure 11-45. Put the if(scaleWatchFaceBitmap) structure inside the if(firstDraw) structure before firstDraw=false*

Now all you have to do is develop bitmap assets for the other watch face modes, which you'll be learning about in Chapter 12, and you will have mastered watch face design from both vector as well as bitmap standpoints!

# Summary

In this chapter, you tested the Java code you have developed so far, using the AVD emulators. You learned the ins and outs of the AVDs, and then got into implementing the onApplyWindowInsets() method so that you can detect the round watch face type.

You learned about the Android classes you will need to implement the bitmap imagery as decorative backgrounds for the watch face design. These included the **Bitmap** class, the **Resources** class, and the **Drawable** class and its subclass the **BitmapDrawable** class.

After that, you learned how to implement these classes to load and display a bitmap asset in the background of the watch face design in the onDraw() method, using a conditional if structure to optimize the processing load on the smartwatch and smartphone device hardware.

In the next chapter, you will use GIMP image editing software to create the different digital image backgrounds to support the different modes the WatchFaces API requires that you support.

# WatchFaces Digital Imaging: Developing Multiple Mode Assets

Now that you have a bitmap asset installed as a background for your watch face design, it is time to get into digital imaging and the work process for creating different mode-compatible versions of a bitmap. You will be using GIMP (GNU Image Manipulation Program) in this chapter, because everyone has free access to it, but you could also use Photoshop CS.

First, I will discuss what digital image processing algorithms GIMP afford us for converting the interactive mode asset, which I am using as a PNG Indexed color (256 colors) asset, into grayscale and black and white modes for use with ambient mode, low-bit ambient mode, and burn-in protect mode.

Once you have created bitmap assets for interactive (PNG8), ambient (PNG3), ambient low-bit (PNG1), and ambient burn-in (PNG1) modes, you will get back into Java coding. You'll modify the custom methods to incorporate switching among these bitmap assets, so that both the vector assets as well as the bitmap assets conform to the mode requirements (or get close) and the vector and raster design components render (work) together seamlessly.

You will rework the .onDraw() method structure so that Bitmap objects will be rescaled whenever mode changes occur, since you will now be implementing a wide range of bitmap image assets across all of the modes.

You'll also overhaul the ensureModeSupport() method to optimize processing, add Bitmap object (background) support, add burn-in protection mode support, and expand the if-else-if structure using another else-if section.

# Ambient Mode Bitmap: GIMP Grayscale Image Mode

If you haven't already, download and install the latest version of GIMP at **gimp.org** and launch it. Use the **File ➤ Open** menu sequence, and access your **Open Image** dialog, shown in Figure 12-1, and open your **prowatchfaceint.png** file, which should be available in the file repository for this book.

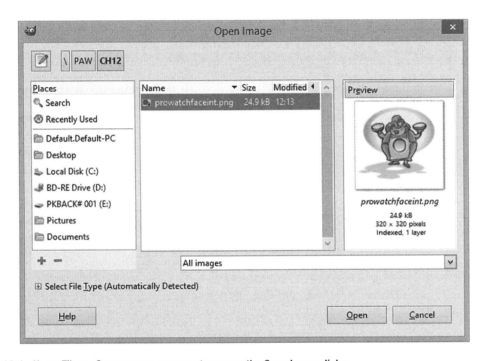

*Figure 12-1. Use a File ➤ Open menu sequence to access the Open Image dialog*

As you can see in the dialog, GIMP will allow you to navigate a disk drive folder hierarchy with the left **Places** pane in the dialog and will show you information about the digital image file you have selected, using the **Preview** pane seen on the right side of the dialog. The file I've selected is shown in the middle section of the dialog. Click the **Open** button in the lower right corner of the dialog and open the file you have selected.

Notice that I have already optimized this interactive mode source imagery using the **PNG8** file format, which uses 256 colors plus dithering. Using **dithering** allows you to simulate more than 256 colors. In this way, when you create the grayscale ambient mode image also using 256 levels of grayscale, this will also have dithering in place, making it appear as though there are more than 256 levels of gray in the ambient mode image. By using this digital image optimization approach, you'll be able to "preoptimize" the image assets for ambient mode as well as for the other required modes.

By preoptimizing the 8-bit imagery using dithering, you will be able to simulate more than 256 levels of grayscale, in ambient mode, allowing it to look like more than 256 colors (or for ambient mode, levels of gray). This is one of the advantages of optimizing 8-bit, indexed color dithered image assets; when you apply the grayscale algorithm to them (for ambient mode), the dithering also comes across, affording the ambient mode asset the same visual upgrade effect that dithering affords to the interactive mode asset with the exact same data footprint optimization (maybe even better).

To create this preoptimized ambient mode grayscale image, look under the **Image** menu in GIMP and find the **Mode** submenu. Click that right-facing arrow at the right side of the Mode menu option and drop down the sub-submenu. Select the **Grayscale** option, as shown at the top of Figure 12-2.

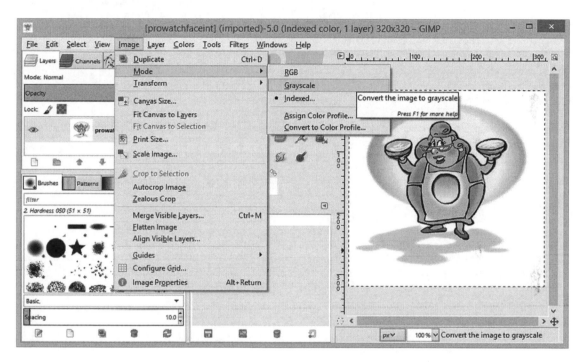

*Figure 12-2. Use an Image ➤ Mode ➤ Grayscale menu sequence to convert a color image to a grayscale image*

As you can see, GIMP has already ascertained that the image selected is an indexed 8-bit image. If the image is 24-bit (PNG24) or 32-bit (PNG32), then the **RGB** option would be bulleted. Once you select this Grayscale option, it will be bulleted, and a GIMP algorithm will be applied that will remove the **Hue** (color) from the image and leave only the **Luminosity** (brightness) values.

Now all you have to do is use the **File ➤ Export As** menu sequence, shown in Figure 12-3 on the left, to access the GIMP **Export Image** dialog.

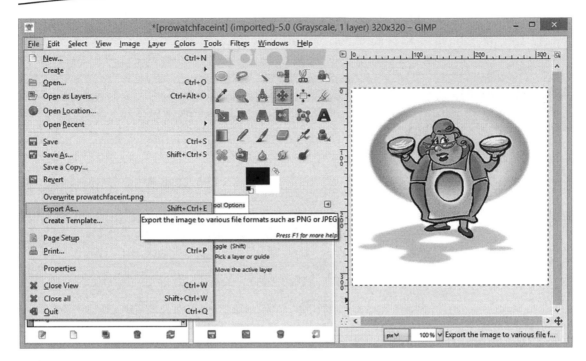

**Figure 12-3.** *Use the GIMP File ➤ Export As menu sequence to access the Export Image dialog (like Save As in Photoshop)*

Once you are in the Export Image dialog, which is shown in Figure 12-4, you can select the prowatchint.png in the center area, so that you don't have to type it all in again, and then change the "int" to "amb." Once you click the **Export** button, you'll get the Export Image as PNG options dialog. Leave all options unchecked to yield the smallest file size.

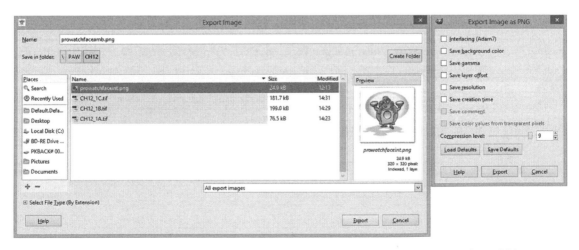

**Figure 12-4.** *To use grayscale ambient mode, name the file prowatchfaceamb.png and select maximum PNG compression*

This will give you the **8-bit grayscale** ambient mode image, which uses the maximum number of gray color values (256) your grayscale ambient mode image can support. Certainly some smartwatches can support 8-bit grayscale, however, some will reduce the image to fewer shades of gray, so I am going to show you how to optimize to lower bit level grayscale imagery in case you are targeting a smartwatch that only uses 16 shades of gray in ambient mode. I will also show you how to create bitmap images that only use eight shades of gray and still look great (and I will even show you how to make four shades of gray look acceptable). I will also cover the 1-bit (two shades of gray or black and white) low-bit ambient mode that is used by the ASUS ZenWatch.

# Low-Bit Mode Bitmaps: GIMP's Posterize Algorithm

The next thing you need to do is create **low-bit level ambient** mode imagery. Some smartwatches when they are not actively in use (being looked at) switch into an "ambient," low-power usage mode. For instance, the Sony SmartWatch 3 (SW3) uses a **transflective screen** (a technology that can be easily read in sunlight), which uses 16-bit (RGB 565) color when it is in interactive mode (as well as a backlight), and turns a backlight off in ambient mode in order to save power. So you could use color in Sony SW3 ambient mode, although the Google WatchFaces API documents suggest using lower-bit level grayscale.

This is why I am detailing this low-bit level grayscale optimization work process in this section of the chapter. Some smartwatch manufacturers will ultimately use fewer levels of gray than the 256 levels I mentioned earlier. Some may use 16 (**PNG4** 4-bit) levels of gray, but it could be even fewer. Check with your smartwatch manufacturer to find out just how low bit their ambient mode really is!

Armed with the knowledge of how many shades of gray (or color) your target smartwatch manufacturer supports in ambient mode, and with a work process that you'll be learning during this section of this chapter, you can even optimize for eight levels of gray (**PNG3**), or even a meager four levels of gray (**PNG2**), and still have the resulting bitmap image asset look good, especially on a smaller smartwatch face, which uses a relatively **fine dot pitch** (i.e., small pixel size).

To reduce the amount of grayscale levels in the 8-bit grayscale image, you will want to access the GIMP **Colors** menu, which can be seen at the top of Figure 12-5. Find the **Posterize** option and select that to access a dialog that will allow you to apply a color (or grayscale) reduction algorithm.

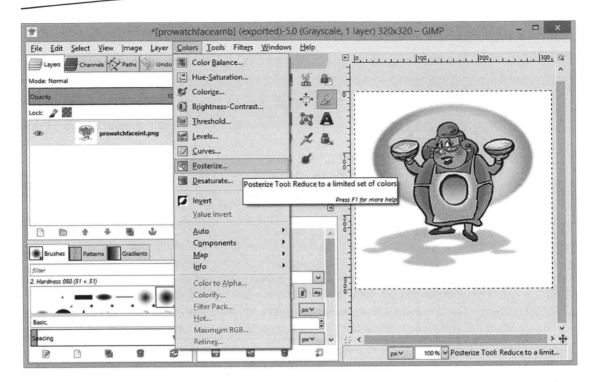

*Figure 12-5. Use GIMP Colors ➤ Posterize menu sequence to access the Posterize dialog to reduce the number of gray colors*

You want to select **even bit level numbers of colors**: **two colors** for **1-bit** or **four colors** for **2-bit** or **eight colors** for **3-bit** or **16 colors** for **4-bit** grayscale.

Yes, even shades of gray, or black and white, are considered colors! Let's launch the Posterize dialog next and create a PNG4 4-bit grayscale image.

As you can see in Figure 12-6, if you select the Preview check box, you'll be able to see the effects of this algorithm's slider setting in real time on the grayscale image.

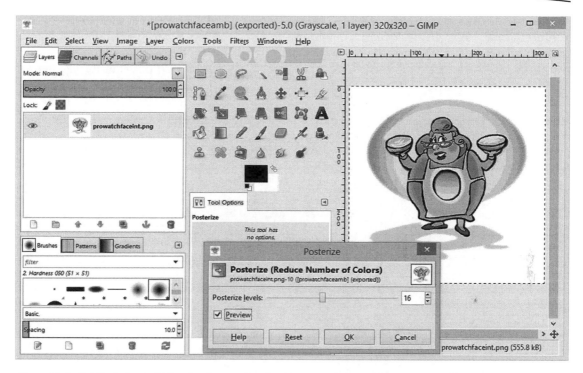

*Figure 12-6. Set Posterize to 16 levels of gray coloration to accommodate 4-bit grayscale ambient mode displays*

If you set the slider value to **16** (4-bit) color values, you will see the visual results are almost as good as the 256 color version, using 16 times less grayscale value data! There is some visible "banding," however, which is not so desirable. Later I will discuss how to mitigate Indexed Color Banding by using the technique called dithering, after I explain the Posterization algorithm. I will explain both work processes so you will know all of the primary ways you can achieve color value reductions using GIMP.

Currently, it is difficult to get physical specifications from a smartwatch manufacturer regarding the bit level used for grayscale (or even color) in ambient mode. Hopefully, manufacturers will release a technical information white paper covering this for Android Wearables developers in the future.

The most "low bit" that this ambient mode can go is the **1-bit** or **low-bit** ambient mode. Here you will be using 1-bit imagery to create your burn-in image.

Next, let's look at a different work process that allows you to access GIMP 2 dithering algorithms by using the **Indexed Color Conversion** dialog.

# Dithering Low-Bit Imagery: Indexed Mode Conversion

Because you can't access a **Floyd-Steinberg dithering algorithm** inside the Posterize dialog, which I feel is an oversight by the developers of GIMP 2, let's look at another work process (and the resulting dialog) that affords us more options in this area of color (grayscale in this case) reduction.

To access the Floyd-Steinberg dithering algorithm, you will need to use the **Indexed Color Conversion** dialog. This is accessed using the **Image ➤ Mode ➤ Indexed** menu sequence, as shown in Figure 12-7. This will change an image back to the Indexed Color mode, which you may recall is where it started. Going to Grayscale mode stripped out **Hue** values, leaving only **Luminosity** values.

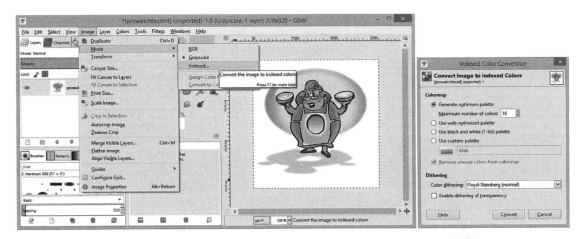

*Figure 12-7. Use the Image ➤ Mode ➤ Indexed menu sequence, and select the Floyd-Steinberg dithering algorithm*

Going back into the Indexed Image mode (in this case, it is grayscale, due to the source image data) will trigger an Indexed Color Conversion dialog. This is where you can find the Floyd-Steinberg dithering algorithm option, which you can see selected in the bottom right-hand corner of Figure 12-7.

Select the **Generate optimum palette** radio button and set a **Maximum number of colors** value of **16**, **8**, **4**, or **2**, and click the **Convert** button. As you can see in Figure 12-8, dithering that will be applied can make a significant quality difference in the resulting low-bit grayscale ambient imagery. The lower-right corner 1-bit ambient mode (nondithered) image has been inverted (I will discuss this work process next in the burn-in mode section) and the algorithm processed, so as to minimize the number of white pixels used.

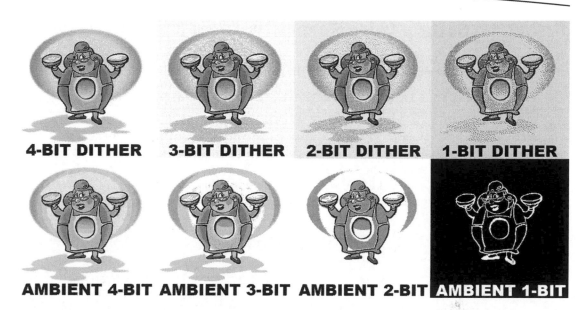

*Figure 12-8. As you can see, dithering will improve low-bit ambient mode image quality by an order of magnitude*

Once you have determined the level of low-bit grayscale supported by your target smartwatch manufacturer, you will export the file to the file name **prowatchfacelow.png**. If you have any doubt as to the number of gray level values that are supported, use the 1-bit approach, invert it (if needed), and then export your file. You want most of your screen to use black (off) pixel values. I will be covering **Invert** later in the **Burn-In Mode** section.

After you have the low-bit grayscale ambient mode Imagery that optimally fits the target smartwatch low-bit ambient mode (or ambient mode), use the GIMP **File ➤ Export As** menu sequence, as shown in Figure 12-3, and name the file **prowatchfacelow.png**, as shown In Figure 12-9 in the Name field, at the top of the dialog. Click the **Export** button to export the indexed color **PNG** file (selecting no options), which will be **PNG4** for 16 gray levels, **PNG3** for eight gray levels, **PNG2** for four gray levels, and **PNG1** for black and white.

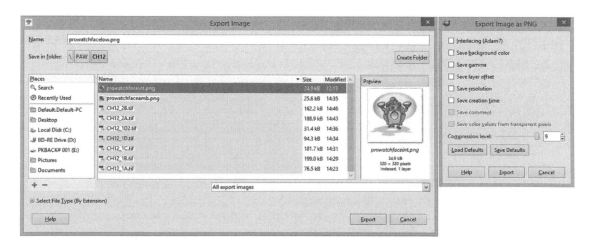

*Figure 12-9. Use a File ➤ Export As menu sequence to use an Export Image dialog to save prowatchfacelow.png*

# Creating a Burn-In Mode Bitmap: Using an Invert Algorithm

The next thing you need to create is the black and white only (1-bit) low-bit ambient mode graphic that will also be used for the burn-in mode.

The first step in this process is to **undo** whatever you did last, which was either the Posterization dialog or the Indexed Color Conversion dialog.

The GIMP Edit ➤ Undo menu customizes itself, based on your last operation, so if you had been using the Posterization dialog, it would be **Edit ➤ Undo Posterize** for this menu sequence. This can be seen in the top left corner of GIMP, as shown in Figure 12-10. The reason you would use Edit ➤ Undo is so you will have the full 8-bit 256 levels of grayscale image going into any algorithm.

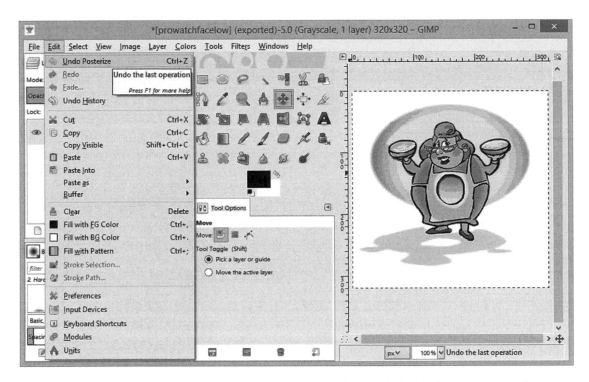

*Figure 12-10.  Use the Edit ➤ Undo work process to return to the 8-bit (256 color) original grayscale image data*

You would want to do this before you "reposterize" the image down to two colors (1-bit or PNG1) because you want to give this posterization algorithm the maximum amount of original grayscale to work with as you can, because the more data the algorithm has to work with, the better results it will produce.

Use the GIMP **Colors ➤ Posterize** menu sequence (as shown in Figure 12-5) and again access the Posterize dialog. This time around, you'll need to select **1-bit** color (**two** colors), which is the lowest possible posterization setting.

The reason for using a posterization algorithm is because you specifically do not want the 1-bit color dithering effect, seen at the top right corner in Figure 12-8. This is because you are trying to get a **line drawing effect** that will provide the desired result once you alpha blend the watch face black background color, which will dim the white pixels to a medium gray. This is to ensure that no burn in will occur in burn-in protect mode.

The setting and its results can be seen in Figure 12-11. As you can see, the results look good, and it will look even better on the smartwatch display, because the pixel pitch dot size screen density is finer. If you want to see what this will look like with .setAlpha(127), take a look at the far right panel in Figure 12-15.

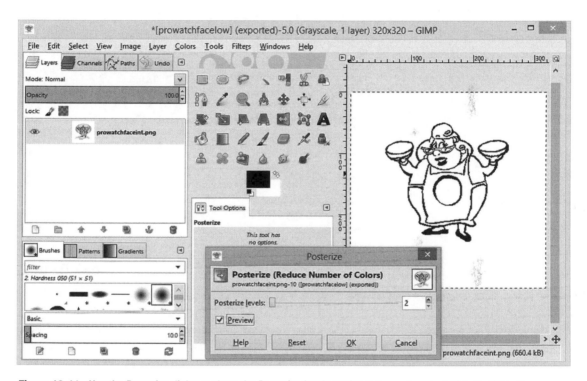

*Figure 12-11. Use the Posterize dialog and set the Posterize levels setting to two colors and click the OK button*

If you want even finer (thinner) lines, you can use the **zoom tool** (it is a magnifying glass) and the **eraser tool** (looks like your old school eraser) to manually erase some of the pixels in the thicker parts of your lines.

As you might have noticed, even though the graphic now uses only black and white color values, and no anti-aliasing, as required by burn-in mode, the problem now is that your watch face is turned on (white) instead of turned off (black). What you ultimately will need to do is the exact opposite result of what you have on your screen now. Fortunately, GIMP has an algorithm that will "flip" or "invert" pixel values, and luckily it works best with black and white imagery, as you might well imagine.

The way that you'll algorithmically handle flipping around white background color values to make the background black, while, at the same time, making the black line drawing white, is to use the GIMP **Invert** algorithm. This is also located under the **Colors** menu, a bit farther down on the menu than the Posterize option, as you can see in the middle of Figure 12-12.

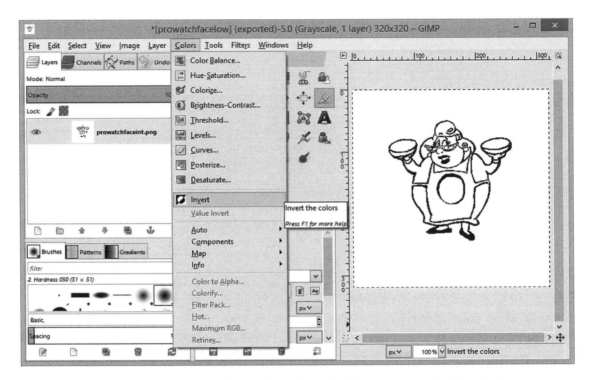

*Figure 12-12. To invert the black lines on white background to a black background, use the Colors ➤ Invert menu*

When you select this option, there is no dialog, as GIMP will simply invert the pixel color values for you, and your image will immediately become the white lines on a black background result you need for burn-in protect mode.

As you can see in Figure 12-13, you are very close to the result you need to have for screen burn-in protection, which is white pixels only in those places where you absolutely need them, with black pixels everywhere else. It's important to notice that you can edit lines in either of these invert modes to make the lines thinner if you wanted less pixels to be turned on in burn-in protection mode.

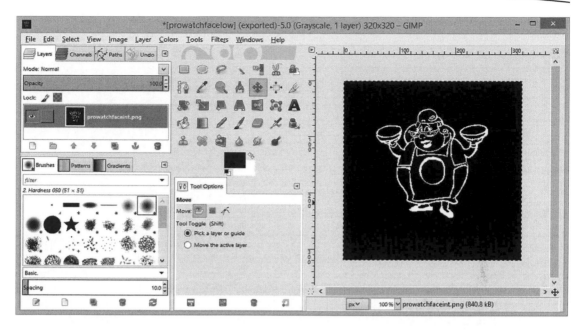

*Figure 12-13.* *The result of the Colors ➤ Invert menu sequence seen on the right preview area of GIMP 2.8.14*

In fact, that might be a great way to get some GIMP 2 digital image editing practice in. To edit these lines, use the magnifying glass tool to zoom in to the image, and then use the GIMP eraser tool to remove pixels until all of the lines in the image are one or two pixels wide.

To be meticulous, you could also remove the color (white) from the interior of those slippers; I'll leave this work for you to do yourself so you can get some practice using GIMP, because this is an important Android watch face development tool for you to master.

It is important to point out that these **BagelToons LLC** images belong to my client Ira H. Harrison-Rubin, and they should be used only to learn and practice within the context of this book, as BagelToons will be releasing all BagelToons artwork, including this one, as Watch Faces apps.

When you are done refining, use a **File ➤ Export As** menu sequence to access the **Export Image** dialog, as shown in Figure 12-14, and then name this digital image **prowatchfacelow.png**. Click the **Export** button (selecting no options), and export this **burn-in protect** image asset in the **PNG1** image file format.

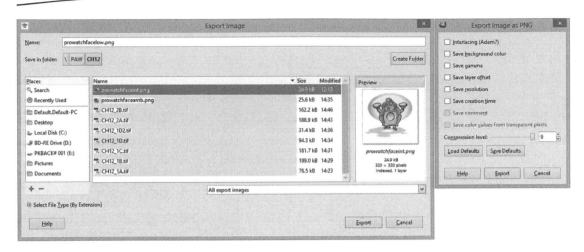

*Figure 12-14.  Use File ➤ Export As menu sequence to use the Export Image dialog to save prowatchfacelow.png*

If you are going to use 1-bit grayscale for **both** ambient low-bit and burn-in modes, then you will save the file as **prowatchfacelow.png** and use only **three bitmaps** to cover four modes. I've shown four bitmaps—interactive (8-bit color), ambient (3-bit, eight level grayscale), low-bit ambient (black and white), and burn-in protection (black and gray)—for one image, as shown in Figure 12-15, so you can compare these all together visually.

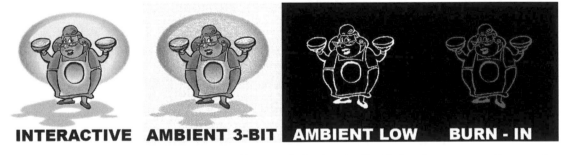

*Figure 12-15.  Four bitmap assets—8-bit color, 3-bit grayscale, black and white, black and gray—cover all your modes*

Now let's switch gears and get into some Java coding, so you can implement the first three bitmap files. Later on, you'll implement the burn-in mode, which can be achieved with a bitmap asset or with alpha blending in code.

# Multimodal Bitmaps: Changing Bitmaps Using Java

The next thing you will need to do to make the watch face app bitmap assets compatible with your mode detection code is to change the onDraw() and the ensureModeSupport() methods to add code that changes the bitmap asset.

First, move the **Resources watchFaceResources = ProWatchFaceService.this.getResources();** Java statement from the onDraw() method to the top of the private Engine class declarations area, as shown in Figure 12-16. Because more than one method is going to be using this Resource object, you have to make it more "visible."

*Figure 12-16. Move the Resources object declaration, naming and loading Java statement to the top of Engine*

Because you will be scaling more than one Bitmap object more than one time, that is, from interactive to ambient mode(s) and back to interactive mode, you need to move the if(scaleWatchFaceBitmap) structure **back outside** the if(firstDraw) conditional if() structure, as shown in Figure 12-17.

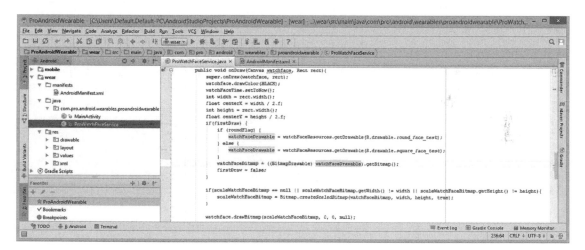

*Figure 12-17. Move if(scaleWatchFaceBitmap) structure outside the if(firstDraw) structure (evaluate on every draw)*

Notice that now the if(scaleWatchFaceBitmap) is its own structure, and you can trigger it to work its bitmap evaluation and scaling magic by setting the scaleWatchFaceBitmap object to the **null** (clearing or emptying its) value.

This is because part of the **Logical OR** structure for the if() conditional evaluator is **scaleWatchFaceBitmap = null**, so if you want what is inside this construct to be invoked, you simply set the object to null to call this rescaling logic for any of the bitmap assets you have created.

Before you get into rewriting the code in the .ensureModeSupport() method, you will need to install the assets you created earlier in the chapter using GIMP into the correct Android Studio project HDPI drawable resource folder.

Copy the prowatchfaceamb.png, prowatchfaceint.png, and prowatchfacelow.png bitmap assets from whichever folder you saved them in into the **/ProAndroidWearable/wear/src/main/res/drawable-hdpi/** folder, as shown in Figure 12-18.

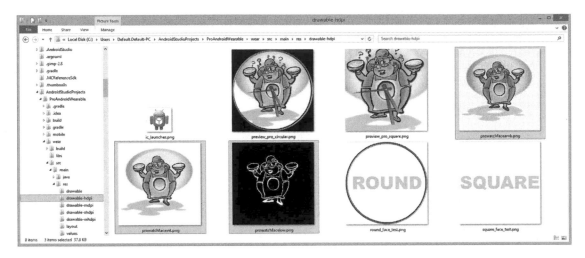

*Figure 12-18.   Copy 8-bit interactive, 3-bit ambient, and 1-bit low-bit ambient bitmaps into the project's /drawable-hdpi folder*

As you can see, I am using the three most highly optimized bitmap assets so that the fewest colors, levels of grayscale, and black and white are used and the smallest file size is achieved for the least power used by the smartwatch to display the imagery. As you can see in Figure 12-18, the visual quality is good, and here I am only using **256 colors** (interactive mode) **eight gray levels** (ambient mode) or **black and white** (low-bit or burn-in mode).

Now you're ready to modify the Java code for ambient mode and low-bit ambient mode so that the correct bitmap assets will be used. White watch face elements that worked well against a black background will be reset to use the Black color for maximum contrast against the White bitmap asset, except for the burn-in protect bitmap asset, where you will use White watch face design elements. Let's start with the grayscale bitmaps and then implement the Java code for indexed color and burn-in protect mode bitmap assets.

## Installing Bitmap Objects into Your Low-Bit Ambient Mode

Copy the **watchFaceDrawable** configuration statement with a **prowatchfacelow** asset reference and the watchFaceBitmap statement from the onDraw() method to the top of the if(enableLowBitAmbientMode) construct. The **Color** values remain **WHITE** as the background is black. The Java code for the if structure is seen, error-free, in Figure 12-19, and should look like the following:

```
if( enableLowBitAmbientMode ) {
    watchFaceDrawable = watchFaceResources.getDrawable(R.drawable.prowatchfacelow);
    watchFaceBitmap = ((BitmapDrawable) watchFaceDrawable).getBitmap();
    scaleWatchFaceBitmap = null;
    pHourHand.setAlpha(255);
```

```
pMinuteHand.setAlpha(255);
pSecondHand.setAlpha(255);
pTickMarks.setAlpha(255);
pHourHand.setColor(Color.WHITE);
pMinuteHand.setColor(Color.WHITE);
pSecondHand.setColor(Color.WHITE);
pTickMarks.setColor(Color.WHITE);
```

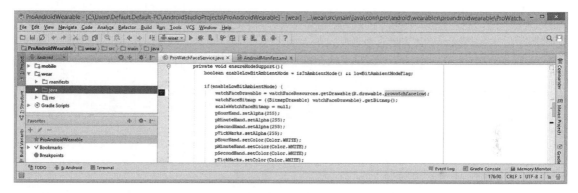

*Figure 12-19. Copy watchFaceDrawable and watchFaceBitmap code and add the scaleWatchFaceBitmap = null*

As you can see, the third line of code is a **scaleWatchFaceBitmap = null;** statement, which will **trigger** the if(scaleWatchFaceBitmap) conditional statement. The mode change that triggers this method will also trigger the image rescale code (if needed) due to this statement being in place after the first two.

Because the background image is now grayscale and primarily white, you will need to change the .setColor() method calls to reference the **Color.BLACK** constant, so that the tick marks and watch face hands will have maximum contrast against a background Bitmap object (grayscale digital image asset).

Next, you'll make changes to the .setAlpha() method call, add .setColor() method calls, and add the Bitmap object–related statements to the second **else-if(isInAmbientMode())** structure. You will again need to use the **BLACK** Color value constant due to the largely white background image used in the ambient mode, and you will also want to make the watch face design elements fully black, for maximum readability, as well as turn off the screen pixels for those watch face design elements. For this reason, you would also want to set your current **127** Alpha value to the fully opaque value of **255**. I have bolded the Java statements in this method structure that have been changed. The Java code, as shown in Figure 12-20, should now look like this:

```
} else if( isInAmbientMode() ) {
    watchFaceDrawable = watchFaceResources.getDrawable(R.drawable.prowatchfaceamb);
    watchFaceBitmap = ((BitmapDrawable) watchFaceDrawable).getBitmap();
    scaleWatchFaceBitmap = null;
    pHourHand.setAlpha(255);
    pMinuteHand.setAlpha(255);
    pSecondHand.setAlpha(255);
```

```
    pTickMarks.setAlpha(255);
    pHourHand.setColor(Color.BLACK);
    pMinuteHand.setColor(Color.BLACK);
    pSecondHand.setColor(Color.BLACK);
    pTickMarks.setColor(Color.BLACK);
```

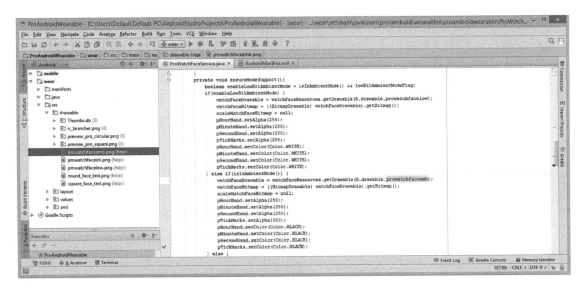

*Figure 12-20.  Add bitmap-related code, change Alpha values to 255, and change color values to Color.BLACK*

Next, let's modify the **else** portion of the if-else-if-else structure to add the Bitmap object–related statements that will set the Indexed Color image asset you're going to use for the watch face when it is in **interactive mode**.

# Refining Interactive Mode: Set Tick Marks Color to Black

The final else section of the conditional if-else structure that makes up a majority of the ensureModeSupport() method is what sets the interactive mode characteristics, if none of the other mode flags have been set. This section of code has the least changes, changing only the **pTickMarks** object to **Color.BLACK** and adding the bitmap-related Java statements that you added in the other sections. Your code, as shown in Figure 12-21, should look like this:

```
} else {
    watchFaceDrawable = watchFaceResources.getDrawable(R.drawable.prowatchfaceint);
    watchFaceBitmap = ((BitmapDrawable) watchFaceDrawable).getBitmap();
    scaleWatchFaceBitmap = null;
    pHourHand.setAlpha(255);
    pMinuteHand.setAlpha(255);
    pSecondHand.setAlpha(255);
    pTickMarks.setAlpha(255);
    pHourHand.setColor(Color.BLUE);
```

```
    pMinuteHand.setColor(Color.GREEN);
    pSecondHand.setColor(Color.RED);
    pTickMarks.setColor(Color.BLACK);
}
```

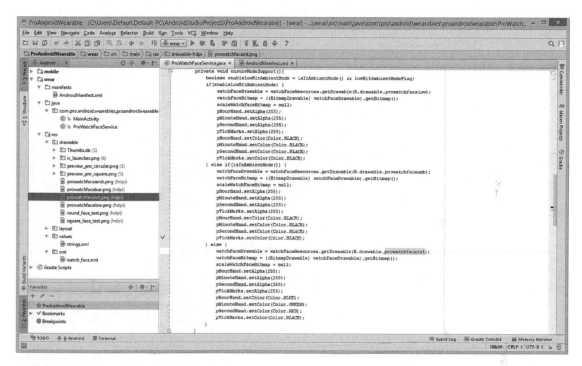

*Figure 12-21.  Add Bitmap object–related code at the top of the else structure, and change the pTickMarks to Color.BLACK*

Now that you have made the bitmap-related additions and Color changes that maximize readability to the existing Java code in the ensureModeSupport() method, let's test the interactive, ambient, and low-bit ambient modes next in the Square AVD emulator.

## Testing Interactive and Ambient Modes in the Square AVD

Make sure you have removed all occurrences of forced flag settings in the private Engine class, in other words, eliminate **lowBitAmbientModeFlag=true;** and **burnInProtectModeFlag=true;** code snippets. Next, use the **Run ➤ Run Wear** menu sequence and launch the Square AVD emulator. You can use the **Run ➤ Edit Configurations** menu sequence if you want to make sure your Square AVD emulator is the one that is currently selected.

Once the emulator starts and you load your Pro Watch Face, you'll see your SQUARE watch face test pattern, because you left that code in the firstDraw part of the .onDraw() method. If you were wondering why I did this, it was to show you how to display a different bitmap (say a legal disclaimer, behind the watch face, the first time it launches) on watch face startup.

It is fairly useful to know how to implement when you add the Round watch face decoration support in Chapter 13 covering watchface configuration dialogs. Optimally you would remove this code entirely and use only square bitmap assets for the watch face background.

However, I wanted to show you that it is possible to do this by using the if(firstDraw) technique, inside the .onDraw() method structure. In any event, once you see the SQUARE test screen, which is still called from the if(firstDraw) code, press the **F7** key and you will see the ambient mode bitmap asset, which is shown on the left-hand side in Figure 12-22.

*Figure 12-22. Use Settings ➤ Change watch face ➤ Pro Watch Face series, and F7 to test ambient mode*

If you toggle the F7 key again, you will trigger the code that is in the **else** construct inside the .ensureModeSupport() method. The color result can be seen on the right-hand side of Figure 12-22, and as you can see, the positioning of the Status Bar icon and the Peek Card with the background artwork is nothing short of perfection.

To test the low-bit (1-bit color in the case of this optimized asset) mode, you need to again install a **lowBitAmbientModeFlag=true;** forced mode switch in the onAmbientModeChanged() method right after the **super.onAmbientModeChanged()** method call statement, as shown in Figure 12-23.

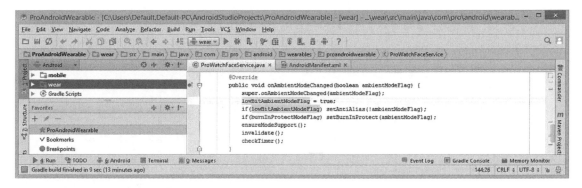

**Figure 12-23.** *Set the lowBitAmbientModeFlag boolean to a true value in the onAmbientModeChanged() method*

Forcing this low-bit, ambient mode flag to be set to the "on" state, which should be done right before the **if(lowBitAmbientModeFlag)** turns off anti-aliasing in the code, as you can see in Figure 12-24, also calls the ensureModeSupport() method, which installs low-bit (1-bit color) graphics.

**Figure 12-24.** *Use Settings ➤ Change watch face ➤ Pro Watch Face series, and F7 to test low-bit ambient mode*

Now, when you use the **Run ➤ Run Wear** and launch the AVD emulator, and then use **Settings ➤ Change watch face ➤ Pro Watch Face ➤ F7 key**, you will get the ambient mode with the low-bit mode enabled, as shown on the left side of Figure 12-24.

The next thing you need to do is create the burn-in mode version of the low-bit ambient mode bitmap, which will use **gray** color values instead of white ones. You will use GIMP to change the white pixels to a **50% gray** color value, which will match the Android **Color.GRAY** constant perfectly, providing a gray "burn-in" version of the low-bit ambient mode.

After that you will add the **if(enableBurnInAmbientMode)** construct into the enableModeSupport() method, which sets the correct Bitmap and Color values.

# Android Wear Burn-In Mode: Bitmap and Java Code

To be thorough about the watch face design, let's implement a burn-in mode image and Java code, creating burn-in protection with this low-bit design!

## Creating Burn-In Mode Bitmaps: GIMP Brightness-Contrast

Open GIMP if it's not still open, and use the **File ➤ Open** menu sequence to open your **prowatchfacelow.png** file. You are going to "dim" the white light intensity for the bitmap by 50%, matching the Android **Color.GRAY** constant.

As you can see in Figure 12-25, the way you are going to achieve this in GIMP is by using the **Colors ➤ Brightness-Contrast** menu sequence, which will open a dialog that will allow you to dim the light (brightness) that is coming out of the white pixels in the watch face design. Pretty cool!

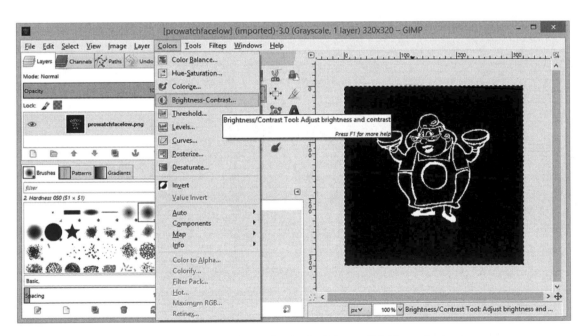

*Figure 12-25. Open the prowatchfacelow.png file and invoke the Colors ➤ Brightness-Contrast menu sequence*

The Brightness-Contrast dialog, which is shown on the right side of Figure 12-26, will allow you to set **Presets** at different brightness (or contrast) settings. This is done by clicking the plus sign (+) icon when you've set a setting you want to save. You could try it now and save a setting as "Android 50% Gray Burn-In Protect Mode Preset," for instance.

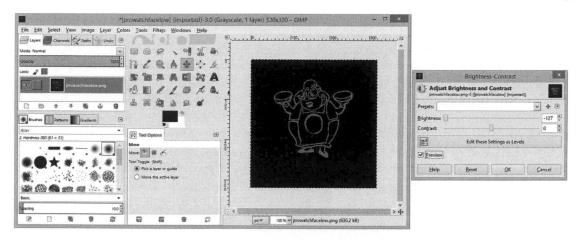

*Figure 12-26. Adjust the Brightness slider all the way to the left to reduce the brightness by 50% (or 127 of 255)*

Drag the **Brightness** slider to the left to the **-127** value, which is really 128, because you count from zero, which is exactly **half** of the 256 values you have with the 8-bit grayscale range. Make sure your **Preview** check box is selected, so you can see the modification in real time, then click the **OK** button, which will complete the operation and apply the algorithm.

Next, you need to save the burn-in mode digital image asset using the GIMP **File ➤ Export As** work process, which is shown in Figure 12-27, and name the file **prowatchfacebur.png** using the same 15-character format.

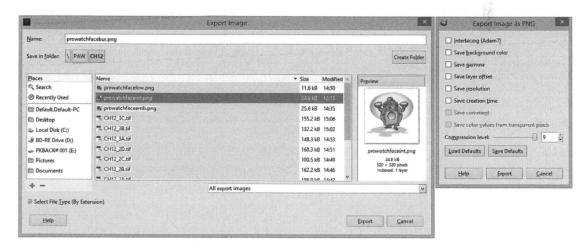

*Figure 12-27. Use File ➤ Export As menu sequence to use the Export Image dialog to save prowatchfacebur.png*

Now you're ready to get back into Java coding and implement burn-in protect mode in the **enableModeSupport()** method by inserting a new **if-else** section.

# Burn-In Protection in Java: if(enableBurnInAmbientMode)

The first thing you will need to do in the ensureModeSupport() method structure is to add a boolean enableBurnInAmbientMode variable at the top of the method structure. You will set it equal to a Logical AND condition, which will return a **true** value if **isInAmbientMode()** returns **true AND** the **burnInProtectModeFlag** is set to a **true** value. Otherwise, this will evaluate to false, as burn-in protection requires ambient mode to be on and the burn-in manufacturer support constant to be in place and specified.

After this new boolean flag is created inside the private method, you will need to add an **if-else** conditional section after the low-bit ambient section and before the ambient mode only section. The end of the method is the final else section, which covers the interactive mode settings.

This **if(enableBurnInAmbientMode)** construct should load a **watchFaceDrawable** object with the **prowatchfacebur.png** image asset you just created and then extract the new burn-in mode Bitmap object from the Drawable with the **.getBitmap()** method, placing that in the **watchFaceBitmap** object. Once this is accomplished, you can set the **scaleWatchFaceBitmap** object to **null**. This will then trigger the rescaling evaluation in your onDraw() method, because you have changed bitmap assets for a new mode, and this may be necessary.

As an optimization technique, instead of using the 127 alpha channel value to create the 50% gray value, as you did previously, I am going to use a 255 (Fully On) Alpha value and the Android OS Color.GRAY constant to set the color value for the watch face hands and tick marks.

In case you are wondering why using this Android Color.GRAY constant is an optimization, if you are using an alpha channel value of 255, it is because Android will not invoke its blending algorithm, which can be processing intensive. Also, you don't want the bright pixels that would be created by blending a White color with the Gray color used in the burn-in protection image you created.

You'll notice in the Java code listing for the ensureModeSupport() method, which I am going to include here in its entirety, since you are now done implementing all of these modes and their Bitmap objects, that you are not using any alpha blending whatsoever with these bitmap image assets, so you have applied this optimization technique across this entire method. If you are going to use background bitmaps, you may decide to remove these calls!

The finished .ensureModeSupport() method can be seen in Figure 12-28, and the Java code should look like the following method structure:

```
private void ensureModeSupport(){
    boolean enableLowBitAmbientMode = isInAmbientMode() && lowBitAmbientModeFlag;
    boolean enableBurnInAmbientMode = isInAmbientMode() && burnInProtectModeFlag;
    if (enableLowBitAmbientMode) {
        watchFaceDrawable = watchFaceResources.getDrawable(R.drawable.prowatchfacelow);
        watchFaceBitmap = ((BitmapDrawable) watchFaceDrawable).getBitmap();
        scaleWatchFaceBitmap = null;
        pHourHand.setAlpha(255);
        pMinuteHand.setAlpha(255);
        pSecondHand.setAlpha(255);
```

```java
        pTickMarks.setAlpha(255);
        pHourHand.setColor(Color.WHITE);
        pMinuteHand.setColor(Color.WHITE);
        pSecondHand.setColor(Color.WHITE);
        pTickMarks.setColor(Color.WHITE);
    } else if (enableBurnInAmbientMode) {
        watchFaceDrawable = watchFaceResources.getDrawable(R.drawable.prowatchfacebur);
        watchFaceBitmap = ((BitmapDrawable) watchFaceDrawable).getBitmap();
        scaleWatchFaceBitmap = null;
        pHourHand.setAlpha(255);
        pMinuteHand.setAlpha(255);
        pSecondHand.setAlpha(255);
        pTickMarks.setAlpha(255);
        pHourHand.setColor(Color.GRAY);
        pMinuteHand.setColor(Color.GRAY);
        pSecondHand.setColor(Color.GRAY);
        pTickMarks.setColor(Color.GRAY);
    } else if ( isInAmbientMode() ) {
        watchFaceDrawable = watchFaceResources.getDrawable(R.drawable.prowatchfaceamb);
        watchFaceBitmap = ((BitmapDrawable) watchFaceDrawable).getBitmap();
        scaleWatchFaceBitmap = null;
        pHourHand.setAlpha(255);
        pMinuteHand.setAlpha(255);
        pSecondHand.setAlpha(255);
        pTickMarks.setAlpha(255);
        pHourHand.setColor(Color.BLACK);
        pMinuteHand.setColor(Color.BLACK);
        pSecondHand.setColor(Color.BLACK);
        pTickMarks.setColor(Color.BLACK);
    } else {
        watchFaceDrawable = watchFaceResources.getDrawable(R.drawable.prowatchfaceint);
        watchFaceBitmap = ((BitmapDrawable) watchFaceDrawable).getBitmap();
        scaleWatchFaceBitmap = null;
        pHourHand.setAlpha(255);
        pMinuteHand.setAlpha(255);
        pSecondHand.setAlpha(255);
        pTickMarks.setAlpha(255);
        pHourHand.setColor(Color.BLUE);
        pMinuteHand.setColor(Color.GREEN);
        pSecondHand.setColor(Color.RED);
        pTickMarks.setColor(Color.BLACK);
    }
}
```

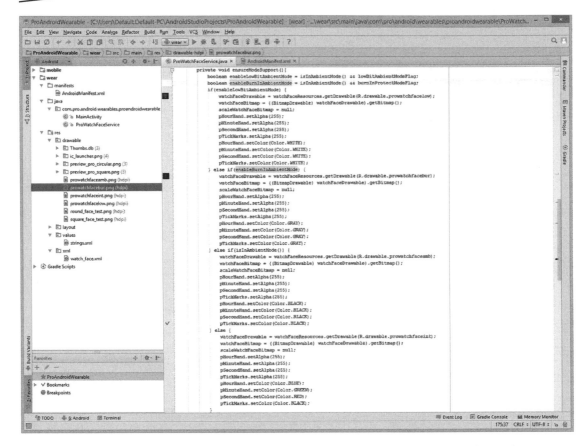

*Figure 12-28.* *Add an else if(enableBurnInAmbientMode) construct with Color.GRAY and prowatchfacebur image*

Now it's time to test the burn-in protection mode's Java code, as well as the bitmap digital asset, which you created earlier in this section using the GIMP Brightness-Contrast dialog.

# Testing the Burn-In Protect Mode Bitmap and Java Code

Open the .onAmbientModeChanged() method structure and remove the forced **lowBitAmbientModeFlag=true;** boolean flag statement, which you used to test low-bit ambient mode. Instead, here you will add in the forced **burnInProtectModeFlag=true;** boolean flag statement, which you'll now utilize to test the burn-in protection mode.

The .onAmbientModeChanged() method structure, which can be seen in Figure 12-29, should look like the following Java method structure:

```
@Override
public void onAmbientModeChanged(boolean ambientModeFlag) {
    super.onAmbientModeChanged(ambientModeFlag);
    if(lowBitAmbientModeFlag) setAntiAlias(!ambientModeFlag);
    burnInProtectModeFlag = true;
```

```
    if(burnInProtectModeFlag) setBurnInProtect(ambientModeFlag);
    ensureModeSupport();
    invalidate();
    checkTimer();
}
```

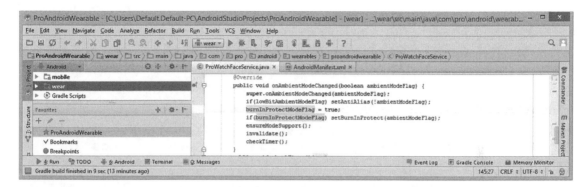

*Figure 12-29.* Set burnInProtectModeFlag equal to true, forcing the Burn-In Protect Mode to test the bitmap

Use a **Run ➤ Run Wear** work process in IntelliJ and test the code and Bitmap object using an Android Wear Square AVD emulator. As you can see in Figure 12-30, you've achieved a 50% dimmed burn-in mode version of low-bit mode.

*Figure 12-30.* Use Settings ➤ Change watch face ➤ Pro Watch Face series, and the F7 key to test ambient burn-in mode

It's important to note that I'll be covering Round AVD emulator and round watch face design principles and techniques by adding additional Java code in the next chapter, which covers how to allow users to customize the watch face design. The reason for this is primarily an optimization-driven decision. Why provide round and square image assets for watch face design when the square asset can be used for both? Round watch face **decorations**, such as a decorative **rim**, for instance, can be added by the end users for their own customization decorations. In this way, even a square watch face can feature round watch face design decorations if the user wishes to make that happen. This adds value to watch face design, via the user interface.

# Summary

In this chapter, you learned how to create, using GIMP, and how to implement, using your enableModeSupport() and onDraw() methods, a plethora of different watch face design modes. Some of these low-power modes will be required by smartwatch manufacturers, depending on the display technology.

First, I discussed how to take an optimized interactive mode bitmap image asset and convert it into a grayscale image, which ambient mode usually requires and Android recommends.

After that, you learned how to reduce the number of gray colors or levels that the image asset uses, so you can optimize this for certain lower-bit modes that some manufacturers smartwatch products require. The Sony SmartWatch 3, for instance, has a 3-bit, or eight levels of gray, ambient mode, and now you know how to perfectly optimize your bitmap for this using a Floyd-Steinberg dithering algorithm.

After you created several digital image assets, you also learned how to add Java code to the .enableModeSupport() method structure, as well as how to modify the onDraw() method structure so that every time the mode changes, the bitmap assets will be reevaluated and rescaled, if necessary, to fit the smartwatch screen if its resolution differs from the image asset.

In the next chapter, you will learn how to use the other side (or component) of an Android Wear application, the "mobile" side, as it is called in Android Studio (IntelliJ). For this topic, the Java coding and XML markup get even more complex. Therefore, the next chapter will serve to "bridge" this watch face design section of the book with the other Android (non-WatchFaces API) Wear topics chapter of the book (Chapter 17).

<br>

Chapter 13

# Watch Face Configuration Companion Activity: Google Mobile Services

Now that you have the basic bitmap and vector watch face design working in all display modes, it's time to switch over to mobile (smartphone) devices and create the watch face "feature selector" application, which will allow your users to customize their very own watch face designs. This will allow you to charge money for your watch faces applications because they will be customized watch face generator applications, not just simple watch faces.

This is as complex as watch face design itself is, but in a different way. In this chapter, you will be learning about the **Google API Client** Java interface, which is used to integrate **Google Play Services** into your watch face wearable apps.

This involves using a series of **com.google.android.gms** packages and their classes, which is the bulk of what I'll be covering during this chapter, along with the creation of one class that will run on the user's smartphone and another that will be a listener class that will reside in the wear section of the project. Google Mobile Services (GMS) is the Android Wear cloud!

You will learn about the Android GMS classes and interfaces that can be used to create Wear Companion smartphone applications. They include APIs such as the **GoogleApiClient**, which allows you to create a Google Play Services "client." Other Wear APIs include the **DataApi**, **DataItem**, **DataMap**, **DataMapItem**, **ComponentName**, **MessageEvent**, **WatchFaceCompanion**, and even the **CompanionResult**. You'll also learn about the Android **AlertDialog** class and the Android **Uri** class and how they are used in WatchFace app development.

# Creating a ProWatchFaceCompanionConfigActivity

In this section, you'll create the foundation for the dialog on the watch face users' phone that will allow them to configure the watch face design characteristics. The more control you give the user over their watch face design, the more you will be able to charge for your watch face application. You will add an **<activity>** tag to the AndroidManifest.xml file that is located in the mobile portion of your Android Studio project. Then you will create an empty **ProWatchFaceCompanionConfigActivity.java** structure in the mobile component of your project, and then learn about the Android **GoogleApiClient** public interface before you actually write Java code to implement this class, which will provide a UI for your watch face.

## The Mobile App: Adding Your Activity to AndroidManifest

Close all your open edit tabs relating to the **wear** portion of your Android Studio project and then open the **mobile** section of the project, as shown in Figure 13-1. In the **manifests** folder, right-click **AndroidManifest.xml** and select the **Jump to Source** option to open this file in an editing tab.

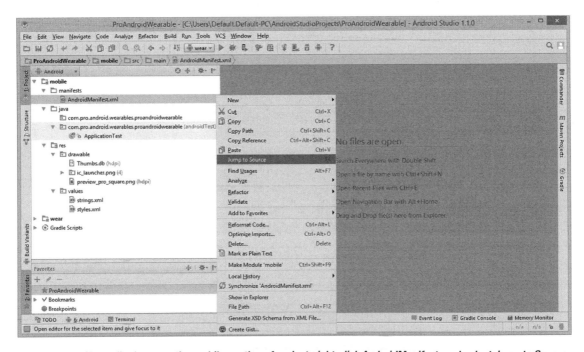

*Figure 13-1. Close all tabs, open the mobile section of project, right-click AndroidManifest, and select Jump to Source*

Add a child **<activity>** tag inside the parent **<application>** tag and name it **ProWatchFaceCompanionConfigActivity** with an **app_name** label. Add a child **<intent-filter>** tag inside the <activity> tag. Inside this add an **<action>** child tag with a **CONFIG_DIGITAL** action constant as well as two **<category>** child tags, with **COMPANION_CONFIGURATION** and **DEFAULT** constants. Notice that I also added a **<uses-sdk>** tag at the top of the manifest, with a **Minimum SDK** Version

API Level **18** and **Target SDK** Version of API Level **21**. The <uses-permission> tags add **PROVIDE_BACKGROUND** and **WAKE_LOCK** functions. Your XML markup, as shown in Figure 13-2, should look like the following:

```
<manifest xmlns:android=http://schemas.android.com/apk/res/android
    package="com.pro.android.wearables.proandroidwearable">
    <uses-sdk android:minSdkVersion="18" android:targetSdkVersion="21" />
    <uses-permission android:name="com.google.android.permission.PROVIDE_BACKGROUND" />
    <uses-permission android:name="android.permission.WAKE_LOCK" />
    <application android:allowBackup="true"
        android:label="@string/app_name" android:icon="@drawable/ic_launcher"
        android:theme="@style/AppTheme" >
        <activity
            android:name=".ProWatchFaceCompanionConfigActivity"
            android:label="@string/app_name" >
            <intent-filter>
                <action android:name="com.pro.android.wearables.proandroidwearable.
                CONFIG_DIGITAL" />
                <category android:name=
                            "com.google.android.wearable.watchface.category.
                            COMPANION_CONFIGURATION" />
                <category android:name="android.intent.category.DEFAULT" />
            </intent-filter>
        </activity>
    </application>
</manifest>
```

*Figure 13-2. Add an <activity> parent tag for ProWatchFaceCompanionConfigActivity and <intent-filter> child tag*

As you may have noticed, IntelliJ is giving a red text error highlight on the android:name parameter value of .ProWatchFaceCompanionConfigActivity, because you have not yet created that Java file. You will be rectifying that in the next section of the chapter, so this will disappear very soon!

While you are at it, let's open the /mobile/res/values/strings.xml file and give the Activity an app_name of Pro WatchFace Options so that the label for the application describes what it does. This is shown in Figure 13-3.

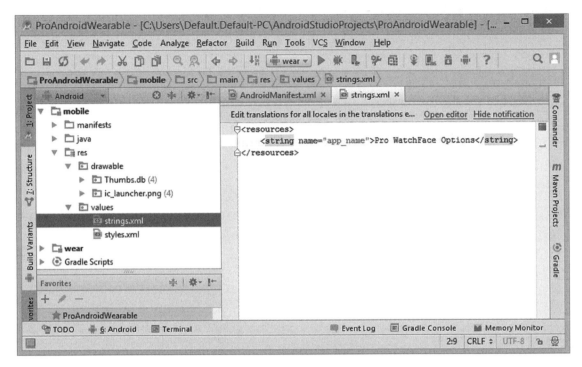

*Figure 13-3. Edit the app_name variable in /res/values/strings.xml and name the Activity Pro WatchFace Options*

Next, you need to create a ProWatchFaceCompanionConfigActivity Java class.

## The Java Class: Creating a WatchFace Companion Activity

Let's create a new Java class by right-clicking the mobile java folder, then selecting the New ➤ Java Class context-sensitive menu sequence, as is shown on the left side of Figure 13-4 (numbered as step 1). In the **Choose Destination Directory** dialog, select the main package (not the androidTest option) and click the **OK** button. In the **Create New Class** dialog, name your class **ProWatchFaceCompanionConfigActivity**, set **Kind** as the **Class**, and click the **OK** button to create a watch face design configuration Activity class.

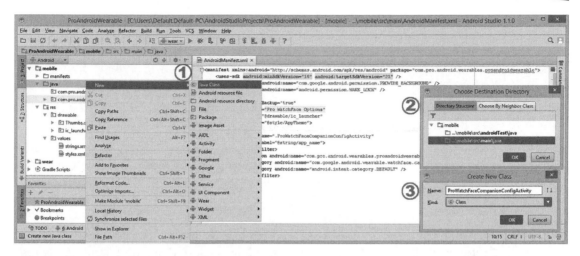

*Figure 13-4.* *Create the ProWatchFaceCompanionConfigActivity.java file to remove the red error highlight*

When I typed in the package name, I got a red error highlight, which can be seen at the top of Figure 13-5. When I looked inside the IntelliJ Project management pane, I noticed that IntelliJ had not followed my instructions, as shown in Figure 13-4 numbered 2, and put my class in the **androidTest** folder where it subsequently generated the "not the correct package path" error.

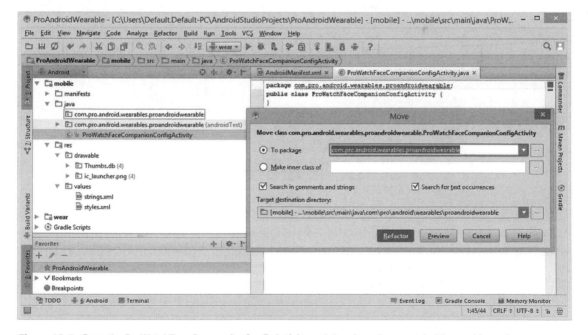

*Figure 13-5.* *Drag the ProWatchFaceCompanionConfigActivity and drop it on the proandroidwearable package*

The way that I rectified this error (on the part of IntelliJ) was to **drag** the Java class file out of the androidTest folder and drop it on the normal (non-androidTest) package folder. This caused the Move Class dialog to appear, where I clicked the **Refactor** button to move the class to the correct folder and set the internal "factors" (pointers) for everything correctly, so that the compiler can "see" how everything goes together. This can be seen in Figure 13-5.

Now you can add the Java **extends** keyword and the **Activity** class that you'll need to extend to make this class into an Android Activity, which is used to hold user interface designs, for the most part.

You will additionally need to add the Java **implements** keyword, because you are going to be specifying three Java interfaces. These will be needed for communication between your smartphone and the smartwatch hardware.

You can see both of these Java keywords in place in Figure 13-6 along with the IntelliJ pop-up helper dialog, which is showing the two interfaces and one nested class that are part of the **GoogleApiClient** interface. You will be learning about GoogleApiClient in the next section after you create this empty code infrastructure so you can see what's required to implement a basic (that is, empty) watch face companion configuration Activity class, public interface, and overridden (@Override keyword) method infrastructure.

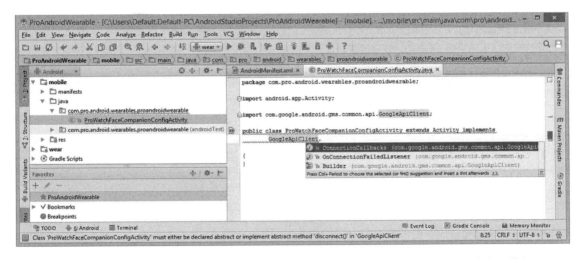

*Figure 13-6. Implement the GoogleApiClient class's ConnectionCallbacks interface using a pop-up helper dialog*

After the implements keyword, type in the GoogleApiClient interface and a period, which will bring up the pop-up helper dialog, where you can select a **ConnectionCallbacks (com.google.android.gms.common.api.GoogleApiClient)** option. Double-click this option if you want IntelliJ to write the code for you. Do the same thing for the **OnConnectionFailedListener** interface as well, which is also shown in the pop-up helper dialog in Figure 13-6.

Once you implement the GoogleApiClient interfaces, you will want to add in the ResultCallback public interface, which you can see I have added in the middle of Figure 13-7. Your completed (empty) Java class declaration would look like the following Java structure, which can also be seen in Figure 13-7:

```
public class ProWatchFaceCompanionConfigActivity extends Activity implements
        GoogleApiClient.ConnectionCallbacks, GoogleApiClient.OnConnectionFailedListener,
        ResultCallback<DataApi.DataItemResult> {  // Your Java class code will go in here  }
```

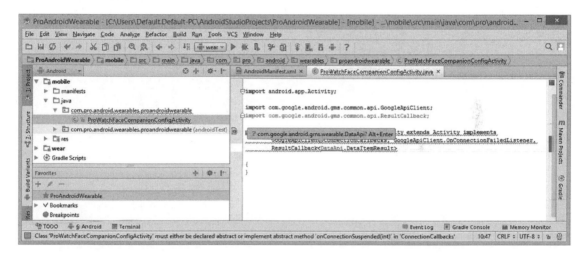

*Figure 13-7.  Add the ResultCallback<DataApi.DataItemResult> interface; import the DataApi class with Alt+Enter*

As you can see in Figure 13-7, you will need to use an **Alt+Enter** keystroke combination to have IntelliJ write the DataApi import statement for you.

As you'll notice in Figure 13-8, as well as in IntelliJ, there is an error suggestion lightbulb icon on the left. Drop down this how-to-correct error suggestion menu and select the **Implement Methods** option, which opens a **Select Methods to Implement** dialog, as shown on the right side of Figure 13-8.

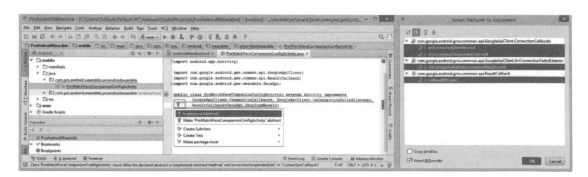

*Figure 13-8.  Drop down the error suggestion, and select the Implement Methods option; implement all methods*

Leave all of the required methods that need to be overridden selected and click the **OK** button, and IntelliJ will write the entire class structure for you. The resulting empty class structure can be seen in Figure 13-9.

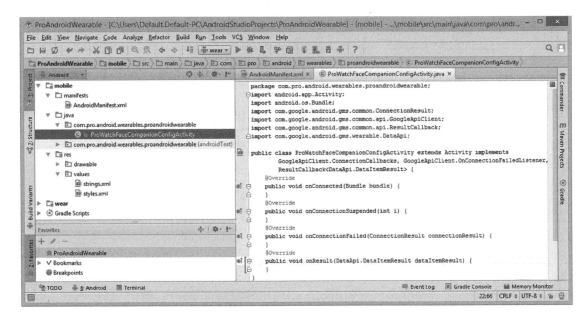

*Figure 13-9. Empty ProWatchFaceCompanionConfigActivity, with six import statements, four required methods*

The next thing you need to do is add the <meta-data> tag to support the CONFIG_DIGITAL constant value, which the CompanionConfigurationAction metadata object holds. This is done in the wear project's AndroidManifest XML definition file, inside the existing parent <service> tag.

# The Wear App: Adding Companion Metadata to Manifest

The next thing you need to do is add a fourth <meta-data> tag into the wear application's parent <service> tag, which is already in an Android Manifest file for the wear application part (section) of your project. The metadata entries define things you're going to use in an application, such as the wallpaper resource, watch face preview image resources, or, in this case, the **CONFIG_WATCH_FACE** ACTION you defined in the mobile AndroidManifest.xml, which launches the Configuration Companion Activity.

The XML markup for this <meta-data> tag can be seen highlighted in the bottom part of Figure 13-10 and should look like the following XML tag structure:

```
<meta-data android:name="com.google.android.wearable.watchface.companionConfigurationAction"
           android:value="com.pro.android.wearables.proandroidwearable.CONFIG_WATCH_FACE" />
```

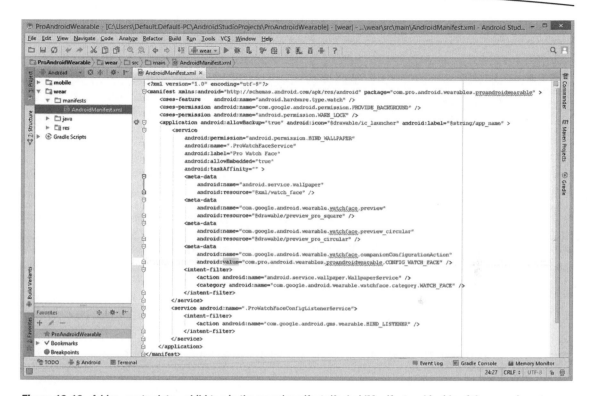

*Figure 13-10. Add a <meta-data> child tag in the wear/manifests/AndroidManifest.xml inside of the <service> tag*

Now that the Android Manifest XML definition files are set up and you have put the empty ProWatchFaceCompanionConfigActivity class structure into place, let's take a quick overview of the GoogleApiClient class and learn about Google Play Services before you get into coding all of these methods.

# Google Play Services: The GoogleApiClient Class

To access the Google Mobile Services and Google Play Services servers, you need to create a GoogleApiClient object for any class that accesses these servers. I like to name my GoogleApiClient object myGoogleApiClient.

## Android's GoogleApiClient: Using Google Mobile Services

The GoogleApiClient public interface is part of the Google Mobile Services API. It's in the com.google.android.gms.common.api.GoogleApiClient package and is the primary app "entry point" for Google Play Services integration.

Before any operation is executed, the GoogleApiClient must be connected to Google Play Services using a **.connect()** method. This is generally done via the **.onStart()** method, which you will be coding a bit later on during this chapter, using the following Java structure:

```
@Override
protected void onStart() {
    super.onStart();
    myGoogleApiClient.connect();
}
```

Your Google Play Services client is not deemed connected until the **public void onConnected(Bundle bundle)** callback method has been called. The empty method for this can be seen in the middle of Figure 13-9.

A GoogleApiClient object can be used with a number of static methods. Some of these methods will require the GoogleApiClient object to be connected, while other methods queue up calls before the GoogleApiClient is connected to the client Activity. Check the current API documentation for each method in order to determine whether or not your client needs to be connected.

When your watch face application is done using the GoogleApiClient object, you will want to call the .disconnect() method. This is generally done via the **.onStop()** method, which you will also be coding a bit later on in this chapter, using the following Java structure:

```
@Override
protected void onStop() {
    if (myGoogleApiClient != null && myGoogleApiClient.isConnected()) {
        myGoogleApiClient.disconnect();
    }
    super.onStop();
}
```

You should instantiate the GoogleApiClient object inside your Activity **onCreate(Bundle savedInstanceState)** method using a **GoogleApiClient.Builder** nested (helper) class. The Java code you will be writing later on in this chapter will look something like this:

```
protected void onCreate(Bundle savedInstanceState) {
        super.onCreate(savedInstanceState);
        setContentView(R.layout.activity_pro_watch_face_config);
        myGoogleApiClient = new GoogleApiClient.Builder(this)
                .addConnectionCallbacks(this)
                .addOnConnectionFailedListener(this)
                .addApi(Wearable.API)
                .build();
    }
```

Interestingly, all of the nested classes I am discussing here are called in the GoogleApiClient instantiation code listed above.

The **GoogleApiClient.Builder** nested class provides a **Builder class**, which is used to configure GoogleApiClient objects using **dot notation chaining**. You can see this in the code above, although the method chains are being aligned using periods, instead of using the period to "chain" the method calls together.

The **GoogleApiClient.ConnectionCallbacks** nested interface provides callback objects that are called when the client is connected or disconnected from the Google Play Service.

A **GoogleApiClient.OnConnectionFailedListener** nested interface will provide a callback object for those scenarios in which Google Play Services access results in a failed attempt to connect the GoogleApiClient object to this Google Play Service.

The GoogleApiClient class contains **15** public methods. I cannot cover all of these here, but I will cover the ones you will be using in your Java code to implement the companion watch face configuration activity.

If you want to get up to speed on all 15 GoogleApiClient method call specifications, you can visit the Android Developer web site with this URL:

```
https://developer.android.com/reference/com/google/android/gms/common/api/
GoogleApiClient.html
```

The abstract void **.connect()** method is used to connect the GoogleApiClient object to a Google Play Service server. You will be implementing this in the .onStart() method in the ProWatchFaceCompanionConfigActivity class.

The abstract void **.disconnect()** method is used to **close the connection** to the Google Play Services server when you are finished using it. You will be using it in an .onStop() method in the ProWatchFaceCompanionConfigActivity class later in the chapter when you start implementing all of your methods.

The abstract boolean **.isConnected()** method is used to check to see if the GoogleApiClient object is **currently connected** to the Google Play Services. If it is, then requests to other Google Play Service methods will succeed.

The abstract boolean **.isConnecting()** method checks if the GoogleApiClient object is **currently attempting to connect** with the Google Play Service.

Next, let's put some of the XML infrastructure in place for the onCreate() method for the ProWatchFaceCompanionConfigActivity class. After these XML assets have been created, you can reference the XML components in the Java code. After that you'll learn about the GoogleApiClient.Builder nested class, and then build the GoogleApiClient object so you can implement Google Play Services in the Pro Watch Face application you are continuing to enhance as you progress throughout this book. There is a ton of code to write and a plethora of Android classes to learn about, so let's get on with it!

# Creating the Play Client: Coding Your .onCreate() method

The most important method in any Android Activity is the onCreate() method, as it always must be in place and it creates the user interface layouts, and in this case, also the GoogleApiClient object and its Peer ID.

The first thing you need to do is override the Activity superclass onCreate() method via a **protected void onCreate(Bundle savedInstanceState)** method structure. Inside the method, you will use the Java super keyword to pass the savedInstanceState Bundle object up to the Activity superclass so that the superclass .onCreate() method can process it. The Java method structure, which can be seen highlighted in yellow in the middle of Figure 13-11, should look like the following Java code:

```java
@Override
protected void onCreate(Bundle savedInstanceState) {
    super.onCreate(savedInstanceState);
}
```

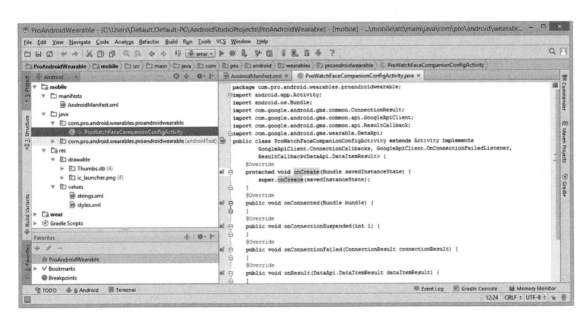

*Figure 13-11. Add a protected void onCreate() method and super.onCreate() superclass method call to the class*

Before you can call the standard Activity **.setContentView()** method, you need to create the **layout** XML directory and put assets in place in this **mobile** part of the project. Right-click the **/mobile/res** folder and select the **New ➤ Android resource directory** menu sequence. Select **layout** using the **Resource type** drop-down; this will also set the folder name, as shown in Figure 13-12.

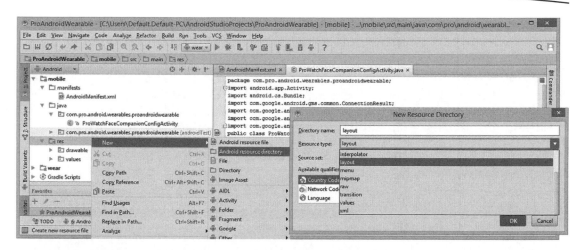

**Figure 13-12.** *Right-click the /res folder and select New ➤ Android resource directory menu option and dialog*

Click the OK button to create the **/mobile/res/layout** folder, and then right-click this new folder in the project navigation pane and select the **New ➤ Android resource file** menu sequence.

This menu sequence can also be seen in Figure 13-12, at the top of the New submenu, so I will only show the **New Resource File** dialog here, which you can see in Figure 13-13. You will name the XML resource file using Android Activity user interface layout file naming conventions (activity first and use underscore characters), so use the name activity_pro_ watch_face_config and select a LinearLayout root element and leave the other two fields with their default settings (main and layout). Click the **OK** button to create a new **activity_pro_watch_face_config.xml** user interface layout definition file. This will hold a user interface definition for the configuration UI.

| New Resource File | |
|---|---|
| File name: | activity_pro_watch_face_config |
| Root element: | LinearLayout |
| Source set: | main |
| Directory name: | layout |
| Available qualifiers: | Chosen qualifiers: |
| Country Code | Nothing to show |
| Network Code | |

**Figure 13-13.** *Right-click the new /res/layout folder and select New ➤ Android Resource File option and dialog*

The bootstrap **&lt;LinearLayout&gt;** parent tag will be configured using a default **vertical** orientation, which is what you want, as well as the default layout constants of **match_parent**. This tells your user interface layout container to fill the screen dimensions, since the display screen is a parent of the LinearLayout user interface layout container XML definition.

Inside the &lt;LinearLayout&gt; parent container, add the child **&lt;TextView&gt;** UI widget, which will contain the **title** for the user interface design. Add a parameter for **ID** with the **@+id/title** value and the **android:text** parameter with the **@string/prowatchface_config** value. Finally, add the **layout_height** and **layout_width** parameters, which Android OS requires to be specified for every user interface element. Set the layout_width to **match_parent** and the layout_height to **wrap_content**. These constant settings will specify the layout parameters for the TextView element, which will force it to span the screen from side to side and constrain it to only be as tall as the text that it contains, which is going to be the title (header) for your UI design.

The basic user interface layout definition XML markup, which is shown in Figure 13-14, should look like the following XML definition structure:

```xml
<?xml version="1.0" encoding="utf-8"?>
<LinearLayout xmlns:android="http://schemas.android.com/apk/res/android"
    android:orientation="vertical" android:layout_width="match_parent"
    android:layout_height="match_parent">
    <TextView
        android:id="@+id/title"
        android:text="@string/prowatchface_config"
        android:layout_width="match_parent"
        android:layout_height="wrap_content" />
</LinearLayout>
```

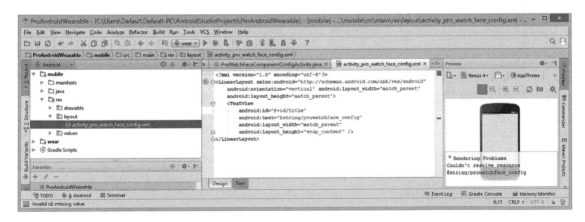

*Figure 13-14. Add a &lt;TextView&gt; inside the parent &lt;LinearLayout&gt; container with the android:id value of title*

Before I get into the Java coding of the onCreate() method, you will need to create the **&lt;string&gt;** constant that is referenced in the user interface layout definition file. Open the **/mobile/res/values/strings.xml** file and add a child &lt;string&gt; tag underneath the parent &lt;resources&gt; tag. Name this **prowatchface_config** with the data value Configure Watch Face, as shown in Figure 13-15, so you can compare these all together visually.

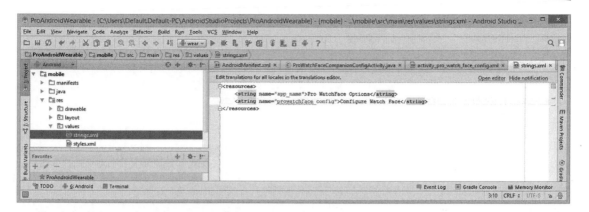

**Figure 13-15.** *Create a <string> constant named prowatchface_config with a data value of Configure Watch Face*

Now you are ready to switch gears and get into some Java coding, so you can implement the rest of the companion app .onCreate() method structure. Add the **setContentView (R.layout.activity_pro_watch_face_config);** statement, as shown in Figure 13-16, as well as declaring a private String watchFacePeerId at the top of the class. As you can see, you will be instantiating the PeerId next, using the WatchFaceCompanion class, the .getIntent(), and .getStringExtra() method calls. You'll be learning about these classes and method calls next.

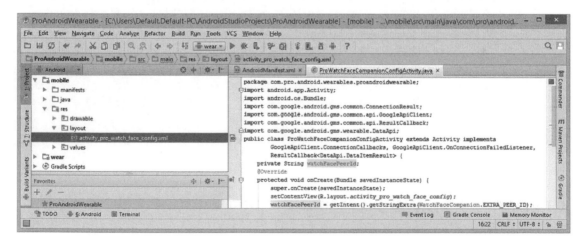

**Figure 13-16.** *Add a private String variable named watchFacePeerId; set it equal to .getIntent()getStringExtra()*

Instantiate the **watchFacePeerId** by using the **.getIntent().getStringExtra()** method chain, then pass in the **WatchFaceCompanion.EXTRA_PEER_ID** constant.

The Java statement, as shown in Figure 13-17, should look like the following:

```
watchFacePeerId = getIntent().getStringExtra(WatchFaceCompanion.EXTRA_PEER_ID);
```

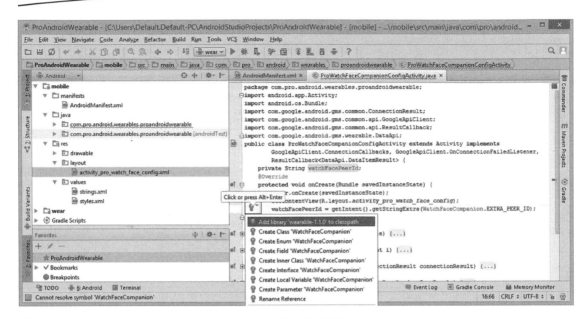

**Figure 13-17.** *Drop down the error suggestion menu; select the Add library 'wearable-1.1.0' to classpath option*

Notice that there is a red error lightbulb at the left of the IDE, so drop down this menu and select the Add library 'wearable-1.1.0' to the classpath option. Usually, the first option is the most optimal. Android Studio will prioritize options, based on what it thinks is the most viable solution.

Interestingly, when I selected this, Android Studio instead wrote an import statement for the WatchFaceCompanion class, so Android Studio will need to correct their pop-up helper user interface code to correct this anomaly, as I looked in the project's Gradle files but did not see any additions.

Let's take a moment to get a high-level overview of the WatchFaceCompanion and ComponentName classes, and after that, you will resume your Java coding.

# The WatchFaceCompanion Class: Configuration Constants

The Android **public final WatchFaceCompanion** class extends **java.lang.Object** and defines **constants** for use by watch face configuration Activity classes. This is why the class is declared using the Java **final** keyword.

The Java class hierarchy for the WatchFaceCompanion class looks like this:

```
java.lang.Object
  > android.support.wearable.companion.WatchFaceCompanion
```

As you've seen already during this chapter, to register your configuration Activity to be started on a companion phone, you will add the **<meta-data>** entry to the watch face component (the wear portion of the project) in an AndroidManifest.xml file. This specifies your Intent ACTION constant, which will be "fired" to start the Activity subclass. You can see this in Figure 13-10, if you want to revisit the XML markup you wrote earlier.

The Activity subclass also needs to have an <intent-filter> specification, which will list the same ACTION constant specified in the metadata block of XML markup, in addition to two WEAR categories, DEFAULT and COMPANION_CONFIGURATION, which were also put into place, as shown in Figure 13-2.

For a watch face configuration dialog Activity class, substitute category com.google.android. wearable.watchface.category.WEARABLE_CONFIGURATION for com.google.android. wearable.watchface.category.COMPANION_CONFIGURATION.

This WatchFaceCompanion class uses two constants, both of which are String values:

> The **EXTRA_PEER_ID** constant contains a key value for a String extra specifying the PeerId for the currently connected device in the phone-side configuration Activity Intent (launching) object.

> The **EXTRA_WATCH_FACE_COMPONENT** constant contains the key value for a String extra specifying the **ComponentName** for the watch face that is being configured using the configuration Activity Intent (launching) object.

Before you get into writing the WatchFaceCompanion-related Java code, let's dig a bit deeper into the Android ComponentName class and see what it offers Android developers, especially where WatchFaces API development is concerned.

## The ComponentName Class: Specify a Component

The Android **public final ComponentName** class is part of an **android.content** package, and it implements the **Parcelable Cloneable Comparable<ComponentName>** interface. This class extends the java.lang.Object master class; therefore, the ComponentName class has the following Java class hierarchy:

```
java.lang.Object
  > android.content.ComponentName
```

This ComponentName class provides an **identifier** for a specific application component. Application components in Android include an **Activity**, **Service**, **BroadcastReceiver**, or **ContentProvider** (DataBase or DataStore) object. This class, therefore, allows developers to specify their Android component type.

In the examples in this book, it's an Activity component type that you are seeking to define for Android OS. Two pieces of information, encapsulated in a ComponentName object, are required to identify any given Android component. The first is the package (String value) a component resides in, and the second is the subclass name (also a String value) for the component type that lives inside that specified package.

This class has one attribute or field specified, which is the **public static final Creator<ComponentName> CREATOR** attribute.

There are four overloaded public constructor methods, none of which you'll be using, as you'll be creating a ComponentName object named componentName by using the **.getIntent().getParcelableExtra()** method chain. You'll do this using the following Java statement in the next section of this chapter:

```
componentName = getIntent().getParcelableExtra(WatchFaceCompanion.EXTRA_WATCH_FACE_
COMPONENT);
```

You can see in this line of Java code the link between the ComponentName class and the WatchFaceCompanion class, which you just learned about.

The ComponentName class has **16** public methods, including the **.clone()** method, which will clone ComponentName objects, a **.compareTo(ComponentName componentName)** method to compare ComponentName objects, an **.equals(Object object)** method, a **.getClassName()** method, a **.getPackageName()** method, a **.toString()** method, and other similar utility methods, which can be used to access ComponentName information. If you wanted to dive into these 16 methods in detail, you will want to visit this Android developer web site URL:

```
http://developer.android.com/reference/android/content/ComponentName.html
```

Next, let's finish writing the Java code that uses the WatchFaceCompanion class, which IntelliJ has already written an import statement for, as seen highlighted at the top of Figure 13-18. After that, you will learn about the GoogleApiClient.Builder nested (helper) class, so you can code the part of the .onCreate() method that instantiates (that is, builds) a GoogleApiClient object. After that, you'll have finished creating your Google Play Services object.

## Setting Watch Face Identity: ComponentName and PeerId

Add a line of code after the setContentView() method call and declare and instantiate the TextView title object using a **.findViewById()** method call, referencing your **title** ID. Set the **watchFacePeerId** String object equal to the getIntent().getStringExtra() method chain, referencing a **EXTRA_PEER_ID** constant from the **WatchFaceCompanion** class.

Declare a ComponentName object named componentName at the top of the class so you can instantiate this object inside the onCreate() method. You'll set the object equal to the getIntent().getParcelableExtra() method chain.

Inside the getIntent().getParcelableExtra() method chain, you will want to reference the **EXTRA_PEER_ID** constant from the **WatchFaceCompanion** class.

The Java code for the .onCreate() method structure so far should look like the following, which can also be seen at the bottom of Figure 13-18:

```
ComponentName componentName;
@Override
protected void onCreate(Bundle savedInstanceState) {
    super.onCreate(savedInstanceState);
    setContentView(R.layout.activity_pro_watch_face_config);
    TextView title = (TextView)findViewById(R.id.title);
    watchFacePeerId = getIntent().getStringExtra(WatchFaceCompanion.EXTRA_PEER_ID);
    componentName = getIntent().getParcelableExtra(WatchFaceCompanion.EXTRA_WATCH_FACE_
    COMPONENT);
}
```

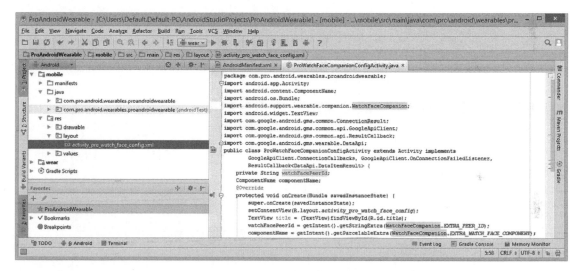

*Figure 13-18. Declare ComponentName object; instantiate a TextView, watchFacePeerId, and componentName*

The only thing you have to do now is declare and instantiate your GoogleApiClient object, which involves using your GoogleApiClient.Builder class, which I will be explaining next.

# The GoogleApiClient.Builder: Building a Google API Client

The Android **public static final GoogleApiClient.Builder** class extends the java.lang.Object master class, creating the following class hierarchy:

```
java.lang.Object
    > com.google.android.gms.common.api.GoogleApiClient.Builder
```

This class creates a **Builder class**, which is used to configure the GoogleApiClient.

To instantiate and build a GoogleApiClient object named myGoogleApiClient, with ConnectionCallbacks and OnConnectionFailedListener support for the Android Wearable API application, you would use the following structure:

```
myGoogleApiClient = new GoogleApiClient.Builder(this)
        .addConnectionCallbacks(this)
        .addOnConnectionFailedListener(this)
        .addApi(Wearable.API)
        .build();
```

The GoogleApiClient.Builder class has two public constructor methods. The first one, which is the one shown above that you will be utilizing, takes the Context object, which you will be passing into the method using the Java **this** keyword. This constructor method takes the following format:

```
GoogleApiClient.Builder( Context context )
```

There is also a more complex (overloaded) constructor method where you can specify a ConnectionCallbacks object and OnConnectionFailedListener object if these objects have already been created in your Java code:

```
GoogleApiClient.Builder( Context context, GoogleApiClient.ConnectionCallbacks connectedListener,
                    GoogleApiClient.OnConnectionFailedListener connectionFailedListener )
```

This GoogleApiClient.Builder class features a dozen methods, which I will cover here (just as I covered all of the WatchFaceStyle.Builder methods), so you can build any type of GoogleApiClient object structure that an application might need to connect to the Google Play Services server:

> The **<O extends Api.ApiOptions.HasOptions> GoogleApiClient.Builder addApi(Api<O> api, O options)** method allows developers to specify which APIs are requested by a client.

> The **GoogleApiClient.Builder addApi(Api<? extends Api.ApiOptions. NotRequiredOptions> api)** method also allows developers to specify which APIs are requested by a client.

> The **GoogleApiClient.Builder addConnectionCallbacks(GoogleApiClien t.ConnectionCallbacks listener)** method allows you to register a listener to receive connection events from your GoogleApiClient object. You will be using this in our watch face application.

> Another method you'll be using in your watch face configuration app is the **GoogleApiClient.Builder addOnConnectionFailedListener(GoogleApiClient. OnConnectionFailedListener listener)** method, which adds your listener to register to receive connection failed events from your GoogleApiClient object.

The **GoogleApiClient.Builder addScope(Scope scope)** method allows developers to specify any OAuth 2.0 scopes that need to be requested by the Wear application.

The **GoogleApiClient build( )** method allows developers to build an GoogleApiClient object for communicating with the Google Play Service server APIs.

The **GoogleApiClient.Builder enableAutoManage(FragmentAc tivity fragmentActivity, int clientId, GoogleApiClient. OnConnectionFailedListener unresolvedConnectionFailedListener)** method allows developers to implement an automatic lifecycle management using the support library FragmentActivity that connects to the GoogleApiClient in the .onStart() method and disconnects from it in the .onStop() method.

The **GoogleApiClient.Builder setAccountName(String accountName)** method allows developers to specify an account name on the hardware device that should be utilized to connect with the Google Play Services server.

The **GoogleApiClient.Builder setGravityForPopups(int gravityForPopups)** method allows developers to specify the general locale on a display screen at which games service pop-ups will be displayed using the Android gravity constants.

The **GoogleApiClient.Builder setHandler(Handler handler)** method allows developers to set a Handler to indicate which thread to use when invoking callbacks.

The **GoogleApiClient.Builder setViewForPopups(View viewForPopups)** method allows developers to set the specified View for use as the content view to use for pop-ups.

The **GoogleApiClient.Builder useDefaultAccount( )** method allows developers to specify that the default account should be used when connecting to the Google Play Services server.

Now that you have a better overview of the Builder class, let's build the GoogleApiClient object using a Java **new** keyword and the basic constructor.

# Building the GoogleApiClient: Using the Wearable API

Let's add the Builder code example, from the previous section, which adds the ConnectionCallbacks and OnConnectionFailed Listener objects, as well as a Wearable. API, and builds the myGoogleApiClient object. The Java code for the onCreate() method is shown in Figure 13-19 and should look like this:

```java
GoogleApiClient myGoogleApiClient;
@Override
protected void onCreate(Bundle savedInstanceState) {
    super.onCreate(savedInstanceState);
    setContentView(R.layout.activity_pro_watch_face_config);
    TextView title = (TextView)findViewById(R.id.title);
    watchFacePeerId = getIntent().getStringExtra(WatchFaceCompanion.EXTRA_PEER_ID);
    componentName = getIntent().getParcelableExtra(WatchFaceCompanion.EXTRA_WATCH_FACE_
    COMPONENT);
    myGoogleApiClient = new GoogleApiClient.Builder(this)
            .addConnectionCallbacks(this)
            .addOnConnectionFailedListener(this)
            .addApi(Wearable.API)
            .build();
}
```

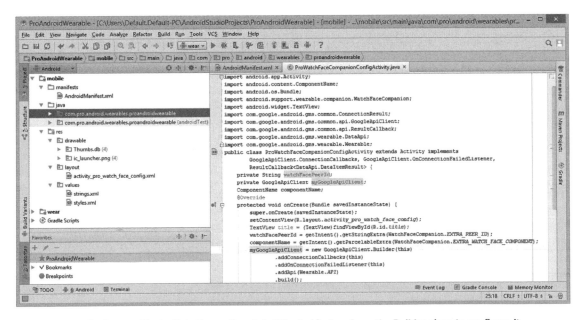

*Figure 13-19. Declare and instantiate the myGoogleApiClient object and use the Builder class to configure it*

Notice that you are passing the **current Context object** for the class via the Java **this** keyword to the GoogleApiClient (class), as well as the nested classes ConnectionCallbacks and OnConnectionFailedListener, which I will be covering in detail later in this chapter. The reason for this is that the Context object contains all of the relevant (system) information about the class, and these classes would need to reference and use **this** information (no pun intended) to be able to perform their related functions optimally.

## Starting and Stopping a Play Client: onStart() and onStop()

Now that you have created the Google Play Services client and a UI layout container inside the onCreate(), the next step is to create the code that starts up your client. Create a **protected void onStart()** method that calls the Activity superclass onStart() method using the Java **super** keyword, and after that, call a .connect() method off the myGoogleApiClient object.

This can be done with the following Java code, which can also be seen in Figure 13-20. I clicked the myGoogleApiClient object to highlight its usage:

```
@Override
protected void onStart() {
    super.onStart();
    myGoogleApiClient.connect();
}
```

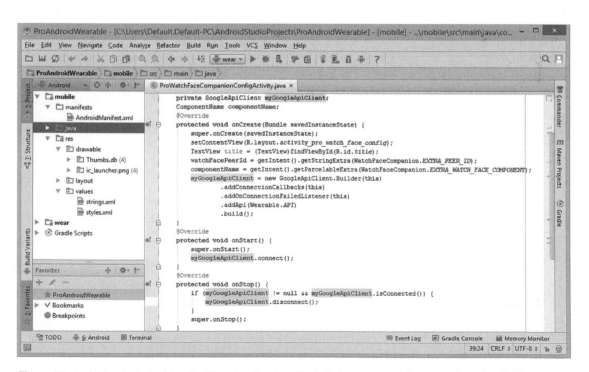

*Figure 13-20.  Add protected void onStart() and onStop() methods that connect and disconnect from Google Play Service*

The onStop() method is a bit more complicated as it involves a conditional if() statement that evaluates the myGoogleApiClient object to see if it is connected. If it is connected, it disconnects it. After that, a Java super keyword is used to pass an onStop() method function call up to an Activity superclass, which removes the application from the device's system memory. The following code accomplishes this:

```
@Override
protected void onStop( ) {
    if (myGoogleApiClient != null && myGoogleApiClient.isConnected( )) {
        myGoogleApiClient.disconnect( );
    }
    super.onStop( );
}
```

Next, create the onConnected() method that will contain the Java code for what you want to do once you are connected to Google Play Services.

## Connect a Client: Creating the onConnected Method

Now let's implement the **onConnected()** method. The method was created for us by IntelliJ using the Java interfaces you specified in your class declaration. The first thing you want to do in your empty bootstrap method is create an empty if-else method that looks at the **watchFacePeerId** and ascertains if it has been used, that is, if it contains a **non-null value**. The (still) empty method structure, as shown in Figure 13-21, looks like this:

```
@Override
public void onConnected(Bundle bundle) {
    if (watchFacePeerId != null) {
        // Things to do if a connection is detected, that is, watchFacePeerId has some ID value
    } else {
        // Things to do if there has not been any connection, that is, watchFacePeerId is empty
    }
}
```

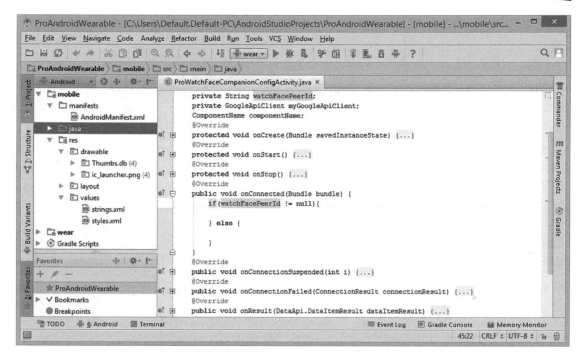

*Figure 13-21. Add an empty if-else conditional structure evaluating the watchFacePeerId String to see if it's used*

Now that you have the evaluation structure in place, I'll provide some information on the **Uri** and **Uri.Builder** classes before you implement the rest of the Java code.

# Android Uri Class: Uniform Resource Identifier Objects

The Android public abstract Uri class extends the java.lang.Object master class and implements a Parcelable Comparable<Uri> interface. It is found in the android.net package. Its class hierarchy looks like the following:

```
java.lang.Object
  > android.net.Uri
```

The Android Uri object contains the immutable Uniform Resource Identifier (URI) reference path. A URI reference includes a URI and a fragment, the component of the URI following a pound sign (#).

Just like the Uri class in the **java.net** package (don't get these confused), the Android Uri class and its Uri.Builder nested class builds, and parses, URI references that conform to the RFC 2396 standard.

In order to maximize performance, the Uri class does not perform data validation on the Uri path content itself. This means that the behavior of the Uri is undefined for invalid Uri path data input. The class is therefore somewhat forgiving; when faced with invalid input data, this class returns garbage, rather than throwing an exception, unless a developer specifies otherwise.

The Android Uri class contains one nested class, the Uri.Builder "helper" class, which is used for building or manipulating URI references. You will be using both of these classes in your onConnect() method, after a short discussion on the Uri.Builder class in the next section.

There are 39 methods in the Android Uri class, and unfortunately I cannot go into all of these in detail, since you're going to be using methods from the Uri.Builder class. However, if you plan to use Uri objects frequently, you can dive into all these methods at your leisure at the following URL:

```
http://developer.android.com/reference/android/net/Uri.html
```

# Android Uri.Builder Class: Building an Android URI Object

The public static final Uri.Builder class extends java.lang.Object, which means the class was scratch-coded and has the following class hierarchy:

```
java.lang.Object
  > android.net.Uri.Builder
```

The Uri.Builder class is a nested or helper class that's used for building or manipulating URI references. It is important to note that this Builder class isn't safe for concurrent use, that is, there is no synchronization provided across threads; use it in one thread only.

If you wanted to build upon a Uri object that already exists, use the **.buildUpon()** method from the Uri class.

The Uri.Builder class has one public constructor method, the Uri.Builder() method, which will construct, or instantiate, a new Uri.Builder object. To declare and instantiate a UriBuilder object named uriBuilder, you would use the following Java programming statement:

```
Uri.Builder uriBuilder = new Uri.Builder();
```

The Uri.Builder class has 17 public methods, all of which I cannot cover here. However, I will cover those methods you will be using to finish the onConnect() method, which you'll do in the next section of the chapter:

A Uri.Builder class **.authority(String authority)** method is used to set the authority for a Uri object. A Uri.Builder class **.path(String path)** method is used to set the path for a Uri object.

A Uri.Builder class **.scheme(String scheme)** method can be used to specify a scheme for a Uri object. A Uri class **.build()** method is used to construct a Uri object, using the other Uri attributes that have been set using the Uri.Builder methods listed on the Android developer website Uri URL listed above.

# Building a Uri for a Client: Finishing the onConnected()

If the watchFacePeerId is not null, that means that it has been assigned a value by Google Play Services, so, in the **if(watchFacePeerId != null)** section of the onConnected() method, you would want to declare and instantiate the uriBuilder Uri.Builder object by using the following line of Java code:

```
Uri.Builder uriBuilder = new Uri.Builder();
```

Once that has been done, you can use the Uri.Builder methods that you just learned about and set the scheme to **wear**, your path to **PATH_WITH_FEATURE**, and the authority to the **watchFacePeerId** value. Be sure to add a **.build()** method call at the end of the method chain, as shown in Figure 13-22 and in the following Java statement:

```
Uri uri = uriBuilder.scheme("wear").path(PATH_WITH_FEATURE).authority(watchFacePeerId).
build();
```

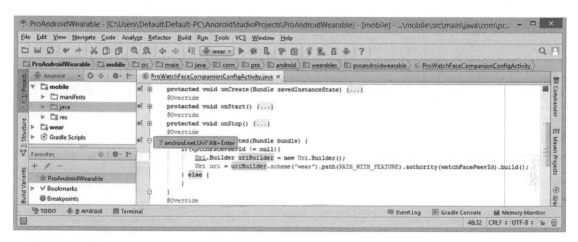

**Figure 13-22.** *Instantiate a Uri.Builder object named uriBuilder; set a Uri object named uri equal to the build scheme, path and authority and then use .build()*

As you can see in Figure 13-22, you'll need to use the **Alt+Enter** keystroke combination and have IntelliJ write an android.net.Uri class import statement for you. That will take care of the red error code highlighting, at least for **Uri** (parent class), **Uri.Builder** (nested class), and **.scheme()** (method) references, as all of those are contained in android.net.Uri and will therefore be properly referenced using the import statement. The only red error text that will remain is the **PATH_WITH_FEATURE** path constant.

To get rid of the final red error highlight, you'll need to add a constant at the top of the class using the Java **private static final** keyword chain to define Java constant values. Use the **String** variable type, name it **PATH_WITH_FEATURE**, and set it equal to **/watch_face_config/ProWatchFace** with the following Java programming statement, as shown in Figure 13-23:

```
private static final String PATH_WITH_FEATURE = "/watch_face_config/ProWatchFace";
```

Now that you have learned about and set up your Uri object, the next thing you need to configure with this custom Uri is the **Wearable.API**, which you created using a

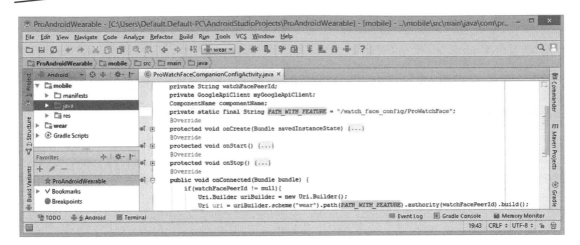

*Figure 13-23. Create private static final PATH_WITH_FEATURE with a /watch_face_config/ProWatchFace value*

GoogleApiClient.Builder class's **.addApi()** method call. This can be seen in Figures 13-19 and 13-20, if you need to visualize it.

# Android's GMS DataApi Interface: Configuring a Data API

This Android Google Mobile Services (GMS) **DataApi public interface** is part of the **com. google.android.gms.wearable.DataApi** package. This interface is used to expose an API for Android Application components to use to read or write **DataItem** or **Asset** objects to GMS, in our case, for use with Wearable applications. A DataApi object contains DataItem as well as Asset (sub) objects.

A DataItem will be synchronized across all the hardware devices in your Android Wear network. It is possible to load, or configure, these DataItem objects when the Wear application is not currently connected to any of the nodes on the network. These DataItem objects will be synchronized when any of the network's nodes appear as being online.

DataItem objects are private to the application that created them. DataItem objects are therefore only accessible by that application on other network nodes. Developers should generally optimize their DataItem objects so they are small in file size.

If you need to transfer large or persistent data objects, such as images, you should use an Asset object, which is the other type of object that can be contained within (inside of) a DataApi object.

Each DataItem object is identified using a URI, accessible with .getUri(). The Uri (object) will contain the DataItem object creator and path. Fully specified URIs should follow the following format:

**wear://<node_id>/<path>**

The <node_id> portion is the **Node ID** of the wearable node that created the DataItem object, and the <path> is an **application-defined path**. This means that given a DataItem object URI, calling the .getHost() method can return the object creator's node ID data value.

In some of the methods for the DataApi class, including the one that you'll be using, the **.getDataItem(GoogleApiClient, Uri)** method, it is possible to leave out (not utilize) a node ID value from the URI, using only the path.

In this particular use case, the Uri object could be utilized to reference **multiple data items**. The reason for this is that multiple nodes can create DataItem objects that use the same exact path value.

Uri objects that contain a partially specified data item URI will utilize a **single forward slash** (/) **character** after wear, in the format **wear:/<path>**.

Concurrent DataItem object modification in different nodes could result in inconsistencies. In our use case, the DataItem object creator will own the DataItem, so DataItem objects will be updated by an original creator node.

A more complicated use case might use what is termed a "producer consumer" approach, where one network node is responsible for producing the DataItem and another network node is responsible for consuming this DataItem, once it has been processed, of course. If you use the more complicated use case, you should make sure that the DataItem objects have unique ID values, and make sure that these DataItem objects are not modified after creation.

The DataApi interface has **four** nested interfaces: a **DataApi.DataItemResult** interface contains the single DataItem, the **DataApi.DataListener** interface is used with an **.addListener(GoogleApiClient, DataApi.DataListener)** method to listen for, and receive, data events, the **DataApi.DeleteDataItemsResult** interface contains the number of deleted DataItem objects, and finally the **DataApi.GetFdForAssetResult** interface contains the **file descriptor** for the requested Asset object.

The DataApi interface contains nine public methods. You will be using the **abstract PendingResult<DataApi.DataItemResult> getDataItem(GoogleApiClient client, Uri uri)** method in the onConnect() method. This method retrieves a single DataItem object from the Android Wear GMS network.

# Using the DataApi Class: Configuring the Wearable.API

Call the **.getDataItem()** off the **Wearable.DataApi** class and pass in your **myGoogleApiClient** and **Uri** object. Create a method chain by adding a method call to the **PendingResult** class's **.setResultCallback()** method, and pass in the current **Context** object with a Java **this** keyword. This is done with the following Java statement, seen highlighted at the bottom of Figure 13-24:

```
Wearable.DataApi.getDataItem(myGoogleApiClient, uri).setResultCallback(this);
```

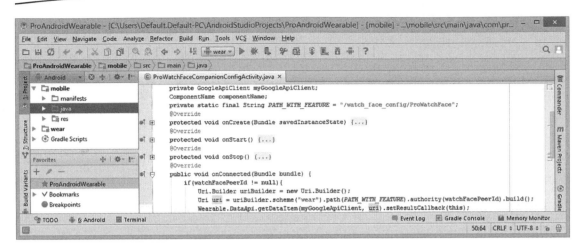

*Figure 13-24. Set Wearable.API to Uri object with .setResultCallback(this), .getDataItem(myGoogleApiClient, uri)*

Let's take a quick look at the Android PendingResult class and then create a method called noConnectedDeviceDialog() that uses the AlertDialog class.

# The Android PendingResult Class: Receiving the Result

The Android GMS **PendingResult public interface** is part of the Wear API, which is included in the **com.google.android.gms.common.api.PendingResult<R extends com.google. android.gms.common.api.Result>** package. This interface has one known indirect subclass: the Batch class.

A PendingResult object contains the pending result from calling a Wear API method from the Google Play Services server. The final result object from a PendingResult is of type **R**, which is the raw data type for Java. The **raw** data packet type can be retrieved in Java by using one of two approaches.

The first approach is to use **blocking calls** to an **.await()** or **.await(long, TimeUnit)** method. The second approach, which is what you will be doing, is to use a ResultCallback interface (object). This is done by passing in an object implementing a ResultCallback public interface to the **.setResultCallback(ResultCallback)** method call.

After the PendingResult has been retrieved using .await(), or delivered to the result callback, if you attempt to retrieve this result again, it will cause an error to be thrown. It is the responsibility of a calling entity, or of the callback receiver, to release any resources associated with the returned result. Some result types may implement **Releasable**, in which case a **.release()** method call should be used to free up associated resources.

The PendingResult public interface has six methods, including the abstract R **.await()** method, which blocks until the PendingResult task is completed; and an abstract R **.await(long time, TimeUnit units)** method, which blocks until the PendingResult task is completed or has timed out a specified number of time units (milliseconds) waiting for a PendingResult.

There is also an abstract void **.cancel()** method, which will request that a PendingResult be canceled. There is an abstract boolean **.isCanceled()** method, which will indicate whether a PendingResult has been canceled either due to calling **{GoogleApiClient#disconnect}** or calling .cancel() directly on the PendingResult object or on an enclosing Batch object.

Finally, there is the abstract void **.setResultCallback(ResultCallback<R> callback)** method, which sets the callback if you want the result object to be delivered via a callback when the result is ready, and an abstract void **.setResultCallback(ResultCallback<R> callback, long time, TimeUnit units)** method, which sets the callback if you want the result to be delivered via a callback when the result is ready or has timed out waiting for the result.

Next, let's create a method that alerts the user if there is no connection.

# Creating a Not Connected Dialog: Using AlertDialog

Add a noConnectedDeviceDialog() method call in the else portion of the onConnected() method if-else structure, which IntelliJ will highlight with red error text, as you can see highlighted at the bottom of Figure 13-25.

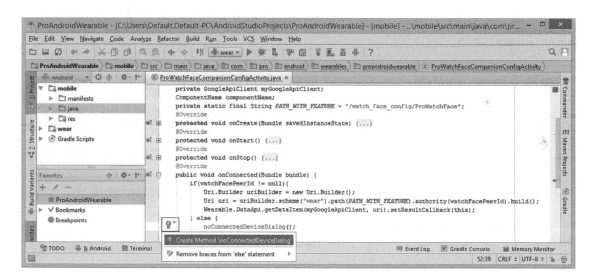

*Figure 13-25. Add a noConnectedDeviceDialog() method call in the else portion and select Create Method option*

Select the Create Method option from the red lightbulb drop-down menu and have IntelliJ create the method structure, which is shown in Figure 13-26. First, declare two String variables named **noConnectText** and **okButtonLabel**.

*Figure 13-26. In this method structure that IntelliJ has created for you, declare and instantiate two String objects*

Next, open the **mobile/res/values/strings.xml** file in its tab in IntelliJ, add the two <string> constants referenced in the noConnectedDeviceDialog() method, and provide a descriptive AlertDialog message and UI Button text for them. This can be seen (highlighted) in Figure 13-27, and should look like the following XML markup:

```
<string name="no_connected_device">Wearable Device Not Connected!</string>
<string name="ok_button_label">OK</string>
```

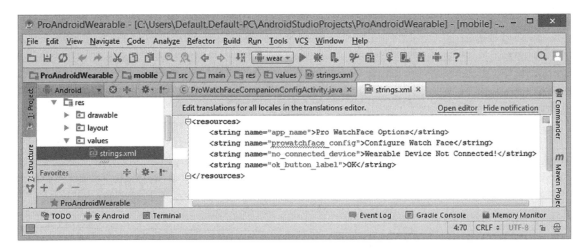

*Figure 13-27. Create text <string> definitions to tell the user that the device is not connected and to click OK*

Before you finish coding the noConnectedDeviceDialog() method, let's take a quick overview of the Android AlertDialog class.

# Android AlertDialog: Creating an Alert Dialog for Your App

The Android **public AlertDialog** class extends the Android Dialog class and implements the **DialogInterface**. It is included in the **android.app** package and has three known direct subclasses: **DatePickerDialog**, **ProgressDialog**, and **TimePickerDialog**. The class hierarchy would look like the following:

```
java.lang.Object
  > android.app.Dialog
    > android.app.AlertDialog
```

The AlertDialog is a special type of Android dialog that can display one, two, or three buttons. If you only want to display a String in the dialog, which you will be doing to tell the user that there is no GMS connection, a **.setMessage()** method would need to be called. If you want to design custom user interface View objects, you should use an **.addView()** method call, and you can later change that View UI design using the **.setView()** method call.

The AlertDialog class contains one nested helper class, which is a builder class aptly called the AlertDialog.Builder class, which you'll be using for constructing the AlertDialog object when you resume the Java coding.

The AlertDialog class supports five Android Theme constants: **THEME_DEVICE_DEFAULT_ DARK**, **THEME_DEVICE_DEFAULT_LIGHT**, **THEME_HOLO_DARK**, **THEME_HOLO_ LIGHT**, and the **THEME_TRADITIONAL** constant, for earlier Android versions prior to Android 4.x, which introduced the HOLO Theme. Android 5.x uses the Material Theme (the first two constants covered above).

The AlertDialog has three protected constructor methods, including the one that you're going to use, **AlertDialog(Context context)**, and a couple more advanced constructors:

> The **AlertDialog(Context context, int theme)** constructor will construct an AlertDialog that uses a completely unique theme you can specify.

> A **AlertDialog(Context context, boolean cancelable, DialogInterface. OnCancelListener cancelListener)** constructor allows you to specify if an AlertDialog is cancelable and attach a cancelListener to it using the constructor method call.

# Android AlertDialog.Builder: Building the Alert Dialog

Android's public static AlertDialog.Builder class extends java.lang.Object and thus was scratch-coded to build alert dialogs. It has the following hierarchy:

```
java.lang.Object
  > android.app.AlertDialog.Builder
```

The class has two public constructor methods. The first one, which you will be using, is the **AlertDialog.Builder(Context context)** method, which will construct an AlertDialog using a Context object, in our case, the Java this keyword, for this AlertDialog.Builder object and the AlertDialog object that it is used to create.

The second constructor is **AlertDialog.Builder(Context context, int theme)**, which allows a different Theme to be specified for the AlertDialog that is being created.

The AlertDialog.Builder class has three dozen public methods, all of which I cannot cover here in detail, but I will cover the methods that you'll be using in the Java code in the next section.

The AlertDialog **.create()** method creates a AlertDialog with the arguments you have supplied to this AlertDialog.Builder class.

The **.setCancelable(boolean cancelable)** method sets whether or not your dialog can be canceled.

The **.setMessage(int messageId)** method will set a message to display, using the given resource ID, in our case, an XML <string> constant.

A **.setPositiveButton(int textId, DialogInterface.OnClickListener listener)** method will set a listener to be invoked, when the positive button of your dialog is pressed.

The **.show()** method displays an AlertDialog using the arguments supplied to the AlertDialog.Builder and overlays the AlertDialog object on the screen.

## Using AlertDialog.Builder: Coding the AlertDialog System

Inside the noConnectedDeviceDialog() method, declare and instantiate an AlertDialog. Builder named alertBuilder using the Java **new** keyword and pass the **Context** (this) object to the basic builder constructor method. Now you can call three methods, using dot notation chaining, off this object to customize the AlertDialog, using the **.setMessage()** and **.setCancelable()** to define the text and UI (Cancel) functions and the **.setPositiveButton()** to implement the UI (Button) element and its onClick() listener and handling. The basic Java code, as shown in Figure 13-28, should look like the following:

```
AlertDialog.Builder alertBuilder = new AlertDialog.Builder(this);
alertBuilder.setMessage(noConnectText)
            .setCancelable(false)
            .setPositiveButton(okButtonLabel, new DialogInterface.OnClickListener()
                          { // handler });
```

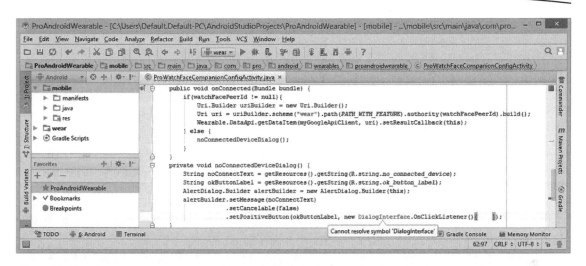

*Figure 13-28. Instantiate the AlertDialog.Builder using .setMessage(), .setCancelable(), and .setPositiveButton()*

As you can see in Figure 13-28, you have some red error code highlighting, which tells you that you need to use an Alt+Enter keystroke combination to have IntelliJ write an import statement for the DialogInterface class. The import of this class triggers IntelliJ to give you another error solution drop-down. Select the first Implement Methods option, as shown in Figure 13-29.

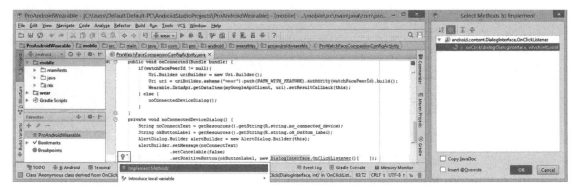

*Figure 13-29. Select the Implement Methods error resolution option to have IntelliJ code an onClick() method*

The IDE will code a **public void onClick(DialogInterface dialog, int which)** method inside the **DialogInterface.OnClickListener()** object, which can be seen in Figure 13-30, along with the code that declares, instantiates, and shows the **AlertDialog** object, which will look like the following code:

```
AlertDialog.Builder alertBuilder = new AlertDialog.Builder(this);
alertBuilder.setMessage(noConnectText).setCancelable(false)
        .setPositiveButton(okButtonLabel, new DialogInterface.OnClickListener() {
            public void onClick(DialogInterface dialog, int which) { }
        });
AlertDialog alertDialog = alertBuilder.create();
alertDialog.show();
```

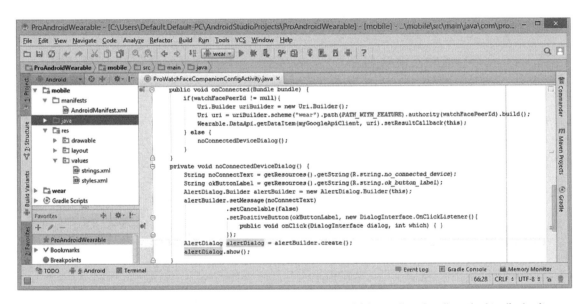

*Figure 13-30.* *Declare and instantiate an AlertDialog object named alertDialog; call a .show() method to display it*

# Coding an onResult Method: DataItem and DataMap

Next you need to code the **onResult()** method, which will contain an if-else structure that evaluates whether or not a DataItemResult has been received by the Activity, hence the method name onResult(). The if() condition uses a **Logical AND** to detect if the **.getStatus(). isSuccess()** method call chain returns **true** AND if the **.getDataItem()** method call does not return anything (null), meaning that there is something inside a DataItemResult object.

An empty DataItemResult processing structure, as shown in Figure 13-31, should look like this (empty) Java conditional if()-else{} processing structure:

```java
public void onResult(DataApi.DataItemResult dataItemResult) {
        if ( dataItemResult.getStatus().isSuccess()  && dataItemResult.getDataItem()
        != null ) {
                // DataItemResult Detected! Processing
        } else {
                // No DataItemResult Detected Processing
        }
}
```

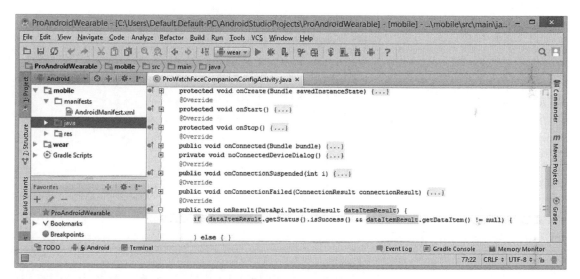

*Figure 13-31. Create an if-else structure inside an onResult() method that evaluates the dataItemResult object*

Now you can write the DataItem, DataMap, and DataMapItem object processing code. This goes inside the if() portion of the statement, since it only gets executed if a DataItemResult object contains data to be worked with.

The next step is to do this coding, in addition to looking at two Android GMS classes and one Android GMS interface in greater detail, so you understand what these data-related objects can be utilized for in your apps.

# Android's DataItem Interface: A Foundation for Wear Data

The Android **public DataItem interface** implements **Freezable<DataItem>** and is part of the **com.google.android.gms.wearable.DataItem** package. A DataItem represents the base (foundation) object of data stored in an Android Wear network. DataItem objects are replicated across all devices in a network.

A DataItem object contains a "blob" of data, as well as associated assets. A DataItem is identified using a Uri that contains its creator and a path. A DataItem class has **four** public methods: the **.getAssets()** method retrieves a **map** of assets contained in the DataItem; the

**.getData()** method retrieves an **array** of data stored at a specified Uri; the **.getUri()** method returns the DataItem **Uri**; and the **.setData(byte[] data)** method sets a **data byte[] array** inside a DataItem. Let's implement a DataItem in our code!

# Loading a DataItem Object: Using a .getDataItem() Method

Let's create a DataItem object named **configDataItem** and set it equal to a **.getDataItem()** method call off the **dataItemResult** DataItemResult object, which was passed into the onResult() method using the following Java code and can be seen highlighted in Figure 13-32. As you can see, you'll need to use the **Alt+Enter** work process so IntelliJ imports the DataItem class:

```
DataItem configDataItem = dataItemResult.getDataItem();
```

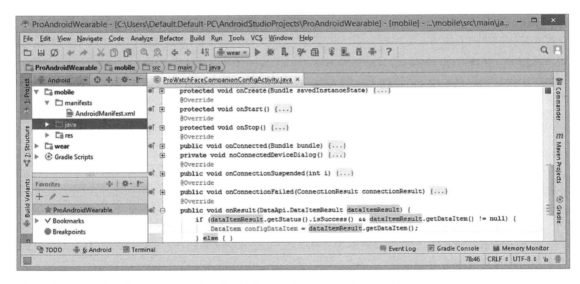

*Figure 13-32.   Declare DataItem named configDataItem and set it equal to a getDataItem() call off dataItemResult*

Let's take a look at the Android GMS DataMapItem class next, since that is the next object you'll be using in the onResult() method if() structure.

# Android's DataMapItem Class: A DataItem with a Map

An Android **public DataMapItem** class extends java.lang.Object. It is included in the **com.google.android.gms.wearable** package and its hierarchy looks like this:

```
java.lang.Object
  > com.google.android.gms.wearable.DataMapItem
```

The DataMapItem class (object) wraps a DataItem object to create advanced mapped DataItem objects called DataMapItem objects. These objects contain more structured data or even serializable data. The class has three public methods: the **static**

**.fromDataItem(DataItem dataItem)** method provides a DataMapItem object that wraps a DataItem object; the **.getDataMap()** method extracts a **DataMap** object, which you will be learning about next; and the **.getUri()** method extracts a Uri object. Let's implement the DataMapItem.

## Using a DataMapItem Object: The .fromDataItem() Method

Declare a DataMapItem named **dataMapItem** and set it equal to the result of a **.fromDataItem(configDataItem)** method call off the DataMapItem object by using the following statement, which is highlighted in Figure 13-33:

```
DataMapItem dataMapItem = DataMapItem.fromDataItem(configDataItem);
```

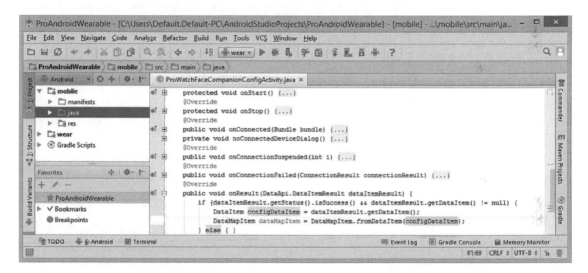

*Figure 13-33. Declare DataMapItem named dataMapItem and set it equal to a fromDataItem(configDataItem) call*

Next, let's take a look at the Android GMS DataMap class, and then you will finish coding the if() portion of the onResult() method structure.

## Android Data Map

The Android GMS public **DataMap** class extends java.lang.Object and is part of the **com.google.android.gms.wearable** package. The GMS DataMap Java class hierarchy looks like the following:

```
java.lang.Object
  > com.google.android.gms.wearable.DataMap
```

A DataMap object contains a map of data supported by **PutDataMapRequest** and **DataMapItem** objects. The DataMap objects can also be converted to and from Bundle objects. It is important to note that this conversion process would drop any data types not explicitly supported by the DataMap object during this data conversion process.

The DataMap class has one public constructor method, DataMap(), and 55 public methods, all of which I cannot cover here. I'll cover some of the more useful methods you may want to use in your Wear app development:

The **.clear()** method will remove all data elements from the mapping for the DataMap object that the method is called off of (so it clears a DataMap).

The **.containsKey(String key)** method will return true if the requested key is contained in a mapping of a DataMap object the method is called off of.

The **.fromByteArray(byte[] bytes)** method will return a DataMap object given an array of bytes, annotated in Java as byte[].

The **.getByte(String key)** method can return a value associated with a given key, or byte 0 if no mapping of the desired type exists for the given key.

The **.getByte(String key, byte defaultValue)** method returns the data value associated with a given key, or defaultValue, if no mapping of the desired type exists for the provided key.

The **.getByteArray(String key)** method will return the value associated with the given key, or null if no mapping of the desired type exists for the given key, or if a null value was explicitly associated with that key.

The **.getDataMap(String key)** method will return a value associated with the given key, or null if no mapping of the desired type exists for a given key, or the null value, if that was explicitly associated with that key.

An **.isEmpty()** method returns true if the mapping of a DataMap is empty. A **.keySet()** method will return a Set, containing the Strings used as keys in the DataMap.

The **.putAll(DataMap dataMap)** method can insert all mappings from the given DataMap into the DataMap. The **.putByte(String key, byte value)** will insert a byte value into the mapping of the DataMap, replacing any existing value for the provided key.

The **.putByteArray(String key, byte[] values)** method will insert a byte array value into the mapping of this dataMap, replacing any currently existing values for the provided key.

The **.putDataMap(String key, DataMap value)** method will insert the DataMap into the mapping of the target DataMap. This replaces any existing DataMap for that provided key value.

The **.toByteArray()** method can return serialized byte[] array objects that represent the contents of a DataMap as an array.

The **.remove(String key)** method selectively removes any data entry with the provided key value from a mapping for a target DataMap.

The **.size()** method will return the number of key-value pairs in the DataMap.

The **.toBundle()** method will return (create) a Bundle object that contains all the elements contained within a target DataMap that this method has been called off of.

## Creating a DataMap Object: Using a .getDataMap() Method

Declare a DataMap object named **configDataMap** and instantiate it using the **.getDataMap()** method, called off of the **dataMapItem** object created in your previous line of code. This is done with the following statement, which is highlighted in Figure 13-34. Don't forget to use an **Alt+Enter** work process and have IntelliJ write the **import DataMap** Java import statement for you:

```
DataMap configDataMap = dataMapItem.getDataMap();
```

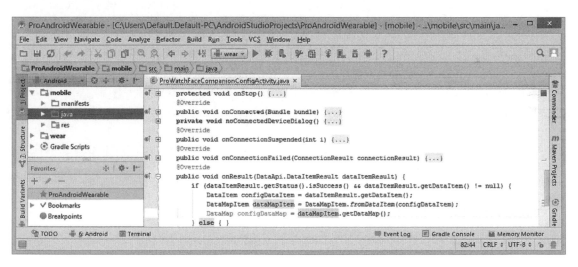

*Figure 13-34. Declare a DataMap named configDataMap, and set it equal to a dataMapItem.getDataMap() call*

Because you are implementing the core Google Mobile Service engine during this chapter, you will finish coding the onMessageReceived() method in the body of your ProWatchFaceConfigListenerService class next.

# Creating a Listener Service: .onMessageReceived( )

Close all of the open editing tabs in IntelliJ and go into the wear/java folder and open the ProWatchFaceConfigListenerService class using a right-click Jump to Source work process, as shown in Figure 13-35.

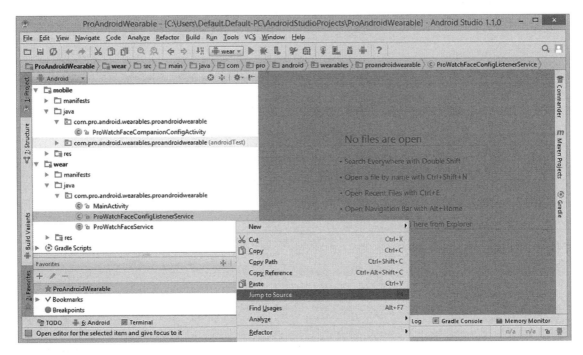

*Figure 13-35.   Close all tabs and go into wear/java and right-click and open ProWatchFaceConfigListenerService*

As you can see in Figure 13-36, because IntelliJ created the empty class for you, you will need to drop down the error helper dialog menu and select an **Implement Methods** option. This will allow IntelliJ to finish creating the empty class, overriding all methods that are required to be implemented.

Interestingly, you will not be adding any new (proprietary) code into these methods, but be aware that this does not mean that these methods do not do anything (the superclass will implement their default behavior code), just that they do not do anything else (custom or new) for this implementation.

Now you can declare the **myGoogleApiClient** GoogleApiClient and get to work!

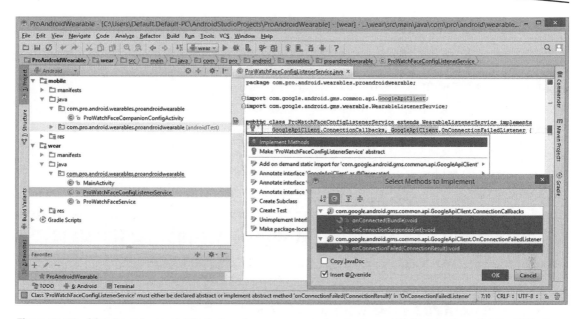

*Figure 13-36.  Click the red error lightbulb drop-down menu, select an Implement Methods option, click the OK button*

Declare the **private myGoogleApiClient** GoogleApiClient object at the top of
the class, as can be seen highlighted in Figure 13-37, so you can build it in an
**onMessageReceived(MessageEvent messageEvent)** method structure, which you are
going to code after a brief discussion about this MessageEvent class.

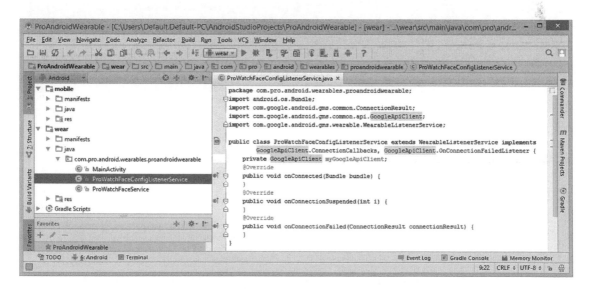

*Figure 13-37.  Add a private GoogleApiClient object named myGoogleApiClient; leave the @Override methods empty*

# The Android MessageEvent Class: Processing a Message

The Android GMS **public MessageEvent interface** handles information about a message received by a listener, in this case a wearable listener service. It is contained within the **com.google.android.gms.wearable** package.

The interface exposes four public methods: the **.getData()** method, which returns the data passed with a message; the **.getPath()** method, which returns the path that a message is being delivered to; the **.getRequestId()** method, which returns the request ID for the message that is generated by the sender; and the **.getSourceNodeId()** method, which returns a node ID for the sender. You'll use the .getData() method next to extract your settings.

# Implementing a MessageEvent Object: Extracting the Data

Let's override an onMessageReceived() method next, as that will be the main method your ConfigListenerService will use to process configuration settings data that will be held inside the MessageEvent object. Create the empty **public void onMessageReceived(MessageEvent messageEvent)** method structure, as shown in Figure 13-38, using the following Java code:

```java
@Override
public void onMessageReceived(MessageEvent messageEvent) {
    // Message Event Processing Code goes in here
}
```

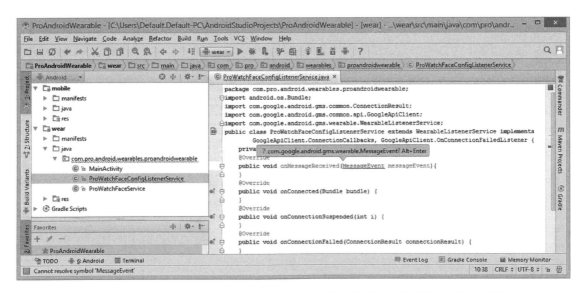

**Figure 13-38.** Add a public void onMessageReceived(MessageEvent) method; use Alt+Enter to import this class

Inside the onMessageReceived() method, declare the **byte[]** array named rawData, and then set it equal to the result of the .getData() method call off the messageEvent MessageEvent object using the following Java code:

```java
byte[] rawData = messageEvent.getData();
```

Remember that this messageEvent object is the object that was passed into the onMessageReceived() method. The next line of Java code will create the DataMap object, let's name it **keysToOverwrite**, and then load it using the **.fromByteArray()** method call, using the following Java code statement:

```java
DataMap keysToOverwrite = DataMap.fromByteArray(rawData);
```

As you can see from the red error code highlight in Figure 13-39, you will have to use the **Alt+Enter** keystroke combination and have IntelliJ import the DataMap class for use in the ProWatchFaceConfigListenerService class.

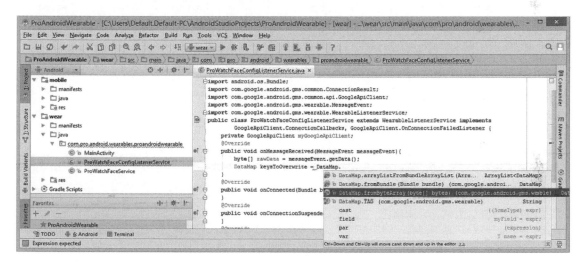

*Figure 13-39. Add a byte array named rawData, and use the .getData() method to load it; add a DataMap object*

The next step in creating the onMessageReceived() method is to create two empty conditional if() structures to hold the condition processing tasks.

One of these would be used when the GoogleApiClient object is empty (null value), and the other would be used if a GoogleApiClient exists but is not currently connected. The Java code for these two conditional if structures can be seen in Figure 13-40, and should look like the following Java code:

```java
if( myGoogleApiClient ==  null ) {
    // Code to Create and Build a GoogleApiClient Object
}
if( !myGoogleApiClient.isConnected() ) {
    // Code to Execute if GoogleApiClient is NOT connected
}
```

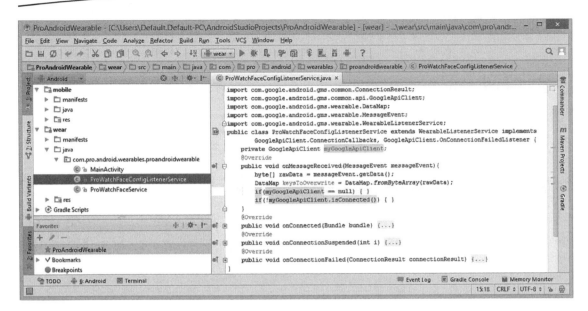

**Figure 13-40.** *Add two conditional if() statements to see if the client object is empty or if the client object is not connected*

If there are no data loaded in the myGoogleApiClient object initially, that is, if a myWatchFaceClient object has a null value, then you would want to create a new GoogleApiClient object using the nested builder helper class.

This is the same exact GoogleApiClient.Builder code you wrote earlier for the ProWatchFaceCompanionConfigActivity.java class, and it should look like the following Java code block, as shown in Figure 13-41:

```
if( myGoogleApiClient == null ) {
    myGoogleApiClient = new GoogleApiClient.Builder(this)
        .addConnectionCallbacks(this)
        .addOnConnectionFailedListener(this)
        .addApi(Wearable.API)
        .build();
}
```

As you can see in Figure 13-41, you'll need to use the **Alt+Enter** keystroke combination and have Intelli-J import the Android Wearable class, so you can use its API inside the GoogleApiClient.Builder method chain .addApi() method call.

Next, you need to write the other conditional if() structure that evaluates the GoogleApiClient object (if it is not null) to see if it is connected to the server. If this is not connected to the Google Play Service server, then you will want to write some code, using the **.blockingConnect()** method, which will connect the Wear application to the Google Play Service server.

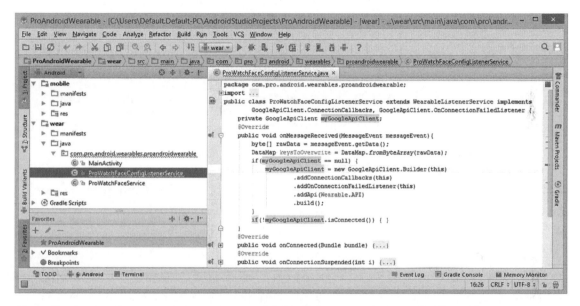

*Figure 13-41.* *Instantiate and .build() a new GoogleApiClient.Builder object if myGoogleApiClient object is null (empty)*

Before you implement the if(!myGoogleApiClient.isConnected()) structure, let's take a closer look at the ConnectionResult class (and object) that you will be using to extract the WatchFaces configuration data from. After that, you can finish implementing the onMessageReceived() method, and then in the next chapter, you will create the Configuration Utility class that pulls it all together.

# The ConnectionResult Class: Connecting to the Network

Android's **public final ConnectionResult** class extends Java.lang.Object and implements **Parcelable**. Its Java class hierarchy looks like the following:

```
java.lang.Object
  > com.google.android.gms.common.ConnectionResult
```

The ConnectionResult class contains all of the possible network connection error codes for use when a client fails to connect to Google Play Service.

The error codes are used by the GoogleApiClient.OnConnectionFailedListener helper class, and they are all listed in Table 13-1 so you can familiarize yourself with them. These are the errors that are generated by the Google Play Service server when something does not work. Working with Google Play will be an important area for Wear developers to master; thus, I wanted to cover a ConnectionResult constant table in detail as you need to know these flags.

The ConnectionResult class has one public constructor method that creates a ConnectionResult object. This public constructor method takes the format **ConnectionResult(int statusCode, PendingIntent pendingIntent)**. This class has ten public methods, including a **.describeContents()** method; **.equals()** method; **.getErrorCode()** method, which indicates the type of error that has interrupted the connection; **.getResolution()** method, containing a pending intent to resolve a failed connection, and **.hasResolution()** method, which will return true if calling **.startResolutionF orResult(Activity, int)** and will start any Intent objects that might require user interaction.

*Table 13-1. ConnectionResult Class Constants and What They Signify Regarding the Network Connection Status*

| ConnectionResult Constant | What It Signifies |
| --- | --- |
| **API_UNAVAILABLE** | API components you attempted to connect to are not available |
| **CANCELED** | The client canceled the connection, by calling .disconnect() |
| **DEVELOPER_ERROR** | The application has somehow been misconfigured |
| **INTERNAL_ERROR** | An internal error occurred |
| **INTERRUPTED** | An interrupt occurred while waiting for connection complete |
| **INVALID_ACCOUNT** | Client attempt to connect service using invalid account name |
| **LICENSE_CHECK_FAILED** | The application is not licensed to the user |
| **NETWORK_ERROR** | A network connection or transport error has occurred |
| **RESOLUTION_REQUIRED** | Completing the connection requires some form of resolution |
| **SERVICE_DISABLED** | Installed version of Google Play Service disabled on device |
| **SERVICE_INVALID** | Google Play Service installed on the device is not authentic |
| **SERVICE_MISSING** | Google Play Service application software missing from device |
| **SERVICE_UPDATE_REQUIRED** | Installed version of Google Play Services is out of date |
| **SIGN_IN_FAILED** | Client attempted to connect to service user is not signed in |
| **SIGN_IN_REQUIRED** | Client attempted to connect to service user is not signed in |
| **SUCCESS** | Your connection has been successfully negotiated |
| **TIMEOUT** | Timeout exceeded while waiting for a connection to complete |

There is an **.isSuccess()** method, which returns true if the connection was a success. A **.sta rtResolutionForResult(Activity activity, int requestCode)** method resolves network errors by starting any Intent objects that require user interaction. There is also a **.toString()** method for converting result data to text and a **.writeToParcel(Parcel out, int flags)** method to write a result to a Parcel object format. Now, let's implement a ConnectionResult!

## Implementing a ConnectionResult: Blocking a Connection

The next conditional if() structure will ascertain whether or not the GoogleApiClient object is connected to the Google Play Service server by using the opposite (a Java NOT operand represented by a preceding exclamation point) of the myGoogleApiClient. isConnected() method call. If the GoogleApiClient object is not connected, you'll declare a **ConnectionResult** object, name it **myConnectionResult**, and set it equal to the **.blockingConnect()** method call off the myGoogleApiClient object. Give the network connection attempt **30 seconds**, using a **30** integer value with the **TimeUnit.SECONDS** constant to retry subsequent connection attempts. This would be accomplished using the following Java code, as is shown highlighted at the bottom of Figure 13-42:

```
if( !myGoogleApiClient.isConnected() ) {
    ConnectionResult myConnectionResult = myGoogleApiClient.blockingConnect(30, TimeUnit.
SECONDS);
}
```

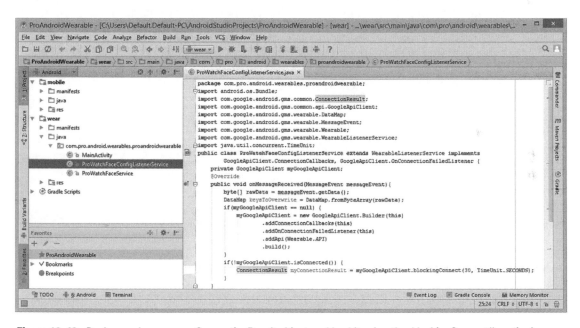

*Figure 13-42. Declare and name a myConnectionResult object, and load it using the .blockingConnect() method*

This is a perfect stopping (resting) point for this chapter covering Google Play Services and the APIs that allow us to connect with and talk to it before I get into coding the configuration constant utility class in the next chapter.

# Summary

In this chapter, you learned about Google Mobile Services (GMS) packages in Android, which is the API that is used to interface with the Google Play Service server. You looked at this in the context of writing two more classes that will be needed to implement a WatchFace Configuration App.

You'll be writing a third class, a utility class, in the next chapter, and then you'll begin testing watch faces on real-world devices and using real-world services!

First, you created the **ProWatchFaceCompanionConfigActivity.java** class and the XML assets needed to make it function, and then you created the GoogleApiClient object, so you could network with Google's Play Services. You learned how to build a client using GoogleApiClient.Builder and how the data are encapsulated with a DataItem, DataMapItem, and DataMap object (classes), as well as how these will related to your watch face configuration data.

Then you created a **ProWatchFaceConfigListenerService.java** class, which will be used in conjunction with the companion Activity class ProWatchFaceCompanionConfigActivity as well as with a utility class, which you will be creating in the next chapter.

In the next chapter, you will create the **ProWatchFaceUtility** class, and you will finish wiring it up to the classes you created in this chapter, as well as to the watch face application you have created in the chapters prior to this one.

# Chapter 14

# Watch Face Configuration Companion Activity Utility and Wearable API

Now that you have coded the foundation Activity class for your watch face companion configuration Activity in the mobile section of your project, it is time to create the **ProWatchFaceUtility** class that will live in the wear section of your project. This class will define the configuration setting constants and house the functions (methods) that manipulate them, using DataMap, DataItem and DataMapItem objects, along with the **Wearable** class's **API**, **DataApi**, **NodeApi**, and **MessageApi** attributes (data fields). You will be learning all about this Wearable class, and its APIs, during this chapter.

You will also be using XML markup during this chapter to create your user interface design for the watch face configuration activity. This UI design will use four **Spinner** widgets, which will allow your user to select one of eight standard system colors for use with your watch face design elements, which include tick marks, an hour hand, a minute hand, and a second hand.

In this chapter you will learn about, and implement in Java code, each of the Android Wearable class data field API attributes. These include the **API**, **DataApi**, **NodeApi**, and **MessageApi**. You'll also learn about the Android **LinearLayout** container class and the Android **Spinner** and **TextView** widgets.

You will implement a complex Android Utility class that talks across a GMS network using a DataAPI, NodeAPI, and MessageAPI. You'll develop key-value data pairs that will define the watch face configuration data for the DataMap, DataItem, and DataMapItem objects, and you'll implement this in Java code.

# The ProWatchFaceUtility Class: Managing the Data

In this first section, you'll create the last class for the companion configuration foundation for the dialog on the watch face user's phone that will allow them to configure their watch face design colors.

The Pro WatchFaces Utility class will live in the **wear/java** portion of the Android Studio project, along with the ProWatchFaceConfigListenerService and the initial ProWatchFaceService class that renders the watch face itself.

After you create the ProWatchFaceUtility.java class structure and constants for the color values you want your users to be able to configure for watch face interactive mode, I will discuss the PutDataMapRequest class, and then you will write the code to implement a utility class, using the classes you have learned about over the past few chapters.

## Creating a ProWatchFaceUtility Class: Defining Constants

Right-click the /wear/java/package folder, as shown in Figure 14-1, and select the **New ➤ Java Class** menu sequence to access a **Create New Class** dialog. Because this is the utility class, let's name it **ProWatchFaceUtility** and select the **Kind** of Class as **Class** from the drop-down in the dialog, as shown in the upper right corner of Figure 14-1. Click the OK button and create the class, which will open in a new editing tab in IntelliJ.

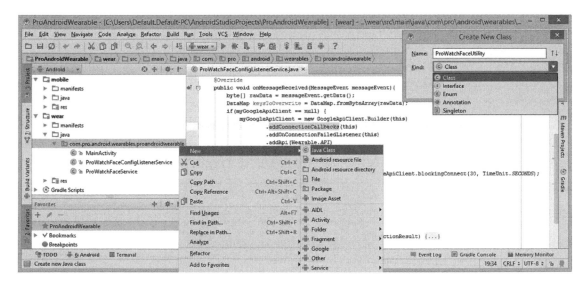

*Figure 14-1. Use the New ➤ Java Class menu sequence and dialog to create your ProWatchFaceUtility class*

Add the Java **final** keyword, after the public keyword and before the class declaration and name, to make your class final. This locks it for use only as your WatchFaces configuration utility.

Next, add five **public static final String** constants. The first should be a **PATH_ WITH_FEATURE** constant that provides a **unique identifier** for the watch face companion application, as you created in your **mobile** app component, WatchFaceCompanionConfigActivity. An ID, which should be unique to each of your

Watch Faces API applications if you create more than one, is how different WatchFaces components know they're talking to a matching application component over the GMS network infrastructure.

The four color constants will allow the user to define the colors used for the watch face design features, that is, the tick marks, hour hand, minute hand, and second hand. You will need **color constants** for the **key-value pairs** used in the DataItem and DataMap objects. Let's create the **key constants** first using **KEY_COLOR** before a design element type, so **KEY_COLOR_TICK_MARK** would represent the key value for your tick mark color configuration data value.

Your final class declaration, along with five Java constant declarations, as seen highlighted in Figure 14-2, should look like the following code:

```java
public final class ProWatchFaceUtility {
    public static final String PATH_WITH_FEATURE = "/watch_face_config/ProWatchFace";
    public static final String KEY_COLOR_TICK_MARK = "COLOR_TICK_MARK";
    public static final String KEY_COLOR_HOUR_HAND = "COLOR_HOUR_HAND";
    public static final String KEY_COLOR_MINUTE_HAND = "COLOR_MINUTE_HAND";
    public static final String KEY_COLOR_SECOND_HAND = "COLOR_SECOND_HAND";
}
```

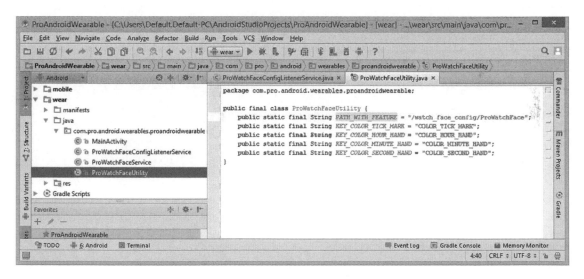

*Figure 14-2. Add the final modifier to the class declaration and constants for the path and interactive mode color values*

Now that you have your key Strings defined (sounds like it could be a country hit: "You Define My Key Strings Babe"), let's define the Android Color class constant for each one, which will define the default color setting. For this app thus far, these would include White (ticks), Blue (hours), Green (minutes), and Red (seconds).

Make sure to utilize the Android System Color constants, as these are already defined inside the OS for you. Later you can use the **.parseColor()** method to turn these into **integer color data values** that Android OS can use. This is shown in the middle portion of Figure 14-3, using the following Java code:

```java
public static final String COLOR_TICK_MARK_INTERACTIVE = "White";
public static final String COLOR_HOUR_HAND_INTERACTIVE = "Blue";
public static final String COLOR_MINUTE_HAND_INTERACTIVE = "Green";
public static final String COLOR_SECOND_HAND_INTERACTIVE = "Red";
```

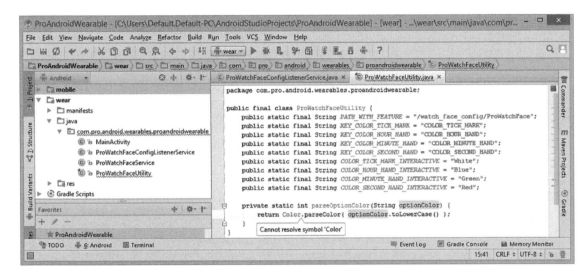

*Figure 14-3.  Create a private static int parseOptionColor() method to convert the color String to the Color class constant*

Let's create a **private static** method called **.parseOptionColor()** and **return** an **int** (integer) data value representing the Android Color class constant.

This method will take in a **String** parameter, which you will name **optionColor**, and return the Color value as an integer, using the **.toLowerCase()** method call, off the **optionColor** parameter. This is done inside the parameter area of the **Color.parseColor()** method call, because you always want to write dense Java code. Your Java method structure, which can be seen highlighted at the bottom of Figure 14-3, should look like the following Java code:

```java
private static int parseOptionColor(String optionColor) {
    return Color.parseColor(optionColor.toLowerCase());
}
```

Make sure to click the red error code highlight and use the **Alt+Enter** work process to have IntelliJ write the import statement you need.

The next step is to use the .parseOptionColor() method you coded to create the **COLOR_VALUE** constants. These will be used for the second part of your key-value pairs, which is used in the DataItem and DataMap objects and will use the same constant names as your default COLOR constants, except you'll be inserting the word **VALUE** after the word COLOR, so that your constant is more descriptive, for instance: **COLOR_VALUE_TICK_MARK_INTERACTIVE**.

The Java code for the four method calls, which set constant values for the value portion of your key-value data pairs, can be seen at the very bottom of Figure 14-4, and should look like the following four Java statements:

```
public static final int COLOR_VALUE_TICK_MARK_INTERACTIVE =
                                      parseOptionColor(COLOR_TICK_MARK_INTERACTIVE);
public static final int COLOR_VALUE_HOUR_HAND_INTERACTIVE =
                                      parseOptionColor(COLOR_HOUR_HAND_INTERACTIVE);
public static final int COLOR_VALUE_MINUTE_HAND_INTERACTIVE =
                                      parseOptionColor(COLOR_MINUTE_HAND_INTERACTIVE);
public static final int COLOR_VALUE_SECOND_HAND_INTERACTIVE =
                                      parseOptionColor(COLOR_SECOND_HAND_INTERACTIVE);
```

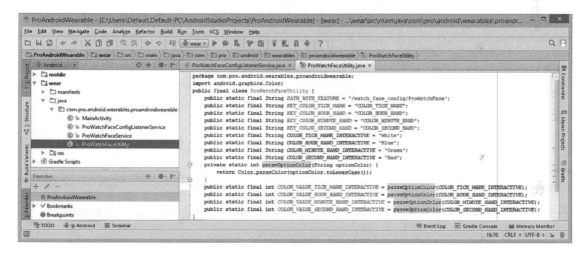

*Figure 14-4. Create the COLOR_VALUE constants that call the parseOptionColor() method to configure themselves*

Now that you have defined over a dozen constants and written one very small but useful utility method, it is time to get into some more complex method coding as well as learn about another Android GMS class related to sending DataItem objects (and DataMap objects) over the network.

The method you'll be creating next loads the constant values into a DataMap object and submits these as a DataItem object to GMS.

## Loading DataItems into a DataMap: .putConfigDataItem()

Let's create a **public static void putConfigDataItem()** method that accepts a GoogleApiClient object and a DataMap object in the parameter list area.

Name the GoogleApiClient object **googleApiClient** and the DataMap object **newConfigData**. Because you haven't used either of these object (class) types yet in this Java class, you will get red error code highlighting, for which you will need to use the **Alt+Enter** work process to get IntelliJ to write the import statements for these classes for you.

The empty Java method structure, which can be seen highlighted in yellow at the bottom of Figure 14-5, should look like the following Java code:

```
public static void putConfigDataItem(GoogleApiClient googleApiClient,
DataMap newConfigData) { }
```

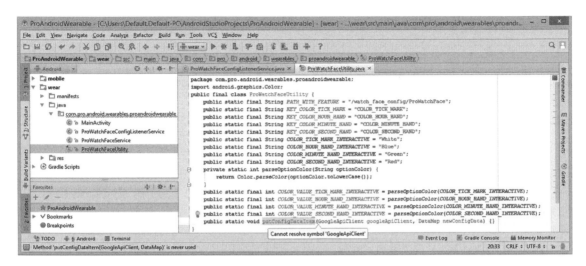

*Figure 14-5. Create a public static void putConfigDataItem(GoogleApiClient, DataMap) empty method structure*

Before you use the PutDataMapRequest class and object, which is central to this method, let's learn a little bit about this Android GMS class next.

## Android PutDataMapRequest Class: Put in a Data Request

The Android GMS **public PutDataMapRequest** class extends java.lang.Object and is contained in the **com.google.android.gms.wearable** package. The Java hierarchy for the class looks like the following:

```
java.lang.Object
  > com.google.android.gms.wearable.PutDataMapRequest
```

A PutDataMapRequest class is a DataMap-aware version of the PutDataRequest class. The class has **six** public methods, which relate to putting in DataMap requests to the Google Play Services server.

The **.asPutDataRequest()** method, which you will be using in the next section of the chapter when you finish writing the putConfigDataItem() method, creates a PutDataRequest object from a PutDataMapRequest object.

You will also be using the **.create(String path)** method, which will create a PutDataMapRequest object using a custom PATH_WITH_FEATURE (constant) path. There's also a **.createFromDataMapItem(DataMapItem source)** method that will create a PutDataMapRequest from a DataMapItem, using a DataMapItem object. A **.createWithAuto AppendedId(String pathPrefix)** method creates an automated PutDataMapRequest, using a randomly generated ID, prefixed with your path.

There's a **.getDataMap()** method, which you will be using to extract a DataMap object from the PutDataMapRequest object, as well as a **.getUri()** method if you want to extract the Uri object from the PutDataMapRequest object.

## Using PutDataMapRequest to Put a Configuration DataItam

Now let's implement a PutDataMapRequest object. I will show you how it is used in the ProWatchFaceUtility.java class to put your configuration DataItem over to Google Play. Declare and instantiate the PutDataMapRequest, naming it **putDataMapRequest**. Set this equal to a call to the **.create()** method off the PutDataMapRequest class, as shown in Figure 14-6, using this Java code:

```
PutDataMapRequest putDataMapRequest = PutDataMapRequest.create(PATH_WITH_FEATURE);
```

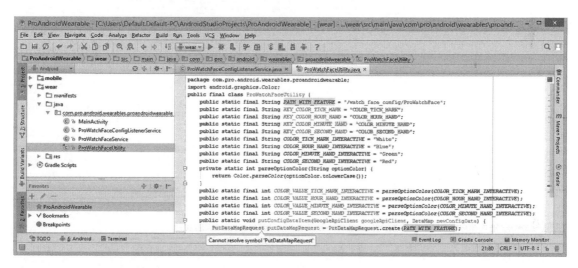

*Figure 14-6. Create a PutDataMapRequest object named putDataMapRequest and instantiate it using .create()*

You will pass the **PATH_WITH_FEATURE** constant into the .create() method to identify this PutDatamapRequest object to the Google Play Service as being related to your specific WatchFaces API application. Think of this kind of like uniquely branding your app, so that GMS does not get things mixed up.

Now that you've created a PutDataMapRequest object branded with your watch face application's unique path specifier, the next step is to create the DataMap object for this PutDataMapRequest object by extracting an "empty" DataMap object from this PutDataMapRequest object, using the **.getDataMap()** method. Your completed (empty) Java class declaration would look like the following Java structure, which can also be seen in Figure 14-7:

```
DataMap configurationToPut = putDataMapRequest.getDataMap();
```

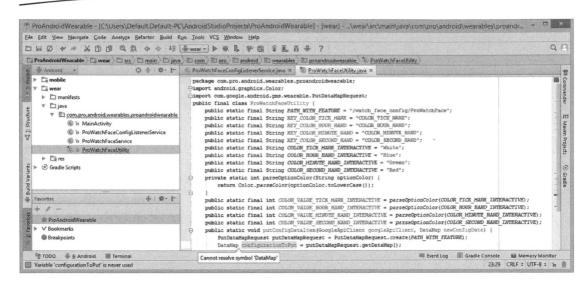

*Figure 14-7.  Create a DataMap object named configurationToPut; load it with putDataMapRequest.getDataMap()*

As you can see in Figure 14-7, you will need to use an **Alt+Enter** keystroke combination to have IntelliJ write the DataMap class import statement for you. Now you can load the empty DataMap object with the configuration data.

To accomplish this, use the **.putAll()** method with the **newConfigData** DataMap object that is passed into the putConfigDataItem() method. This is how the DataMap containing your configuration parameters will replace this empty configurationToPut DataMap that lives inside the PutDataMapRequest:

**configurationToPut**.putAll(**newConfigData**);

As you'll notice in Figure 14-8, this line of code requires no imports and is error free, so you can now get into the most complex Java statement you will be coding for this putConfigDataItem() method relating to putting the PutDataMapRequest in a **Wearable** class **DataApi** object using **.putDataItem()**.

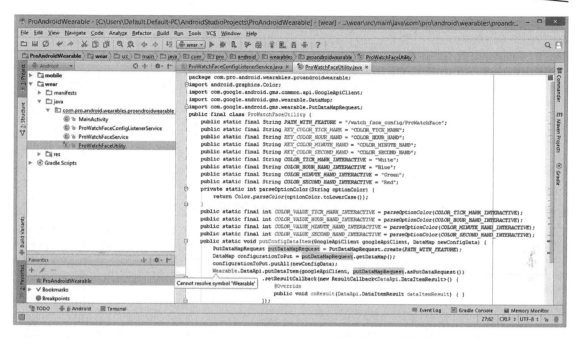

*Figure 14-8.  Use .putAll() to load newConfigData DataMap into configurationToPut DataMap, and call .putDataItem()*

Let's take a closer look at the Android Wearable class before you use it in the rest of your Java code to access its various APIs. In this way you will be familiar with its API types, data fields, and nested classes.

# Android Wearable Class: Android's Wearable APIs

The Android **public Wearable** class extends java.lang.Object and is part of the **com.google. android.gms.wearable** package. It is important to notice that the Wearable class and the wearable package use the same name, so wearable for Android is both a package and a class, as well as the smartwatch platform.

The Wearable class (and object) contains the wearable APIs for the Android Wear platform. Your class hierarchy for this Wearable class looks like the following, indicating that this Wearable class was scratch-coded for Android Wear:

```
java.lang.Object
  > com.google.android.gms.wearable.Wearable
```

There's one nested helper class, the **Wearable.WearableOptions** class, which contains the API configuration parameters for the Android Wearable API.

The four properties, attributes, or data fields that the Wearable class or object contains represent the Primary API, as well as a Network Node API, a Messaging API, and the Data API.

The **public static final Api<Wearable.WearableOptions> API** field contains a Token object to pass over to an **.addApi(Api)** method to enable the Wearable Options (features) outlined in a WearableOptions object. The **public static final DataApi** DataApi field contains the Data API, while the **public static final MessageApi** MessageApi field contains a Message API and the **public static final NodeApi** NodeApi field contains a Network Node API.

# Using the Wearable Class: Putting a DataApi Data Request

The next seven lines of Java code that you are about to write are actually a complex Java statement that features both method (dot) chaining as well as a nested onResult() method inside the .setResultCallback() method! The construct starts with a **Wearable** class, referencing its **DataApi** field, off of which a **.putDataItem()** method is called.

Inside the .putDataItem() parameter area, you pass the GoogleApiClient object named **googleApiClient** as well as the result of an **.asPutDataRequest()** method call off the **putDataMapRequest** object, which transmutes it into a **PutDataRequest** object. The PutDataRequest class (and the object) is used to create new DataItem objects in the Android Wear network.

The .putDataItem() method call requires the GoogleApiClient object and the PutDataRequest object to be passed in as parameters. This portion of the Java statement submits the request to the GMS server.

The next portion of the statement, connected to the .putDataItem() method using **dot chaining**, is the **.setResultCallback()** method, which sets up the application to listen for the Data Request response from the GMS server.

Inside the .setResultCallback() method parameter area, you instantiate a **new ResultCallback<DataApi.DataItemResult>** object. Inside the construct, you @Override the **public void onResult()** method, leaving it empty, so that it performs its default processing of the DataItemResult object (contained inside the ResultCallback object). The Java statement, as shown in Figure 14-8, should look like the following Java code construct:

```java
Wearable.DataApi.putDataItem(googleApiClient, putDataMapRequest.asPutDataRequest())
        .setResultCallback(new ResultCallback<DataApi.DataItemResult>() {
            @Override
            public void onResult(DataApi.DataItemResult dataItemResult) {
                // an empty method represents using the default onResult()
                functionality
            }
        });
```

Now that you have the DataApi request taken care of, let's look at Node Api.

# Using Android's Node API: .fetchConfigDataMap() Method

Let's create a **.fetchConfigDataMap()** method that will use the Node API to fetch (retrieve) the configuration DataMap object. Declare a **public static void fetchConfigDataMap()** method, with the **final GoogleApiClient** object named **client** and a **final FetchConfigDataMapCallback** object named **callback**.

The resulting empty class structure can be seen in Figure 14-9, and would utilize the following Java code:

```
public static void
fetchConfigDataMap( final GoogleApiClient client, final FetchConfigDataMapCallback
callback ) {
    // Empty Method
}
```

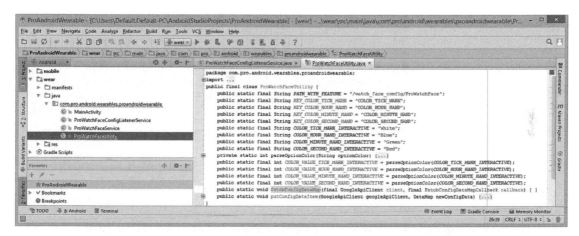

*Figure 14-9. Create an empty public static void fetchConfigDataMap() method structure right after the constants*

As you can see in Figure 14-9, the FetchConfigDataMapCallback has red code error highlighting, because the public interface it references has not yet been created.
If you drop down an error suggestion option list, you'll see "Create public interface FetchConfigDataMapCallback," so let's do just that now. Add a **public interface FetchConfigDataMapCallback** after the constants at the top of the class. Inside the public interface, declare the **void onConfigDataMapFetched(DataMap config)** method required for implementation.

The Java structure for the FetchConfigDataMapCallback interface can be seen highlighted in the bottom part of Figure 14-10 and should look like the following Java public interface structure:

```
public interface FetchConfigDataMapCallback {
    void onConfigDataMapFetched(DataMap config);
}
```

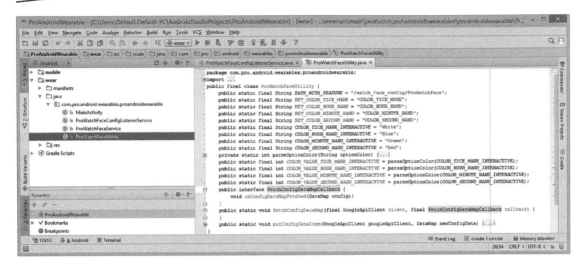

*Figure 14-10. Create the public interface FetchConfigDataMapCallback with an onConfigDataMapFetched() method*

Inside the FetchConfigDataMap() method, you will be using a **NodeApi** class and object, so let's do a quick overview of this Android GMS class first.

## The Android NodeApi Interface: Searching for Connected Nodes

The Android **public NodeApi interface** exposes the API for your Wear apps to utilize **poll** (i.e., search) for **local or connected Nodes**. This NodeApi interface is a part of the **com. google.android.gms.wearable.NodeApi** package. Node API **events** can be delivered to all applications on a device, and you'll be learning how to listen for and take advantage of these Node events. This NodeApi interface has **three** nested (also known as helper) interfaces:

The **NodeApi.GetConnectedNodesResult** interface contains a list of connected nodes on the Wear GMS network.

The **NodeApi.GetLocalNodeResult** interface contains a unique name and an ID, which will uniquely represent the user's hardware device. You will be using this interface in your Java code in the next section of this chapter.

A **NodeApi.NodeListener** interface is intended to be utilized with Android's **.addListener(GoogleApiClient, NodeApi.NodeListener)** method to receive Node API events so that they can be processed.

This NodeApi interface has **four** public methods:

The PendingResult<Status> **.addListener(GoogleApiClient client, NodeApi.NodeListener listener)** method registers a listener that is able to receive (filter) all Node API events.

The abstract PendingResult<NodeApi.GetConnectedNodesResult> **.getCo nnectedNodes(GoogleApiClient client)** method will obtain a list of nodes the user's hardware device is currently connected to.

The abstract PendingResult<NodeApi.GetLocalNodeResult> **.getLocalNode(GoogleApiClient client)** method will obtain the Node that refers to the user's current hardware device. You will be using this method in your Java code in the next section of this chapter.

The abstract PendingResult<Status> **.removeListener(GoogleApiClient client, NodeApi.NodeListener listener)** method will remove the listener that was previously added by using the .addListener(GoogleApiClient, NodeListener).

Now let's finish the Java coding for the .fetchConfigDataMap() method, which uses NodeApi-related methods and classes.

## Harness NodeApi: Using getLocalNode() and getLocalNodeResult()

Inside an empty fetchConfigDataMap() method structure, access Android's **Wearable** class **NodeApi** interface, using dot notation. Call **.getLocalNode()** off this construct and pass in the GoogleApiClient object named **client**, which is passed into this fetchConfigDataMap() method.

Next, use Java method chaining and add a **.setResultCallback()** method call. Inside this, instantiate the ResultCallback object, using the Java **new** keyword, to create a **ResultCallback** object for the **<NodeApi.GetLocalNodeResult>** object type, which is designated using a ResultCallback<NodeApi.GetLocalNodeResult> Java construct. Inside this construct, you will @Override an onResult() method, which you will be completing next, using Java code, which will determine what you want to happen when you get a LocalNode result back.

The Java structure for the fetchConfigDataMap() method thus far, including the **Wearable. NodeApi** structure, getting the **LocalNodeResult**, and setting a result callback, as well as your (currently) empty **onResult()** method body, can be seen in Figure 14-11, and should look like the following Java code:

```
public static void
fetchConfigDataMap(final GoogleApiClient client, final FetchConfigDataMapCallback callback)
{
    Wearable.NodeApi.getLocalNode(client)
                .setResultCallback(new ResultCallback<NodeApi.GetLocalNodeResult>() {
                    @Override
                    public void onResult(NodeApi.GetLocalNodeResult getLocalNodeResult) {
                        // Java code to be executed when a LocalNodeResult object appears
                    }
                });
}
```

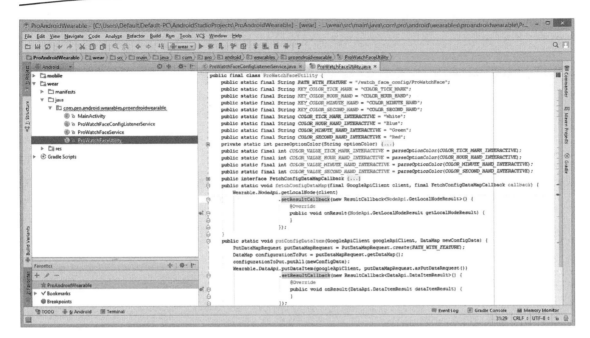

*Figure 14-11. Call a .getLocalNode() and .setResultCallback() off a NodeApi, and override an onResult() method*

Inside the onResult(NodeApi.GetLocalNodeResult getLocalNodeResult) method, you will declare the String object named **myLocalNode** and load it with the result of a **.getNode(). getId()** method chain, off the **getLocalNodeResult** object, which has been passed into this onResult() method structure.

Once myLocalNode is loaded with this NodeApi identification data, you will declare a Uri object named **uri** and instantiate it using a **Uri.Builder** class constructor method in conjunction with the new keyword. Using method chaining, you will set the URI scheme to **wear**, the path to **PATH_WITH_FEATURE**, and the authority to the ID data in the **myLocalNode** String object, as shown in Figure 14-12. Your Java code thus far should look just like the following:

```java
Wearable.NodeApi.getLocalNode(client)
        .setResultCallback(new ResultCallback<NodeApi.GetLocalNodeResult>() {
            @Override
            public void onResult(NodeApi.GetLocalNodeResult getLocalNodeResult) {
                String myLocalNode = getLocalNodeResult.getNode().getId();
                Uri uri = new Uri.Builder()
                                .scheme("wear")
                                .path(ProWatchFaceUtility.PATH_WITH_FEATURE)
                                .authority(myLocalNode)
                                .build();
            }
        });
```

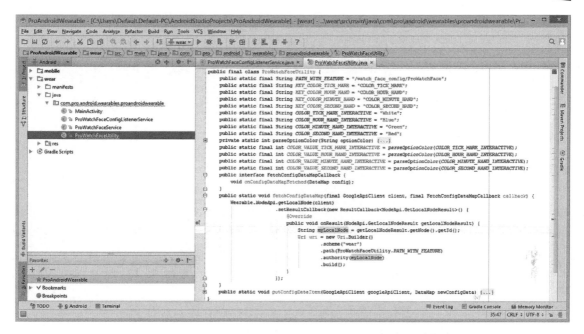

*Figure 14-12. Add a myLocalNode String to extract the LocalNodeResult node data and build a Uri object with it*

Now that you have the GoogleApiClient and Uri objects, you can use them in a
.getDataItem() method call, off the Wearable.DataApi. Then chain the .setResultCallback()
method, requesting a new DataItemResultCallback() constructor that passes
over a FetchConfigDataMapCallback object callback, which is passed into this
fetchConfigDataMap() method construct. As you'll see in Figure 14-13, your finished Java
method structure looks like this:

```
public static void
fetchConfigDataMap(final GoogleApiClient client, final FetchConfigDataMapCallback callback)
{
  Wearable.NodeApi.getLocalNode(client)
              .setResultCallback(new ResultCallback<NodeApi.GetLocalNodeResult>() {
                  @Override
                  public void onResult(NodeApi.GetLocalNodeResult getLocalNodeResult) {
                      String myLocalNode = getLocalNodeResult.getNode().getId();
                      Uri uri = new Uri.Builder()
                                      .scheme("wear")
                                      .path(ProWatchFaceUtility.PATH_WITH_FEATURE)
                                      .authority(myLocalNode)
                                      .build();
                      Wearable.DataApi.getDataItem(client, uri)
                                      .setResultCallback(new
                                      DataItemResultCallback(callback));
                  }
              });
}
```

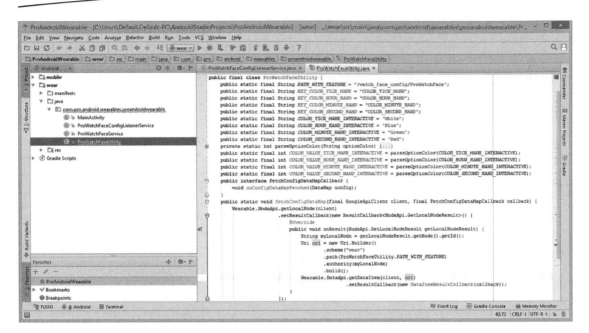

*Figure 14-13.  Call the .getDataItem() method off the Wearable.DataApi, passing it to the client and new Uri object*

As shown in Figure 14-13, there's still one red error code highlight that you will need to address, so let's do that next, so you can get this method error free and move on to create the other needed methods.

Click this line of code, preferably on that red error code highlighting itself, and you should then get a red error lightbulb drop-down arrow, on the left side of the IDE.

Click the down-arrow to drop down a menu list of error-fixing suggestions that IntelliJ thinks will solve the code continuity problem it sees. There are two options: create an entirely separate class, or create a private or inner class inside the ProWatchFaceUtility.java class. In the interests of keeping the number of classes needed to implement your watch faces apps compact, select the second "Create Inner Class 'DataItemResultCallback'" option, as can be seen highlighted at the bottom of Figure 14-14.

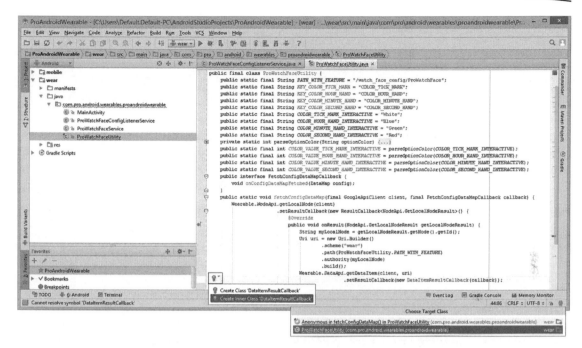

*Figure 14-14.  Select a "Create Inner Class" error drop-down menu option and ProWatchFaceUtility target class*

This will pop open a second chooser dialog with a list of two more options that allow you to specify a **Target Class** in which you want the inner class to be contained. You want the private static inner class inside the ProWatchFaceUtility class, so select this by double-clicking it, and IntelliJ will code a **private static** class **DataItemResultCallback** that implements the **ResultCallback<DataApi.DataItemResult>** interface. This will have some red error highlighting until you implement the required methods, which you will be doing in the next section of this chapter.

IntelliJ will create the private static (inner) class at the bottom of the ProWatchFaceUtility class, as can be seen at the bottom of Figure 14-15.

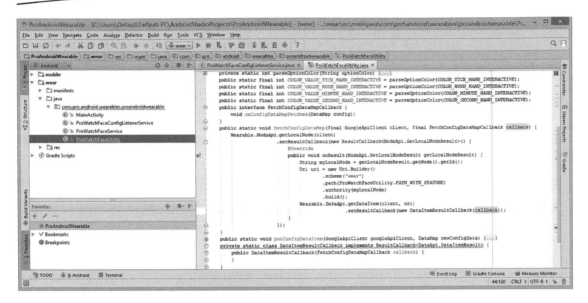

*Figure 14-15. Now your callback object reference is in place and private static inner class created*

Let's write the Java code that will make up the body of this method, which will extract the Watch Face Configuration DataMap from the DataItem using a DataMapItem, as you have done before using the .fromDataItem() method.

## Using Wearable DataApi: DataItemResultCallback() Class

The first thing you'll want to do in this DataItemResultCallback class is declare a private final FetchConfigDataMapCallback object and then name it mCallback. Next, create a public DataItemResultCallback() method, which takes a FetchConfigDataMapCallback object named callback as the parameter.

Inside this method, set the mCallback object created at the top of this class equal to a callback object passed into this DataItemResultCallback() method. The code, as shown in Figure 14-16, should look like the following:

```
private static class DataItemResultCallback implements ResultCallback<DataApi.
DataItemResult> {
    private final FetchConfigDataMapCallback mCallback;
    public DataItemResultCallback(FetchConfigDataMapCallback callback) {
        mCallback = callback;
    }
}
```

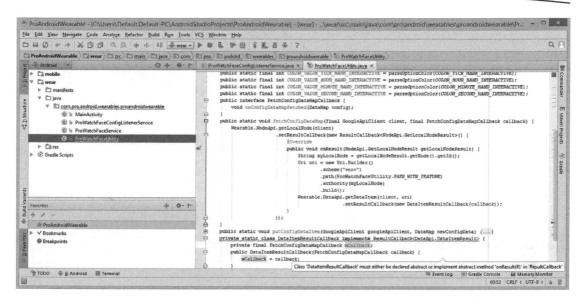

*Figure 14-16.* Add the private final mCallback variable; set it equal to the callback passed into
DataItemResultCallback()

Notice in Figure 14-16 that the wavy red error highlighting is still present, so mouse-over
the error highlight and reveal the error message, which says "Class must either be declared
abstract or implement method onResult(R)."

Override the public void .onResult(DataApi.DataItemResult dataItemResult) method, at the
end of the DataItemResultCallback() method, which will add an empty method (for now)
and remove that red error highlighting. The Java method, shown error free in Figure 14-17,
should look like the following:

```
private static class DataItemResultCallback implements ResultCallback<DataApi.
DataItemResult> {
    private final FetchConfigDataMapCallback mCallback;
    public DataItemResultCallback(FetchConfigDataMapCallback callback) {
        mCallback = callback;
    }
    @Override
    public void onResult(DataApi.DataItemResult dataItemResult) { // empty method removes
    error }
}
```

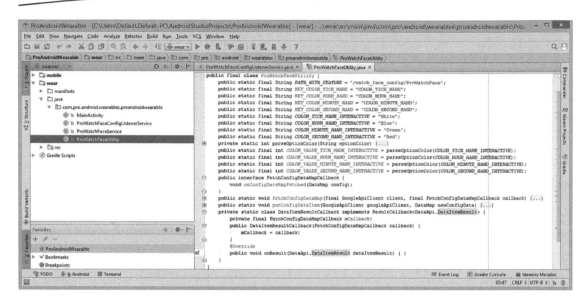

*Figure 14-17. Add an @Override onResult() method to remove red error highlighting on DataItemResultCallback*

Next, you need to create conditional if() structures, which determine if this onResult() method has returned a DataItemResult (an outer if() structure), and a second, inner conditional if() structure, which will determine if the DataItemResult has been used or is not empty (that is, it is != null).

The first outer conditional if() structure uses a **.getStatus().isSuccess()** method chain off the **dataItemResult** DataItemResult object, which you've seen used before to obtain the successful result status flag (true value).

A second inner conditional if() structure then uses a getDataItem() method call off the dataItemResult object and compares it to a null value. If the DataItemResult object has something inside it, the if portion is processed. If it's empty (null), then the else portion of the construct is processed.

The first line of code inside the nested if() structure also relates to the DataItemResult processing, so I am going to include this here as well. This **.getDataItem()** method is again used to get the valid DataItem result, and it is installed into a **DataItem** object named **configDataItem** in one single Java statement that declares, names, and instantiates that DataItem so it can receive a **dataItemResult.getDataItem()** method call object transfer.

The Java code for the .onResult() method structure, which can also be seen highlighted at the bottom of Figure 14-18, should look like the following:

```java
public void onResult(DataApi.DataItemResult dataItemResult) {
    if (dataItemResult.getStatus().isSuccess()) {
        if (dataItemResult.getDataItem() != null) {
            DataItem configDataItem = dataItemResult.getDataItem();
        } else {
        }
    }
}
```

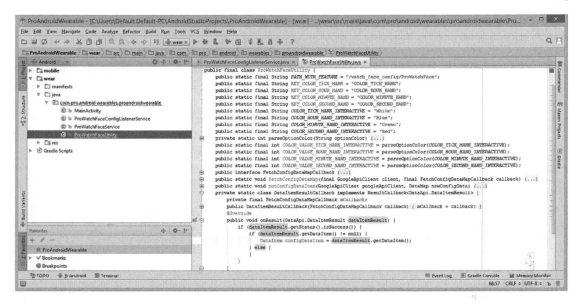

*Figure 14-18.   Create an if() and nested if-else structure inside onResult(); use .getDataItem() to extract the result*

The next thing you want to do, now that all the DataItemResult object processing is in place, is to transmute the DataItem into a DataMapItem so later you can transmute the DataMapItem into the DataMap object you need.

The code for loading a DataMapItem object with a DataItem object is shown in Figure 14-19 and should look just like the following two lines of code:

```
DataItem configDataItem = dataItemResult.getDataItem();
DataMapItem dataMapItem = DataMapItem.fromDataItem(configDataItem);
```

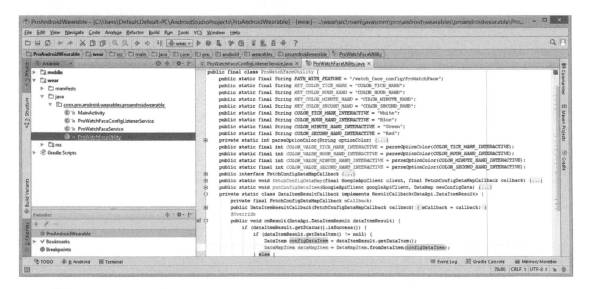

*Figure 14-19.   Declare a DataMapItem, name it dataMapItem, and set it equal to the result of .fromDataItem()*

The next thing you want to do, now that all of the DataMapItem object processing is in place, is to transmute the DataMapItem into a DataMap, so later you can pass the DataMap object into an onConfigDataMapFetched() method call. This transmution of DataItem to DataMapItem to DataMap can be seen in Figure 14-20, and should be done using these three lines of Java code:

```java
DataItem configDataItem = dataItemResult.getDataItem();
DataMapItem dataMapItem = DataMapItem.fromDataItem(configDataItem);
DataMap config = dataMapItem.getDataMap();
```

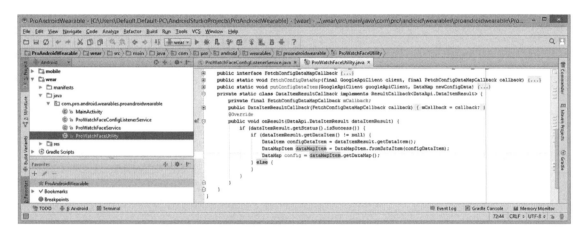

*Figure 14-20. Declare a DataMap named config, set it equal to the result of a .getDataMap() call off dataMapItem*

The final step in this if portion of the conditional statement is to pass the **config DataMap** object into the **mCallback FetchConfigDataMapCallback** object by using the **.onConfigDataMapFetched()** method call.

In the **else** portion of the conditional if-else statement, if the DataItem object is indeed empty (null), you would then simply instantiate a new DataMap object by using the Java **new** keyword and the **DataMap()** constructor method call inside the .onConfigDataMapFetched() method, called off the mCallback FetchConfigDataMapCallback object. The finished onResult() method structure, as shown in Figure 14-21, should look like the following:

```java
public void onResult(DataApi.DataItemResult dataItemResult) {
        if (dataItemResult.getStatus().isSuccess()) {
            if (dataItemResult.getDataItem() != null) {
                DataItem configDataItem = dataItemResult.getDataItem();
                DataMapItem dataMapItem = DataMapItem.fromDataItem(configDataItem);
                DataMap config = dataMapItem.getDataMap();
                mCallback.onConfigDataMapFetched(config);
            } else {
                mCallback.onConfigDataMapFetched(new DataMap());
            }
        }
}
```

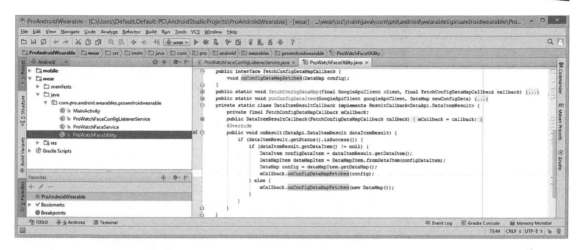

*Figure 14-21. Set the FetchConfigDataMapCallback object to the DataMap using .onConfigDataMapFetched()*

Notice that I clicked the .onConfigDataMapFetched() method in the code to track its implementation back to the FetchConfigDataMapCallback Java interface, which is shown highlighted in blue at the top of Figure 14-21.

Next, let's create the last major method you'll need to code for this class. The .overwriteKeysInConfigDataMap() method will replace any changed key-data pairs that a user specifies, creating an all-new DataMap object.

## Replacing Changed Data: overwriteKeysInConfigDataMap

Let's create the **public static void overwriteKeysInConfigDataMap()** method with a **final** GoogleApiClient, which you will name **googleApiClient**, and the **final** DataMap object, which you will name **configKeysToOverwrite**, as shown in Figure 14-22. The Java code should look like this empty method body declaration:

```
public static void overwriteKeysInConfigDataMap(final GoogleApiClient googleApiClient, final
DataMap configKeysToOverwrite) {  // empty method: your method body will go in here  }
```

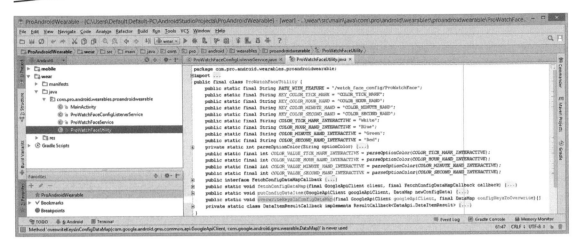

**Figure 14-22.** *Create empty public static void overwriteKeysInConfigDataMap() method*

The first thing you are going to code inside this method body is a method call to one of the methods you created earlier in this chapter. This will be referenced with the ProWatchFaceUtility class name, a period, and the method name, as shown in Figure 14-23.

Inside the method call parameter area, you will pass the **GoogleApiClient** object and instantiate a new **fetchConfigDataMapCallback** object using the Java **new** keyword. The Java code for the empty method declaration should look like the following code:

```
ProWatchFaceUtility.fetchConfigDatamap(googleApiClient, new fetchConfigDataMapCallback() {
empty method });
```

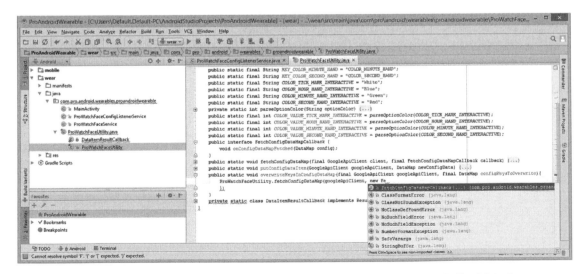

**Figure 14-23.** *Use the IntelliJ pop-up helper dialog to implement your FetchConfigDataMapCallback interface*

The **fetchConfigDatamap(GoogleApiClient, FetchConfigDataMapCallback)** method is currently being designated (colored) as unused by the IntelliJ IDEA, as you can see in Figure 14-22. Unused methods or variables are defined using gray code text coloration, and once they're referenced in other code, they will turn black. As you can see in Figure 14-23, IntelliJ can help code an empty method body; for instance, if you type in a Java new keyword and the **Fe** characters, an IntelliJ helper dialog will pop up, where you can select the FetchConfigDataMapCallback interface from the drop-down list of options.

When you select the FetchConfigDataMapCallback interface, IntelliJ will also implement the required **.onConfigDataMapFetched(DataMap config)** method for you, which can be seen in Figure 14-24, producing the following Java code:

```
ProWatchFaceUtility.fetchConfigDatamap(googleApiClient, new fetchConfigDataMapCallback() {
    @Override
    public void onConfigDataMapFetched(DataMap config) { // an empty method created by
    IntelliJ }
});
```

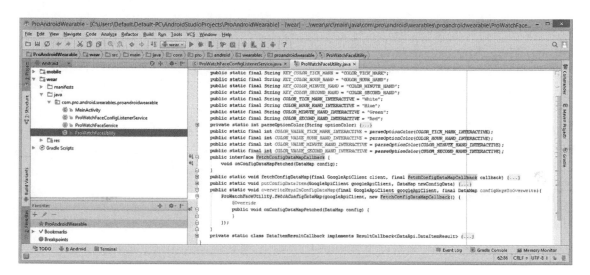

*Figure 14-24. IntelliJ will implement the complete (empty) FetchConfigDataMapCallback infrastructure for you*

Now all you have to do is to write the Java statements that create the new DataMap, which will hold the latest (updated) configuration data array by overwriting the current (or default, if this is the first update) DataMap.

## Updating a DataMap Object: onConfigDataMapFetched()

Inside this public void onConfigDataMapFetched() method, which IntelliJ has created for you, change the name of the DataMap parameter passed into the method to **currentConfig**. This is done to more accurately reflect what is being passed into this method structure.

Next, declare and instantiate a **new** DataMap object, named **overwriteConfig**, which is used to hold the DataMap and will contain the modified configuration parameters. To load that object with the currentConfig DataMap passed into this method, call the **.putAll()** method using the **currentConfig** object as a parameter, off the overwriteConfig DataMap object.

The Java method structure thus far, which you can see highlighted at the bottom of Figure 14-25, should look just like the following Java code:

```java
ProWatchFaceUtility.fetchConfigDatamap(googleApiClient, new fetchConfigDataMapCallback() {
    @Override
    public void onConfigDataMapFetched(DataMap currentConfig) {
        DataMap overwriteConfig = new DataMap();
        overwriteConfig.putAll(currentConfig);
    }
});
```

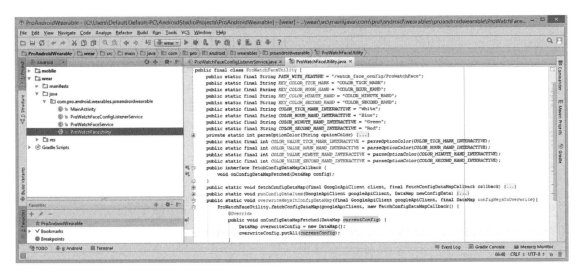

*Figure 14-25.  Declare and instantiate a DataMap named overwriteConfig and use a .putAll() method to load it*

Now that your current settings, or default settings if this is your first configuration parameters update, are in an overwriteConfig DataMap, you'll then use the same putAll() method to overwrite (replace) new configuration parameters passed into this overwriteKeysInConfigDataMap() method.

This work process ensures that if there are any incomplete or missing key-data pairs in the incoming (updates or changes) DataMap after the two .putAll() method are called, they will be processed and there'll be a complete DataMap object with all of the parameters, both changed as well as unchanged (or default).

The Java method structure thus far, which you can see highlighted at the bottom of Figure 14-26, should look just like the following Java code:

```
ProWatchFaceUtility.fetchConfigDatamap(googleApiClient, new fetchConfigDataMapCallback() {
    @Override
    public void onConfigDataMapFetched(DataMap currentConfig) {
        DataMap overwriteConfig = new DataMap();
        overwriteConfig.putAll(currentConfig);
        overwriteConfig.putAll(configKeysToOverwrite);
    }
});
```

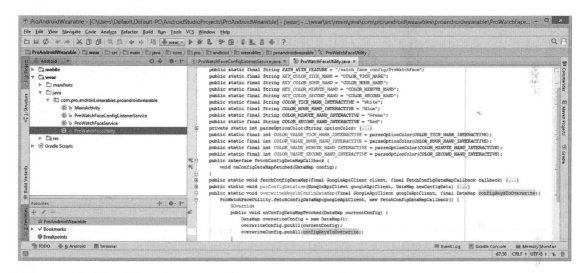

**Figure 14-26.**  *Use another .putAll() method call to overwrite the updated configuration data over the current data*

The final programming "move" that you need to make is to write the updated **overwriteConfig** DataMap object, by passing it to the **.putConfigDataItem()** method, which you coded earlier in this chapter. Because you are calling this method outside the current method body, you'll preface this method name with the class name, like this: **ProWatchFaceUtility.putConfigDataItem()**. Inside the parameter area, pass the GoogleApiClient object and DataMap object containing the updated (overwritten) watch face configuration data.

The final Java code for this method structure can be seen highlighted at the bottom of Figure 14-27 and should look like the following:

```
ProWatchFaceUtility.fetchConfigDatamap(googleApiClient, new fetchConfigDataMapCallback() {
    @Override
    public void onConfigDataMapFetched(DataMap currentConfig) {
        DataMap overwriteConfig = new DataMap();
        overwriteConfig.putAll(currentConfig);
        overwriteConfig.putAll(configKeysToOverwrite);
        ProWatchFaceUtility.putConfigDataItem(googleApiClient, overwriteConfig);
    }
});
```

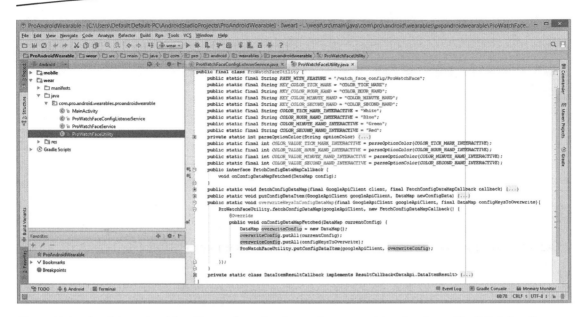

*Figure 14-27.  Send the updated DataMap configuration data to the smartwatch, using the .putConfigDataItem()
method called off the ProWatchFaceUtility class*

The next thing you need to do is call the ProWatchFaceUtility class from the
ProWatchFaceConfigListenerService class, wiring the two classes together.

# Connect the Maps: Call the Utility from the Listener

Click the **ProWatchFaceConfigListenerService.java** tab, or open it if it isn't open
in the IDE. Add a final line of code to the **onMessageReceived()** method, which
will send the **keysToOverwrite** DataMap object into the ProWatchFaceUtility class
**.overwriteKeysInConfigDataMap()** method. The Java statement, as shown in Figure 14-28,
should look just like the following:

```
ProWatchFaceUtility.overwriteKeysInConfigDataMap(myGoogleApiClient, keysToOverwrite);
```

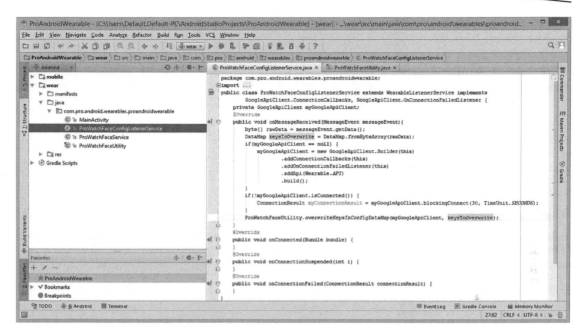

**Figure 14-28.** *Open the Listener class and call the overwriteKeysInConfigDataMap method off the ProWatchFaceUtility class passing over keysToOverwrite*

As you'll see in Figure 14-29, the utility class Java code is error free, and no Java code (other than constants, which I'll address next) is **gray**.

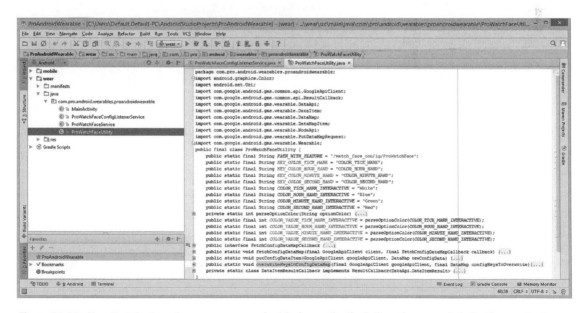

**Figure 14-29.** *Now that the two classes are cross-wired (using each other), the only gray code is for the constants*

Now you are ready to go back into the ProWatchFaceCompanionConfigActivity, which you coded originally when you started developing all of this code in Chapter 13. You will finish up by creating the key-value data pairs that you need in the other classes you have created, as well as doing all the UI design work that is needed to create the color selection user interface design for your watch face users to use to customize their watch face app.

# Finishing the Configuration Companion: UI Design

Open the **ProWatchFaceCompanionConfigActivity.java** class (in the mobile section of your project) and add in the same four KEY_COLOR constants you declared at the top of the ProWatchFaceUtility.java class.

The only difference in these constants are that they will be declared with a Java private keyword because they're only used in the class, rather than a public keyword, as in ProWatchFaceUtility. These constant declarations can be seen in Figure 14-30 and will look like the following Java statements:

```
private static final String PATH_WITH_FEATURE = "/watch_face_config/ProWatchFace";
private static final String KEY_COLOR_TICK_MARK = "COLOR_TICK_MARK";
private static final String KEY_COLOR_HOUR_HAND = "COLOR_HOUR_HAND";
private static final String KEY_COLOR_MINUTE_HAND = "COLOR_MINUTE_HAND";
private static final String KEY_COLOR_SECOND_HAND = "COLOR_SECOND_HAND";
```

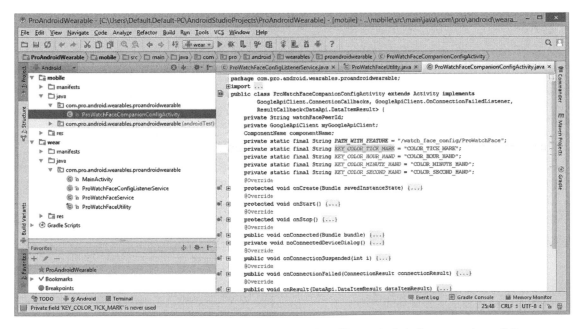

*Figure 14-30. Declare private KEY_COLOR constants matching the utility constants in the companion activity*

Now that all of the Java code is in place for passing DataMap and DataItem objects around between all of the classes, let's switch gears and go into UI design mode. Let's write some XML markup to define the user experience on the smartphone for your WatchFaces Configuration Companion Activity.

# Choosing Color Using the Spinner Widget: XML UI Layout

Open the **mobile/res/activity_pro_watch_face_config.xml** file in an editing tab and add
a nested <LinearLayout> tag under the <TextView> tag. Set the orientation parameter to
horizontal, so the Text widget will be next to the Spinner widget. Inside this LinearLayout
container, nest a TextView tag and reference the <string> constant using @string/pro_config_
tick_mark. Then set the layout_width parameter to zero and the layout_weight parameter to
one. The XML markup, as shown in Figure 14-31, should look like the following:

```
<?xml version="1.0" encoding="utf-8"?>
<LinearLayout xmlns:android="http://schemas.android.com/apk/res/android"
    android:orientation="vertical" android:layout_width="match_parent"
    android:layout_height="match_parent">
    <TextView android:id="@+id/title" android:text="@string/prowatchface_config"
        android:layout_width="match_parent" android:layout_height="wrap_content" />
    <LinearLayout android:layout_width="match_parent" android:layout_height="wrap_content"
        android:orientation="horizontal" >
        <TextView android:text="@string/pro_config_tick_mark" android:layout_width="0dp"
            android:layout_height="wrap_content" android:layout_weight="1" />
    </LinearLayout>
</LinearLayout>
```

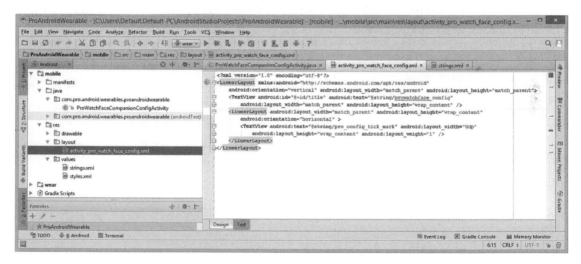

*Figure 14-31. Add a nested <LinearLayout> and inside that, nest a <TextView> tag to hold the first UI construct*

The reason you set the layout_width parameter to zero density pixels, or density
independent pixels (DIP), is because this setting tells Android OS to allow the **layout_weight**
parameter to determine the relative layout percentage of screen allocation. If you set a
Spinner widget layout_weight to two, your TextView would get one-third of the screen,
calculated as 1/(1+2). A Spinner layout_weight of three, which is what you are going to
implement next, gives your TextView 25% of the screen and the Spinner 75% of the screen.

Let's get rid of the red error code highlighting seen in Figure 14-31, and open the **mobile/res/values/strings.xml** file and add the <string> constant named **pro_config_tick_mark** using a data value of **Tick Marks**. While you are at it, add the other <string> constants for the hour, minute, and second hands. The XML markup, as shown in Figure 14-32, should look like the following:

```
<string name="pro_config_tick_mark">Tick Marks</string>
<string name="pro_config_hour_hand">Hour Hand</string>
<string name="pro_config_minute_hand">Minute Hand</string>
<string name="pro_config_second_hand">Second Hand</string>
```

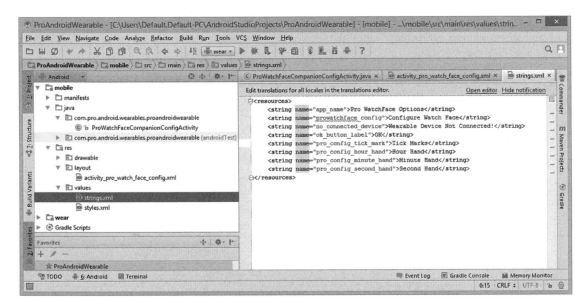

***Figure 14-32.*** *Create <string> constants for UI labels to use for tick marks and hour, minute, and second hands*

Inside this initial child horizontal <LinearLayout> construct, add the <Spinner> widget, right underneath the <TextView> widget. Give it an ID of tickMarks using the format **@+id/tickMarks**, and again set the layout_width to 0dp (or 0dip if you prefer) and the layout_weight to 3.

To load the Spinner widget with color values, add the **entries** parameter set to an **array** named **color_array**, using the format **@array/color_array**.

Your XML markup thus far, which can be seen highlighted in Figure 14-33, should look like the following XML layout definition construct:

```
<LinearLayout xmlns:android="http://schemas.android.com/apk/res/android"
    android:orientation="vertical" android:layout_width="match_parent"
    android:layout_height="match_parent">
    <TextView android:id="@+id/title" android:text="@string/prowatchface_config"
        android:layout_width="match_parent" android:layout_height="wrap_content" />
    <LinearLayout android:layout_width="match_parent" android:layout_height="wrap_content"
        android:orientation="horizontal" >
```

```
            <TextView android:text="@string/pro_config_tick_mark" android:layout_width="0dp"
                android:layout_height="wrap_content" android:layout_weight="1" />
            <Spinner android:id="@+id/tickMarks" android:entries="@array/color_array"
                android:layout_width="0dp" android:layout_height="wrap_content"
                android:layout_weight="3" />
        </LinearLayout>
    </LinearLayout>
```

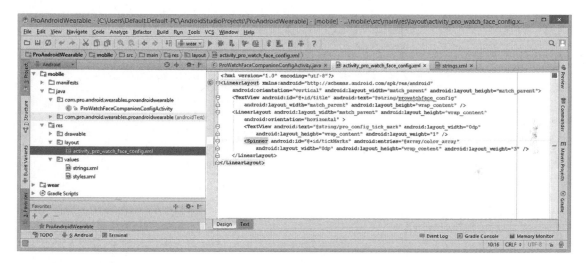

*Figure 14-33. Add a <Spinner> widget child tag underneath the <TextView> tag referencing a color_array*

To get rid of the red error text highlight, click the **strings.xml** tab and add color data value constants, which you must put in place before you can create an array object that references these color constant values.

I am going to use the eight primary Color constants from the Android Color class. These are the most standardized colors that are defined within the Android OS, and these will look great against the black background color.

This will give your users **1,680** different (nonunique) color combinations, which means that the same color could be used for more than one watch face design element. The way you would calculate the number of variations is C! (number of colors factorial) over E! (number of elements factorial).

There are eight different color possibilities, or eight factorial **8!**, which is **8*7*6*5*4*3*2*1=40320**. You then divide this by the four different watch face design elements, or four factorial **4!**, which is **4*3*2*1=24**. This gives you 1,680 potential color combinations!

The XML markup to define the eight colors, which is shown in Figure 14-34, should look like the following:

```
<string name="color_yellow">Yellow</string>
<string name="color_blue">Blue</string>
<string name="color_red">Red</string>
<string name="color_green">Green</string>
```

```xml
<string name="color_cyan">Cyan</string>
<string name="color_magenta">Magenta</string>
<string name="color_gray">Gray</string>
<string name="color_white">White</string>
```

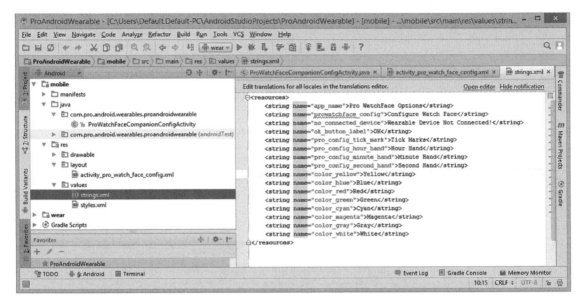

***Figure 14-34.*** *Add eight <string> constant definitions referencing the most common Android OS Color constants*

After the color constant <string> XML definitions are in place, you'll add a <string-array> object XML definition, which will create the Array object construct that will hold the Color Constant String Values.

What this <string-array> tag does is create a String Array object using XML by nesting **<item>** tags that reference <string> constants inside the <string-array> Array object definition construct.

The XML markup that you need to code to achieve the creation of the String Array structure can be seen in Figure 14-35, and should look like the following:

```xml
<string-array name="color_array">
    <item>@string/color_yellow</item>
    <item>@string/color_blue</item>
    <item>@string/color_red</item>
    <item>@string/color_green</item>
    <item>@string/color_cyan</item>
    <item>@string/color_magenta</item>
    <item>@string/color_gray</item>
    <item>@string/color_white</item>
</string-array>
```

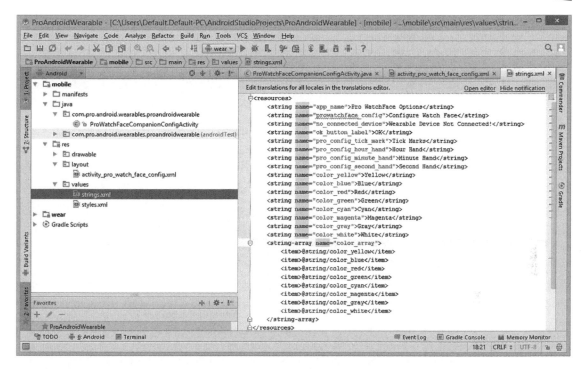

***Figure 14-35.*** *Add a <string-array> structure filled with eight <item> child tags that reference the eight Colors*

As you will see in Figure 14-36, now that you have created the XML String Color constants and the Array, there are no red error code highlights, and you are ready to copy and paste your first nested <LinearLayout> structure and create the second one for an Hour Hand Color Selection Spinner UI element.

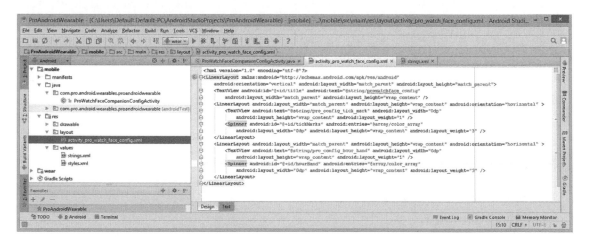

***Figure 14-36.*** *Copy and paste the first nested LinearLayout UI container to create a second one for the hour hand*

Select the child <LinearLayout> XML structure and its two child UI widgets and right-click and select **Copy**, or use the **CTRL+C** keystroke combination. Next, click the mouse to insert the insertion bar (cursor) right before the final </LinearLayout> closing tag for the parent LinearLayout, and right-click and select **Paste**, or use your **CTRL+V** keystroke combination to paste. The results can be seen in Figure 14-36 and should look like the following:

```
<LinearLayout xmlns:android="http://schemas.android.com/apk/res/android"
    android:orientation="vertical" android:layout_width="match_parent"
    android:layout_height="match_parent">
    <TextView android:id="@+id/title" android:text="@string/prowatchface_config"
        android:layout_width="match_parent" android:layout_height="wrap_content" />
    <LinearLayout android:layout_width="match_parent" android:layout_height="wrap_content"
        android:orientation="horizontal" >
        <TextView android:text="@string/pro_config_tick_mark" android:layout_width="0dp"
            android:layout_height="wrap_content" android:layout_weight="1" />
        <Spinner android:id="@+id/tickMarks" android:entries="@array/color_array"
            android:layout_width="0dp" android:layout_height="wrap_content"
            android:layout_weight="3" />
    </LinearLayout>
    <LinearLayout android:layout_width="match_parent" android:layout_height="wrap_content"
        android:orientation="horizontal" >
        <TextView android:text="@string/pro_config_hour_hand" android:layout_width="0dp"
            android:layout_height="wrap_content" android:layout_weight="1" />
        <Spinner android:id="@+id/hourHand" android:entries="@array/color_array"
            android:layout_width="0dp" android:layout_height="wrap_content"
            android:layout_weight="3" />
    </LinearLayout>
</LinearLayout>
```

Because you want to allow your users to configure colors for four watch face design elements, you will need to again perform this time-saving, copy and paste work process, and select both of these nested LinearLayout container XML markup blocks and paste them at the bottom of the UI definition.

What you'll end up with in the end is a master parent **vertical** LinearLayout container arranging nested child **horizontal** LinearLayout containers, which contain the **TextView** (labels), **Spinner** (color selector), and UI elements.

The final **activity_pro_watch_face_config.xml** user interface layout design XML definition, which can be seen, error free, in Figure 14-37, should use the following XML markup:

```
<?xml version="1.0" encoding="utf-8"?>

<LinearLayout xmlns:android="http://schemas.android.com/apk/res/android"
    android:orientation="vertical" android:layout_width="match_parent"
    android:layout_height="match_parent">
    <TextView android:id="@+id/title" android:text="@string/prowatchface_config"
        android:layout_width="match_parent" android:layout_height="wrap_content" />

    <LinearLayout android:layout_width="match_parent" android:layout_height="wrap_content"
        android:orientation="horizontal" >
        <TextView android:text="@string/pro_config_tick_mark" android:layout_width="0dp"
            android:layout_height="wrap_content" android:layout_weight="1" />
```

```xml
        <Spinner android:id="@+id/tickMarks" android:entries="@array/color_array"
            android:layout_width="0dp" android:layout_height="wrap_content"
            android:layout_weight="3" />
    </LinearLayout>

    <LinearLayout android:layout_width="match_parent" android:layout_height="wrap_content"
        android:orientation="horizontal" >
        <TextView android:text="@string/pro_config_hour_hand" android:layout_width="0dp"
            android:layout_height="wrap_content" android:layout_weight="1" />
        <Spinner android:id="@+id/hourHand" android:entries="@array/color_array"
            android:layout_width="0dp" android:layout_height="wrap_content"
            android:layout_weight="3" />
    </LinearLayout>

    <LinearLayout android:layout_width="match_parent" android:layout_height="wrap_content"
        android:orientation="horizontal" >
        <TextView android:text="@string/pro_config_minute_hand" android:layout_width="0dp"
            android:layout_height="wrap_content" android:layout_weight="1" />
        <Spinner android:id="@+id/minuteHand" android:entries="@array/color_array"
            android:layout_width="0dp" android:layout_height="wrap_content"
            android:layout_weight="3" />
    </LinearLayout>

    <LinearLayout android:layout_width="match_parent" android:layout_height="wrap_content"
        android:orientation="horizontal" >
        <TextView android:text="@string/pro_config_second_hand" android:layout_width="0dp"
            android:layout_height="wrap_content" android:layout_weight="1" />
        <Spinner android:id="@+id/secondHand" android:entries="@array/color_array"
            android:layout_width="0dp" android:layout_height="wrap_content"
            android:layout_weight="3" />
    </LinearLayout>

</LinearLayout>
```

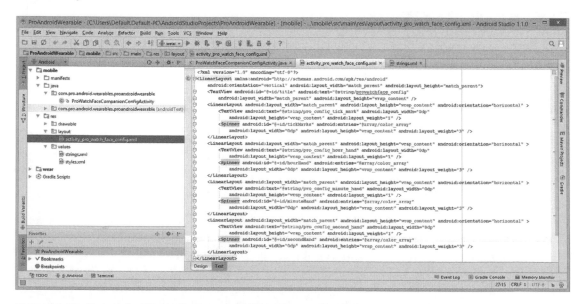

*Figure 14-37. Copy and paste the first two nested LinearLayout UI containers to create the minute and second hands*

Now that the XML UI Layout Definition is built, let's switch back to Java programming mode and write the methods that make these Spinners function.

## Setting the Spinner Widget: setUpColorPickerSelection()

In the next few sections, you will be coding the Java methods that relate to the back-end processing (Java code; XML markup is the front-end design) for your Color Selection Widgets. These are implemented using the Spinner class (object) definitions you put in place using the <Spinner> tag.

Click the ProWatchFaceCompanionConfigActivity.java tab (or open it) and add a private void setUpColorPickerSelection() method at the bottom of the class before the ending curly brace ( } ). You'll need to pass four parameters into this method: one for the Spinner ID parameter you created in the XML UI definition, a String holding configuration data key, a DataMap with the key-value pairs, and the Resource ID integer for a default Color constant. The Java code, as shown in Figure 14-38, should look like the following:

```
private void setUpColorPickerSelection(int spinnerId, final String configKey, DataMap
config,
                                       int defaultColorNameResId) {
    String defaultColorName = getString(defaultColorNameResId);
    int defaultColor = Color.parseColor(defaultColorName);
    int color;
}
```

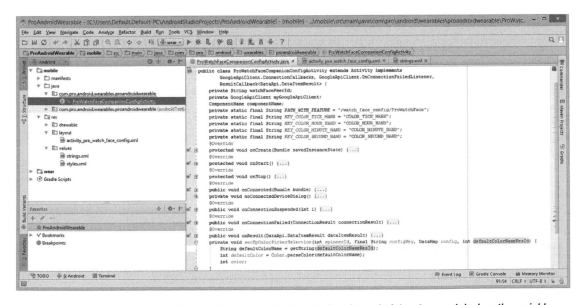

*Figure 14-38.  Add private void setUpColorPickerSelection() method at the end of the class and declare the variables*

The next Java construct you will need to put into place in this method is an if-else conditional statement that will ascertain if the DataMap has been loaded (used) or if it is a virgin (unutilized) DataMap.

The way that you ascertain this is by using the if(config != null) condition, as a non-null DataMap contains a map of data! If the DataMap is "live," you use the **.getInt(String, integer)**, called off the **config DataMap** object. This will extract an integer value associated with a configKey String key. This is assigned to the color integer variable you declared earlier.

On the other hand, within an else portion of the construct, if the DataMap is empty (null value), you'll simply set the color integer variable to the defaultColor value, which you extracted from the defaultColorName variable using the .getString() method call. The Java code for the construct, as shown in Figure 14-39, should look like the following method structure:

```java
private void setUpColorPickerSelection(int spinnerId, final String configKey, DataMap config,
                                       int defaultColorNameResId) {
    String defaultColorName = getString(defaultColorNameResId);
    int defaultColor = Color.parseColor(defaultColorName);
    int color;
    if (config != null) {
        color = config.getInt(configKey, defaultColor);
    } else {
        color = defaultColor;
    }
}
```

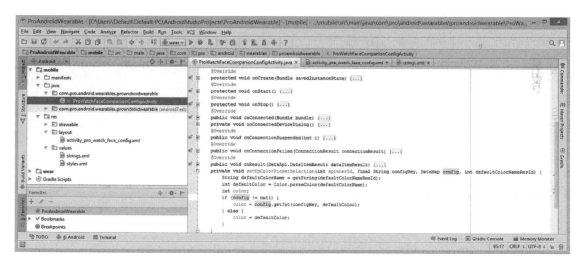

*Figure 14-39. Add an if-else conditional structure, evaluating the config DataMap, and processing it accordingly*

The final step in completing the method is to create a Java **Spinner** object named **spinner** and **inflate** it using the <Spinner> XML definition using the **findViewById()** method. The process of inflation in Android is populating a Java object using an XML object definition that you've created previously. You then create a **colorNames String[]** Array and populate it using the data you created using the XML **<string-array>** construct and the

**.getStringArray()** method chained off a **getResources()** method. Use a **for loop** and load the colorNames Array with your Color constant values. The Java code to do this can be seen in Figure 14-40 and should look like the following:

```
private void setUpColorPickerSelection(int spinnerId, final String configKey, DataMap config,
                                       int defaultColorNameResId) {
    String defaultColorName = getString(defaultColorNameResId);
    int defaultColor = Color.parseColor(defaultColorName);
    int color;
    if (config != null) {
        color = config.getInt(configKey, defaultColor);
    } else {
        color = defaultColor;
    }
    Spinner spinner = (Spinner) findViewById(spinnerId);
    String[] colorNames = getResources().getStringArray(R.array.color_array);
    for (int i = 0; i < colorNames.length; i++) {
        if (Color.parseColor(colorNames[i]) == color) {
            spinner.setSelection(i);
            break;
        }
    }
}
```

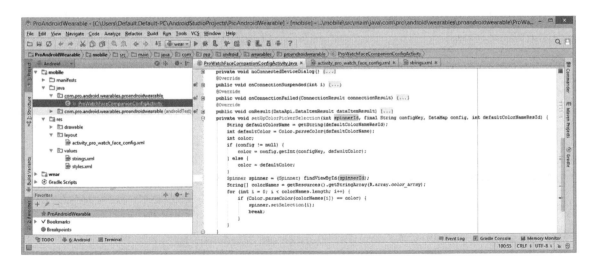

*Figure 14-40. Create a Spinner object named spinner; load it with String[] Array data, defined in your XML array*

Now that you have loaded your Spinner object with the Color values, the next step us to set up the Color Picker Listener object to listen for user selection changes.

# Setting Up a Spinner Listener: setUpColorPickerListener()

Now that you've populated the Spinner object with the Color constant values in the <string-array> that you created earlier, you also need to set up the Listener object, which will listen for any changes your user makes to the Spinner default (or previous) Color constant selection.

Create a **private void setUpColorPickerListener()** method at the end of your class that takes in the **Spinner ID integer** and **configKey KEY_COLOR String** Color constant values as its two method parameters.

Inside the method, declare a **Spinner** object named **spinner** and inflate it using the **findViewById(spinnerId)** method call and parameter. You did this in the previous method you just created; however, notice that both of these are **local** (or private) variables for use inside each of the methods, and as such, they don't conflict. You need a unique Spinner object for this method, because you are going to construct a Listener structure off of it.

The Java method structure thus far, which can be seen highlighted at the bottom of Figure 14-41, should look like the following Java code:

```java
private void setUpColorPickerListener(int spinnerId, final String configKey) {
    Spinner spinner = (Spinner) findViewById(spinnerId);
}
```

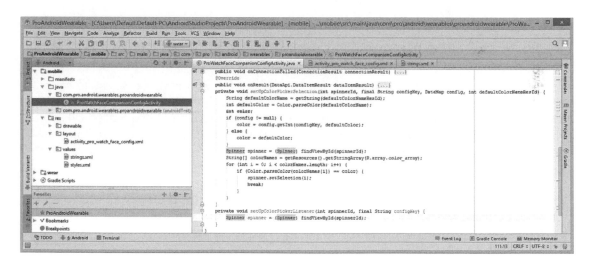

**Figure 14-41.** Create a public void setUpColorPickerListener() method at the bottom of the class; then inflate the Spinner

The next thing you need to do is use the .setOnItemSelectedListener() method to create an AdapterView Listener. The Spinner class is subclassed from the **AdapterView** class, so the Spinner object is also an AdapterView object. It uses an **AdapterView.OnItemSelectedListener()**

constructor method call, in conjunction with the Java new keyword. Create this Listener using the following Java code, as shown highlighted at the bottom of Figure 14-42:

```java
private void setUpColorPickerListener(int spinnerId, final String configKey) {
    Spinner spinner = (Spinner) findViewById(spinnerId);
    spinner.setOnItemSelectedListener(new AdapterView.OnItemSelectedListener() { // empty
method });
}
```

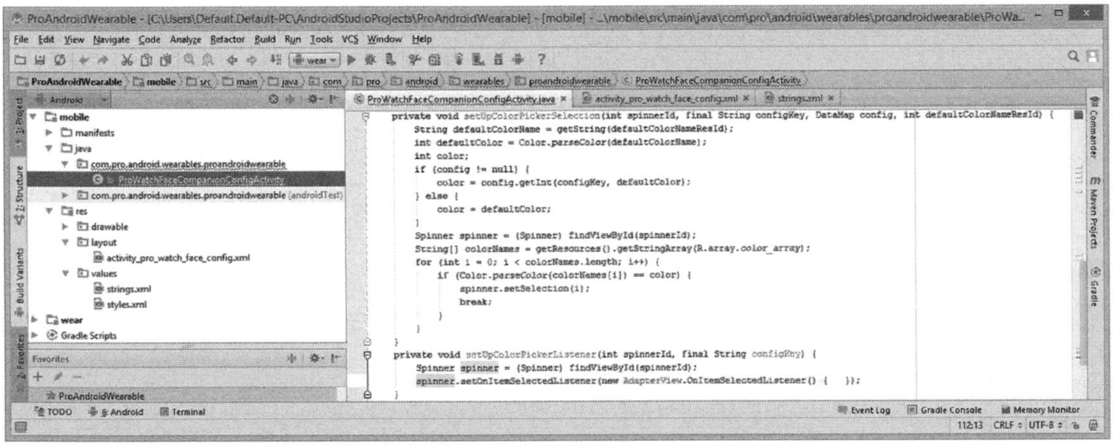

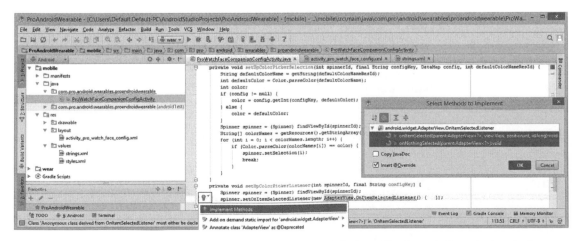

***Figure 14-42.*** *Call a .setOnItemSelectedListener() method off the spinner and construct a new AdapterView Listener*

As you can see in Figure 14-42, you will need to use the **Alt+Enter** work process to have IntelliJ write an import statement for the AdapterView class. Once IntelliJ does this, it will reevaluate your code and give you a wavy red error highlight under the AdapterView. OnItemSelectedListener() constructor method. In the error drop-down shown in Figure 14-43, select the **Implement Methods** option, and implement both required methods, with **Insert @ Override** selected. IntelliJ will then create an **onItemSelected()** construct for you.

***Figure 14-43.*** *Use error suggestion drop-down, select Implement Methods, and implement all required methods*

Inside the empty onItemSelected() method, shown highlighted in Figure 14-44, create a **final String colorName** variable and call the **.getItemAtPosition()** method off the **AdapterView** object named **parent**, which is passed into this method structure. You can use an IntelliJ pop-up helper dialog if you wish.

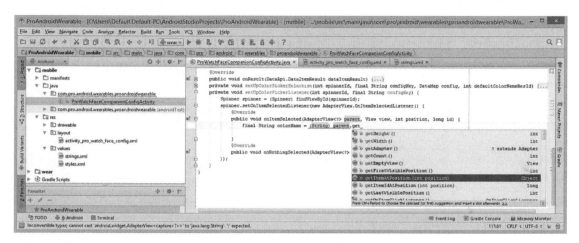

**Figure 14-44.** *Create a final String variable named colorName and use the .getItemPosition() method to load it*

After you have the Color constant that has been selected in the Spinner by the user, call a **sendConfigUpdateMessage()** method with a **configKey** DataMap and an integer result from a **Color.parseColor(colorName)** nested statement.

As you can see in Figure 14-45, this sendConfigUpdateMessage() method does not yet exist, so use the error suggestion drop-down and select the **Create Method** option to have IntelliJ code the empty method structure for you in **ProWatchFaceCompanionConfigActivity** (a **Choose Target Class** dialog option).

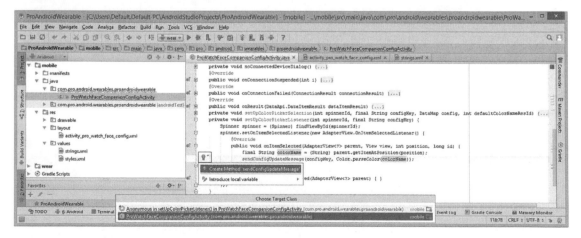

**Figure 14-45.** *Call the sendConfigUpdateMessage() method with DataMap and Color Key; then select Create Method*

Edit the **private void .sendConfigUpdateMessage(String configKey, int i)** method structure that IntelliJ wrote for you to more accurately reflect what is going on inside the method by changing **int i** to **int color**. Now you can code the inside of this sendConfigUpdateMessage() method structure and then finish up this class by coding the .setUpAllPickers() method.

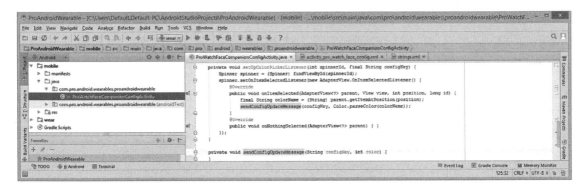

*Figure 14-46. IntelliJ will create the sendConfigUpdateMessage(String configKey, int i) method; then rename i to color*

Everything in this method is executed if there is a watchFacePeerId value.

The first thing to do inside the **if(watchFacePeerId != null)** structure is to construct a DataMap named **newConfig**, and then use a .putInt() method to load it with the **configKey** and **Color** constant passed into this method. The Java code, as shown in Figure 14-47, should look like the following:

```
If ( watchFacePeerId != null ) { DataMap newConfig = new DataMap();
                                  newConfig.putInt(configKey, color); }
```

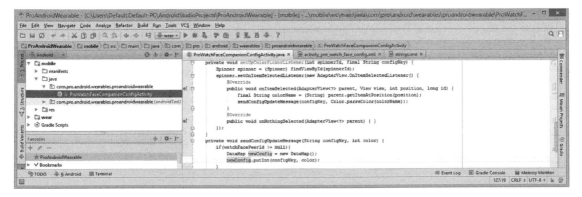

*Figure 14-47.  Create the if() condition to see if watchFacePeerId exists; inside it, create a DataMap and load it with the key-value pair*

The next two lines of code will declare a **byte[]** Array named **rawConfigData** and use a **.toByteArray()** method call to extract the data from the DataMap named newConfig. The heavy lifting is done by the Wearable.MessageApi and the .sendMessage() method call, which passes the rawConfigData byte[] Array to the GMS server, along with the unique watchFacePeerId, GoogleApiClient object, and PATH_WITH_FEATURE constant, using the following code, as shown in Figure 14-48:

```
byte[] rawConfigData = newConfig.toByteArray();
Wearable.MessageApi.sendMessage(myGoogleApiClient,watchFacePeerId,
PATH_WITH_FEATURE,rawConfigData);
```

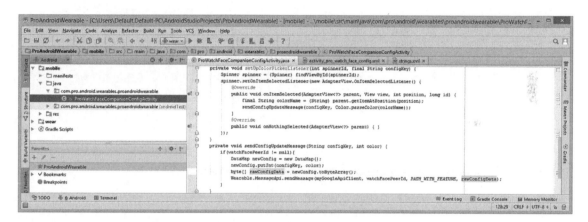

*Figure 14-48.   Create a byte[] Array from the DataMap and use the .sendMessage() method to submit it to Wearable*

Next, you need to create a method that sets up all four Spinner UI elements, which will allow the application to set up color picking for all of the watch face design elements.

## Setting Up All Four Spinners: A .setUpAllPickers() Method

Add a line of code after the public void onResult() method and declare a **private void setUpAllPickers()** method. The last method you're going to code will call those setUpColorPickerSelection() and setUpColorPickerListener() methods you just finished coding. It takes in one **DataMap** parameter, which holds the DataMap object, and will pass that, along with watch face design elements to be configured and chosen default color values for those elements, to the setUpColorPickerSelection() method.

As you know from coding this .setUpColorPickerSelection() method, you will need to pass the **ID** reference for the Spinner object, the **KEY_COLOR** String constant for the data you want to set up, a **configData DataMap** object that contains the key-value data pairs, and the **default Color String** reference.

The Java method structure, which can be seen in Figure 14-49, should look like the following code, once you declare it and add the four method calls to configure each of the four Spinner objects for the watch face elements:

```
private void setUpAllPickers(DataMap configData) {
    setUpColorPickerSelection(R.id.tickMarks, KEY_COLOR_TICK_MARK, configData, R.string.
    color_gray);
    setUpColorPickerSelection(R.id.hourHand, KEY_COLOR_HOUR_HAND, configData, R.string.
    color_blue);
    setUpColorPickerSelection(R.id.minuteHand,KEY_COLOR_MINUTE_HAND,configData,R.string.
    color_green);
    setUpColorPickerSelection(R.id.secondHand,KEY_COLOR_SECOND_HAND,configData,R.string.
    color_red);
}
```

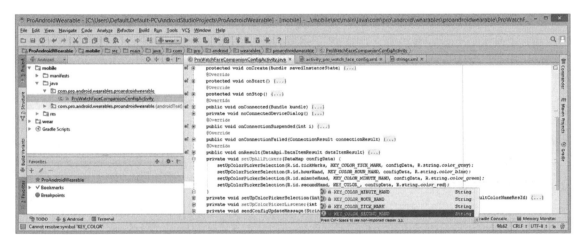

**Figure 14-49.** *Call setUpColorPickerSelection() method for the watch face design elements, passing the configData*

Now that you've configured all of your Spinner UI widgets as to what Color they will display initially (as the default), the next thing you will need to do is set up a **Listener** so that if your user changes this Color setting, your app code can process this new setting and send that Color to the watch face application. The listener needs to know which Spinner (ID) to listen for and which KEY_COLOR constant to process if it is triggered.

The Java code for calling the setUpColorPickerListener() method four times to set up each Spinner Is shown highlighted in Figure 14-50, and it should look like the following finished Java method structure:

```
private void setUpAllPickers(DataMap configData) {
    setUpColorPickerSelection(R.id.tickMarks, KEY_COLOR_TICK_MARK, configData, R.string.
    color_gray);
    setUpColorPickerSelection(R.id.hourHand, KEY_COLOR_HOUR_HAND, configData, R.string.
    color_blue);
    setUpColorPickerSelection(R.id.minuteHand,KEY_COLOR_MINUTE_HAND,configData,R.string.
    color_green);
    setUpColorPickerSelection(R.id.secondHand,KEY_COLOR_SECOND_HAND,configData, R.string.
    color_red);
```

```
    setUpColorPickerListener(R.id.tickMarks, KEY_COLOR_TICK_MARK);
    setUpColorPickerListener(R.id.hourHand, KEY_COLOR_HOUR_HAND);
    setUpColorPickerListener(R.id.minuteHand, KEY_COLOR_MINUTE_HAND);
    setUpColorPickerListener(R.id.secondHand, KEY_COLOR_SECOND_HAND);
}
```

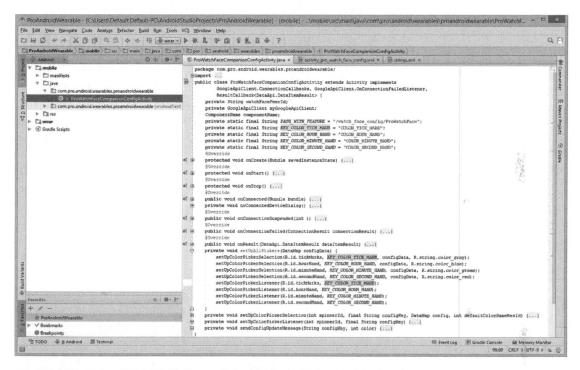

*Figure 14-50.* Call setUpColorPickerListener() method for watch face design elements; then pass the Spinner ID and KEY

Now that you have everything in place, let's try to run the mobile component of the watch face application in the Nexus 5 AVD emulator and see if your UI design is working.

# Testing the WatchFaceCompanion Activity: Nexus 5

Let's run the mobile component of the WatchFaces application you have been developing in the default AVD emulator in Android Studio, which happens to be Google's Nexus 5 running Android 5.0. Use the **Run ➤ Edit Configurations** menu sequence to access the **Run/Debug Configurations** dialog seen in Figure 14-51, and set the IntelliJ **Module** drop-down to **mobile** and the **Prefer Android Virtual Device** drop-down to **Nexuas 5 API 21**. In the **Activity** section, set the **Launch** radio button to the **ProWatchFaceCompanionConfigActivity** class. Click the **Apply** button and then the **OK** button to make your settings final.

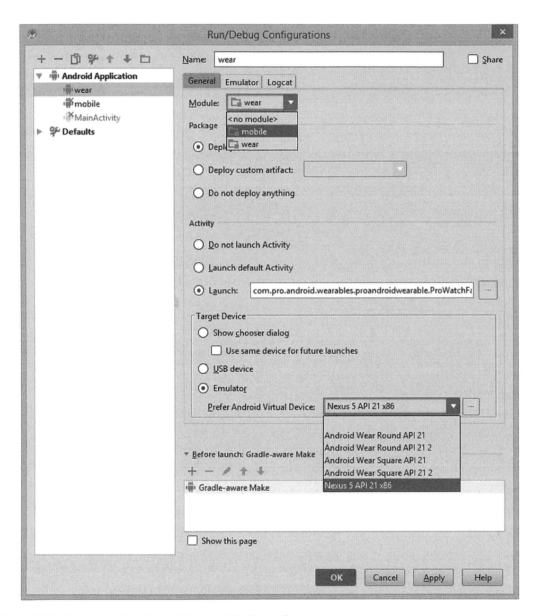

**Figure 14-51.** *Use the Configurations dialog to set the Run options*

Use the **Run ➤ Run 'ProWatchFaceCompanionConfigActivity'** menu sequence and run the application code thus far to see if it runs and to check the UI.

As you can see in Figure 14-52, I got a **package error** saying that "package android. support.wearable.companion does not exist" and that a Gradle Build "cannot find symbol variable WatchFaceCompanion." What a bummer!

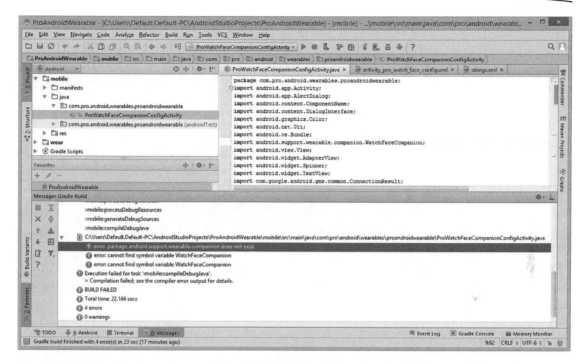

*Figure 14-52. Four errors have appeared in the Gradle Build Messages pane, regarding the companion package*

The WatchFaceCompanion class is referenced in the code, which is where the error was thrown. I know the class (and package) does exist because I have reviewed its information on the Android Developer web site extensively.

Because the android.support.wearable.companion package seems to be missing, as Gradle Build has highlighted the import statement for you in yellow, as shown in Figure 14-52, the logical place for you to check the **compile statements** is the **Gradle configuration** file for the **mobile** component of the application.

The way you do this is to click the right-facing arrow next to the **Gradle Scripts** section of the Project pane. This will drop down (open) the content in the Gradle Scripts folder, including the **build.gradle** scripts.

Find the **build.gradle (Module: mobile)** configuration file, right-click it, and select the **Jump to Source** option, to open it in an editing pane.

What you'll be looking for is a **dependencies** section for the configuration where **compile statements** are added, providing a path for support libraries.

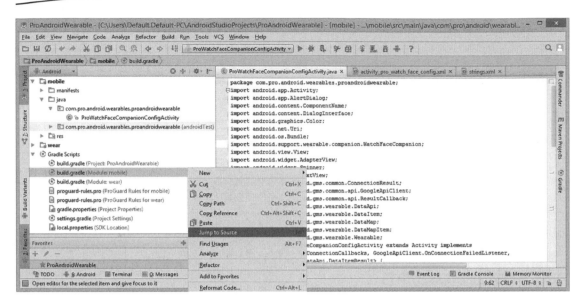

*Figure 14-53. Open the Gradle Scripts drop-down arrow and right-click it, then select Jump to Source for the mobile module*

As you can see in the **dependencies** section, at the bottom of Figure 14-54. I have the **appcompat-v7** and **play-services** installed, but not the **wearable**. Add the **compile "com.google.android.wearable:1.1.+"** statement to fix this.

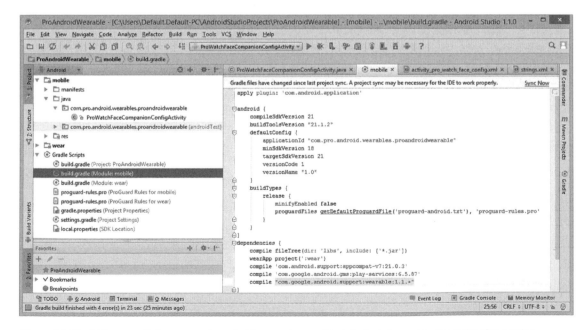

*Figure 14-54. Add a compile "com.google.android.support:wearable:1.1.+" statement in dependencies section*

The next time I tested the application, I noticed that IntelliJ was using a Wear Round AVD, which was strange, so I used a **Run ➤ Edit Configuration** menu sequence to check the settings IntelliJ was currently using.

Sure enough, as you can see in Figure 14-55, the Target Device > Emulator drop-down setting was blank (unset), so I selected the Nexus 5 API 21 default Android Studio AVD emulator.

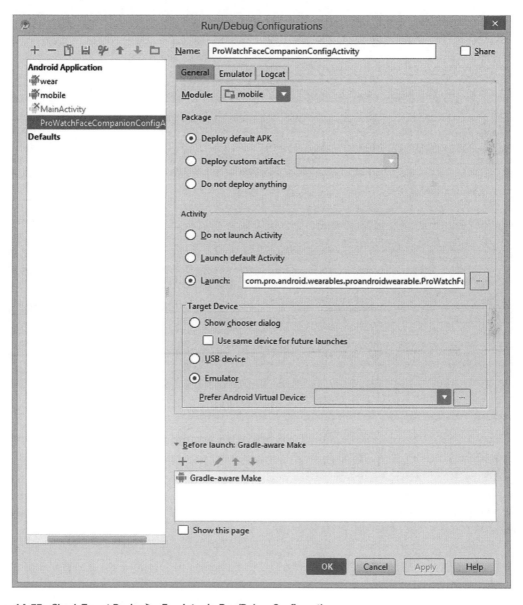

*Figure 14-55. Check Target Device ➤ Emulator in Run/Debug Configurations*

This time the compiler did not throw an error, meaning that I had fixed the build.gradle configuration file problem, but then I was getting an AVD error, relating to not having Intel hardware, since I am using an AMD-64 8-core processor, as you can see at the bottom of Figure 14-56.

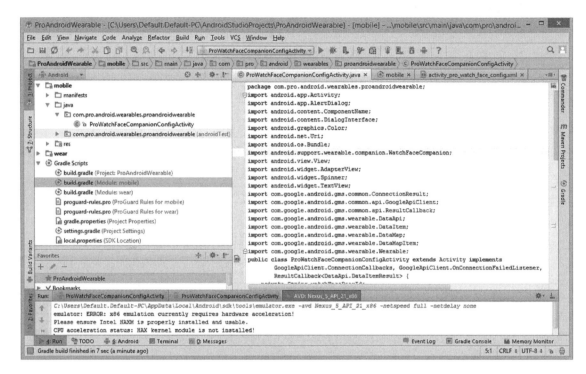

*Figure 14-56. Again Run the application, if you are on an AMD-64 system, you may get these Intel Hardware Accelerated Execution Manager (HAXM) errors*

You need to be diligent and ready for anything when developing for Android OS, so I used the **Tools ➤ Android ➤ AVD Manager** to change my AVD emulator.

I needed to change the configuration to use an **ARM emulator** version, just as I did when I set up emulators for Wear, and I made sure you had both x86 and ARM versions, as not everyone uses Intel architecture.

Open the **Tools ➤ Android ➤ AVD Manager** dialog and select the Nexus 5 API 21, then click the **green pencil Icon** at the far right. This will open a **Virtual Device Configuration** dialog, where you can change core settings.

Notice in the top section of this dialog that you can change your AVD name, and you might want to do this for your Wear AVD emulators at some point in time, renaming Android Wear Square and Round 2 AVDs to Android Wear Square and Round ARM, for instance. Always take some time to customize your IDEA, so everything is crystal clear to you during your application development.

In the third section of the dialog, you will see the software platform, for this AVD that is Lollipop, and this hardware (software) emulator currently set is x86 (Intel), which I would have to change to be an ARM so I can test on my AMD-64 system.

Look for the **Change** button on the right side of the section, which you can use to access a dialog that allows you to select the ARM hardware emulator if you need to do so. As you'll see in Figure 14-57, I needed to change the AVD to use ARM hardware emulation rather than Intel hardware emulation, so another error that I was encountering in the testing process has now been solved. You're getting close to being able to see this Multi-Spinner UI Design!

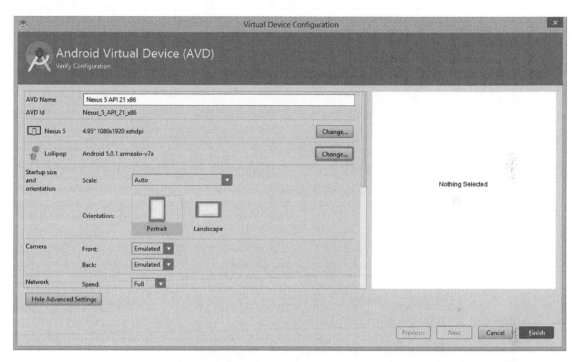

*Figure 14-57. Use a Virtual Device Configuration dialog to rename or reconfigure hardware emulation settings*

Click the Finish button, and make sure that the **CPU/ABI** column has the new setting listed in it, in my case this would be **ARM**, as shown highlighted in Figure 14-58. Now you're ready to try and run the application and test it.

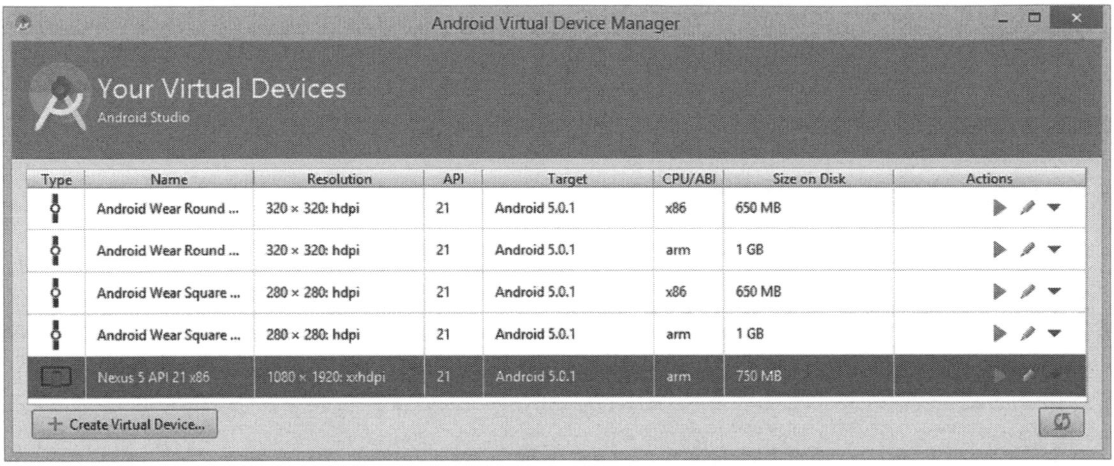

*Figure 14-58. Be sure to check your new emulator settings in the Android Virtual Device Manager home screen*

As you can see in Figure 14-59, the Nexus 5 emulator is now launching, and you can see that I forgot to rename this emulator with the _ARM extension, so I'll had to go back and do that! On the left is the initial launch screen, in the middle are the icons, and because an app icon isn't available, I am going to use the Run command in IntelliJ again, which will place this app into the emulator, now that it has been launched inside system memory.

*Figure 14-59. Run the Companion Configuration Activity in the Nexus 5 API 21 AVD emulator to check the UI design*

As you can see on the right-hand side of Figure 14-59, the <LinearLayout> UI design filled with the nested <LinearLayout> containers with <TextView> and <Spinner> widgets are rendering correctly and have the <string-array> data in them as expected. The reason that the defaults haven't been set via the Java code you have written is because the AVD emulator can only go so far, and connecting with the Google Play GMS server is not a current capability of the AVD environment in IntelliJ.

For this reason, I will take the entire next chapter to explain how you test WatchFaces API-based Android applications on real-world hardware products, like Samsung Gear S or Sony SmartWatch 3, using real-world network providers (I use T-Mobile) and using a real-world smartphone (I use T-Mobile's Samsung Note4). This is getting more and more exciting with each progressive chapter!

# Summary

In this chapter, you learned about the **wearable package** as well as the **Wearable** class in Android, which contains the APIs that are used to communicate across a GMS network. These include the **API**, **DataAPI**, **NodeAPI**, and **WearableAPI**, all of which you utilized in the Java code you wrote during this chapter to implement the final ProWatchFaceUtility.java class.

After creating the utility class and defining the constants, you coded the **putConfigDataItems()** method to load the DataItem objects into the DataMap object. You learned about the **PutDataMapRequest** class and how to put in a DataMap request, and then you learned about the Android **Wearable** class and its four API data fields.

Next, you created a **fetchConfigDataMap()** method to ask the GMS network for a DataMapResult. This uses the **fetchConfigDataMapCallback()** interface that you coded to set up the **ResultCallback** and processes it with an **onResult()** method structure.

Then you created the **dataItemResultCallback()** method, which utilizes the fetchDataMapCallback() method and processes a DataItem object to extract a DataMapItem object used to create a DataMap object inside the onResult() method structure. If the fetched DataItem is empty (null), an empty DataMap is created.

Next, you created the **overwriteKeysInDataMap()** method to update existing configuration DataMap objects. This implements an **onConfigDataMapFetched()** method, which was defined as needing to be implemented inside the fetchConfigDataMapCallback() interface and uses the **.putAll()** method call to overwrite the keys in the current (or new) DataMap with the user's latest configuration preferences.

You then switched gears and opened the **ProWatchFaceCompanionConfigActivity** class and added constants to match those used in the ProWatchFaceUtility class. Then you designed your user interface for the four **Spinner** widgets, using XML markup, in an **activity_pro_watch_face_config.xml** definition file.

Next, you added Java methods that set up the color picker (Spinner) widgets and then tested the mobile side of the application using the AVD emulator. You looked at some of the issues that might get in the way of testing the application and how to solve these. You made sure that your UI design was working, and you are now ready to test on real-world hardware and a live network.

You will take a closer look at how to test your watch face application on an actual hardware device in the next chapter, including using the Java **Singleton** Design Pattern, which is the last coding step in the watch faces API implementation, before I get into how to set up the hardware, Gradle build, and running and testing your application.

# Chapter 15

# Wearables Application Testing: Using Hardware Devices in Android Studio

Now that you have the majority of the coding and design completed for your watch faces application, you need to begin testing your application on **real-world hardware devices**, which can be a very involved work process.

The first step will be to get the computer, smartphone, and smartwatch hardware working together, and that is the primary objective of this chapter, to **bridge** the software development environment (Android SDK and IntelliJ IDE) with your hardware device(s) environment. I have already discussed using only a computer (with AVDs), so now I'll discuss using the computer and the smartphone with the AVD, and finally I'll discuss using your computer with your smartphone and your smartwatch at the same time.

This will involve using your manufacturer's **USB driver** software, unless you're using Google hardware devices, which are also the devices that are used for the emulator. If your hardware does not have a USB driver, you'll learn how to use Google's USB driver to get your Android smartwatch device to interface with the computer. You'll also install the **Google Wear App** on your smartphone and learn how to configure it for **pairing** and **debugging**.

After that, you will learn about the **Android Debug Bridge**, or **ADB**, and how to use that command-line utility to establish **communication ports** between your computer and USB or Bluetooth-connected devices. You'll then learn how to get the **Android Studio** IDE to recognize, and build to, the hardware device using features in IntelliJ and its **Gradle Build System**. Let's get started!

# Interfacing a Device with a Computer: USB Drivers

The first thing you'll want to do, unless you're using a **Google Nexus** device (in which case you can use the USB Driver, the **SDK Manager**, installed for you when you installed Android Studio), is to go to the **OEM USB Drivers** page on the Android Developer web site, which is at the following URL:

`http://developer.android.com/tools/extras/oem-usb.html`

Once you have arrived at the page, right-click the manufacturer driver URL for your Android device. This will open a context-sensitive menu, seen encircled in red in the top right corner of Figure 15-1. Select the first context menu option, **Open link in new tab**, and open your Android device manufacturer web site in a second tab in your browser (I'm using Google Chrome browser).

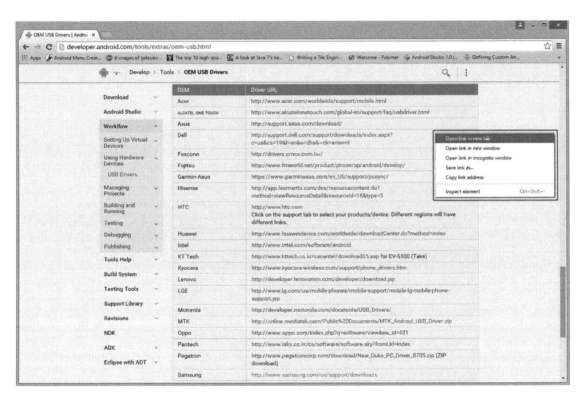

*Figure 15-1. Go to developer.android.com/tools/extras/oem-usb.html and right-click and open the manufacturer's web site*

Because I'm currently using a **Samsung Galaxy Note 3** running **Android 4.4** from **T-Mobile**, I will show my Samsung Note 3 work process over the next several screenshots, which should be similar to your manufacturer's work process.

Find the support section on your manufacturer's web site, if the Android link does not take you there, as it did in my case. Click your device type, in my case, this was labeled "Cell Phones." The link I clicked can be seen encircled in red at the bottom left portion of Figure 15-2.

*Figure 15-2. Find the section of the manufacturer's web site that matches the type of Android device you're using*

This should take you to the page where you can find your exact smartphone product, usually using some sort of search application dialog or possibly using a process of refinement over a series of pages to find your device.

On the Samsung web site, this is a series of drop-down (spinner) UI control elements that allow you to refine your search from Genre (mobile, preset), to Hardware Device (Cell Phones, preset), to Choose the Cell Phone Carrier.

My carrier is the popular T-Mobile service, therefore, I selected T-Mobile for that option, as is seen in Figure 15-3 on the bottom left. T-Mobile is an excellent network for Android development and testing as they support a wide variety of Android hardware and feature modern, lightning-fast 4G LTE and, recently, a wide-band 4G LTE network. T-Mobile now has 4G LTE technology installed everywhere, even here on the Point Conception Peninsula, next to a famous space technology company (Space-X) and Vandenberg Air Force Base.

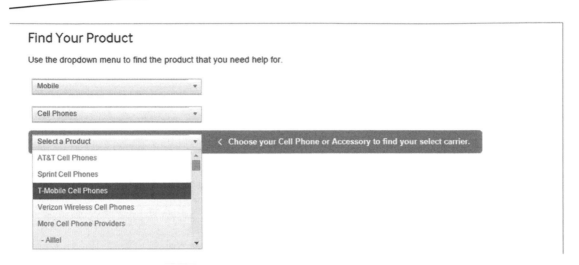

*Figure 15-3.* *Find your product; on the Samsung web site this was under the Mobile ➤ Cell Phones ➤ T-Mobile Cell Phones drop-down*

As you can see in Figure 15-4, once I specified T-Mobile as the carrier, I was then able to access a fourth drop-down spinner UI element where all of the Samsung phones supported by T-Mobile are listed. I found the SM-N900T, which stands for Samsung Manufacturing Note 900 Telephone (I'm guessing).

*Figure 15-4.* *Find the model number on your device, and find that exact product, and download the USB driver*

Notice that there is a W (White) and a K (Black, for those of you who are not familiar with print, and with the CMYK color model) version. Because the color of the case does not affect the driver, I could have selected either of these options, but I went with the technically correct Black version so I could show off an image of my smartphone inside the screenshot shown in Figure 15-4. As you can see in the right side of Figure 15-4 (don't let the pretty hardware device distract you), once you have selected a hardware model number, you will be provided a "GET DOWNLOADS" (or similar) button. Click the download button and open your driver software download page.

Look for the **DOWNLOAD** (.EXE) or similar button on the downloads page and click it to begin the download process. Once you do, there should be a progress tab at the bottom of the browser, which is shown at the bottom of Figure 15-5. Once the download is completed, use the drop-down options menu for the download file and select a **Show in folder** option, which will give you the file in a file management utility where you have the most control.

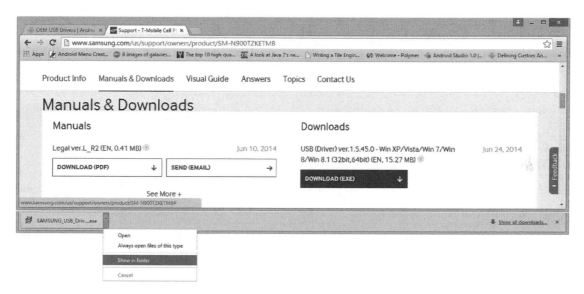

*Figure 15-5.  Download USB Driver (top); when the Download finishes, select Show in folder from the drop-down menu*

As you can see in Figure 15-6, once you are in the file management utility you can right-click this downloaded file and again get a context-sensitive menu full of options, one of which will be a **Run as administrator** option, which will allow you to run the file using full OS (read and write) permissions.

*Figure 15-6.  Right-click the driver installer executable file and select the Run as Administrator menu option*

Go through the installation process. As you can see in Figure 15-7, I chose **US English** and accepted a default **C:/Program Files/SAMSUNG/USB Drivers** as my installation directory. I then used an **Install** button and installed the drivers on my 64-bit Windows 8.1 AMD-64 system, as shown in Figure 15-7.

*Figure 15-7. Progress through the installation configuration dialogs using the Next button; then click the Install button*

It's important to note that you are not actually installing the USB Driver into your OS configuration at this point; you are only installing your USB driver software on your hard drive so that the **Computer Management** dialog can find it and make it part of your current OS hardware configuration.

As you can see in Figure 15-8, the way you access this dialog is by right-clicking your **Computer**, **My Computer**, or in the case of Windows 8.1 the icon called **This PC**. On the context-sensitive menu, you will find a Manage option that will open the Computer (Hardware) Management dialog.

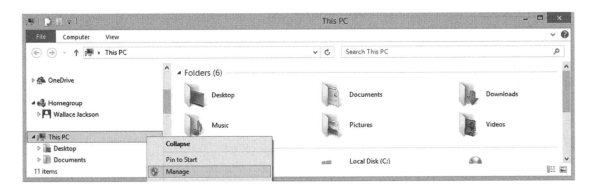

*Figure 15-8. Right-click This PC (Computer) icon; select Manage option, to open Computer Management dialog*

The Windows 8.1 **Computer Management** dialog should more accurately be named the Computer Hardware Device Manager Utility, since that is what it's used for. If you feel like exploring your computer set up, you can click the right-facing arrows in the left pane and open all of the areas in your System Tools listing. Click the **Device Manager** entry to show all of the hardware devices connected to your computer, as shown in Figure 15-9.

This should include the smartphone, which you should have attached to your USB port using the USB charging cable. I keep mine attached to my computer all the time, so I always have a full charge. You can see it in the middle pane, it is highlighted and says: **Wallace Jackson (SM-N9)**, which represents the owner's name and the first few letters of the model name. If your smartphone is not attached, plug it in now, and it should be detected and appear.

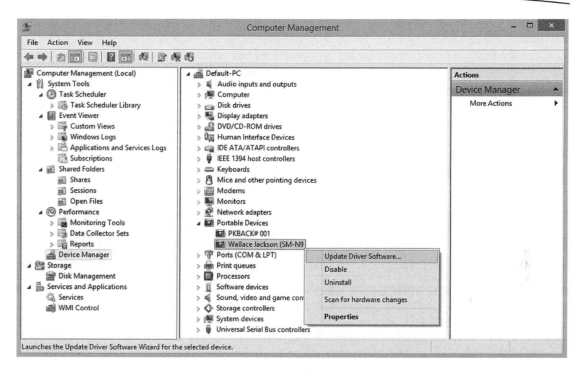

*Figure 15-9.  Select Device Manager in the left pane; find the USB driver; right-click and select Update Driver Software*

Again use a right-click to access a context-sensitive menu and select the **Update Driver Software** menu option. This opens your Update Driver Software dialog, as shown in Figure 15-10. Click **Search automatically for updated driver software** to make sure you have the latest version of the USB driver.

*Figure 15-10.  Select Search automatically for the latest driver version to make sure you have the latest driver revision*

Now that you have made sure you have the latest USB driver version, select the other option, Browse my computer for driver software. Your OS will then find the latest USB driver software, which you have downloaded, and will start the installation process, which can be seen in the series of dialogs shown in Figure 15-11. Now your computer can transfer data to your smartphone, and your smartphone will be visible to IntelliJ IDEA.

**Figure 15-11.** *Browse your computer for the USB driver software and install the USB driver on your operating system*

Now when you look in your File Explorer (file management) utility, you'll be able to see an Android Hardware Device, as shown in Figure 15-12.

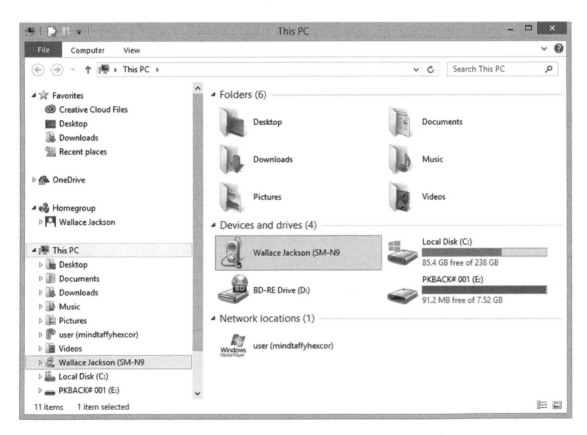

**Figure 15-12.** *Showing my Galaxy Note 3 Smartphone mounted to my PC using the USB driver*

# Installing Wear API: Linking Smartwatch with Phone

Now that you have set up the Wear development workstation with the correct software, the next step is to make sure you have Android Wear installed on the mobile devices you are going to use with your wearable hardware.

This includes the smartphone (or tablet) and smartwatch you are going to be using to test your various Pro Android Wearables applications. These will include your watch face application, which you will be testing on real-world hardware devices.

Because your smartwatch has Android 5.0 and Wear already on it, this amounts to installing these Wear APIs on your smartphone, and then interfacing the smartwatch with your smartphone. This is what you will be doing in this section of the chapter, so that you have your mobile hardware set up.

## Downloading and Installing Wear API: Google Play Store

The way you will be downloading and installing the Wear API is on the smartphone itself, through the service provider (in my case, that would be the T-Mobile 4G LTE service). Find your Google Play Store icon on the smartphone you are going to use to test your applications and launch the Play Store. In your Google Play Store search bar, type the word "wear" so you can find Android Wear-related software.

One of the first results that appears will be the **Android Wear** application itself. The application will indicate that it is free for you to download. The download section of your Android devices should look similar to what's shown in Figure 15-13, with statistics that reflect current use, of course.

*Figure 15-13.  Android Wear after the Install (before Wear is opened)*

The Android Wear app essentially installs the wearable APIs you have been learning about onto any end-user's smartphone, so they can run a Wear application. The Wear application gives the smartphone the ability to "pair" with any Wear-compatible smartwatch hardware, by using technologies such as Bluetooth 4.x, NFC, or Wi-Fi, if smartwatch hardware supports it.

Because the Apple Watch supports Wi-Fi, it won't be long before Android Wear SmartWatch products support it. In fact, the Sony SmartWatch 3 already supports it. It's interesting to note that the Google app (the main Google app, which includes all things/apps Google) also wanted to update itself right after I installed Android Wear on my Note 3, so I updated this app as well.

Now that you have upgraded your smartphone to work with Android Wear SmartWatches, it is time to set up the smartwatch itself and pair it with your smartphone so you can get into setting up IntelliJ to work with these.

## Setting Up the Smartwatch: Sony SmartWatch 3

Next I am going to set up my Sony SmartWatch 3, which I just received for use in Wear development for this book. I plugged in the SW3 as instructed for 30 minutes to charge it, and then turned it on before pairing it with the Galaxy Note 3, which now has the Wear application installed on it.

Interestingly, I got the exact same start-up animation as shown in the AVD emulator (spinning Google colored dots) and then a language menu selector. I selected English (United States) and then the "Install Android Wear on your phone" notification.

Next, I launched the Android Wear application and got a "Let's get you set up" screen, where I tapped the proceed (right arrow in a blue circle) icon so that I could continue with the smartwatch pairing process.

The next screen has information about the Google Location Service, the Google Fit Service, as well as an Accept option. Once you select this, you indicate (agree) that you accept the Privacy Policy and Terms of Service.

The next screen I got was the "Turn on Bluetooth" screen, so I swiped down the top of my screen and tapped the Bluetooth button, turning that feature on for my Note 3. I selected (checked) My Device (Wallace Jackson (SM-N9).

This Bluetooth dialog also showed me the SmartWatch 3 804D as an available device. Next I selected the **Scan** button, just to make sure everything was set up correctly.

When I went back to the Wear App, I was able to then select a SmartWatch 3 804D option and got a "Pairing" dialog, giving me a 224433 pairing code.

On my SmartWatch 3, I selected (touched) the **check mark** UI option, and then got a **downloading** screen while the two devices paired themselves together.

This process took quite a while, because I was on the 2G connection at the time. If you have a 3G or 4G connection, it would proceed much faster. The point is that the update process goes over the Google Mobile (GMS) Network, so the speed will be predicated upon the connection speed at the time.

On my smartphone, I got a "Turn on Watch Notifications" screen where I was told to go to the SmartWatch Notification Settings and select the check box next to Android Wear, so I tapped this notification, and it took me to the screen where I could put a check mark next to this option. I then finished this set up by using the Back button at the bottom of that screen.

It's important to note that the Turn on Watch Notifications is part of the Wear App and not a part of the SmartWatch UI, so make sure you aren't looking for it there, because you won't find it! (I made this time consuming mistake.)

When I first used the smartwatch after the Wear update (download), it had a series of how-to screens that matched those seen in the AVD exactly. Let's get into how to interface all of this hardware with Android Studio next.

# Using ADB: Linking a Smartphone with the AVD

In this section of the chapter, I will explain how to use the IntelliJ AVD emulator as a smartphone. You will do this by hooking it up to a smartphone using the USB cable and set it up so that the AVD acts as your smartwatch.

The primary purpose of the **ADB**, or **Android Debug Bridge**, is to provide the real-time connection of Android Device Hardware. This bridge allows you to make your device hardware an extension of Android Studio (IntelliJ), which will allow seamless interaction between a development system, in this case Android Studio, and device hardware for testing.

This data connection will allow AVD emulators and physical Android devices to "see" each other using a USB (universal serial bus) port, going in both "directions," for the purposes of running and debugging applications.

First, let's look at how to implement the **Hardware ➤ IDEA** direction so you can use your Wear AVD as a smartwatch, and then I'll get into using the Android Device Hardware instead of the AVD for testing, which would equate to the **IDEA ➤ Hardware** direction.

To enable the Android hardware to "see" the USB hardware, you will need to enable the developer settings option on the smartphone. Once this is done, you will be able to select the Enable USB Debugging setting, allowing your phone to communicate with your workstation and, ultimately, with your IDE.

To do this, go into the **Apps area** of the smartphone (a 16-square grid icon labeled Apps) and click the **Gear Icon** labeled "Settings." Click the **General** tab at the top and scroll down to the **About** option, then click that. In the **About** section you will find a **Build Number** entry, which you will click seven consecutive times. This will unlock an **Android developer mode** for the smartphone, and a new **Developer Options** section will appear under your General tab. Inside of this section are a plethora of developer options.

Select the **USB debugging** option to enable debugging (communication with Android Studio) when the USB connection between your smartphone and your workstation is detected to be active (in place, or plugged in). Now that you have installed the USB driver on the computer and enabled the use of USB on your smartphone, all you have left to do is configure the software on your workstation to manage this connection using something called ADB.

Next, let's take a detailed overview of the Android Debug Bridge functionality. This is important because ADB is a real-time networking (data connectivity) link between the development workstation Android Studio IDEA and any Android device hardware that you may want to test your application with to see how it looks and functions. IntelliJ can access many advanced features of connected hardware, allowing you to benchmark your application usage of the CPU, system memory, screen real estate, and similar information.

# Android Debug Bridge: Networking Hardware and Software

ADB is a **command-line tool** that lets you communicate with an AVD emulator instance or connected Android-powered device. You can find it on your hard disk drive by using your file manager **search** feature.

To do this, open your file manager (in Windows 8.1, it is called **Explorer**), and in the left pane, click the topmost OS level (This PC, My Computer, Computer, etc.) inside your file management utility. This will show the search utility what level you want to search (down) from.

Next, enter the **adb.exe** executable file you're looking for into the search bar, as shown in Figure 15-14 on the top right of the screenshot, encased in red. Once you hit the Enter key on your keyboard to "initiate" your search, the file management utility will search your entire hard disk drive so you can find the file. More importantly, this will show you a **path** you will need to use (next) in order to access and run this ADB file using the Command Prompt utility. The path (folder address) is seen on the right side of the search result, as shown highlighted in blue in Figure 15-14.

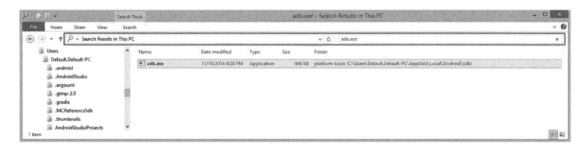

*Figure 15-14.  Using a Search Results in This PC feature of the File Explorer with an adb.exe search specification*

ADB.exe is a client portion of a client-server architecture that includes three primary components, including the client that runs on a development machine and a server that runs as a background process on a development machine. This server will manage all communication between your client and the **ADB daemon**, which will either be running on your emulator, on your device, or both, depending on what you are doing and which direction you are going in your development (IDEA ➤ Device, or Device ➤ AVD) process.

You can invoke the client from a shell, in the case of Windows this is the DOS Command Line Utility, which you'll be using soon. To issue an adb command, you should invoke the ADB executable and give it a series of switches and commands and, optionally, data input options, using a command-line prompt.

Other Android tools such as the ADT plug-in or DDMS will also automatically create adb clients, so that modules like AVDs and hardware can communicate with them as one, seamless development environment. This is why ADB stands for **Android Device Bridge** because it allows you to connect or bridge things into the IDE.

The third component is the ADB daemon, which runs as a background process on each AVD emulator and is active on each hardware device instance.

You can find the adb tool in the **<sdk-install-folder>/platform-tools/** folder, but this is usually a hidden folder, at least in Windows. As you can see in Figure 15-14, the search utility found **adb.exe** in the **/AppData/** folder, which is **not visible in the folder hierarchy** pane shown on the left side.

It is important to note that if you're still using Eclipse IDE and have an ADT plug-in installed, you do not need to use adb directly to install your application on the emulator or device because the ADT plug-in handles the packaging and installation of the application. However, Eclipse was discontinued for Android Studio development more than a year ago, so you may want to switch to IntelliJ IDE version 14 (Android Studio) and Gradle as soon as you can.

# Using AVD Inside Android Studio: ADB Port Forwarding

To send data between your smartphone hardware and the AVD emulator, you'll need to set up something called **ADB port forwarding**. This would be done by using the **adb -d forward** command-line entry and specifying your TCP port.

Let's go over the process in detail so you can interface your hardware devices. Launch Android Studio, access **Run ➤ Edit Configurations** and specify a **Wear Module**, the **Do Not Launch Activity** option, and the **Android Wear Round** AVD **Emulator**, as shown in Figure 15-15, and click the **Apply** button and then **OK**.

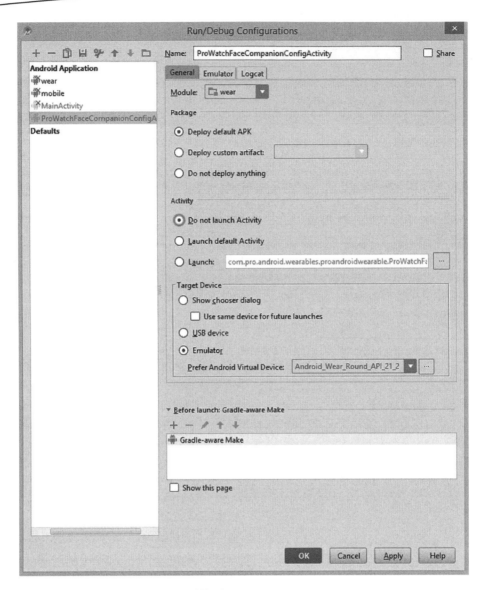

*Figure 15-15.  Set wear Module and Wear_Round Emulator*

Next, make sure the **Enable ADB Integration** option is checked in the **Tools ➤ Android** submenu, as shown highlighted in Figure 15-16.

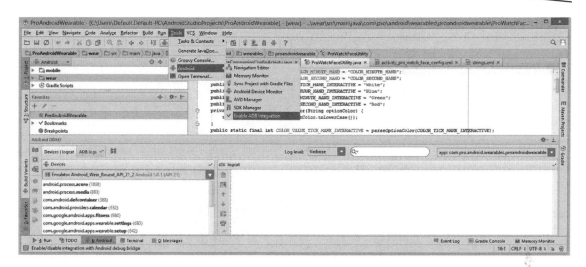

**Figure 15-16.** *Make sure that Tools ➤ Android ➤ Enable ADB Integration submenu item has been selected*

Next, make sure your smartphone has the Wear App and is connected via the USB to your workstation, and that the Wear App has been launched on the phone, then click the **Play** icon at the top of IntelliJ, or use **Run ➤ Run Wear** to launch the AVD emulator. You could also use **Run ➤ Debug Wear** to launch the emulator in Debug mode. Either approach should work for the purposes of this example (I tested it both ways and it worked).

Wait until the Wear AVD emulator initializes, showing an Android Wear home screen, and then you can "pair" the smartphone with the AVD emulator. This is done by **forwarding** the AVD communication port to the connected hand-held device, using the following command sequence:

**adb -d forward tcp:5601 tcp:5601**

It is important to note that you would perform this step every single time you connect your smartphone to your workstation with the USB port (or if you turn your workstation off or unplug your smartphone).

The way that this is done under Windows 8.1 is to **right-click** the **Start menu** (looks like a window pane) and then select the **Command Prompt (Admin)** option from the context-sensitive menu, as shown highlighted in Figure 15-17.

This will open the Command Prompt (Windows Shell or Command Line) utility, which is what you'll use to run the **adb.exe** utility and send it **switches**, **commands**, and **parameters**, like the adb -d forward tcp:5601 tcp:5601 command outlined above. The -d is a switch (d means device), forward is a command, and the tcp:5601 is a parameter (TCP is a transmission control protocol or Internet protocol and 5601 is a port location or "address"). There are two of these TCP port addresses, one for each side (workstation and device) of the network connection "equation" that is being created in memory by using this ADB device forwarding command-line sequence.

*Figure 15-17. Right-click Start Menu, and select Command Prompt (Admin)*

When your Administrator: Command Prompt window appears, the command prompt will show the directory where this **cmd.exe** utility "lives," so you'll know where on the computer hard disk drive you're "standing." This will be **C:\WINDOWS\system32>** as you can see at the top left, as shown in Figure 15-18. Type in a **cd\** command, which means "Change Directory: Root" and hit **Enter**. The prompt will now read **C:\>** and you can use the **CD** (or cd) command to change the directory (folder) to your **platform-tools** folder, which you located in Figure 15-14. The **change directory** (cd) command uses a cd command and then the **Users\Default.Default-PC\AppData\Local\Android\sdk\platform-tools** path, which specifies the folder on the hard drive you want to "stand" in.

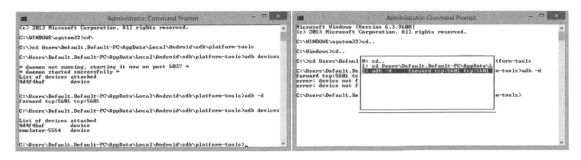

*Figure 15-18. Navigate to the platform-tools folder, list attached devices, forward adb port, and list more attached devices*

The prompt now shows that you are in the platform-tools folder and can run the adb.exe file because it is in the same folder you're now standing in. You can now list all devices that are attached to a workstation using an **adb devices** command-line entry. This outputs a **List of devices attached** and as you can see in Figure 15-18, my AVD has not yet launched, so only my Note 3 is shown.

In my case, the smartphone device is listed as **4d4f4baf**, which most likely is a memory location. I entered a adb -d forward tcp:5601 tcp:5601 command and then once the AVD had finished loading into memory, I ran the adb devices command again, as you can see in Figure 15-18 at the bottom, and an AVD is now visible in the attached devices list, specified as **emulator-5554**.

The next step is to launch the Android Wear app on your Android device and connect to the emulator, which can also be difficult because the menu item you need to find is not directly visible on the Android Wear Settings menu, and the work process isn't outlined in too many places on the Internet, so pay close attention to this step in the process! It's important to note that the Android Wear App might change the UI design in the future to make this "Pair with emulator" option easier to locate.

Select the functions menu for Android Wear, this was accessed via the menu button in the lower left-hand corner of my Note 3 smartphone hardware. This will look like a square icon with two horizontal bars inside and therefore looks like a drop-down menu. Click it, and a menu will appear on the screen.

On the top of the menu there's a "Pair with a new wearable" option. Select this, and there is a "Choose a Device" screen, which does not list the AVD at all, only paired smartwatch devices, in my case this was the Sony SmartWatch 3. Once this screen is visible, again click the hardware **menu** button, and then you will see the "Pair with emulator" option that you need to select.

To test the ADB connection and send data to the AVD, again access the Wear functions menu (on my Note 3, this was using the menu hardware key). Midway down this menu you will see an option to select the **Demo Cards** feature.

You can use this feature to test your AVD that is set up as a smartwatch. Simply select some of the demo cards, and make sure they appear to be transferred for display on your AVD as notifications on the home screen of the Wear Round AVD emulator. I selected the Sports, Hotel, and Stocks demo cards to test the workstation to device interface established using an ADB connection protocol over the USB bus (ports), as shown in Figure 15-19.

*Figure 15-19.  Testing the smartphone to AVD (through Android Studio, on the workstation) ADB connection link*

Next, the process will get even more complex, and you'll attach the smartwatch hardware as well, so your workstation talks to the smartwatch through your smartphone.

# Bluetooth Debugging: Linking to your Smartwatch

The reason I covered how to link from smartphone to AVD first is because those steps will need to be performed, in this same order, to connect your IDE to hardware devices, going in the other direction. You will need to be able to send your apps from Android Studio through the USB cable into your smartphone, and then over to the smartwatch. Let's go through the steps to pair a smartwatch to a smartphone and then establish a real-time link from Android Studio through the USB, to the smartphone to the smartwatch.

It is important to note that you do not need to do all this if you wish to plug both the smartwatch and smartphone into USB ports on the workstation. Some smartwatches, such as the MOTO 360, do not permit USB connection, and because all smartwatches have Bluetooth Debugging, I'm going to show the more complex way to get everything working without a smartwatch USB connection.

## Smartwatch Set Up: Pair and Enable Bluetooth Debugging

The three primary steps you need to do is **pairing** the smartwatch with your smartphone, enabling **Bluetooth Debugging** for the smartwatch, and then enabling Bluetooth Debugging on your smartphone. The first is done via the Wear App on your smartphone, the second is done on the smartwatch, and the third is done on the smartphone. After all of that is done, you will use an ADB forward and connect the command sequence to make everything visible to the ADB daemon.

Start the Wear App on your smartphone and make sure it is paired with your smartwatch, or use the **Pair with a new wearable** on the Wear functions menu, which you used in the previous section. The first time you do the pairing, the Android Wear companion app will suggest you take a short tutorial that introduces the Wearable UI and its basic functions. After that you will be able to access a standard Wear UI, where you can select watch faces, enable voice actions, and browse suggested Wear apps in the Google Play Store.

The next step is to enable Bluetooth debugging for your smartwatch device. All wearable devices will disable USB debugging as a default setting, thus you will have to manually enable it on the smartwatch. An option to enable Bluetooth Debugging will be hidden just like it is on the smartphone. This is so "normal" end users do not accidentally enable debugging modes.

You will need to open Settings, select About, and then click Build Number, seven times in a row. This new Settings menu then includes the Developer options, where you can enable debugging over Bluetooth. On my SmartWatch 3 (Sony), the Debugging over Bluetooth option was grayed out (disabled) until I selected the ADB Debugging option first. So for each smartwatch hardware device, the sequence needed to turn on the Debugging over Bluetooth may be different.

The next step is to return to your smartphone device where you can start a "Device Debugging Session." This is done by again opening the Android Wear application and going to the Wear Settings (Gear) Icon in the upper right-hand corner of the application.

Tap the Settings icon to open the Settings menu, scroll to the bottom, and find the Debugging over Bluetooth option and place a check mark next to it to enable this feature (function).

Underneath the Debugging over Bluetooth feature title there should be some smaller font text, which indicates that the **Host** (your workstation running **ADB** connecting to Android Studio) is **disconnected**, and that a **Target** (your smartwatch) is **connected**.

The next step involves using the **Command Prompt** utility to access your ADB daemon and configure it to see the smartwatch using a Bluetooth link. This is done by entering two commands, the forward, and then a connect, via the DOS Command Prompt. The first **adb forward** command should look like this:

`adb forward tcp:4444 localabstract:/adb-hub`

The second adb connect command is simpler and should look like this:

`adb connect localhost:4444`

As you can see in Figure 15-20, I still had the AVD emulator running so I got an error.

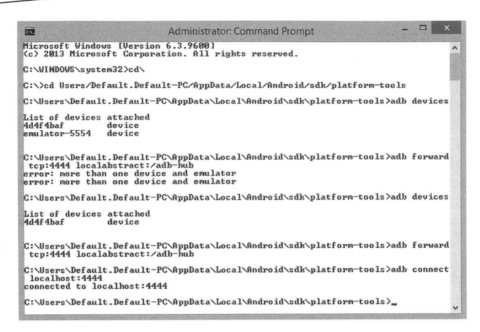

*Figure 15-20.*  *Invoke adb forward and adb connect commands, to connect the smartwatch*

Once this is successful, you will get an "Allow USB Debugging?" message on your Wear app, along with a **This Computer's RSA encryption key fingerprint is: <key string here>** message. Hit the **OK** button to complete this set up. There's also an "Always allow from this computer" option, which I selected.

After you do this, the smaller font text under the Debugging over Bluetooth option in Wear application Settings will change to display the following:

**Host:    connected**
**Target: connected**

Now that you have "wired" everything together, you should be able to access both your smartphone and your smartwatch from your workstation. You're now set up to test the Watch Faces API classes and functionality you have built thus far during this book.

Before you get into testing and debugging in Android Studio, I would like to cover one additional topic, the **Java Singleton Design Pattern**. You'll add one last **private constructor method** to the ProWatchFaceUtility.java class, and then you'll be ready to test and debug your new application.

# Java Singleton: ProWatchFaceUtility() Constructor

In Java software development, a singleton pattern is a design pattern that restricts an instantiation of a class to one single object. This is useful when exactly one object is needed to coordinate actions across the system, as in your ProWatchFaceUtility class. This concept is often generalized to scenarios that operate more efficiently when only one object exists, such as Wear (wear or smartwatch-side) components that have limited resources.

The first step in doing this is to create your class's default constructor method as private. This will prevent a direct instantiation of this object by other classes. Add the empty **private ProWatchFaceUtility(){ }** constructor method at the end of your ProWatchFaceUtility.java class, as shown highlighted at the bottom of Figure 15-21.

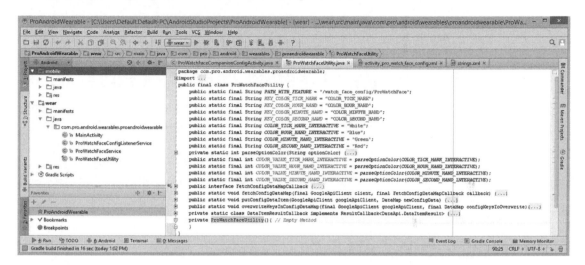

*Figure 15-21. Add a private ProWatchFaceUtility() constructor method at end of your ProWatchFaceUtility class*

This makes this private method a class-level method, which means that your ProWatchFaceUtility can be accessed statically without creating an object. As you might well imagine, this is a memory and CPU optimization technique.

In fact, you will see this IntelliJ suggestion **Add on demand static import for 'com.pro. android.wearable.proandroidwearables.ProWatchFaceUtility'** via a yellow lightbulb on the left side of the IDEA, as shown in Figure 15-22.

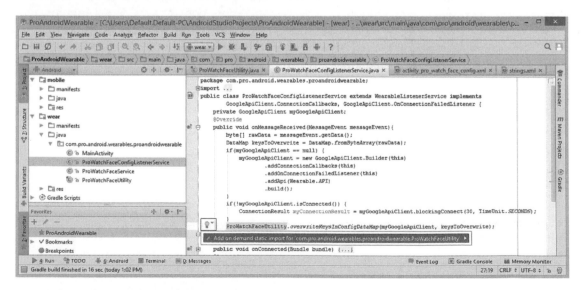

*Figure 15-22. Use ProWatchFaceUtility.overwriteKeysInConfigDataMap() for static access (ProWatchFaceUtility)*

By using the singleton pattern here, you will now be able to access methods in your ProWatchFaceUtility class (as you have in your onMessageReceived() method structure inside your ProWatchFaceConfigListenerService.java class) using the ProWatchFaceUtility. overwriteKeysInConfigDataMap() methodology, no pun intended, as can be seen highlighted at the bottom of Figure 15-22.

Next, let's get into testing and debugging your Watch Faces Apps!

# Testing and Debugging: Creating Your .APK Files

In order to test, and if necessary, debug your wear application inside Android Studio using external hardware devices, you need to generate **.APK** files. You can also test these debug and release "builds" using your AVDs.

You use the **debug build version** to test your attached hardware devices, using AVD emulators, and you use a **release build version** to distribute your application in the Google Play Store once you "sign" (serialize) it.

## The Android Studio Build System: An Overview

Android Studio's build system is built on top of the advanced **Gradle** build system, as previously discussed. It is an **integrated** toolkit you will utilize to build, test, run, and ultimately package (publish) an app.

The Gradle build system can run as an integrated toolkit using the Android Studio menuing system, as well as independently from the command line. You can use features of this build system to configure, customize, and extend this Gradle build process to suit your specific application development needs.

It's possible to create multiple APK versions for your app using different features inside the same project and its modules. You will reuse both code assets and resources, across different application source "sets." The flexibility of Android's Gradle build system enables developers to achieve all these optimization perks without modifying core source files for apps.

The Android build process involves many tools and processes that generate a significant number of "intermediate" files, like .java, .class, .dex, and .apk, along the way to produce a signed, memory optimized .apk that you can put in the Google Play Store. If you are developing apps using Android Studio, a complete build process will be undertaken every time you run the Gradle build task for a project and its modules. It's useful to understand what's happening during various stages in the process, because much of the build process is configurable and is even extensible.

For this reason, I'll present a detailed look at various components involved in the Gradle build system, and then I'll explain how to create builds in your Android Studio projects, which is a fairly involved work process.

## Components of a Build System: AAPT, AIDL, DEX, CLASS, and APK

The way that a Gradle build process works is that an **APPT** (Android Asset Packaging Tool) will collect all of your application's resource files, such as XML files, that are needed for UI design, the application manifest, and new media assets. AAPT compiles all of these nonprogramming-logic assets and produces the R.java module that you will reference in your Java code as R., which is really a dot notation path through this R.java file to the asset, as in the following code:

```
watchFaceDrawable=watchFaceResources.getDrawable(R.drawable.prowatchfacelow);
//ProWatchFaceService
```

This will access the **prowatchfacelow.png** PNG BitmapDrawable asset from the proper resolution density folder (/res/drawable-hdpi) in your project **/res** resource folder, where your R.java resources are organized for the AAPT to compile into a format that can be used at runtime.

The **AIDL** (Android Interface Definition Language) tool converts your .aidl interfaces, which are used to implement IPC (inter-process communication) into Java interfaces. IPC is not commonly used in Wear applications and is not within the scope of this book, but if you need to utilize it, you will be able to get more information at the following developer web site URL:

```
http://developer.android.com/guide/components/aidl.html
```

As you can see in the hierarchy shown in Figure 15-23, all custom Java code, including the R.java generated by AAPT and AIDL generated .aidl files, are compiled by a **Java compiler** to create intermediate **.class** files, which you have also referenced in your AndroidManifest. XML application definition.

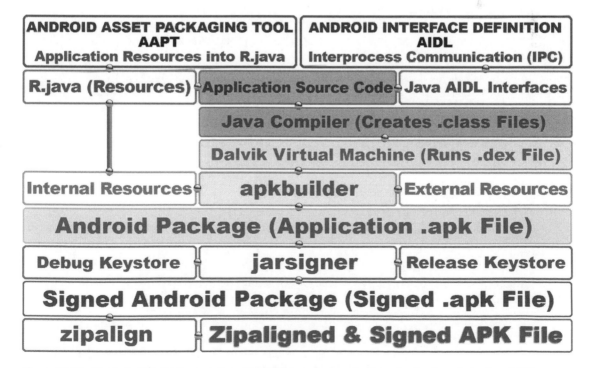

*Figure 15-23. The Android Build Process, from the AAPT down to .java, to .class, to .dex, to .apk, to signed APK*

The next step in the build process is the conversion of the Java bytecode in the .class file into an optimized .dex file format, using the Dalvik VM tool. All third-party libraries and .class files that you've included in the project module build will also be converted into .dex files. This is so that these can be packaged into the final .apk file.

All noncompiled resources, which are generally placed into your project's **/res/raw** folder, as well as all compiled resources (R.java) and your .dex files are then sent to the **apkbuilder** tool to be packaged into your APK.

Once your .apk is built, it must be **signed**, using either a **debug** or **release key**, before it can be installed on an Android hardware device for testing (debug) or usage (release). I'll be covering the release portion of the equation in the next chapter, where I'll explain the last row (step) in a Gradle build process, as shown in Figure 15-23.

Just to finish explaining the build process, if your application was being signed in a release mode, you must **align** the .apk using the **zipalign** tool. In case you are wondering, aligning your final .apk will **decrease memory usage** when your application is run on an Android hardware device.

## Android Application Java Code Limitation: 64 Kilobytes of Methods

Android applications have a code limit of 64 kilobytes allocated to method references—64 KB represents 65,536 characters of code. If your app reaches this limit, the Gradle build process will not get past the .dex conversion.

As the Android API libraries, which developers can pull on to create apps, have ballooned in size, so too has the resulting size of Android apps created using these Java classes or methods. When applications and the libraries they reference reach a certain size, you will encounter build errors that indicate the app has reached the 64 KB Android app build limitation.

Early versions of the Android 4 build system report this error as follows:

```
Conversion to Dalvik format failed:
Unable to execute dex: method ID not in [0, 0xffff]: 65536
```

The recent versions of the Android 5 (Android Studio) Gradle build system may display a different error, which is an indication of the same problem:

```
Trouble writing output:
Too many field references: 128000; max is 65536.
You may try using --multi-dex option.
```

Both error conditions display the decimal equivalent for 64 KB: 65,536. This number represents the total number of references that can be invoked by your Java code inside a single Dalvik Executable (DEX) bytecode file. If you build Android Wear applications that "throw" this error, you probably have a plethora of Java code and may want to look at code optimization.

There's a way to get around this limitation, which is what this section of the chapter explains. I included this in case your apps need to be complex. Android Application Packages (or APK) files contain **executable bytecode** files. These will take the form of **Dalvik Executable** (DEX) files, which contain the Dalvik VM optimized Java bytecode needed to run the app.

The current Dalvik Executable optimization specification limits the total number of methods that can be referenced in a single .dex file to 65,536. This is an even "Power of 2" memory boundary and can include your Android API framework methods, library methods, and custom methods that you create for your application's functionality.

It's possible to go past this 64 KB limit by "chaining" .dex files together. This requires you to configure your application's Gradle build process to generate more than one .dex file. This is commonly referred to in Android as the **multidex** application distribution configuration.

Android platform versions prior to Android 5 use the **Dalvik VM** runtime for executing app code, whereas version 5 and later using the **ART** (Android Run Time) customized for Android. The Dalvik VM limits apps to one **classes.dex** bytecode file in each .apk file. To get around the limitation, you can use the **multidex support library**. This library will become part of the primary .dex file of your app and will then manage access to your additional .dex files, effectively chaining over to the bytecode they contain.

Android 5 and later uses the Android runtime (ART), which natively supports loading multiple .dex files, using a single .apk file. This is because ART does its precompilation at the time that users install their application, so ART can therefore scan for multiple classes.dex files and compile them into a single **.oat** file for execution by the Android device. An .oat file stores native C++ code for an application designed for the new Android RunTime (ART) that is available in Android 4.4 and higher.

Before you configure an app to use more than 65,536 method references, you should try to optimize the total number of references called by the app's Java code. This includes methods defined in the application's Java code or more likely by reducing the number of API library package imports.

To accomplish this, optimize your app's direct and transitive dependencies by ensuring any large libraries you include in your app are used in a fashion that outweighs the amount of code being added to your application.

A mistake developers sometimes make is to include large libraries when a few utility methods are seldom used. Reducing your Java code dependencies can usually accomplish avoiding this 64 KB .dex method reference limitation.

You can also remove unused code using ProGuard. To do this, configure your ProGuard settings for an app to run ProGuard and ensure that you have **shrinking** enabled for your APK release Gradle builds. Enabling shrinking will ensure that you are not including any unused Java classes or methods with an APK.

Using these optimization techniques may help avoid the build configuration changes required to allow more method references in your app. Optimization can also decrease the size of an APK. This could be particularly important for those markets where bandwidth costs are high, making the running of your apps less expensive!

## Configuring Gradle Builds: Creating Different APK Types

The Gradle build will generate a specific .apk file for each build variant in your app/build folder. Generally this will be a **debug** variant, used for your testing work process, and a **release** variant, used for publishing your app to the Google Play Store for distribution.

You could create any other "flavors" of your application that you need for your Wear application publishing endeavors. For instance, you could create a "limited feature demo" version in a **/src/demo** folder and instruct Gradle to create a **ProWatchFace-demo-release.apk** file for you, using the contents of that folder.

The APK files generated into the **app/build/outputs/apk/** directory will contain packages named using the following APK file naming convention:

```
<application name>-<flavor>-<buildtype>.apk
```

As an example, ProWatchFace-full-release.apk would be your release APK, or the ProWatchFace-full-debug.apk would be the debug version for your full watch face application demo version.

Next, let's check to make sure you have the latest version of Android Studio before I get into at the discussion of ProGuard and the Gradle build system. After you do this, you can actually use Android Studio to generate a build, and you can start looking at the process of building and testing your Watch Face app.

Launch Android Studio and use the **Help ➤ Check for Updates** menu sequence to make sure there are no new Android components that have been released. Hopefully, you will get the "You already have the latest version of Android Studio installed" dialog, as shown in Figure 15-24, along with the Help ➤ Check for Updates menu sequence. If needed, update Android Studio before proceeding here!

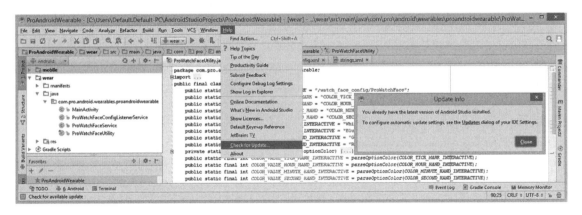

*Figure 15-24. Before starting the build, debug and testing phase, always use the IDE's Check for Update feature*

Next, let's take a closer look at your Gradle build configuration file for your mobile module (component) and learn about some of the other sections (besides the Android and dependencies sections, which I've already covered in some detail) inside your build.gradle file.

## Configuring Gradle Build: Anatomy of a build.gradle Configuration

First, let's take an in-depth look at the **gradle.build** file for the **mobile** module of the application. Open the **Gradle Scripts** section of your app and right-click the **build.gradle (Module: mobile)** and select **Jump to Source** (or press the **F4** function key) to open this Gradle script in an editing tab, as shown in Figure 15-25.

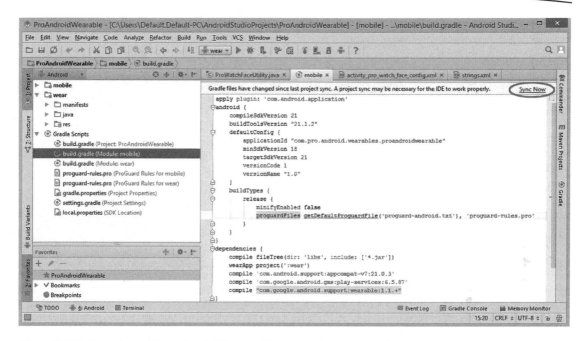

***Figure 15-25.*** *Open the mobile module build.gradle file and use the Sync Now feature to make sure it's up to date*

If you get a yellow "Gradle files have changed" message at the top of your build.gradle editing pane, click the **Sync Now** link option at the right. This will sync your project, which you always need to do before you build.

The first apply plug-in statement allows an android {} section of the build configuration to reference the com.android.application definition on Google's Android Maven repository. This allows the android {…} section of the file to exist (that is, to have meaning) and therefore to be parsed correctly.

The **android** section defines your versioning and package naming conventions, as you already know, and your **dependencies** section references external API libraries, which Gradle will need to pull into your application compilation process. Notice there is a wearApp project entry, which connects the **wear** module of your application, as well as a compile fileTree entry, which will include any third-party JAR files (i.e., physics or 3D render libraries) that you might place in the /ExternalJarFiles directory of your project.

At build time, the buildTypes{} section is what is of primary concern. The buildTypes{} section in Figure 15-25 shows the nested **release{}** subsection of the buildTypes{} section. In case you are wondering which coding format build.gradle files are using, it is a programming language called Groovy.

You may be wondering why there is no debug{} subsection, since there are two primary build types that are always generated. This is because debug build specifications are generated automatically (as defaults) without having to have an explicit build configuration specification implemented. That said, you can use a debug{} subsection if you like.

For instance, you could add the **applicationIdSuffix** of ".debug" to further identify your debug file version, if you wish, using the following Groovy code:

```
debug {
        applicationIdSuffix ".debug"
        }
```

The release{} section of your buildTypes{} section will optimize your .APK file release version, using the ProGuard utility and minification flag, by using the following Groovy code, which does not use a semicolon character to terminate its statements! This can be seen highlighted in Figure 15-25:

```
buildTypes {
    release {
        minifyEnabled false
        proguardFiles getDefaultProguardFile('proguard-android.txt'), 'proguard-rules.pro'
    }
}
```

Next, let's take a look at the ProGuard utility and the minification flag in detail, so you know exactly what they are and why they should be utilized for your release APK file builds.

## Using ProGuard: Compacting, Optimizing, and Obfuscating Code

The ProGuard tool optimizes your code, making it more compact, and it also makes the code harder to reverse engineer, a process called "obfuscation." It accomplishes this by removing unused code and renaming classes, fields, and methods with obscure names, making code difficult to reverse engineer.

The result is a more compact release .apk file, which is more difficult to reverse engineer. Because ProGuard makes your applications harder to reverse engineer, it is important that you implement ProGuard when the application utilizes features that are sensitive to security, for instance when you're licensing an application or when it contains proprietary or valuable IP.

ProGuard is integrated into the Android build system, as shown in Figure 15-25, so you do not have to manually code the call to implement it, using Groovy. ProGuard should be invoked only when you build your application in the release mode. This is so you don't have to debug using obfuscated code when you build your application using debug mode, which would be confusing to say the least!

Running the ProGuard process is optional, however, it's highly recommended. To turn on ProGuard, set the **minifyEnabled** flag equal to a **true** value, and to disable (turn off) ProGuard, set the minifyEnabled flag equal to false. This minifyEnabled property is part of the buildTypes{} section inside the release{} subsection, which controls the settings applied to your release build. Set the minifyEnabled property to true to enable ProGuard when you are ready to have your Java code compacted (compressed) and obfuscated.

It's important to note that even though Android wants you to use ProGuard, which is why these two Groovy statements are installed for you by Android Studio, Android stops one step short of implementing it for you by setting minifyEnabled to a false value, which turns ProGuard off initially.

The **getDefaultProguardFile()** method sets a 'proguard-android.txt' ProGuard configuration definition, which is shown highlighted in Figure 15-25. This is your default ProGuard configuration setting, and this file can be found in the Android <SDK>/tools/proguard/ folder.

There is also a **proguard-android-optimize.txt** file, which is also available in the Android **<SDK>/tools/proguard/** folder. The file implements identical rules, but it also enables "bytecode-level" optimization. These optimizations will perform additional optimization analysis at the Java bytecode level. This is done both inside and across methods to help make your app smaller and run faster when it's run as Java bytecode by the Android RunTime (ART) engine.

Finally, also note in the highlighted line of Groovy code in Figure 15-25, Android Studio uses a comma at the end of the proguardFiles entry and adds the **'proguard-rules.pro'** file reference at the root of this module. This is so you can easily add your own, customized, ProGuard rules if you need to, which should be specific to the release module, that you would add into this file so they will be sure to take effect.

Next, let's take a look at your **build.gradle (Module: wear)** and make sure it does not need to be synchronized before you build your app.

Right-click the **build.gradle (Module: mobile)** and select **Jump to Source** (or press the **F4** function key) to open this Gradle script in an editing tab, as shown in Figure 15-26. If you get the yellow "Gradle files have changed" message at the top of your build.gradle editing pane, click **Sync Now**.

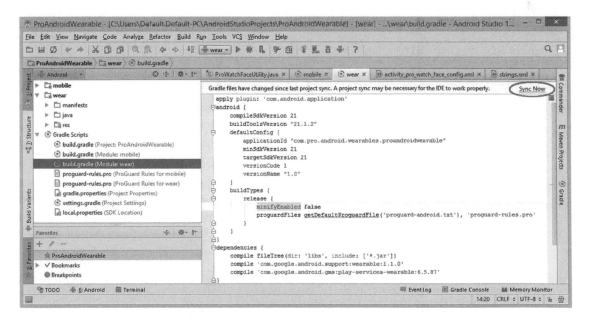

*Figure 15-26. Open the build.gradle file for the wear module and use the Sync Now link to synchronize to your project*

Now it's time to look at the Gradle build process and create the debug APK, so you can start the long testing, debugging, and publishing process, which will span the rest of this chapter as well as the next one.

# Building Your Project: Using the Gradle Build Engine

Although you can test project components internally using an AVD emulator, in order to really test your project components at the next level requires that you "build" them into an Android Package, or .APK for short, file format. This format can also be tested using an AVD. More importantly, it can be tested on real-world hardware, usually at the end of the app development process.

## Running the Make Project Utility: Using the Gradle Build Console

Open your project in Android Studio and use the **Build ➤ Make Project** menu sequence and invoke the Gradle build process, as shown in Figure 15-27.

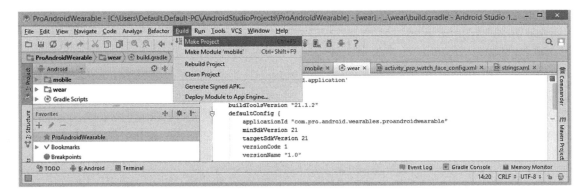

*Figure 15-27.  Use Build ➤ Make Project to create Android Package APK files for the ProAndroidWearable project*

As you can see in the menu shown in Figure 15-27, you could just build the mobile module, but because this is a Wear book, you will build the project, which will build both the mobile (phone) and wear (smartwatch) components.

To see what Gradle is doing inside the build process for the mobile and wear sections of your project, click the **Gradle Console** tab, located at the bottom right corner of Android Studio. As you can see in Figure 15-28, I had to use two screens (in one figure) to show the 24 mobile build steps and 24 wear build steps resulting in a successful APK build in 29 seconds.

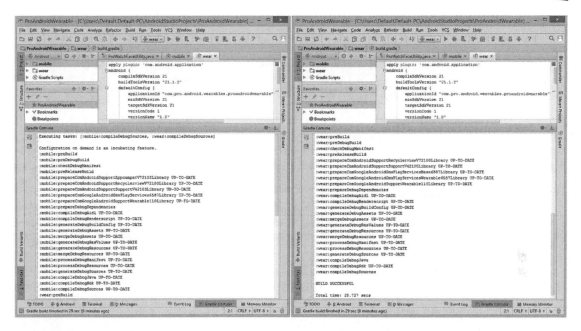

*Figure 15-28.  Click the Gradle Console tab at the bottom right and review the build tasks being done by Gradle*

Now that you have built your project, the next step is running the project modules to see how they work, via USB connected, Android hardware devices.

## Running Your APK: Using a USB Device Target Device Setting

When you run a module as an Android Application (APK), Android Studio will automatically create your run configuration. The default run configuration will launch the default project Activity and use Automatic Target Mode for device selection. **Automatic Target Device Mode** will have the **Emulator** selected with **none** of the (preferred) AVDs selected (empty drop-down menu area).

A **Manual Target Device Mode** is what you have been using thus far during this book, where you selected Nexus or Wear AVDs that you want to launch. Now you are going to select the **USB device** option for the **Target Device** section of the **General** tab in your **Run/Debug Configurations** dialog, as shown in Figure 15-29 (left side is the mobile module, right side is wear module).

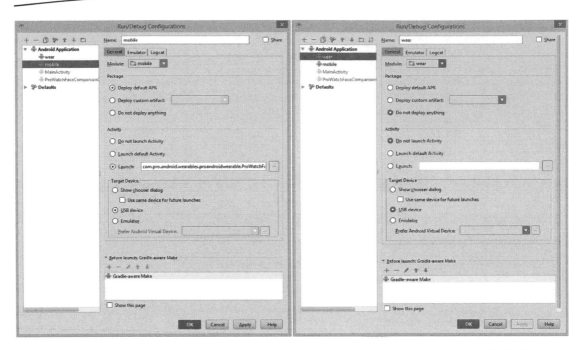

*Figure 15-29. Use the Run/Debug Configuration dialog to set the mobile and wear modules to use a USB device*

I had to reestablish the hardware interface over USB, so I included my DOS Command Prompt window in Figure 15-30 to show you how I used adb devices to see if there is a device connected, and how once I got the device visible, I used the forward and connect commands to access the smartphone and smartwatch.

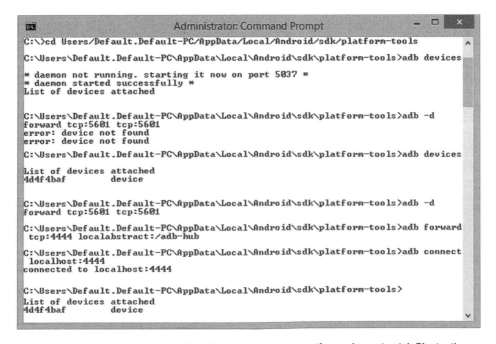

*Figure 15-30. Use ADB commands to set up the USB smartphone connection and smartwatch Bluetooth*

After this was set up, I used the **Run Project** (not Run wear) to run both a mobile module and wear module so I could test them together. I got the **Allow Google to Check Device for Viruses** and **Wear Not Connected** messages on my device, even though the Wear application was running. I got a couple of errors and warnings in the LogCat pane, as shown in Figure 15-31.

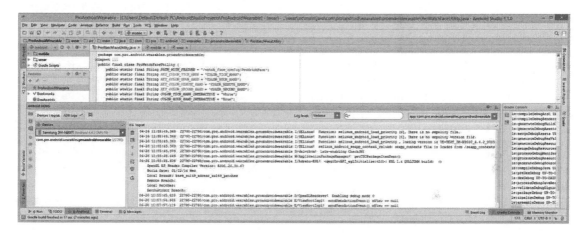

*Figure 15-31. Devices and LogCat panes will open up next to the Gradle Console showing warnings and errors*

I addressed the error messages in red first, using Google search, to see if any other developers were getting this **sendUserActionEvent() mView == null** error message. Turns out this is an issue with Samsung hardware, and because I am using the Galaxy Note 3 currently, I ruled this out as a bug that I'll need to look for a solution for in my code base.

I wanted to address the other warning that there is no sepolicy file to find out what a sepolicy file was, so I did a Google search on that as well and found that this error was related to running more than one build session and had nothing to do with the watch face not coming up on the smartwatch.

The next thing to try in this situation would be to connect the smartwatch via USB cable directly so that both smartphone and smartwatch are directly connected and Bluetooth debugging (which is slower and may be the problem) can be turned off, taking a layer of complexity out of the equation. It is important to note that smartwatches without a USB port such as the MOTO360 must use Bluetooth debugging, which is why I have covered it in detail.

## Hardwired USB Connection: Setting Up a Smartwatch USB Driver

Because I could not find a dedicated Sony SmartWatch 3 USB driver, this will be a great opportunity to show you how to use the Google USB driver, which you installed using the Android SDK Manager, to accomplish the connection.

Because you have installed the Google USB driver, the only thing you'll need to do is to locate it in your **AppData/Local/Android/sdk** folder. It is not in the /platform-tools folder, instead it is in a different directory, called **/extras/google/usb_driver** and is named **android_winusb**.

Perform the same steps you did earlier for the smartphone USB driver, which can be seen in Figures 15-8 through 15-10, except this time, specify the Google USB driver for Windows, which you just located. It is important to note that if you're using Linux or Macintosh, you don't have to install any USB driver.

Now the ADB command sequence becomes easier as you do not have to use that adb forward and adb connect Bluetooth sequence; you would only use the **adb devices** command to see that the hardware devices are connected. You do not need the **adb -d forward tcp:5601 tcp:5601** command enabling port forwarding through the smartphone to the smartwatch either.

As you can see in Figure 15-32, the new ADB command line sequence is quite a bit shorter, because you do not have to set up a Bluetooth port and then connect to it.

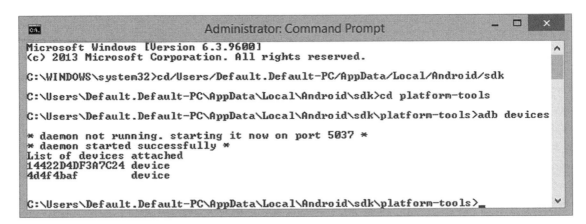

*Figure 15-32.* *The ADB command-line sequence is much shorter when both hardware devices connect via USB*

When you go into Android Studio and look in the Android pane next to the Gradle Console pane, you will see that there are now two hardware devices, as shown in the drop-down menu that is highlighted on the left side of the screen in Figure 15-33.

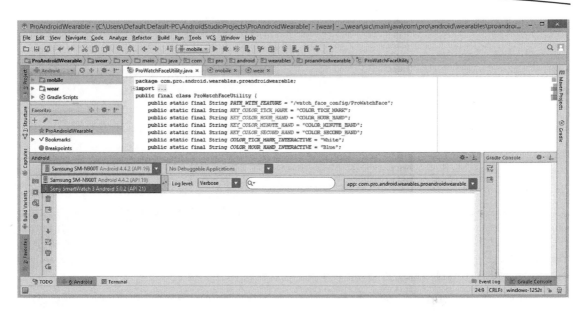

**Figure 15-33.** *In the Android tab, at the bottom of IntelliJ, you will find both hardware devices on the drop-down menu*

When you use the Run ➤ Project, Run ➤ Wear, or Run ➤ Mobile sequence, the **Choose Device** dialog, as shown in Figure 15-34, will pop up so that you can select the hardware device you want that build to be pushed onto.

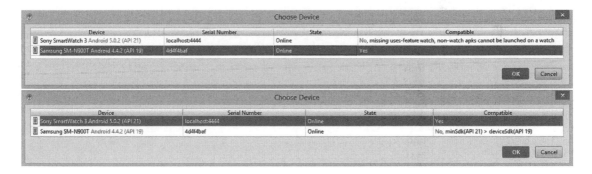

**Figure 15-34.** *When you select Run ➤ wear or Run ➤ mobile, you'll get a Choose Device dialog with the hardware listed*

However, whereas my companion app was launching just fine on a smartphone, my watch face component was not showing up on the smartwatch. On a whim, I checked for updates and learned that Android 5.2 had just been released.

The 5.2 release proved to be a major one and made significant API changes. This affected the ProWatchFaceService class and the methods I am using. So I decided to end this chapter here and add another chapter on how to deal with these major OS update changes, so you can see the entire process in case it happens to you, which it invariably will, as Android is a "moving target."

# Summary

In this chapter, you learned how to get your computer, smartphone, and smartwatch hardware working together, to **bridge** a software development environment (Android Studio) with your hardware device(s) environment.

This involved getting a manufacturer **USB driver** software and learning how to use Google's USB driver if you needed to get your Android smartwatch device to interface with the computer.

You learned how to make sure a **Google Wear App** is installed on your phone and how to configure it for **pairing** and **debugging** purposes.

You learned about the **Android Debug Bridge (ADB)** command-line utility and how to access it using a DOS command prompt to establish **communication ports** between your computer, a USB, or Bluetooth-connected devices. Then you got into using the **Android Studio** IDE to recognize and build to your hardware devices, using the various panes and dialog features in IntelliJ and its **Gradle build system**.

In the next chapter, you will upgrade to Android 5.2 and take a deprecated method call out of your BitmapDrawable code, and learn how developing in Android can be a moving target and how best to deal with this!

# Wear API Deprecation: Updating Apps to Use New Classes or Methods

In Chapter 15, you set up the hardware devices so that they could talk with Android Studio by using the Android Debug Bridge. Then you attempted to get the wear component to show up on a smartwatch so you could test the configuration companion activity. One of the things I tried in my work process was to check for updates to Android Studio and Android SDK.

There had been a major OS update, **Android Studio 1.2** (Android 5.2), made available! So I decided to make the process for this update and the deprecated code update part of its own chapter. This chapter will cover the process of updating this project's wear component, which thus far has not run as expected on the smartwatch device hardware. I will cover this entire process, spanning from dealing with an unexpected major SDK upgrade to recoding any deprecated classes or methods. In this case, these will involve the ProWatchFaceService.java class.

Therefore, during this chapter, you will learn more about the **Calendar** and **GregorianCalendar** classes, which will be used to replace the use of the Time class, which was deprecated in Android 5.2. You will also implement a different version of the **.getDrawable()** method, as one of the two versions of this method call was deprecated in this Android 5.2 API (SDK) upgrade.

As I was finishing up the code upgrades, an **Android Studio 1.2.1.1** upgrade was also released, which created some problems with the integration of the Gradle build system with IntelliJ (Android Studio). So I'll explain more about Gradle and IntelliJ to help you learn how to solve this problem.

# Dealing with the Unexpected Update: Android 5.2

When I checked for updates, I got the series of dialogs, as shown in Figure 16-1. I then proceeded around dialogs shown in Figure 16-1 to update Android. I clicked the **Update and Restart** button, I got the **Downloading Patch File** and the **Update** progress bar dialogs, and finally, I selected the **I want to import my settings from a previous version** radio button, and the **OK** button to finish the process. A couple of weeks later, 1.2.1 came out, and then 1.2.2 a week after that, so I had to do it all over again!

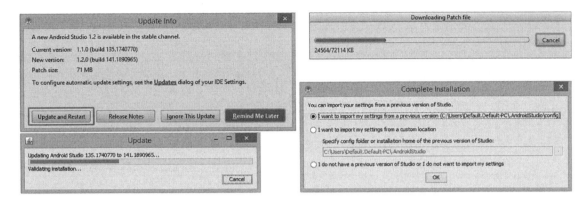

*Figure 16-1. Dialogs for updates, showing a major 71MB update was available to update to Android Studio 1.2*

As you can see in Figure 16-2, this update is a major one, with **28 API SDK packages** to install. I clicked the Install 28 packages button and updated.

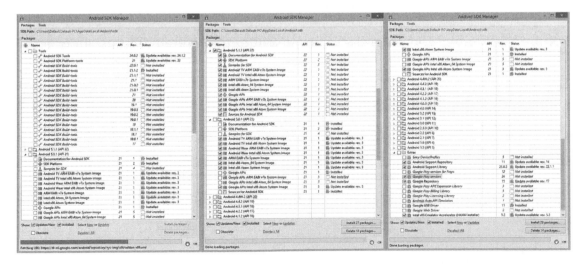

*Figure 16-2. This installation autoselected 28 SDK packages, libraries, and system images, to install or update*

An Android SDK Manager Log shows the download and installation of revision 24.1.2 of Android SDK Tools and revision 22 of Android SDK platform tools, which as you now know includes the **ADB server** and utility. The install can stop the ADB server if it is running, which it did, and then the installer tried to rename the current **/platform-tools** folder in order to back it up. This failed because I had a command prompt open, so the installer stopped and generated an error message, which is shown in red in Figure 16-3.

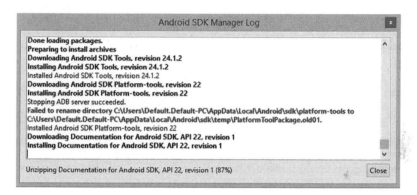

*Figure 16-3. I had to close the command prompt utility for install to continue*

Once I closed the command prompt, the install finished, as shown in Figure 16-4.

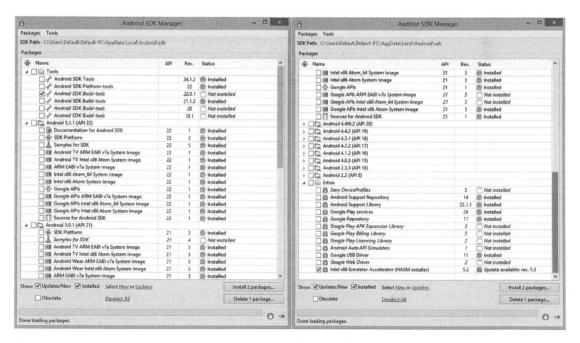

*Figure 16-4. Select the latest Android SDK Build-tools; update the Intel x86 emulator to see if it will work on AMD*

As you can see, the latest version of Android Build Tools (22.0.1) was not selected for installation. I selected this as well, as I'm trying to solve this problem of the watch face (wear) side of my project not showing up on the smartwatch, and the solution might be in this new Build Tools 22 code.

I also selected the update to the Intel x86 Emulator Accelerator (HAXM) to see if any support for the AMD64 line of processors had been added. Next I clicked an Install 2 packages button and installed these packages that didn't get installed on the first OS platform update, which you will often have to do in order to get everything you need installed in your IDE.

Now that I have updated to the next major version of Android (5.2), it is time to look at the ProWatchFaceService.java file (class) to see if there is anything in the code that may be preventing the watch face (wear) side of the application from running on the smartwatch device hardware.

# Dealing with Deprecation: .getDrawable() and Time

As you can see in Figure 16-5, there are now highlights in your code that weren't there prior to the latest version update. **Deprecated** code is lined out (this uses the **strike-thru** font), which can be somewhat unnerving, but it visually informs developers that the code they are using is **no longer supported** by the Android 5.x platform, which is what deprecated means. You can mouse-over the highlighted (and lined-out) code and you will get a pop-up note, which will tell you that this **.getDrawable(int)** method call is deprecated. This means you need to go to the developer's web site and review the API.

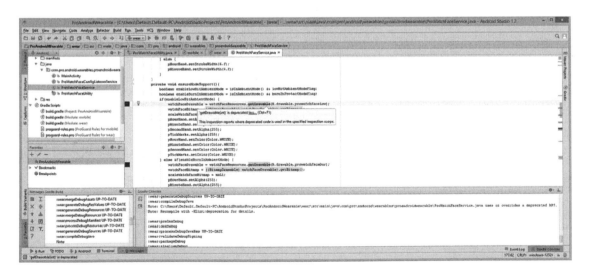

*Figure 16-5. Open the ProWatchFaceService class, which is not working on the smartwatch, to review the code*

You can see the color-highlighted note in the Gradle Console, shown at the bottom of Figure 16-5, that advises you that if you want to use deprecated code, you need to use the compile switch called **-Xlint:deprecation**. I want to use **100% clean** (bug-free and current) code for this book, so I am going to take the more difficult path here and rework the Java code.

There are two major deprecations in Android 5.2 (Android Studio 1.2) that affect the code you have been writing. One is the **Time** class and the other is the .getDrawable(int) method. In this section of the chapter, I'll discuss the classes and methods that can be used instead of the deprecated classes and methods you have been using. It's important to note that you could still use the code you've added earlier in the book, however, over time deprecated code will eventually become discontinued code, so it is best to deal with upgrading (replacing) deprecated Java statements right away!

## Android's Resources Class: Two .getDrawable() Methods

I have already explained the Android Resources class, so I won't revisit that material here. I will just cover what applies to the necessary Java code upgrade, which will get rid of your strike-thru (lined out) code in IntelliJ (Android Studio 1.2).

In order to upgrade the deprecated .getDrawable(int) method call, you will need to look at Android's **Resources** class on the developer's web site. You need to do this to ascertain whether there are other versions of these **.getDrawable()** method calls that will allow you to retrieve the background image Drawable assets from the /res/drawable-hdpi/ folder. The Resources class technical information page can be found at the following URL:

http://developer.android.com/reference/android/content/res/**Resources.html**

Notice there are two .getDrawable() methods listed in the Resources class, and one is now deprecated, so you'll have to use the newer one, which is what is suggested in the online documentation. The technical information regarding these .getDrawable() method structures online should look like this:

```
Drawable        getDrawable(int id)
This method was deprecated in API level 22. Use getDrawable(int, Theme) instead.

Drawable        getDrawable(int id, Resources.Theme theme)
Return Drawable object associated with a particular resource ID and styled for the specified
theme.
```

Therefore, your solution to this Android 5.2 upgrade deprecation is to use a different version of .getDrawable(), which uses a **Resources.Theme** object named **theme**. If you want to keep using your currently specified Theme, use a **null** value. Let's take a look at the Resources.Theme nested class next.

## The Resources.Theme Nested Class: Theme Attributes

The Resources class has a nested **public final Resources.Theme** class, which extends the java.lang.Object master class and has the following hierarchy:

```
java.lang.Object
  > android.content.res.Resources.Theme
```

This nested **helper class** was created to hold your current attribute values for a particular Theme object definition. As you know, a Theme is a set of values defining a user's interface look and feel, using resource attributes.

The Theme objects encapsulate a **TypedArray** object, which holds these Theme attributes. The TypedArray can be utilized to resolve the final values for an attribute using an **int[]** array and **AttributeSet**. You would normally use the **.obtainStyledAttributes(AttributeSet, int[], int, int)** API to retrieve the XML-defined Theme attributes with style and theme information applied using parent and child user interface attribute definition tags. Wear apps don't usually change Themes, at least not the Watch Face app you're coding.

When you want to leave a default or current Theme in place, you will use a **null** value for the Resources.Theme object in a .getDrawable() method call.

The Theme object's attributes come into play in two ways. The first is via the styled attribute, which can explicitly reference any value in the Theme by using a **themeParameterName="?them eAttribute"** syntax in the XML tag parameters.

The second way you can reference a Theme object attribute is in your Java code using the **.obtainStyledAttributes(AttributeSet, int[], int, int)** API method call to retrieve the XML-defined Theme attributes. If you want to maintain **backward compatibility**, there is also a **ResourcesCompat** class.

Let's take a look at the ResourcesCompat class next, as adding a backward compatibility feature could prevent this from happening again. This class also has a .getDrawable() method, allowing you to pass in the **Resource R** reference, a **Drawable index** integer, and a **Theme**, all in one method call.

# The ResourcesCompat Class: Backward Compatibility

Android's **public ResourcesCompat** class also extends java.lang.Object and was thus scratch-coded to provide backward compatibility for Resources. A Java class hierarchy for this class would look like the following code:

```
java.lang.Object
  > android.support.v4.content.res.ResourcesCompat
```

This class was created to be a helper class that developers can utilize to access features in Resources that were introduced after API level 4. This is done in a **backward compatible** way, so that Android developers can avoid exactly what happened during the process of this book on out into the future. You don't need to use this for wear development as Wear was introduced in 4.4 and is quickly progressing to primarily utilize 5.0 through 5.2 (so far).

This class features one public constructor method, **ResourcesCompat()**, which is used to create an object. There are two public method calls in this class as well. One is **.getDrawable(Resources res, int id, Resources.Theme theme)**, which returns the Drawable object that is associated with the referenced resource ID and will be styled using the specified Theme object.

The other is the **getDrawableForDensity(Resources res, int id, int density, Resources. Theme theme)** method call. This could be used to access different **density** Drawable assets. Most smartwatch products range from 320 to 400 pixels (I hope that this may increase to 480 to 640 pixels by 2016), so you won't need to use this version of the method call for now, which adds in a variable for the **density** (folder) to access the Drawable asset(s).

Because the Resources class is a more often used and standard class for Wear applications, and what you have already been using, I'm going to use that. Let's take a look at the other major deprecation next, an entire class!

# Dealing with Deprecated Classes: The Time Class

You may have also noticed at the top of the ProWatchFaceService class that the Time class (object) reference is lined out in the code, which means it too is deprecated. This class can still be used, at least until 2038, when the date (time) range that it covers runs out (expires). This is, most likely, the primary reason that this class is being deprecated in the first place, although no specified reason is given on the Android developer's web site.

This is another major deprecation in this Android 5.2 update that affects the ProWatchFaceService class Java code, meaning you will have to recode to fix the problem.

This time, an entire class, the Time class, will need to be replaced using either the **Calendar** or **GregorianCalendar** classes or a combination thereof. As you'll soon learn, these classes are closely related, as well as being related to the Android **Date** and **TimeZone** classes.

The Android Calendar class is an **abstract** class that is used to create the GregorianCalendar **concrete** class, and the Date and TimeZone objects can be accessed (utilized) by this Calendar abstract class and the GregorianCalendar concrete class. You will be using the Calendar class (object) directly with the .getInstance() method call, which you will be learning about next.

## The Calendar Class: An Abstract Class for Date and Time

The Android **public abstract Calendar** class extends java.lang.Object and it implements the **Serializable Cloneable Comparable<Calendar>** Java interface. The Java class hierarchy for this Calendar class looks like the following:

```
java.lang.Object
  > java.util.Calendar
```

The Calendar class has one known direct subclass, **GregorianCalendar**, which I'll cover in the next section. The Calendar class is an abstract class that was used to create the GregorianCalendar class. It provides the method calls that can be used to extract data from a **Date** object and the set of **integer fields** this Date object contains.

These include YEAR, MONTH, DAY, HOUR, SECOND, MINUTE and MILLISECOND. A Date object represents an instant in time and has the capability of using millisecond precision, if you need it. You'll be using this data extraction capability in your new code base soon, so I'm covering this class and its related methods in detail here.

Similar to other Android 5 location-sensitive classes, this Calendar class provides a method call named **.getInstance()**. This can be used to create an instance of this Calendar class for general usage. A .getInstance() method will return a Calendar object whose location's fine tuning is based on the application user's system settings. This object's time data fields will be initialized using a user's **current system date** and **system time**.

Object declaration and instantiation can be accomplished in one unified statement, and this could be done by using the following Java statement:

```
Calendar calendar = Calendar.getInstance(); // Declare a Calendar object named calendar and
load it
```

You will be using a Calendar object in your new code, and this will be done a little bit differently using the following Java code:

```
Calendar watchFaceTime = Calendar.getInstance(); // Create/Load Calendar object named
watchFaceTime
```

You'll then access the Calendar object's attributes with **Calendar.ATTRIBUTE** constants via the **.get()** method call, using the following Java statements:

```
int hour   = watchFaceTime.get(Calendar.HOUR);
int minute = watchFaceTime.get(Calendar.MINUTE);
int second = watchFaceTime.get(Calendar.SECOND);
```

Calendar objects can be defined as being **lenient** or **nonlenient**. A lenient Calendar object accepts a wider range of field values than it produces. As an example, if you're using a lenient GregorianCalendar object, if you use MONTH == APRIL, DAY_OF_MONTH == 31, it would interpreted the day to be May 1.

A **nonlenient** GregorianCalendar would throw an exception in this scenario, due to the attempt to set an **out-of-range** data field value. When a Calendar object recomputes a field value for return as a result of a .get() method call, your Calendar object will "normalize" it. As an example, the Android GregorianCalendar will always produce a DAY_OF_MONTH value that is between 1 and the length of the current month, taking leap year rules into account as well. A Calendar object defines location-specific seven-day weeks using two parameters. The first is the first day of the week and the second is a number of "minimal days" in the first week (1 to 7). The numbers are taken from the location resource data when your Calendar object is instantiated.

Location-specific data parameters may also be specified explicitly by the Android developer by utilizing methods in this Calendar API. If you would like to dive deeper into information regarding all the ins and outs of the Calendar object (class), peruse the Android Developer page using this URL:

```
http://developer.android.com/reference/java/util/Calendar.html
```

One final point that I would like to make is that this Calendar class has two constructor methods: **Calendar()** and **Calendar(TimeZone timezone Locale locale)**. Why would an abstract class have a constructor method if it can't be instantiated? Not only can an abstract class have a constructor method, but it always will have one. If you don't specify a constructor, the class will have a default, no argument object constructor, just like other class types such as nested and anonymous classes. In the case of anonymous classes, it's impossible to specify a constructor, so you'll always get the default constructor. The constructor method is always accessed using the subclass, so you can't say **Calendar calendar = new Calendar();** but you can create a Calendar object by utilizing a **Calendar calendar = Calendar.getInstance();** Java statement.

This Calendar class is an excellent example of an abstract class that has a constructor method. You will be creating your Calendar object by calling Calendar.getInstance(), but Calendar has constructors that are **protected**.

The reason Calendar constructors are protected (not private) is so it can be extended by a subclass, like GregorianCalendar. Because Calendar's constructors are protected, only other classes in their package can extend Calendar. As of Java 7, which was used for Android 5, the GregorianCalendar class is the only subclass that can access the two Calendar constructors.

Next, it's time to take a closer look at the GregorianCalendar subclass of the Calendar class, so that you have complete knowledge of both viable Calendar classes. You will be using the top-level Calendar class in the new code to eliminate the deprecated code in ProWatchFaceService, however, the GregorianCalendar class (object) is recommended to use in lieu of the Time class (object), so I am including this next section to provide complete topic coverage. In this way, you'll have a comprehensive overview of both of the Android (Java 7) calendar utility classes you can use in your apps.

## The GregorianCalendar Class: A Concrete Class for Date and Time

The **public GregorianCalendar** class is a **concrete subclass** of **Calendar**, and it provides a standard calendar representation utilized across most of the world. It is contained in a **java. util** package, and its Java class hierarchy would therefore look something like the following:

```
java.lang.Object
  > java.util.Calendar
    > java.util.GregorianCalendar
```

In case you're wondering what a concrete class is and how it differs from an abstract class, a concrete class will be instantiated, using a Java **new** keyword along with a constructor method, whereas an abstract class cannot be instantiated using the Java new (instance) keyword, as you now know.

I use abstract classes in the 2014 Apress *Beginning Java 8 Games Development* title to create the game actor classes, if you wish to review this concept in greater detail. In Java, a concrete class is designed to be subclassed, like abstract classes, but it can also be instantiated, unlike an abstract class, which cannot be directly used in your compiled (final) code base.

The standard **Gregorian** calendar supports two "eras," **BC** and **AD**. The Android implementation handles a single discontinuity that corresponds by default to the date the Gregorian calendar was implemented, on October 15, 1582, in most countries, although this could be later in other countries. This "cutover date" can be changed in Android by the developer by calling the **.setGregorianChange()** method. In countries that adopted the Gregorian calendar first, October 4, 1582, will be followed by October 15, 1582. This Calendar subclass will therefore model this date anomaly correctly.

Before this Gregorian cutover date, the Android GregorianCalendar class will implement the **Julian** calendar. The difference between a Gregorian and a Julian calendar is its **leap year rules**. The Julian calendar will specify a leap year every four years, no matter what.

A Gregorian calendar will omit leap years in every even century year for those century years that are not evenly divisible by 400.

The Android GregorianCalendar class implements both a Gregorian and Julian calendar at the same time. Dates are computed by extrapolating the current rules backward as well as forward in time using a specified cutoff date.

Due to this fact, the GregorianCalendar class can be used for all years to generate meaningful and consistent date results for your watch faces apps and can also be used to access the system time, accurate to a millisecond.

The date obtained by accessing a GregorianCalendar object is "historically accurate" only from March 1, 4 AD and onward. This is when a modern Julian calendar rule was adopted. Before this date, the leap year rule was applied irregularly. Note that before 45 BC, a Julian calendar did not exist. Prior to the institution of the Gregorian calendar, New Year's Day was March 25!

To avoid any confusion, the Calendar subclass will always use January 1. Manual adjustments can be made by developers if needed, for dates that are prior to the Gregorian cutoff and fall between January 1 and March 24.

A GregorianCalendar class accesses data fields (properties, or attributes) from its Calendar superclass, which I will discuss next. They include constant names, such as MONTH, DAY_OF_MONTH, WEEK_OF_MONTH, HOUR, HOUR_OF_DAY, MINUTE, SECOND, MILLISECOND, DAY_OF_WEEK, DAY_OF_YEAR, AM_PM, WEEK_OF_YEAR, and DAY_OF_WEEK_IN_MONTH.

In a sense, you can use this deprecation from using a Time class to using one of the Calendar classes to your advantage. By accessing the system time through a Calendar object, you will be putting in the infrastructure to allow a cool date readout in your watch face design, if that is needed.

Now it is time to start morphing the previous use of the Time class to use the Calendar class in your ProWatchFaceService Java code.

# Upgrading Your Code: Calendar and .getDrawable()

To get rid of the strike-through font (lined out code), you need to replace a Time object instantiation with a Calendar.getInstance() object and upgrade the .getDrawable(int) usage with the .getDrawable(int, Theme) method call.

You will do the class replacement first, since this is the major change, and then add a null value to the .getDrawable() method calls. This will do the same thing as your previous method call, but it won't generate deprecated code highlighting. As you know, a null tells this method to use the current Theme object definition. You defined this earlier using an XML definition.

# Upgrading the Time Class Code: Using the Calendar Class

As you can see in Figure 16-6, the Android **Time** class has been discontinued for use (deprecated), in API level 22. First, you would need to mouse-over this to see if there is any advice regarding what to do to make your Java code completely up to date. As you can see, in Figure 16-6, there is not a lot of information in the suggestion tool tip even if you click the more link, which states the same exact thing as the pop-up yellow tool tip. This means you will have to look at your Android Time class documentation.

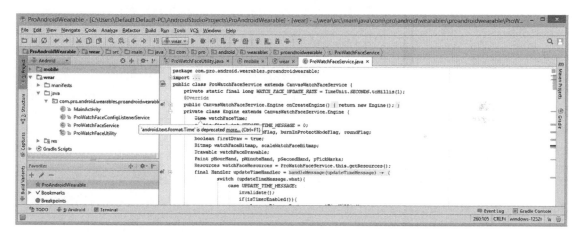

*Figure 16-6. You can see a deprecated Time class declaration (reference) at the top of the private Engine class*

Change the **Time watchFaceTime;** Java object declaration statement to instead use the Calendar class. This will make it a **Calendar watchFaceTime;** Java statement.

As you can see, highlighted in the middle of Figure 16-7, you will need to use the **Alt+Enter** keystroke work process and have Android Studio code your import statement for you at the top of your ProWatchFaceService class. Make sure to delete the Time class import statement.

*Figure 16-7. Change the Time class reference to a Calendar class reference in the watchFaceTime declaration*

The next thing you'll need to do is to load this Calendar object in the onCreate() method, using the Calendar.getInstance() structure that you learned about in the previous section. Use the following Java statement, which can be seen highlighted in pale yellow in the middle of Figure 16-8:

```
watchFaceTime = Calendar.getInstance();
```

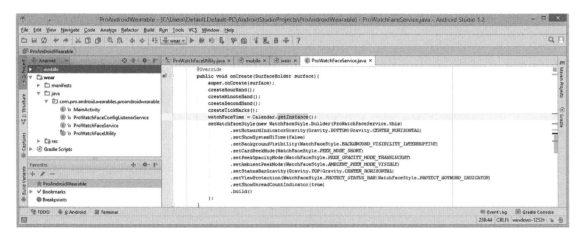

*Figure 16-8.* *Set a watchFaceTime Calendar object to a Calendar.getInstance() inside of the onCreate() method*

This will create a watchFaceTime Calendar object and load it with a valid Calendar object, in this case, that would be a GregorianCalendar subclass.

In this way, you're setting up your code so that you will not have to **cast** GregorianCalendar to Calendar or vice versa, and you can just use Calendar in your code. Because GregorianCalendar is the concrete class, this is what will be created (since Calendar is the static class) and this is what a recommendation in the Time class suggests you use to replace Time.

Now that you have the watchFaceTime GregorianCalendar object that replaces the watchFaceTime Time object, you will need to change the .clear() method call and .setToNow() method call for the Time class with some method calls that work with the GregorianCalendar and Calendar classes. These include a .setTimeInMillis() method call, a .get() method call, and a .setTimeZone() method call. Let's do this for the **timeZoneReceiver** BroadcastReceiver now.

# Upgrading timeZoneReceiver: The .setTimeZone() Method

Click the plus (+) icon in the left margin and open your timeZoneReceiver object structure. Comment out the .clear() and .setToNow() method call structures, as shown in Figure 16-9, so you can use deprecated code if you want to later on (the Time class will still work if you want to use it).

*Figure 16-9.  In the BroadcastReceiver onReceive() method, use the .setTimeZone() method, instead of .clear()*

To replace these, use a **.setTimeZone()** method, with a call to the **TimeZone** class **.getDefault()** method, to replace the **.clear(intent.getStringExtra("time-zone")** and then call the **invalidate()** method to update the watch face time onDraw logic. This would be done using the following updated Java structure:

```java
public void onReceive(Context context, Intent intent) {
    watchFaceTime.setTimeZone( TimeZone.getDefault() );
    invalidate();
}
```

Next, let's work on upgrading the code that is in the onDraw() method, as that is the next most important code. You will get the current time at the top of the method, using a new Calendar .setTimeInMillis() method call.

## Upgrading the onDraw() Method: Using .setTimeInMillis()

First, let's comment out the **super.onDraw(watchface, rect);** because you are replacing the onDraw() logic completely, and your **watchFaceTime.setToNow();** Java statement, because you are going to replace that with a different Calendar class method call. Type in the watchFaceTime GregorianCalendar object and hit the period key, then start to type ".setTi" and double-click the **.setTimeInMillis(long milliseconds)** option, as shown in the drop-down method selection helper in Figure 16-10.

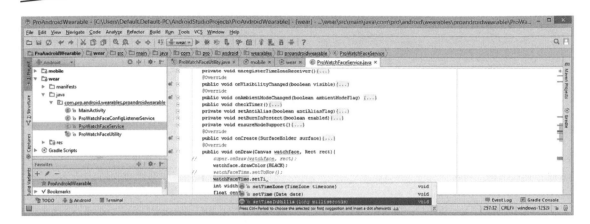

*Figure 16-10.  In the onDraw() method, replace the .setToNow() method call with a .setTimeInMillis() method call*

Inside the method parameter area, type the System class and a period, and then double-click the **currentTimeMillis()** option and insert it into your Java statement, as shown in Figure 16-11. The resulting Java statement should look like the following:

```
watchFaceTime.setTimeInMillis(System.currentTimeMillis()); // Load Calendar object with
current time
```

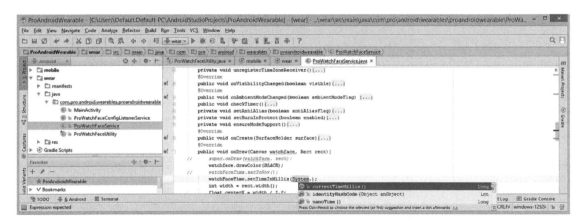

*Figure 16-11.  Inside the .setTimeInMillis() method, access the System.currentTimeMillis() method to set the time*

Now that your GregorianCalendar object has been loaded with a current time value using the System.currentTimeMillis() getter method, you will upgrade the hour, minute, and second integer variables to extract the time values from the Calendar constants you learned about in the section of the chapter covering the Calendar class.

# Loading Your Time Variables: Using the .get() Method

To extract the system time values from the watchFaceTime GregorianCalendar object, you will use the **.get()** method call and pass in the Calendar.VALUE constant that you want the data for, in this case, **HOUR**, **MINUTE,** and **SECOND,** which will give you the values that the rest of the onDraw() logic you have in place will need to position the hour hand, minute hand, and second hand, respectively.

The Java statements that replace your watchFaceTime Time object's simpler method calls to the Time object's .hour(), .minute(), and .second() method calls are shown highlighted in Figure 16-12 and should look like the following three Java programming statements:

```
int hours = watchFaceTime.get(Calendar.HOUR);
int minutes = watchFaceTime.get(Calendar.MINUTE);
int seconds = watchFaceTime.get(Calendar.SECOND);
```

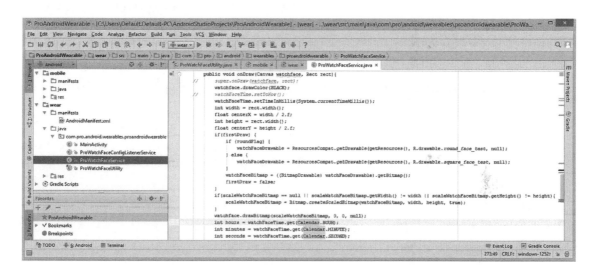

*Figure 16-12.  Convert the hours, minutes, and seconds integers to use a .get(Calendar.TIME_UNIT) method call*

An advantage here is that you can also use .get() for other Date or TimeZone data!

Now that your onDraw() method has been updated to the latest code, you can move on to upgrade the onVisibilityChanged() method to use .setTimeZone().

# Upgrade the onVisibilityChanged() Method: .setTimeZone()

Click the plus (+) icon in the left margin to open the onVisibilityChanged() method structure and comment out the .clear() and .setToNow() method call structures, as shown in Figure 16-13, so you can use deprecated code, if you want to, later on. Notice that this is the same modification you made in the onReceive() method of the BroadcastReceiver object.

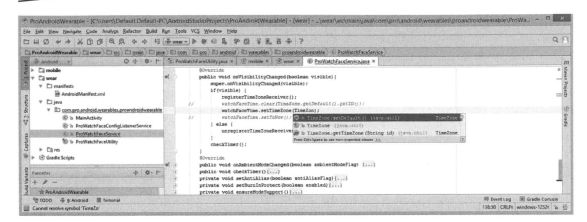

**Figure 16-13.** *Inside the onVisibilityChanged() method, change the .clear() and .setToNow() to .setTimeZone()*

It is important to note that you will not need to include the invalidate() method call as this was already done in the onReceive() method update.

# Upgrading the Code: Using the .getDrawable(int, Theme)

Let's go back into the onDraw() method and upgrade the BitmapDrawable code to use a nondeprecated .getDrawable(int, Theme) method version by adding a comma and a null value inside the method call parameter area. This is a fairly basic Java statement upgrade, and it can be seen highlighted in Figure 16-14. The new Java statement should look like the following:

```
if(firstDraw) {
    if (roundFlag) {
        watchFaceDrawable = watchFaceResources.getDrawable(R.drawable.round_face_test, null);
    } else {
        watchFaceDrawable = watchFaceResources.getDrawable(R.drawable.square_face_test, null);
    }
    watchFaceBitmap = ((BitmapDrawable) watchFaceDrawable).getBitmap();
    firstDraw = false;
}
```

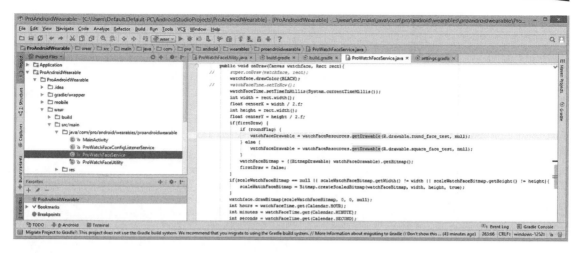

*Figure 16-14. Upgrade .getDrawable() method call to use a null to instruct Android to keep using the current Theme*

As you can see in Figure 16-15, you will also need to make this exact same upgrade to the .getDrawable(int) method call in the ensureModeSupport() method, which is needed to convert this method to the still-supported .getDrawable(int, Theme) version.

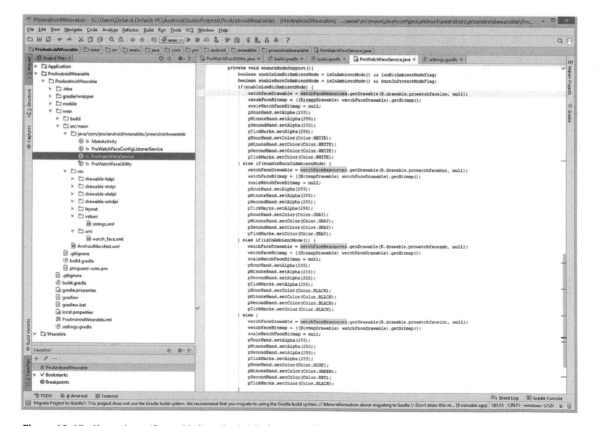

*Figure 16-15. Upgrade .getDrawable() method calls in ensureModeSupport() method to use the null value as well*

This will also need to be done for the four BitmapDrawable assets used for the prowatchfacelow.png, prowatchfacebur.png, prowatchfaceamb.png, and prowatchfaceint. png watchFaceResources object asset loader Java statements.

This finishes the deprecated code upgrades for the old Time class, as well as the older .getDrawable(int) method call. The next logical step would be to test this code, but Android Studio threw us a 1.2.1.1 upgrade curve ball!

# Solving IDE Problems Introduced by SDK Upgrades

Right when I was about to start testing, I checked for updates, as I'll always do before I start any serious application testing. I found the Android Studio 1.2.1.1 update was available, as shown in Figure 16-16. I again went through the steps shown in Figures 16-1 through 16-4.

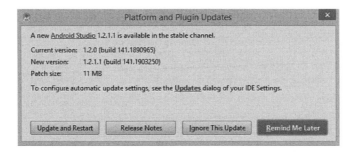

*Figure 16-16. Another rapid fire Android Studio upgrade from 1.2.0 to 1.2.1.1 requires the upgrade process again*

I applied the patch to Android Studio (IntelliJ plus the Android SDK plug-ins) and then used the Android SDK Manager to make sure I had all the upgrades to APIs, tools, documentation, system images, and the like that I needed in place. Then I restarted Android Studio and launched the new 1.2.1.1 version.

As you can see in Figure 16-17, I encountered a fairly major problem. This was clearly not my fault, as I had only changed Java code, nothing else. I received a message in the upper right corner of IntelliJ that asked me if I wanted to **Migrate Project to Gradle?** Because the project has always been a Gradle build system project, I needed to find out what was causing this problem. This caused me to add this section to the chapter on how I figured this out, as this is likely to happen to you at some time. So here I'll go deeper into the Gradle build system, projects integrated in IntelliJ, and how to use Invalidate and Restart, Import a Project, and the most drastic solution, how to create your project from scratch. After I explain how to solve this problem and turn the project back into Gradle build system compatibility, which the 1.2.1.1 upgrade seems to have altered.

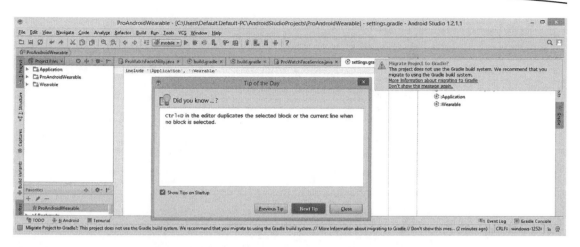

*Figure 16-17.  Upon restart after upgrading, the project no longer thinks that it is using the Gradle build system*

I'll show you the order in which I tried things, from the necessary Gradle build definitions upgrades, to using Invalidate and Restart, to the Import Project work process, to completely re-creating an Android Wear project.

## Upgrading Gradle Files: Adding Build Definition Sections

The first logical thing that I tried to fix the Migrate Project to Gradle warning was to upgrade the build.gradle (wear, mobile, and project) build definition files.

As you can see in Figure 16-18, I added a buildscript definitions section, containing subsections for repositories and dependencies, shown at the top of the definition file for wear, and compileOptions specifying Java 7, and sourceSets, specifying Java and resources locations, as shown at the bottom.

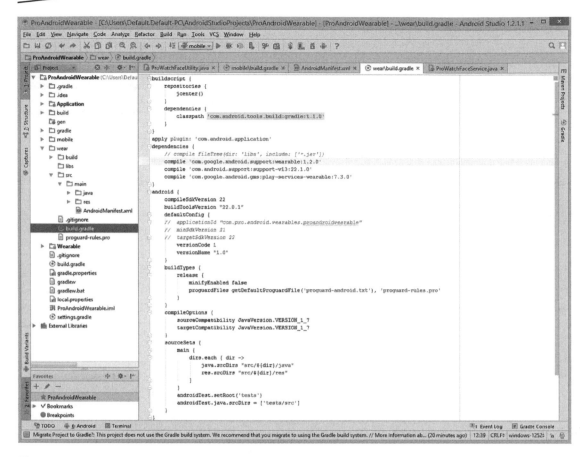

*Figure 16-18. Upgrade wear gradle.build definition to include buildscript, compileOptions and sourceSets section*

Next, I added these same sections to the mobile gradle.build file, as shown in Figure 16-19. I upgraded my compile dependencies and added a couple more.

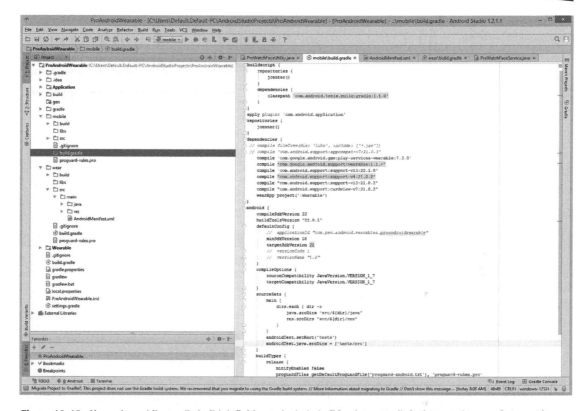

*Figure 16-19.   Upgrade mobile gradle.build definition to include buildscript, compileOptions, and sourceSets sections*

Because I didn't have the insight as to which compile dependencies to use for WatchFaces API, I used https://github.com/googlesamples/android-WatchFace as a guide to what the internal development team at Google has found works for version 1.2.1.1. These compile dependencies will accommodate any features you decide to add to your WatchFace API design. It is important to note an unused compile dependency will not cause any problem if you do not use it.

The GitHub WatchFace code no longer features the root (ProAndroidWearable) gradle.build file, so I simply upgraded mine from the Gradle 1.0 classpath to the 1.2.3 classpath using the following statement, and is shown in Figure 16-20:

```
buildscript {
    repositories { jcenter() }
    dependencies { classpath 'com.android.tools.build:gradle:1.2.3' }
}
```

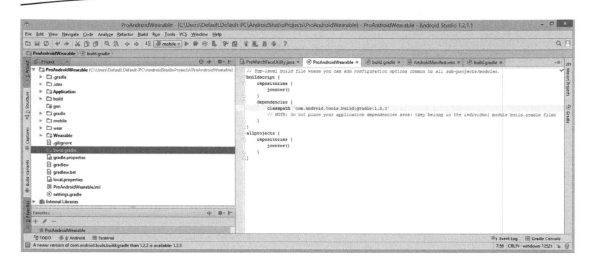

**Figure 16-20.** *Upgrade the classpath dependency for the root gradle.build to use com.android.tools.gradle:1.2.3*

The new gradle.settings file references the Wearable and Application folders:

```
include ':Application', ':Wearable'
```

After I restarted Android Studio, I opened the AndroidManifest, and as you can see in Figure 16-21 on the left side of the screenshot, the referencing errors still exist. These errors cause the Run/Debug Configurations dialog to not be able to run (build, execute) the project, so it can't be tested, as you can see on the right side of Figure 16-21.

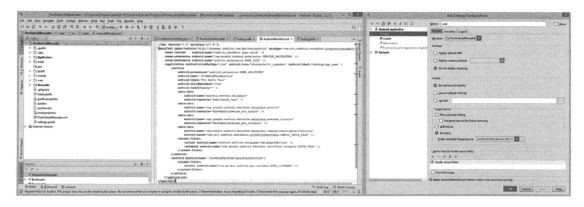

**Figure 16-21.** *Upgrading the Gradle build system definitions did not fix the AndroidManifest referencing problem*

Since upgrading the Gradle configuration files did not solve this problem, the next thing that I tried, which is the next easiest solution, was to use the Invalidate function, which is found under the File menu.

If this does not work, try the next most difficult solution, which is to Import the Project and then see if it will build and run. If that does not work, you would have to re-create the project from scratch, which would fix any Android Studio (IntelliJ 14) file referencing problems.

# Using Invalidate and Restart: Rebuilding Project Structure

Click the **File** menu in Android Studio, as shown in Figure 16-22. Select the **Invalidate Caches / Restart** menu option, and click **Invalidate and Restart**.

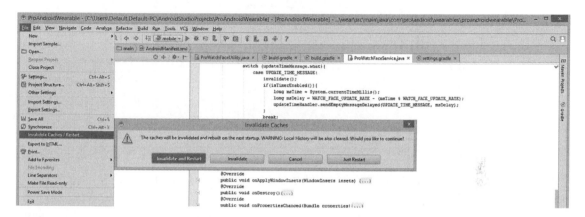

*Figure 16-22. Fixing the project referencing by using the File ➤ Invalidate Caches and Restart Utility*

The IDEA will disappear and relaunch itself. Open AndroidManifest, and you will see if the red referencing errors have disappeared. My AndroidManifest.xml was still showing the red error highlights, which can be seen in Figure 16-21.

The next most difficult work process involves moving the project to a backup folder, launching IntelliJ as you did the first time, with no new project, and using the Import Project feature to hopefully import the code and XML from a project that's been corrupted into a new IntelliJ file and project hierarchy structure that does not have these referencing errors.

# Using Import Project

The work process I used to import this project was to back up the project, using Cut and Paste, as shown in Figure 16-23. I right-clicked the project folder and used **Cut** to remove it from the AndroidStudioProjects folder and then right-clicked the **C:/Back-Up/AndroidStudioProjects** folder and used Paste to move an entire project hierarchy folder location on my C:\ drive.

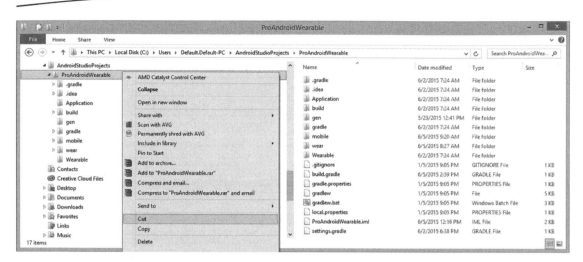

**Figure 16-23.** *Empting the AndroidStudioProjects folder using Cut and Paste to move the project to C:\Back-Up*

What this will do is make Android Studio think there is no current project in use, since there is nothing in the AndroidStudioProjects folder.

This will then produce an IntelliJ dialog that contains the Import Project option. This is what I needed to use to try to create a new IntelliJ project infrastructure, which will hopefully fix this asset referencing problem.

Figure 16-24 shows the ProAndroidWearable project backed up to my C:\ drive.

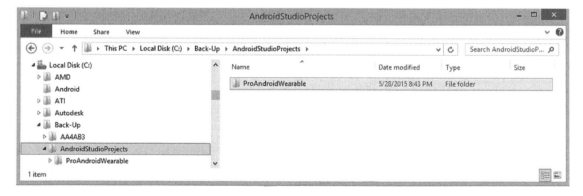

**Figure 16-24.** *I created a Back-Up\AndroidStudioProjects folder, using Paste, to move ProAndroidWearable there*

Once your project folder hierarchy is backed up (and hidden from IntelliJ), start up Android Studio and you will get the original menu that allows you to Start a New Project, Open Existing Projects, Import Code Samples, Check Out Projects from Version Control, and Import a Project.

Select the **Import Project** option, as shown in Figure 16-25, then select the **C:/Back-Up/ AndroidStudioProjects/ProAndroidWearable/gradle.build** file, and click the **OK** button. You will see a **Building Project** progress bar, and the new project will finally open in an empty Android Studio IntelliJ IDEA.

**Figure 16-25.** *Launch Android Studio with no project, use Import Project, and select build.gradle, rebuilt project*

Right-click the AndroidManifest.xml file in the wear component (folder) of the project hierarchy and use the Jump to Source option to inspect the file.

As you can see in Figure 16-26, I still have referencing errors highlights in my AndroidManifest XML file. They are different referencing errors than I had before, and I additionally have a new **Frameworks detected** warning at the top right of the IDE, along with a **Configure** link. This opens a dialog called **Setup Frameworks**, seen highlighted in Figure 16-26, which is what corrupted my project in the first place. It does not matter which of these drop-down menu options you select, type or directory, your end result is the same. In my case, this equated to different AndroidManifest referencing errors in the XML file, so it looks like I will be re-creating the project!

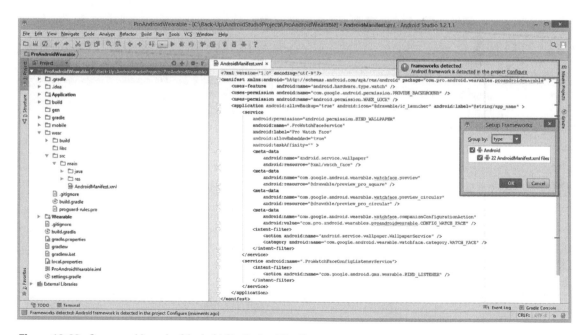

**Figure 16-26.** *On second launch of Android Studio, I get the Frameworks detected warning that changed the project*

As you can see in Figure 16-27, this new project now has the same problems that the project I imported had, so I'll need to create a new Android Wear project and copy all of my Java code, XML markup, and assets over into it.

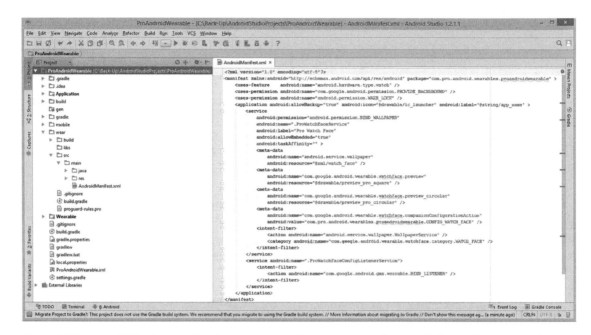

**Figure 16-27.** *AndroidManifest now has the same referencing errors I had before, so this is what broke the project*

Because the original project was created under Android Studio 1.0 and the IDE is now at 1.2.1.1, there are probably some new features, possibly relating to the WatchFaces API, that can be used to shortcut the Java coding or XML markup tasks. I am going to leave the coding from the first 15 chapters in this book as they are, because they show you how to create a Watch Faces Application from absolute scratch, so you have the maximum learning experience in learning how to fix the coding.

## Re-creating a Project from Scratch: Copy Code and Assets

Cut and paste any subfolders under the AndroidStudioProjects folder as you did in the previous section and in the startup menu shown in Figure 16-25, then select the Start a New Android Studio Project option. It will give you the dialog seen in Figure 4-16, where you will use the same **ProAndroidWearable** and **wearables.android.pro.com** entries. Make sure the project is in a User's folder and in an AndroidStudioProjects subfolder. After you click the **Next** button, you'll get a Target Android Devices dialog, as shown in Figure 16-28. This dialog can also be seen in Figure 4-17, using older Wear API Levels.

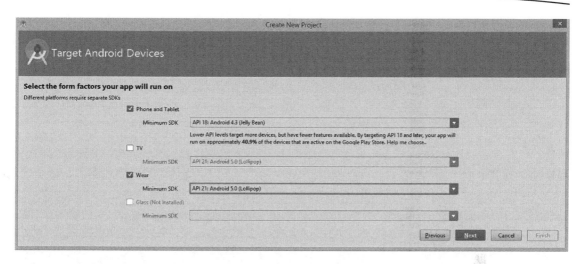

*Figure 16-28. Select an API Level 18 for the Phone and Tablet, and an API Level 21 for the Wear component*

Select **Android 4.3 API 18** for the Phone and Tablet App and **Android 5.0 API 21** for the Wear App component. Then click the Next button to access an **Add an activity to Wear** dialog, which is shown in Figure 16-29. If you want to see the older version of this dialog, reference Figure 4-19.

*Figure 16-29. Select the WatchFace option to have Android Studio write your WatchFace API code infrastructure*

Notice that there are two options in this dialog that were not available in Android Studio 1.0: the Display Notification and the WatchFace API. I will select the WatchFace API option to show you that Android Studio will write the WatchFace API code for you, as you're going to replace this soon.

In the **Service Name** data field, type in the **ProWatchFaceService** Java class name and select your **Analog** WatchFace Style option in the drop-down menu, as shown in Figure 16-30, and then click **Finish** to create your project.

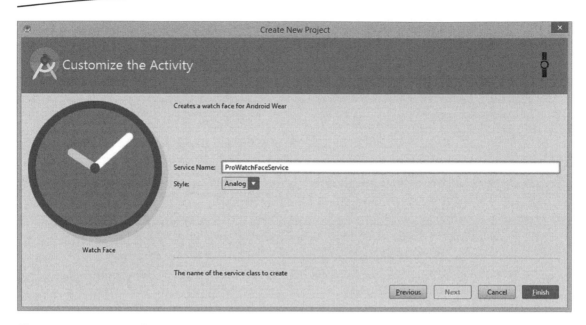

*Figure 16-30. Name your Service ProWatchFaceService and select the Analog WatchFace Style and click Finish*

After building your new project, the IntelliJ IDEA will now open up, using the standard bootstrap WatchFace API code, which is not nearly as detailed, or complex, as the code you had been developing over the course of this book. I have also used more descriptive object and variable names so you can visualize what each of these objects and data fields are doing for your WatchFace API code base as a whole.

It's important to note that none of this code will be used! What I'm doing here is using this new project structure, primarily, new **.IML**, or **IntelliJ Mark-Up Language** project structure definitions, to fix the problem I have been encountering. All the Java code, XML, and assets will be copied over.

I noticed in the bootstrap code base that the deprecated Time class hasn't been replaced with the Calendar class code, as you can see highlighted in yellow near the top of Figure 16-31. I guess they will get to that in the Android Studio 1.3 update, which is supposed to be out sometime later in 2015, hopefully by the time you get this book.

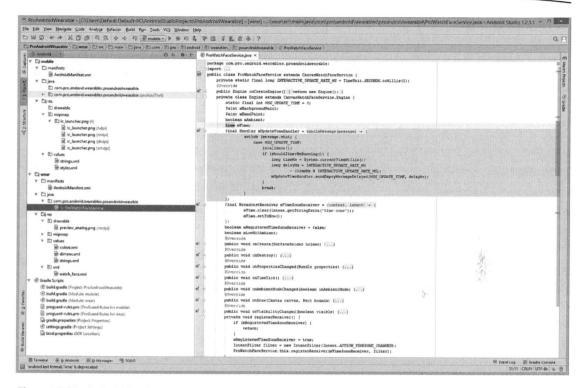

*Figure 16-31.   Android Studio creates the basic Analog WatchFace Service class and all the basic methods for you*

These rapid updates are getting to be really a bear!.

The first thing I did was to restart the IDE, rebuild the project, and make sure everything is as it should be in the Gradle Console tab. I'm glad I took this step, because as you can see in Figure 16-32, there is an error present in the Gradle Console for this bootstrap project structure! Let's click the **Open File Encoding Settings** link and fix this right away. In the **Project Encoding** drop-down, select **UTF-8**, and click the **OK** button to set a suggested UTF-8 project encoding format for the entire Wear project.

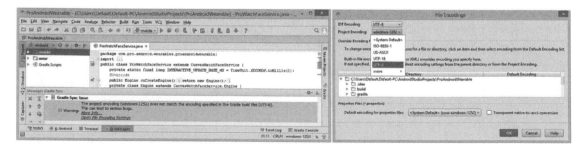

*Figure 16-32.   Fixing a Gradle sync issue project encoding problem (left), using the File Encodings dialog (right)*

As you can see in Figure 16-33, after I clicked the Gradle Project **Refresh** icon shown at the upper right, my Gradle Console was now clear of all error or warning messages. I also show you the menu sequence you will use if you want to get back into this File Encodings dialog again on the left side of the figure. This is done using **File ➤ Settings ➤ Editor ➤ File Encodings**.

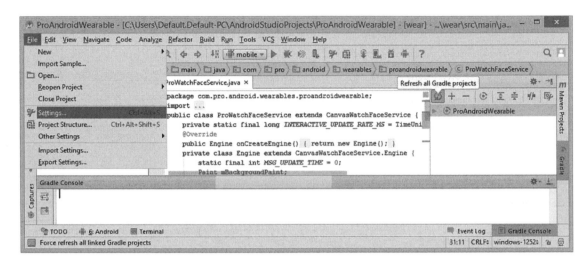

**Figure 16-33.** *Open (click) the Gradle tab (right) and use the Refresh Gradle Project icon to clear Gradle Console*

I am going to follow the order you did things during this book in this rebuild of the project that you are doing, so the next thing that you did in Chapter 5 was to create the AVD emulator infrastructure for the project. I looked in the Run/Debug Configurations dialog and the Round and Square AVD emulators that I created in Chapter 5 were still a part of Android Studio, which makes sense as these are independent of projects, so let's move on.

Chapter 7 covered gradle.build and XML definition files, so let's put them in place now. Copy the build.gradle file text from your ProAndroidWearable folder, wear and mobile folders, and replace the build.gradle file text for the new bootstrap project. The **wear/res/xml/ watch_face.xml** file is already in place, so copy and paste the values in the strings.xml file in a backup wear/res/values folder to the new project **wear/res/values/strings.xml** file, replacing your bootstrap <string> values. Do the same for your strings.xml values in your **mobile/res/values/strings.xml** so the color array and values are in place for the WatchFace Companion App.

Next let's transfer the Activity UI design. Create the **/layout** folder in your **mobile/res** folder and then create an **activity_pro_watch_face_config.xml** file. Copy and paste your Configuration Activity UI definition. Before you can replace both AndroidManifest.xml files, you will need to copy your **PNG** assets that the Manifest files access, or you'll get error highlights.

The PNG files are fortunately all in the **wear/res/drawable-hdpi** folder, so next, you need to copy and paste these into your new project as well, into the res/drawable-dpi folders for scaling or res/drawable-nodpi for fixed use.

It's interesting to note that as I was researching these new Android 1.2.1 and 1.3 WatchFaces API upgrades and updates that I found a new recommended WatchFaces background bitmap image size of **400 pixels** and a recommendation that images go in the **/wear/res/drawable-nodpi/** folder, so I am pasting my bitmap assets into this folder. My guess is a new 400-pixel recommendation is because a new Huawei SmartWatch that features a 400-pixel screen. This means that once a 480-pixel smartwatch comes out, which will be in 2015 or 2016, this recommended NODPI resolution for the WatchFaces Bitmap will change to 480.

Another thing that I noticed is that the res/drawable-dpi folders had been replaced by **res/mipmap-dpi** folders. A mipmap capability was introduced for use with icons in Android 4.3, and mipmaps have their origins in 3D. These are precalculated to fit Android DPI icon resolutions using preoptimized PNG32 images, each of which is a lower resolution representation resampled from the highest resolution version of that same application icon image. I would use these folders for your application icons only, and use /drawable folders for BitmapDrawable assets you use inside your Wear apps.

Because your AndroidManifest.xml files also reference the Java classes you have created, you will need to create these Java classes using the IDEA New ➤ Java class feature, and copy and paste your Java logic into these next.

Let's start with your **ProWatchFaceService.java** file first, because this Java class was created by the **New Project** series of dialogs. Copy and paste the code into your ProWatchFaceService tab, replacing the bootstrap code. Next right-click the **/wear/java/com.pro.android.wearables.proandroidwearable** folder and use the **New ➤ Java Class** dialog to create the ConfigListener **ProWatchFaceConfigListenerService.java** file. Then copy and paste the Java code you wrote during the book into your ProWatchFaceConfigListenerService tab, replacing the empty Java class code. There will be an error until you create the ProWatchFaceUtility.java class file, so let's do that next.

Right-click the **/wear/java/com.pro.android.wearables.proandroidwearable** folder and use the **New ➤ Java Class** dialog to create your Utility class **ProWatchFaceUtility.java** file. Then copy and paste the Java code you wrote during this book into the ProWatchFaceUtility tab, replacing the empty Java class code. Let's finish up by adding in the mobile component's Java code.

Right-click the **/mobile/java/com.pro.android.wearables.proandroidwearable** folder and use the **New ➤ Java Class** dialog to create the ConfigActivity class **ProWatchFaceCompanionConfigActivity.java** file. Then copy and paste the Java code for this class into the ProWatchFaceCompanionConfigActivity tab, replacing the empty Java class. Now you can copy and paste the wear and mobile AndroidManifest.xml files. Change your icon referencing to use the mipmap with this line of code:

```
android:icon="@mipmap/ic_launcher"   // Replace the @drawable reference with an @mipmap
reference
```

Now that the **mobile AndroidManifest.xml** is copied over, with only a single reference change, it is time to copy the more complex wear AndroidManifest, which may have some upgrades, since you created it under Android Studio 1.0.

Besides the mipmap reference change, the **wear AndroidManifest.xml** is error free, and I am also adding a **<uses-sdk>** tag specifying **API Level 21** at the top of the Manifest, inside the <manifest> parent tag. This can be seen highlighted at the top of Figure 16-34 and uses the following XML markup:

```
<uses-sdk android:minSdkVersion="21" android:targetSdkVersion="21" />
```

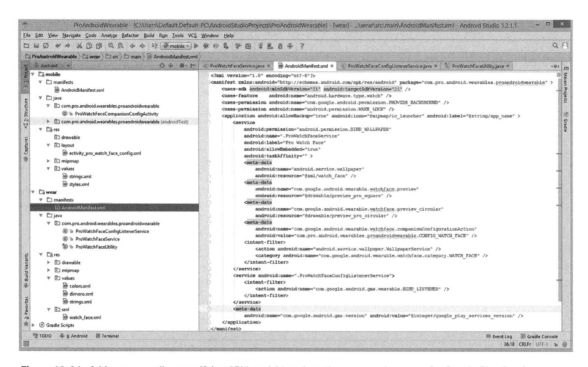

*Figure 16-34. Add a <uses-sdk> specifying API Level 21 and another <meta-data> tag for Google Play Services*

I am also adding a **<meta-data>** child tag, right before the </application> closing tag, to define a Google Mobile Services (GMS) version for this app. This can be seen highlighted in yellow at the bottom of Figure 16-34 and uses the following XML markup:

```
<meta-data android:name="com.google.android.gms.version"
           android:value="@integer/google_play_services_version" />
```

Next I did a Run ➤ Run Wear, and the project build was again working using the Gradle build system, so I was back to having a working IDEA, although it took an extreme work process to get there!

# The Moral of the Story: Android Is More than Java or XML

It's important to remember that programming these days is a moving target, involving multiple and integrated components such as the IDE (IntelliJ), a build system (Gradle), an SDK (Android Studio), programming language (Java 7), a markup language (XML), new media codecs (MPEG4, JPEG, PNG, MP3, GIF, WebM, WebP, etc.), technology APIs (WebKit, OpenGL, SQLite), and operating system (Windows, Linux, and Mac) platforms, and that's just on the Android application development side of the equation, which I covered in this book.

On the device side of the equation, you also have a Dalvik Virtual Machine (DVM) or Android Run Time (ART) engine, Android OS, and Linux 64 Kernel, so developing and publishing Android applications of any type, whether they are generic Android or more specialized Android Wear (this book), Android TV, Android Auto, or Android Glass (the Apress *Pro Android IoT* book), is never going to be a walk in the park by any stretch of the imagination!

All of the components are maintained by literally hundreds of programmers, working at multiple companies (Google and Oracle, for instance) and open source organizations (MPEG LA, Khronos, Apache, and W3C, for instance). We have even experienced an occurrence where a brand new, 100% Android Studio-generated project had a Gradle build system error, which had to be fixed immediately!

# Summary

In this chapter, you learned how to upgrade your deprecated code to use new, recommended classes and methods of more current API classes. I also showed you how to fix noncode-related, in this case, IntelliJ IDEA-related problems that will inevitably arise due to OS API upgrades.

This required that you learn about a **Calendar** superclass, and its subclass the **GregorianCalendar** class, and the new methods you will need to use to replace the Time class and its methods that had been used originally to implement a Watch Faces API. The deprecated classes and methods will still work, if you don't mind having lined-out (strike-thru) code in your IDEA.

You also learned how to use a more advanced **getDrawable(int, Theme)** method call, which Android deprecated the simpler getDrawable(int) version of, in my opinion to force developers to incorporate a Theme into their code usage.

In the next chapter, you will take a look at the other Android APIs, as well as some of the other cool things such as GPS location awareness and voice recognition capabilities that you can add to your Wear applications.

# The Future of Android IoT APIs: Android TV, Glass, Auto, and Wear

Because there's no possible way to cover all of Android, or any of the niche hardware device SDKs that have become available for Android, I thought I would leave you with a chapter that gives you some ideas regarding what to take a look at next on your Android hardware device development journey.

Android is intelligently organizing these APIs, matching API function with hardware product genres or types, such as interactive television sets (iTV sets) running **Android TV**, Smart Eyeglasses running **Android Glass**, which is not released but is shown in the New Project dialog (see Figure 16-28), or Automobile Dashboards running **Android Auto**, and let's not forget the smartwatches running **Android Wear**, which is what this book explores.

I will be writing a book on Android IoT next year, which will cover these other APIs, as well as any other Internet of Things APIs that might materialize in the meantime. As other consumer electronic genres grow more popular and are adopted by major hardware manufacturers, Android will release other customized APIs.

For example, many manufacturers have virtual reality headsets, which could run an **Android VR** API. Android-driven robots, and even drones, are growing in popularity, so an **Android Robot** API would allow developers to create an application customizing their robot or drone. Another growing area is home appliances, so do not be surprised to see an **Android Home** API. During this chapter, I'll discuss some of these other Android APIs as well as some of the other features of Wear you should take a look at implementing.

# HD and UHD Android TV: The Opposite of Wear

Android TV SDK addresses the opposite end of the consumer electronics size spectrum than the Android Wear SDK, which is optimized for small square or round screens. Android TV is geared for developing apps for big widescreen displays that have **True HD**, or 1920-by-1080 resolution, or the newer **UHD**, or 4096-by-2160 resolution. These displays range from 60 to 80 inches for their diagonal screen size, whereas smartwatches range from 1 to 2 inches!

Logical Android TV application types include 2D and 3D Games, Live Content Streaming, Television Playback, Interactive Television, and Content Search.

Android TV applications need to have a **320-by-180** pixel home screen **banner** in the **res/drawable-xhdpi** project folder and should include localized text identifying the application. This banner is declared and referenced in the AndroidManifest.xml **application** definition, using the following parameter:

```
<application android:banner="@drawable/png_banner_name" >
    // Nested Tags for the TV Application will go in here
</application>
```

Android TV apps intended to run on iTV set devices will need to declare an iTV Launcher Activity for the Android TV API in the AndroidManifest, using the **CATEGORY_LEANBACK_ LAUNCHER** constant in the **<intent-filter>** child tag.

This Intent Filter will serve to identify iTV apps as being TV compatible. This is required for Google Play to correctly categorize an iTV set app to be in the Android TV app section of the store. This Intent also identifies the Activity to launch when a user selects the icon on an iTV home screen. The following XML markup shows how to code an intent filter in a Manifest:

```
<application android:banner="@drawable/banner" >
  <activity android:name="com.example.android.MainActivity" android:label="@string/app_name" >
    <intent-filter>
      <action android:name="android.intent.action.MAIN" />
      <category android:name="android.intent.category.LAUNCHER" />
    </intent-filter>
  </activity>
  <activity
    android:name="com.example.android.iTVsetActivity"
    android:label="@string/itv_app_name"
    android:theme="@style/Theme.Leanback">
    <intent-filter>
      <action android:name="android.intent.action.MAIN" />
      <category android:name="android.intent.category.LEANBACK_LAUNCHER" />
    </intent-filter>
  </activity>
</application>
```

Android has a support library for iTV user interface design called the **V17 Leanback Library**. This provides standard themes for iTV activities, called Theme.Leanback, as you can see applied (in bold) in the above XML markup.

The Theme.Leanback android: theme parameter can implement consistent visual UI styles for the iTV set apps. Use of this leanback theme is recommended for most iTV apps. The Theme.Leanback should be used with iTV UI design classes that are from the V17 Leanback Library, which also supports TV media playback classes.

Other classes that can be used for Android TV development include the **V7 RecyclerView Library**, which offers classes for memory-efficient management and display of long lists. A number of classes in the V17 Leanback Library depend on the classes in the V7 RecyclerView Library. There is also the **V7 CardView Library**, which offers developers additional user interface widgets for displaying content information cards that contain media item pictures and media item text description. The V7 Leanback Library is also dependent on the V4 Support Library, so just like with Wear apps, many older versions of support libraries may need to be included in the build.gradle dependencies section for the Android TV applications.

You will also need to declare that your app uses a Leanback user interface at the **<manifest>** level of your Android Manifest XML file. If you set this required **<uses-feature>** attribute to a **true** value, the Android TV app will only run on iTV set devices that implement an Android TV Leanback UI. The XML markup for this would look like the following:

```
<manifest>
    <uses-feature android:name="android.software.leanback" android:required="true" />
    // Other Manifest Child Tags will go in here
</manifest>
```

If you are developing apps that run on mobile phones, wearables, tablets, e-book readers, and the like, in addition to running on Android TV, you will set this required attribute to a **false** value, using the following markup:

```
<manifest>
    <uses-feature android:name="android.software.leanback" android:required="false" />
    // Other Manifest Child Tags will go in here
</manifest>
```

Android TV apps that you intend to run on iTV sets use a remote and don't rely on touchscreens for input, at least until major manufacturers release touchscreen iTV sets, which they probably will at some point in time.

In order to clarify the use of touch for your users, the Manifest for your iTV applications needs to declare this **android.hardware.touchscreen** feature as not being required. This is done by using a **false** setting inside the **<uses-feature>** tag. The following XML markup shows how to include this in the Android Manifest application settings and privileges declaration file:

```
<manifest>
    <uses-feature android:name="android.hardware.touchscreen" android:required="false" />
    // Other Manifest Child Tags will go in here
</manifest>
```

This setting will identify your iTV application as being able to work with an Android TV device, and it is required for the app to be considered an Android TV application and listed in the correct iTV area in Google Play.

It is important to note that currently an iTV application must be declared in this fashion, that is, that touchscreen support is not required in your app manifest, as shown in this example code, or your app cannot appear in the Google Play Store under TV devices.

Besides interactive television shows, one of the most popular types of iTV set applications will surely be iTV games. Unlike smartphone apps designed for portrait orientation or smartwatch apps designed for square and round screens, Android TV apps are designed in landscape orientation. The normal aspect ratio for an HDTV (1920 by 1080) is 16:9, but super-wide 16:8 WHD screens that feature a 2160-by-1080 resolution are also appearing as well.

Unlike most multiplayer games, shared over a network, which use their own display, system memory, and processors, iTV games do not need any network, reducing latency, but they also share the same screen, system memory, and multicore processor, and thus they require careful design and optimization. A shared screen can also present some unique multiplayer game design challenges as all of your players can see everything, which is especially difficult when designing card games and similar strategy games that rely on the player's proprietary (undisclosed) game play strategy information.

A possible solution to this would be a companion app, also called a second screen display app. This would be running on Bluetooth-connected phones or tablets. This would enable the player to conceal game strategy information that only they can view, using this second screen Bluetooth-connected app.

An Android TV home screen lists games in a different area than regular iTV apps. To cause a game to appear in this list of games, set android:isGame attribute to "true" in your Manifest <application> tag, using this markup:

```
<application android:isGame="true" >
```

In order to advise users that a game requires or supports game controllers, you must include the following <uses-feature> entry in the Manifest file:

```
<uses-feature android:name="android.hardware.gamepad" />
```

If your iTV game uses, but does not absolutely require, a game controller, you will additionally include an **android:required="false"** parameter inside the <uses-feature> tag. This XML markup would look like the following:

```
<uses-feature android:name="android.hardware.gamepad" android:required="false" />
```

# Android Auto: Android Apps for the Car Dashboard

The Android Auto SDK (API) platform enables you to extend your application to work with automobile console systems that are using Android Auto. These Android Auto console devices provide basic Android user interfaces for car apps. These car apps will allow users to take app functionality along with them on the way to work, shopping, entertainment, on dates, or a road trip.

Just like with Android Wear, apps that work with Android Auto consoles run on the Bluetooth-connected device, for instance, a phone or tablet. The app communicates via specific APIs with the dashboard's Android console, which provides the Android Auto user interface for a connected Android Auto app that is specifically designed for use inside the car environment.

Android Auto application users interact with the apps and services through voice recognition-invoked actions and the vehicle input controls, such as the in-dashboard touchscreen or even physical dashboard hardware buttons.

Android Auto SDK currently supports two types of applications: **Audio apps**, which allow the user to browse, preview, and play music, as well as spoken audio content, such as audiobooks, inside a car stereo environment, or **Messaging apps**, which receive incoming notifications, read messages aloud using text-to-speech synthesis, or send replies via voice input in the car using microphones built into the automobile or the dashboard.

You can configure current audio or messaging apps developed for phones and tablets to work under Android Auto without having to accommodate vehicle-specific hardware differences. To enable these applications to use Android Auto, the app must use a targetSdk setting of Android 5.0 API level 21 or higher. The application Manifest must declare the car capabilities that it uses, such as audio playback or messaging services. This is done in a very similar way to how you would do this in Android Wear for the Watch Faces API.

In the application Manifest, you should provide a reference to the Android Auto XML configuration file **automotive_app_desc.xml**, which you will create in the **/res/xml** folder, just like you did for the res/xml/watch_face.xml file.

To do this, you'll use a **<meta-data>** child tag inside the <application> parent tag. This <meta-data> tag references the **android:name** parameter set to "com.google.android.gms.car.application" and **android:resource** parameter set to "@xml/automotive_app_desc" by using the following XML markup:

```
<application>
    <meta-data android:name="com.google.android.gms.car.application"
     android:resource="@xml/automotive_app_desc"/>
    // Other Application Child Tags will be nested inside of the parent <application> tag
</application>
```

You will specify the Android Auto capabilities that the car app uses using the XML file you placed in the project XML resources directory, which you will probably have to create (res/xml) just like you did for Wear.

To declare an audio application for use with Android Auto, create the file called automotive_ app_desc.xml, saving it under the project res/xml folder, and make sure the XML definition contains the **<automotiveApp>** and **<uses>** tags:

```
<automotiveApp>
    <uses name="media" />
</automotiveApp>
```

The child <uses> tag declares the Android Auto feature that an application intends to utilize. Multiple <uses> tags will be added if your application needs to use multiple Android Auto SDK capabilities. The name="" attribute is used to specify the capability the application is going to utilize.

The <uses name="value"> constants that are supported include **media**, used for playing music in a vehicle (enables audio app), and **notification**, used to display message notifications via a car Overview screen, which allows users to select a message to be read aloud and lets the user respond through voice input to the message (enables an Android Auto messaging app).

For this media constant, Android Auto console devices expect to connect to a Media Browser Service to browse audio track listings. You should declare this MediaBrowserService subclass in the Manifest. This will allow a car's dashboard device hardware to discover the service and connect to the app.

The XML markup needed to declare the MediaBrowserService object as well as the Intent object used to start it and would look much like the following:

```
<application>
    <service android:name=".ProAutoMediaBrowserService" android:exported="true">
        <intent-filter>
            <action android:name="android.media.browse.MediaBrowserService"/>
        </intent-filter>
    </service>
    // Other Application Child Tags will be nested inside of the parent <application> tag
<application>
```

As you can see, the **ProAutoMediaBrowserService** object, as I named it, that the application provides for browsing audio tracks must extend the Android **MediaBrowserService** class, which will become the ProAutoMediaBrowserService class's superclass.

Android Auto hardware devices also use Intent objects for the notification constant as well, to indicate that a user has read or replied to a message provided by an app. An app defines Intent types for reading or replying to messages and adds this information to messaging notifications, so that the dashboard system can notify an app when a user takes one of these actions.

You'll need to define both a heard Action Intent and a reply Action Intent for the application. These are used by the BroadcastReceiver classes, which handle the Intents defined in the application Manifest definition file. An example of the XML markup to implement these Intents, and their associated BroadcastReceiver objects, should look something like the following:

```
<application>
    <receiver android:name=".ProAutoMessageHeardReceiver">
        <intent-filter>
          <action android:name="com.myapp.messagingservice.PRO_AUTO_ACTION_MESSAGE_HEARD"/>
        </intent-filter>
    </receiver>
    <receiver android:name=".ProAutoMessageReplyReceiver">
        <intent-filter>
          <action android:name="com.myapp.messagingservice.PRO_AUTO_ACTION_MESSAGE_REPLY"/>
        </intent-filter>
    </receiver>
</application>
```

In this XML "ProAutoMessageReadReceiver" and "ProAutoMessageReplyReceiver" are the names of the BroadcastReceiver subclasses you code to handle your Intents. You can choose to define any constant you like as the Action object name. Make sure that all of the Action names are completely unique.

Building the notifications for use with Android Auto console devices will require classes from the Android V4 Support Library. Use the Android SDK Manager to update the Extras > Android Support Repository to version 9 or higher and update the Extras > Android Support Library to version 21.0.2 or a higher version numbering, if a later version has become available.

After you have updated these Android Support Libraries, import these into the Android Studio development project by adding this dependency to your Android Auto application's build.gradle file, using the following Groovy code:

```
dependencies { compile 'com.android.support:support-v4:21.0.2' }
```

Android Auto SDK uses standard user interfaces and user interaction models, which work across all consoles, so you don't need to worry about different dashboard hardware. Android takes driver distraction seriously, and it has specific design requirements to qualify Auto apps for sale in the Google Play Store.

When users connect to Android Auto, they first encounter an Overview screen, which displays context cards based on the user's location and time of day. The user can use this screen to view notifications from messaging apps and select messages to send responses via voice input. Tap on a headphone icon in an Activity Bar to see the audio apps installed on a hand-held device. After the user selects the audio app, the display shows this primary app UI. The media control card in the primary app UI supports up to four main actions, as well as four auxiliary actions (on overflow bar) and the Return action.

Android Auto uses a drawer UI paradigm for List browsing actions, and your car console's display will show the contents of a data list using a drawer transition. For media (audio) applications, a customized List UI shows the media containers and audio files provided by the media service in the app. You can customize data entries in the drawers, using icons for list items.

The standard Android Auto user interfaces describe different color schemes for daytime vs. nighttime usage. The Android Auto platform provides the state (daytime or nighttime) variable and automatically sets this state.

As far as Android Auto color themes go, your application is allowed to use colors from the **Material Theme's color palette**. The Material color palette comprises 500 primary and accent colors that can be used for illustration or to develop your application color schema. They've been designed to work harmoniously with one another and can be seen at the following Google URL:

`http://www.google.com/design/spec/style/`**`color.html`**

This color palette starts with 20 primary colors of white, red, green, blue, purple, pink, indigo, cyan, teal, lime, yellow, amber, orange, gray, blue gray, brown, deep orange, deep purple, light green, and light blue. If you consider black as a color, there are actually 21 colors in all.

The other 480 colors fill in this spectrum to create a complete and usable palette for Android or WebKit. Google suggests using the 500 colors as the primary color selections for your apps and then using other custom colors as your accent colors. Your Android Auto applications will be permitted to specify two colors for the system palette. These are defined in the Android OS using the **colorPrimaryDark** and the **colorAccentNext** data field constants.

The Android Auto platform is designed to maximize safety and to reduce any distractions, and this color palette is only a small part of that process.

Android Auto app user interfaces need to be quick and easy to navigate, and each Android Auto app must pass formal reviews and meet minimum safety and driver distraction requirements and regulations. Android Auto apps need to be completely predictable and inherently intuitive to ensure that drivers will always keep their eyes on the road, as lives could be at stake here.

Your application needs to be customized for Android Auto. Don't specify an Android Auto compatibility in the Android Manifest XML file without making user interface, usability, and design adjustments for a driving experience. Complex actions, such as creating an account, signing in, or even creating a playlist, should be performed on a phone or tablet, not an Auto display.

Android Auto application design should conform to the principles that this platform implements in its own Auto platform UI, including a glanceable UI design and predictable application functionality, have continuously connected user experiences, and offer an integrated application environment to users.

# Google Glass: Develop Apps for Smart Eyeglasses

Google Glass Development Kit, also known as GDK, is the add on for Android SDK that lets you build Glassware (Glass apps) that runs directly on Google Glass. The Google Glass 1 was discontinued as of the time of the writing of the book; however, Google Glass 2 is scheduled for release sometime during 2015. If Google is smart, instead of making Glass 2 an external API for Android, it will do the same thing that was done for Wear, TV, and Auto and make it an Android Glass API and SDK that is far more integrated with the Android OS and available to all smart eyeglass manufacturers, such as Luxottica, LGE, Sony, six15, Vuzix, Samsung, GlassUp, PivotHead, Meta AR, and many others.

Google Glass 1 featured a screen resolution of 640 by 360. This is quarter pseudo-HD, since a 1280-by-720 screen has four 640-by-360 rectangular areas. Like Android TV or Auto, Glass has a unique UI paradigm that specifically fits your hardware device. This is designed around a timeline UI paradigm.

This timeline is the main user interface that is presented to users. It is comprised of 640-by-360 resolution cards. The Glass UI provides some linear features, such as a common way to review animated and static cards, invoke voice recognition commands, and launch your Android Glass applications.

Android Glass users can scroll linearly between different sections of this timeline UI, revealing card UI elements from the past, present, and future, which equate to on-screen (present), previously reviewed (past), and yet to have been reviewed (future). The most recently reviewed (past) items would remain closest to the Home card. This is the default card users see when they resume using Android Glass or use it for the first time.

In addition to navigating timeline cards, this Android Glass UI provides a response to user input. Users navigate the timeline UI using the touchpad and can launch Android Glass applications using voice commands. Cards also are allowed to feature menu items, thus Android Glass applications will be able to give control over to users so that they may complete actions, such as replying to an incoming text message or even share a photo or video.

The Android Glass timeline UI and its cards are organized into a number of different functional sections, including **Home**, **Past**, **Present**, and **Future**. A default Home card features an Android Glass clock. This Home card occupies the center of the timeline user interface, and it appears whenever the user starts using an Android Glass device. This Home card remains in the center area of the timeline UI because it provides access to the rest of the UI.

Android Glass provides either voice or touch commands, allowing Glass users to start other operating system components of or custom applications for Android Glass. Voice commands allow hands-free operation of Android Glass.

On the right side of the Android Glass Home screen (clock) is the **history** section, representing the **past** and displaying static data cards. The reason for this is because live cards are always considered to be in the present, so they will never appear in this history section of the Android Glass UI.

Static cards will naturally "decay" in this history section if they aren't refreshed by revisiting them. As newer cards end up in this past section, they will be positioned closest to the Home screen (clock). Android Glass will position the oldest card the farthest to the right. The Glass OS will remove any card older than seven days, or when the 200 card limit is reached.

On the left side of the Android Glass Home screen (clock) are the **present** and **future** sections, which contain both static as well as live cards. Live cards always display current information that is relevant to users and is happening in real time. Live cards should always appear in the present and future sections. When a live card has **focus** and Android Glass goes to sleep, that card will be the one that becomes the default card that will appear when Android Glass comes back on. Static cards that contain future "timestamps" or that are "pinned" will also appear in the present and future sections.

For instance, a Google Now weather card might show relevant information automatically in the present and future sections, even though it is a static card. Static information can be updated dynamically, at predefined times.

At the far left of the timeline UI are the **Settings** cards. With these, you are able to configure Android Glass operating system settings, like volume or what Wi-Fi network you are connecting with.

Live cards are clearly the central feature of Android Glass, because these will always contain rich, real-time content, or content the user has requested to be periodically updated and remain on the present section of the screen. Live cards should be updated frequently using custom graphics that will show the user's compelling, real-time information. This functionality is necessary for animated user interfaces that need to constantly update, based on some user data or on external data the user is consuming.

Live cards have access to low-level sensor data like the accelerometer and GPS. This allows cutting-edge types of user interactions and features that are not possible with static cards, because sensors such as these stream out dynamic data in real time and, therefore, require a live card format.

Live cards are capable of running inside the Android Glass timeline UI. Users can scroll left or right to view and interact with other live cards, while each of these live cards is running. This allows users to multitask and seamlessly maintain each live card's run-time state in the background.

Static cards can only display text, imagery, and video content, which will be able to be loaded into memory once (static) and contain data that does not change (is not dynamic). Video is animated, but it is a series of images. Therefore, digital video, although it looks dynamic, is not, as it does not change over time and is the same series of imagery each time it is played! Static cards contain information you can build with HTML, text, images, or video. Static cards do not update their data frequently, if at all, and they should be designed for content display and quick notifications.

Static cards are allowed to have a share menu item, which allows your users to share the card with other people, called contacts, or even with another Android Glass application. You can declare these Android Glass timeline UI cards to be "shareable," and you can also define a contact for the Android Glass application that can accept shared timeline UI static card items.

When you need full user interface control for your user experience, Android Glass has something called "immersions." These would be run outside the typical Android Glass timeline user interface or user experience.

Immersions allow you to render your own user interfaces, processing all of the user input inside the Android Glass application programming logic. Immersions are needed for Android Glass applications that cannot function within the rigid linear constraints of a timeline user interface paradigm and required a freeform, nonlinear, or object-oriented GUI approach.

It is important to note that both timeline cards as well as immersions can contain menu items. These carry out associated actions, such as replying, configuring, dismissing, sharing, data entry, and many more user actions.

The original Google Glass 1 API (called Mirror API and Glassware GDK) was not 100% Android specific, although it did support Java 1.6 and, therefore, 32-bit Android 4.x. Glass Mirror also supported Python and PHP as well. An Android Glass API, which would naturally be part of the new Glass 2.0, would be 64-bit Android 5.x or even 6.x, and use Java 1.7 (Java 7) or Java 1.8 (Java 8) or even Java 1.9 (Java 9).

Because this API is currently under development and not available yet, I'll just cover the basics of Google Glass 1 in this section of the chapter and cover Android Glass (or Google Glass 2.0) in my next Pro Android title, *Pro Android IoT* (Apress, 2016).

# Android Wear: Interesting API Elements to Explore

For the rest of the chapter, I am going to cover some other important features of Android Wear that I did not cover earlier in the book. You can use most of these on top of your Watch Face code infrastructure, which will allow you to make Android Wear applications that are also watch face compatible at the same time, which is going to be a trend for Android Wear as the smartwatch hardware device is first and foremost used for a digital wristwatch. This is why I made sure I covered Watch Faces API completely during this book.

## Detecting Location: GPS Data from Google Play Services

Some Wear applications will need to be aware of their **location** in order to be able to calculate distances traveled (fitness and travel apps) or even ascertain where the user is on the face of the planet. Some users, such as myself, tend to turn **GPS** features on smartphones off, for privacy reasons, unless there's a compelling reason to allow one's self to be tracked. Keep this in mind, as well, when considering Wear apps that utilize GPS data.

Many wearable devices include a GPS **sensor** that can retrieve location data without being tethered to another device such as a tablet or a smartphone. Fortunately, when you request the location data in the wearable app, there is no need to worry about where this location data originates. Android can ascertain location data and update the data using a power-efficient method on either the smartphone or the smartwatch.

A Wear application should be able to handle any loss of the location data, in case the wear hardware device loses the connection with a paired device and does not happen to have the GPS sensor hardware on board.

GPS location data on a wearable device will be obtained through Google Play Services (location API), which you've already learned how to utilize during this book. For GPS, you would utilize the **FusedLocationProviderApi**, and its accompanying classes, to obtain this location data. To access GPS location Services, create your instance of **GoogleApiClient**, which is the main entry point for any of the Google Play Services APIs, just like you did for your Android Wear Watch Faces API implementation during this book.

To connect to Google Play Services, create an instance of GoogleApiClient and create an Activity that specifies an implementation for the interfaces **ConnectionCallbacks**, **OnConnectionFailedListener**, and the **LocationListener**. To manage the connection lifecycle, call connect() in an onResume() method and disconnect() in an onPause() method, similar to the following Java code:

```java
public class WearableMainActivity extends Activity implements GoogleApiClient.
ConnectionCallbacks,
    GoogleApiClient.OnConnectionFailedListener, LocationListener {
    private GoogleApiClient myGoogleApiClient;
    @Override
    protected void onCreate(Bundle savedInstanceState) {
        super.onCreate(savedInstanceState);
        myGoogleApiClient = new GoogleApiClient.Builder(this)
                .addApi(LocationServices.API)
                .addApi(Wearable.API)           // used for the data layer API
                .addConnectionCallbacks(this)
                .addOnConnectionFailedListener(this)
                .build();
    }
    @Override
    protected void onResume() {
        super.onResume();
        mGoogleApiClient.connect();
    }
    @Override
    protected void onPause() {
        super.onPause();
        mGoogleApiClient.disconnect();
    }
}
```

After an app connects to Google Play Services, it is ready to receive location updates. When Android invokes the .onConnected() callback for the client, you'll build the location data request by creating a LocationRequest object and setting options using methods such as **.setPriority()**. You would request location updates using **.requestLocationUpdates()** in onConnected() or remove location updates using **.removeLocationUpdates()** in the onPause() method, as can be seen in the following implemented methods example code:

```java
@Override
public void onConnected(Bundle bundle) {
    LocationRequest locationRequest = LocationRequest.create()
            .setPriority(LocationRequest.PRIORITY_HIGH_ACCURACY)
            .setInterval(UPDATE_INTERVAL_MS)
            .setFastestInterval(FASTEST_INTERVAL_MS);
```

```
LocationServices.FusedLocationApi
        .requestLocationUpdates(myGoogleApiClient, locationRequest, this)
        .setResultCallback(new ResultCallback() {
            @Override
            public void onResult(Status status) {
                if (status.getStatus().isSuccess()) {
                    if (Log.isLoggable(TAG, Log.DEBUG)) {
                        Log.d(TAG, "Successfully requested location updates");
                    }
                } else { Log.e(TAG, "Failed in requesting location updates, "
                                    + "status code: " + status.getStatusCode()
                                    + ", message: " + status.getStatusMessage());
                }
            }
        });
}
@Override
protected void onPause() {
    super.onPause();
    if (myGoogleApiClient.isConnected()) {
        LocationServices.FusedLocationApi.removeLocationUpdates(myGoogleApiClient, this);
    }
    myGoogleApiClient.disconnect();
}
@Override
public void onConnectionSuspended(int i) {
    if (Log.isLoggable(TAG, Log.DEBUG)) {
        Log.d(TAG, "connection to location client suspended");
    }
}
}
```

Once you enable location updates, the system calls an **.onLocationChanged()** method with the updated location using the interval value you specify using the **.setInterval()** method call.

Not all smartwatch hardware will feature the GPS sensor. If a user goes out for a spin and leaves their phone or tablet behind, the wearable app can't receive GPS location data using the tethered connection. If the smartwatch hardware doesn't feature a GPS sensor, you could detect this situation and warn users the GPS location functionality is not currently available. This is accomplished by using the .hasSystemFeature() method call. This example Java code polls a device to see if it has GPS when it starts the Activity:

```
protected void onCreate(Bundle savedInstanceState) {
    super.onCreate(savedInstanceState);
    setContentView(R.layout.main_activity);
    if ( !hasGpsData() ) {
        // Fall-back functionality, for use without location data (Or warn user: No location
        data!)
    }
}
private boolean hasGpsData() {
    return getPackageManager().hasSystemFeature(PackageManager.FEATURE_LOCATION_GPS);
}
```

It's also possible that smartwatch hardware devices that rely on tethered connections for their location data could lose the connection abruptly. If your smartwatch app processes a constant stream of GPS data, you will need to handle disconnections based on where the data is interrupted or becomes unavailable. On smartwatch hardware that does not feature a GPS sensor, a loss of GPS location data may occur when the smartwatch loses its tethered data connection.

In cases where your app depends on a tethered data connection for location data and the wear device does not have a GPS sensor, you should detect the connection loss, warn the user, and change the functionality for the app.

To detect a loss of a tethered data connection, you would need to extend a WearableListenerService. This service will allow you to process data layer events. To do this, declare an <intent-filter> in the AndroidManifest that notifies Android about the WearableListenerService. This filter will allow the operating system to bind to your WearableListenerService when needed.

Your XML markup for the <service> parent tag defining the ListenerService class and a **BIND_LISTENER** child <intent-filter> tag should look like this:

```
<service android:name=".MyNodeListenerService">
    <intent-filter>
        <action android:name="com.google.android.gms.wearable.BIND_LISTENER" />
    </intent-filter>
</service>
```

Inside the MyNodeListenerService subclass of WearableListenerService, you would then implement the **.onPeerDisconnected()** method to handle cases pertaining to whether or not a smartwatch hardware device features built-in GPS. The Java code would look something like the following:

```
public class MyNodeListenerService extends WearableListenerService {
    @Override
    public void onPeerDisconnected(Node peer) {
        if( !hasGpsData() ) {
            // Fall-back to functions that don't use location or notify user to bring their
            handset
        }
    }
}
```

If it loses GPS data (signal), you should retrieve the last known location by using the .getLastLocation() method call. This method can be helpful in scenarios where you're not able to get GPS data or when a smartwatch does not feature a built-in GPS and loses its connection with a phone or a tablet. Here's how you would use the .getLastLocation() method call (remember to request GPS location permission in your Manifest XML file) in order to retrieve the last known GPS location data, if it is available:

```
Location location = LocationServices.FusedLocationApi.getLastLocation(myGoogleApiClient);
```

If your smartwatch application records data using an on-watch GPS, you can also synchronize the smartwatch location data with the smartphone location data. Using the LocationListener, you can implement an **.onLocationChanged()** method in order to detect, and record, the GPS location data as it changes by using the following Java programming structures:

```
@Override
public void onLocationChanged(Location location) {
    addLocationEntry(location.getLatitude(), location.getLongitude());
}
private void addLocationEntry(double latitude, double longitude) {
    if (!mySavedGpsLocation || !myGoogleApiClient.isConnected()) { return; }
    mCalendar.setTimeInMillis(System.currentTimeMillis());
    String path = Constants.PATH + "/" + mCalendar.getTimeInMillis();
    PutDataMapRequest putDataMapRequest = PutDataMapRequest.create(path);
    putDataMapRequest.getDataMap().putDouble(Constants.KEY_LATITUDE, latitude);
    putDataMapRequest.getDataMap().putDouble(Constants.KEY_LONGITUDE, longitude);
    putDataMapRequest.getDataMap().putLong(Constants.KEY_TIME, mCalendar.getTimeInMillis());
    PutDataRequest request = putDataMapRequest.asPutDataRequest();
    Wearable.DataApi.putDataItem(myGoogleApiClient, request)
            .setResultCallback(new ResultCallback() {
                @Override
                public void onResult(DataApi.DataItemResult dataItemResult) {
                    if (!dataItemResult.getStatus().isSuccess()) {
                        Log.e(TAG, "Failed to set the data, "
                                + "status: " + dataItemResult.getStatus()
                                .getStatusCode());
                    }
                }
            });
}
```

The other major feature that is supported more and more in Wear smartwatch hardware is a **microphone**, so let's take a look at speech recognition next!

## Voice Actions: Using Speech Recognition Technology

We all remember (or do we?) the vanguard Dick Tracy (when is someone going to remake this as a hit film?) comic series where hero Dick Tracy was able to talk into his smartwatch and elicit miracles that always saved the day.

Now you too can allow your user to talk to your smartwatch app and have it work miracles for them, because **voice actions** have become an integral part of the Android Wear user experience, allowing users to trigger app actions hands free and relatively quickly.

Android Wear allows developers two types of voice actions. **System-provided** voice actions are OS task based and are built into the Wear platform. You use IntentFilter objects to define them for the Activity you wish to start when a particular voice action is invoked using a speech recognition engine in Android, which I will be discussing later on. Some examples of system-provided voice actions would include "Take a note," and "Set an alarm," or "Call a Taxi" and even "Start Stopwatch" and many more.

The second type of voice action is the **application-provided** voice actions. These voice actions are application based, and you declare them much like a launcher icon. To utilize these actions, the user will state "Start" and an action (specified as a label) in order to utilize the voice actions, and an Activity subclass that you specify will subsequently launch (start).

The Android Wear platform provides a number of voice Intent constants that are based on user actions and allow users to say what they want to do and let the system figure out the best Activity to launch. These are contained in the android.speech package's RecognizerIntent class and can be found at the following Android developer web site URL, if you want to research them:

http://developer.android.com/reference/android/speech/**RecognizerIntent**.html

When users invoke a voice action, your app can filter for the Intent that is utilized to launch the associated Activity, as defined in your Manifest.

If you want to start a Service instead, show the Activity as a visual cue, and start the Service inside that Activity. Make sure to call **.finish()** when you want to get rid of the Activity's (Service's) visual cue wrapper.

As an example, the XML markup block that should be utilized to implement the "Take a Note to Self" command declares a child <intent-filter> inside a parent <activity> that will start the Activity subclass named SelfNote, as follows:

```
<activity android:name="SelfNoteActivity">
  <intent-filter>
    <action android:name="android.intent.action.SEND" />
    <category android:name="com.google.android.voicesearch.SELF_NOTE" />
  </intent-filter>
</activity>
```

If none of the voice Intent constants apply to your app, you can start your app directly with a customized "Start Activity [Name Here]" voice action. The way to register your application to use a custom "Start" action is the same as registering your launcher icon. Instead of requesting the application icon in the launcher XML construct, an app will request a voice action instead, using the **android:label** parameter. To specify a voice command for the user to use after "Start:", specify the label attribute for the Activity you wish to launch. For example, this <intent-filter> construct recognizes the "Start: Voice Control App" voice action, launching StartVoiceActivity:

```
<application>
  <activity android:name="StartVoiceActivity" android:label="VoiceControlApp">
    <intent-filter>
      <action android:name="android.intent.action.MAIN" />
      <category android:name="android.intent.category.LAUNCHER" />
    </intent-filter>
  </activity>
</application>
```

In addition to using voice actions in conjunction with the built-in speech recognition constants in Android Wear to launch activities, you could also process "free-form" or nonstandard speech input, using a **SpeechRecognizer** class, which accesses the **RecognitionService** class and the **RecognizerIntent** class that accessed the predefined voice action constants covered earlier.

These are just some of the components of the **android.speech** package. This Speech Recognizer class and related classes will be utilized to obtain hands-free voice input from users and process that voice input, providing a result.

An example of this might entail sending a short text message or specifying a search term for a search engine. It is important to note that the speech APIs are not intended to be used for continuous voice recognition, such as you would have with a professional speech software package like the Dragon Naturally Speaking Premium software from Nuance Communications. There also is a speech recognition capability built into Microsoft Windows 8.1.

The reason you don't want to do continuous voice (speech) recognition with Android Wear is because Android OS, although quite powerful, is still just an embedded device OS and does not currently possess the CPU cores, memory, and clock speeds to perform continuous speech recognition and translation.

Trying to accomplish this level of speech recognition inside a Wear app would consume a significant amount of battery life, processing overhead and network bandwidth. The SpeechRecognizer methods need to be invoked using the main application thread. You call **startActivityForResult()** using an **ACTION_RECOGNIZE_SPEECH** action, launching a speech recognition Activity. You would then handle the result in an onActivityResult() method, using the following Java structure:

```
private static final int SPEECH_REQUEST_CODE = 0;
private void displaySpeechRecognizer() {
    Intent intent = new Intent(RecognizerIntent.ACTION_RECOGNIZE_SPEECH);
    // Create an Intent object
    intent.putExtra(RecognizerIntent.EXTRA_LANGUAGE_MODEL,
                    RecognizerIntent.LANGUAGE_MODEL_FREE_FORM);
    startActivityForResult(intent, SPEECH_REQUEST_CODE);                // Start the Activity
}
@Override // The callback which is invoked when the Speech Recognizer returns
protected void onActivityResult(int requestCode, int resultCode, Intent data) {
// Process Intent    if (requestCode == SPEECH_REQUEST_CODE && resultCode == RESULT_OK) {
        List<String> results = data.getStringArrayListExtra(RecognizerIntent.EXTRA_RESULTS);
        String spokenWord = results.get(0);
        // Process Voice Recognition Result
    }
    super.onActivityResult(requestCode, resultCode, data);
}
```

Adding Location Awareness and Speech Recognition can make your apps aware!

# Summary

Congratulations, you've finished this Pro Android Wearables book, and with flying colors at that! You're well on your way to creating innovative Wear applications primed and ready to spark this Internet of Things revolution!

In this final chapter, you learned about some of the additional Internet of Things APIs that Android OS has recently introduced, in addition to Wear. You took a look at Android TV, which allows you to create applications for the massive 64- to 96-inch screens users are now installing in their living rooms.

Next, you got an overview of the new Android Auto API, which allows you to create applications that work seamlessly inside an automobile dashboard environment and leverage built-in automobile hardware like audio speakers.

You also took a look at Google Glass 1, soon to be Android Glass 2, and at some of the other features of Android Wear that you should consider using.

Next, you took a look at implementing location based services, using the GPS sensor hardware data, along with Google Mobile Services (GMS), and Google Play Services.

The chapter concluded with a look at use of the latest speech recognition technology as well as internal voice action commands provided by Android.

# Index

**D**

**H**

**I**

# ▇P, Q

# Get the eBook for only $5!

Why limit yourself?

Now you can take the weightless companion with you wherever you go and access your content on your PC, phone, tablet, or reader.

Since you've purchased this print book, we're happy to offer you the eBook in all 3 formats for just $5.

Convenient and fully searchable, the PDF version enables you to easily find and copy code—or perform examples by quickly toggling between instructions and applications. The MOBI format is ideal for your Kindle, while the ePUB can be utilized on a variety of mobile devices.

To learn more, go to www.apress.com/companion or contact support@apress.com.

Druck: KN Digital Printforce GmbH · Schockenriedstraße 37 · 70565 Stuttgart